ELEVENTH EDITION

►►► BECOMING A MASTER STUDENT

Tools, techniques, hints, ideas, illustrations, examples, methods, procedures, processes, skills, resources, and suggestions for success.

DAVE ELLIS

DOUG TOFT
Contributing Editor

DEAN MANCINA
Faculty Advisor

ADVISORY BOARD
MARY HALE BARRY
Corinthian Colleges, Inc., CA
RAY EMETT
Salt Lake Community College, UT
SANDRA M. KARMAN
The Chubb Institute, NJ
LOIS PASPANE
Palm Beach Community College, FL
M. ELAINE RICHARDSON
Clemson University, SC
DR. KAREN N. VALENCIA
South Texas Community College, TX
DR. JOYCE WEINSHEIMER
University of Minnesota-Twin Cities, MN
DR. MARTHA W. WILLIAMS
Valencia Community College, FL

HOUGHTON MIFFLIN COMPANY
Boston   New York

Publisher: Patricia A. Coryell
Senior Sponsoring Editor: Mary Finch
Development Editor: Shani B. Fisher
Editorial Associate: Andrew Sylvester
Senior Project Editor: Cathy Labresh Brooks
Editorial Assistant: Neil Reynolds
Composition Buyer: Sarah L. Ambrose
Art and Design Manager: Jill Haber
Manufacturing Manager: Karen Banks
Marketing Manager: Elinor Gregory
Marketing Assistant: Evelyn Yang

Cover Design: Majel Peters
Cover Images: www.navy.mil; Chief Petty Officer Jim Melton

College Survival
A Program of Houghton Mifflin Company
2075 Foxfield Drive, Suite 100
St. Charles, IL 60174

Photo and illustration credits are listed on page 400.

Custom Publishing Editor: Kyle Henderson
Custom Publishing Production Manager: Kathleen McCourt
Project Coordinator: Kimberly Gavrilles

This book contains select works from existing Houghton Mifflin Company resources and was produced by Houghton Mifflin Custom Publishing for collegiate use. As such, those adopting and/or contributing to this work are responsible for editorial content, accuracy, continuity and completeness.

Printed in the United States of America.

ISBN: 0-618-56538-8
N-04275

1 2 3 4 5 6 7 8 9 – PP – 07 06 05

Houghton Mifflin
Custom Publishing

222 Berkeley Street • Boston, MA 02116

Address all correspondence and order information to the above address.

advisory board

brief table of contents

table of contents

Making Transitions

First Steps

2 Planning

3 Memory

4 Reading

5 Notes

6 Tests

7 Thinking

8 Communicating

9 Diversity

10 Technology

11 Health

12   What's Next?

INTRODUCTION
Making Transitions

Change and growth take place when a person has risked himself and dares to become involved with experimenting with his own life.

HERBERT OTTO

The human ability to learn and remember is virtually limitless.

SHEILA OSTRANDER AND LYNN SCHROEDER

why
the Introduction matters . . .

Acquiring learning strategies will help you make a smooth and successful transition to the world of higher education, help you feel more at ease in this new world, and help you succeed.

what
is included . . .

This book is worthless—if you just read it
Get the most out of this book
The Discovery and Intention Journal Entry system
Discovery and Intention Statement guidelines
Making the transition to higher education
The art of re-entry: Going back to school as an adult learner
Connect to school resources
Connect to community resources
Extracurricular activities
Following instructions
Link to the world of work
Ways to change a habit
Power Process: "Discover what you want"

how
you can use this Introduction . . .

Discover a way to interact with books that multiplies their value.
Use writing to translate personal discoveries into powerful new behaviors.
Connect with people and organizations that can support your success.

As you read, ask yourself
what if . . .

I could use the ideas in this Introduction to master any transition in my life?

This book is worthless—if you just read it

The first edition of this book began with the sentence *This book is worthless*. Many students thought this was a trick to get their attention. It wasn't. Others thought it was reverse psychology. It wasn't that, either. Still others thought it meant that the book was worthless if they didn't read it. It's more than that.

This book is worthless *even if you read it*—if reading is all you do. What was true of that first edition is true of this one. Until you take action and use the ideas in it, *Becoming a Master Student* really is worthless.

The purpose of this book is to help you make a successful transition to higher education by setting up a pattern of success that will last the rest of your life. You probably won't take action and use the ideas in this book until you are convinced that you have something to gain. That's the reason for this introduction—to persuade you to use this book actively.

Before you stiffen up and resist this sales pitch, remember that you have already bought the book. Now you can get something for your money by committing yourself to take action—in other words, by committing yourself to becoming a master student. Here's what's in it for you.

Pitch #1: You can save money now and make more later. Start with money. Your college education is one of the most expensive things you will ever buy. Typically, it costs students $30 to $70 an hour to sit in class. Unfortunately, many students think their classes aren't worth even 50 cents an hour.

As a master student, you control the value you get out of your education, and that value can be considerable. The joy of learning aside, college graduates make more money during their lifetimes than their nondegreed peers.[1] The income advantage you gain through higher education could total over half a million dollars. It pays to be a master student.

Pitch #2: You can rediscover the natural learner in you. Joy is important, too. As you become a master student, you will learn to gain knowledge in the most effective way possible by discovering the joyful, natural learner within you.

Children are great natural students. They quickly master complex skills, such as language, and they have fun doing it. For them, learning is a high-energy process involving experimentation, discovery, and sometimes broken dishes. Then comes school. For some students, drill and drudgery replace discovery and dish breaking.

Learning can become a drag. You can use this book to reverse that process and rediscover what you knew as a child—that laughter and learning go hand in hand.

Sometimes learning does take effort, especially in college. As you become a master student, you will learn many ways to get the most out of that effort.

Pitch #3: You can choose from hundreds of techniques. *Becoming a Master Student* is packed with hundreds of practical, nuts-and-bolts techniques. And you can begin using them immediately. For example, during the textbook reconnaissance on page 2, you can practice three powerful learning techniques in one 15-minute exercise. Even if you doze in lectures, drift during tests, or dawdle on term papers, you'll find ideas in this book that you can use to become a more effective student.

Not all of these ideas will work for you. That's why there are so many of them in *Becoming a Master Student*. You can experiment with the techniques. As you discover what works, you will develop a unique style of learning that you can use for the rest of your life.

Pitch #4: You get the best suggestions from thousands of students. The concepts and techniques in this book are here not because learning theorists, educators, and psychologists say they work. They are here because tens of thousands of students from all kinds of backgrounds have tried them and say that they work. These are people who dreaded giving speeches, couldn't read their own notes, and fell behind in their course work. Then they figured out how to solve these problems. Now you can use their ideas.

Pitch #5: You can learn about you. The process of self-discovery is an important theme in *Becoming a Master Student*. Throughout the book you can use Discovery and Intention Statements for everything from organizing your desk to choosing long-term goals. Studying for an organic chemistry quiz is a lot easier with a clean desk and a clear idea of the course's importance to you.

Pitch #6: You can use a proven product. The first ten editions of this book have proved successful for hundreds of thousands of students. In schools where it was widely used, the dropout rate decreased as much as 25 percent, and in some cases, 50 percent. Student feedback has been positive. In particular, students with successful histories have praised the techniques in this book.

Pitch #7: You can learn the secret of student success. If this sales pitch still hasn't persuaded you to use this book actively, maybe it's time to reveal the secret of student success. (Provide your own drum roll here.) The secret is—that there are no secrets. Perhaps the ultimate formula is to give up formulas and keep inventing.

The strategies and tactics that successful students use are well known. You have hundreds of them at your fingertips right now, in this book. Use them. Modify them. Invent new ones. You're the authority on what works for you.

However, what makes any technique work is commitment—and action. Without them, the pages of *Becoming a Master Student* are just 2.1 pounds of expensive mulch. Add your participation to the mulch, and these pages are priceless. ▨

This book is worth $1,000

Houghton Mifflin Student Success is proud to present three students each year with a $1,000 scholarship for tuition reimbursement. Any post-secondary school in the United States and Canada can nominate one student for the scholarship. In order to be considered, students must write an essay that answers the question "How do you define success?"

For more details, go to (masterstudent.college.hmco.com)

exercise 1

TEXTBOOK RECONNAISSANCE

Start becoming a master student this moment by doing a 15-minute "textbook reconnaissance." Here's how.

First, read the table of contents. Do it in three minutes or less. Next, look at every page in the book. Move quickly. Scan headlines. Look at pictures. Notice forms, charts, and diagrams. Don't forget the last few pages in back, which include extra copies of planning forms that you might find useful.

A textbook reconnaissance shows you where a course is going. It gives you the big picture. That's useful because brains work best when going from the general to the specific. Getting the big picture before you start makes it easier to recall and understand details later on.

Your textbook reconnaissance will work even better if, as you scan, you look for ideas you can use. When you find one, write the page number and a short description of it in the space below. If you run out of room, just continue your list on a separate sheet of paper. Or use Post-it Notes to flag the pages that look useful. You could even use notes of different colors to signal priority, such as green for ideas to use right away and yellow for those to apply later. The idea behind this technique is simple: It's easier to learn when you're excited, and it's easier to get excited about a course if you know it's going to be useful, interesting, or fun.

Remember, look at every page, and do it quickly. And here's another useful tip for the master student: Do it now.

Page number   *Description*

_____

_____

_____

_____

_____

_____

_____

_____

_____

_____

Get the most out of this book

1. Rip 'em out. The pages of *Becoming a Master Student* are perforated because some of the information here is too important to leave in the book and some your instructor might want to see. For example, Journal Entry #2 asks you to list some important things you want to get out of your education. To keep yourself focused, you could rip that page out and post it on your bathroom mirror or some other place where you'll see it several times a day.

You can reinsert the page later by sticking it into the spine of the book. A piece of tape will hold it in place.

2. Skip around. You can use this book in several different ways. Read it straight through. Or pick it up, turn to any page, and find an idea you can use. Look for ideas you can use right now. For example, if you are about to choose a major or are considering changing schools, skip directly to the articles on these topics in Chapters Seven and Twelve, respectively.

3. If it works, use it. If it doesn't, lose it. If there are sections of the book that don't apply to you at all, skip them—unless, of course, they are assigned. Then see if you can gain value from these sections anyway. When you are committed to getting value from this book, even an idea that seems irrelevant or ineffective at first can turn out to be a powerful tool.

4. Put yourself into the book. As you read about techniques in this book, create your own scenarios, starring yourself in the title role. For example, when reading through Exercise #1: "Textbook reconnaissance," picture yourself using this technique on your world history textbook.

5. Listen to your peers. Throughout this book you will find Student Voices, short features that contain quotations from students who used *Becoming a Master Student* to promote their success. As you dig into the following chapters, think about what you would say if you could add your voice to theirs. Look for tools and techniques that can make a huge difference in your life.

6. Own this book. Right now, put your name, address, and related information on the inside cover of this book, and don't stop there. Determine what you want to get out of school and create a record of how you intend to get it by reading the Power Process and completing the Journal Entries in this Introduction. Every time your pen touches a page, you move closer to mastery of learning.

 7. Do the exercises. Action makes this book work. To get the most out of an exercise, read the instructions carefully before you begin. To get the most out of this book, do most of the exercises. More important, avoid feeling guilty if you skip some. And by the way, it's never too late to go back and do the ones you skipped.

These exercises invite you to write, touch, feel, move, see, search, ponder, speak, listen, recall, choose, commit, and create. You might even sing and dance. Learning often works best when it involves action.

8. Practice critical thinking. Throughout this book are Practicing Critical Thinking activities. Their purpose is to reinforce contemplation and problem solving. Note that other elements of this text, including the exercises and Journal Entries, also promote critical thinking.

 **9. Learn about learning styles.** Check out the Learning Styles Application in each chapter. These exercises are included to increase your awareness of your preferred learning styles and to help you explore new styles. Each application will guide you through experiencing four specific modes of learning as applied to the content of the chapter. The modes can be accessed by asking four basic questions: *Why? What? How?* and *What if?* You'll find more details in the Learning Style Inventory in Chapter One.

10. Navigate through learning experiences with the Master Student Map. You can orient yourself for maximum learning every time you open this book by asking those same four questions. That's the idea behind the

Master Student Map included on the first page of each chapter. Eventually, you'll be able to use the four-part structure of this map to guide yourself in effectively learning anything.

11. Link to the Web. Throughout this book, you'll notice reminders to visit the Web site for *Becoming a Master Student*:

> masterstudent.college.hmco.com

Check regularly for articles, online exercises, and links to other useful Web sites.

12. Sweat the small stuff. Look for sidebars—short bursts of words and pictures placed between longer articles—throughout this book. These short pieces might offer an insight that transforms your experience of higher education. Remember this related point: Shorter chapters in this book are just as important as longer chapters.

13. Take this book to work. With a little tweaking in some cases, you can apply nearly all of the techniques in this book to your career. For more details, see the Put It to Work articles in each chapter. Use them to make a seamless transition from success in school to success on the job.

14. Get used to a new look and tone. This book looks different from traditional textbooks. *Becoming a Master Student* presents major ideas in magazine-style articles. You will discover lots of lists, blurbs, one-liners, pictures, charts, graphs, illustrations, and even a joke or two.

Even though this book is loaded with special features, you'll find some core elements. For example, the two pages that open each chapter include a "lead" article and an introductory Journal Entry. And at the end of each chapter you'll find a Power Process, Put It to Work article, chapter quiz, Learning Styles Application, and Master Student Profile—all noted in a toolbar at the top of the page.

Note: As a strategy for avoiding sexist language, this book alternates the use of feminine and masculine pronouns.

COMMITMENT

This book is worthless unless you actively participate in its activities and exercises. One powerful way to begin taking action is to make a commitment. Conversely, without commitment, sustained action is unlikely, and the result is again a worthless book. Therefore, in the interest of saving your valuable time and energy, this exercise gives you a chance to declare your level of involvement up front. From the choices below, choose the sentence that best reflects your commitment to using this book. Write the number in the space provided at the end of the list.

1. "Well, I'm reading this book right now, aren't I?"
2. "I will skim the book and read the interesting parts."
3. "I will read the book and think about how some of the techniques might apply to me."
4. "I will read the book, think about it, and do the exercises that look interesting."
5. "I will read the book, do some exercises, and complete some of the Journal Entries."
6. "I will read the book, do some exercises and Journal Entries, and use some of the techniques."
7. "I will read the book, do most of the exercises and Journal Entries, and use some of the techniques."
8. "I will study this book, do most of the exercises and Journal Entries, and use some of the techniques."
9. "I will study this book, do most of the exercises and Journal Entries, and experiment vigorously with most of the suggestions in order to discover what works best for me."
10. "I promise myself to get value from this book, beginning with Exercise #1: 'Textbook reconnaissance,' even if I have to rewrite the sections I don't like and invent new techniques of my own."

Enter your commitment level and today's date here:

Commitment level _____ Date _____

If you selected commitment level 1 or 2, you might consider passing this book on to a friend. If your commitment level is 9 or 10, you are on your way to terrific success in school. If your level is somewhere in between, experiment with the techniques and learning strategies in this book. If you find that they work, consider returning to this exercise and raising your level of commitment.

The Discovery and Intention Journal Entry system

AIRPORT

One way to become a better student is to grit your teeth and try harder. There is another way. Using familiar tools and easily learned processes, the Discovery and Intention Journal Entry system can help increase your effectiveness by showing you how to focus your energy.

The Discovery and Intention Journal Entry system is a little like flying a plane. Airplanes are seldom exactly on course. Human and automatic pilots are always checking positions and making corrections. The resulting flight path looks like a zigzag. The plane is almost always flying in the wrong direction, but because of constant observation and course correction, it arrives at the right destination.

A similar system can be used by students. Most Journal Entries throughout this book are labeled as either Discovery Statements or Intention Statements—some are Discovery/Intention Statements. Each Journal Entry will contain a short set of suggestions that involve writing.

Through Discovery Statements, you can assess "where you are." These statements are a record of what you are learning about yourself as a student—both strengths and weaknesses. Discovery Statements can also be declarations of your goals, descriptions of your attitudes, statements of your feelings, transcripts of your thoughts, and chronicles of your behavior.

Sometimes Discovery Statements chronicle an "aha!" moment—a flash of insight that results when a new idea connects with your prior experiences, preferred styles of learning, or both. Perhaps a solution to a long-standing problem suddenly occurs to you, or a life-changing insight wells up from the deepest recesses of your mind. Don't let such moments disappear. Capture them in Discovery Statements.

Intention Statements can be used to alter your course. They are statements of your commitment to do a specific task or take a certain action. An intention arises out of your choice to direct your energy toward a particular goal. While Discovery Statements promote awareness, Intention Statements are blueprints for action. The two processes reinforce each other.

The purpose of this system is not to get you pumped up and excited to go out there and try harder. Rather, Discovery and Intention Statements are intended to help you focus on what you want to accomplish and how you plan to achieve your goals.

GOAL

→ Rewrite this book

Some books should be preserved in pristine condition. This isn't one of them.

Something happens when you interact with your book by writing in it. *Becoming a Master Student* is about learning, and learning is an active pursuit, not a passive one. When you make notes in the margin, you can hear yourself talking with the author. When you doodle and underline, you can see the author's ideas taking shape. You can even argue with the author and come up with your own theories and explanations. In all of these ways, you become a coauthor of this book. You rewrite it to make it yours.

While you're at it, you can create symbols or codes that will help when reviewing the text later on, such as "Q" for questions or exclamation points for important ideas. You can also circle words to look up in a dictionary.

Remember, if any idea in this book doesn't work for you, you can rewrite it. Change the exercises to fit your needs. Create a new technique by combining several others. Create a technique out of thin air!

Find something you agree or disagree with on this page and write a short note in the margin about it. Or draw a diagram. Better yet, do both. Let creativity be your guide. Have fun.

Begin rewriting now.

immediately. Do not be concerned. Stay with the cycle. Use Discovery Statements to get a clear view of your world and what you want out of it. Then use Intention Statements to direct your actions. When you notice progress, record it.

The following statement might strike you as improbable, but it is true: It often takes the same amount of energy to get what you want in school as it takes to get what you *don't* want. Sometimes getting what you don't want takes even more effort. An airplane burns the same amount of fuel flying away from its destination as it does flying toward it. It pays to stay on course.

You can use the Discovery and Intention Journal Entry system to stay on your own course and get what you want out of school. Consider the guidelines for Discovery and Intention Statements that follow, and then develop your own style. Once you get the hang of it, you might discover you can fly. ✖

The Journal Entry process is a cycle. First, you write Discovery Statements about where you are now and where you want to be. Next, you write Intention Statements about the specific steps you will take to get there. Then you follow up with Discovery Statements about whether you completed those steps and what you learned in the process, followed by more Intention Statements, and so on. Sometimes a statement will be long and detailed. Usually, it will be short—maybe just a line or two. With practice, the cycle will become automatic.

While Discovery Statements promote awareness, Intention Statements are blueprints for action. The two processes reinforce each other.

Don't panic when you fail to complete an intended task. Straying off course is normal. Simply make the necessary corrections. Miraculous progress might not come

voices

student

I found completing the Discovery and Intention Statements very rewarding. The questions were very thought provoking and often had me thinking long after I had written an answer.

—AMY GUY

The Discovery and Intention Statements have really helped me see things that I could possibly improve on or fix when needed.

—AUBREY YOUNG

Discovery and Intention Statement guidelines

Discovery Statements

1 Record the specifics about your thoughts, feelings, and behavior. Thoughts include inner voices. We talk to ourselves constantly in our heads. When internal chatter gets in the way, write down what you are telling yourself. If this seems difficult at first, just start writing. The act of writing can trigger a flood of thoughts.

Thoughts also include mental pictures. These are especially powerful. Picturing yourself flunking a test is like a rehearsal to do just that. One way to take away the power of negative images is to describe them in detail.

Also notice how you feel when you function well. Use Discovery Statements to pinpoint exactly where and when you learn most effectively.

In addition, observe your actions and record the facts. If you spent 90 minutes chatting online with a favorite cousin instead of reading your anatomy text, write about it and include the details, such as when you did it, where you did it, and how it felt. Record your observations quickly, as soon as you make them.

2 Use discomfort as a signal. When you approach a daunting task, such as a difficult accounting problem, notice your physical sensations—a churning stomach, perhaps, or shallow breathing or yawning. Feeling uncomfortable, bored, or tired might be a signal that you're about to do valuable work. Stick with it. Tell yourself you can handle the discomfort just a little bit longer. You will be rewarded.

You can experience those rewards at any time. Just think of a problem that poses the biggest potential barrier to your success in school. Choose a problem that you face right now, today. (Hint: It might be the thing that's distracting you from reading this article.) If you have a lot of emotion tied up in this problem, that's even better. Write a Discovery Statement about it.

3 Suspend judgment. When you are discovering yourself, be gentle. Suspend self-judgment. If you continually judge your behaviors as "bad" or "stupid" or "galactically imbecilic," sooner or later your mind will revolt. Rather than put up with the abuse, it will quit making discoveries. For your own benefit, be kind.

4 Tell the truth. Suspending judgment helps you tell the truth about yourself. "The truth will set you free" is a saying that endures for a reason. The closer you get to the truth, the more powerful your Discovery Statements will be. And if you notice that you are avoiding the truth, don't blame yourself. Just tell the truth about it.

Intention Statements

1 Make intentions positive. The purpose of writing intentions is to focus on what you want rather than what you don't want. Instead of writing "I will not fall asleep while studying accounting," write "I intend to stay awake when studying accounting."

Also avoid the word *try*. Trying is not doing. When we hedge our bets with *try*, we can always tell ourselves, "Well, I *tried* to stay awake." We end up fooling ourselves into thinking we succeeded.

2 Make intentions observable. Experiment with an idea from educational trainer Robert Mager, who suggests that goals be defined through behaviors that can be observed and measured.[2] Rather than writing "I intend to work harder on my history assignments," write "I intend to review my class notes, and I intend to make summary sheets of my reading." Then, when you review your progress, you can determine more precisely whether you have accomplished what you intended.

3 Make intentions small and keepable. Give yourself opportunities to succeed by setting goals you can meet. Break large goals into small, specific tasks that can be accomplished quickly. If you want to get an A in biology, ask yourself, What can I do today? You might choose to study biology for an extra hour. Make that your intention.

When setting your goals, anticipate self-sabotage. Be aware of what you might do, consciously or unconsciously, to undermine your best intentions. If you intend to study differential equations at 9 p.m., notice when you sit down to watch a two-hour movie that starts at 8 p.m.

Also, be careful of intentions that depend on others. If you write that you intend for your study group to complete an assignment by Monday, then your success depends on the other students in the group.

4 Set timelines that include rewards. Timelines can focus your attention. For example, if you are assigned to write a paper, break the assignment into small tasks and set a precise due date for each one. You might write "I intend to select a topic for my paper by 9 a.m. Wednesday."

Timelines are especially useful when your intention is to experiment with a technique suggested in this book. The sooner you act on a new idea, the better. Consider practicing a new behavior within four hours after you first learn about it.

Remember that you create timelines for your own benefit, not to set yourself up to feel guilty. And you can always change the timeline.

When you meet your goal on time, reward yourself. Rewards that are an integral part of a goal are powerful. For example, your reward for earning a degree might be the career you've always dreamed of. External rewards, such as a movie or an afternoon in the park, are valuable, too. These rewards work best when you're willing to withhold them. If you plan to take a nap on Sunday afternoon whether or not you've finished your English assignment, the nap is not an effective reward.

Another way to reward yourself is to sit quietly after you have finished your task and savor the feeling. One reason why success breeds success is that it feels good. ◪

journal entry 1

Discovery Statement

Welcome to the first Journal Entry in this book. You'll find Journal Entries in every chapter, all with a similar design that allow space for you to write.

In the space below, write a description of a time in your life when you learned or did something well. This experience does not need to be related to school. Describe the details of the situation, including the place, time, and people involved. Describe how you felt about it, how it looked to you, how it sounded. Describe the physical sensations you associate with the event. Also describe your emotions.

I discovered that . . .

_____

_____

_____

_____

_____

_____

_____

_____

_____

_____

_____

_____

You share one thing in common with other students at your vocational school, college, or university: Entering higher education represents a major change in your life. You've joined a new culture with its own set of rules, both spoken and unspoken.

Making the transition to higher education

Whether they've just graduated from high school or have been out of the classroom for decades, students new to higher education immediately face many differences between secondary and post-secondary education. The sooner you understand such differences, the sooner you can deal with them. Some examples include:

- *New academic standards.* Often there are fewer tests in higher education than in high school, and the grading might be tougher. You'll probably find that teachers expect you to study more than you did in high school. At the same time, your instructors might give you less guidance about what or how to study, and less feedback about how you are doing.

- *Differences in teaching styles.* Instructors at colleges, universities, and vocational schools are often steeped in their subject matter. Many did not take courses on how to teach and might not be as interesting as some of your high school teachers. And some professors might seem more focused on research than on teaching.

- *A larger playing field.* The institution you've just joined might seem immense, impersonal, and even frightening. The sheer size of the campus, the variety of courses offered, the large number of departments—all of these can add up to a confusing array of options.

- *More students and more diversity.* The school you're attending right now might enroll hundreds or thousands more students than your high school. And the range of diversity among these students might surprise you.

There's an opportunity that comes with all of these changes: a greater degree of freedom. Higher education presents you with a new world of choices. You are now responsible for deciding what classes to take, how to structure your time, and with whom to associate. Perhaps more than ever before, you'll find that your education is your own creation. When making decisions that lead to the future of your dreams, keep the following in mind.

Decrease the unknowns. Before classes begin, get a map of the school property and walk through your first day's schedule, perhaps with a classmate or friend. Visit your instructors in their offices and introduce yourself. Anything you can do to get familiar with the new routine will help.

Admit your feelings—whatever they are. School can be an intimidating experience for new students. People of diverse cultures, adult learners, commuters, and people with disabilities can feel excluded. Anyone can feel anxious, isolated, homesick, or worried about doing well academically.

Those emotions are common among new students, and there's nothing wrong with them. Simply admitting the truth about how you feel—to yourself and to someone else—can help you cope. And you can almost always do something constructive, no matter how you feel.

If your feelings about this transition make it hard for you to carry out the activities of daily life—going to class, working, studying, and relating to people—then get professional help. Start with a counselor at the student health service on your campus. The mere act of seeking help can make a difference.

Access resources. A supercharger increases the air supply to an internal combustion engine. The resulting difference in power can be dramatic. You can make just as powerful a difference in your education by using all of the resources available to students. In this case, your "air supply" includes people, campus clubs and organizations, and school and community services.

Of all resources, people are the most important. You can isolate yourself, study hard, and get a good education. When you make the effort to establish relationships with teachers, staff members, fellow students, and employers, you can get a *great* education.

Meet with your academic advisor. One person in particular can help you access resources and make the transition to higher education—your academic advisor. Meet with this person regularly. Advisors generally have a big picture of course requirements, options for declaring majors, and the resources available at your school. Peer advisory programs might also be available.

When you work with an advisor, remember that you're a paying customer and have a right to be satisfied with the service you get. Don't be afraid to change advisors when that seems appropriate.

Learn the language of higher education. Terms such as *grade point average (GPA), prerequisite, accreditation, matriculation, tenure,* and *syllabus* might be new to you. Ease your transition to higher education by checking your school catalog for definitions of these words and others that you don't understand. Also ask your academic advisor for clarification.

Perhaps more than ever before, you'll find that your education is your own creation.

Attend class. In higher education, teachers generally don't take attendance. Yet you'll find that attending class is essential to your success. The amount that you pay in tuition and fees makes a powerful argument for going to classes regularly and getting your money's worth. In large part, the material that you're tested on comes from events that take place in class.

"Showing up" for class occurs on two levels. The most visible level is being physically present in the classroom. Even more important is showing up mentally. This includes taking detailed notes, asking questions, and contributing to class discussions.

Don't assume that you already know how to study. You can cope with increased workloads and higher academic expectations by putting all of your study habits on the table and evaluating them. Keep the habits that serve you, drop those that hold you back, and adopt new ones to promote your success. On every page of this book, you'll find helpful suggestions.

Become a self-regulated learner. Psychologists use the term *self-regulation* to describe people who set specific goals, monitor their progress toward those goals, and regularly change their behavior to produce the desired results. These people have a clear idea of their objectives and their capabilities.

Becoming a Master Student promotes self-regulation through the ongoing cycle of discovery, intention, and action. Write Discovery Statements to monitor yourself and evaluate the results you're currently creating in life. Create Intention Statements to determine exactly what you want. And use the exercises throughout the book to experience the power of putting your ideas into practice.

Take the initiative in meeting new people. Promise yourself to meet one new person each week, then write an Intention Statement describing specific ways to do this. Introduce yourself to classmates. Just before or after class is a good time to do so. Realize that most of the people in this new world of higher education are waiting to be welcomed. You can help them and help yourself at the same time. ⊠

For more strategies on mastering the art of transition, visit the Master Student Web site at

masterstudent.college.hmco.com

If you're returning to school after a long break from the classroom, there's no reason to feel out of place. Returning adults and other nontraditional students are already a majority in some schools.

The art of re-entry
Going back to school as an adult learner

Being an adult learner puts you on strong footing. With a rich store of life experience on which to draw, you can ask meaningful questions and more easily make connections between course work and daily life. Many instructors will especially enjoy working with you.

Following are some suggestions for returning adult students. Even if you don't fit into this category, you can look for ways to apply these ideas.

Ease into it. If you're new to higher education, consider easing into it. You can choose to attend school part-time before making a full-time commitment.

Plan your week. Many adult learners report that their number one problem is time. One solution is to plan your week. By planning ahead a week at a time, you get a bigger picture of your multiple roles as a student, an employee, and a family member. For more suggestions on managing time, see Chapter Two: Planning.

Add 15 minutes to your day. If you're pressed for time, plan to get up 15 minutes earlier or stay up 15 minutes later. Chances are, the lost sleep won't affect your alertness during the day. You can use the extra time to scan a reading assignment or outline a paper. Stretching each day by just 15 minutes yields 91 extra hours in a year. That's time you can use to promote your success in school.

Delegate tasks. Consider hiring others to do some of your household work or errands. Yes, this costs money.

It's also an investment in your education and future earning power.

If you have children, delegate some of the chores to them. Or start a meal co-op in your neighborhood. Cook dinner for yourself and someone else one night each week. In return, ask that person to furnish you with a meal on another night. A similar strategy can apply to childcare and other household tasks.

Get to know younger students. You share a central goal with younger students: succeeding in school. It's easier to get past the generation gap when you remember this. Consider pooling resources with younger students. Share notes, form study groups, or edit each other's term papers.

Get to know other returning students. Introduce yourself to other adult learners. Being in the same classroom gives you an immediate bond. You can exchange work, home, or cell phone numbers and build a network of mutual support. Some students adopt a buddy system, pairing up with another student in each class to complete assignments and prepare for tests.

Find common ground with instructors. Many of your teachers might be juggling academic careers, work schedules, and family lives, too. Finding common ground gives you one more way to break the ice with instructors.

Enlist your employer's support. Employers often promote continuing education. Further education can increase your skills in a specific field while enhancing your ability to work with people. That makes you a more valuable employee or consultant.

Let your employer in on your educational plans. Point out how the skills you gain in class will help you meet work objectives. Offer informal "seminars" at work to share what you're learning in school.

Get extra mileage out of your current tasks. You can look for specific ways to merge your work and school lives. Some schools will offer academic credit for work and life experience. Your company might reimburse its employees for some tuition costs or even grant time off to attend classes.

Experiment with combining tasks. For example, when you're assigned a research paper, choose a topic that relates to your current job tasks.

Look for childcare. For some students, returning to class means looking for childcare outside the home. Many schools offer childcare facilities at reduced rates for students.

Review your subjects before you start classes. Say that you're registered for trigonometry and you haven't taken a math class since high school. Consider brushing up on the subject before classes begin. Also talk with future instructors about ways to prepare for their classes.

Prepare for an academic environment. If you're used to an efficient corporate setting, school life might present some frustrations. A lack of advanced computer systems might slow down your class registration. Faculty members might take a little longer to return your calls or respond to letters, especially during holiday and summer breaks. Knowing the rhythm of academic life can help you plan around these possibilities.

Be willing to adopt new study habits. Rather than returning to study habits from previous school experiences, many adult learners find it more effective to treat their school assignments exactly as they would treat a project at work. They use the same tactics in the library as they do on the job, which often helps them learn more actively.

Integrate class work with daily experiences. According to psychologist Malcolm Knowles, adult learners in particular look for ways to connect classroom experience with the rest of their life.[3] This approach can promote success in school for students of any age. You can start by remembering two words: *why* and *how*. *Why* prompts you to look for a purpose and benefit in what you're learning.

> *The theory of self-actualization could clarify your goals and help you get the most out of school.*

Say that your psychology teacher lectures about Abraham Maslow's ideas on the hierarchy of human needs. Maslow stated that the need for self-actualization is just as important as the need for safety, security, or love.[4]

As you learn what Maslow meant by *self-actualization,* ask yourself why this concept would make a difference in your life. Perhaps your reason for entering higher education is connected to your own quest for self-actualization, that is, for maximizing your fulfillment in life and living up to your highest potential. The theory of self-actualization could clarify your goals and help you get the most out of school.

How means looking for immediate application. Invent ways to use and test concepts in your daily life—the sooner, the better. For example, how could you restructure your life for greater self-actualization? What would you do differently on a daily basis? What would you have that you don't have now? And how would you be different in your moment-to-moment relationships with people?

"Publish" your schedule. After you plan your study and class sessions for the week, hang your schedule in a place where others who live with you will see it. You could make it look like an "official" document. Laminate a daily calendar, fill in your schedule with a magic marker, and post this in a high-traffic area in your house. Designate open slots in your schedule where others can sign up for "appointments" to see you. If you use an on-line calendar, print out copies to put in your school binder or on your refrigerator door, bathroom mirror, or kitchen cupboard.

Share your educational plans. The fact that you're in school will affect the key relationships in your life. Attending classes and doing homework will mean less time to spend with others. You can prepare family members and help prevent problems by discussing these issues ahead of time. You can also involve your spouse, partner, children, or close friends actively in your schooling. Offer to give them a tour of the campus, introduce them to your instructors and classmates, and encourage them to attend social events at school with you.

Take this a step further and ask the key people in your life for help. Ask them to think of ways that they can support your success in school and to commit to those actions. Make your own education a joint mission that benefits everyone. ✖

More resources are available for adult learners on the *Becoming a Master Student* web site at

mastersstudent.college.hmco.com

Connect to school resources

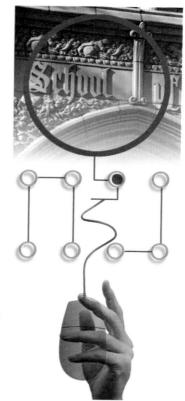

When you entered higher education, you also signed up for a world of student services. Any of them can help you succeed in school. Many of them are free. Following are a few examples of school resources. Check your school catalog, newspaper, and Web site for the specific resources available to you. Your school fees pay for them. Now use them.

Academic advisors can help you with selecting courses, choosing majors, planning your career, and adjusting in general to the culture of higher education.

Alumni organizations aren't just for graduates. Alumni publications and alumni themselves can be good sources of information about the benefits and potential pitfalls of being a student at your school.

Arts resources can include museums, galleries, special libraries, and music and film recording and editing equipment. Music practice rooms are often available to nonmusic students.

Athletic centers and *gymnasiums* often open weight rooms, swimming pools, indoor tracks, basketball courts, and racquet-sport courts to all students.

Car-pooling maps provide information on getting across town or across the country. Connect with a car pool, and you might discover new study group partners or lifelong friends.

Chapels are usually open to students of any religion. They are quiet places to pray or meditate in peace.

Childcare is sometimes made available to students at a reasonable cost through the early childhood education department.

Computer labs where students can go 24 hours a day to work on projects and access the Internet are usually free. Instruction on computer use might also be offered.

Counseling centers help students deal with the emotional pressures of school life, usually for free or at low cost. If you need help that is not available on campus, ask for a referral to an appropriate agency off campus.

The *financial aid office* assists students with loans, scholarships, and grants. To find ways to finance your education, visit this office.

Job placement offices can help you find part-time employment while you are in school and a job after you graduate.

The *registrar* handles information about transcripts, grades, changing majors, transferring credits, and dropping or adding classes. You'll probably contact this office after you graduate when employers or other schools ask to receive transcripts of your courses and grades.

The *school catalog* lists course descriptions and tuition fees, requirements for graduation, and information on everything from the school's history to its grading practices.

The *school newspaper* provides information about activities, services, and policies. You can advertise in it for a job, a roommate, or a ride to Dubuque. Larger schools also might have their own radio and television stations.

School security agencies can tell you what's safe and what's not. They can also provide information about parking, bicycle regulations, and traffic rules. Some offer safe escorts at night for female students.

Student government can help you develop skills in leadership and teamwork. If you have experience with student government, many employers will take notice.

Student health clinics often provide free or inexpensive treatment for minor problems. Many offer information about alcohol and drug abuse and addiction.

Student organizations present an opportunity to explore fraternities, sororities, service clubs, veterans' organizations, religious groups, sports clubs, political groups, and programs for special populations. The last includes women's centers, multicultural student centers, and organizations for international students, disabled students, and gay and lesbian students.

Student unions are hubs for social activities, special programs, and free entertainment. Clubs and organizations often meet there, too.

Tutoring can help, even if you think you are hopelessly stuck in a course. It is usually free and is available through academic departments or counseling centers.

Resources such as the following often go unused—even when people pay taxes to fund them. You can demonstrate an alternative. Taking advantage of community resources and letting others know about them is an act of service.

Arts organizations allow you to attend a play, see an independent film, hear live jazz, visit an art gallery, or groove on a poetry jam. Explore local museums, concert venues, clubs, and stadiums.

Chambers of commerce provide information about local attractions, organizations, clubs, and businesses. Larger chambers of commerce have committees that deal with specific issues such the environment or economic development.

Childcare is provided by both public and private organizations. Some charge for childcare on a sliding scale, based on income.

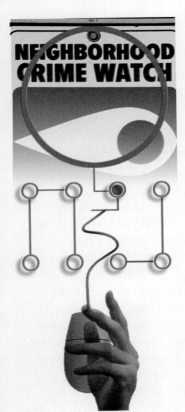

Churches, synagogues, mosques, and temples have members happy to welcome fellow worshippers who are away from home.

Community education classes are usually offered by local school districts. Use them to learn about anything from tax planning to ballroom dancing.

Consumer credit counseling can help even if you've really blown your budget. And it's usually free. Remember, no matter how bad your financial picture, you are probably in better shape than most governments.

Counseling centers in the community can assist you with a problem when you can't get help at school. Look for job and career planning services, rehabilitation offices, veterans' outreach programs, church and social service agencies, and mental health clinics.

Governments (city, county, state, and federal) often have programs for students. Check the government listings in your local telephone directory.

Health care centers provide inexpensive birth control, gynecological exams, disease diagnosis and treatment, and vaccinations.

Hot lines can save your life during a crisis. Professionals or trained volunteers are often available for help 24 hours a day, whether the situation involves physical abuse, AIDS, rape, potential suicide, or another emergency.

Legal aid services provide free or inexpensive assistance to low-income people.

Libraries are a treasure in any community. Even small libraries can have access to the Internet, and most employ people who are happy to help you locate information.

Local newspapers list community events and services that are free or inexpensive. Reading a local newspaper also helps you get a feel for a new city.

Money is sometimes available in a real emergency from the Salvation Army, the Red Cross, local churches, or a county relief agency. Be prepared to document the exact nature of your need.

Political parties always want volunteers. Working for a candidate you believe in is one way to learn organizational skills, meet people, and make a difference in the world.

Public transportation, such as a bus, train, trolley, subway, or an occasional horse-drawn carriage, offers money-saving alternatives to owning a car.

Recreation departments of the city or county, YWCAs, YMCAs, and other organizations provide free or inexpensive ways to exercise and have fun.

Specialty clubs and organizations promote everything from public speaking (Toastmasters) to conservation (the Sierra Club).

Support groups exist for people with almost any problem, from drug addiction to cancer. You can find people with problems who meet every week to share suggestions, information, and concerns. Some examples are groups for single parents, newly widowed people, alcoholics or drug addicts, breast cancer survivors, and parents who have lost a child. ⊠

Connect to community resources

Extracurricular activities
Reap the benefits

Many students in higher education are busier than they've ever been before. Often that's due to the variety of extracurricular activities available to them: athletics, fraternities, sororities, student newspapers, debate teams, study groups, political action groups, and many more.

With this kind of involvement come potential benefits. People involved in extracurricular activities are often excellent students. Such activities help them bridge the worlds inside and outside the classroom. Through student organizations they develop new skills, explore possible careers, build contacts for jobs, and add experiences to their résumés. They make new friends among both students and faculty, work with people from other cultures, and sharpen their skills at conflict resolution.

Involvement in campus activities can ease the transition to higher education.

Getting involved in such organizations comes with some risks as well. When students don't balance extracurricular activities with class work, their success in school can suffer. They can also compromise their health by losing sleep, neglecting exercise, skipping meals, or relying on fast food. These costs are easier to avoid if you keep a few suggestions in mind:

- *Make conscious choices* about how to divide your time between schoolwork and extracurricular activities. Decide up front how many hours each week or month you can devote to a student organization. Leave room in your schedule for relaxing and for unplanned events.

- *Look to the future* when making commitments. Write down three or four of the most important goals you'd like to achieve in your lifetime. Then choose extracurricular activities that directly support those goals.

- *Recognize reluctance* to follow through on a commitment. You might agree to attend meetings and find yourself forgetting them or consistently showing up late. If that happens, write a Discovery Statement about the way you're using time. Follow that with an Intention Statement about ways to keep your agreements—or consider renegotiating your agreements.

- *Say no* to activities that fail to create value for you. Avoid joining groups only because you feel guilty or obligated to do so.

- *Check out the rules* before joining any student organization. Ask about dues and attendance requirements.

- *Do a trial run* by attending one or two meetings of an organization. Explain that you want to find out what the group is about before making a commitment.

- *Learn new skills* in managing your time. Many students reap the benefits of extracurricular activities while staying on course with their academic workload. Chapter Two is teeming with ideas. ▨

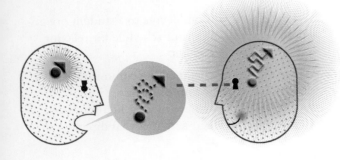

Following instructions

Think for a moment about the importance of instructions. Teachers give instructions. Managers and supervisors give instructions. Architects give instructions for making buildings, and playwrights give instructions for staging a play. Lawyers and accountants, coaches and therapists, parents and priests—all give instructions. Even friends and lovers give each other instructions on how they want to be treated. You could argue, as author Richard Saul Wurman does, that "the motivation of all communication is the giving and receiving of instructions."[5] Many students assume that they're experts in following instructions. Soon after entering higher education, they discover that this assumption is misguided. Following instructions is often far more complicated than it appears. And the costs of misunderstanding instructions can range from missing a few points on a test to missing out on acceptance from the university where you want to transfer.

The steps below can help you follow directions successfully.

Prepare to follow instructions. Begin by gathering all relevant materials. When filling out an application for financial aid, for example, you might need detailed income and expense records along with last year's income tax return. If the directions are written, read slowly. If the directions are verbal, listen carefully. One quick way to focus your attention is to remind yourself that following instructions usually helps you get something you want.

Distinguish between outcomes and tasks. At work, your supervisor might ask you to increase sales of a certain product by 20 percent. Her statement of a desired outcome might be the sum total of her instruction. Or she might give you a detailed list of tasks designed to *produce* that 20 percent increase.

These two scenarios pose quite different implications for you as an instruction follower. When your focus is on the outcome, you might have the freedom to choose from several different paths to achieve that result. If your instruction is to follow a sequence of tasks, you might have less flexibility. Skilled instruction followers look for this difference and clarify what's expected before they move into action.

Distinguish between sequential instructions and lists of options. In many cases, you'll benefit by seeing instructions as a series of steps to perform in a certain order. These are called sequential instructions, and they often apply to tasks such as following a recipe, assembling furniture, or troubleshooting a computer problem.

In other cases, instructions consist of a list of options that you can apply in almost any order. *Becoming a Master Student* frequently gives this kind of instruction. Teachers can assign chapters, journal entries, and exercises in a number of different sequences. And when reading an article such as this one, you can choose one suggestion to apply now and come back for more later. The suggestion you start with does not have to appear first in the list.

Make sure that you understand all of the instructions. Take notes on the directions, or, if written, highlight key points. Reread for clarification. If the directions are numerous or complex, make a checklist to ensure that you don't miss a step. Ask questions when you are unsure about what to do. Anticipate possible problems and plan what you'll do to solve them.

On the other hand, don't make instructions any harder than they need to be. When following instructions, estimate the time you'll take to complete a task. If a one-hour project starts looking like a full day's enterprise, it's time to adjust your estimate—or review the instructions and weed out unnecessary steps.

Look for instructions everywhere. Use the above suggestions to boost your opportunities in everything from petitioning a closed class to getting the grade you want on a final exam. Remember that these suggestions can also be used outside of school. Job applications, loan applications, and contracts all come with instructions. As you master the art of following instructions, you maximize your chances for success in every area of life. ✖

Link to the world of work

The suggestions in this book can help you succeed both inside and outside the classroom. Apply the techniques you gain from this course to any learning situation you encounter, whether at home, at school, or at work.

Staying current in the job market means continually expanding your knowledge and skills. You might change careers several times during your working life—a possibility that calls for continuous learning. As a master student, you can gain favor with employers by getting up to speed quickly on new jobs and new projects.

Starting now, read this book with a mental filter in place. Ask yourself: How can I use this idea to meet my career goals? How can I apply this technique to my current job or the next job I see for myself? The answers can help you thrive in any job, whether you work full- or part-time. To stimulate your thinking, look for the Put It to Work article located in each chapter. In addition, invent techniques of your own based on what you read and test them at work. There's no limit to the possibilities.

For example, you can use the Discovery and Intention Journal Entry system while you're in the work force. Write Discovery Statements to note your current job skills as well as areas for improvement. Also use Discovery Statements to describe what you want from your career.

Follow up with Intention Statements that detail specifically what you want to be doing one year, five years, and ten years or more from today. Write additional Intention Statements about specific actions you can take right now to meet those career goals.

Below is a textbook reconnaissance that lists articles in this book with workplace applications. These are just a few examples. As you read, look for more.

- The skills you learn as you are *making the transition to higher education* (page 9) can help you make the transition to a new job. For example, you can decrease unknowns by working for a company on a temporary, part-time, or contract basis. These positions can lead to an offer of full-time employment. If that happens, you'll already know a lot about the company.

- The article *25 ways to get the most out of now* (page 80) is packed with ideas you can transfer to the workplace. For example, tackle difficult tasks first in the day, or at any other time when your energy peaks. Also find five-minute tasks that you can complete while waiting for a meeting to start.

- The article *20 memory techniques* (page 112) will come in handy as you learn the policies and procedures for a new job.

- Techniques presented in *Remembering names* (page 121) can help as you meet people during your job search and as you are being introduced to new coworkers.

- Use *Muscle Reading* (page 135) to keep up with journals and books in your field. This set of techniques can also help you

scan Web sites for the information you want, keep up with ever increasing volumes of e-mail, and reduce mountains of interoffice memos to manageable proportions.

- The article *Record* (page 163) explains different formats for taking notes—mind maps, concept maps, the Cornell format, and more. These are tools you can use to document what happens at work-related meetings.

- Adapt the ideas mentioned in *Cooperative learning—studying with people* (page 191) in order to cooperate more effectively with members of a project team.

- Use the thinking skills presented in *Gaining skill at decision making* (page 230) when it comes time to choose a career, weigh job offers, or make work-related decisions.

- Ideas from *The fine art of conflict management* (page 254) can help you defuse tensions among coworkers.

- The suggestions in *Communicating across cultures* (page 284) can assist you in adapting to the culture of a new job. Each company, large or small, develops its own culture—a set of shared values and basic assumptions. Even if you are self-employed, you can benefit by discovering and adapting to a client's corporate culture.

Ways to change a habit

  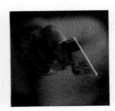

Consider a new way to think about the word *habit*. Imagine for a moment that many of our most troublesome problems and even our most basic traits are just habits.

That expanding waistline that is being blamed on a spouse's cooking—maybe that's just a habit called overeating.

That fit of rage that a student blames on a teacher—maybe that's just the student's habit of closing the door to new ideas.

Procrastination, stress, and money shortages might just be names that we give to collections of habits—scores of simple, small, repeated behaviors that combine to create a huge result. The same goes for health, wealth, love, and many of the other things that we want from life.

One way of thinking about success is to focus on habits. Behaviors such as failing to complete reading assignments or skipping class might be habits leading to an outcome that "couldn't" be avoided—dropping out of school.

When you confront a behavior that undermines your goals or creates a circumstance that you don't want, consider a new attitude: It's just a habit. And it can be changed.

Thinking about ourselves as creatures of habit actually gives us power. Then we are not faced with the monumental task of changing our very nature. Rather, we can take on the doable job of changing our habits. One change in behavior that seems insignificant at first can have effects that ripple throughout your life.

After interviewing hundreds of people, psychologists James Prochaska, John Norcross, and Carlo DiClemente identified stages that people typically go through when adopting a new behavior.[6] These stages take people from *contemplating* a change and making a clear *determination* to change to taking *action* and *maintaining* the new behavior. Following are ways to help yourself move successfully through each stage.

Tell the truth

Telling the truth about any habit—from chewing our fingernails to cheating on tests—frees us. Without taking this step, our efforts to change might be as ineffective as rearranging the deck chairs on the *Titanic*. Telling the truth allows us to see what's actually sinking the ship.

When we admit what's really going on in our lives, our defenses are down. We're open to accepting help from others. The support we need to change the habit has an opportunity to make an impact.

Choose and commit to a new behavior

It often helps to choose a new habit to replace an old one. First, make a commitment to practice the new habit. Tell key people in your life about your decision to change. Set up a plan for when and how. Answer questions such as these: When will I apply the new habit? Where will I be? Who will be with me? What will I be seeing, hearing, touching, saying, or doing? Exactly how will I think, speak, or act differently?

Take the student who always snacks when he studies. Each time he sits down to read, he positions a bag of potato chips within easy reach. For him, opening a book is a cue to start chewing. Snacking is especially easy, given the place he chooses to study: the kitchen. He decides to change this habit by studying at a desk in his bedroom instead of at the kitchen table. And every time he feels the urge to bite into a potato chip, he drinks from a glass of water instead.

Affirm your intention

You can pave the way for a new behavior by clearing a mental path for it. Before you apply the new behavior, rehearse it in your mind. Mentally picture what actions you will take and in what order.

Say that you plan to improve your handwriting when taking notes. Imagine yourself in class with a blank notebook poised before you. See yourself taking up a finely crafted pen. Notice how comfortable it feels in your hand. See yourself writing clearly and legibly. You can even picture how you will make individual letters—the *e*'s, *i*'s, and *r*'s. Then, when class is over, see yourself reviewing your notes and taking pleasure in how easy they are to read.

Such scenes are more vivid if you include all of your senses. Round out your mental picture by adding sounds, textures, and colors.

You can act as if your intention is already a reality, as if the new habit is already a part of you. Be the change you want to see—today. In some cases, this might be enough to change the old habit completely.

Start with a small change

You can sometimes rearrange a whole pattern of behaviors by changing one small habit. If you have a habit of always being late for class, and if you want to change that habit, then be on time for one class. As soon as you change the old pattern by getting ready and going on time to one class, you'll likely find yourself arriving at all of your classes on time. You might even start arriving everywhere else on time.

If you know that you are usually nervous, you don't have to change how you react in all situations at all times. Just change your nervous behavior in one setting. Like magic, watch the rest of your nervousness lessen or even disappear. The joy of this process is watching one small change of habit ripple through your whole life.

Get feedback and support

This is a crucial step and a point at which many plans for change break down. It's easy to practice your new behavior with great enthusiasm for a few days. After the initial rush of excitement, however, things can get a little tougher. We begin to find excuses for slipping back into old habits: "One more cigarette won't hurt." "I can get back to my diet tomorrow." "It's been a tough day. I deserve this beer."

One way to get feedback is to bring other people into the picture. Ask others to remind you that you are chang-

ing your habit. If you want to stop an old behavior, such as cramming for tests, then it often works to tell everyone you know that you intend to stop. When you want to start a new behavior, though, consider telling only a few people—those who truly support your efforts. Starting new habits might call for the more focused, long-lasting support that close friends or family members can give.

Support from others can be as simple as a quick phone call: "Hi. Have you started that outline for your research paper yet?" Or it can be as formal as a support group that meets once weekly to review everyone's goals and action plans.

You are probably the most effective source for your own support and feedback. You know yourself better than anyone else does and can design a system to monitor your behavior. You can create your own charts or diagrams to track your behavior or you can write about your progress in your journal. Figure out a way to monitor your progress.

Practice, practice, practice—without self-judgment

Psychologists such as B. F. Skinner define learning as a stable change in behavior that comes as a result of practice.[7] This idea is key to changing habits. Act on your intention. If you fail or forget, let go of any self-judgment. Just keep practicing the new habit and allow whatever time it takes to make a change.

Accept the feelings of discomfort that might come with a new habit. Keep practicing the new behavior, even if it feels unnatural. Trust the process. You will grow into the new behavior. Keep practicing until it becomes as natural as breathing. However, if this new habit doesn't work, simply note what happened (without guilt or blame), select a new behavior, and begin this cycle of steps over again.

Making mistakes as you practice doesn't mean that you've failed. Even when you don't get the results you want from a new behavior, you learn something valuable in the process. Once you understand ways to change one habit, you understand ways to change almost any habit.

journal entry 2

Discovery Statement

Success is a choice—your choice. To *get* what you want, it helps to *know* what you want. That is the purpose of this Journal Entry, which has two parts.

You can begin choosing success right now by setting a date, time, and place to complete this Journal Entry. Write your choices here, then block out the time on your calendar.

Date: _____

Time: _____

Place: _____

Part 1

Select a time and place when you know you will not be disturbed for at least 20 minutes. (The library is a good place to do this.) Relax for two or three minutes, clearing your mind. Next, complete the following sentences—and then keep writing.

When you run out of things to write, stick with it just a bit longer. Be willing to experience a little discomfort. Keep writing. What you discover might be well worth the extra effort.

What I want from my education is . . .

_____

_____

_____

When I complete my education, I want to be able to . . .

_____

_____

_____

I also want . . .

_____

_____

_____

_____

Part 2

After completing Part 1, take a short break. Reward yourself by doing something that you enjoy. Then come back to this Journal Entry.

Now, review the above list of things that you want from your education. See if you can summarize them in a one-sentence, polished statement. This will become a statement of your purpose for taking part in higher education.

Allow yourself to write many drafts of this mission statement, and review it periodically as you continue your education. With each draft, see if you can capture the essence of what you want from higher education and from your life. State it in a vivid way—a short sentence that you can easily memorize, one that sparks your enthusiasm and makes you want to get up in the morning.

You might find it difficult to express your purpose statement in one sentence. If so, write a paragraph or more. Then look for the sentence that seems most charged with energy for you.

Following are some sample purpose statements:

- My purpose for being in school is to gain skills that I can use to contribute to others.

- My purpose for being in school is to live an abundant life that is filled with happiness, health, love, and wealth.

- My purpose for being in school is to enjoy myself by making lasting friendships and following the lead of my interests.

Write at least one draft of your purpose statement below:

_____

_____

_____

_____

_____

_____

_____

power process

Discover what you want

Imagine a person who walks up to a counter at the airport to buy a plane ticket for his next vacation. "Just give me a ticket," he says to the reservation agent. "Anywhere will do."

The agent stares back at him in disbelief. "I'm sorry, sir," he replies. "I'll need some more details. Just minor things—such as the name of your destination city and your arrival and departure dates."

"Oh, I'm not fussy," says the would-be vacationer. "I just want to get away. You choose for me."

Compare this with another traveler who walks up to the counter and says, "I'd like a ticket to Ixtapa, Mexico, departing on Saturday, March 23 and returning Sunday, April 7. Please give me a window seat, first class, with vegetarian meals."

Now, ask yourself which traveler is more likely to end up with a vacation that he'll enjoy.

The same principle applies in any area of life. Knowing where we want to go increases the probability that we will arrive at our destination. Discovering what we want makes it more likely that we'll attain it. Once our goals are defined precisely, our brains reorient our thinking and behavior to align with those goals—and we're well on the way there.

Mastery lies in the details

The example about the traveler with no destination seems far-fetched. Before you dismiss it, do an informal experiment: Ask three other students what they want to get out of their education. Be prepared for hemming and hawing, vague generalities, and maybe even a helping of pie-in-the-sky à la mode.

That's amazing, considering the stakes involved. Our hypothetical vacationer is about to invest a couple weeks of his time and hundreds of dollars—all with no destination in mind. Students routinely invest years of their lives and thousands of dollars with an equally hazy idea of their destination in life.

Suppose that you ask someone what she wants from her education and you get this answer: "I plan to get a degree in journalism with double minors in earth science and Portuguese so that I can work as a reporter covering the environment in Brazil." Chances are you've found a master student. The details of a person's vision offer a clue to mastery.

Discover the benefits

Discovering what you want greatly enhances your odds of succeeding in higher education. Many students quit school simply because they are unsure of their goals. With well-defined objectives in mind, you can constantly look for connections between what you want and what you study. The more connections you discover, the more likely you'll stay in school—and the more likely you'll benefit from higher education.

Having a clear idea of your goals makes many decisions easier. Knowing what you want from your education helps you choose the school you'll attend, the courses you'll take, the major you'll declare, and the next career you'll pursue.

Discovering what you want also enhances your study skills. An example is memorizing. A skydiver will not become bored learning how to pack her parachute. Her reward for learning the skill is too important. Likewise, when information helps you get something you want, it becomes easier to remember.

You can have more energy when your daily activities lead to what you want. If you're bogged down in quadratic equations, stand back for a minute. Think about how that math course ties in with your goal of becoming an electrical engineer, how your philosophy course relates to your aim of becoming a minister, or how your English course can help you become a better teacher.

Succeeding in higher education takes effort. When you follow the path of getting what you truly want, you can enjoy yourself even if the path is uphill. You can expend great energy and still feel fresh and eager to learn. When you take on courses that you care about and prepare for a career that you look forward to, you can play full out. You can work even to the point of exhaustion at times, and do it happily.

That's one purpose of discovering what you want. Your vision is not meant to be followed blindly—it's meant to pull you forward.

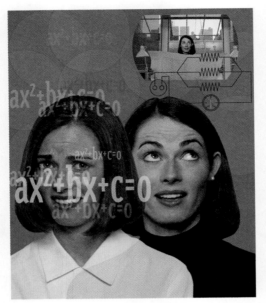

Perhaps you want to restore the integrity of the ozone layer or eliminate racism through international law. Or perhaps you simply want to be more physically fit, more funny, or more loving. Whatever you want, write it down.

Later, if you want, you can let go of some goals. First, though, live with them for a while. Goals that sound outlandish right now might seem more realistic in a few weeks, months, or years. Time often brings a more balanced perspective, along with an expanded sense of possibility.

Put it in writing

For maximum clarity, write down what you want. Goals that reside strictly in your head can remain fuzzy. Writing them down brings them into sharper focus.

As you write about what you want, expand your imagination to many different time frames. Define what you want to be, do, and have next week, next month, and next year. Write about what you want five years from now— and five minutes from now.

Approach this process with a sense of adventure and play. As you write, be willing to put any option on the table. List the most outrageous goals—those that sound too wonderful to ever come true.

You might want to travel to India, start a consulting business, or open a library in every disadvantaged neighborhood. Write those goals down.

You might want to own a ranch in a beautiful valley, become a painter, or visit all of the hot springs in the world. Write those down, too.

With well-defined objectives in mind, you can constantly look for connections between what you want and what you study.

Move from discovery to action

Discovering what you want can be heady fun. And it can quickly become an interesting but irrelevant exercise unless you take action to get what you want. Most discoveries come bundled with hints to *do* something—perhaps to change a habit, contact someone, travel, get educated, or acquire a new skill. Dreams that are not followed with action tend to die on paper. On the other hand, dreams that lead to new behaviors can lead to new results in your life.

To move into action, use this book. It's filled with places to state what you want to accomplish and how you intend to go about it. Every Journal Entry and exercise exists for this purpose. Fill up those pages. Take action and watch your dreams evolve from fuzzy ideals into working principles.

With your dreams and new behaviors in hand, you might find that events fall into place almost magically. Start telling people about what you want, and you'll eventually find some who are willing to help. They might offer an idea or two or suggest a person to call or an organization to contact. They might even offer their time or money. The sooner you discover what you want, the sooner you can create the conditions that transform your life.

Excerpts from *Creating Your Future*. Copyright © 1998 by David B. Ellis. Reprinted by permission of Houghton Mifflin Company. All rights reserved.

Name _____ Date _____/_____/_____

1. List three common differences between secondary and post-secondary education.

2. According to the text, one way to master the transition to higher education is to remind yourself that you already know how to study. True or False? Explain your answer.

3. Explain how you would respond differently to task-based compared to outcome-based instructions.

4. List two arguments for regularly attending classes in higher education.

5. Define the term *self-regulation*.

6. The purpose of the Discovery and Intention Journal Entry system is to increase the amount of effort you put into succeeding in higher education. True or False? Explain your answer.

7. Describe in your own words the necessary steps to complete a textbook reconnaissance.

8. List at least two benefits of discovering what you want from your education.

9. List five examples of community resources that could help you get the most from higher education.

10. The process of changing habits is effective only if you concentrate on making major changes in behavior. True or False? Explain your answer.

1

First Steps

You either change things or you don't. Excuses rob you of power and induce apathy.

AGNES WHISTLING ELK

In oneself lies the whole world, and if you know how to look and learn, then the door is there and the key is in your hand. Nobody on earth can give you either that key or the door to open, except yourself.

J. KRISHNAMURTI

why
this chapter matters. . .

Visible measures of success—such as top grades and résumés filled with accomplishments—start with invisible assets called attitudes.

what
is included. . .

First Step: Truth is a key to mastery
If you skipped the Introduction . . .
The Discovery Wheel
Learning styles: Discovering how you learn
Learning Style Inventory
Using your learning style profile to succeed in school
Claim your multiple intelligences
Learning by seeing, hearing, and moving: The VAK system
The Master Student
Motivation
Attitudes, affirmations, and visualizations
The value of higher education
Power Process: "Ideas are tools"
Master Student Profile: Suny Urrutia Moore

how
you can use this chapter. . .

Experience the power of telling the truth about your current skills.
Discover your preferred learning styles and develop new ones.
Consciously choose attitudes that promote your success.

As you read, ask yourself
what if. . .

I could create attitudes that would help me achieve my goals?

First Step: Truth is a key to mastery

The First Step technique is simple: Tell the truth about who you are and what you want. End of discussion. Now proceed to Chapter Two.

Well, it's not *quite* that simple.

The First Step is one of the most valuable tools in this book. It magnifies the power of all the other techniques. It is a key to becoming a master student. Unfortunately, a First Step is easier to explain than it is to use. Telling the truth sounds like pie-in-the-sky moralizing, but there is nothing pie-in-the-sky or moralizing about a First Step. It is a practical, down-to-earth way to change our behavior. No technique in this book has been field-tested more often or more successfully—or under tougher circumstances.

Success starts with telling the truth about what *is* working—and what *isn't*—in our lives right now. When we acknowledge our strengths, we gain an accurate picture of what we can accomplish. When we admit that we have a problem, we free up energy to find a solution. Ignoring the truth, on the other hand, can lead to problems that stick around for decades. The principle of telling the truth is applied universally by people who want to turn their lives around. For members of Alcoholics Anonymous, the First Step is acknowledging that they are powerless over alcohol. For people who join Weight Watchers, the First Step is admitting how much they weigh.

It's not easy to tell the truth about ourselves. And for some of us, it's even harder to recognize our strengths. Maybe we don't want to brag. Maybe we're attached to poor self-images. The reasons don't matter. The point is that using the First Step technique in *Becoming a Master Student* means telling the truth about our positive qualities, too.

Many of us approach a frank evaluation of ourselves about as enthusiastically as we'd anticipate an audit by the IRS. There is another way to think about self-evaluations. If we could see them as opportunities to solve problems and take charge of our lives, we might welcome them. Believe it or not, we can begin working with our list of weaknesses by celebrating them.

Consider the most accomplished, "together" people you know. If they were totally candid with you, you'd soon hear about their mistakes and regrets. The more successful people are, the more willing they are to look at their flaws.

It might seem natural to judge our own shortcomings and feel bad about them. Some people believe that such feelings are necessary in order to bring about change. Others think that a healthy dose of shame can turn

journal entry 3

Discovery/Intention Statement

Take five minutes to skim the Discovery Wheel exercise starting on page 28. Find one statement that describes a skill you already possess—a personal strength that will promote your success in school. Write that statement here:

_____

_____

_____

_____

_____

The Discovery Wheel might also prompt some thoughts about skills you want to acquire. Describe one of those skills by completing the following sentence:

I discovered that . . .

_____

_____

_____

_____

Now, skim the appropriate chapter in this book for at least three articles that could help you develop this skill. For example, if you want to take more effective notes, turn to Chapter Five. List the names of your chosen articles here and a time when you will read them in more detail.

I intend to . . .

_____

_____

_____

_____

negatives into positives. There is an alternative. We can discover a way to gain skill without feeling rotten about the past. By taking a First Step, we can change the way things *are* without having to be upset about the way things *have been*. We can learn to see shame or blame as excess baggage and just set it aside. It might also help to remember that weaknesses are often strengths taken to an extreme. The student who carefully revises her writing can make significant improvements in a term paper. If she hands in the paper late, though, her grade might suffer. Any success strategy carried too far can backfire. Whether written or verbal, First Steps are more powerful when they are specific. For example, if you want to improve your note-taking skills, you might write, "I am an awful note taker." It would be more effective to write, "I can't read 80 percent of the notes I took in Introduction to Psychology last week, and I have no idea what was important in that class." Be just as specific about what you plan to achieve. You might declare, "I want to take legible notes that help me predict what questions will be on the final exam."

Complete the exercises in this chapter, and your courage will be rewarded. The Discovery Wheel exercise and the rest of the activities in this book can help you tap resources you never knew you had. They're all First Steps—no kidding. It's just that simple. The truth has power. ⊠

Refresh

If you skipped the Introduction...

Some people think introductions have little to offer and are a waste of time. The Introduction to *Becoming a Master Student* is important. It suggests ways to get your money's worth out of this book— and out of your education.

Here are some of the informative articles that await you:

- Get the most out of this book
- The Discovery and Intention Journal Entry system
- Making the transition to higher education
- The art of re-entry: Going back to school as an adult learner
- Connect to school resources
- Connect to community resources
- Extracurricular activities: Reap the benefits
- Following instructions
- Link to the world of work
- Ways to change a habit
- Power Process: "Discover what you want"

Please go back and read the Introduction now. ⊠

voices

student

A personal interest in pursuing the unknown, digging deeper, and taking that one extra step makes the difference between an ordinary student and a master student. A master student has a desire to learn and absorb, and to find the essence that exists in the world around her. Every master student also knows that time is not limitless and that the quest for knowledge is retained in a lifetime.

—JENNIFER FAY

TAKING THE FIRST STEP

The purpose of this exercise is to give you a chance to discover and acknowledge your own strengths, as well as areas for improvement. For many students, this is the most difficult exercise in the book. To make the exercise worthwhile, do it with courage.

Some people suggest that looking at areas for improvement means focusing on personal weaknesses. They view it as a negative approach that runs counter to positive thinking. Well, perhaps. Positive thinking is a great technique. So is telling the truth, especially when we see the whole picture—the negative aspects as well as the positive ones.

If you admit that you can't add or subtract and that's the truth, then you have taken a strong, positive First Step toward learning basic math. On the other hand, if you say that you are a terrible math student and that's not the truth, then you are programming yourself to accept unnecessary failure.

The point is to tell the truth. This exercise is similar to the Discovery Statements that appear in every chapter. The difference is that in this case, for reasons of confidentiality, you won't write down your discoveries in the book.

Be brave. If you approach this exercise with courage, you are likely to disclose some things about yourself that you wouldn't want others to read. You might even write down some truths that could get you into trouble. Do this exercise on separate sheets of paper; then hide or destroy them. Protect your privacy.

To make this exercise work, follow these suggestions:

Be specific. It is not effective to write "I can improve my communication skills." Of course you can. Instead, write down precisely what you can *do* to improve your communication skills, for example, "I can spend more time really listening while the other person is talking, instead of thinking about what I'm going to say next."

Look beyond the classroom. What goes on outside of school often has the greatest impact on your ability to be an effective student.

Be courageous. This exercise is a waste of time if it is done half-heartedly. Be willing to take risks. You might open a door that reveals a part of yourself that you didn't want to admit was there. The power of this technique is that once you know what is there, you can do something about it.

Part 1

Time yourself, and for 10 minutes write as fast as you can, completing each of the following sentences at least 10 times with anything that comes to mind. If you get stuck, don't stop. Just write something—even if it seems crazy.

> I never succeed when I . . .
> I'm not very good at . . .
> Something I'd like to change about myself is . . .

Part 2

When you have completed the first part of the exercise, review what you have written, crossing off things that don't make any sense. The sentences that remain suggest possible goals for becoming a master student.

Part 3

Here's the tough part. Time yourself, and for 10 minutes write as fast as you can, completing the following sentences with anything that comes to mind. As in Part 1, complete each sentence at least 10 times. Just keep writing, even if it sounds silly.

> I always succeed when I . . .
> I am very good at . . .
> Something I like about myself is . . .

Part 4

Review what you have written and circle the things that you can fully celebrate. This is a good list to keep for those times when you question your own value and worth.

THE DISCOVERY WHEEL

The Discovery Wheel is another opportunity to tell the truth about the kind of student you are and the kind of student you want to become.

This is not a test. There are no trick questions, and the answers will have meaning only for yourself.

Here are two suggestions to make this exercise more effective. First, think of it as the beginning of an opportunity to change. There is another Discovery Wheel at the end of this book. You will have a chance to measure your progress, so be honest about where you are now. Second, lighten up. A little laughter can make self-evaluations a lot more effective.

Here's how the Discovery Wheel works. By the end of this exercise, you will have filled in a circle similar to the one on this page. The Discovery Wheel circle is a picture of how you see yourself as a student. The closer the shading comes to the outer edge of the circle, the higher the evaluation of a specific skill. In the example to the right, the student has rated her reading skills low and her note-taking skills high.

The terms *high* and *low* are not meant to reflect a negative judgment. The Discovery Wheel is not a permanent picture of who you are. It is a picture of how you view your strengths and weaknesses as a student today. To begin this exercise, read the following statements and award yourself points for each one, using the point system described below. Then add up your point total for each section and shade the Discovery Wheel on page 31 to the appropriate level.

5 points
This statement is always or almost always true of me.

4 points
This statement is often true of me.

3 points
This statement is true of me about half the time.

2 points
This statement is seldom true of me.

1 point
This statement is never or almost never true of me.

Do this exercise online at (masterstudent.college.hmco.com)

1. _____ I enjoy learning.
2. _____ I understand and apply the concept of multiple intelligences.
3. _____ I connect my courses to my purpose for being in school.
4. _____ I make a habit of assessing my personal strengths and areas for improvement.
5. _____ I am satisfied with how I am progressing toward achieving my goals.
6. _____ I use my knowledge of learning styles to support my success in school.
7. _____ I am willing to consider any idea that can help me succeed in school—even if I initially disagree with that idea.
8. _____ I regularly remind myself of the benefits I intend to get from my education.

_____ Total score (1) *Motivation*

1. _____ I set long-term goals and periodically review them.
2. _____ I set short-term goals to support my long-term goals.
3. _____ I write a plan for each day and each week.

4. _____ I assign priorities to what I choose to do each day.

5. _____ I plan regular recreation time.

6. _____ I adjust my study time to meet the demands of individual courses.

7. _____ I have adequate time each day to accomplish what I plan.

8. _____ I am confident that I will find the resources to finance my education.

_____ Total score (2) *Planning*

1. _____ I am confident of my ability to remember.

2. _____ I can remember people's names.

3. _____ At the end of a lecture, I can summarize what was presented.

4. _____ I apply techniques that enhance my memory skills.

5. _____ I can recall information when I'm under pressure.

6. _____ I remember important information clearly and easily.

7. _____ I can jog my memory when I have difficulty recalling.

8. _____ I can relate new information to what I've already learned.

_____ Total score (3) *Memory*

1. _____ I preview and review reading assignments.

2. _____ When reading, I ask myself questions about the material.

3. _____ I underline or highlight important passages when reading.

4. _____ When I read textbooks, I am alert and awake.

5. _____ I relate what I read to my life.

6. _____ I select a reading strategy to fit the type of material I'm reading.

7. _____ I take effective notes when I read.

8. _____ When I don't understand what I'm reading, I note my questions and find answers.

_____ Total score (4) *Reading*

1. _____ When I am in class, I focus my attention.

2. _____ I take notes in class.

3. _____ I am aware of various methods for taking notes and choose those that work best for me.

4. _____ I distinguish important material and note key phrases in a lecture.

5. _____ I copy down material that the instructor writes on the chalkboard or overhead projector.

6. _____ I can put important concepts into my own words.

7. _____ My notes are valuable for review.

8. _____ I review class notes within 24 hours.

_____ Total score (5) *Notes*

1. _____ I feel confident and calm during an exam.

2. _____ I manage my time during exams and am able to complete them.

3. _____ I am able to predict test questions.

4. _____ I adapt my test-taking strategy to the kind of test I'm taking.

5. _____ I understand what essay questions ask and can answer them completely and accurately.

6. _____ I start reviewing for tests at the beginning of the term.

7. _____ I continue reviewing for tests throughout the term.

8. _____ My sense of personal worth is independent of my test scores.

_____ Total score (6) *Tests*

1. _____ I have flashes of insight and often think of solutions to problems at unusual times.

2. _____ I use brainstorming to generate solutions to a variety of problems.

3. _____ When I get stuck on a creative project, I use specific methods to get unstuck.

4. _____ I see problems and tough decisions as opportunities for learning and personal growth.

5. _____ I am willing to consider different points of view and alternative solutions.

6. _____ I can detect common errors in logic.

7. _____ I construct viewpoints by drawing on information and ideas from many sources.

8. _____ As I share my viewpoints with others, I am open to their feedback.

_____ Total score (7) *Thinking*

1. _____ I am candid with others about who I am, what I feel, and what I want.

2. _____ Other people tell me that I am a good listener.

3. _____ I can communicate my upset and anger without blaming others.

4. _____ I can make friends and create valuable relationships in a new setting.

5. _____ I am open to being with people I don't especially like in order to learn from them.

6. _____ I can effectively plan and research a large writing assignment.

7. _____ I create first drafts without criticizing my writing, then edit later for clarity, accuracy, and coherence.

8. _____ I know ways to prepare and deliver effective speeches.

_____ Total score (8) *Communicating*

1. _____ I am aware of my biases and am open to understanding people from other cultures, races, and ethnic groups.

2. _____ I build rewarding relationships with people from other backgrounds.

3. _____ I can point out examples of discrimination and sexual harassment and effectively respond to them.

4. _____ I am learning ways to thrive with diversity—attitudes and behaviors that will support my career success.

5. _____ I can effectively resolve conflict with people from other cultures.

6. _____ My writing and speaking are free of sexist expressions.

7. _____ I can recognize bias and discrimination in the media.

8. _____ I am aware of the changing demographics in my country and community.

_____ Total score (9) *Diversity*

1. _____ I learn effectively from course materials and activities that are posted online.

2. _____ I can efficiently find information on the Internet.

3. _____ I think critically about information and ideas that I access online.

4. _____ I write clear and concise e-mail messages that generate the results I want.

5. _____ My online communication is fair and respectful to other people.

6. _____ I monitor new technology that can support my success in school.

7. _____ I monitor new technology that can support my success in my career.

8. _____ I effectively use libraries to find the resources and information I want.

_____ Total score (10) *Technology*

1. _____ I have enough energy to study and still fully enjoy other areas of my life.

2. _____ If the situation calls for it, I have enough reserve energy to put in a long day.

3. _____ The food I eat supports my long-term health.

4. _____ The way I eat is independent of my feelings of self-worth.

5. _____ I exercise regularly to maintain a healthful weight.

6. _____ My emotional health supports my ability to learn.

7. _____ I notice changes in my physical condition and respond effectively.

8. _____ I am in control of any alcohol or other drugs I put into my body.

_____ Total score (11) *Health*

1. _____ I see learning as a lifelong process.

2. _____ I relate school to what I plan to do for the rest of my life.

3. _____ I learn by contributing to others.

4. _____ I revise my plans as I learn, change, and grow.

5. _____ I am clear about my purpose in life.

6. _____ I know that I am responsible for my own education.

7. _____ I take responsibility for the quality of my life.

8. _____ I am willing to accept challenges even when I'm not sure how to meet them.

_____ Total score (12) *Purpose*

Filling in your Discovery Wheel

Using the total score from each category, shade in each section of the Discovery Wheel. Use different colors, if you want. For example, you could use green to denote areas you want to work on. When you have finished, complete the Journal Entry on the next page.

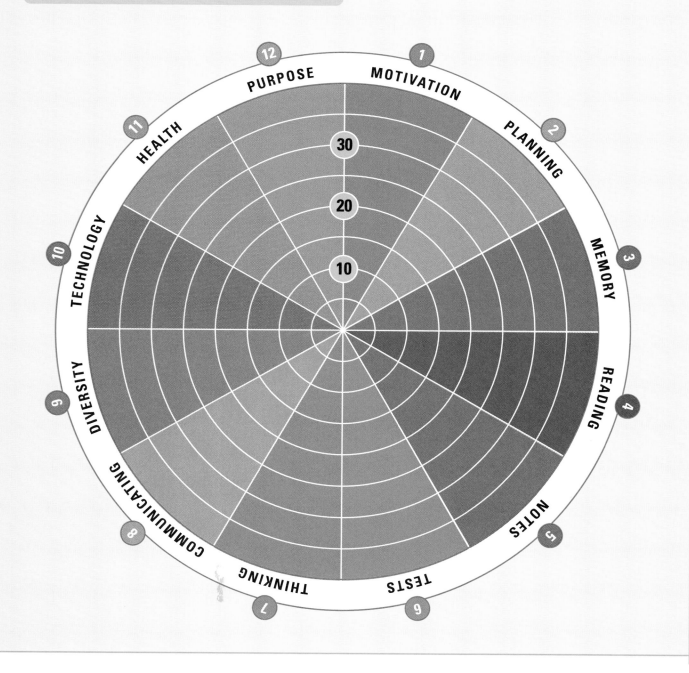

journal entry 4

Discovery/Intention Statement

Now that you have completed your Discovery Wheel, spend a few minutes with it. Get a sense of its weight, shape, and balance. Can you imagine running your hands around it? If you could lift it, would it feel light or heavy? How would it sound if it rolled down a hill? Would it roll very far? Would it wobble? Make your observations without judging the wheel as good or bad. Simply be with the picture you have created.

After you have spent a few minutes studying your Discovery Wheel, complete the following sentences in the space below. Don't worry if you can't think of something to write. Just put down whatever comes to mind. Remember, this is not a test.

This wheel is an accurate picture of my ability as a student because . . .

_____

_____

My self-evaluation surprises me because . . .

_____

_____

_____

The two areas in which I am strongest are . . .

_____

_____

_____

The areas in which I want to improve are . . .

_____

_____

_____

I want to concentrate on improving these areas because . . .

_____

_____

_____

Now, select one of your discoveries and describe how you intend to benefit from it. Complete the statement below.

To gain some practical value from this discovery, I will . . .

_____

_____

_____

→ Textbook reconnaissance, take two

The first chapter of a textbook usually includes key material—ideas that the author wants you to have up front. Likewise, this book is packed with articles that could benefit you right now. There just wasn't enough room to put them all in the first chapter.

While skimming the book for Exercise #1: "Textbook reconnaissance," you might have spotted the following articles in later chapters. If not, consider sampling them right now.

The seven-day antiprocrastination plan, page 77

More ways to stop procrastination, page 78

25 ways to get the most out of now, page 80

20 memory techniques, page 112

Muscle Reading, page 135

The note-taking process flows, page 159

Disarm tests, page 187

Gaining skill at decision making, page 230

Writing and delivering speeches, page 270

Communicating across cultures, page 284

Becoming an online learner, page 318

Take care of your machine, page 334

Transferring to another school, page 368

Career planning: Begin the process now, page 370

learning styles

what if

why

how

what

Discovering
how you learn

When we learn, two things initially happen. First, we notice new information. We *perceive* and take in what's before us. Second, we make sense of the information. We *process* it in a way that helps us understand what's going on and makes the information our own. *Learning styles* is a term that takes into account differences in how people prefer to perceive and process information.

Knowing your preferred learning style helps you understand why some courses appeal to you while others seem dull or boring. Figuring out when to use your preferences—and when it might be helpful to include another style of learning—can help you create value from any class and function successfully as a student in many different settings.

Perceiving information

The ways that people perceive information typically range from a preference for concrete experience (CE) to a preference for abstract conceptualization (AC):

■ People who favor perceiving by concrete experience like to absorb information through their five senses. They learn by getting directly involved in new experiences. When solving problems, they rely on their intuition as much as their intellect. These people

typically function well in unstructured learning classes that allow them to take the initiative.

■ People who favor perceiving by *abstract conceptualization* take in information best when they can think about it as a subject separate from themselves. They analyze, intellectualize, and create theories. Often these people take a scientific approach to problem solving and excel in traditional classrooms.

Processing information

The ways that people process information typically range from a preference for active experimentation (AE) to a preference for reflective observation (RO):

■ People who favor processing information by *active experimentation* prefer to jump in and start doing things immediately. They do not mind taking risks as they attempt to make sense of things, because this helps them learn. They are results-oriented and look for practical ways to apply what they have learned.

■ People who favor processing information by *reflective observation* prefer to stand back, watch what is going on, and think about it. Often they consider several points of view as they attempt to make sense of things and can generate many ideas about how something happens. They value patience, good judgment, and a thorough approach to understanding information.

According to David Kolb, a psychologist who developed the theory of experiential learning, learners have natural preferences for how they perceive and process information.[1] Yet they benefit most fully if they allow themselves to participate in all four points of the continuums described above. Successful learners:

1. involve themselves fully, openly, and without bias in new experiences (CE);

2. observe and reflect on these experiences from many points of view (RO);

3. integrate these observations into logically sound theories (AC) that include predictions about the consequences of new behaviors; and

4. use these theories to make decisions, solve problems, and take effective action (AE). This view of learning is quite flexible. You can start learning at any one of the four points listed above and cycle through the rest. In any case, the power of your learning derives from testing theories in your daily life—and in changing those theories based on the feedback you get from concrete experiences.

You can use Kolb's ideas to increase your skills at learning anything. First, start by understanding your natural preferences. Then balance them with activities that you consciously choose to support your learning.

Taking your Learning Style Inventory

To help you become more aware of what you currently do to support your learning, David Kolb has developed the Learning Style Inventory (LSI), which is included on the next few pages. Completing this inventory will help you discover more about how you learn.

Step 1 Keep in mind that this is not a test. There are no right or wrong answers. Your goal is to develop a profile of your learning. Take the inventory quickly. There's no need to agonize over your responses. Recalling a recent situation in which you learned something new at school, at work, or in your life might make it easier for you to focus and answer the questions.

Step 2 Remove the sheet of paper following page LSI-2. When you're ready to write on the inventory, press firmly so that your answers will show up on the page underneath the questions.

Step 3 Note that the LSI consists of 12 sentences, each with four different endings. You will read each sentence, then write a "4" next to the ending that best describes the way you currently learn. Then you will continue ranking the other endings with a "3," "2," or "1." This is a forced choice inventory, so you must rank each ending; no items can be left out. *Look at the example provided at the top of page LSI-1 before you begin.*

When you understand the example, you're ready to respond to the 12 sentences of the LSI:

- After you answer item #1, check to be sure that you wrote one "1," one "2," one "3," and one "4."

- Also check to make sure that your markings are showing through onto the scoring page (LSI-3).

- After you have responded to the 12 items, go to page LSI-3, which has instructions for computing your results.

Learning Style Inventory

Fill in the following blanks like this example:

A. When I learn: ___2___ I am happy.   ___3___ I am fast.   ___4___ I am logical.   ___1___ I am careful.

Remember: **4** = Most like you   **3** = Second most like you   **2** = Third most like you   **1** = Least like you

Remove the sheet of paper following this page. Press firmly while writing.

1. When I learn: _____ I like to deal with my feelings. _____ I like to think about ideas. _____ I like to be doing things. _____ I like to watch and listen.

2. I learn best when: _____ I listen and watch carefully. _____ I rely on logical thinking. _____ I trust my hunches and feelings. _____ I work hard to get things done.

3. When I am learning: _____ I tend to reason things out. _____ I am responsible about things. _____ I am quiet and reserved. _____ I have strong feelings and reactions.

4. I learn by: _____ feeling. _____ doing. _____ watching. _____ thinking.

5. When I learn: _____ I am open to new experiences. _____ I look at all sides of issues. _____ I like to analyze things, break them down into their parts. _____ I like to try things out.

6. When I am learning: _____ I am an observing person. _____ I am an active person. _____ I am an intuitive person. _____ I am a logical person.

7. I learn best from: _____ observation. _____ personal relationships. _____ rational theories. _____ a chance to try out and practice.

8. When I learn: _____ I like to see results from my work. _____ I like ideas and theories. _____ I take my time before acting. _____ I feel personally involved in things.

9. I learn best when: _____ I rely on my observations. _____ I rely on my feelings. _____ I can try things out for myself. _____ I rely on my ideas.

10. When I am learning: _____ I am a reserved person. _____ I am an accepting person. _____ I am a responsible person. _____ I am a rational person.

11. When I learn: _____ I get involved. _____ I like to observe. _____ I evaluate things. _____ I like to be active.

12. I learn best when: _____ I analyze ideas. _____ I am receptive and open-minded. _____ I am careful. _____ I am practical.

Interpreting your Learning Style Graph

NOTE: **Before you read this page,** score your inventory by following the directions on page LSI-3. Then complete the Learning Style Graph on page LSI-5. The following information appears on this page so that you can more easily compare your completed graph to the samples below. You will make this comparison *after* you remove page LSI-3.

Four modes of learning

When we're learning well, we tend to search out the answers to four key questions: *Why? What? How?* and *What if?* Each of these questions represents a different *mode of learning*. The modes of learning are patterns of behavior—unique combinations of concrete experience, reflective observation, abstract conceptualization, and active experimentation. When you are in a learning situation, you might find that you continually ask yourself one of these key questions more than the others. Or you might routinely ask several of these questions. Read the descriptions below to get a better idea of how you approach learning.

Mode 1: Why? Some of us question why we are learning things. We seek a purpose for information and a personal connection with the content. We want to know a rationale for what we're learning—why the course content matters and how it challenges or fits in with what we already know.

Mode 2: What? Some of us crave information. When learning something, we want to know critical facts. We seek a theory or model to explain what's happening and follow up to see what experts have to say on the topic. We break a subject down into its key components or steps and master each one.

Mode 3: How? Some of us hunger for an opportunity to try out what we're studying. We ask ourselves: Does this idea make sense? Will it work, and, if so, *how* does it work? How can I make use of this information? We want to apply and test theories and models. We excel at taking the parts or key steps of a subject and assembling them into a meaningful sequence.

Mode 4: What if? Some of us get excited about going beyond classroom assignments. We aim to adapt what we're learning to another course or to a situation at work or at home. By applying our knowledge, we want to make a difference in some area that we care about. We ask ourselves: What if we tried…? or What if we combined…?

Your preferred learning mode

When you examine your completed Learning Style Graph on page LSI-5, you will notice that your learning style profile (the "kite" that you drew) might be located primarily in one part of the graph. This will give you an idea of your preferred mode of learning, that is, the kind of behaviors that feel most comfortable and familiar to you when you are learning something. Using the descriptions below and the sample graphs, identify your preferred learning mode.

Mode 1: Why? If the majority of your learning style profile is in the upper right-hand corner of the Learning Style Graph, you probably prefer Mode 1 learning. You like to consider a situation from many different points of view and determine why it is important to learn a new idea or technique.

Mode 2: What? If your learning style profile is mostly in the lower right-hand corner of the Learning Style Graph, you probably prefer Mode 2 learning. You are interested in knowing what ideas or techniques are important. You enjoy learning lots of facts and then arranging these facts in a logical and concise manner.

Mode 3: How? If most of your learning style profile is in the lower left-hand corner of the Learning Style Graph, you probably prefer Mode 3 learning. You get involved with new knowledge by testing it out. You investigate how ideas and techniques work, and you put into practice what you learn.

Mode 4: What if? If most of your learning style profile is in the upper left-hand corner of the Learning Style Graph, you probably prefer Mode 4 learning. You like to take what you have practiced and find other uses for it. You seek ways to apply this newly gained skill or information at your workplace or in your personal relationships.

Combinations. Some learning style profiles combine all four modes. The profile to the right reflects a learner who is focused primarily on gathering information—lots of information! People with this profile tend to ask for additional facts from an instructor, or they want to know where they can go to discover more about a subject.

The profile to the right applies to learners who focus more on understanding what they learn and less on gathering lots of information. People with this profile prefer smaller chunks of data with plenty of time to process it. Long lectures can be difficult for these learners.

The profile to the right indicates a learner whose preferences are fairly well balanced. People with this profile can be highly adaptable and tend to excel no matter what the instructor does in the classroom. These people enjoy learning in general and do well in school.

Remove this sheet before completing the Learning Style Inventory.

This page is inserted to ensure that the other writing you do in this book doesn't show through on page LSI-3.

Remove this sheet before completing the Learning Style Inventory.

This page is inserted to ensure that the other writing you do in this book doesn't show through on page LSI-3.

Scoring your Inventory

Now that you have taken the Learning Style Inventory, it's time to fill out the Learning Style Graph (page LSI-5) and interpret your results. To do this, please follow the next five steps.

1 First, add up all of the numbers you gave to the items marked with brown **F** letters. Then write down that total to the right in the blank next to "**Brown F**." Next, add up all of the numbers for "**Teal W**," "**Purple T**," and "**Orange D**," and also write down those totals in the blanks to the right.

2 Add the four totals to arrive at a GRAND TOTAL and write down that figure in the blank to the right. (*Note:* The grand total should equal 120. If you have a different amount, go back and re-add the colored letters; it was probably just an addition error.) Now remove this page and continue with Step 3 on page LSI-5.

continue with Step 3 on page LSI-5

scorecard

Brown **F**	total	_____
Teal **W**	total	_____
Purple **T**	total	_____
Orange **D**	total	_____
GRAND TOTAL		_____

F	T	D	W
W	T	F	D
T	D	W	F
F	D	W	T
F	W	T	D
W	D	F	T
W	F	T	D
D	T	W	F
W	F	D	T
W	F	D	T
F	W	T	D
T	F	W	D

Remove this page after you have completed Steps 1 and 2 on page LSI-3. Then continue with Step 3 on page LSI-5.

Once you have completed Step 3, discard this page so that you can more easily compare your completed Learning Style Graph with the examples on page LSI-2.

Learning Style Graph

3 Remove the piece of paper that follows this page and then transfer your totals from Step 2 on page LSI-3 to the lines on the Learning Style Graph below. On the brown (F) line, find the number that corresponds to your "**Brown F**" total from page LSI-3. Then write an X on this number. Do the same for your "**Teal W**," "**Purple T**," and "**Orange D**" totals.

4 Now, pressing firmly, draw four straight lines to connect the four X's and shade in the area to form a "kite." This is your learning style profile. Each X that you placed on these lines indicates your preference for a different aspect of learning:

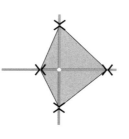

Concrete experience ("Feeling"). The number where you put your X on this line indicates your preference for learning things that have personal meaning. The higher your score on this line, the more you like to learn things that you feel are important and relevant to yourself.

Reflective observation ("Watching"). Your number on this line indicates how important it is for you to reflect on the things you are learning. If your score is high on this line, you probably find it important to watch others as they learn about an assignment and then report on it to the class. You probably like to plan things out and take the time to make sure that you fully understand a topic.

Abstract conceptualization ("Thinking"). Your number on this line indicates your preference for learning ideas, facts, and figures. If your score is high on this line, you probably like to absorb many concepts and gather lots of information on a new topic.

Active experimentation ("Doing"). Your number on this line indicates your preference for applying ideas, using trial and error, and practicing what you learn. If your score is high on this line, you probably enjoy hands-on activities that allow you to test out ideas to see what works.

5 Read page LSI-2 to understand further your preferences for learning.

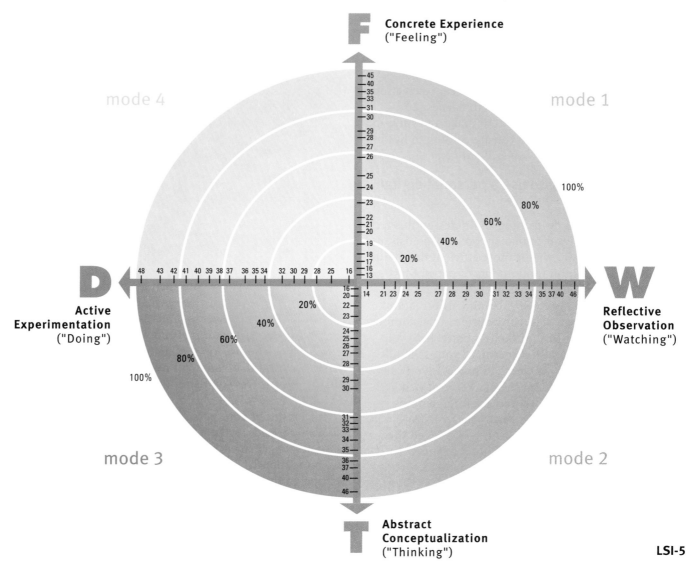

Cycle of learning

These examples show how the learning cycle works. You're interested in something (Mode 1), so you gather information about it (Mode 2). You try out what you're learning (Mode 3), then you integrate it into your day-to-day life (Mode 4). You go through this cycle many times as one learning experience generates another.

Example 1 Learning about a historical issue

You're required to take an elective in history, and you decide to take a course on the history of immigration in the United States. Your great-grandparents came to this country as immigrants, and immigration is still taking place today. You conclude that this topic is interesting—in part, because of your family background (Mode 1: *Why?*).

Soon you're in class, and you learn that from the early years of the country's history, many Americans have had misconceptions and fears about immigration that persist to the present day (Mode 2: *What?*).

You find yourself re-evaluating your own beliefs and assumptions. You wonder whether new immigrants in your city are experiencing some of the same stereotyping that was commonplace in earlier times. You decide to become more active in a community organization that deals firsthand with the impact of immigration policies (Mode 3: *How?*).

You also start to consider what it would be like to become an attorney and devote your career to creating a system that treats all immigrants with fairness and respect. You realize that you want to make a positive difference in the lives of people who are coming to live in the United States today (Mode 4: *What if?*).

Example 2 Learning to use a personal digital assistant (PDA)

Learning begins with developing an interest in this technology. Maybe you want to manage your to-do lists and appointments in a way that is more efficient than writing notes to yourself on random bits of paper. Maybe you never want to buy another pocket calendar. Or maybe you want to store your planning information digitally and exchange files with your personal computer. You conclude that this technology could help you finally get organized and feel on top of your schedule (Mode 1: *Why?*). Next, you learn as much as you can about the different PDAs on the market. You visit Web sites, go to a computer store, and ask for a demonstration. You also talk to friends who swear by PDAs—and those who swear never to use them—and weigh their advice and differing opinions (Mode 2: *What?*).

After you gather this information, you decide to buy your own PDA. You take the handwritten information from your pocket calendar and to-do lists and enter it all into your new PDA. This takes several hours, including the time spent learning to write with a stylus (Mode 3: *How?*).

Once you've conquered the mechanics of using a PDA, you begin to use it on a daily basis—and encounter some unexpected hassles. For one thing, writing with the stylus requires you to form individual letters in a special way. Also, your friends who stick with paper-based planning can simply open up their pocket calendars and quickly pencil in appointments. Meanwhile, you have to turn on your PDA and wait for it to boot up before you can use it. Instead of feeling more organized, you end up feeling behind. You wonder what it would be like to switch back to paper-based planning. After your experiences with a PDA, you decide to do just that. This time, however, you introduce a change in your behavior. Instead of recording your to-do items on any scrap of paper that is lying around, you put a pen and some 3x5 index cards in your pocket and carry them with you at all times. Whenever you want to make a note to yourself, you simply pull out a card and jot down your thoughts. Cards are easy to store and sort. This new system, while it seems so simple and so "low-tech," finally helps you achieve that sense of organization you've been craving (Mode 4: *What if?*).

Example 3 Thinking about the effects of television

Your sociology instructor asks you to write a 2,000-word paper about the impact of television on our society. As part of the assignment, you're asked to envision a society without television. This interests you, since you've often wondered what it would be like to give up television (Mode 1: *Why?*).

One of your first steps in writing this paper is to ask what purposes television serves. You conclude that, based on the varieties of programming, several purposes are involved: entertainment, news and information, documentaries, sports, and, of course, advertising. To research the paper, you also read two books on the history of American television (Mode 2: *What?*).

Still wondering how your own life would change if you were to give up television, you choose to do so on a trial basis—for two weeks—and observe the effects. This change in your behavior frees up several hours each week, which you use for reading newspapers and magazines. You find that you don't miss television news and that reading leaves you better informed about the world (Mode 3: *How?*).

As a result of your personal experiment with television, you wonder what it would be like to give up television news permanently. You choose to do this for at least six more months. You also volunteer for a local literacy campaign that encourages people to go television-free for one month each year and devote the time they save to reading (Mode 4: *What if?*).

Remove this sheet before completing the Learning Style Graph.

This page is inserted to ensure that the other writing you do in this book doesn't show through on page LSI-7.

Remove this sheet before completing the Learning Style Graph.

This page is inserted to ensure that the other writing you do in this book doesn't show through on page LSI-7.

Name _____ Date _____/_____/_____

journal entry 5

Discovery/Intention Statement

To make this concept of the learning cycle more useful, start applying it right away. You can begin with the content of this book. For example, as you read the Master Student Profiles, ask questions based on each mode of learning: *Why* is this person considered a master student? *What* attitudes or behaviors helped to create her mastery? *How* can I develop those qualities? *What if* I could use her example to create significant new results in my own life? (Or, *What if* I ignore the lessons to be learned from this Master Student Profile and experience significant costs as a result?) Also see the Master Student Map at the beginning of each chapter for sample answers to *Why? What? How?* and *What if?* questions.

Regarding my preferences for learning, I discovered that...

_____

Given my preferences for learning, I intend to...

_____

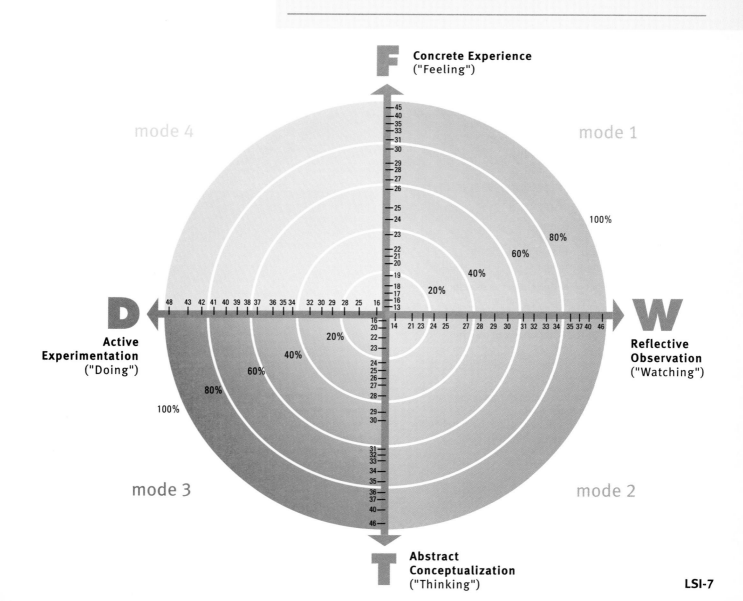

F   **Concrete Experience** ("Feeling")

mode 4   mode 1

D   **Active Experimentation** ("Doing")

W   **Reflective Observation** ("Watching")

mode 3   mode 2

T   **Abstract Conceptualization** ("Thinking")

Balancing your preferences

The chart below identifies some of the natural talents as well as challenges for people who have a strong preference for any one mode of learning. For example, if most of your "kite" is in Mode 2 of the Learning Style Graph, then look at the lower right-hand corner of the following chart to see if this is an accurate description of yourself.

After reviewing the description of your preferred learning mode, read all of the sections that start with the words "People with other preferred modes." These sections explain what actions you can take to become a more balanced learner.

Concrete Experience

mode 4

Strengths:
Getting things done
Leadership
Risk taking

Too much of this mode can lead to:
Trivial improvements
Meaningless activity

Too little of this mode can lead to:
Work not completed on time
Impractical plans
Lack of motivation to achieve goals

People with other preferred modes can develop Mode 4 by:
• Making a commitment to objectives
• Seeking new opportunities
• Influencing and leading others
• Being personally involved
• Dealing with people

mode 1

Strengths:
Imaginative ability
Understanding people
Recognizing problems
Brainstorming

Too much of this mode can lead to:
Feeling paralyzed by alternatives
Inability to make decisions

Too little of this mode can lead to:
Lack of ideas
Not recognizing problems and opportunities

People with other preferred modes can develop Mode 1 by:
• Being aware of other people's feelings
• Being sensitive to values
• Listening with an open mind
• Gathering information
• Imagining the implications of ambiguous situations

Active Experimentation

Reflective Observation

Strengths:
Problem solving
Decision making
Deductive reasoning
Defining problems

Too much of this mode can lead to:
Solving the wrong problem
Hasty decision making

Too little of this mode can lead to:
Lack of focus
Reluctance to consider alternatives
Scattered thoughts

People with other preferred modes can develop Mode 3 by:
• Creating new ways of thinking and doing
• Experimenting with fresh ideas
• Choosing the best solution
• Setting goals
• Making decisions

mode 3

Strengths:
Planning
Creating models
Defining problems
Developing theories

Too much of this mode can lead to:
Vague ideals ("castles in the air")
Lack of practical application

Too little of this mode can lead to:
Inability to learn from mistakes
No sound basis for work
No systematic approach

People with other preferred modes can develop Mode 2 by:
• Organizing information
• Building conceptual models
• Testing theories and ideas
• Designing experiments
• Analyzing quantitative data

mode 2

Abstract Conceptualization

Using your learning style profile
to succeed in school

what if · why · how · what

To get the most value from knowing your learning style profile, look for ways to apply this knowledge in school and at work. Remember that in this exercise the term *preferred learning mode* refers to the way you've typically approached learning in the past. It does not describe the way you have to learn in the future. No matter what aspects of learning you've tended to prefer, you can develop the ability to use all four modes. Doing so offers many potential benefits. For example, you can excel in different types of courses, seize more opportunities for learning outside the classroom, and expand your options for declaring a major and choosing a career. In addition, you can more fully understand people who learn differently from you, decreasing the potential for conflict while increasing the effectiveness of your working relationships. Exploring all of the learning modes provides more opportunities for you to achieve your goals. Consider the suggestions that follow.

Tolerate discomfort. Discomfort is a natural part of the learning process. As you participate in modes of learning that do not energize you, allow yourself to notice your struggle with a task or your lack of interest in completing it. Realize that you are balancing your learning preferences. Resist the temptation to skip a mode of learning or move too quickly through it. By tolerating discomfort and using all of the modes, you increase your chances for success.

Match activities to your learning style profile. You might want to examine your learning style profile when choosing your major and planning your career. You could focus on courses or jobs that suit your preferred modes of learning. Consulting with people who have different learning preferences can also be beneficial when you approach course work or other learning situations.

Ask for what you want. You might find that the way an instructor teaches is not the way you prefer to learn, and that teachers don't always promote all four modes of learning. Once you know your learning preferences, you can take a more active role in ensuring that your learning needs are met.

- *If you have a strong preference for Mode 1,* you are likely to spend time observing others and planning out your course of action. You probably also enjoy working with other students. To assist yourself in

> ### ➔ When learning styles conflict, you have options
>
> When they experience difficulty in school, some students say: "The classroom is not conducive to the way I learn." Or "This teacher creates tests that are too hard for me." Or "In class, we never have time for questions." Or "The instructor doesn't teach to my learning style."
>
> Such statements can become mental crutches—a set of beliefs that prevent you from taking responsibility for your education. To stay in charge of your learning, consider adopting attitudes such as the following:
>
> *I will discover the value in learning this information.*
> *I will find out more details and facts about this information.*
> *I will discover how I can experiment with this information.*
> *I will discover new ways to use this information in my life.*
> *I will study this information with modes of learning that are not my preferred style.*
>
> Note that you can base your behaviors on such statements even if you don't fully agree with them. One way to change your attitudes is to adopt new behaviors and watch for new results in your life.

school, ask questions that help you understand why it is important for you to learn about a specific topic. You might also want to form study group.

- *If you have a strong preference for Mode 2,* you are skilled in understanding theories and concepts. When in learning situations, you are likely to enjoy lectures and individual class assignments. Chances are that you also enjoy solitary time and are not fond of working in groups. To assist yourself in school, ask questions that help you gather enough information to understand what you are learning. You might also increase your effectiveness by choosing not to concentrate equally on all of the material in a chapter, focusing primarily on specific parts of the text.

- *If you have a strong preference for Mode 3,* you probably excel at working with your hands and at laboratory stations. When in a learning situation, you are interested in knowing how things work. In addition, you probably enjoy working alone or with a small group. To assist yourself in school, ask questions that help you understand how something works and how you can experiment with these new ideas. Also allow time to practice and apply what you learn. You can conduct experiments, create presentations, tabulate findings, or even write a rap song that summarizes key concepts. Such activities provide an opportunity to internalize your learning through hands-on practice.

- *If you have a strong preference for Mode 4,* you are skilled at teaching others what you have learned and helping them see the importance of these concepts. Whether in a learning situation or in everyday life, you like to apply facts and theories. You probably enjoy carrying out plans and having new and challenging experiences. You also prefer working with others and are likely to have a large social circle. To assist yourself in school, ask questions that help you determine where else in your life you can apply what you have just learned. Also seek opportunities to demonstrate your understanding. You could coach a classmate about what you have learned, present findings from your research, explain how your project works, or perform a rap song that someone else might have written.

Associate with students who have different learning style profiles. If your instructor asks your class to form groups to complete an assignment, avoid joining a group in which everyone shares your preferred modes of learning. Get together with people who both complement and challenge you. This is one way you can develop skills in all four learning modes and become a more well-rounded student.

Use this book with the modes of learning in mind. The four modes of learning are part of a natural cycle. Master students learn in all four ways. If you strongly prefer one mode, then experiment with the others. Becoming a Master Student can help. This book is designed to move you through all four modes of learning.

- At the beginning of each chapter, you are asked to complete a Journal Entry designed to stimulate your thinking and connect the chapter content to your current life experience—to help you see why learning this material is beneficial (a Mode 1 activity).

- Next, you read articles that are filled with ideas, information, and suggestions that can help you succeed in school (a Mode 2 activity).

- You are also asked to practice new skills with exercises provided throughout each chapter (a Mode 3 activity).

- Finally, at the end of each chapter Discovery and Intention Statements and Learning Styles Applications help you tie all of this information together and suggest ways that you can use it in your future (a Mode 4 activity).

This article and the previous one were written following the same four-mode learning cycle. The previous article, "Learning styles: Discovering how you learn," first reviewed the value of knowing about learning styles (Mode 1). Then facts and theories about learning styles were discussed (Mode 2). Next, you took action and did the Learning Style Inventory (Mode 3). Finally, this article invites you to apply your newfound knowledge of learning styles in your daily life (Mode 4). ▨

Claim your multiple intelligences

People often think that being smart means the same thing as having a high IQ, and that having a high IQ automatically leads to success. However, psychologists are finding that IQ scores do not always foretell which students will do well in academic settings—or after they graduate.

Howard Gardner of Harvard University believes that no single measure of intelligence can tell us how smart we are. Instead, Gardner identifies many types of intelligence, as described below.[2] Gardner's theory of several types of intelligence complements the discussion in this chapter on different learning styles—both recognize that there are alternative ways for people to learn and assimilate knowledge. You can use Gardner's concepts to explore additional methods for achieving success in school, work, and relationships. People using **verbal/linguistic intelligence** are adept at language skills and learn best by speaking, writing, reading, and listening. They are likely to enjoy activities such as telling stories and doing crossword puzzles.

Those using **mathematical/logical intelligence** are good with numbers, logic, problem solving, patterns, relationships, and categories. They are generally precise and methodical, and are likely to enjoy science.

When people learn visually and by organizing things spatially, they display **visual/spatial intelligence.** They think in images and pictures, and understand best by seeing the subject. They enjoy charts, graphs, maps, mazes, tables, illustrations, art, models, puzzles, and costumes.

People using **bodily/kinesthetic intelligence** prefer physical activity. They enjoy activities such as building things, woodworking, dancing, skiing, sewing, and crafts. They generally are coordinated and athletic, and would rather participate in games than just watch.

Those using **musical/rhythmic intelligence** enjoy musical expression through songs, rhythms, and musical instruments. They are responsive to various kinds of sounds, remember melodies easily, and might enjoy drumming, humming, and whistling. People using **intrapersonal intelligence** are exceptionally aware of their own feelings and values. They are generally reserved, self-motivated, and intuitive.

Evidence of **interpersonal intelligence** is seen in outgoing people. They do well with cooperative learning and are sensitive to the feelings, intentions, and motivations of others. They often make good leaders.

Those using **naturalist intelligence** love the outdoors and recognize details in plants, animals, rocks, clouds, and other natural formations. These people excel in observing fine distinctions among similar items.

Each of us has all of these intelligences to some degree. And each of us can learn to enhance them. Experiment with learning in ways that draw on a variety of intelligences—including those that might be less familiar. When we acknowledge all of our intelligences, we can constantly explore new ways of being smart. The following chart summarizes the multiple intelligences discussed in this article and suggests ways to apply them. This is not an exhaustive list or a formal inventory, so take what you find merely as points of departure. You can invent strategies of your own to cultivate different intelligences. ▧

Type of intelligence	Possible characteristics	Possible learning strategies	Possible careers
Verbal/linguistic	• You enjoy writing letters, stories, and papers. • You to prefer to write directions rather than draw maps. • You take excellent notes from textbooks and lectures. • You enjoy reading, telling stories, and listening to them.	• Highlight, underline, and write other notes in your textbooks. • Recite new ideas in your own words. • Rewrite and edit your class notes. • Talk to other people often about what you're studying.	Librarian, lawyer, editor, journalist, English teacher, radio or television announcer
Mathematical/logical	• You enjoy solving puzzles. • You prefer math or science class over English class. • You want to know how and why things work. • You make careful step-by-step plans.	• Analyze tasks into a sequence of steps. • Group concepts into categories and look for underlying patterns. • Convert text into tables, charts, and graphs. • Look for ways to quantify ideas—to express them in numerical terms.	Accountant, auditor, tax preparer, mathematician, computer programmer, actuary, economist, math or science teacher
Visual/spatial	• You draw pictures to give an example or clarify an explanation. • You understand maps and illustrations more readily than text. • You assemble thing from illustrated instructions. • You especially enjoy books that have a lot of illustrations.	• When taking notes, create concept maps, mind maps, and other visuals (see Chapter Five). • Code your notes by using different colors to highlight main topics, major points, and key details. • When your attention wanders, focus it by sketching or drawing. • Before you try a new task, visualize yourself doing it well.	Architect, commercial artist, fine artist, graphic designer, photographer, interior decorator, engineer, cartographer
Bodily/kinesthetic	• You enjoy physical exercise. • You tend not to sit still for long periods of time. • You enjoy working with your hands. • You use a lot of gestures when talking.	• Be active in ways that support concentration; for example, pace as you recite, read while standing up, and create flash cards. • Carry materials with you and practice studying in several different locations. • Create hands-on activities related to key concepts; for example, create a game based on course content. • Notice the sensations involved with learning something well.	Physical education teacher, athlete, athletic coach, physical therapist, chiropractor, massage therapist, yoga teacher, dancer, choreographer, actor

(continued)

Type of intelligence	Possible characteristics	Possible learning strategies	Possible careers
Musical/rhythmic	• You often sing in the car or shower. • You easily tap your foot to the beat of a song. • You play a musical instrument. • You feel most engaged and productive when music is playing.	• During a study break, play music or dance to restore energy. • Put on background music that enhances your concentration while studying. • Relate key concepts to songs you know. • Write your own songs based on course content.	Professional musician, music teacher, music therapist, choral director, musical instrument sales representative, musical instrument maker, piano tuner
Intrapersonal	• You enjoy writing in a journal and being alone with your thoughts. • You think a lot about what you want in the future. • You prefer to work on individual projects over group projects. • You take time to think things through before talking or taking action.	• Connect course content to your personal values and goals. • Study a topic alone before attending a study group. • Connect readings and lectures to a strong feeling or significant past experience. • Keep a journal that relates your course work to events in your daily life.	Minister, priest, rabbi, professor of philosophy or religion, counseling psychologist, creator of a home-based or small business
Interpersonal	• You enjoy group work over working alone. • You have plenty of friends and regularly spend time with them. • You prefer talking and listening over reading or writing. • You thrive in positions of leadership.	• Form and conduct study groups early in the term. • Create flash cards and use them to quiz study partners. • Volunteer to give a speech or lead group presentations on course topics. • Teach the topic you're studying to someone else.	Manager, school administrator, salesperson, teacher, counseling psychologist, arbitrator, police officer, nurse, travel agent, public relations specialist, creator of a mid-size to large business
Naturalist	• As a child, you enjoyed collecting insects, leaves, or other natural objects. • You enjoy being outdoors. • You find that important insights occur during times you spend in nature. • You read books and magazines on nature-related topics.	• During study breaks, take walks outside. • Post pictures of outdoor scenes where you study and play recordings of outdoor sounds while you read. • Invite classmates to discuss course work while taking a hike or going on a camping trip. • Focus on careers that hold the potential for working outdoors.	Environmental activist, park ranger, recreation supervisor, historian, museum curator, biologist, criminologist, mechanic, woodworker, construction worker, construction contractor or estimator

Learning by seeing, hearing, and moving:

The VAK system

You can approach the topic of learning styles with a simple and powerful system—one that focuses on just three ways of perceiving through your senses:

- Seeing, or *visual* learning
- Hearing, or *auditory* learning
- Movement, or *kinesthetic* learning

To recall this system, remember the letters *VAK*, which stand for **v**isual, **a**uditory, and **k**inesthetic. The theory is that each of us prefers to learn through one of these sense channels. And we can enrich our learning with activities that draw on the other channels.

To reflect on your VAK preferences, answer the following questions. Each question has three possible answers. Circle the answer that best describes how you would respond in the stated situation. This is not a formal inventory—just a way to prompt some self-discovery.

When you have problems spelling a word, you prefer to:
1. *Look it up in the dictionary.*
2. *Say the word out loud several times before you write it down.*
3. *Write out the word with several different spellings and choose one.*

You enjoy courses the most when you get to:
1. *View slides, overhead transparencies, videos, and readings with plenty of charts, tables, and illustrations.*
2. *Ask questions, engage in small-group discussions, and listen to guest speakers.*
3. *Take field trips, participate in lab sessions, or apply the course content while working as a volunteer or intern.*

When giving someone directions on how to drive to a destination, you prefer to:
1. *Pull out a piece of paper and sketch a map.*
2. *Give verbal instructions.*
3. *Say, "I'm driving to a place near there, so just follow me."*

When planning an extended vacation to a new destination, you prefer to:

1. *Read colorful, illustrated brochures or articles about that place.*
2. *Talk directly to someone who's been there.*
3. *Spend a day or two at that destination on a work-related trip before taking a vacation there.*

You've made a commitment to learn to play the guitar. The first thing you do is:
1. *Go to a library or music store and find an instruction book with plenty of diagrams and chord charts.*
2. *Pull out your favorite CDs, listen closely to the guitar solos, and see if you can sing along with them.*
3. *Buy or borrow a guitar, pluck the strings, and ask someone to show you how to play a few chords.*

You've saved up enough money to lease a car. When choosing from among several new models, the most important factor in your decision is:
1. *The car's appearance.*
2. *The information you get by talking to people who own the cars you're considering.*
3. *The overall impression you get by taking each car on a test drive.*

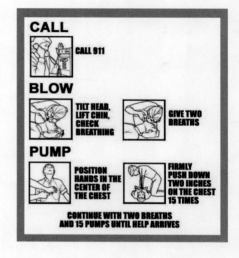

You've just bought a new computer system—monitor, central processing unit, keyboard, CD burner, cable modem, and external speakers. When setting up the system, the first thing you do is:
1. *Skim through the printed instructions that come with the equipment.*
2. *Call up someone with a similar system and ask her for directions.*
3. *Assemble the components as best as you can, see if everything works, and consult the instructions only as a last resort.*

You get a scholarship to study abroad next semester, which starts in just three months. You will travel to a country where French is the most widely spoken language. To learn as much French as you can before you depart, you:
1. *Buy a video-based language course that's recorded on a DVD.*

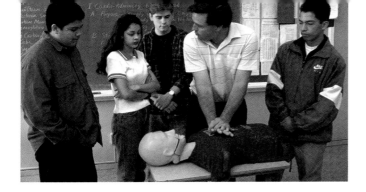

2. Set up tutoring sessions with a friend who's fluent in French.

3. Sign up for a short immersion course in an environment in which you speak only French, starting with the first class.

Now take a few minutes to reflect on the meaning of your responses. All of the answers numbered "1" are examples of visual learning. The "2's" refer to auditory learning, and the "3's" illustrate kinesthetic learning. Finding a consistent pattern in your answers indicates that you prefer learning through one sense channel more than the others. Or you might find that your preferences are fairly balanced.

Listed below are suggestions for learning through each sense channel. Experiment with these examples and create more techniques of your own. Use them to build on your current preferences and develop new options for learning.

To enhance *visual* learning:

- Preview reading assignments by looking for elements that are highlighted visually—bold headlines, charts, graphs, illustrations, and photographs.

- When taking notes in class, leave plenty of room to add your own charts, diagrams, tables, and other visuals later.

- Whenever an instructor writes information on a blackboard or overhead projector, copy it exactly in your notes.

- Transfer your handwritten notes to your computer. Use word processing software that allows you to format your notes in lists, add headings in different fonts, and create visuals in color.

- Before you begin an exam, quickly sketch a diagram on scratch paper. Use this diagram to summarize the key formulas or facts you want to remember.

- During tests, see if you can visualize pages from your handwritten notes or images from your computer-based notes.

To enhance *auditory* learning:

- Reinforce memory of your notes and readings by talking about them. When studying, stop often to recite key points and examples in your own words.

- After doing several verbal summaries, record your favorite version or write it out.

- Read difficult passages in your textbooks slowly and out loud.

- Join study groups and create short presentations about course topics.

- Visit your instructors during office hours to ask questions.

To enhance *kinesthetic* learning:

- Look for ways to translate course content into three-dimensional models that you can build. While studying biology, for example, create a model of a human cell using different colors of clay.

- Supplement lectures with trips to museums, field observations, lab sessions, tutorials, and other hands-on activities.

- Recite key concepts from your courses while you walk or exercise.

- Intentionally set up situations in which you can learn by trial and error.

- Create a practice test and write out the answers in the room where you will actually take the exam.

Note: This chapter introduces several approaches to learning styles: the Learning Style Inventory, multiple intelligences, and the VAK system. That's a lot of information to absorb. Remember that each approach presents an option, not the final word on learning styles. Above all, look for ideas from any of these methods that you can put to immediate use. When you write Intention Statements, keep these questions in mind: How can I use this idea to *be* more successful in school? What will I *do* differently as a result of reading about learning styles? If I develop new learning styles, what skill will I *have* that I don't have now? ▨

The magic of metacognition

It's pronounced "metta-cog-ni-shun." "Meta" means *beyond* or *above*, "cognition" refers to everything that goes on inside your brain—thinking, perceiving, and learning. Metacognition is thinking about thinking, learning about learning. It's your ability to stand "above" your mental processes—to observe them and to take conscious control of them.

Metacognition is one of the main benefits of higher education. Mastering this skill allows you to learn anything you want, any time. Among other things, metacognition includes:

- *Planning*—the ability to determine your purpose, choose from alternative behaviors, predict their consequences, and monitor your progress in meeting your goals

- *Analysis*—the ability to separate a whole subject into its parts

- *Synthesis*—the ability to combine parts to form a meaningful whole

- *Application*—the ability to transfer new concepts and skills from one life situation to another

Each aspect of metacognition dovetails nicely with a mode of learning. Mode 1 involves planning—connecting the content of a course to your personal interests and goals. In Mode 2, you analyze by taking key ideas apart, separating skills into their component steps, and learning each step in turn. In Mode 3, you synthesize—that is, combine all of the separate ideas, facts, and skills you learned to see how they work in a real-life situation. And in Mode 4, you take what you have learned in one course and apply it in other courses and outside the classroom.

Students who master metacognition can do things such as:

- state the ways that they'll benefit from learning a subject;

- describe their preferred learning styles and develop new ones;

- make accurate statements about their current abilities;

- monitor their behavior and change their habits;

- choose and apply various strategies for reading, writing, speaking, listening, managing time, and related tasks; and

- modify strategies so that they work in several contexts.

Remember that the teachers in your life will come and go. Some are more skilled than others. None of them are perfect. With metacognition, you can view any course as one step along the path to learning what you want to learn—in the way that you prefer to learn it. The magic of metacognition is that you become your own best teacher.

voices

student

At first I was very angry about being left behind and was discouraged because of my learning style. In fact, I spent a lot of energy resenting my lost opportunities. Then I realized that the energy I was spending on resentment could be turned into something positive. I wrote a speech and shared my experiences; I addressed problems that can result from not recognizing learning styles. In the speech, I pointed out ways to identify learning styles and ways to get those styles met. I received a lot of good feedback from the speech, and I think it actually helped other students.

—REBECCA GULLEDGE

In 1482, **Leonardo da Vinci** wrote a letter to a wealthy baron, applying for work. In excerpted form, he wrote,

"I can contrive various and endless means of offense and defense.... I have all sorts of extremely light and strong bridges adapted to be most easily carried.... I have methods for destroying every turret or fortress.... I will make covered chariots, safe and unassailable.... In case of need I will make big guns, mortars, and light ordnance of fine and useful forms out of the common type." And then he added, almost as an afterthought, *"In times of peace I believe I can give perfect satisfaction and to the equal of any other in architecture ... can carry out sculpture ... and also I can do in painting whatever may be done."*

The **Mona Lisa**, for example.

The Master Student

This book is about something that cannot be taught. It's about becoming a master student.

A master is a person who has attained a level of skill that goes beyond technique. For a master, methods and procedures are automatic responses to the needs of the task. Work is effortless; struggle evaporates. The master carpenter is so familiar with her tools, they are part of her. To a master chef, utensils are old friends. Because these masters don't have to think about the details of the process, they bring more of themselves to their work.

Mastery can lead to flashy results—an incredible painting, for example, or a gem of a short story. In basketball, mastery might result in an unbelievable shot at the buzzer. For a musician, it might be the performance of a lifetime, the moment when everything comes together. Often the result of mastery is a sense of profound satisfaction, well-being, and timelessness. Work seems self-propelled. The master is *in* control by being *out* of control. He lets go and allows the creative process to take over. That's why after a spectacular performance, it is often said of an athlete or a performer, "He was playing out of his mind."

Likewise, the master student is one who "learns out of her mind." Of course, that statement makes no sense. Mastery, in fact, doesn't make sense. It cannot be captured with words. It defies analysis. Mastery cannot be taught, only learned and experienced.

Examine the following list of characteristics of master students in light of your own experience. The list is not complete. It merely points in a direction. Look in that direction, and you'll begin to see the endless diversity of master students. These people are old and young, male and female. They exist in every period of history. And they come from every culture, race, and ethnic group.

Also remember to look to yourself. No one can teach us to be master students; we already *are* master students. We are natural learners by design. As students, we can discover that every day.

Following are some traits shared by master students.

Inquisitive. The master student is curious about everything. By posing questions she can generate interest in the most mundane, humdrum situations. When she is bored during a biology lecture, she thinks to herself, "I always get bored when I listen to this instructor. Why is that? Maybe it's because he reminds me of my boring Uncle Ralph, who always tells those endless fishing stories. He even looks like Uncle Ralph. Amazing! Boredom is certainly interesting." Then she asks herself, "What can I do to get value out of this lecture, even though it seems boring?" And she finds an answer.

Able to focus attention. Watch a 2-year-old at play. Pay attention to his eyes. The wide-eyed look reveals an energy and a capacity for amazement that keep his attention absolutely focused in the here and now. The master student's focused attention has a childlike quality. The world, to a child, is always new. Because the master student can focus attention, to him the world is always new, too.

Willing to change. The unknown does not frighten the master student. In fact, she welcomes it—even the unknown in herself. We all have pictures of who we think we are, and these pictures can be useful. They also can prevent learning and growth. The master student is open to changes in her environment and in herself.

Able to organize and sort. The master student can take a large body of information and sift through it to discover relationships. He can play with information, organizing data by size, color, function, timeliness, and hundreds of other categories.

Competent. Mastery of skills is important to the master student. When she learns mathematical formulas, she studies them until they become second nature. She practices until she knows them cold, then puts in a few extra minutes. She also is able to apply what she learns to new and different situations.

Joyful. More often than not, the master student is seen with a smile on his face—sometimes a smile at nothing in particular other than amazement at the world and his experience of it.

Able to suspend judgment. The master student has opinions and positions, and she is able to let go of them when appropriate. She realizes she is more than her thoughts. She can quiet her internal dialogue and listen to an opposing viewpoint. She doesn't let judgment get in the way of learning. Rather than approaching discussions with a "Prove it to me and then I'll believe it" attitude, she asks herself, What if this is true? and explores possibilities.

Energetic. Notice the student with a spring in his step, the one who is enthusiastic and involved in class. When he reads, he often sits on the very edge of his chair, and he plays with the same intensity. He is a master student.

Well. Health is important to the master student, though not necessarily in the sense of being free of illness. Rather, she values her body and treats it with respect. She tends to her emotional and spiritual health, as well as her physical health.

Self-aware. The master student is willing to evaluate himself and his behavior. He regularly tells the truth about his strengths and those aspects that could be improved.

Responsible. There is a difference between responsibility and blame, and the master student knows it well. She is willing to take responsibility for everything in her life—even for events that most people would blame on others.

For example, if a master student is served cold eggs in the cafeteria, she chooses to take responsibility for getting cold eggs. This is not the same as blaming herself for cold eggs. Rather, she looks for ways to change the situation and get what she wants. She could choose to eat breakfast earlier, or she might tell someone in the kitchen that the eggs are cold and request a change. The cold eggs might continue. Even then, the master student takes responsibility and gives herself the power to choose her response to the situation.

Willing to take risks. The master student often takes on projects with no guarantee of success. He participates in class dialogues at the risk of looking foolish. He tackles difficult subjects in term papers. He welcomes the risk of a challenging course.

Willing to participate. Don't look for the master student on the sidelines. She's in the game. She is a player who can be counted on. She is willing to make a commitment and to follow through on it.

A generalist. The master student is interested in everything around him. He has a broad base of knowledge in many fields and can find value that is applicable to his specialties.

Willing to accept paradox. The word *paradox* comes from two Greek words, *para* (beyond) and *doxen* (opinion). A paradox is something that is beyond opinion or, more accurately, something that might seem contradictory or absurd yet might actually have meaning.

For example, the master student can be committed to managing money and reaching her financial goals. At the same time, she can be totally detached from money, knowing that her real worth is independent of how much money she has. The master student recognizes the limitations of the mind and is at home with paradox. She can accept that ambiguity.

Courageous. The master student admits his fear and fully experiences it. For example, he will approach a tough exam as an opportunity to explore feelings of anxiety and tension related to the pressure to perform. He does not deny fear; he embraces it.

Self-directed. Rewards or punishments provided by others do not motivate the master student. Her motivation to learn comes from within.

Spontaneous. The master student is truly in the here and now. He is able to respond to the moment in fresh, surprising, and unplanned ways.

Relaxed about grades. Grades make the master student neither depressed nor euphoric. She recognizes that sometimes grades are important, and grades are not the only reason she studies. She does not measure her worth as a human being by the grades she receives.

Intuitive. The master student has an inner sense that cannot be explained by logic. He has learned to trust his feelings, and he works to develop this intuitive sense.

Creative. Where others see dull details and trivia, the master student sees opportunities to create. She can gather pieces of knowledge from a wide range of subjects and put them together in new ways. The master student is creative in every aspect of her life.

Willing to be uncomfortable. The master student does not place comfort first. When discomfort is necessary to reach a goal, he is willing to experience it. He can endure personal hardships and can look at unpleasant things with detachment.

Accepting. The master student accepts herself, the people around her, and the challenges that life offers.

Willing to laugh. The master student might laugh at any moment, and his sense of humor includes the ability to laugh at himself.

Going to school is a big investment. The stakes are high. It's OK to be serious about that, but you don't have to go to school on the deferred-fun program. A master student celebrates learning, and one of the best ways to do that is to have a laugh now and then.

Hungry. Human beings begin life with a natural appetite for knowledge. In some people it soon gets dulled. The master student has tapped that hunger, and it gives her a desire to learn for the sake of learning.

Willing to work. Once inspired, the master student is willing to follow through with sweat. He knows that genius and creativity are the result of persistence and work. When in high gear, the master student works with the intensity of a child at play.

Caring. A master student cares about knowledge and has a passion for ideas. She also cares about people and appreciates learning from others. She flourishes in a community that values "win-win" outcomes, cooperation, and love.

The master student in you. The master student is in all of us. By design, human beings are learning machines. We have an innate ability to learn, and all of us have room to grow and improve.

It is important to understand the difference between learning and being taught. Human beings can resist being taught anything. Carl Rogers goes so far as to say that anything that can be taught to a human being is either inconsequential or just plain harmful.[3] What is important in education, Rogers asserts, is *learning*. And everyone has the ability to learn.

Unfortunately, people also learn to hide that ability. As they experience the pain that sometimes accompanies learning, they shut down. If a child experiences embarrassment in front of a group of people, he could learn to avoid similar situations. In doing so, he restricts his possibilities.

Some children "learn" that they are slow learners. If they learn it well enough, their behavior comes to match that label.

As people grow older, they sometimes accumulate a growing list of ideas to defend, a catalog of familiar experiences that discourages them from learning anything new.

Still, the master student within survives. To tap that resource, you don't need to acquire anything. You already have everything you need. Every day you can rediscover the natural learner within you. 🔯

Motivat

In large part, this chapter is about your motivation to succeed in school. And a First Step in creating motivation is getting some definitions straight.

The terms *self-discipline, willpower,* and *motivation* are often used to describe something missing in ourselves. Time after time we invoke these words to explain another person's success—or our own shortcomings: "If I were more motivated, I'd get more involved in school." "Of course she got an A. She has self-discipline." "If I had more willpower, I'd lose weight." It seems that certain people are born with lots of motivation, while others miss out on it.

An alternative is to stop assuming that motivation is mysterious, determined at birth, or hard to come by. Perhaps what we call *motivation* is something that you already possess—or simply a habit that you can develop with practice. The following suggestions offer ways to do that.

Promise it. Motivation can come simply from being clear about your goals and acting on them. Say that you want to start a study group. You can commit yourself to inviting people and setting a time and place to meet. Promise your classmates that you'll do this, and ask them to hold you accountable. Self-discipline, willpower, motivation—none of these mysterious characteristics needs to get in your way. Just make a promise and keep your word.

Befriend your discomfort. Sometimes keeping your word means doing a task you'd rather put off. The mere thought of doing laundry, reading a chapter in a statistics book, or proofreading a term paper can lead to discomfort. In the face of such discomfort, we can procrastinate. Or we can use this barrier as a means to get the job done.

Begin by investigating the discomfort. Notice the thoughts running through your head and speak them out loud: "I'd rather walk on a bed of coals than do this." "This is the last thing I want to do right now."

Also observe what's happening with your body. For example, are you breathing faster or slower than usual? Is your breathing shallow or deep? Are your shoulders tight? Do you feel any tension in your stomach?

Once you're in contact with your mind and body, stay with the discomfort a few minutes longer. Don't judge it as good or bad. Accepting the thoughts and body sensations robs them of power. They might still be there, but in time they can stop being a barrier for you.

Discomfort can be a gift—an opportunity to do valuable work on yourself. On the other side of discomfort lies mastery.

Change your mind—and your body. You can also get past discomfort by planting new thoughts in your mind or changing your physical stance. For example, instead of slumping in a chair, sit up straight or stand up. You can also get physically active by taking a short walk. Notice what happens to your discomfort.

Work with thoughts, also. Replace "I can't stand this" with "I'll feel great when this is done" or "Doing this will help me get something I want."

Sweeten the task. Sometimes it's just one aspect of a task that holds us back. We can stop procrastinating merely by changing that aspect. If distaste for our physical environment keeps us from studying, we can change that environment. Reading about social psychology might seem like a yawner when we're alone in a dark corner of the house. Moving to a cheery, well-lit library can sweeten the task.

Talk about how bad it is. One way to get past negative attitudes is to take them to an extreme. When faced with an unpleasant task, launch into a no-holds-barred gripe session. Pull out all the stops: "There's no way I can start my income taxes now. This is terrible beyond words, an absolute disaster. This is a catastrophe of global proportions!" Griping taken this far can restore perspective. It shows how self-talk can turn inconveniences into crises.

Turn up the pressure. Sometimes motivation is a luxury. Pretend that the due date for your project has been moved up one month, one week, or one day. Raising the stress level slightly can spur you into action. Then the issue of motivation seems beside the point, and meeting the due date moves to the forefront.

"I'm just not in the MOOD"

Turn down the pressure. The mere thought of starting a huge task can induce anxiety. To get past this feeling, turn down the pressure by taking "baby steps." Divide a large project into small tasks. In 30 minutes or less, you could preview a book, create a rough outline for a paper, or solve two or three math problems. Careful planning can help you discover many such steps to make a big job doable.

Ask for support. Other people can become your allies in overcoming procrastination. For example, form a support group and declare what you intend to accomplish before each meeting. Then ask members to hold you accountable. If you want to begin exercising regularly, ask another person to walk with you three times weekly. People in support groups ranging from Alcoholics Anonymous to Weight Watchers know the power of this strategy.

Adopt a model. One strategy for succeeding at any task is to hang around the masters. Find someone you consider successful and spend time with her. Observe this person and use her as a model for your own behavior. You can "try on" this person's actions and attitudes. Look for tools that feel right for you. This person can become a mentor for you.

Compare the payoffs to the costs. Behaviors such as cramming for exams or neglecting exercise have payoffs. Cramming might give us more time that's free of commitments. Neglecting exercise can give us more time to sleep.

One way to let go of such unwanted behaviors is first to celebrate them—even embrace them. We can openly acknowledge the payoffs.

Celebration can be especially powerful when we follow it up with the next step—determining the costs. For example, skipping a reading assignment can give you time to go to the movies. However, you might be unprepared for class and have twice as much to read the following week.

Maybe there is another way to get the payoff (going to the movies) without paying the cost (skipping the reading assignment). With some thoughtful weekly planning, you might choose to give up a few hours of television and end up with enough time to read the assignment *and* go to the movies.

Comparing the costs and benefits of any behavior can fuel our motivation. We can choose new behaviors because they align with what we want most.

Do it later. At times, it's effective to save a task for later. For example, writing a résumé can wait until you've taken the time to analyze your job skills and map out your career goals. This is not a lack of motivation—it's planning.

When you do choose to do a task later, turn this decision into a promise. Estimate how long the task will take and schedule a specific date and time for it on your calendar.

Motivation can come simply from being clear about your goals and acting on them.

Heed the message. Sometimes lack of motivation carries a message that's worth heeding. An example is the student who majors in accounting but seizes every chance to be with children. His chronic reluctance to read accounting textbooks might not be a problem. Instead, it might reveal his desire to major in elementary education. His original career choice might have come from the belief that "real men don't teach kindergarten." In such cases, an apparent lack of motivation signals a deeper wisdom trying to get through. ⬕

Attitudes, affirmations, and visualizations

"I have a bad attitude." Some of us say this as if we were talking about having the flu. An attitude is certainly as strong as the flu, but it isn't something we have to succumb to or accept.

Some of us see our attitudes the way we see our height or eye color: "I might not like it, but I might as well accept it."

Acceptance is certainly a worthwhile approach to things we cannot change. When it comes to attitudes, acceptance is not necessary—attitudes can change. We don't have to live our lives with an attitude that doesn't work.

Attitudes are powerful. They create behavior. If your attitude is that you're not very interesting at a party, then your behavior will probably match your attitude, and you might act like a bore. If your attitude is that you are fun at a party, then your behavior is more likely to be playful. Soon you are the life of the party. All that has to change is attitude.

Success in school starts with attitudes. Some attitudes will help you benefit from all the money and time you invest in higher education. Other attitudes will render your investment worthless.

You can change your attitudes through regular practice with affirmations and visualizations.

Affirm it. An affirmation is a statement describing what you want. The most effective affirmations are personal, positive, and written in the present tense.

Affirmations have an almost magical power.

They are used successfully by athletes and actors, executives and ballerinas, and thousands of people who have succeeded in their lives. Affirmations can change your attitudes and behaviors.

To use affirmations, first determine what you want, then describe yourself as if you already have it. To get what you want from your education, you could write, "I, Malika Jones, am a master student. I take full responsibility for my education. I learn with joy, and I use my experiences in each course to create the life that I want."

If you decide that you want a wonderful job, you might write, "I, Susan Webster, have a wonderful job. I

Decide what you want to improve, and write down what it would look like, sound like, and feel like to have that improvement in your life.

respect and love my colleagues, and they feel the same way about me. I look forward to going to work each day."

Or if money is your desire, you might write, "I, John Henderson, am rich. I have more money than I can spend. I have everything I want, including a six-bedroom house, a new sports car, a 200-watt sound system, and a large-screen television with a satellite dish receiver."

What makes the affirmation work is detail. Use brand names, people's names, and your own name. Involve all of your senses—sight, sound, smell, taste, touch. Take a positive approach. Instead of saying, "I am not fat," say, "I am slender."

Once you have written the affirmation, repeat it. Practice saying it out loud several times a day. This works best if you say it at a regular time, such as just before you go to sleep or just after you wake up.

Sit in a chair in a relaxed position. Take a few deep and relaxing breaths, and then repeat your affirmation with emotion. It's also effective to look in a mirror while saying the affirmation. Keep looking and repeating until you are saying your affirmation with conviction.

Visualize it. It would be difficult to grow up in our culture without hearing the maxim that "practice makes perfect." The problem is that most of us limit what we consider to be practice. Effective practice can occur even when we are not moving a muscle.

You can improve your golf swing, tennis serve, or batting average while lying in bed. You can become a better driver, speaker, or cook while sitting silently in a chair. In line at the grocery store, you can improve your ability to type or to take tests. This is all possible through visualization—the technique

of seeing yourself be successful.

Here's one way to begin. Decide what you want to improve, and write down what it would look like, sound like, and feel like to have that improvement in your life. If you are learning to play the piano, write down briefly what you would see, hear, and feel if you were playing skillfully. If you want to improve your relationships with your children, write down what you would see, hear, and feel if you were communicating with them successfully.

A powerful visualization involves other senses besides seeing. Feel the physical sensations. Hear the sounds. Note any smells, tastes, textures, or qualities of light that accompany the scene in your mind.

Once you have a sketch of what it

→ Attitude replacements

You can use affirmations to replace a negative attitude with a positive one. There are no limitations, other than your imagination and your willingness to practice. Here are some sample affirmations. Modify them to suit your individual hopes and dreams, and then practice them. The article "Attitudes, affirmations, and visualizations" explains ways to use these attitude replacements.

I, _____, am healthy.

I, _____, have abundant energy and vitality throughout the day.

I, _____, exercise regularly.

I, _____, work effectively with many different kinds of people.

I, _____, eat wisely.

I, _____, plan my days and use time wisely.

I, _____, have a powerful memory.

I, _____, take tests calmly and confidently.

I, _____, have a sense of self-worth that is independent of my test scores.

I, _____, am a great speller.

I, _____, fall asleep quickly and sleep soundly.

I, _____, am smart.

I, _____, learn quickly.

I, _____, am creative.

I, _____, am aware of and sensitive to other people's moods.

I, _____, have relationships that are mutually satisfying.

I, _____, work hard and contribute to other people through my job.

I, _____, am wealthy.

I, _____, know ways to play and have fun.

I, _____, am attractive.

I, _____, focus my attention easily.

I, _____, like myself.

I, _____, am liked by other people.

I, _____, am a worthwhile person even though I am _____.

I, _____, have a slim and attractive body.

I, _____, am relaxed in all situations, including _____.

I, _____, make profitable financial investments.

I, _____, have an income that far exceeds my expenses.

I, _____, live a life of abundance and prosperity.

I, _____, always live my life in positive ways for the highest good of all people.

To hear an online version of these affirmations, link to ⟨ masterstudent.college.hmco.com ⟩

would be like to be successful, practice it in your imagination—successfully. As you play out the scenario, include as many details as you can. Always have your practices be successes. Whenever you toss the basketball, it swishes through the net. Every time you invite someone out on a date, the person says yes. Each test the teacher hands back to you is graded an A. Practice at least once a day.

You can also use visualizations to replay errors. When you make a mistake, replay it in your imagination. After a bad golf shot, stop and imagine yourself making that same shot again, this time very successfully. If you just had a discussion with your roommate that turned into a fight, replay it successfully. Get all of your senses involved. See yourselves calmly talking things over together. Hear the words and feel the pleasure of a successful interaction.

Visualizations and affirmations can restructure your attitudes and behaviors. Be clear about what you want—and then practice it. 🗵

REPROGRAM YOUR ATTITUDE

Affirmations and visualizations can be employed successfully to reprogram your attitudes and behaviors. Use this exercise to change your approach to any situation in your life.

Step 1

Pick something in your life that you would like to change. It can be related to anything—relationships, work, money, or personal skills. Below, write a brief description of what you choose to change.

_____

_____

_____

Step 2

Add more details about the change you described in Step 1. Write down how you would like the change to come about. Be outlandish. Imagine that you are about to ask your fairy godmother for a wish that you know she will grant. Be detailed in your description of your wish.

_____

_____

_____

Step 3

Here comes the fairy godmother. Use affirmations and visualizations to start yourself on the path to creating ex-

actly what you wrote about in Step 2. Below, write at least two affirmations that describe your dream wish. Also, briefly outline a visualization that you can use to picture your wish. Be specific, detailed, and positive.

_____

_____

_____

Step 4

Put your new attitudes to work. Set up a schedule to practice them. Let the first time be right now. Then set up at least five other times and places that you intend to practice your affirmations and visualizations.

I intend to relax and practice my affirmations and visualizations for at least five minutes on the following dates and at the times and location(s) given.

Date	Time	Location
1.		
2.		
3.		
4.		
5.		

When you're waist-deep in reading assignments, writing papers, and studying for tests, you might well ask yourself: Is all this effort going to pay off someday?

The value of higher education

That's a fair question. And it addresses a core issue—the value of getting an education beyond high school.

Be reassured. The potential benefits of higher education are enormous. To begin with, there are economic benefits. Over their lifetimes, college graduates on average earn much more than high school graduates.

That's just one potential payoff. Consider the others explained below.

Gain a broad vision

It's been said that a large corporation is a collection of departments connected only by a plumbing system. This quip makes a point: As workers in different fields become more specialized, they run the risk of forgetting how to talk to each other.

Higher education can change that. One benefit of studying the liberal arts is the chance to gain a broad vision. People with a liberal arts background are aware of the various kinds of problems tackled in psychology and theology, philosophy and physics, literature and mathematics. They understand how people in all of these fields arrive at conclusions and how these fields relate to each other.

Master the liberal arts

According to one traditional model of education, there are two essential tasks for people to master—the use of language and the use of numbers. To acquire these skills, students once immersed themselves in seven subjects: grammar, rhetoric, logic, arithmetic, geometry, music, and astronomy. These subjects were called the "liberal" arts. They complemented the fine arts, such as poetry, and the practical arts, such as farming.

This model of liberal arts education still has something to offer. Today we master the use of language through the basic processes of communication: reading, writing, speaking, and listening. In addition, courses in mathematics and science help us understand the world in quantitative terms. The abilities to communicate and calculate are essential to almost every profession. Excellence at these skills has long been considered an essential characteristic of an educated person.

The word *liberal* comes from the Latin verb *libero*, which means "to free." Liberal arts are those that promote critical thinking. Studying them can free us from irrational ideas, half-truths, racism, and prejudice. The liberal arts grant us freedom to explore alternatives and create a system of personal values. These benefits are priceless, the very basis of personal fulfillment and political freedom.

Discover your values

We do not spend all of our waking hours at our jobs. That leaves us with a decision that affects the quality of our lives: how to spend leisure time. By cultivating our interest in the arts and community affairs, the liberal arts provide us with many options for activities outside of work. These studies add a dimension to life that goes beyond having a job and paying the bills.

Practical people are those who focus on time and money. And managing these effectively calls for a clear sense of values. Our values define what we commit our time and money to.

Vocational education is about *how to do* things that we can get paid for. Through a liberal arts education, we discover *what's worth doing*—what activities are worthy of our energy and talents. Both types of education are equally important. No matter where they've attended school, liberally educated people can state what they're willing to bet their lives on.

Discover new interests

Taking a broad range of courses has the potential to change your direction in life. A student previously committed to a career in science might try out a drawing class and eventually switch to a degree in studio arts. Or a person who swears that she has no aptitude for technical subjects might change her major to computer science after taking an introductory computer course.

To make effective choices about your long-term goals, base those choices on a variety of academic and personal experiences. Even if you don't change majors or switch career directions, you could discover an important avocation or gain a complementary skill. For example, science majors who will eventually write for professional journals can benefit from taking English courses.

Hang out with the great

Today we enjoy a huge legacy from our ancestors. The creative minds of our species have given us great works of art, systems of science, and technological advances that defy the imagination. Through higher education we can gain firsthand knowledge of humanity's greatest creations. The poet Ezra Pound defined literature as "news that stays news."[4] Most of the writing in newspapers and magazines becomes dated quickly. In contrast, many of the books you read in higher education have passed the hardest test of all—time. Such works have created value for people for decades, sometimes for centuries. These creations are inexhaustible. We can return to them time after time and gain new insights. These are the works we

can justifiably deem great. Hanging out with them transforms us. Getting to know them exercises our minds, just as running exercises our bodies.

By studying the greatest works in many fields, we raise our standards. We learn ways to distinguish what is superficial and fleeting from what is lasting and profound.

The criteria for a great novel, poem, painting, or piece of music or dance might vary among individuals. Differences in taste reflect the differences in our backgrounds. The point is to discover those works that have enduring value—and enjoy them for a lifetime.

Learn skills that apply across careers

Jobs that involve responsibility, prestige, and higher incomes depend on self-management skills. These include knowing ways to manage time, resolve conflicts, set goals, learn new skills, and control stress. Higher education is a place to learn and practice such skills.

Judging by recent trends, most of us will have multiple careers in our lifetimes. In this environment of constant change, it makes sense to learn skills that apply across careers.

Join the conversation

Long ago, before the advent of printing presses, televisions, and computers, people educated themselves by conversing with each other. Students in ancient Athens were often called *peripatetic* (a word that means "walking around") because they were frequently seen strolling around the city, engaged in heated philosophical debate. Since then, the debate has deepened and broadened. The world's finest scientists and artists have joined voices in a conversation that spans centuries and crosses cultures. This is a conversation about the nature of truth and beauty, knowledge and compassion, good and evil—ideas that form the very basis of human society. Robert Hutchins, former president of the University of Chicago, called this the "great conversation."[5] By studying this conversation, we take on the most basic human challenges: coping with death and suffering, helping create a just global society, living with meaning and purpose. Our greatest thinkers have left behind tangible records. You'll find them in libraries, concert halls, museums, and scientific laboratories across the world. Through higher education, you gain a front-row seat for the great conversation— and an opportunity to add your own voice. ◪

PRACTICING CRITICAL THINKING

1

Review the article *The Master Student* in this chapter. Then skim the master student profiles throughout this book. Finally, choose one of the people profiled and describe in the space below how this person embodies qualities of a master student.

_____

_____

_____

_____

_____

_____

_____

_____

_____

_____

_____

_____

The Practicing Critical Thinking exercises that appear throughout this book incorporate ideas from Peter Facione, Dean of the College of Arts and Sciences, Santa Clara University, and creator of the California Critical Thinking Disposition Inventory. Mr. Facione provided substantial suggestions for these exercises and edited them. He can be contacted through the California Academic Press on the World Wide Web at **http://www.insightassessment.com/about.html.**

Adapted with permission from Critical Thinking: What It Is and Why It Counts *by Peter Facione (Millbrae, CA: The California Academic Press, 1996).*

→ Master Student Profiles

In each chapter of this text there is an example of a person who embodies several qualities of a master student. As you read about these people and others like them, ask yourself: How can I apply this? Look for the timeless qualities in the people you read about. Many of the strategies used by master students from another time or place are tools that you can use today.

The master students in this book were chosen because they demonstrate unusual and effective ways to learn. Re-member that these are just 12 examples of master students (one for each chapter). You can read more about them in the Master Student Hall of Fame at **masterstudent.college.hmco.com.** Also reflect on other master students you've read about or know personally. As you meet new people, look for those who excel at learning. The master student is not a vague or remote ideal. Rather, master students move freely among us.

In fact, there's one living inside your skin.

power process

Ideas are tools

There are many ideas in this book. When you first encounter them, don't believe any of them. Instead, think of them as tools.

For example, you use a hammer for a purpose—to drive a nail. When you use a new hammer, you might notice its shape, its weight, and its balance. You don't try to figure out whether the hammer is "right." You just use it. If it works, you use it again. If it doesn't work, you get a different hammer.

This is not the attitude most people adopt when they encounter new ideas. The first thing most people do with new ideas is to measure them against old ones. If a new idea conflicts with an old one, the new one is likely to be rejected.

People have plenty of room in their lives for different kinds of hammers, but they tend to limit their capacity for different kinds of ideas. A new idea, at some level, is a threat to their very being—unlike a new hammer, which is simply a new hammer.

Most of us have a built-in desire to be right. Our ideas, we often think, represent ourselves. And when we identify with our ideas, they assume new importance in our lives. We put them on our mantels. We hang them on our walls. We wear them on our T-shirts and display them on our bumpers. We join associations of people who share our most beloved ideas. We make up rituals about them, compose songs about them, and write stories about them. We declare ourselves dedicated to these ideas.

Some ideas are worth dying for. But please note: This book does not contain any of those ideas. The ideas on these pages are strictly "hammers."

Imagine someone defending a hammer. Picture this person holding up a hammer and declaring, "I hold this hammer to be self-evident. Give me this hammer or give me death. Those other hammers are flawed. There are only two kinds of people in this world: people who believe in this hammer and people who don't."

That ridiculous picture makes a point. This book is not a manifesto. It's a toolbox, and tools are meant to be used. This viewpoint is much like one advocated by psychologist and philosopher William James. His approach to philosophy, which he called "pragmatism," emphasized the usefulness of ideas as a criterion of truth.[6] James liked to talk about the "cash value" of an idea—whether it leads to new actions and new results.

If you read about a tool in this book that doesn't sound "right" or one that sounds a little goofy, remember that the ideas here are for using, not necessarily for believing. Suspend your judgment. Test the idea for yourself.

If it works, use it. If it doesn't, don't.

Ask: What if it's true?

When presented with a new idea, some of us take pride in being critical thinkers. We look for problems. We probe for weaknesses. We continue to doubt the idea until there's clear proof. Our main question seems to be "What's wrong with this idea?"

This approach can be useful when it is vital to expose flaws in ideas or reasoning. On the other hand, when we constantly look for what's wrong with new ideas, we might not recognize their value. A different and potentially more powerful approach is to ask yourself: What if that idea is true? This opens up all sorts of new possibilities and variations. Rather than looking for what's wrong, we can look for what's potentially valuable. Faced with a new idea, we can stay in the inquiry, look deeper, and go further.

Keep looking for answers

The light bulb, the airplane, the computer chip, the notion of the unconscious—these and many other tools became possible when their inventors practiced the art of continually looking for additional answers.

Another way to expand your toolbox is to keep on looking for answers. Much of your education will be about finding answers to questions. Every subject you study—from algebra to history to philosophy—poses a unique set of questions. Some of the most interesting questions are those that admit many answers: How can we create a just society? How can we transmit our values to the next generation? What are the purposes of higher education? How can we prevent an environmental crisis?

Other questions are more personal: What career shall I choose? Shall I get married? Where shall I live and how shall I spend my leisure time? What shall I have, do, and be during my time on earth?

Perhaps you already have answers to these questions. Answers are wonderful, especially when they relate to our most persistent and deeply felt questions. Answers can

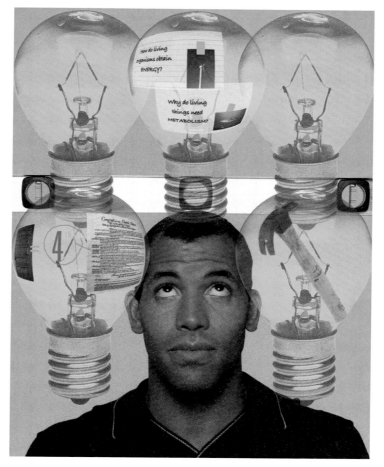

also get in the way. Once we're convinced that we have the "right" answer, it's easy to stop looking for more answers. We then stop learning. Our range of possible actions becomes limited.

Instead of latching on to one answer, we can look for more. Instead of being content with the first or easiest options that come to mind, we can keep searching. Even when we're convinced that we've finally handled a problem, we can brainstorm until we find five more solutions.

When we keep looking for answers, we uncover fresh possibilities for thinking, feeling, and behaving. Like children learning to walk, we experience the joy of discovery.

A caution

A word of caution: Any tool—whether it's a hammer, a computer program, or a study technique—is designed to do a specific job. A master mechanic carries a variety of tools because no single tool works for all jobs. If you throw a tool away because it doesn't work in one situation, you won't be able to pull it out later when it's just what you need. So if an idea doesn't work for you and you are satisfied that you gave it a fair

This book is not a manifesto. It's a toolbox, and tools are meant to be used.

chance, don't throw it away. File it away instead. The idea might come in handy sooner than you think.

And remember, this book is not about figuring out the "right" way. Even the "ideas are tools" approach is not "right."

It's a hammer . . . (or maybe a saw). ⊠

put it to work

At work, you can benefit by remembering the concept of learning styles. In the workplace, people act in a variety of ways that express their preferences for perceiving information, processing ideas, and acting on what they learn.

The worker who's continually moving might prefer concrete experience over memos and meetings. She likes to learn by doing. The person who's usually on the phone might prefer to learn by listening and talking. She likes to reflect on her experiences and forge relationships.

You might have a supervisor who enjoys working with concepts as much as working with people. She might prefer to decide on a long-range goal and a detailed plan before taking action.

Discover learning styles in your workplace. You can learn a lot about your coworkers' learning styles simply by observing them during the workday. Just look for clues.

One clue is how they *approach a learning task*. Some people process new information or ideas by sitting quietly and reading or writing. When learning to use a piece of equipment, such as a new computer, they'll read the instruction manual first. Those who use a trial-and-error approach will skip the manual, unpack all the boxes, and start setting up equipment. Other coworkers might ask a more experienced colleague to guide them in person, step by step.

Another clue is *word choice*. Some people like to process information visually. You might hear them say, "I'll look into that" or "Give me the big picture first." Those who like to solve problems verbally might say, "Let's talk though this problem" or "I hear you!" In contrast, some of your coworkers express themselves using body sensations ("This product feels great") or action ("Let's run with this idea and see what happens").

In addition, notice *process preferences*—patterns in the way that your coworkers meet goals. When attending meetings, for example, some might stick closely to the agenda and keep an eye on the clock. Others might prefer to "go with the flow," even if it means working an extra hour or scrapping the agenda.

Once you've discovered such differences among your coworkers, look for ways to accommodate their learning styles.

Gear presentations to different learning styles. When you want coworkers to agree to a new procedure or promote a new product, you'll probably make a speech or give a presentation. To persuade more people, gear your presentation to several learning styles.

For example, some people want to see the overall picture first. You can start by saying "This product has four major features." Then explain the benefits of each feature in order.

Also allow time for verbally oriented people to ask questions and make comments. For those who prefer a hands-on approach, offer a chance to try out the new product for themselves—to literally "get the feel of it."

Finish with a handout that includes plenty of illustrations, charts, and step-by-step instructions. Visual learners and people who like to think abstractly will appreciate it.

Gear projects to different learning styles. When working on project teams, look for ways to combine complementary skills. If you're adept at planning, find someone who excels at active experimentation. Also seek people who can reflect on and interpret the team members' experiences. Pooling different learning styles allows you to draw on everyone's strengths.

Remember that a person's learning style is both stable and dynamic. People gravitate toward the kinds of tasks they've succeeded at in the past. They can also broaden their learning styles by taking on new tasks to reinforce different aspects of learning. For example, ask people who enjoy taking immediate action to step back more often and reflect on the overall purpose of a project. ▨

Name _____ Date _____/_____/_____

quiz

1. Explain three ways that you can use knowledge of your learning styles to succeed in school.

2. Define the term *mastery* as it is used in this chapter.

3. The First Step technique refers only to telling the truth about your areas for improvement. True or False? Explain your answer.

4. The four modes of learning are associated with certain questions. List the appropriate question for each mode.

5. According to the text, motivation is mysterious and hard to develop. True or False? Explain your answer.

6. Give three examples of the benefits of getting an education beyond high school.

7. Briefly describe how being aware of your own multiple intelligences can help you thrive in higher education.

8. According to the Power Process: "Ideas are tools," if you want the ideas in this book to work, you must believe in them. True or False? Explain your answer.

9. Students who are skilled in metacognition can do which of the following:
   (a) Choose and apply various strategies for reading, writing, speaking, listening, managing time, and related tasks.
   (b) Modify strategies so that they work in several contexts.
   (c) Monitor their behavior and change habits.
   (d) State the ways that they'll benefit from learning a subject.
   (e) All of the above.

10. List two strategies that you can use to enhance kinesthetic learning.

learning styles application

Even though you have preferred ways to learn new ideas or skills, you can benefit from using several learning styles. The questions below will "cycle" you through four styles, or modes, of learning as explained in the article "Learning styles: Discovering how you learn" in Chapter One. Each question will help you explore a different mode. You can answer the questions in any order.

Remember that you do not have to start with Why? of Mode 1. Any of the four questions can serve as your point of entry into the cycle of learning.

Look for a similar Learning Styles Application at the end of every chapter in this book. Also notice that the first page of each chapter includes a preview based on the four questions that represent the four modes of learning: *Why? What? How?* and *What if?*

what if
Review this chapter and the Introduction, looking for ideas that could help you make the transition from being in school to working in your next career. List two or three suggestions, stating each one in a short sentence.

why
Think about why the subject of transitions matters to you. Describe a major transition that you have experienced in the past. Examples might include changing schools, moving to a new city, starting a job, or going to college. In a sentence or two, describe what you did to cope with this change in your life.

how
In a short paragraph, explain how you can use one suggestion from this book to master a future transition that you will experience in education. Examples include declaring a major, changing majors, or transferring to a new school.

what
Review this chapter and the Introduction, looking for ideas that could help you make a major transition in your life. List two or three suggestions, stating each one in a short sentence.

master student

profile

SUNY URRUTIA MOORE

As a student at Aims Community College in Fort Lupton-Love-land, Colorado, wrote an essay that won her a scholarship from Houghton Mifflin.

Asmall child attends a rural parochial school in a Third World country in South America. In order to get to school, she has to walk a mile on a dirt road twice daily. Her supplies are a note-book, pencil, an eraser, and a yellow-brown old book borrowed from the school. The beginning of her educa-tion comes at a price. Can there be a "master student" in her?

Because education is important to her family, they make arrangements for her to finish elementary grades in a city school. To continue her educa-tion, the child attends the Superior Institute of Commerce, which is a combination of high school and business school. Throughout the seven-year program, memorization is the main strategy for learning, which awards her a "C" average grade. She could excel, but this education system doesn't teach any strategies to suc-ceed as a student. In fact, this defi-ciency will carry through into later years. The small child becomes a young adult, and the small child is me, the author of this essay.

In the late 1970s, I was offered the opportunity to come to the United States of America. This was to be a radical change, which involved not only leaving my native country, Chilé, but also family and friends, a success-ful accounting career, and familiar surroundings. All of my possessions would be exchanged for a different country and society, unfamiliar envi-ronment, and a strange language. So I took the opportunity to move, and when I arrived in this country, I real-ized that I had a problem: I couldn't communicate with others! I accepted this problem and experienced the lan-guage barrier, but I did what was nec-essary to learn how to speak English and become fully bilingual.... For the last 14 years, my main focus has been taking care of my family. In addition, I have held a position as a bilingual paraprofessional for the last few years. Being willing to change, accepting the discomforts that come with it, and taking risks are qualities of the "master student." Without realizing it, I was exercising these qualities all along.

When I had the opportunity to at-tend college in the summer of 1999, it wasn't an easy decision to make as I had planned to spend a relaxed summer with my children. As a non-traditional student, I felt insecure, not only about my learning ability because I had been away from school for 28 years, but also because I had never learned good study skills. Be-sides, I would have to study in my second language. For these reasons, it took courage for me to return to school and experience something new. This is the way the "master stu-dent" would respond....

The "master student" class opened up to me many strategies that I use daily. For instance, I enjoy learning actively, by reading aloud or walking as I read. I study when I'm rested and my mind is fresh and receptive. In addition, when I have the opportu-nity, I enjoy studying with groups. As I continue my studies toward an As-sociate of Arts degree with an em-phasis in bilingual education, I feel confident and better equipped to meet the demands of my present and future courses.

The "master student" strategies are not only applied to studying; they are all-encompassing tools that I use for success in life. Applying time management skills has helped me set priorities. For instance, I have learned to postpone doing chores that aren't indispensable and to elim-inate nonproductive activities (such as watching television or long phone conversations) in order to have enough time for studying or cooking nutritious meals for my family....

The young adult grasped at op-portunities and was open to changes in her environment and herself. As an adult, I now eagerly pursue higher education and continue to discover the natural learner within. I will walk joyfully through the doors of oppor-tunity and taste success. ◪

2

Planning

Even if you are on the right track, you'll get run over if you just sit there.

WILL ROGERS

Dost thou love life, then do not squander time, for that's the stuff life is made of.

BENJAMIN FRANKLIN

why

this chapter matters . . .

Your ability to manage time and money is a major predictor of your success in school.

What

is included . . .

how

you can use this chapter . . .

Know exactly what you want to accomplish today, this month, this year—and beyond.
Eliminate stress due to poor planning and procrastination.
Gain freedom from money worries.

As you read, ask yourself

what if . . .

I could have more than enough time and money to accomplish whatever I choose?

You've got the time

The words *planning* and *time management* can call forth images of restriction and control. You might visualize a prune-faced Scrooge hunched over your shoulder, stopwatch in hand, telling you what to do every minute. Bad news.

Good news: You do have enough time for the things you want to do. All it takes is learning to plan.

Planning is about time, and time is an equal opportunity resource. All of us, regardless of gender, race, creed, or national origin, have exactly the same number of hours in a week. No matter how newsworthy we are, no matter how rich or poor, we get 168 hours to spend each week—no more, no less.

Time is also an unusual commodity. It cannot be saved. You can't stockpile time like wood for the stove or food for the winter. It can't be seen, felt, touched, tasted, or smelled. You can't sense time directly. Even scientists and philosophers find it hard to describe. Because time is so elusive, it is easy to ignore. That doesn't bother time at all. Time is perfectly content to remain hidden until you are nearly out of it. And when you are out of it, you are out of it.

Time is a nonrenewable resource. If you're out of wood, you can chop some more. If you're out of money, you can earn a little extra. If you're out of love, there is still hope. If you're out of health, it can often be restored. But when you're out of time, that's it. When this minute is gone, it's gone. Time seems to pass at varying speeds. Sometimes it crawls and sometimes it's faster than a speeding bullet. On Friday afternoons, classroom clocks can creep. After you've worked a 10-hour day, reading the last few pages of an economics assignment can turn minutes into hours. A year in school can stretch out to an eternity. At the other end of the spectrum, time flies. There are moments when you are so absorbed in what you're doing that hours disappear like magic.

Approach time as if you are in control. Sometimes it seems that your friends control your time, that your boss controls your time, that your teachers or your parents or your kids or somebody else controls your time. Maybe that is not true. When you say you don't have enough time, you might really be saying that you are not spending the time you *do* have in the way that you want.

This chapter used to be called *Time*. The new title—*Planning*—puts this material in a bigger context. Planning involves determining what you want to achieve and how you intend to go about it. You can state your wants as written goals. Then use your time management skills to schedule activities that will help you meet those goals.

As you plan, be willing to include all areas of your life. In addition to setting academic goals, write down goals relating to your career, family life, social life, or anything else that matters to you. Since money is a concern for many students, this chapter includes specific suggestions for financial planning.

Planning gives you a chance to spend your most valuable resource in the way you choose. Start by observing how you use time. The next exercise gives you this opportunity. ✖

journal entry 6

Discovery/Intention Statement

Think back to a time during the past year when you rushed to finish a project or when you did not find time for an activity that was important to you. List one thing you might have done to create this outcome.

I discovered that I . . .

_____

_____

_____

Take a few minutes to skim this chapter. Find three to five articles that might help you avoid such outcomes in the future and list them below.

Title	*Page number*

If you don't have time to read these articles in depth right now, schedule a time to do so.

I intend to . . .

_____

_____

_____

THE TIME MONITOR/TIME PLAN PROCESS

The purpose of this exercise is to transform time into a knowable and predictable resource. You can do this by repeating a two-phase cycle of monitoring and planning.

This exercise takes place over two weeks. During the first week, you can monitor your activities to get a detailed picture of how you spend your time. Then you can plan the second week thoughtfully. Monitor your time during the second week, compare it to your plan, and discover what changes you want to make in the following week's plan.

Monitor your time in 15-minute intervals, 24 hours a day, for seven days. Record how much time you spend sleeping, eating, studying, attending lectures, traveling to and from class, working, watching television, listening to music, taking care of the kids, running errands—everything.

If this sounds crazy, hang on for a minute. This exercise is not about keeping track of the rest of your life in 15-minute intervals. It is an opportunity to become conscious of how you spend your time, your life. Use the Time Monitor/Time Plan process only for as long as it is helpful to do so.

When you know how your time is spent, you can find ways to adjust and manage it so that you spend your life doing the things that are most important to you. Monitoring your time is a critical first step toward putting you in control of your life.

Some students choose to keep track of their time on 3x5 cards, calendars, campus planners, or software designed for this purpose. You might even develop your own form for monitoring your time.

1. Get to know the Time Monitor/Time Plan. Look at the Time Monitor/Time Plan on page 63. Note that each day has two columns, one labeled "monitor" and the other labeled "plan." During the first week, use only the "monitor" column. After that, use both columns simultaneously to continue the monitor-plan process.

To become familiar with the form, look at the example on page 63. When you begin an activity, write it down next to the time you begin and put a line just above that spot. Round off to the nearest 15 minutes. If, for example, you begin eating at 8:06, enter your starting time as 8:00. Over time, it will probably even out. In any case, you will be close enough to realize the benefits of this exercise. (Note that you can use the blank spaces in the "monitor"

Do this exercise online at

masterstudent.college.hmco.com

and "plan" columns to cover most of the day.)

On Monday, the student in this example got up at 6:45 a.m., showered, and got dressed. He finished this activity and began breakfast at 7:15. He put this new activity in at the time he began and drew a line just above it. He ate from 7:15 to 7:45. It took him 15 minutes to walk to class (7:45 to 8:00), and he attended classes from 8:00 to 11:00.

Keep your Time Monitor/Time Plan with you every minute you are awake for one week. Take a few moments every two or three hours to record what you've done. Or enter a note each time you change activities.

Here's an eye opener for many students. If you think you already have a good idea of how you manage time, predict how many hours you will spend in a week on each category of activity listed in the form on page 64. (Four categories are already provided; you can add more at any time.) Do this before your first week of monitoring. Write your predictions in the margin to the left of each category. After monitoring your time for one week, see how accurate your predictions were.

2. Remember to use your Time Monitor/Time Plan. It might be easy to forget to fill out your Time Monitor/Time Plan. One way to remember is to create a visual reminder for yourself. You can use this technique for any activity you want to remember.

Relax for a moment, close your eyes, and imagine that you see your Time Monitor/Time Plan. Imagine that it has arms and legs and is as big as a person. Picture the form sitting at your desk at home, in your car, in one of your classrooms, or in your favorite chair. Visualize it sitting wherever you're likely to sit. When you sit down, the Time Monitor/Time Plan will get squashed.

You can make this image more effective by adding sound effects. The Time Monitor/Time Plan might scream, "Get off me!" Or since time can be related to money, you might associate the Time Monitor/Time Plan with the sound of an old-fashioned cash register. Imagine that every time you sit down, a cash register rings.

3. Evaluate the Time Monitor/Time Plan. After you've monitored your time for one week, group your activities together by categories. The form on page 64 lists the categories "sleep," "class," "study," and "meals." Think of other categories you could add. "Grooming" might include showering, putting on makeup, brushing teeth, and getting dressed. "Travel" can include walking, driving, taking the bus, and

MONDAY 9 / 12

Time	Monitor	Plan
	Get up	
	Shower	
7:00	———	7:00
7:15	Breakfast	
7:30		
7:45	Walk to	
8:00	class	8:00
8:15		
8:30	Econ 1	
8:45		
9:00		9:00
9:15		
9:30		
9:45		
10:00	Bio 1	10:00
10:15		
10:30		
10:45		
11:00		11:00
11:15	Study	
11:30		
11:45		
12:00		12:00
12:15	Lunch	
12:30		
12:45		
1:00		1:00
1:15	Eng. Lit	
1:30		
1:45		
2:00		2:00
2:15	Coffeehouse	
2:30		
2:45		
3:00		3:00
3:15		
3:30		
3:45		
4:00		4:00
4:15	Study	
4:30		
4:45		
5:00		5:00
5:15	Dinner	
5:30		
5:45		
6:00		6:00
6:15		
6:30	Babysit	
6:45		
7:00		7:00

TUESDAY 9 / 13

Time	Monitor	Plan
	Sleep	
7:00		7:00
7:15		
7:30		
7:45	Shower	
8:00	Dress	8:00
8:15	Eat	
8:30		
8:45		
9:00	Art	9:00
9:15	Apprec.	
9:30	Project	
9:45		
10:00		10:00
10:15		
10:30		
10:45		
11:00	Data	11:00
11:15	process	
11:30		
11:45		
12:00		12:00
12:15		
12:30		
12:45		
1:00		1:00
1:15	Lunch	
1:30		
1:45		
2:00	Work	2:00
2:15	on book	
2:30	report	
2:45		
3:00	Art	3:00
3:15	Apprec.	
3:30		
3:45		
4:00		4:00
4:15		
4:30		
4:45		
5:00	Dinner	5:00
5:15		
5:30		
5:45		
6:00	Letter to	6:00
6:15	Uncle Jim	
6:30		
6:45		
7:00		7:00

riding your bike. Other categories might be "exercise," "entertainment," "work," "television," "domestic," and "children."

Write in the categories that work for you, and then add up how much time you spent in each of your categories. Put the totals in the "monitored" column on page 64. Make sure that the grand total of all categories is 168 hours.

Now take a minute and let these numbers sink in. Compare your totals to your predictions and notice your reactions. You might be surprised. You might feel disappointed or even angry about where your time goes. Use those feelings as motivation to plan your time differently. Go to the "planned" column and decide how much time you want to spend on various daily activities. As you do so, allow yourself to have fun. Approach planning in the spirit of adventure. Think of yourself as an artist who's creating a new life.

In several months you might want to take another detailed look at how you spend your life. You can expand the two-phase cycle of monitoring and planning to include a third phase: evaluating. Combine this with planning your time, following the suggestions in this chapter. You can use a continuous cycle: monitor, evaluate, plan; monitor, evaluate, plan. When you make it a habit, this cycle can help you get the full benefits of time management for the rest of your life. Then time management becomes more than a technique. It's transformed into a habit, a constant awareness of how you spend your lifetime.

Planning is a broad word that refers to all aspects of creating a vision for your future. Goal setting, time management, budgeting—all are tools that allow you to maximize your freedom and live a full life. Few architects propose a building project without a blueprint. Few entrepreneurs get venture capital without a sound business plan. And few film producers begin shooting a movie without a script. In each case, the rationale is to avoid actions that waste time, money, effort, and talent. In this light, it's amazing that so many people lack a plan for something as important as their own lives.

Planning and motivation are mutually reinforcing. When your goals connect to your deepest desires, you discover new reserves of energy. Moving into action becomes almost effortless. When you clearly define a goal, your mind and body start to operate more consistently in ways to achieve your dreams. As you meet goals and cross them off your list, you experience the satisfaction of success.

Look for extra copies of the Time Monitor/Time Plan at the back of this book.

WEEK OF ___ / ___ / ___ /		
Category	Monitored	Planned
Sleep		
Class		
Study		
Meals		

MONDAY ___ / ___ / ___ /		TUESDAY ___ / ___ / ___ /		WEDNESDAY ___ / ___ / ___ /	
Monitor	**Plan**	**Monitor**	**Plan**	**Monitor**	**Plan**
7:00	7:00	7:00	7:00	7:00	7:00
7:15		7:15		7:15	
7:30		7:30		7:30	
7:45		7:45		7:45	
8:00	8:00	8:00	8:00	8:00	8:00
8:15		8:15		8:15	
8:30		8:30		8:30	
8:45		8:45		8:45	
9:00	9:00	9:00	9:00	9:00	9:00
9:15		9:15		9:15	
9:30		9:30		9:30	
9:45		9:45		9:45	
10:00	10:00	10:00	10:00	10:00	10:00
10:15		10:15		10:15	
10:30		10:30		10:30	
10:45		10:45		10:45	
11:00	11:00	11:00	11:00	11:00	11:00
11:15		11:15		11:15	
11:30		11:30		11:30	
11:45		11:45		11:45	
12:00	12:00	12:00	12:00	12:00	12:00
12:15		12:15		12:15	
12:30		12:30		12:30	
12:45		12:45		12:45	
1:00	1:00	1:00	1:00	1:00	1:00
1:15		1:15		1:15	
1:30		1:30		1:30	
1:45		1:45		1:45	
2:00	2:00	2:00	2:00	2:00	2:00
2:15		2:15		2:15	
2:30		2:30		2:30	
2:45		2:45		2:45	
3:00	3:00	3:00	3:00	3:00	3:00
3:15		3:15		3:15	
3:30		3:30		3:30	
3:45		3:45		3:45	
4:00	4:00	4:00	4:00	4:00	4:00
4:15		4:15		4:15	
4:30		4:30		4:30	
4:45		4:45		4:45	
5:00	5:00	5:00	5:00	5:00	5:00
5:15		5:15		5:15	
5:30		5:30		5:30	
5:45		5:45		5:45	
6:00	6:00	6:00	6:00	6:00	6:00
6:15		6:15		6:15	
6:30		6:30		6:30	
6:45		6:45		6:45	
7:00	7:00	7:00	7:00	7:00	7:00
7:15		7:15		7:15	
7:30		7:30		7:30	
7:45		7:45		7:45	
8:00	8:00	8:00	8:00	8:00	8:00
8:15		8:15		8:15	
8:30		8:30		8:30	
8:45		8:45		8:45	
9:00	9:00	9:00	9:00	9:00	9:00
9:15		9:15		9:15	
9:30		9:30		9:30	
9:45		9:45		9:45	
10:00	10:00	10:00	10:00	10:00	10:00
10:15		10:15		10:15	
10:30		10:30		10:30	
10:45		10:45		10:45	
11:00	11:00	11:00	11:00	11:00	11:00
11:15		11:15		11:15	
11:30		11:30		11:30	
11:45		11:45		11:45	
12:00	12:00	12:00	12:00	12:00	12:00

THURSDAY ___ / ___ / ___ /

Monitor	Plan
7:00	7:00
7:15	
7:30	
7:45	
8:00	8:00
8:15	
8:30	
8:45	
9:00	9:00
9:15	
9:30	
9:45	
10:00	10:00
10:15	
10:30	
10:45	
11:00	11:00
11:15	
11:30	
11:45	
12:00	12:00
12:15	
12:30	
12:45	
1:00	1:00
1:15	
1:30	
1:45	
2:00	2:00
2:15	
2:30	
2:45	
3:00	3:00
3:15	
3:30	
3:45	
4:00	4:00
4:15	
4:30	
4:45	
5:00	5:00
5:15	
5:30	
5:45	
6:00	6:00
6:15	
6:30	
6:45	
7:00	7:00
7:15	
7:30	
7:45	
8:00	8:00
8:15	
8:30	
8:45	
9:00	9:00
9:15	
9:30	
9:45	
10:00	10:00
10:15	
10:30	
10:45	
11:00	11:00
11:15	
11:30	
11:45	
12:00	12:00

FRIDAY ___ / ___ / ___ /

Monitor	Plan
7:00	7:00
7:15	
7:30	
7:45	
8:00	8:00
8:15	
8:30	
8:45	
9:00	9:00
9:15	
9:30	
9:45	
10:00	10:00
10:15	
10:30	
10:45	
11:00	11:00
11:15	
11:30	
11:45	
12:00	12:00
12:15	
12:30	
12:45	
1:00	1:00
1:15	
1:30	
1:45	
2:00	2:00
2:15	
2:30	
2:45	
3:00	3:00
3:15	
3:30	
3:45	
4:00	4:00
4:15	
4:30	
4:45	
5:00	5:00
5:15	
5:30	
5:45	
6:00	6:00
6:15	
6:30	
6:45	
7:00	7:00
7:15	
7:30	
7:45	
8:00	8:00
8:15	
8:30	
8:45	
9:00	9:00
9:15	
9:30	
9:45	
10:00	10:00
10:15	
10:30	
10:45	
11:00	11:00
11:15	
11:30	
11:45	
12:00	12:00

SATURDAY ___ / ___ / ___ /

Monitor	Plan

SUNDAY ___ / ___ / ___ /

Monitor	Plan

Discovery Statement

After one week of monitoring my time, I discovered that . . .

_____

_____

_____

I want to spend more time on . . .

_____

_____

_____

I want to spend less time on . . .

_____

_____

_____

I was surprised that I spent so much time on . . .

_____

_____

_____

I was surprised that I spent so little time on . . .

_____

_____

_____

I had strong feelings about my use of time when (describe the feeling and the situation) . . .

_____

_____

_____

Setting and achieving goals

Many of us have vague, idealized notions of what we want out of life. These notions float among the clouds in our heads. They are wonderful, fuzzy, safe thoughts such as "I want to be a good person," "I want to be financially secure," or "I want to be happy."

Such outcomes are great possible goals. Left in a generalized form, however, these goals can leave us confused about ways to actually achieve them.

If you really want to meet a goal, translate it into specific, concrete behaviors. Find out what that goal looks like. Listen to what it sounds like. Pick it up and feel how heavy that goal is. Inspect the switches, valves, joints, cogs, and fastenings of the goal. Make your goal as real as a chain saw.

There is nothing vague or fuzzy about chain saws. You can see them, feel them, and hear them. They have a clear function. Goals can be every bit as real and useful.

Writing down your goals exponentially increases your chances of meeting them. Writing exposes undefined terms, unrealistic time frames, and other symptoms of fuzzy thinking. If you've been completing Intention Statements as explained in the Introduction to this book, then you've already had experience writing goals. Goals and Intention Statements both address changes you want to make in your behavior, your values, your circumstances—or all of these. To keep track of your goals, write each one on a separate 3x5 card or key them all into a word processing file on your computer.

There are many useful methods for setting goals. Following is one of them. This method is based on writing specific goals in several time frames and areas of your life. Experiment with it and modify it as you see fit. You're also encouraged to reflect regularly on your goals. The key words to remember are *specific, time, areas*, and *reflect*. Combine the first letter of each word and you get the acronym *STAR*. Use this acronym to remember the suggestions that follow.

Write specific goals. In writing, state your goals as observable actions or measurable results. Think in detail about how things will be different once your goals are attained. List the changes in what you'd see, feel, touch, taste, hear, be, do, or have.

Suppose that one of your goals is to become a better student by studying harder. You're headed in a powerful direction; now go for the specifics. Translate that goal into a concrete action, such as "I will study two hours for every hour I'm in class." Specific goals make clear what actions are needed or what results are expected. Consider these examples:

Vague goal	Specific goal
Get a good education.	Graduate with B.S. degree in engineering, with honors, by 2009.
Enhance my spiritual life.	Meditate for 15 minutes daily.
Improve my appearance.	Lose six pounds during the next six months.

When stated specifically, a goal might look different to you. If you examine it closely, a goal you once thought you wanted might not be something you want after all. Or you might discover that you want to choose a new path to achieve a goal that you are sure you want.

Write goals in several time frames. To get a comprehensive vision of your future, write down:

- *Long-term goals.* Long-term goals represent major targets in your life. These goals can take five to 20 years to achieve. In some cases, they will take a lifetime. They can include goals in education, careers, personal relationships, travel, financial security—whatever is important to you. Consider the answers to the following questions as you create your long-term goals: What do you want to accomplish in your life? Do you want your life to make a statement? If so, what is that statement?

- *Mid-term goals.* Mid-term goals are objectives you can accomplish in one to five years. They include goals such as completing a course of education, paying off a car loan, or achieving a specific career level. These goals usually support your long-term goals.

- *Short-term goals.* Short-term goals are the ones you can accomplish in a year or less. These goals are specific achievements, such as completing a particular course or group of courses, hiking down the Appalachian Trail, or organizing a family reunion. A fi-

nancial goal would probably include an exact dollar amount. Whatever your short-term goals are, they will require action now or in the near future.

Write goals in several areas of life. People who set goals in only one area of life—such as their career—can find that their personal growth becomes one-sided. They could experience success at work while neglecting their health or relationships with family members and friends.

To avoid this outcome, set goals in a variety of categories. Consider what you want to experience in your:

- education
- career
- financial life
- family life
- social life
- spiritual life
- level of health

Add goals in other areas as they occur to you.

Reflect on your goals. Each week, take a few minutes to think about your goals. You can perform the following "spot checks":

- *Check in with your feelings.* Think about how the process of setting your goals felt. Consider the satisfaction you'll gain in attaining your objectives. If you don't feel a significant emotional connection with a written goal, consider letting it go or filing it away to review later.

- *Check for alignment.* Look for connections between your goals. Do your short-term goals align with your mid-term goals? Will your mid-term goals help you achieve your long-term goals? Look for a "fit" between all of your goals and your purpose for taking part in higher education, as well as your overall purpose in life.

- *Check for obstacles.* All kinds of things can come between you and your goals, such as constraints on time and money. Anticipate obstacles and start looking now for workable solutions.

- *Check for immediate steps.* Here's a way to link goal setting to time management. Decide on a list of small, achievable steps you can take right away to accomplish each of your short-term goals. Write these small steps down on a daily to-do list. If you want to accomplish some of them by a certain date, enter them in a calendar that you consult daily. Then, over the coming weeks, review your to-do list and calendar. Take note of your progress and celebrate your successes. ✖

GET REAL WITH YOUR GOALS

One way to make goals effective is to examine them up close. That's what this exercise is about. Using a process of brainstorming and evaluation, you can break a long-term goal into smaller segments until you have taken it completely apart. When you analyze a goal to this level of detail, you're well on the way to meeting it.

For this exercise, you will use a pen, extra paper, and a watch with a second hand. (A digital watch with a built-in stopwatch is even better.) Timing is an important part of the brainstorming process, so follow the stated time limits. This entire exercise takes about an hour.

Part one: Long-term goals

Brainstorm. Begin with an eight-minute brainstorm. For eight minutes write down everything you think you want in your life. Write as fast as you can and write whatever comes into your head. Leave no thought out. Don't worry about accuracy. The object of a brainstorm is to generate as many ideas as possible. Use a separate sheet of paper for this part of the exercise.

Evaluate. After you have finished brainstorming, spend the next six minutes looking over your list. Analyze what you wrote. Read the list out loud. If something is missing, add it. Look for common themes or relationships between goals. Then select three long-term goals that are important to you—goals that will take many years to achieve. Write these goals below in the space provided.

_____

_____

_____

Before you continue, take a minute to reflect on the process you've used so far. What criteria did you use to select your top three goals? For example, list some of the core values (such as love, wealth, or happiness) underlying these goals.

Part two: Mid-term goals

Brainstorm. Read out loud the three long-term goals you selected in Part One. Choose one of them. Then brainstorm a list of goals you might achieve in the next one to five years that would lead to the accomplishment of that

Do this exercise online at

masterstudent.college.hmco.com

one long-term goal. These are mid-term goals. Spend eight minutes on this brainstorm. Remember, neatness doesn't count. Go for quantity.

Evaluate. Analyze your brainstorm of mid-term goals. Then select three that you determine to be important in meeting the long-term goal you picked. Allow yourself six minutes for this part of the exercise. Write your selections below in the space provided.

_____

_____

Again, pause for reflection before going on to the next part of this exercise. Why do you see these three goals as more important than the other mid-term goals you generated? Write about your reasons for selecting these three goals.

Part three: Short-term goals

Brainstorm. Review your list of mid-term goals and select one. In another eight-minute brainstorm, generate a list of short-term goals—those you can accomplish in a year or less that will lead to the attainment of that mid-term goal. Write down everything that comes to mind. Do not evaluate or judge these ideas yet. For now, the more ideas you write down, the better.

Evaluate. Analyze your list of short-term goals. The most effective brainstorms are conducted by suspending judgment, so you might find some bizarre ideas on your list. That's fine. Now is the time to cross them out. Next evaluate your remaining short-term goals and select three that you are willing and able to accomplish. Allow yourself six minutes for this part of the exercise, then write your selections below in the space provided.

_____

_____

The more you practice, the more effective you can be at choosing goals that have meaning for you. You can repeat this exercise, employing the other long-term goals you generated or creating new ones. By using this brainstorm and evaluation process, you can make goals come to life in the here and now.

One of the most effective ways to stay on track and actually get things done is to use a daily to-do list. While the Time Monitor/Time Plan gives you a general picture of the week, your daily to-do list itemizes specific tasks you want to complete within the next 24 hours.

The ABC daily to-do list

One advantage of keeping a daily to-do list is that you don't have to remember what to do next. It's on the list. A typical day in the life of a student is full of separate, often unrelated tasks—reading, attending lectures, reviewing notes, working at a job, writing papers, researching special projects, running errands. It's easy to forget an important task on a busy day. When that task is written down, you don't have to rely on your memory.

The following steps present one method for to-do lists. Experiment with these steps, modify them as you see fit, and invent new techniques that work for you.

Step 1 Brainstorm tasks.
To get started, list all of the tasks you want to get done tomorrow. Each task will become an item on a to-do list. Don't worry about putting the entries in order or scheduling them yet. Just list everything you want to accomplish on a sheet of paper or a planning calendar, or in a special notebook. You can also use 3x5 cards, writing one task on each card. Cards work well because you can slip them into your pocket or rearrange them, and you never have to copy to-do items from one list to another.

Step 2 Estimate time.
For each task you wrote down in step 1, estimate how long it will take you to complete it. This can be tricky. If you allow too little time, you end up feeling rushed. If you allow too much time, you become less productive. For now, give it your best guess. Your estimates will improve with practice. Now pull out your calendar or Time Monitor/Time Plan. You've probably scheduled some hours for activities such as classes or work. This leaves the unscheduled hours for tackling your to-do lists.

Add up the time needed to complete all your to-do items. Also add up the number of unscheduled hours in your day. Then compare the two totals. The power of this step is that you can spot overload in advance. If you have eight hours' worth of to-do items but only four unscheduled hours, that's a potential problem. To solve it, proceed to step 3.

Step 3

Rate each task by priority. To prevent overscheduling, decide which to-do items are the most important given the time you have available. One suggestion for doing this comes from the book *Take Control of Your Time and Life* by Alan Lakein: Simply label each task A, B, or C.[1]

The A's on your list are those things that are the most critical. These are assignments that are coming due or jobs that need to be done immediately. Also included are activities that lead directly to your short-term goals.

The B's on your list are important, but less so than the A's. B's might someday become A's. For the present, these tasks are not as urgent as A's. They can be postponed, if necessary, for another day.

The C's do not require immediate attention. C priorities include activities such as "shop for a new blender" and "research genealogy on the Internet." C's are often small, easy jobs with no set timeline. These, too, can be postponed.

Once you've labeled the items on your to-do list, schedule time for all of the A's. The B's and C's can be done randomly during the day when you are in between tasks and are not yet ready to start the next A.

Step 4

Cross off tasks. Keep your to-do list with you at all times, crossing off activities when you finish them and adding new ones when you think of them. If you're using 3x5 cards, you can toss away or recycle the cards with completed items. Crossing off tasks and releasing cards can be fun—a visible reward for your diligence. This step fosters a sense of accomplishment.

When using the ABC priority method, you might experience an ailment common to students: C fever. This is the uncontrollable urge to drop that A task and begin crossing C's off your to-do list. If your history paper is due tomorrow, you might feel compelled to vacuum the rug, call your third cousin in Tulsa, and make a trip to the store for shoelaces. The reason C fever is so common is that A tasks are usually more difficult or time-consuming to achieve, with a higher risk of failure.

If you notice symptoms of C fever, ask: Does this job really need to be done now? Do I really need to alphabetize my CD collection, or might I better use this time to study for tomorrow's data processing exam? Use your to-do list to keep yourself on task, working on your A's. Don't panic or berate yourself when you realize that in the last six hours, you have completed 11 C's and not a single A. Calmly return to the A's.

Step 5

Evaluate. At the end of the day, evaluate your performance. Look for A priorities you didn't complete. Look for items that repeatedly turn up as B's or C's on your list and never seem to get done. Consider changing these to A's or dropping them altogether. Similarly, you might consider changing an A that didn't get done to a B or C priority. When you're done evaluating, start on tomorrow's to-do list. Be willing to admit mistakes. You might at first rank some items as A's only to realize later that they are actually C's. Some of the C's that lurk at the bottom of your list day after day might really be A's. When you keep a daily to-do list, you can adjust these priorities *before* they become problems.

The ABC system is not the only way to rank items on your to-do list. Some people prefer the "80-20" system. This is based on the idea that 80 percent of the value of any to-do list comes from only 20 percent of the tasks on that list. So on a to-do list of 10 items, find the two that will contribute most to your life, and complete those tasks without fail.

Another option is to rank items as "yes," "no," or "maybe." Do all of the tasks marked "yes." Ignore those marked "no." And put all of the "maybe's" on the shelf for later. You can come back to the "maybe's" at a future point and rank them as "yes" or "no."

Or you can develop your own style for to-do lists. You might find that grouping items by categories such as "errands" or "reading assignments" works best. Be creative.

Keep in mind the power of planning a whole week or even two weeks in advance. Planning in this way can make it easier to put activities in context and see how your daily goals relate to your long-term goals. Weekly planning can also free you from feeling that you have to polish off your whole to-do list in one day. Instead, you can spread tasks out over the whole week.

In any case, make starting your own to-do list an A priority.

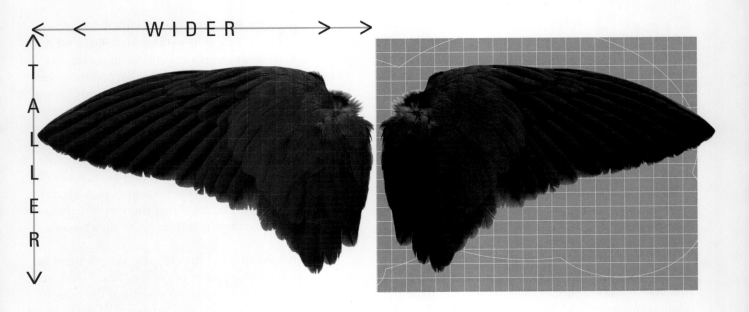

WIDER

TALLER

Planning
sets you free

When you plan, you can
create freedom. This contradicts
the common notion of planning:
"Me? Plan? No way. I don't want
to be uptight. I don't want to be
restrained. I don't want to lose
my spontaneity. I don't want
to be some tense person who
never gets to have any fun.
I want to be free."

Rather than being a restraint, planning is a way of living life to the fullest. One path to feeling calm, peaceful, fun-loving, joyful, and powerful is to have a plan. When we are uptight, worried, and hassled—when we're not feeling free—we often have no plan.

You set the plan

One freedom in planning stems from the simple fact that you set the plan. The course and direction are yours.

Often, particularly at work or in school, people do not feel this way. They feel that the plan is coming from someone else—an employer, a supervisor, or a teacher.

Consider that this view is inaccurate. If we look ahead into the future, we can choose to see any circumstance as part of a plan for our whole lives. Even when we don't like aspects of a job, for example, working provides income and helps us develop useful skills for the next job. When we plan far enough in advance, a job no longer has to feel limiting.

You can change the plan

Another freedom in planning is the freedom to make changes. An effective plan is flexible, not carved in stone.

Tell people that you have a 20-year plan for your career. They might ask, "Well, if the economy changes, would you consider changing your plan?" "Yes," you reply. "I change it every year." Then comes the laughter: "Well, it really isn't a 20-year plan if you change it every year. It's actually a one-year plan."

In reality, we can change our plans frequently and still preserve the advantages of long-range planning. Those advantages come from choosing our overall direction and taking charge of our lives.

You choose how to achieve the plan

Suppose you take a new job and with it comes a detailed agenda of goals to achieve in one year. You might say, "I didn't choose these goals. I guess I'll just have to put up with them."

There is another point of view you can take in this situation: Even when others select the goals, you can choose whether to accept them. You can also choose your own way to achieve any goal. The outcome might be determined for you, but the way you produce that outcome can be up to you.

When there's a plan, there's a chance

Planning to meet a goal doesn't ensure accomplishment, but it does boost the odds of success. Your clearly defined goals and carefully chosen action plans increase the probability that you'll achieve what you want. You have a goal. You've laid out the necessary actions in logical sequence. And you've set a due date to perform each action. Now the goal seems possible, whereas before it might have seemed impossible.

Much of what people undertake at school, at work, in relationships, and at home is simply "digging in"—frantic action with no plan. "Sure, we might never reach the goal," they say, "but at least we're out there trying." In this statement we hear a loss of hope. Planning can replace despair with a purpose and a timeline.

Planning frees you from constant decisions

When we operate without a plan, we might change our minds often: "Hmmm.... That chocolate cake smells great. Maybe I'll have a piece—but maybe I shouldn't. It's a lot of calories. I don't know...." That kind of debate takes up a lot of time and energy.

But suppose you plan to stop eating chocolate cake. You write down this plan. You speak about this plan to friends, even commit yourself to it in their presence. Temptation still occurs: "Gee, that cake smells great." But then you remember: "Wait. I don't have to make this decision now. I'll just follow my plan and avoid chocolate cake."

Planning makes adjustments easier

Suppose you are scheduled to give a talk in your speech class next week. Suddenly you find out there was a misprint in the course schedule. You're supposed to speak two days from now, not seven. Without a plan, you would face a lengthy mental process, a whole series of questions: What will I do now? When will I have time to get that speech done? How will this affect the rest of my schedule?

With a plan, things are different. You might say, "I don't have to worry about this. I've done my plan for the week, and I know I have free time tomorrow night between 7 and 10 p.m. I can finish the speech then."

Planning enables you to respond to crises—or opportunities. With a plan, you are free to handle unexpected change. With a plan, you can take initiative rather than merely react. When you plan, you *give* your time to things instead of allowing things to *take* your time.

Rather than being a restraint, planning is a way of living life to the fullest.

Planning and action create your life

Of course, planning by itself is ineffective. Nothing in our lives will change until we take action. The value of planning is that it promotes actions that we consciously choose.

Planning is about creating your own experience. When you plan, your life does not just "happen." When you plan, you are the equal of the greatest sculptor, painter, or playwright. More than creating a work of art, you are designing a life. ◪

Strategies for scheduling

Schedule fixed blocks of time first. Start with class time and work time, for instance. These time periods are usually determined in advance. Other activities must be scheduled around them. Then schedule essential daily activities such as sleeping and eating. No matter what else you do, you will sleep and eat. Be realistic about how much time you need for these functions.

Include time for errands. The time we spend buying toothpaste, paying bills, and doing laundry is easy to overlook. These little errands can destroy a tight schedule and make us feel rushed and harried all week. Plan for them and remember to allow for travel time between locations.

Schedule time for fun. Fun is important. Brains that are constantly stimulated by new ideas and new challenges need time off to digest them. Take time to browse aimlessly through the library, stroll with no destination, ride a bike, or do other things you enjoy. Recreation deserves a place in your priorities. It's important to "waste" time once in a while.

Set realistic goals. Don't set yourself up for failure by telling yourself you can do a four-hour job in two hours. There are only 168 hours in a week. If you schedule 169 hours, you've already lost before you begin.

Allow flexibility in your schedule. Recognize that unexpected things will happen and plan for the unexpected. Leave some holes in your schedule; build in blocks of unplanned time. Consider setting aside time each week marked "flex time" or "open time." Use these hours for emergencies, spontaneous activities, catching up, or seizing new opportunities.

Study two hours for every hour in class. In higher education, it's standard advice to allow two hours of study time for every hour spent in class. Students making the transition from high school to college are often unaware that more is expected of them.

If you are taking 15 credit hours, plan to spend 30 hours a week studying. The benefits of following this advice will be apparent at exam time.

This guideline is just that—a guideline, not an absolute rule. Consider what's best for you. If you do the Time Monitor/Time Plan exercise in this chapter, note how many hours you actually spend studying for each hour of class. Then ask how your schedule is working. You might want to allow more study time for some subjects.

Also keep in mind that the "two hours for one" rule doesn't distinguish between focused time and unfocused time. In one four-hour block of study time, it's possible to use up two of those hours with phone calls, breaks, daydreaming, and doodling. When it comes to scheduling time, quality counts as much as quantity.

Avoid scheduling marathon study sessions. When possible, study in shorter sessions. Three three-hour sessions are usually far more productive than one nine-hour session. In a nine- or 10-hour study marathon, the percentage of time actually spent on a task can be depressingly small. With 10 hours of study ahead of you, the temptation is to tell yourself, "Well, it's going to be a long day. No sense rushing into it. Better sharpen about a dozen of these pencils and change the light bulbs." In a nine-hour sitting you might spend only six or seven hours studying, whereas three shorter sessions will likely yield more productive study time. When you do study in long sessions, stop and rest for a few minutes every hour. Give your brain a chance to take a break.

If you must study in a large block of time, work on several subjects and avoid studying similar topics one after the other. For example, if you plan to study sociology, psychology, and computer science, schedule computer science in between psychology and sociology.

Set clear starting and stopping times. Tasks often expand to fill the time we allot for them. "It always takes me an hour just to settle into a reading assignment" might become a self-fulfilling prophecy.

Try scheduling a certain amount of time for a reading assignment—set a timer, and stick to it. Students often find that they can decrease study time by forcing themselves to read faster. This can usually be done without sacrificing comprehension.

The same principle can apply to other tasks. Some people find they can get up 15 minutes earlier in the morning and still feel alert throughout the day. Plan 45 minutes for a trip to the grocery store instead of one hour. Over the course of a year, those extra minutes can add up to hours.

Feeling rushed or sacrificing quality is not the goal here. The point is to push ourselves a little and discover what our time requirements really are.

Plan for the unexpected.
The best-laid plans can be foiled by the unexpected. Children and day care providers get sick. Cars break down. Subway trains run late. The electric power shuts off, silencing alarm clocks.

That's when it pays to have a backup plan. You can find someone to care for your children when the babysitter gets the flu. You can plan an alternative way to get to work. You can set the alarm on your watch as well as the one on your bedside clock. Giving such items five minutes of careful thought today can save you hours in the future.

Involve others when appropriate.
Sometimes the activities we schedule depend on gaining information, assistance, or direct participation from other people. If we neglect to inform them of our plans or forget to ask for their cooperation at the outset—surprise! Our schedules can crash.

Statements such as these often follow the breakdown: "I just assumed you were going to pick up the kids from school on Tuesday." "I'm working overtime this week and hoped that you'd take over the cooking for a while."

When you schedule a task that depends on another person's involvement, let that person know—the sooner, the better.

Back up to a bigger picture.
When scheduling activities for the day or week, take some time to lift your eyes to the horizon. Step back for a few minutes and consider your longer-range goals—what you want to accomplish in the next six months, the next year, the next five years, and beyond. Ask whether the activities you've scheduled actually contribute to those goals. If they do, great. If not, ask whether you can delete some items from your calendar to make room for goal-related activities.

You can make this kind of adjustment to your schedule even when your goals are not precisely defined. You might suddenly sense that this is the time in your life to start a new relationship, take a long trip, or move to a new house. Pay attention to these intuitions; allow space in your daily and weekly schedules to explore and act on your dreams.

Aim to free up at least one hour each day for doing something you love instead of putting it off to a more "reasonable" or "convenient" time.

"Filter" tasks before scheduling them.
To trim the "fat" from your schedule, ask some questions before you add an activity to your calendar or to-do list. For example: What do I need to accomplish before I can schedule this item? If I choose never to take this action, could I live with the consequences? What would be the outcome if I put this task off for a month? Six months? One year?

Consider technology carefully.
Today you can choose from a constantly expanding line of devices to assist with scheduling. These range from time management software for your desktop computer to personal digital assistants. You might enjoy experimenting with this technology. And if your budget is tight, you can always rely on some old-fashioned technology—pencil and paper. ◩

For updates on useful technology for scheduling, visit this book's Web site at

masterstudent.college.hmco.com

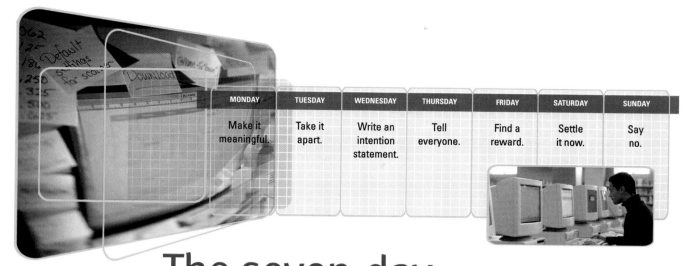

MONDAY	TUESDAY	WEDNESDAY	THURSDAY	FRIDAY	SATURDAY	SUNDAY
Make it meaningful.	Take it apart.	Write an intention statement.	Tell everyone.	Find a reward.	Settle it now.	Say no.

The seven-day
antiprocrastination plan

Listed here are seven strategies you can use to reduce or eliminate many sources of procrastination. The suggestions are tied to the days of the week to help you remember them. Use this list to remind yourself that each day of your life presents an opportunity to stop the cycle of procrastination.

MONDAY **Make it meaningful.** What is important about the task you've been putting off? List all the benefits of completing it. Look at it in relation to your short-, mid-, or long-term goals. Be specific about the rewards for getting it done, including how you will feel when the task is completed. To remember this strategy, keep in mind that it starts with the letter *M*, like the word *Monday*.

TUESDAY **Take it apart.** Break big jobs into a series of small ones you can do in 15 minutes or less. If a long reading assignment intimidates you, divide it into two-page or three-page sections. Make a list of the sections and cross them off as you complete them so you can see your progress. Even the biggest projects can be broken down into a series of small tasks. This strategy starts with the letter *T*, so mentally tie it to *Tuesday*.

WEDNESDAY **Write an intention statement.** For example, if you can't get started on a term paper, you might write, "I intend to write a list of at least 10 possible topics by 9 p.m. I will reward myself with an hour of guilt-free recreational reading." Write your intention on a 3x5 card and carry it with you, or post it in your study area where you can see it often. In your memory, file the first word in this strategy—*write*—with *Wednesday*.

THURSDAY **Tell everyone.** Publicly announce your intention to get a task done. Tell a friend that you intend to learn 10 irregular French verbs by Saturday. Tell your spouse, roommate, parents, and children. Include anyone who

> ## voices
>
> **student**
>
> *Making lists has been one of my favorite tools to stay on track and prioritize. Not much gives me more pleasure than to cross off duties one by one and to see the number of items left to do shrink to nothing, or what can be put off until another time.*
>
> — LAURIE MURRAY

will ask whether you've completed the assignment or who will suggest ways to get it done. Make the world your support group. Associate *tell* with *Thursday*.

FRIDAY

Find a reward. Construct rewards to yourself carefully. Be willing to withhold them if you do not complete the task. Don't pick a movie as a reward for studying biology if you plan to go to the movie anyway. And when you legitimately reap your reward, notice how it feels. Remember that *Friday* is a fine day to *find* a reward. (Of course, you can find a reward on any day of the week. Rhyming *Friday* with *fine day* is just a memory trick.)

SATURDAY

Settle it now. Do it now. The minute you notice yourself procrastinating, plunge into the task. Imagine yourself at a cold mountain lake, poised to dive. Gradual immersion would be slow torture. It's often less painful to leap. Then be sure to savor the feeling of having the task behind you. Link *settle* with *Saturday*.

SUNDAY

Say no. When you keep pushing a task into a low-priority category, re-examine your purpose for doing it at all. If you realize that you really don't intend to do something, quit telling yourself that you will. That's procrastinating. Just say no. Then you're not procrastinating. You don't have to carry around the baggage of an undone task. *Sunday*—the last day of this seven-day plan—is a great day to finally let go and just *say* no. ⊠

More ways to stop procrastination

Perhaps you didn't get around to using the seven-day antiprocrastination plan. Well, there's plenty more where that plan came from. Consider seven more suggestions.

Observe your procrastination. Instead of rushing to fix your procrastination problem, take your time. Get to know your problem well. Avoid judgments. Just be a scientist and record the facts. Write Discovery Statements about the specific ways you procrastinate and the direct results. Find out if procrastination keeps you from getting what you want. Clearly seeing the costs of procrastination can help you kick the habit.

Discover your procrastination style. Psychologist Linda Sapadin identifies different styles of procrastination.[2] For example, *dreamers* have big goals that they seldom translate into specific plans. *Worriers* focus on the "worst case" scenario and are likely to talk more about problems than about solutions. *Defiers* resist new tasks or promise to do them and then don't follow through. *Overdoers* create extra work for themselves by refusing to delegate tasks and neglecting to set priorities.

Awareness of procrastination styles is a key to changing your behavior. For example, if you exhibit the characteristics of an overdoer, then say no to new projects. Also ask for help in completing your current projects.

Trick yourself into getting started. Practice being a con artist—and your own unwitting target. If you have a 50-page chapter to read, grab the book and say to yourself, "I'm not really going to read this chapter right now. I'm just going to flip through the pages and scan the headings for ten minutes." If you have a paper due next week, say, "I'm not really going to outline this paper today. I'll just spend five minutes writing anything that comes into my head about the assigned topic."

Tricks like these can get you started on a task you've been dreading. Once you get started, you might find it easy to keep going.

Let feelings follow action. If you put off exercising until you feel energetic, you might wait for months. Instead, get moving now and watch your feelings change. After five minutes of brisk walking, you might be in the mood for a 20-minute run. This principle—action generates motivation—can apply to any task that's been delegated to the back burner.

Choose to work under pressure. Sometimes people thrive under pressure. As one writer put it, "I don't do my *best* work because of a tight timeline. I do my *only* work with a tight timeline." Used selectively, this strategy might also work for you.

Put yourself in control. You might consciously choose to work with a timeline staring you in the face. If you do, then schedule a big block of time right before your project is due. Until then, enjoy!

Step back to the big picture. If you plan just a day or two ahead, you might lose sight of what's coming up over the next few weeks or months. Discover the benefits of backing up to a bigger picture of your life. For example, use the monthly calendar on page 88 or the long-term planner on page 91 to list due dates for assignments in all your courses. Using these tools, you can anticipate heavy demands on your time and take action to prevent last-minute crunches. Make *Becoming a Master Student* your "home base": the first place to turn in taking control of your schedule.

Take it easy. You can find shelves full of books with techniques for overcoming procrastination. Resist the temptation to use all of these techniques at once. You could feel overwhelmed, give up, and sink back into the cycle of procrastination.

Instead, make one small, simple change in behavior—today. Tomorrow, make the change again. Take it day by day until the new behavior becomes a habit. One day you might wake up and discover that procrastination is part of your past. ⬛

PRACTICING CRITICAL THINKING

Some thoughts fuel procrastination and keep you from experiencing the rewards in life that you deserve. Psychologists Jane Burka and Lenora Yuen list these examples:[3]

> *I must be perfect.*
> *Everything I do should go easily and without effort.*
> *It's safer to do nothing than to take a risk and fail.*
> *If it's not done right, it's not worth doing at all.*
> *If I do well this time, I* must *always* do well.*
> *If I succeed, someone will get hurt.*

Choose one of these statements—or think of a similar one—and write a sentence or two about how it could promote procrastination.

In the space below, create an alternative to the statement you just wrote about. Write a sentence that puts you back in charge of your time and no longer offers an excuse for procrastination. For example: "Even if I don't complete a task perfectly, I can give it my best shot and learn from my mistakes."

25
ways to
get the most out of **now**

The following time-management techniques are about:

- **When to study**
- **Where to study**
- **Ways to handle the rest of the world**
- **Things to ask yourself if you get stuck**

Don't feel pressured to use all of the techniques listed below or to tackle them in order. As you read, note the suggestions you think will be helpful. Pick one technique to use now. When it becomes a habit, come back to this article and select another one. Repeat this cycle and enjoy the results as they unfold in your life.

When to study

1 Study difficult (or "boring") subjects first. If your chemistry problems put you to sleep, get to them first, while you are fresh. We tend to give top priority to what we enjoy studying, yet the courses we find most difficult often require the most creative energy. Save your favorite subjects for later. If you find yourself avoiding a particular subject, get up an hour earlier to study it before breakfast. With that chore out of the way, the rest of the day can be a breeze.

Continually being late with course assignments indicates a trouble area. Further action is required. Clarify your intentions about the course by writing down your feelings in a journal, talking with an instructor, or asking for help from a friend or counselor. Consistently avoiding study tasks can also be a signal to re-examine your major or course program.

2 Be aware of your best time of day. Many people learn best in daylight hours. If this is true for you, schedule study time for your most difficult subjects before nightfall.

Unless you grew up on a farm, the idea of being conscious at 4 a.m. might seem ridiculous. Yet many successful business people begin the day at 5 a.m. or earlier. Athletes and yogis use this time, too. Some writers complete their best work before 9 a.m.

For others, the same benefits are experienced by staying up late. They flourish after midnight. If you aren't convinced, then experiment. When you're in a time crunch, get up early or stay up late. You might even see a sunrise.

3 Use waiting time. Five minutes waiting for a subway, 20 minutes waiting for the dentist, 10 minutes in between classes—waiting time adds up fast. Have short study tasks ready to do during these periods. For example, you can carry 3x5 cards with facts, formulas, or definitions and pull them out anywhere.

A tape recorder can help you use commuting time to your advantage. Make tape cassettes of yourself reading your notes. Then play these tapes in a car stereo as you drive, or listen through your headphones as you ride on the bus or subway.

Where to study

4 Use a regular study area. Your body and your mind know where you are. Using the same place to study, day after day, helps train your responses. When you arrive at that particular place, you can focus your attention more quickly.

5 Study where you'll be alert. In bed, your body gets a signal. For most students, that signal is more likely to be "Time to sleep!" than "Time to study!" Just as you train your body to be alert at your desk, you also train it to slow down near your bed. For that reason, don't study where you sleep.

Easy chairs and sofas are also dangerous places to study. Learning requires energy. Give your body a message that energy is needed. Put yourself in a situation that supports this message.

Some schools offer empty classrooms as places to study. Many students report finding themselves studying effectively in a classroom setting.

6 Use a library. Libraries are designed for learning. The lighting is perfect. The noise level is low. A wealth of material is available. Entering a library is a signal to focus the mind and get to work. Many students can get more done in a shorter time frame at the library than anywhere else. Experiment for yourself.

Ways to handle the rest of the world

7 Pay attention to your attention. Breaks in concentration are often caused by internal interruptions. Your own thoughts jump in to divert you from your studies. When this happens, notice these thoughts and let them go.

Perhaps the thought of getting something else done is distracting you. One option is to handle that other task now and study later. Or you can write yourself a note about it, or schedule a specific time to do it.

8 Agree with living mates about study time. This includes roommates, spouses, and children. Make the rules clear, and be sure to follow them yourself. Explicit agreements—even written contracts—work well. One student always wears a colorful hat when he wants to study. When his wife and children see the hat, they respect his wish to be left alone.

9 Get off the phone. The telephone is the ultimate interrupter. People who wouldn't think of distracting you might call at the worst times because they can't see that you are studying. You don't have to be a telephone victim. If a simple "I can't talk, I'm studying" doesn't work, use dead silence. It's a conversation killer. Or short-circuit the whole problem: Unplug the phone. Other solutions include getting an answering machine and studying at the library.

10 Learn to say no. This is a timesaver and a valuable life skill for everyone. Some people feel it is rude to refuse a request. But saying no can be done effectively and courteously. Others want you to succeed as a student. When you tell them that you can't do what they ask because you are busy educating yourself, most people will understand.

11 Hang a "do not disturb" sign on your door. Many hotels will give you a free sign, for the advertising. Or you can create a sign yourself. They work. Using signs can relieve you of making a decision about cutting off each interruption—a timesaver in itself.

12 Get ready the night before. Completing a few simple tasks just before you go to bed can help you get in gear the next day. If you need to make some phone calls first thing in the morning, look up those numbers, write them on 3x5 cards, and set them near the phone. If you need to drive to a new location, make note of the address and put it next to your car keys. If you plan to spend the next afternoon writing a paper, get your materials together: dictionary, notes, outline, paper, and pencil (or disks and portable computer or computer disks). Pack your lunch or gas up the car. Organize your diaper bag, briefcase, or backpack.

13 Call ahead. We often think of talking on the telephone as a prime time-waster. Used wisely, the telephone can actually help manage time. Before you go shopping, call the store to see if it carries the items you're looking for. If you're driving, call for directions to your destination. A few seconds on the phone can save hours in wasted trips and wrong turns.

14 Avoid noise distractions. To promote concentration, avoid studying in front of the television and turn off the radio. Many students insist that they study better with background noise, and this might be true. Some students report good results with carefully selected and controlled music. For many others, silence is the best form of music to study by.

At times noise levels might be out of your control. A neighbor or roommate might decide to find out how far he can turn up his boom box before the walls crumble. Meanwhile, your ability to concentrate on the principles of sociology goes down the drain. To avoid this scenario, schedule study sessions during periods when your living environment is usually quiet. If you live in a residence hall, ask if study rooms are available. Or go somewhere else where it's quiet, such as the library. Some students have even found refuge in quiet cafés, self-service laundries, and places of worship.

15 Notice how others misuse your time. Be aware of repeat offenders. Ask yourself if there are certain friends or relatives who consistently interrupt your study time. If avoiding the interrupter is impractical, send a clear message. Sometimes others don't realize that they are breaking your concentration. You can give them a gentle yet firm reminder. If this doesn't work, there are methods to make your message more effective. For more ideas, see Chapter Eight: Communicating.

Things to ask yourself if you get stuck

16 Ask: What is one task I can accomplish toward achieving my goal? This is a helpful technique to use when faced with a big, imposing job. Pick out one small accomplishment, preferably one you can complete in about five minutes; then do it. The satisfaction of getting one thing done can spur you on to get one more thing done. Meanwhile, the job gets smaller.

17 Ask: Am I being too hard on myself? If you are feeling frustrated with a reading assignment, if your attention wanders repeatedly, or if you've fallen behind on math problems that are due tomorrow, take a minute to listen to the messages you are giving yourself. Are you scolding yourself too harshly? Lighten up. Allow yourself to feel a little foolish and then get on with the task at hand. Don't add to the problem by berating yourself.

Worrying about the future is another way people beat themselves up: How will I ever get all this done? What if every paper I'm assigned turns out to be this hard? If I can't do the simple calculations now, how will I ever pass the final? Instead of promoting learning, such questions fuel anxiety.

Keep on going?

Some people keep on going, even when they get stuck or fail again and again. To such people belongs the world. Consider the hapless politician who compiled this record:

- Failed in business, 1831
- Defeated for legislature, 1832
- Second failure in business, 1833
- Suffered nervous breakdown, 1836
- Defeated for Speaker, 1838
- Defeated for Elector, 1840
- Defeated for Congress, 1843
- Defeated for Senate, 1855
- Defeated for Vice President, 1856
- Defeated for Senate, 1858
- Elected President, 1860

Who was the fool who kept on going in spite of so many failures?

Answer: The fool was Abraham Lincoln.

Labeling and generalizing weaknesses are other ways people are hard on themselves. Being objective and specific will help eliminate this form of self-punishment and will likely generate new possibilities. An alternative to saying "I'm terrible in algebra" is to say "I don't understand factoring equations." This rewording suggests a plan to improve.

18 **Ask: Is this a piano?** Carpenters who construct rough frames for buildings have a saying they use when they bend a nail or accidentally hack a chunk out of a two-by-four: "Well, this ain't no piano." It means that perfection is not necessary. Ask yourself if what you are doing needs to be perfect. Perhaps you don't have to apply the same standards of grammar to lecture notes that you would apply to a term paper. If you can complete a job 95 percent perfectly in two hours and 100 percent perfectly in four hours, ask yourself whether the additional 5 percent improvement is worth doubling the amount of time you spend.

Sometimes it *is* a piano. A tiny miscalculation can ruin an entire lab experiment. A misstep in solving a complex math problem can negate hours of work. Computers are notorious for turning little errors into nightmares. Accept lower standards only when appropriate.

A related suggestion is to weed out low-priority tasks. The to-do list for a large project can include dozens of items, not all of which are equally important. Some can be done later, while others could be skipped altogether, if time is short.

Apply this idea when you study. In a long reading assignment, look for pages you can skim or skip. When it's appropriate, read chapter summaries or article abstracts. As you review your notes, look for material that might not be covered on a test and decide whether you want to study it.

19 **Ask: Would I pay myself for what I'm doing right now?** If you were employed as a student, would you be earning your wages? Ask yourself this question when you notice that you've taken your third snack break in 30 minutes. Most students are, in fact, employed as students. They are investing in their own productivity and paying a big price for the privilege of being a student. Sometimes they don't realize that doing a mediocre job now might result in fewer opportunities for the future.

20 **Ask: Can I do just one more thing?** Ask yourself this question at the end of a long day. Almost always you will have enough energy to do just one more short task. The overall increase in your productivity might surprise you.

21 **Ask: Am I making time for things that are important but not urgent?** If we spend most of our time putting out fires, we can feel drained and frustrated. According to Stephen R. Covey, this happens when we forget to take time for things that are not urgent but are truly important.[4] Examples include exercising regularly, reading, praying or meditating, spending quality time alone or with family members and friends, traveling, and cooking nutritious meals. Each of these can contribute directly to a long-term goal or life mission. Yet when schedules get tight, we often forgo these things, waiting for that elusive day when we'll "finally have more time."

That day won't come until we choose to make time for what's truly important. Knowing this, we can use some of the suggestions in this chapter to free up more time.

22 **Ask: Can I delegate this?** Instead of slogging through complicated tasks alone, you can draw on the talents and energy of other people. Busy executives know the value of delegating tasks to coworkers. Without delegation, many projects would flounder or die.

You can apply the same principle. Instead of doing all the housework or cooking by yourself, for example, you can assign some of the tasks to family members or roommates. Rather than making a trip to the library to look up a simple fact, you can call and ask a library assistant to research it for you. Instead of driving across town to deliver a package, you can hire a delivery service to do so. All of these tactics can free up extra hours for studying.

It's not practical to delegate certain study tasks, such as writing term papers or completing reading assignments. However, you can still draw on the ideas of others in completing such tasks. For instance, form a writing group to edit and critique papers, brainstorm topics or titles, and develop lists of sources.

If you're absent from a class, find a classmate to summarize the lecture, discussion, and any upcoming assignments. Presidents depend on briefings. You can use this technique, too.

23 **Ask: How did I just waste time?** Notice when time passes and you haven't accomplished what you had planned to do. Take a minute to review your actions and note the specific ways you wasted time. We tend to operate by habit, wasting time in the same ways over and over again. When you are aware of things you do that drain your time, you are more likely to catch yourself in

→ Remember cultural differences

There are as many different styles for managing time as there are people. These styles vary across cultures.

In the United States and England, for example, business meetings typically start on time. That's also true in Scandinavian countries such as Norway and Sweden. However, travelers to Panama might find that meetings start about a half-hour late. And people who complain about late meetings while doing business in Mexico might be considered rude.

Cultural differences can get even more pronounced. In her book *Freedom and Culture*, anthropologist Dorothy Lee writes about a group of people in the Trobriand Islands east of New Guinea.[5] Their language has no verb tenses—no distinction between past, present, and future. The Trobrianders celebrate each event as an end in itself, not as a means to achieve some future goal. In this culture, the whole concept of time management would have little meaning.

When you study or work with people of different races and ethnic backgrounds, look for differences in their approach to time. A behavior that you might view as rude or careless—such as showing up late for appointments—could simply result from seeing the world in a different way.

Find additional articles about cultural differences online at **masterstudent.college.hmco.com**

---

the act next time. Observing one small quirk might save you hours. But keep this in mind: Asking you to notice how you waste time is not intended to make you feel guilty. The point is to increase your skill by getting specific information about how you use time.

24 Ask: Could I find the time if I really wanted to? The way people speak often rules out the option of finding more time. An alternative is to speak about time with more possibility.

The next time you're tempted to say "I just don't have time," pause for a minute. Question the truth of this statement. Could you find four more hours this week for studying? Suppose that someone offered to pay you $10,000 to find those four hours. Suppose, too, that you will get paid only if you don't lose sleep, call in sick for work, or sacrifice anything important to you. Could you find the time if vast sums of money were involved?

Remember that when it comes to school, vast sums of money *are* involved.

25 Ask: Am I willing to promise it? This might be the most powerful time-management idea of all. If you want to find time for a task, promise yourself—and others—that you'll get it done.

To make this technique work, do more than say that you'll try or that you'll give it your best shot. Take an oath, as you would in court. Give it your word.

One way to accomplish big things in life is to make big promises. There's little reward in promising what's safe or predictable. No athlete promises to place seventh in the Olympic games. Chances are that if we're not making big promises, we're not stretching ourselves.

The point of making a promise is not to chain ourselves to a rigid schedule or to impossible expectations. We can also promise to reach goals without unbearable stress. We can keep schedules flexible and carry out our plans with ease, joy, and satisfaction.

At times we can go too far. Some promises are truly beyond us, and we might break them. However, failing to keep a promise is just that—failing to keep a promise. A broken promise is not the end of the world.

Promises can work magic. When our word is on the line, it's possible to discover reserves of time and energy we didn't know existed. Promises can push us to exceed our expectations. ⊠

Time management for right-brained people (...or what to do if **to-do lists** are not your style)

Ask some people about managing time, and a dreaded image appears in their minds.

They see a person with a 50-item to-do list clutching a calendar chock full of appointments. They imagine a robot who values cold efficiency, compulsively accounts for every minute, and is too rushed to develop personal relationships. Often this image is what's behind the comment "Yeah, there are some good ideas in those time-management books, but I'll never get around to using them. Too much work."

These stereotypes about time management hold a kernel of truth. Sometimes people who pride themselves on efficiency are merely keeping busy. In their rush to check items off their to-do lists, they might be fussing over things that don't need doing—insignificant tasks that create little or no value in the first place. If this is one of your fears, relax. The point of managing time is not to overload your schedule with extra obligations. Instead, the aim is to get the important things done and still have time to be human. An effective time manager is productive and relaxed at the same time.

Personal style enters the picture, too. Many of the suggestions in this chapter appeal to "left-brained" people—those who thrive on making lists, scheduling events, and handling details. These suggestions might not work for people who like to see wholes and think visually. Remember that the strategies discussed in this chapter represent just one set of options for managing time.

The trick is to discover what works for you. Do give time-management strategies a fair chance. Some might be suitable, with a few modifications. Instead of writing a conventional to-do list, for instance, you can plot your day on a mind map. (Mind maps are explained in Chapter Five: Notes.) Or write to-do's, one per 3x5 card, in any order in which tasks occur to you. Later you can edit, sort, and rank the cards, choosing which items to act on.

Strictly speaking, time cannot be managed. Time is a mystery, an abstract concept that cannot be captured in words. The minutes, hours, days, and years march on whether we manage anything or not. What we can do is manage ourselves in respect to time. A few basic principles can do that as well as a truckload of cold-blooded techniques.

Know your values. Begin by managing time from a bigger picture. Instead of thinking in terms of minutes or hours, view your life as a whole. Consider what that expanse of time is all about.

As a thought-provoking exercise, write your own obituary. Describe the way you want to be remembered. List the contributions you intend to make during your lifetime. If this is too spooky, write a short mission statement for your life—a paragraph that describes your values and the kind of life you want to lead. Periodically during the day, stop to ask if what you're doing is contributing to those goals.

Do less. Managing time is as much about dropping worthless activities as about adding new and useful ones. The idea is to weed out those actions that deliver little reward.

Decide right now to eliminate activities with a low payoff. When you add a new item to your schedule, consider dropping a current one.

Slow down. Sometimes it's useful to hurry, such as when you're late for a meeting or about to miss a train. At other times, haste is a choice that serves no real purpose. If you're speeding through the day like a launched missile, consider what would happen if you got to your next destination a little bit later than planned. Rushing to stay a step ahead might not be worth the added strain.

Remember people. Few people on their deathbed ever say, "I wish I'd spent more time at the office." They're more likely to say, "I wish I'd spent more time with my family and friends." The pace of daily life can lead us to neglect the people we cherish.

Efficiency is a concept that applies to things—not people. When it comes to maintaining and nurturing relationships, we can often benefit from loosening up our schedules. We can allow extra time for conflict management, spontaneous visits, and free-ranging conversations.

Focus on outcomes. You might feel guilty when you occasionally stray from your schedule and spend two hours napping or watching soap operas. But if you're regularly meeting your goals and leading a fulfilling life, there's probably no harm done. When managing time, the overall goal of personal effectiveness counts more than the means used to achieve it. This can be true even when your time-management style differs from that recommended by experts.

Likewise, there are many methods for planning your time. Some people prefer a written action plan that carefully details each step leading to a long-range goal. Others just note the due date for accomplishing a goal and periodically assess their progress. Either strategy can work.

Visualizing the desired outcome can be as important as having a detailed action plan. Here's an experiment. Write a list of goals you plan 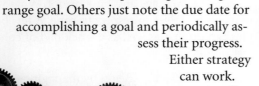 to accomplish over the next six months. Then create a vivid mental picture of yourself attaining them and enjoying the resulting benefits. Visualize this image several times in the next few weeks. File the list away, making a note on your calendar to review it in six months. When six months have passed, look over the list and note how many of your goals you have actually accomplished.

Handle it now. A backlog of unfinished tasks can result from postponing decisions or procrastinating. An alternative is to handle the task or decision immediately. Answer that letter now. Make that phone call as soon as it occurs to you.

You can also save time by graciously saying no immediately to projects that you don't want to take on. Saying "I'll think about it and get back to you later" might mean that you'll have to take more time to say no later.

Buy less. Before you purchase an item, estimate how much time it will take to locate, assemble, use, repair, and maintain it. You might be able to free up hours by doing without. If the product comes with a 400-page manual or 20 hours of training, beware. Before rushing to the store to add another possession to your life, see if you can reuse or adapt something you already own.

Forget about time. Schedule "downtime"—a period when you're accountable to no one else and have nothing to accomplish—into every day. This is time to do nothing, free of guilt. Even a few minutes spent in this way can yield a sense of renewal.

Also experiment with decreasing your awareness of time. Leave your watch off for a few hours each day. Spend time in an area that's free of clocks. Notice how often you glance at your watch, and make a conscious effort to do so less often.

If you still want some sense of time, then use alternatives to the almighty, unforgiving clock. Measure your day with a sundial, hourglass, or egg timer. Or synchronize your activities with the rhythms of nature, for example, by rising at dawn. You can also plan activities to harmonize with the rhythms of your body. Schedule your most demanding tasks for times when you're normally most alert. Eat when you're hungry, not according to the clock. Toss out schedules when it's appropriate. Sometimes the best-laid plans are best laid to rest.

Take time to retreat from time. Create a sanctuary, a haven, a safe place in your life that's free from any hint of schedules, lists, or accomplishments. One of the most effective ways to manage time is periodically to forget about it. ⊠

MASTER MONTHLY CALENDAR

This exercise will give you an opportunity to step back from the details of your daily schedule and get a bigger picture of your life. The more difficult it is for you to plan beyond the current day or week, the greater the benefit of this exercise.

Your basic tool is a one-month calendar. Use it to block out specific times for upcoming events, such as study group meetings, due dates for assignments, review periods before tests, and other time-sensitive tasks.

To get started, you might want to copy the blank monthly calendar on pages 88–89 onto both sides of a sheet of paper. Or make several copies of these pages and tape them together so that you can see several months at a glance.

Also be creative. Experiment with a variety of uses for your monthly calendar. For instance, you can note day-to-day changes in your health or moods, list the places you visit while you are on vacation, or circle each day that you practice a new habit. For examples of filled-in monthly calendars, see below.

MONDAY	TUESDAY	WEDNESDAY	THURSDAY	FRIDAY	SATURDAY	SUNDAY

Name

Month

MONDAY	TUESDAY	WEDNESDAY	THURSDAY	FRIDAY	SATURDAY	SUNDAY

Name _____

Month _____

Gearing up:
Using a long-term planner

Planning a day, a week, or a month ahead is a powerful practice. Using a long-term planner—one that displays an entire quarter, semester, or year at a glance—can yield even more benefits.

With a long-term planner, you can eliminate a lot of unpleasant surprises. Long-term planning allows you to avoid scheduling conflicts—the kind that obligate you to be in two places at the same time three weeks from now. You can also anticipate busy periods, such as finals week, and start preparing for them now. Good-bye, all-night cram sessions. Hello, serenity.

Find a long-term planner, or make your own. Many office supply stores carry academic planners in paper form that cover an entire school year. Computer software for time management offers the same feature. You can also be creative and make your own long-term planner. A big roll of newsprint pinned to a bulletin board or taped to a wall will do nicely.

Enter scheduled dates that extend into the future. Use your long-term planner to list commitments that extend beyond the current month. Enter test dates, lab sessions, days that classes will be canceled, and other events that will take place over this term and next term.

Create a master assignment list. Find the syllabus for each course you're currently taking. Then, in your long-term planner, enter the due dates for all of the assignments in all of your courses. This can be a powerful reality check.

The purpose of this technique is to not to make you feel overwhelmed with all the things you have to do. Rather, its aim is to help you take a First Step toward recognizing the demands on your time. Armed with the truth about how you use your time, you can make more accurate plans.

Include nonacademic events. In addition to tracking academic commitments, you can use your long-term planner to mark significant events in your life outside of school. Include birthdays, doctor's appointments, concert dates, credit card payment due dates, and car maintenance schedules.

Use your long-term planner to divide and conquer. Big assignments such as term papers or major presentations pose a special risk. When you have three months to do a project, you might say to yourself, "That looks like a lot of work, but I've got plenty of time. No problem." Two months, three weeks, and six days from now, it could suddenly be a problem.

For some people, academic life is a series of last-minute crises punctuated by periods of exhaustion. You can avoid that fate. The trick is to set due dates *before* the final due date.

When planning to write a term paper, for instance, enter the final due date in your long-term planner. Then set individual due dates for each milestone in the writing process—creating an outline, completing your research, finishing a first draft, editing the draft, and preparing the final copy. By meeting these interim due dates, you make steady progress on the assignment throughout the term. That sure beats trying to crank out all those pages at the last minute. ◫

Week of	Monday	Tuesday	Wednesday	Thursday	Friday	Saturday	Sunday
9 / 5							
9 / 12		English quiz					
9 / 19			English paper due		Speech #1		
9 / 26	Chemistry test					Skiing at the lake	
10 / 3		English quiz			Speech #2		
10 / 10				Geography project due			
10 / 17				--- No classes ---			

LONG-TERM PLANNER ___ / ___ / ___ to ___ / ___ / ___

Week of	Monday	Tuesday	Wednesday	Thursday	Friday	Saturday	Sunday
___ / ___							
___ / ___							
___ / ___							
___ / ___							
___ / ___							
___ / ___							
___ / ___							
___ / ___							
___ / ___							
___ / ___							
___ / ___							
___ / ___							
___ / ___							
___ / ___							
___ / ___							
___ / ___							
___ / ___							
___ / ___							
___ / ___							
___ / ___							
___ / ___							
___ / ___							
___ / ___							
___ / ___							
___ / ___							
___ / ___							
___ / ___							
___ / ___							
___ / ___							
___ / ___							
___ / ___							
___ / ___							
___ / ___							
___ / ___							

Name _____

LONG-TERM PLANNER ___ / ___ / ___ to ___ / ___ / ___

Week of	Monday	Tuesday	Wednesday	Thursday	Friday	Saturday	Sunday
___ / ___							
___ / ___							
___ / ___							
___ / ___							
___ / ___							
___ / ___							
___ / ___							
___ / ___							
___ / ___							
___ / ___							
___ / ___							
___ / ___							
___ / ___							
___ / ___							
___ / ___							
___ / ___							
___ / ___							
___ / ___							
___ / ___							
___ / ___							
___ / ___							
___ / ___							
___ / ___							
___ / ___							
___ / ___							
___ / ___							
___ / ___							
___ / ___							
___ / ___							
___ / ___							
___ / ___							
___ / ___							

Strategies for even *longer*-term planning

The following suggestions can help you plan anything in your life, from getting an education or managing money to finding a job or developing new relationships. You can do all this by lifting your eyes to the horizon and thinking years—even decades—into the future.

Keep in mind that there's really no "right" way to do longer-term planning. The main thing is to immerse yourself in the process of planning. Then you can see for yourself the benefits it brings. Begin by planning to plan—setting aside time to put down your goals in writing. From there you can launch your future.

Remember the difference between measurements and values. In planning, it's possible to get the intended results yet still miss the purpose. Say that you want to learn Spanish. One way to state that goal in measurable terms is to write "I will sign up for a Spanish course and attend at least 98 percent of the class meetings." However, merely showing up for class every time does not guarantee completing the assigned work—or enjoying Spanish.

Ideals, values, emotions, and other nonmeasurable factors are the "fuel" for our plans. Often they're what inspired us in the first place. "I want to be a better student," "I want to become a more loving person," or "I want to enjoy music"—none of these is stated as a measurable goal. Yet it's useful to keep such values in mind. They help us remember the purpose of our planning.

Work backward, from the future to the present. When you plan, consider working from the general to the specific. Short-range goals are often easier to plan when they flow naturally from long-range objectives.

To apply this idea, start planning as far in the future as you can and work backward to the present. The specific length of time doesn't matter. For some people, long-range might mean starting out at 10, 20, or even 50 years from now. For others, imagining three years ahead might feel like reaching into the distant future. Any of these alternatives is fine.

Once you have stated your long-range goals, work backward until you get to a one-day plan. Suppose your 30-year goal is to retire and maintain your present standard of living. Ask yourself: In order to accomplish that goal, what needs to be in place in 20 years? To get to that point, what is needed in 10 years? In one year? In one month? In one week? With the answers to such questions, you can make an informed choice about what step to take today.

Write out your plan. Writing uncovers holes in a plan—gaps in logic, hidden assumptions, contradictions, and other forms of fuzzy thinking. Writing a plan down keeps it specific and powerful.

You can also use other media to shape your plans. For example, make a drawing that represents where you want to be in 20 years. Draw yourself, the people you want in your life, and the things you want to be, have, and do. Capturing your plans in a painting, a sculpture, or a collage can also help shape your future.

Be willing to act—even if the plan is not complete. Many careers, successful businesses, and enduring social changes have begun with the most simple intention or sketchy plan. One African American woman, Rosa Parks, sparked the civil rights movement by refusing to sit at the back of a bus. Albert Schweitzer first considered doing medical relief work in Africa when he saw a magazine article about the needs of people in the Belgian Congo.

Complete, detailed plans are powerful. At the same time, taking action on an incomplete plan is one way to fill in the gaps. An unfinished plan is no excuse for missing a rewarding experience or for ignoring a worthy idea.

Just open your mouth and talk planning. Conversations about planning can bring our intentions into focus. We can even start talking about a plan before we really have one.

In planning, you don't have to go it alone. Talk to others about your dreams, wishes, fantasies, and goals. You can speak of your desire to take charge of your learning, your life, and your career. The more you speak about your goals, the more real they become. Your plan might start out as a hazy ideal. That's fine. By speaking about it with others, you can fill in the details.

Look boldly for things to change. To create new goals, open up your thinking about what aspects of your life can be changed and what cannot. Be willing to put every facet of your life on the table.

It's fascinating to note the areas that are off-limits when people set goals. Money, sex, spirituality, career, marriage, and other topics can easily fall into the category "I'll just have to live with this."

For example, you might think that you have to live with the face you have now. Maybe not. There are ways to change your face even without plastic surgery. Physical therapists tell us that there are dozens of muscles in the face. Learning to relax them and bring more of them under conscious control will change the way you look. Even something as simple as a smile can go a long way toward changing your appearance.

When creating your future by setting goals, consider the whole range of your experience. Staying open-minded can lead to a future you never dreamed was possible.

Look for what's missing in your life. Goals usually arise from a sense of what's missing in our lives. Goal setting is fueled by unresolved problems, incomplete projects, relationships we want to develop, and careers we still want to pursue. When nothing's missing, goals can seem irrelevant. Affluent people rarely set a goal of eating three meals a day.

To create the life of your dreams, release negative judgments about what's missing from your life. Forgive yourself for not attaining some of the things you want. Instead of talking about your shortcomings or deficiencies, talk about your potential. The person with a bulging belly and weak knees can honestly say, "There's a lot of potential in this body!"

Maintain what you love about your life. Not all goals need to spring from a sense of need. You can also make it a goal to maintain things that you already have or to keep doing the effective things that you already do. If you exercise vigorously three times each week, you can set a goal to keep exercis-

ing. If you already have a loving relationship with your spouse, you can set a goal to nurture that relationship for the rest of your life.

Remember to remember. A key part of making any plan work is simply remembering the plan. Yet this can be a challenge. In the midst of an active life, we can easily lose sight of our goals.

To avoid this outcome, include your goals on a monthly calendar or daily to-do list. Post notes on your refrigerator. Write your goals on 3x5 cards and tape them to your desk or bathroom mirror, or tack them to a wall. Think of these as flash cards for the future. Do whatever it takes to keep the vision alive.

exercise 9

CREATE A LIFELINE

On a large sheet of paper, draw a horizontal line. This line will represent your lifetime. Now add key events in your life to this line in chronological order. Examples are birth, first day at school, graduation from high school, and enrollment in higher education.

Now extend the lifeline into the future. Write down key events you would like to see occur in one year, five years, and 10 or more years from now. Choose events that align with your core values. Work quickly in the spirit of a brainstorm, bearing in mind that this is not a final plan.

Afterward, take a few minutes to review your lifeline. Select one key event for the future and list any actions you could take in the next month to bring yourself closer to that goal. Do the same with the other key events on your lifeline. You now have the rudiments of a comprehensive plan for your life.

Finally, extend your lifeline another 50 years beyond the year when you would reach age 100. Describe in detail what changes in the world you'd like to see as a result of the goals you attained in your lifetime.

Do this exercise online at

masterstudent.college.hmco.com

Financial planning

Meeting your money goals

You've probably heard the saying, "Time is money." There's wisdom in that time-worn saying.

Many of the skills that help you plan—such as monitoring your behavior and setting priorities—can also help you manage money. An important part of planning is setting and meeting financial goals.

Some people shy away from setting financial goals. They think that money is a complicated subject. Yet most money problems result from spending more than is available. It's that simple, even though often we do everything we can to make the problem much more complicated.

The solution also is simple: *Don't spend more than you have.* If you are spending more money than you have, increase your income, decrease your spending, or do both. This idea has never won a Nobel Prize in economics, but you won't go broke applying it.

Starting today, you can take three simple steps to financial independence:

- Tell the truth about how much money you have and how much you spend.

- Make a commitment to spend no more than you have.

- Begin saving money.

If you do these three things consistently, you could meet your monetary goals and even experience financial independence. This does not necessarily mean having all of the money you could ever desire. Rather, you can be free from money worries by living within your means. Soon you will control money instead of letting money control you.

Increase money in

For many of us, making more money is the most appealing way to fix a broken budget. This approach is reasonable—and it has a potential problem: When our income increases, most of us continue to spend more than we make. Our money problems persist, even at higher incomes. You can avoid this dilemma by managing your expenses no matter how much money you make.

There are several ways to increase your income while you go to school. One of the most obvious ways is to get a job. You could also apply for scholarships and grants. You might borrow money, inherit it, or receive it as a gift. You could sell property, collect income from investments, or use your savings. Other options—such as lotteries and gambling casinos—pose obvious risks. Stick to making money the old-fashioned way: Earn it.

Work while you're in school. If you work while you go to school, you can earn more than money. Working helps you gain experience, establish references, and expand your contacts in the community. Doing well at a work-study position or an internship while you're in school can also help you land a good job after you graduate.

Regular income, even at a lower wage scale, can make a big difference. Look at your monthly budget to see how it would be affected if you worked just 15 hours a week (times 4 weeks a month) for $8 an hour.

Find a job. Make a list of several places that you would like to work. Include places that have advertised job openings and those that haven't. Then go to each place on your list and tell someone that you would like a job. This will yield more results than depending on the want ads alone. The people you speak to might say that there isn't a job available, or that the job is filled. That's OK. Ask to see the person in charge of hiring and tell him that you want to be considered for future job openings. Then ask when you can check back.

Keep your job in perspective. If your job is in your career field, great. If it is meaningful and contributes to society, great. If it involves working with people you love and respect, fantastic. If not—well, remember that almost any job can help you reach your educational goals.

It's also easy to let a job eat up time and energy that you need for your education. You can avoid this by managing your time effectively. If you are a full-time student, try to limit your work commitment to 20 hours per week. That leaves 148 hours to focus on your most important present goal—becoming a master student.

Decrease money out

You do not have to live like a miser, pinching pennies and saving used dental floss. There are many ways to decrease the amount of money you spend and still enjoy life. Consider the ideas that follow.

Look to the big-ticket items. Your choices about which school to attend, what car to buy, and where to live can save you tens of thousands of dollars. When you look for places to cut expenses, start with the items that cost

the most. For example, there are several ways to keep your housing costs reasonable. Sometimes a place a little farther from your school or a smaller house will be much less expensive. You can cut your housing costs in half by finding a roommate. Also look for opportunities to house-sit rather than paying rent. Some homeowners will even pay a responsible person to live in their house when they are away.

Look to the small-ticket items. Decreasing the money you spend on small purchases can help you balance your budget. A three-dollar cappuccino is tasty, but the amount that some of people spend on such treats over the course of a year could give anyone the jitters.

Monitor money out. Each month, review your checkbook, receipts, and other financial records. Sort your expenditures into major categories such as school expenses, housing, personal debt, groceries, eating out, and entertainment. At the end of the month, total up how much you spend in each category. You might be surprised. Once you discover the truth, it might be easier to decrease unnecessary spending.

Create a budget. When you have a budget and stick to it, you don't have to worry about whether you can pay your bills on time. The basic idea is to project how much money is coming in and how much is going out and to make sure that those two amounts balance.

Creating two kinds of budgets is even more useful. A monthly budget includes regularly recurring income and expense items such as paychecks, food costs, and housing. A long-range budget includes unusual monetary transactions such as annual dividends, grants, and tuition payments that occur only a few times a year. With an eye to the future, you can make realistic choices about money today.

Do comparison shopping. Prices vary dramatically on just about anything you want to buy. You can clip coupons and wait for sales or shop around at second-hand stores, mill outlets, or garage sales. When you first go shopping, leave your checkbook and credit cards at home, a sure way to control impulse buying. Look at all of the possibilities, then make your decision later when you don't feel pressured. To save time, money, and gas, you can also search the Internet for sites that compare prices on items.

Use public transportation or car pools. Aside from tuition, a car can be the biggest financial burden in a student's budget. The purchase price is often only the tip of the iceberg. Be sure to consider the cost of parking, insurance, repairs, gas, maintenance, and tires. When you add up all of those items, you might find it makes more sense to car-pool or to take the bus or a cab instead.

Notice what you spend on "fun." Blowing your money on fun is fun. It is also a quick way to ruin your budget. When you spend money on entertainment, ask yourself what the benefits will be and whether you could get the same benefits for less money. You can read or borrow magazines for free at the library. Most libraries also loan CDs, DVDs, and videotapes at no cost. Student councils often sponsor activities, such as dances and music performances, for which there is no fee. Schools with sports facilities set aside times when students can use them for free. Meeting your friends for a pick-up basketball game at the gym can be more fun than meeting at a bar, where there is a cover charge.

Free entertainment is everywhere. However, it usually isn't advertised, so you'll have to search it out. Start with your school bulletin boards and local newspapers.

Redefine money. Reinforce all of the above ideas by understanding money in a new way. According to authors Joe Dominguez and Vicki Robin, money is what we accept in exchange for the time, passion, and effort that we put into our work.[6] When you take this view of money, you might naturally find yourself being more selective about how often you spend it and what you spend it on. It's not just cash you're putting on the line—it's your life energy.

Remember that education is worth it ...

A college degree is one of the safest and most worthwhile investments you can make. Money invested in land, gold, oil, or stocks can be lost, but your education will last a lifetime. It can't rust, corrode, break down, or wear out. Once you have an education, it becomes a permanent part of you.

Think about all of the services and resources that your tuition money buys: academic advising; access to the student health center and counseling services; career planning and job placement offices; athletic, arts, and entertainment events; and a student center where you can meet people and socialize. If you live on campus, you get a place to stay with meals provided. By the way, you also get to attend classes.

In the long run, education pays off in increased income, job promotions, career satisfaction, and more creative use of your leisure time. These are benefits that you can sustain for a lifetime.

... and you can pay for it

Most students can afford higher education. If you demonstrate financial need, you can usually get financial aid. In general, financial need equals the cost of your schooling minus the amount that you can reasonably be expected to pay. Receiving financial assistance has little to do with "being poor." Your prospects for aid depend greatly on the costs of the school you attend.

Financial aid includes money you don't pay back (grants and scholarships), money you do pay back (low-interest loans), and work-study programs that land you a job while you're in school. Most students receive aid awards that include several of these elements. Visit the financial aid office on campus to find out what's available.

In applying for financial aid, you'll need to fill out a form called the Free Application for Federal Student Aid (FAFSA). You can access it on the World Wide Web at **http://www.fafsa.ed.gov**. For links to a wealth of information about financial aid in general, access **http://www.students.gov**. Create a master plan—a long-term budget listing how much you need to complete your education and where you plan to get the money. Having a plan for paying for your entire education makes completing your degree work a more realistic possibility.

Once you've lined up financial aid, keep it flowing. Find out the requirements for renewing your loans, grants, and scholarships.

Create money for the future

You don't have to wait until you finish school to begin saving and investing. You can start now, even if you are in debt and living on a diet of macaroni.

Start saving. Saving is one of the most effective ways to reach your money goals. Aim to save at least 10 percent of your monthly take-home pay. If you can save more, that's even better.

One possible goal is to have savings equal to at least six months of living expenses. Build this nest egg first as a cushion for financial emergencies. Then save for major, long-term expenses.

Put your money into insured savings accounts, money market funds, savings bonds, or certificates of deposit. These are low-risk options that you can immediately turn into cash. Even a small amount of money set aside each month can grow rapidly. The sooner you begin to save, the more opportunity your money has to grow. Time allows you to take advantage of the power of compound interest.

Invest after you have a cushion. Remember that investing is risky. Invest only money that you can afford to lose. Consider something safe, such as Treasury securities (bills, notes, and bonds backed by the federal government), bonds, no-load mutual funds, or blue chip stocks.

Avoid taking a friend's advice on how to invest your hard-earned money. Be wary, too, of advice from someone who has something to sell, such as a stockbroker or a realtor. See your banker or an independent certified financial planner instead.

Save on insurance. Insuring yourself now is a wise investment for the future. Shop around for insurance. Benefits, premiums, exclusions, and terms vary considerably from policy to policy, so study each one carefully. Buy health, auto, and life insurance with high deductibles to save on premiums. Also ask about safe driver, non-smoker, or good student discounts.

Be careful with contracts. Before you sign anything, read the fine print. If you are confused, ask questions and keep asking until you are no longer confused. After you sign a contract, policy, or lease, read the entire document again. If you think you have signed something that you will regret, back out quickly and get your release in writing. Purchase contracts in many states are breakable if you act quickly.

Use credit wisely. If you don't already have one, you can begin to establish a credit rating now. Borrow a small amount of money and pay it back on time. Also pay your bills on time. Avoid the temptation to let big companies wait for their money. Develop a good credit rating so that you can borrow large amounts of money if you need to.

Before you take out a loan to buy a big-ticket item, find out what that item will be worth *after* you buy it. A brand-new $20,000 car might be worth only $15,000 the minute you drive it off the lot. To maintain your net worth, don't borrow any more than $15,000 to buy the car.

If you're in trouble. If you find yourself in over your financial head, get specific data about your present situation. Find out exactly how much money you owe, earn, and spend on a monthly basis. If you can't pay your bills in full, be honest with creditors. Many will allow you to pay off a large debt in small installments. Also consider credit counseling with professional advisors who can help you straighten out your financial problems. You can locate these people through your campus or community phone directories.

→ Places to find money for school

- Grants: Pell Grants, Supplemental Educational Opportunity Grants, state government grants

- Scholarships from federal, state, and private organizations

- Loan programs: Perkins Loans, Stafford Loans, Supplemental Loans, Consolidation Loans, Ford Direct Student Loans, and PLUS (Parent Loans for Undergraduate Students)

- Part-time or full-time jobs, including work-study programs

- Military programs: funds from the Veterans Administration and financial aid programs for active military personnel

- Programs to train the unemployed, such as JTPA (Job Training Partnership Act) and WIN (Work Incentive)

- Company assistance programs

- Social security payments

- Relatives

- Personal savings

- Selling a personal possession, such as a car, boat, piano, or house

Note: Programs change constantly. In some cases, money is limited and application deadlines are critical. Be sure to get the most current information from the financial aid office at your school.

voices

student

I made a goal to make it to college. And here I am, even though in high school I was told that it wouldn't happen and there wasn't enough money to go. I achieved my goal and am working to support myself as well as working hard at my grades to get a better education.

— TRICIA MILLS

Take charge
of your credit card

A credit card is compact and convenient. That piece of plastic seems to promise peace of mind. Low on cash this month? Just whip out your card, slide it across the counter, and relax. Your worries are over—that is, until you get the bill.

Credit cards often come with a hefty interest rate, sometimes as high as 27 percent. That can be over one-fifth of your credit card bill. Imagine working five days a week and getting paid for only four: You'd lose one-fifth of your income. Likewise, when people rely on high-interest credit cards to get by from month to month, they lose one-fifth of their monthly payments to interest charges. In a 2000 survey by Nellie Mae, a student loan corporation, 78 percent of undergraduate students had credit cards. Their average credit card debt was $2,748. Suppose that a student with this debt used a card with an annual percentage rate of 18 percent. Also suppose that

he pays only the minimum balance due each month. He'll be making payments for 15 years and will pay an additional $2,748 in interest fees.

Credit cards do offer potential benefits. Getting a card is one way to establish a credit record. Many cards offer rewards, such as frequent flier miles and car rental discounts. Your monthly statement also offers a way to keep track of your expenses.

Used wisely, credit cards can help us become conscious of what we spend. Used unwisely, they can leave us with a load of debt that takes decades to repay. That load can seriously delay other goals—paying off student loans, financing a new car, buying a home, or saving for retirement.

Use the following three steps to take control of your credit cards before they take control of you. Write these steps on a 3x5 card and don't leave home without it.

Do a First Step about money. See your credit card usage as an opportunity to take a financial First Step. If you rely on credit cards to make ends meet every month, tell the truth about that. If you typically charge up to the maximum limit and pay just the minimum balance due each month, tell the truth about that, too.

Write Discovery Statements focusing on what doesn't work—and what does work—about the way you use credit cards. Follow up with Intention Statements regarding steps you can take to use your cards differently. Then take action. Your bank account will directly benefit.

Scrutinize credit card offers. Beware of cards offering low interest rates. These rates are often only temporary. After a few months, they could double or triple. Also look for annual fees and other charges buried in the fine print.

To simplify your financial life and take charge of your credit, consider using only one card. Choose one with no annual fee and the lowest interest rate. Don't be swayed by offers of free T-shirts or coffee mugs. Consider the bottom line and be selective.

Pay off the balance each month. Keep track of how much you spend with credit cards each month. Then save an equal amount in cash. That way, you can pay off the card balance each month and avoid interest charges. Following this suggestion alone might transform your financial life.

If you do accumulate a large credit card balance, ask your bank about a "bill-payer" loan with a lower interest rate. You can use this loan to pay off your credit cards. Then promise yourself never to accumulate credit card debt again. ◪

exercise 10

EDUCATION BY THE HOUR

Determine exactly what it costs you to go to school. Fill in the blanks below using totals for a semester, quarter, or whatever term system your school uses.

Note: Include only the costs that relate directly to going to school. For example, under "Transportation," list only the amount that you pay for gas to drive back and forth to school—not the total amount you spend on gas for a semester.

Tuition	$_____
Books	$_____
Fees	$_____
Transportation	$_____
Clothing	$_____
Food	$_____
Housing	$_____
Entertainment	$_____
Other (such as insurance, medical, childcare)	$_____
Subtotal	$_____
Salary you could earn per term if you weren't in school	$_____
Total (A)	$_____

Now figure out how many classes you attend in one term. This is the number of your scheduled class periods per week multiplied by the number of weeks in your school term. Put that figure below:

Total (B) _____

Divide the **Total (B)** into the **Total (A)** and put that amount here:

$_____

This is what it costs you to go to one class one time.

On a separate sheet of paper, describe your responses to discovering this figure. Also list anything you will do differently as a result of knowing the hourly cost of your education.

The articles in this chapter about money are based on three core ideas:

- Money problems have a simple source: You spend more than you have.

- The solution to money problems is also simple: Spend less than you have.

- You can implement this solution with three broad strategies: Increase your income, decrease your expenses, or both.

In this exercise, you will think critically about these ideas by completing the following four steps:

1. First, test the logic of these assertions. Are they clear? Are they consistent with one another? And are they based on sound assumptions?

For example, the first assertion is based on the assumption that problems can have a single cause. You might argue that this is simplistic and that most problems have more than one cause.

Summarize your thinking about the logic of the assertions in the space below:

_____

_____

_____

_____

_____

2. Next, consider the evidence for these assertions. See if you can think of examples to support them. Also see if you can think of any counterexamples. For instance, you might be able to list money problems that are not due to spending more than you have.

Summarize your evidence for and against the assertions here:

_____

_____

_____

_____

_____

3. The third assertion states three broad financial goals that you could adopt: increase your income, decrease your expenses, or both. Consider which of these goals you are willing to adopt. Then plan to meet the goal by taking a specific action. For example, you could decrease your expenses by finding a cheaper place to live or spending less on entertainment.

In the space below, state your financial goal and your plan to meet it:

_____

_____

_____

_____

4. Finally, make a note on your calendar to return to this exercise in one month and assess the results. Did you take your planned action? If so, do the results support or contradict the assertions listed above?

Summarize your experience in the space below:

_____

_____

_____

_____

_____

power process

Be here now

Being right here, right now is such a simple idea. It seems obvious. Where else can you be but where you are? When else can you be there but when you are there?

The answer is that you can be somewhere else at any time—in your head. It's common for our thoughts to distract us from where we've chosen to be. When we let this happen, we lose the benefits of focusing our attention on what's important to us in the present moment.

To "be here now" means to do what you're doing when you're doing it and to be where you are when you're there. Students consistently report that focusing attention on the here and now is one of the most powerful tools in this book.

Leaving the here and now

We all have a voice in our head that hardly ever shuts up. If you don't believe it, conduct this experiment: Close your eyes for 10 seconds and pay attention to what is going on in your head. Please do this right now.

Notice something? Perhaps your voice was saying, "Forget it. I'm in a hurry." Another might have said, "I wonder when 10 seconds is up." Another could have been saying, "What little voice? I don't hear any little voice." That's the voice.

This voice can take you anywhere at any time—especially when you are studying. When the voice takes you away, you might appear to be studying, but your brain is at the beach.

All of us have experienced this voice, as well as the absence of it. When our inner voices are silent, time no longer seems to exist. We forget worries, aches, pains, reasons, excuses, and justifications. We fully experience the here and now. Life is magic. There are many benefits of such a state of consciousness. It is easier to discover the world around us when we are not chattering away to ourselves about how we think it ought to be, has been, or

will be. Letting go of inner voices and pictures—being totally in the moment—is a powerful tool. Do not expect to be rid of daydreams entirely. That is neither possible nor desirable. Inner voices serve a purpose. They enable us to analyze, predict, classify, and understand events out there in the "real" world.

Your stream of consciousness serves a purpose. When you are working on a term paper, your inner voices might suggest ideas. When you are listening to your sociology instructor, your inner voices can alert you to possible test questions. When you're about to jump out of an airplane, they could remind you to take a parachute. The trick is to consciously choose when to be with your inner voices and when to let them go.

Returning to the here and now

A powerful step toward returning to the here and now is to notice when we leave it. Our mind has a mind of its own, and it seems to fight back when we try to control it too much. If you doubt this, for the next 10 seconds do not, under any circumstances, think of a pink elephant. Please begin not thinking about one now.

Persistent image, isn't it? Most ideas are this insistent when we try to deny them or force them out of our consciousness.

For example, during class you might notice yourself thinking about a test you took the previous day, or a party planned for the weekend, or the DVD player you'd like to have.

Instead of trying to force a stray thought out of your head—a futile enterprise—simply notice it. Accept it. Tell yourself, "There's that thought again." Then gently return your attention to the task at hand. That thought, or another, will come back. Your mind will drift. Simply notice again where your thoughts take you and gently bring yourself back to the here and now.

Another way to return to the here and now is to notice your physical sensations. Notice the way the room looks or smells. Notice the temperature and how the chair feels. Once you've regained control of your attention by becoming aware of your physical surroundings, you can more easily take the next step and bring your full attention back to your present task.

We can often immediately improve our effectiveness—and our enjoyment—by fully entering into each of our activities, doing one thing at a time.

For example, take something as simple as peeling and eating an orange. Carefully notice the color, shape, and texture of the orange. Hold it close to your nose and savor the pungent, sweet smell. Then slowly peel the orange and see if you can hear every subtle sound that results. Next take one piece of the orange and place it in your mouth. Notice the feel of the fruit on your tongue. Chew the piece slowly, letting the delicious juice bathe your taste buds. Take note of each individual sensation of pleasure that ripples through your body as you sample this delicious treat.

"Be here now" can turn the act of eating an orange into a rich experience. Imagine what can happen when you bring this quality of attention to almost everything that you do.

Choose when to be here now

Remember that no suggestion is absolute—including the suggestion to do one thing at a time with full, focused attention. Sometimes choosing to do two or more things at once is useful, even necessary. For example, you might study while doing laundry. You might ask your children to quiz you with flash cards while you fix dinner.

The key to this Power Process is to *choose*. When you choose, you overcome distractions and stay in charge of your attention.

Experiment with noticing your inner voices. Let go of the ones that prevent you from focusing on learning. Practice the process. Be here now, moment by moment.

To "be here now" means to do what you're doing when you're doing it and to be where you are when you're there.

The here and now in your future

You also can use this Power Process to keep yourself pointed toward your goals. In fact, one of the best ways to get what you want in the future is to realize that you do not have a future. The only time you have is right now.

The problem with this idea is that some students might think: "No future, huh? Terrific! Party time!" Being in the here and now, however, is not the same as living for today and forgetting about tomorrow.

Nor is the "be here now" idea a call to abandon goals. Goals are merely tools we create to direct our actions right now. They are useful only in the present. Goals, like our ideas of the past and future, are creations of our minds. The only time they are real is in the here and now.

The power of this idea lies in a simple but frequently overlooked fact: The only time to do anything is now. You can think about doing something next Wednesday. You can write about doing something next Wednesday. You can daydream, discuss, ruminate, speculate, and fantasize about what you will do next Wednesday.

But you can't do anything on Wednesday until it is Wednesday.

Sometimes students think of goals as things that exist in the misty future. And it's easy to postpone action on things in the misty future, especially when everyone else is going to a not-so-misty party.

However, the word *goal* comes from the Anglo-Saxon *gaelan,* which means "to hinder or impede," as in the case of a boundary. That's what a goal does. It restricts, in a positive way, our activity in the here and now. It channels our energy into actions that are more likely to get us what we really want. That's what goals are for. And they are useful only when they are directing action in the here and now.

The idea behind this Power Process is simple. When you plan for the future, plan for the future. When you listen to a lecture, listen to a lecture. When you read this book, read this book. And when you choose to daydream, daydream. Do what you're doing when you're doing it.

Be where you are when you're there. Be here now . . . and now . . . and now. ▨

put it to work

Being skilled at managing time and money will serve you in any career you choose. Following are ways that you can transfer techniques from this chapter to the workplace.

Monitor work time. Use the Time Monitor/ Time Plan process to analyze the way you currently use your time at work. With this awareness, you can minimize downtime and boost your productivity. Look for low-value activities to eliminate. Also note your peak periods of energy during the workday and schedule your most challenging tasks for these times.

Use a long-term planner to manage major projects at work. Besides scheduling a due date for the final product, set interim due dates—what you'll produce at key points leading up to that final date. For example, you're planning to launch a new in-house training program in one year. Set individual due dates for finishing each major component of the program, such as manuals, Web sites, and videotapes.

Avoid the perils of multi-tasking. Our effectiveness often decreases when we try to do several things at once, such as talking on a cell phone while driving. When you get busy at work, you might feel tempted to multi-task. Yet studies indicate that multi-tasking reduces metabolic activity in the brain, lowers ability to complete tasks efficiently, and increases the number of errors made in following a procedure.[7] Turn to the Power Process: "Be here now" to find a solution. Plan your workday as a succession of tasks, then do each task with full attention. Use the ABC priority system to weed out tasks of lower importance. This can give you more time to focus on the A's.

Overcome procrastination. This problem is as widespread in the workplace as it is on any campus. Apply the suggestions from "The seven-day antiprocrastination plan" and "More ways to stop procrastination" to work tasks as well as academic tasks.

Calculate the cost of attending meetings. Meetings are a way of life for countless people in the workplace. In fact, if you're in a management or supervisory position, meetings can take up most of your workday. See if you can modify the "Education by the hour" exercise to calculate what it costs you to attend a one-hour business meeting. With this data in hand, write an Intention Statement about how you plan to get the most value out of the meetings you will attend in the future.

Use a lifeline to chart your career path. Your career plan can extend decades into the future. Below are some possible lifeline entries for a person focusing on a career in education.

May 2009	Graduate with a teaching degree
August 2010	Begin teaching high school physics
September 2017	Begin saving 5 percent of income to fund a personal sabbatical
September 2021	Return to school for a graduate degree in school administration
September 2023	Begin career as a high school principal
September 2027	Take a one-year sabbatical to live and work part-time in New Zealand
September 2028	Return to job as a high school principal
January 2031	Begin a home-based consulting business, advising teachers and principals about ways to avoid job burnout

Do long-term planning for your organization. The strategies for long-term planning in this chapter can help you set goals for your company that extend well into the future. For example, create a lifeline for your organization, listing specific outcomes to achieve during each of the next five years. ◪

Name _____ Date _____/_____/_____

1. Name three ways you can control interruptions when you study.

2. It is effective to leave holes in your schedule to allow for the unexpected. True or False? Explain your answer.

3. Suppose that after you choose where to focus your attention, your mind wanders. The Power Process: "Be here now" suggests that one of the most effective ways to bring your focus back to the here and now is to:
   (a) Slap your cheek and shout "Attention" as loudly as you can.
   (b) Notice that your thoughts have wandered and gently bring them back.
   (c) Sleep.
   (d) Concentrate as hard as you can to force distracting thoughts out of your head.
   (e) Ignore physical sensations.

4. What are at least five of the 25 ways to get the most out of now?

5. In time-management terms, what is meant by "This ain't no piano"?

6. Define "C fever" as it applies to the ABC priority method.

7. Scheduling marathon study sessions once in a while is generally an effective strategy. True or False? Explain your answer.

8. Describe at least three strategies for overcoming procrastination.

9. According to this chapter, most money problems have a simple source. What is it?

10. List the three steps toward financial independence explained in the text.

learning styles application

The questions below will "cycle" you through four styles, or modes, of learning as explained in the article "Learning styles: Discovering how you learn" in Chapter One. Each question will help you explore a different mode. You can answer the questions in any order.

what if Describe exactly how you will change your behavior to free up four additional hours each week for the upcoming month. (That's a total of 16 extra hours over the next four weeks.) Choose from the techniques presented in this chapter or any that you have created yourself.

why Suppose that you could use the techniques in this chapter to free up four additional hours each week to do whatever you please. Describe the things you would do with this extra time and why these activities matter to you.

how Describe exactly how you will change your behavior to free up four additional hours in the next week. Choose from the techniques presented in this chapter or any that you have created yourself.

what Choose three techniques from this chapter that you could use to free up four additional hours in the next week. Summarize those techniques in a single phrase or sentence and list them here.

master student profile

GREG LOUGANIS

Four-time Olympic Gold Medal diving champion, published his autobiography in 1995 to tell his story of facing challenges of fear and discrimination regarding his Samoan heritage, dyslexia, substance abuse, sexual orientation, domestic violence, and living with AIDS.

Going into 1980, Ron and I talked about what we thought was possible for me at the upcoming Olympics in Moscow. Ron wasn't someone who talked about expectations, but based on how well I'd been doing at competitions, he thought it was possible for me to win both 3-meter springboard and 10-meter platform at the Olympic trials and at the Moscow Games. Ron [Louganis' coach] didn't expect me to do it, but he thought it was possible, and we both thought it was something we could work toward. It was a goal to reach for...

It didn't matter how much effort I made in preparing for the Olympics, because history intervened and there was no 1980 Olympics for the U. S. Olympic team. The Soviet Union invaded Afghanistan in December 1979, and President Carter demonstrated the U. S. government's displeasure by deciding to boycott the Moscow Olympics.

Despite the boycott, we still had the Olympic trials. At first it was like we were just going through the motions. The trials were held at the end of June, in Austin, Texas, at the Texas Swimming Center at the University of Texas. Fifty-three of the top men and women divers from around the country came to compete.

Success in diving is never guaranteed. All it takes is one mistake, and you can blow your entire lead. I had to concentrate from my first dive to my last.

In the springboard competition, I was happiest with my seventh dive of the final round, a reverse two-and-a-half pike, which is a difficult dive. I got six 10's and a 9.5, an almost-perfect score. My total score at the end of the final round was 940 points, 28 points ahead of the second-place finisher. Then on platform I finished 65 points ahead of the next diver. I scored several 10's in that round despite the fact that I cut my palm on a pipe at the bottom of the 18-foot pool on my first dive.

When you dive off the 10-meter platform, you're going at 32 miles per hour when you hit the water, and your hands hit the water first. So with a cut palm, it really hurt. But by that point in my career, I didn't let a minor injury get in the way of a good dive.

Ron once told me that I dove with more pain and suffering and sickness than any diver he had ever had. A lot of my injuries were just routine, sprains and stomach viruses, but sometimes I did klutzy things. One time I sat down on a glass when I was in a boat and cut my butt. That doesn't sound like anything big, but when you're in the middle of a dive and you're pulling your legs up to your chest, the stitches hurt like crazy.

A week later, I was diving on springboard and I slipped going up the ladder and gashed and bruised my leg right on the spot where I had to grab my leg and squeeze hard during the dive. Each time I dove I wanted to scream.

One time I almost didn't get through it. At the national championships in Indianapolis in 1986, I caught a stomach virus. I was very sick, but I did a few dives, went into the bathroom, threw up, and came back out and did a few more dives. I don't know how, but I won.

I may cry easily, but I never give up.

From *Breaking the Surface* by Greg Louganis with Eric Marcus. Copyright © 1995 by Greg Louganis. Reprinted by permission of Random House, Inc.

For more biographical information about Greg Louganis, visit the Master Student Hall of Fame on the *Becoming a Master Student* Web site at

masterstudent.college.hmco.com

3

Memory

The art of true memory is the art of attention.
SAMUEL JOHNSON

Memory is the mother of imagination, reason and skill.... This is the companion, this is the tutor, the poet, the library with which you travel.
MARK VAN DOREN

why

this chapter matters . . .

Learning memory techniques can boost your skills at test taking, reading, note taking, and many other academic tasks.

what

is included . . .

Take your memory out of the closet
The memory jungle
20 memory techniques
Pay attention to your attention
Set a trap for your memory
Remembering names
Mnemonic devices
Power Process: "Love your problems (and experience your barriers)"
Master Student Profile: Cesar Chavez

how

you can use this chapter . . .

Focus your attention.
Make conscious choices about what to remember.
Recall facts and ideas with more ease.

As you read, ask yourself
what if . . .

I could use my memory to its full potential?

Take your memory out of the closet

Once upon a time, people talked about human memory as if it were a closet. You stored individual memories there like old shirts and stray socks. Remembering something was a matter of rummaging through all that stuff. If you were lucky, you found what you wanted.

This view of memory creates some problems. For one thing, closets can get crowded. Things too easily disappear. Even with the biggest closet, you eventually run out of space. If you want to pack some new memories in there—well, too bad. There's no room. Brain researchers have shattered this image to bits. Memory is not a closet. It's not a place or a thing. Instead, memory is a *process*.

On a conscious level, memories appear as distinct and unconnected mental events: words, sensations, images. They can include details from the distant past—the smell of cookies baking in your grandmother's kitchen or the feel of sunlight warming your face through the window of your first-grade classroom. On a biological level, each of those memories involves millions of nerve cells, or neurons, firing chemical messages to each other. If you could observe these exchanges in real time, you'd see regions of cells all over the brain glowing with electrical charges at speeds that would put a computer to shame.

When a series of cells connects several times in a similar pattern, the result is a memory. Psychologist Donald Hebb uses the aphorism "Neurons which fire together, wire together" to describe this principle.[1] This means that memories are not really "stored." Instead, remembering is a process in which you *encode* information as links between active neurons that fire together and *decode*, or reactivate, neurons that wired together in the past. Memory is the probability that certain patterns of brain activity will occur again in the future. In effect, you re-create a memory each time you recall it.

Whenever you learn something new, your brain changes physically by growing more connections between neurons. The more you learn, the greater the number of connections. For all practical purposes, there's no limit to how many memories your brain can encode.

There's a lot you can do to wire those neural networks into place. That's where the memory techniques described in this chapter come into play. Step out of your crowded mental closet into a world of infinite possibilities. ⬧

journal entry 8

Discovery/Intention Statement

Write a sentence or two describing the way you feel when you want to remember something but have trouble doing so. Think of a specific incident in which you experienced this problem, such as trying to remember someone's name or a fact you needed during a test.

I discovered that I . . .

_____

_____

_____

Now spend five minutes skimming this chapter and find three to five memory strategies you think could be helpful. List the strategies below and note the page numbers where they are explained. Then write an Intention Statement scheduling a time to study them in more detail.

Strategy   *Page number*

_____

_____

_____

_____

I intend to . . .

_____

_____

_____

_____

The memory jungle

Think of your memory as a vast, overgrown jungle. This memory jungle is thick with wild plants, exotic shrubs, twisted trees, and creeping vines. It spreads over thousands of square miles— dense, tangled, forbidding.

The more often you recall information, and the more often you put the same information into your memory, the easier it is to find.

Imagine that the jungle is encompassed on all sides by towering mountains. There is only one entrance to the jungle, a small meadow that is reached by a narrow pass through the mountains.

In the jungle there are animals, millions of them. The animals represent all of the information in your memory. Imagine that every thought, mental picture, or perception you ever had is represented by an animal in this jungle. Every single event ever perceived by any of your five senses—sight, touch, hearing, smell, or taste—has also passed through the meadow and entered the jungle. Some of the thought animals, such as the color of your seventh-grade teacher's favorite sweater, are well hidden. Other thoughts, such as your cell phone number or the position of the reverse gear in your car, are easier to find.

There are two rules of the memory jungle. Each thought animal must pass through the meadow at the entrance to the jungle. And once an animal enters the jungle, it never leaves.

The meadow represents short-term memory. You use this kind of memory when you look up a telephone number and hold it in your memory long enough to make a call. Short-term memory appears to have a limited capacity (the meadow is small) and disappears fast (animals pass through the meadow quickly).

The jungle itself represents long-term memory. This is the kind of memory that allows you to recall information from day to day, week to week, and year to year. Remember that thought animals never leave the long-term memory jungle. The following visualizations can help you recall useful concepts about memory.

Visualization #1: A well-worn path

Imagine what happens as a thought, in this case we'll call it an elephant, bounds across short-term memory and into the jungle. The deer leaves a trail of broken twigs and hoof prints that you can follow. Brain research suggests that thoughts can wear paths in the memory.[2] These paths are called *neural traces*. The more well-worn the neural trace, the easier it is to retrieve (find) the thought. In other words, the more often the elephant retraces the path, the clearer the path becomes. The more often you recall information, and the more often you put the same information into your memory, the easier it is to find. When you buy a new car, for example, the first few times you try to find reverse, you have to think for a moment. After you have found reverse gear every day for a week, the path is worn into your memory. After a year, the path is so well-worn that when you dream about driving your car backward, you even dream the correct motion for putting the gear in reverse.

Visualization #2: A herd of thoughts

The second picture you can use to your advantage is the picture of many animals gathering at a clearing—like thoughts gathering at a central location in the memory. It is easier to retrieve thoughts that are grouped together, just as it is easier to find a herd of animals than it is to find a single elephant.

Pieces of information are easier to recall if you can associate them with similar information. For example,

you can more readily remember a particular player's batting average if you can associate it with other baseball statistics.

Visualization #3: Turning your back

Imagine releasing the elephant into the jungle, turning your back, and counting to 10. When you turn around, the elephant is gone. This is exactly what happens to most of the information you receive.

Generally, we can recall only 50 percent of the material we have just read. Within 24 hours, most of us can recall only about 20 percent. This means that 80 percent of the material has not been encoded and is wandering around, lost in the memory jungle.

The remedy is simple: Review quickly. Do not take your eyes off the thought animal as it crosses the short-

term memory meadow, and review it soon after it enters the long-term memory jungle. Wear a path in your memory immediately.

Visualization #4: You are directing the animal traffic

The fourth picture is one with you in it. You are standing at the entrance to the short-term memory meadow, directing herds of thought animals as they file through the pass, across the meadow, and into your long-term memory. You are taking an active role in the learning process. You

are paying attention. You are doing more than sitting on a rock and watching the animals file past into your brain. You have become part of the process, and in doing so, you have taken control of your memory. ✖

Experience these visualizations online at mastersudent.college.hmco.com

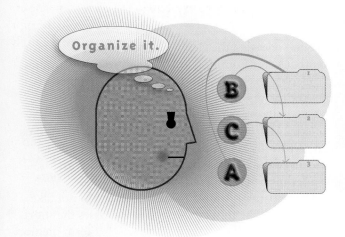

20 memory techniques

Experiment with these techniques to develop a flexible, custom-made memory system that fits your style of learning.

The 20 techniques are divided into four categories, each of which represents a general principle for improving memory. Briefly, the categories are:

Organize it. Organized information is easier to find.

Use your body. Learning is an active process; get all of your senses involved.

Use your brain. Work *with* your memory, not *against* it.

Recall it. This is easier when you use the other principles efficiently to notice and elaborate on incoming information.

The first three categories, which include techniques #1 through #16, are about storing information effectively. Most memory battles are won or lost here.

To get the most out of this article, first survey the following techniques by reading each heading. Then read the techniques. Next, skim them again, looking for the ones you like best. Mark those and use them.

Organize it

1 Be selective. There's a difference between gaining understanding and drowning in information. During your stay in higher education, you will be exposed to thousands of facts and ideas. No one expects you to memorize all of them. To a large degree, the art of memory is the art of selecting what to remember in the first place.

As you dig into your textbooks and notes, make choices about what is most important to learn. Imagine that you are going to create a test on the material and consider the questions you would ask.

When reading, look for chapter previews, summaries, and review questions. Pay attention to anything printed in bold type. Also notice visual elements—tables, charts, graphs, and illustrations. All of these are clues pointing to what's important. During lectures, notice what the instructor emphasizes. Anything that's presented visually—on the board, on overheads, or with slides—is probably key.

2 Make it meaningful. One way to create meaning is to learn from the general to the specific. Before you begin your next reading assignment, skim it to locate the main idea. You can use the same techniques you learned in Exercise #1: "Textbook reconnaissance" on page 2. If you're ever lost, step back and look at the big picture. The details might make more sense.

You can organize any list of items—even random ones—in a meaningful way to make them easier to remember. In his book *Information Anxiety*, Richard Saul Wurman proposes five principles for organizing any body of ideas, facts, or objects:[3]

Principle	Example
Organize by **time**	Events in history or in a novel flow in chronological order.
Organize by **location**	Addresses for a large company's regional offices are grouped by state and city.
Organize by **category**	Nonfiction library materials are organized by subject categories.
Organize by **continuum**	Products rated in *Consumers Guide* are grouped from highest in price to lowest in price, or highest in quality to lowest in quality.
Organize by **alphabet**	Entries in a book index are listed in ABC order.

3 Create associations. The data already encoded in your neural networks is arranged according to a scheme that makes sense to you. When you introduce new data, you can remember it more effectively if you associate it with similar or related data.

Think about your favorite courses. They probably relate to subjects that you already know something about. If you know a lot about the history of twentieth-century music, you'll find it easier to remember facts about music recorded since 2000. If you've already passed an advanced algebra course, you're primed to remember calculus formulas. And if you've enjoyed several novels by your favorite author, you've already cleared a memory path for another book from that writer.

Even when you're tackling a new subject, you can build a mental store of basic background information—the raw material for creating associations. Preview reading assignments, and complete those readings before you attend lectures. Before taking upper-level courses, master the prerequisites.

Use your body

4 Learn it once, actively. Action is a great memory enhancer. You can test this theory by studying your assignments with the same energy that you bring to the dance floor or the basketball court.

This technique illustrates the practical advantage of knowing about learning styles. In Chapter One, the article "Learning styles: Discovering how you learn" explains four aspects of learning: concrete experience, abstract conceptualization, active experimentation, and reflective observation. Many courses in higher education lean heavily toward abstract conceptualization, emphasizing lectures, papers, and textbook assignments. These courses might not give you the chance to act on ideas, to experiment with them and test them in situations outside the classroom.

You can create those opportunities yourself. For example, your introductory psychology book probably offers some theories about how people remember information. Choose one of those theories and test it on yourself. See if you can turn that theory into a new memory technique.

Your English teacher might tell you that one quality of effective writing is clear organization. To test this idea, examine the texts you come in contact with daily—newspapers, popular magazines, Web sites, and textbooks. Look for examples of clear organization *and* unclear organization. Then write Intention Statements about ways to organize your own writing more clearly.

Your sociology class might include a discussion about how groups of people resolve conflict. See if you can apply any of these ideas to resolving conflict in your own family. Then write Discovery Statements about your experiences.

The point behind each of these examples is the same: To remember an idea, go beyond thinking about it. *Do* something with it.

You can use simple, direct methods to infuse your learning with action. When you sit at your desk, sit up straight. Sit on the edge of your chair, as if you were about to spring out of it and sprint across the room.

Also experiment with standing up when you study. It's harder to fall asleep in this position. Some people insist that their brains work better when they stand.

Pace back and forth and gesture as you recite material out loud. Use your hands. Get your whole body involved in studying.

5 Relax. When you're relaxed, you absorb new information quickly and recall it with greater ease and accuracy. Students who can't recall information under the stress of a final exam can often recite the same facts later when they are relaxed.

Relaxing might seem to contradict the idea of active learning as explained in technique #4, but it doesn't. Being relaxed is not the same as being drowsy, zoned out, or asleep. Relaxation is a state of alertness, free of tension, during which your mind can play with new information, roll it around, create associations with it, and apply many of the other memory techniques. You can be active *and* relaxed.

6 Create pictures. Draw diagrams. Make cartoons. Use these images to connect facts and illustrate relationships. Associations within and among abstract concepts can be "seen" and recalled more easily when they are visualized. The key is to use your imagination.

For example, Boyle's law states that at a constant temperature, the volume of a confined ideal gas varies inversely with its pressure. Simply put, cutting the volume in half doubles the pressure. To remember this concept, you might picture someone "doubled over" using a bicycle pump. As she increases the pressure in the pump by decreasing the volume in the pump cylinder, she seems to be getting angrier. By the time she has doubled the pressure (and halved the volume) she is boiling ("Boyle-ing") mad.

Another reason to create pictures is that visual information is associated with a part of the brain that is different from the part that processes verbal information. When you create a picture of a concept, you are anchoring the information in a second part of your brain. This increases your chances of recalling that information.

To visualize abstract relationships effectively, create an action-oriented image, such as the person using the pump. Make the picture vivid, too. The person's face could be bright red. And involve all of your senses. Imagine how the cold metal of the pump would feel and how the person would grunt as she struggled with it. (Most of us would have to struggle. It would take incredible strength to double the pressure in a bicycle pump, not to mention a darn sturdy pump.)

7 Recite and repeat. When you repeat something out loud, you anchor the concept in two different senses. First, you get the physical sensation in your throat, tongue, and lips when voicing the concept. Second, you hear it. The combined result is synergistic, just as it is when you create pictures. That is, the effect of using two different senses is greater than the sum of their individual effects.

The "out loud" part is important. Reciting silently in your head can be useful—in the library, for example—but it is not as effective as making noise. Your mind can trick itself into thinking it knows something when it doesn't. Your ears are harder to fool.

The repetition part is important, too. Repetition is a common memory device because it works. Repetition blazes a trail through the pathways of your brain, making the information easier to find. Repeat a concept out loud until you know it, then say it five more times.

Recitation works best when you recite concepts in your own words. For example, if you want to remember that the acceleration of a falling body due to gravity at sea level equals 32 feet per second per second, you might say, "Gravity makes an object accelerate 32 feet per second faster for each second that it's in the air at sea level." Putting it in your own words forces you to think about it.

Have some fun with this technique. Recite by writing a song about what you're learning. Sing it in the shower. Use any style you want ("Country, jazz, rock, or rap—when you sing out loud, learning's a snap!").

Or imitate someone. Imagine your textbook being read by Bill Cosby, Madonna, or Clint Eastwood ("Go ahead, punk. Make my density equal mass over volume").

Recite and repeat. It's a technique you can use anywhere.

8 Write it down. This technique is obvious, yet easy to forget. Writing a note to yourself helps you remember an idea, even if you never look at the note again.

You can extend this technique by writing down an idea not just once, but many times. Let go of the old image of being forced to write "I will not throw paper wads" 100 times on the chalkboard after school. When you choose to remember something, repetitive writing is a powerful tool.

Writing engages a different kind of memory than speaking. Writing prompts us to be more logical, coherent, and complete. Written reviews reveal gaps in knowledge that oral reviews miss, just as oral reviews reveal gaps that written reviews miss.

Another advantage of written reviews is that they more closely match the way you're asked to remember materials in school. During your academic career, you'll probably take far more written exams than oral exams. Writing can be an effective way to prepare for such tests.

Finally, writing is physical. Your arm, your hand, and your fingers join in. Remember, learning is an active process—you remember what you *do*.

Use your brain

9 Engage your emotions. One powerful way to enhance your memory is to make friends with your amygdala. This is an area of your brain that lights up with extra neural activity each time you feel a strong emotion. When a topic excites love, laughter, or fear, the amygdala sends a flurry of chemical messages that say, in effect: *This information is important and useful. Don't forget it.*

You're more likely to remember course material when you relate it to a goal—whether academic, personal, or career—that you feel strongly about. This is one reason why it pays to be specific about what you want. The more goals you have and the more clearly they are defined, the more channels you create for incoming information.

You can use this strategy even when a subject seems boring at first. If you're not naturally interested in a topic, then create interest. Find a study partner in the class—if possible, someone you know and like—or form a study group. Also consider getting to know the instructor personally. When a course creates a bridge to human relationships, you engage the content in a more emotional way.

10 Overlearn. One way to fight mental fuzziness is to learn more than you need to know about a

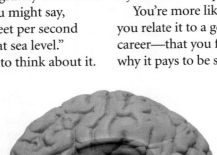

•Amygdala

The amygdala, highlighted in this illustration, is an area of your brain that sends neural messages associated with strong emotions. When you link new material to something that you feel strongly about, you activate this part of your brain. In turn, you're more likely to remember that material.

subject simply to pass a test. You can pick a subject apart, examine it, add to it, and go over it until it becomes second nature.

This technique is especially effective for problem solving. Do the assigned problems, and then do more problems. Find another textbook and work similar problems. Then make up your own problems and solve them. When you pretest yourself in this way, the potential rewards are speed, accuracy, and greater confidence at exam time.

11 Escape the short-term memory trap. Short-term memory is different from the kind of memory you'll need during exam week. For example, most of us can look at an unfamiliar seven-digit phone number once and remember it long enough to dial it. See if you can recall that number the next day.

Short-term memory can fade after a few minutes, and it rarely lasts more than several hours. A short review within minutes or hours of a study session can move material from short-term memory into long-term memory. That quick minireview can save you hours of study time when exams roll around.

12 Use your times of peak energy. Study your most difficult subjects during the times when your energy peaks. Many people can concentrate more effectively during daylight hours. The early morning hours can be especially productive, even for those who hate to get up with the sun. Observe the peaks and valleys in your energy flow during the day and adjust study times accordingly. Perhaps you will experience surges in memory power during the late afternoon or evening.

13 Distribute learning. As an alternative to marathon study sessions, experiment with shorter, spaced-out sessions. You might find that you can get far more done in three two-hour sessions than in one six-hour session.

For example, when you are studying for your American history exam, study for an hour or two and then wash the dishes. While you are washing the dishes, part of your mind will be reviewing what you studied. Return to American history for a while, then call a friend. Even when you are deep in conversation, part of your mind will be reviewing history.

You can get more done if you take regular breaks. You can even use the breaks as minirewards. After a productive study session, give yourself permission to log on and check your e-mail, listen to a song, or play 10 minutes of hide-and-seek with your kids.

Distributing your learning is a brain-friendly thing to do. You cannot absorb new information and ideas during all of your waking hours. If you overload your brain, it will find a way to shut down for a rest—whether you plan for it or not. By taking periodic breaks while studying, you allow information to sink in. During these breaks, your brain is taking the time to literally rewire itself by growing new connections between cells. Psychologists call this process *consolidation*.[4]

There is an exception to this idea of allowing time for consolidation. When you are so engrossed in a textbook that you cannot put it down, when you are consumed by an idea for a term paper and cannot think of anything else—keep going. The master student within you has taken over. Enjoy the ride.

14 Be aware of attitudes. People who think history is boring tend to have trouble remembering dates and historical events. People who believe math is difficult often have a hard time recalling mathematical equations and formulas. All of us can forget information that contradicts our opinions.

If you think a subject is boring, remind yourself that everything is related to everything else. Look for connections that relate to your own interests.

For example, consider a person who is fanatical about cars. She can rebuild a motor in a weekend and has a good time doing so. From this apparently specialized interest, she can explore a wide realm of knowledge. She can relate the workings of an engine to principles of physics, math, and chemistry. Computerized parts in newer cars can lead her to the study of data processing. She can research how the automobile industry has changed our cities and helped create suburbs, a topic that includes urban planning, sociology, business, economics, psychology, and history.

Being aware of attitudes is not the same as fighting them or struggling to give them up. Acknowledge them. Notice them. Simple awareness can deflate an attitude that is blocking your memory.

15 Give your "secret brain" a chance. Sometimes the way you combine studying with other activities can affect how well you remember information. The trick is to avoid what psychologists call *retroactive inhibition*, something that happens when a new or unrelated activity interferes with previous learning. Say that you've just left your evening psychology class, which included a fascinating lecture on Sigmund Freud's theory of dreams. When you arrive home, you decide to sneak in a few pages of that mystery novel you've wanted to finish. After you find out who poisoned the butler, you settle in for a well-deserved rest. In this scenario, the key concepts of the psychology lecture are pushed aside by the gripping drama of the whodunit. Consider another scenario instead. You have arranged to car-pool with a classmate, and on the way home, you talk about the lecture. The discussion ignites into a debate as you and your friend take opposite stands on a principle of Freud's theory. Later, just before going to sleep, you mull over the conversation. While you sleep, your brain can now process the key points of the lecture—something that will come in handy for the mid-term exam.

16 **Combine techniques.** All of these memory techniques work even better in combination. Choose two or three techniques to use on a particular assignment and experiment for yourself. For example, after you take a few minutes to get an overview of a reading assignment, you could draw a quick picture or diagram to represent the main point. Or you could overlearn a chemistry equation by singing a jingle about it all the way to work. If you have an attitude that calculus is difficult, you could acknowledge that. Then you could distribute your study time in short, easy-to-handle sessions. Combining memory techniques involves using sight, sound, and touch when you study. The effect is synergistic.

Recall it

17 **Remember something else.** When you are stuck and can't remember something that you're sure you know, remember something else that is related to it.

If you can't remember your great-aunt's name, remember your great-uncle's name. During an economics exam, if you can't remember anything about the aggregate demand curve, recall what you do know about the aggregate supply curve. If you cannot recall specific facts, remember the example that the instructor used during her lecture. Information is encoded in the same area of the brain as similar information. You can unblock your recall by stimulating that area of your memory.

You can take this technique one step further with a process that psychologists call *elaboration*.[5] The key is to ask questions that prompt you to create more associations. For example, when you meet someone new, ask yourself: What are the distinctive features of this person's face? Does she remind me of someone else?

A brainstorm is a good memory jog. If you are stumped when taking a test, start writing down lots of answers to related questions, and—pop!—the answer you need is likely to appear.

18 **Notice when you do remember.** Everyone has a different memory style. Some people are best at

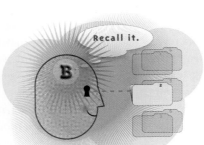

recalling information they've read. Others have an easier time remembering what they've heard, seen, or done.

To develop your memory, notice when you recall information easily and ask yourself what memory techniques you're using naturally. Also notice when it's difficult to recall information. Be a reporter. Get the facts and then adjust your learning techniques. And remember to congratulate yourself when you remember.

19 **Use it before you lose it.** Even information encoded in long-term memory becomes difficult to recall when we don't use it regularly. The pathways to the information become faint with disuse. For example, you can probably remember your current phone number. What was your phone number 10 years ago?

This points to a powerful memory technique. To remember something, access it a lot. Read it, write it, speak it, listen to it, apply it—find some way to make contact with the material regularly. Each time you do so, you widen the neural pathway to the material and make it easier to recall the next time.

Another way to make contact with the material is to teach it. Teaching demands mastery. When you explain the function of the pancreas to a fellow student, you discover quickly whether you really understand it yourself.

Study groups are especially effective because they put you on stage. The friendly pressure of knowing that you'll teach the group helps focus your attention.

20 **Adopt the attitude that you never forget.** You might not believe that an idea or a thought never leaves your memory. That's OK. In fact, it doesn't matter whether you agree with the idea or not. It can work for you anyway.

Test the concept. Instead of saying, "I don't remember," you can say, "It will come to me." The latter statement implies that the information you want is encoded in your brain and that you can retrieve it—just not right now.

People who use the flip side of this technique often get the opposite results. "I never remember anything," they say over and over again. "I've always had a poor memory. I'm such a scatterbrain." That kind of negative talk is self-fulfilling.

Instead, use positive affirmations that support you in developing your memory: "I recall information easily and accurately." "At any time I choose, I will be able to recall key facts and ideas." "My memory serves me well."

Or even "I never forget!" ⊠

Pay attention to your attention

Many of the memory glitches of everyday life result from simple absent-mindedness and a failure to concentrate. Often, the results are minor inconveniences, such as misplacing an umbrella or entering a room and forgetting why. Sometimes, though, the consequences are serious—missing an important meeting, forgetting to answer key questions on a final exam, or running a stop sign and causing an accident.

When you notice your mind heading off on an unscheduled vacation, use any of the following techniques to return to the here and now.

Reduce interference. Turn down the music—or turn it off—when you study. Find a quiet place that is free from distractions. If there's a party at your house, go to the library. If you like to snack, don't tempt yourself by studying next to the refrigerator. Two hours of studying in front of the television might be worth 10 minutes of studying where it is quiet. If you have two hours in which to study *and* watch television, it's probably better to study for an hour and then watch television for an hour. Doing one activity at a time increases your ability to remember.

Think out loud. You can also train your attention by noticing unconscious actions and making them conscious. An example is the sequence of actions you might take before you leave home for the day—grabbing your keys, turning off lights, and locking the front door. If you go through this series in a robotic trance of semiattention, you might get to campus and wonder, Did I remember to lock the door? You can eliminate such worries by saying to yourself before you leave home: "Now I am turning out the lights....Now I am checking the stove...Now I am turning the lock." Instead of coasting through large portions of your life on automatic pilot, you'll wake up and pay attention.

Bring your attention to your body—or your body to attention. In any given moment, your mind can be in two or more places at once. Your body, however, is always parked in one spot and dwells contentedly in the present moment. To focus your attention instantly, simply return to your body. Notice simple sensations—the air passing in and out of your nostrils, or your clothes gently resting on your skin. Then redirect your attention to the task at hand. Another option is to bring your body to a state of attention. Stand erect or sit with a straight spine on the edge of your chair. Visualize yourself on a tennis court, poised to return a serve. Repeat this process whenever your mind drifts.

Use a concentration cheat sheet. Each time that your attention wanders during a class or meeting, make a tick mark in the margins of your note paper. Creating a visible record of your distractions is one way to reduce them. Also, the physical act of writing re-engages your attention.

Note: This technique works only if you release any self-judgment about how often your mind wanders. At first, you might end up with row after row of tick marks. That's OK. With time and consistent practice, they will decrease.

Deal with distraction. One source of distraction is an urgent task that constantly resurfaces in your mind. Perhaps there is an important phone call to make, an errand to run, or a pressing problem to solve. When time and circumstances allow, deal with the distraction by taking care of the matter now.

If that's not feasible, write a detailed Intention Statement that describes exactly what you will do to handle the distraction. With your intention safely recorded in writing, you can now zero in on studying, working, or whatever else is most important in the present moment.

Know when to get help. A condition called attention deficit/hyperactivity disorder (ADHD) interferes with the ability to concentrate. People with ADHD consistently experience negative consequences—missed due dates, low grades, poor work performance, strained relationships with friends and family, and more—as a result of being unable to focus their attention.

If you find that none of the above techniques helps you take charge of your attention, then meet with an academic advisor or counselor and ask for help. ADHD can be reliably diagnosed and treated. ▧

> *Doing one activity at a time increases your ability to remember.*

USE Q-CARDS TO REINFORCE MEMORY

One memory strategy you might find useful involves a special kind of flash card. It's called a *Question Card*, or *Q-Card* for short.

To create a standard flash card, you write a question on one side of a 3x5 card and its answer on the other side. Q-Cards have a question on *both* sides. Here's the trick: The question on each side of the card contains the answer to the question on the other side.

The questions you write on Q-Cards can draw on both lower- and higher-order thinking skills. Writing these questions forces you to encode material in different ways. You activate more areas of your brain and burn the concepts even deeper into your memory.

For example, say that you want to remember the subject of the 18th Amendment to the United States Constitution, the one that prohibited the sale of alcohol. On one side of a 3x5 card, write *What amendment prohibited the sale of alcohol?* Turn the card over and write *What did the 18th Amendment do?*

To get the most from Q-Cards:

- Add a picture to each side of the card. This helps you learn concepts faster and develop a more visual learning style.

- Read the questions and recite the answers out loud. Two keys to memory are repetition and novelty, so use a different voice whenever you read and recite. Whisper the first time you go through your cards, then shout or sing the next time. Doing this develops an auditory learning style.

- Carry Q-Cards with you and pull them out during waiting times. To develop a kinesthetic learning style, handle your cards often.

- Create a Q-Card for each new and important concept within 24 hours after attending a class or completing an assignment. This is your *active stack* of cards. Keep answering the questions on these cards until you learn each new concept.

- Review all of the cards from the term for a certain subject on one day each week. For example, on Monday, review all cards from biology; on Tuesday, review all cards from history. These cards make up your *review stacks*.

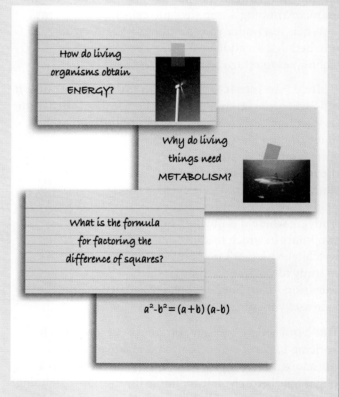

Set a trap for your memory

When you want to remind yourself to do something, link this activity to another event you know will take place. The key is to "trap" your memory by picking events that are certain to occur.

Say that you're walking to class and suddenly remember that your accounting assignment is due tomorrow. Switch your watch to the opposite wrist. Now you're "trapped." Every time you glance at your wrist and remember that you have switched your watch, it becomes a reminder that you were supposed to remember something else. (You can do the same with a ring.)

If you empty your pockets every night, put an unusual item in your pocket in the morning to remind yourself to do something before you go to bed. For example, to remember to call your younger sister on her birthday, pick an object from the playpen—a teething toy, perhaps—and put it in your pocket. When you empty your pocket that evening and find the teething toy, you're more likely to make the call.

Everyday rituals that are seldom neglected, such as feeding a pet, listening to the weather report, and unlacing shoes, provide opportunities for setting traps. For example, tie a triple knot in your shoelace as a reminder to set the alarm for your early morning study group meeting. You can even use imaginary traps. To remember to write a check for the phone bill, picture your phone hanging on the front door. In your mind, create the feeling of reaching for the doorknob and grabbing the phone instead. When you get home and reach to open the front door, the image is apt to return to you.

Link two activities together, and make the association unusual. ▧

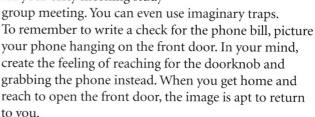

→ Keep your brain fit for life

Your brain is an organ that needs regular care and exercise. Higher education gives you plenty of chances to exercise that organ. Don't let those benefits fade after you leave school. Starting now, adopt habits to keep your brain lean and fit for life.

Seek out new experiences. If you sit at a desk most of the workday, take a dance class. If you seldom travel, start reading maps of new locations and plan a cross-country trip. Seek out museums, theaters, concerts, and other cultural events. Even after you graduate, consider learning another language or taking up a musical instrument. Your brain thrives on novelty. Build it into your life.

Shaking up your routines might involve some initial discomfort. Hang in there. Remind yourself that new experiences give your brain a workout just like sit-ups condition your abs.

Take care of your health. Exercising regularly, staying tobacco-free, and getting plenty of sleep can reduce your risk of cancer, heart disease, stroke, and other conditions that interfere with memory. Eating well also helps. A diet rich in fruits and vegetables boosts your supply of antioxidants—natural chemicals that nourish your brain.

Drink alcohol moderately, if at all. A common definition of moderate consumption for people of legal drinking age is no more than one drink per day for women and no more than two drinks per day for men. Heavier drinking can affect memory. In fact, long-term alcoholics tend to develop conditions that impair memory. One is Korsakoff's syndrome, a disorder that causes people to forget incidents immediately after they happen.

For more suggestions on maintaining health, see Chapter Eleven.

Engage life fully. Research sponsored by the MacArthur Foundation indicates that engagement with life acts as a strong predictor of successful aging.[6] Researchers define engagement as maintaining close relationships with friends and family, and staying productive in paid or volunteer work. Both loving and working help keep your brain fit to handle a lifetime of memories.

→ Notable failures, part one

You might feel discouraged about your failure to remember information at critical moments, such as during a test. Before you despair over your test scores or grade point average, remember that history is filled with examples of people who struggled academically and then went on to achieve great things. These notable failures, some of whom are listed below, are emblazoned in our collective memory, while their detractors are long forgotten.

Einstein was four years old before he could speak and seven before he could read. **Isaac Newton** did poorly in grade school. **Beethoven**'s music teacher once said of him, "As a composer he is hopeless."

When **Thomas Edison** was a boy, his teachers told him he was too stupid to learn anything. **F. W. Woolworth** got a job in a dry goods store when he was 21, but his employers would not let him wait on customers because he "didn't have enough sense."

A newspaper editor fired **Walt Disney**, claiming that he had "no good ideas." **Caruso**'s music teacher told him,

"You can't sing. You have no voice at all." The director of the Imperial Opera in Vienna told **Madame Schumann-Heink** that she would never be a singer and advised her to buy a sewing machine. **Leo Tolstoy** flunked out of college. **Wernher von Braun** flunked ninth-grade algebra. Admiral **Richard E. Byrd** had been retired from the navy as "unfit for service" until he flew over both Poles.

Louis Pasteur was rated as "mediocre" in chemistry when he attended the Royal College. **Abraham Lincoln** entered the Black Hawk War as a captain and came out as a private. **Louisa May Alcott** was told by an editor that she could never write anything that would have popular appeal. **Fred Waring** was once rejected for high school chorus. **Winston Churchill** failed the sixth grade.

"Humbling Cases for Career Counselors," by Dr. Milton E. Larson, from *Phi Delta Kappan* February 1973 issue, Volume LVI, no. 6, p. 374. © 1973. Reprinted by permission.

exercise 12

REMEMBERING YOUR CAR KEYS— OR ANYTHING ELSE

Pick something you frequently forget. Some people chronically lose their car keys or forget to write down checks in their check register. Others let anniversaries and birthdays slip by.

Pick an item or a task you're prone to forget. Then design a strategy for remembering it. Use any of the techniques from this chapter, research others, or make up your own from scratch. Describe your technique and the results in the space below.

_____

_____

_____

_____

In this exercise, as in most of the exercises in this book, a failure is also a success. Don't be concerned with whether your technique will work. Design it, and then find out. If it doesn't work for you this time, use another method.

journal entry 9

Discovery Statement

Take a minute to reflect on the memory techniques in this chapter. You probably use some of them already without being aware of it. In the space below, list at least three techniques you have used in the past and describe how you used them.

_____

_____

_____

_____

_____

_____

_____

_____

_____

_____

Remembering names

One powerful way to immediately practice memory techniques is to use them to remember names.

Recite and repeat in conversation. When you hear a person's name, repeat it. Immediately say it to yourself several times without moving your lips. You could also repeat the name out loud in a way that does not sound forced or artificial: "I'm pleased to meet you, Maria."

Ask the other person to recite and repeat. You can let other people help you remember their names. After you've been introduced to someone, ask that person to spell the name and pronounce it correctly for you. Most people will be flattered by the effort you're making to learn their names.

Visualize. After the conversation, construct a brief visual image of the person. For a memorable image, make it unusual. Imagine the name painted in hot pink fluorescent letters on the person's forehead.

Admit you don't know. Admitting that you can't remember someone's name can actually put people at ease. Most of them will sympathize if you say, "I'm working to remember names better. Yours is right on the tip of my tongue. What is it again?" (By the way, that's exactly what psychologists call that feeling—the "tip of the tongue" phenomenon.)

Introduce yourself again. Most of the time we assume introductions are one-shot affairs. If we miss a name the first time around, our hopes for remembering it are dashed. Instead of giving up, reintroduce yourself: "Hello, again. We met earlier. I'm Jesse, and please tell me your name again."

Use associations. Link each person you meet with one characteristic that you find interesting or unusual. For example, you could make a mental note: "Vicki Cheng— long, black hair" or "James Washington—horn-rimmed glasses." To reinforce your associations, write them on 3x5 cards as soon as you can.

Limit the number of new names you learn at one time. Occasionally, we find ourselves in situations where we're introduced to many people at the same time: "Dad, these are all the people in my Boy Scout troop." "Let's take a tour so you can meet all 32 people in this department."

When meeting a group of people, concentrate on remembering just two or three names. Free yourself from feeling obligated to remember everyone. Few of the people in mass introductions expect you to remember their names. Another way to avoid memory overload is to limit yourself to learning just first names. Last names can come later.

Ask for photos. In some cases, you might be able to get photos of all the people you meet. For example, a small business where you apply for a job might have a brochure with pictures of all the employees. Ask for individual or group photos and write in the names if they're not included. You can use these photos as "flash cards" as you drill yourself on names.

Go early. Consider going early to conventions, parties, and classes. Sometimes just a few people show up on time at these occasions. That's fewer names for you to remember. And as more people arrive, you can overhear them being introduced to others—an automatic review for you.

Make it a game. In situations where many people are new to one another, consider pairing up with another person and staging a contest. Challenge each other to remember as many new names as possible. Then choose an "award"—such as a movie ticket or free meal—for the person who wins.

Intend to remember. The simple act of focusing your attention at key moments can do wonders for your memory. Test this idea for yourself. The next time you're introduced to someone, direct 100 percent of your attention to hearing that person's name. Do this consistently and see what happens to your ability to remember names.

The intention to remember can be more powerful than any single memory technique. ▨

It's pronounced *ne-mon´-ik*. The word refers to tricks that can increase your ability to recall everything from grocery lists to speeches.

Mnemonic devices

Some entertainers use mnemonic devices to perform "impossible" feats of memory, such as recalling the names of everyone in a large audience after hearing them just once. Waiters use mnemonics to take orders from several tables without the aid of pad and pencil. Using mnemonic devices, speakers can go for hours without looking at their notes. The possibilities for students are endless.

There is a catch. Mnemonic devices have three serious limitations.

First, they don't always help you understand or digest material. Instead of encouraging critical thinking skills, mnemonics rely only on rote memorization.

Second, the mnemonic device itself is sometimes complicated to learn and time-consuming to develop. It

might take more energy to create such a device than to memorize something by using a more traditional memory technique, such as repetition.

Third, mnemonic devices can be forgotten. Recalling a mnemonic device might be as hard as recalling the material itself.

In spite of their limitations, mnemonic devices can be powerful. There are five general categories: new words, creative sentences, rhymes and songs, the loci system, and the peg system.

New words

Acronyms are words created from the initial letters of a series of words. Examples include NASA (**N**ational

Aeronautics and Space Administration), radar (**ra**dio **d**etecting **an**d **r**anging), scuba (**s**elf-**c**ontained **u**nderwater **b**reathing **a**pparatus), and laser (**l**ight **a**mplification by **s**timulated **e**mission of **r**adiation). You can make up your own acronyms to recall series of facts. A common mnemonic acronym is Roy G. Biv, which has helped thousands of students remember the colors of the visible spectrum (**r**ed, **o**range, **y**ellow, **g**reen, **b**lue, **i**ndigo, and **v**iolet). IPMAT helps biology students remember the stages of cell division (**i**nterphase, **p**rophase, **m**etaphase, **a**naphase, and **t**elophase).

Creative sentences

Acrostics are sentences that help you remember a series of letters that stand for something. For example, the first letters of the words in the sentence "Every good boy does fine" (E, G, B, D, and F) are the music notes of the lines of the treble clef staff.

Rhymes and songs

Madison Avenue advertising executives spend billions of dollars a year on commercials designed to burn their messages into your memory. Coca-Cola's song, "It's the Real Thing," practically stands for Coca-Cola, despite the fact that the soda contains artificial ingredients.

Rhymes have been used for centuries to teach children basic facts: "In fourteen hundred and ninety-two, Columbus sailed the ocean blue" or "Thirty days hath September."

The loci system

The word *loci* is the plural of *locus*, a synonym for *place* or *location*. Use this system to create visual associations with familiar locations. Unusual associations are the easiest to remember.

Example 1

The loci system is an old one. Ancient Greek orators used it to remember long speeches. For example, if an orator's position was that road taxes must be raised to pay for school equipment, his loci visualizations might have looked like the following.

First, as he walks in the door of his house, he imagines a large *porpoise* jumping through a hoop. This reminds him to begin by telling the audience the *purpose* of his speech.

Next, he visualizes his living room floor covered with paving stones, forming a road leading into the kitchen. In

the kitchen, he pictures dozens of school children sitting on the floor because they have no desks.

Now it's the day of the big speech. The Greek politician is nervous. He is perspiring, and his toga sticks to his body. He stands up to give his speech, and his mind goes blank. Then he starts thinking to himself:

I am so nervous that I can hardly remember my name. But no problem—I can remember the rooms in my house. Let's see, I'm walking in the front door and—wow! I see the porpoise. That reminds me to talk about the purpose of my speech. And then there's that road leading to the kitchen. Say, what are all those kids doing there on the floor? Oh, yeah, now I remember—they have no desks! We need to raise taxes on roads to pay for their desks and the other stuff they need in classrooms.

Example 2

The loci system can also be based on parts of your body. When studying biology, for instance, use the loci system to memorize the order of structures of living things.

Start with your toes, the lowest points of your body. Associate them with the lowest structure of living things—*atoms*.

The top of your head is the highest point on your body. So associate it with the highest order of living things—*biosystems*, or groups of species.

exercise 13

BE A POET

Construct your own mnemonic device for remembering some of the memory techniques in this chapter. Make up a poem, jingle, acronym, or acrostic, or use another mnemonic system. Describe your mnemonic device in the space below.

_____

_____

_____

_____

_____

_____

4th Amendment

protection from unlawful search and seizure

Then associate the intermediate structures with points on your body between your head and toes.

Link *molecules* to your feet.
Link *cells* to your ankles.
Link *tissues* with your knees.
Link *organs* with your waist.
Link *organ systems* with your chest.
Link *organisms* with your neck.

The peg system

This technique employs key words that are paired with numbers. Each word forms a "peg" on which you can "hang" mental associations. To use this system effectively, learn the following peg words and their associated numbers well:

bun goes with 1
shoe goes with 2
tree goes with 3
door goes with 4
hive goes with 5
sticks goes with 6
heaven goes with 7
gate goes with 8
wine goes with 9
hen goes with 10

Believe it or not, you can use the peg system to remember the Bill of Rights (the first ten amendments to the United States Constitution). For example, amendment number *four* is about protection from unlawful search and seizure. Imagine people knocking at your *door* who are demanding to search your home. This amendment means that you do not have to open your door unless those people have a proper search warrant.

voices

student

I didn't realize how useful the mnemonic devices were until I used them. They have actually helped me out in all my classes. I have especially used them in my medical terminology class. I especially like using the creative sentences. That one worked the best for me!

—COURTNEY MEYER

Albert Einstein's parents thought he was retarded. He spoke haltingly until age nine, and after that he answered questions only after laboring in thought about them. He was advised by a teacher to drop out of high school: "You'll never amount to anything, Einstein."

Charles Darwin's father said to his son, "You will be a disgrace to yourself and all your family." (Darwin did poorly in school.)

Henry Ford barely made it through high school.

Sir Isaac Newton did poorly in school and was allowed to continue only because he failed at running the family farm.

Pablo Picasso was pulled out of school at age 10 because he was doing so poorly. A tutor hired by Pablo's father gave up on Pablo.

Giacomo Puccini's first music teacher said that Puccini had no talent for music. Later Puccini composed some of the world's greatest operas.

The machines of the world's greatest inventor, **Leonardo da Vinci**, were never built, and many wouldn't have worked anyway.

Clarence Darrow became a legend in the courtroom as he lost case after case.

Edwin Land's attempts at instant movies (Polarvision) failed completely. He described his efforts as trying to use an impossible chemistry and a nonexistent technology to make an unmanufacturable product for which there was no discernible demand.

After the success of the show *South Pacific,* composer **Oscar Hammerstein** put an ad in *Variety* that listed over a dozen of his failures. At the bottom of the ad, he repeated the credo of show business, "I did it before, and I can do it again."

Asked about how he felt when his team lost a game, **Joe Paterno**, coach of the Penn State University football team, once replied that losing was probably good for them since that was how the players learned what they were doing wrong.

R. Buckminster Fuller built his geodesic domes by starting with a deliberately failed dome and making it "a little stronger and a little stronger ... a little piece of wood here and a little piece of wood there, and suddenly it stood up."

Igor Stravinsky said, "I have learned throughout my life as a composer chiefly through my mistakes and pursuits of false assumptions, not by my exposure to the founts of wisdom and knowledge."

Charles Goodyear bungled an experiment and discovered vulcanized rubber.

Before gaining an international reputation as a painter, **Paul Gauguin** was a failed stockbroker.

The game Monopoly was developed by **Charles Darrow**, an unemployed heating engineer. Darrow presented his first version of the game to a toy company in 1935. That company originally rejected the game for containing 52 "fundamental errors." Today the game is so successful that its publisher, Parker Brothers, prints more than $40 billion of Monopoly money each year. That's twice the amount of real money printed annually by the United States Mint.

Robert Pirsig's best-selling book, *Zen and the Art of Motorcycle Maintenance*, was rejected by 121 publishers.

Spike Lee applied for graduate study at the top film schools in the country, including the University of Southern California and the University of California at Los Angeles. Due to his scores on the Graduate Record Exam, both schools turned Lee down.

Jaime Escalante is a nationally known educator and the subject of the film *Stand and Deliver*. When he first tried to get a teaching job in California, the state refused to accept his teaching credentials from Bolivia.

Before **Alan Page** became the first African American to sit on the Minnesota Supreme Court, he played in the American Football League. Seeking a career change, he entered law school. After three weeks he dropped out and did not enroll again for another eight years.

Before the career-planning book *What Color Is Your Parachute?* became a perennial best-seller, author **Richard Nelson Bolles** got laid off from a job and ended up broke. One Friday in 1971, his cash reserves included only the $5.18 in his pocket. Bolles sold two copies of his book that day and was able to survive through the weekend. Today, *What Color Is Your Parachute?* sells nearly 20,000 copies every month.

Reprinted with permission by Stillpoint Publishing, Walpole, NH (USA) 03608 from the book *Diet for a New America* by John Robbins. Copyright © 1987. From *Information Anxiety* by Richard Saul Wurman, copyright © 1989 by Richard Saul Wurman. Used by permission of Doubleday, a division of Bantam Doubleday Dell Publishing Group, Inc.

PRACTICING CRITICAL THINKING

4

Take five minutes to remember a time when you enjoyed learning something. In the space below, describe that experience in a sentence or two. Then make a brief list of the things you found enjoyable about that experience.

_____

_____

_____

_____

_____

_____

_____

_____

_____

Within the next 24 hours, compare your list with those of other classmates. Look for similarities and differences in the descriptions of your learning experiences.

Based on your comparison, form a tentative explanation about what makes learning enjoyable for people. Summarize your explanation here:

_____

_____

_____

_____

_____

_____

_____

_____

_____

_____

_____

_____

_____

voices

student

I am now 37 years old and have returned to college. I am very apprehensive about this experience. However, I am not trying to conquer my fear. My fear has become my friend. When I embraced my fear it was a moment of enlightenment. I thought I would appear foolish, old, and unsuccessful. By recognizing these feelings and taking away their powers over me, they become harmless. They also became the fuel for my drive for success.

— RICHARD HERBERT

The one technique of Becoming a Master Student *that has helped me the most is definitely going over and repeating the material within 24 hours. After reading about it, I decided to try it and it truly made a difference when the time came to take a test. Studying seemed much easier because I recalled a lot more of the information.*

— MACHEALA JACQUEZ

MOVE FROM PROBLEMS TO SOLUTIONS

Students who enter higher education immediately face the decision about whether to *stay* in higher education. You can promote your chances of thriving in school by anticipating possible barriers to your success and putting solutions in place now.

Many students find it easy to complain about school and dwell on problems. This exercise gives you an opportunity to change that habit and respond creatively to any problem you're currently experiencing.

The key is to dwell more on solutions than on problems. Do that by inventing as many solutions as possible for any given problem. Shifting the emphasis of your conversation from problems to solutions raises your sense of possibility and unleashes the master learner within you.

In the space below, describe at least three problems that could interfere with your success as a student. The problems can be related to courses, teachers, personal relationships, finances, or anything else that might get in the way of your success.

My problem is that . . .

_____

_____

_____

My problem is that . . .

_____

_____

_____

_____

My problem is that . . .

_____

_____

_____

_____

_____

_____

Next, brainstorm at least five possible solutions to each of those problems. Ten is even better. You might find it hard to come up with that many ideas. That's OK. Stick with it. Stay in the inquiry, give yourself time, and ask other people for ideas.

I could solve my problem by . . .

_____

_____

_____

_____

I could solve my problem by . . .

_____

_____

_____

_____

I could solve my problem by . . .

_____

_____

_____

Now go online to [masterstudent.college.hmco.com]

Look for links to discussion groups with other students and share your responses to this exercise. By reviewing other students' postings, you could discover many more possible solutions to your own problems. While you're there, offer some possible solutions to the problems that others have posted.

power process

Love your problems
(and experience your barriers)

We all have problems and barriers that block our progress or prevent us from moving into new areas. Often, the way we respond to our problems puts boundaries on our experiences. We place limitations on what we allow ourselves to be, do, and have.

Our problems might include fear of speaking in front of a group, anxiety about math problems, or reluctance to sound ridiculous when learning a foreign language. We might have a barrier about looking silly when trying something new. Some of us even have anxiety about being successful.

Problems often work like barriers. When we bump up against one of our problems, we usually turn away and start walking along a different path. And all of a sudden—bump!—we've struck another barrier. And we turn away again. As we continue to bump into problems and turn away from them, our lives stay inside the same old boundaries. Inside these boundaries, we are unlikely to have new adventures. We are unlikely to improve or to make much progress.

The word *problem* is a wonderful word coming from the ancient Greek word *proballein,* which means "to throw forward." In other words, problems are there to provide an opportunity for us to gain new skills. If we respond to problems by loving them instead of resisting them, we can expand the boundaries in which we live our lives. When approached with acceptance, and even love, problems can "throw" us forward.

Three ways to handle a barrier

It's natural to have barriers, but sometimes they limit our experience so much that we get bored, angry, or frustrated with life. When this happens, consider the following three ways of dealing with a barrier. One way is to pretend it doesn't exist. Avoid it, deny it, lie about it. It's like turning your head the other way, putting on a fake grin, and saying, "See, there's really no problem at all. Everything is fine. Oh, that problem. That's not a problem—it's not really there."

In addition to making us look foolish, this approach leaves the barrier intact, and we keep bumping into it. We deny the barrier and might not even be aware that we're bumping into it. For example, a student who has a barrier about math might subconsciously avoid enriching experiences that include math.

A second approach is to fight the barrier, to struggle against it. This usually makes the barrier grow. It increases the barrier's magnitude. A person who is obsessed with weight might constantly worry about being fat. She might struggle with it every day, trying diet after diet. And the more she struggles, the bigger the problem gets.

The third alternative is to love the barrier. Accept it. Totally experience it. Tell the truth about it. Describe it in detail. When you do this, the barrier loses its power. You can literally love it to death.

The word *love* might sound like an overstatement. In this Power Process, the word means to accept your problems, to allow and permit them. When we fight a problem, it grows bigger. The more we struggle against it, the stronger it seems to become. When we accept the fact that we have a problem, we are more likely to find effective ways to deal with it.

Suppose one of your barriers is being afraid of speaking in front of a group. You can use any of these three approaches.

First, you can get up in front of the group and pretend that you're not afraid. You can fake a smile, not admitting to yourself or the group that you have any concerns about speaking—even though your legs have turned to rubber bands and your mind to jelly. The problem is that everyone in the room, including you, will know you're scared when your hands start shaking, your voice cracks, and you forget what you were going to say.

The second way to approach this barrier is to fight it. You can tell yourself, "I'm not going to be scared," and then try to keep your knees from knocking. Generally, this doesn't work. In fact, your knee-knocking might get worse.

The third approach is to go to the front of the room, look out into the audience, and say to yourself, "I am scared. I notice that my knees are shaking and my mouth feels dry, and I'm having a rush of thoughts about what might happen if I say the wrong thing. Yup, I'm scared, and that's OK. As a matter of fact, it's just part of me, so I accept it and I'm not going to try to fight it. I'm going to give this speech even though I'm scared." You might not actually eliminate the fear; however, your barrier about the fear—which is what inhibits you—might disappear. And you might discover that if you examine the fear, love it, accept it, and totally experience it, the fear itself also disappears.

Applying this process

Applying this process is easier if you remember three ideas. First, loving a problem is not necessarily the same as enjoying it. Love in this sense means total and unconditional acceptance.

This can work even with problems as thorny as physical pain. When we totally experience pain, it often diminishes and sometimes it disappears. This strategy can work with emotions and even with physical pain. Make it your aim to love the pain, that is, to fully accept the pain and know all the details about it. Most pain has a wavelike quality. It rises, reaches a peak of intensity, and then subsides for a while. See if you can watch the waves as they come and go.

Second, unconditional acceptance is not the same as unconditional surrender. Accepting a problem does not mean escaping from it or giving up on finding a solution. Rather, this process involves freeing ourselves from the

When we accept the fact that we have a problem, we are more likely to find effective ways to deal with it.

grip of the problem by diving *into* the problem headfirst and getting to know it in detail.

Third, love and laughter are allies. It's hard to resist a problem while you are laughing at it. Sure, that incident when you noticed the spinach in your teeth only *after* you got home from a first date was a bummer. But with the passage of time, you can admit that it was kind of funny. You don't have to wait weeks to gain that perspective. As long as you're going to laugh anyway, why wait? The sooner you can see the humor in your problems, the sooner you can face them.

When people first hear about loving their problems, they sometimes think it means being resigned to problems. Actually, loving a problem does not need to stop us from solving it. In fact, fully accepting and admitting the problem usually helps us take effective action—which can free us of the problem once and for all. ⬙

put it to work

Meeting your professional goals might call for continual training to update your skills—perhaps even an advanced degree. The memory techniques in this chapter can serve you at every stage of your career. Following are examples of ways to transfer those techniques to the workplace.

Focus on solving problems.
When applying for jobs, review the Power Process: "Love your problems." Present yourself as someone who can spot an organization's areas for improvement and take appropriate action. During the hiring process, transform yourself from a faceless job applicant to a potent problem solver. For example, you might say, "I've found it difficult to order products from your Web site. Five people have told me the same thing. I have a list of ideas that could solve this problem." Then explain one item from your list. You'll get an employer's attention.

If some of your solutions fail, return to the "Notable failures" articles in this chapter to renew your inspiration. Many of the people featured in these articles experienced career-related snafus.

Organize your workspace to promote memory. When personal computers first became standard fixtures in office cubicles, some futurists predicted the imminent arrival of the "paperless office." It didn't happen. Data might be stored digitally, but workers in the twenty-first century still handle reams of paper—letters, memos, manuals, meeting minutes, training materials, newsletters, magazines, technical journals, and books. That's all in addition to e-mail, Web pages, and other Internet-based documents.

Faced with such an information glut, you might find it challenging to remember where you *put* a particular document, let alone remember what's *in* it. Memory techniques from this chapter can help:

- **Be selective.** Instead of letting paper-based and digital documents pile up and telling yourself you'll get to them later, make quick decisions about which documents to keep. You might know right away that you'll never refer to some of them again. Be bold and trash them immediately. If only one article out of a magazine interests you, tear it out and toss the rest. Out of the millions of words and images that filter into your life at work, extract the gems and commit those to memory. A recycling bin that's full of paper is one sign of a healthy brain at work.

- ***Create a meaningful organization for your files.*** Take the documents you decide to keep and consider your options for filing them. You can group them alphabetically by subject, chronologically by date, or on a continuum from high to low priority. Documents that call for immediate action can go in a file that you check daily. Put lower-priority items in other files to review weekly, monthly, or quarterly. You don't have to memorize everything that's in these documents—even the most urgent ones. Just know where to find them on a moment's notice.

- ***Create a personal system of cues and reminders.*** In 1999, the winner of the U.S. National Memory Championship was a 27-year-old woman, Tatiana Cooley. To gain her title, she memorized lists of hundreds of randomly organized numbers and words. Yet Cooley confessed to a CNN reporter that she is absent-minded at work and plasters her office with handwritten Post-it Notes to aid her memory.[7] The same approach can work for you. This is a highly kinesthetic memory system. ✉

Name _____ Date _____/_____/_____

1. Explain how the "recite and repeat" memory technique leads to synergy.

2. Give a specific example of "setting a trap" for your memory.

3. Describe a visualization that can help you remember Boyle's law.

4. Define *acronym* and give an example.

5. Memorization on a deep level can take place if you:
   (a) Repeat the idea.
   (b) Repeat the idea.
   (c) Repeat the idea.
   (d) All of the above.

6. Mnemonic devices are tricks that can increase your ability to:
   (a) Manage your time.
   (b) Understand or digest material.
   (c) Recall information that you already understand.

7. Briefly describe at least three memory techniques.

8. There are five general categories of mnemonic devices given in the text. Explain two of them.

9. Briefly describe two ideas that can help you unconditionally accept a problem you're having right now.

10. Explain a strategy that can help transfer information from your short-term memory into your long-term memory.

learning styles application

The questions below will "cycle" you through four styles, or modes, of learning as explained in the article "Learning Styles: Discovering how you learn" in Chapter One. Each question will help you explore a different mode. You can answer the questions in any order.

what if *Describe how you intend to use a technique from this chapter in a situation outside school where memory skills are important.*

why *List some important situations in which you could be more effective by improving your memory skills.*

how *Describe how you intend to use a technique from this chapter in a class where memory skills are important.*

what *List the three most useful memory techniques you learned from this chapter.*

master student profile

CESAR CHAVEZ

(1927–1993) leader of the United Farm Workers (UFW), organized strikes, boycotts, and fasts to improve conditions for migrant workers.

A *few men and women have* engraved their names in the annals of change through nonviolence, but none have experienced the grinding childhood poverty that Chavez did after the Depression-struck family farm on the Gila River was foreclosed in 1937. Chavez was 10. His parents and the five children took to the picking fields as migrant workers.

Chavez's faith sustained him, but it is likely that it was both knowing and witnessing poverty and the sheer drudgery and helplessness of the migrant life that drove him.

He never lost the outreach that he had learned from his mother, who, despite the family's poverty, told her children to invite any hungry people in the area home to share what rice, beans and tortillas the family had.

He left school to work. He attended 65 elementary schools but never graduated from high school . . . .

It was in the fields, in the 1950s, that Chavez met his wife, Helen. The couple and their eight children gave much to "La Huelga," the strike call that became the UFW trademark, from their eventual permanent home near Bakersfield. Chavez did not own

the home . . . but paid rent out of his $900 a month as a union official.

Yet, in the fields in the 1930s, something happened that changed Chavez's life. He was 12 when a Congress of Industrial Organizations union began organizing dried-fruit industry workers, including his father and uncle. The young boy learned about strikes, pickets and organizing.

For two years during World War II, Chavez served in the U.S. Navy; then it was back to the fields and organizing. There were other movements gaining strength in the United States during those years, including community organizing.

From 1952 to 1962, Chavez was active outside the fields, in voter registration drives and in challenging police and immigration abuse of Mexicans and Mexican-Americans.

At first, in the 1960s, only one movement had a noticeable symbol: the peace movement. By the time the decade ended, the United Farm Workers, originally established as the National Farm Workers Association, gave history a second flag: the black Aztec eagle on the red background.

In eight years, a migrant worker son of migrants helped change a nation's perception through nonviolent resistance. It took courage, imagination, and the ability to withstand physical and other abuse.

The facts are well-known now. During the 1968 grape boycott, farmers and growers fought him, but

Chavez stood firm. Shoppers hesitated, then pushed their carts past grape counters without buying. The growers were forced to negotiate.

The UFW as a Mexican-American civil rights movement in time might outweigh the achievements of the UFW as a labor movement, for Chavez also represented something equally powerful to urban Mexican-Americans and immigrants—a nonviolent leader who had achieved great change from the most humble beginnings.

Yet, through the UFW, Chavez and his colleagues brought Americans face-to-face with the true costs, the human costs, of the food on their tables and brought Mexican-Americans into the political arena and helped keep them there. . . .

Word of Chavez's death spread to the union halls decorated with the Virgin of Guadalupe and UFW flag, to the fields, to the small towns and larger cities. And stories about the short, compact man with the ready smile, the iron determination, the genuine humility and the deep faith were being told amid the tears.

Reprinted by permission of the *National Catholic Reporter*, Kansas City, MO 64111.

For more biographical information about Cesar Chavez, visit the Master Student Hall of Fame on the *Becoming a Master Student* Web site at

masterstudent.college.hmco.com

4

Reading

Reading furnishes our mind only with materials of knowledge; it is thinking that makes what we read ours.

JOHN LOCKE

There would seem to be almost no limit to what people can and will misunderstand when they are not doing their utmost to get at a writer's meaning.

EZRA POUND

why

this chapter matters . . .

Higher education requires extensive reading that results in comprehension of facts, figures, and concepts.

what

is included . . .

Muscle Reading
How Muscle Reading works
Phase one: Before you read
Phase two: While you read
Phase three: After you read
Read with a dictionary in your lap
Reading fast
When reading is tough
English as second language
Reading with children underfoot
Power Process: "Notice your pictures and let them go"
Master Student Profile: Helen Keller

how

you can use this chapter . . .

Analyze what effective readers do and experiment with new techniques.
Increase your vocabulary and adjust your reading speed for different types of material.
Comprehend difficult texts with more ease.

As you read, ask yourself

what if . . .

I could finish my reading with time to spare and easily recall the key points?

Muscle Reading

Picture yourself sitting at a desk, a book in your hands. Your eyes are open, and it looks as if you're reading. Suddenly your head jerks up. You blink. You realize your eyes have been scanning the page for 10 minutes, and you can't remember a single thing you have read.

Or picture this: You've had a hard day. You were up at 6 a.m. to get the kids ready for school. A coworker called in sick, and you missed your lunch trying to do his job as well as your own. You picked up the kids, then had to shop for dinner. Dinner was late, of course, and the kids were grumpy.

Finally, you get to your books at 8 p.m. You begin a reading assignment on something called "the equity method of accounting for common stock investments." "I am preparing for the future," you tell yourself, as you plod through two paragraphs and begin the third. Suddenly, everything in the room looks different. Your head is resting on your elbow, which is resting on the equity method of accounting. The clock reads 11:00 p.m. Say good-bye to three hours.

Sometimes the only difference between a sleeping pill and a textbook is that the textbook doesn't have a warning on the label about operating heavy machinery.

Muscle Reading is a technique you can use to avoid mental minivacations and reduce the number of unscheduled naps during study time, even after a hard day. More than that, Muscle Reading is a way to decrease effort and struggle by increasing energy and skill. Once you learn this technique, you can actually spend less time on your reading and get more out of it.

This is not to say that Muscle Reading will make your education a breeze. Muscle Reading might even look like more work at first. Effective textbook reading is an active, energy-consuming, sit-on-the-edge-of-your-seat business. That's why this strategy is called Muscle Reading. ⬙

journal entry 10

Discovery/Intention Statement

Recall a time when you encountered problems with reading, such as words you didn't understand or paragraphs you paused to reread more than once. Sum up the experience and how you felt about it by completing the following statement.

I discovered that I . . .

_____

_____

_____

_____

_____

Now list three to five specific reading skills you want to gain from this chapter.

I intend to . . .

_____

_____

_____

_____

_____

_____

_____

_____

_____

How Muscle Reading works

Muscle Reading is a three-phase technique you can use to extract the ideas and information you want.

Phase one includes steps to take *before* you read.
Phase two includes steps to take *while* you read.
Phase three includes steps to take *after* you read.
Each phase has three steps.

Phase one: Before you read
Step 1: Preview
Step 2: Outline
Step 3: Question

Phase two: While you read
Step 4: Read
Step 5: Underline
Step 6: Answer

Phase three: After you read
Step 7: Recite
Step 8: Review
Step 9: Review again

A nine-step reading strategy might seem cumbersome and unnecessary for a two-page reading assignment. It is. Use the steps appropriately. Choose which ones to apply as you read.

To assist your recall of Muscle Reading strategies, memorize three short sentences:

Pry Out Questions.
Root Up Answers.
Recite, Review, and Review again.

These three sentences correspond to the three phases of the Muscle Reading technique. Each sentence is an acrostic. The first letter of each word stands for one of the nine steps listed above.

Take a moment to invent images for each of those sentences.

For *phase one*, visualize or feel yourself prying out questions from a text. These are questions you want answered based on a brief survey of the assignment. Make a mental picture of yourself scanning the material, spotting a question, and reaching into the text to pry it out. Hear yourself saying, "I've got it. Here's my question." Then for *phase two*, get your muscles involved. Feel the tips of your fingers digging into the text as you root up the answers to your questions.

Finally, you enter *phase three*. Hear your voice reciting what you have learned. Listen to yourself making a speech or singing a song about the material as you review it.

To jog your memory, write the first letters of the Muscle Reading acrostic in a margin or at the top of your notes. Then check off the steps you intend to follow. Or write the Muscle Reading steps on 3x5 cards and then use them for bookmarks.

Muscle Reading could take a little time to learn. At first you might feel it's slowing you down. That's natural when you're gaining a new skill. Mastery comes with time and practice.

Before you read

Step 1 Preview

Before you start reading, preview the entire assignment. You don't have to memorize what you preview to get value from this step. Previewing sets the stage for incoming information by warming up a space in your mental storage area.

If you are starting a new book, look over the table of contents and flip through the text page by page. If you're going to read one chapter, flip through the pages of that chapter. Even if your assignment is merely a few pages in a book, you can benefit from a brief preview of the table of contents.

Keep the preview short. If the entire reading assignment will take less than an hour, your preview might take five minutes. Previewing is also a way to get yourself started when an assignment looks too big to handle. It is an easy way to step into the material.

Keep an eye out for summary statements. If the assignment is long or complex, read the summary first. Many textbooks have summaries in the introduction or at the end of each chapter.

Read all chapter headings and subheadings. Like the headlines in a newspaper, these are usually printed in large, bold type. Often headings are brief summaries in themselves.

When previewing, seek out familiar concepts, facts, or ideas. These items can help increase comprehension by linking new information to previously learned material. Look for ideas that spark your imagination or curiosity. Inspect drawings, diagrams, charts, tables, graphs, and photographs. Imagine what kinds of questions will show up on a test. Previewing helps to clarify your purpose for reading. Ask yourself what you will do with this material and how it can relate to your long-term goals. Are you reading just to get the main points? Key supporting details? Additional details? All of the above? Your answers will guide what you do with each step that follows.

Step 2 Outline

With complex material, take time to understand the structure of what you are about to read. Outlining actively organizes your thoughts about the assignment and can help make complex information easier to understand.

If your textbook provides chapter outlines, spend some time studying them. When an outline is not provided, sketch a brief one in the margin of your book or at the beginning of your notes on a separate sheet of paper. Later, as you read and take notes, you can add to your outline.

Headings in the text can serve as major and minor entries in your outline. For example, the heading for this article is "Phase one: Before you read," and the subheadings list the three steps in this phase. When you outline, feel free to rewrite headings so that they are more meaningful to you.

The amount of time you spend on this step will vary. For some assignments, a 10-second mental outline is all you might need. For other assignments (fiction and poetry, for example), you can skip this step altogether.

Step 3 Question

Before you begin a careful reading, determine what you want from an assignment. Then write down a list of questions, including any that resulted from your preview of the materials.

Another useful technique is to turn chapter headings and subheadings into questions. For example, if a heading is "Transference and suggestion," you can ask yourself, "What are *transference* and *suggestion*? How does *transference* relate to *suggestion*?" Make up a quiz as

if you were teaching this subject to your classmates. If there are no headings, look for key sentences and turn these into questions. These sentences usually show up at the beginnings or ends of paragraphs and sections.

Have fun with this technique. Make the questions playful or creative. You don't need to answer every question that you ask. The purpose of making up questions is to get your brain involved in the assignment. Take your unanswered questions to class, where they can be springboards for class discussion.

Demand your money's worth from your textbook. If you do not understand a concept, write specific questions about it. The more detailed your questions, the more powerful this technique becomes.

PHASE TWO
While you read

Step 4   **Reflect**   At last! You have previewed the assignment, organized it in your mind, and formulated questions. Now you are ready to begin reading.

Before you dive into the first paragraph, take a few moments to reflect on what you already know about this subject. Do this even if you think you know nothing. This technique prepares your brain to accept the information that follows.

As you read, be conscious of where you are and what you are doing. Use the Power Process: "Be here now" in Chapter Two. When you notice your attention wandering, gently bring it back to the present moment.

One way to stay focused is to avoid marathon reading sessions. Schedule breaks and set a reasonable goal for the entire session. Then reward yourself with an enjoyable activity for five or 10 minutes every hour or two.

For difficult reading, set more limited goals. Read for a half-hour and then take a break. Most students find that shorter periods of reading distributed throughout the day and week can be more effective than long sessions. You can use the following four techniques to stay focused as you read.

First, visualize the material. Form mental pictures of the concepts as they are presented. If you read that a voucher system can help control cash disbursements, picture a voucher handing out dollar bills. Using visual imagery in this way can help deepen your understanding of the text, while allowing information to be transferred into your long-term memory.

Second, read the material out loud, especially if it is complicated. Some of us remember better and understand more quickly when we hear an idea.

Third, get a "feel" for the subject. For example, let's say you are reading about a microorganism, a paramecium, in your biology text. Imagine what it would feel like to run your finger around the long, cigar-shaped body of the organism. Imagine feeling the large fold of its gullet on one side and the tickle of the hairy little cilia as they wiggle in your hand.

Fourth, remember that a goal of your reading is to answer the questions you listed during phase one. After you've identified the key questions, predict how the author will answer them. Then read to find out if your predictions were accurate.

A final note: It's easy to fool yourself about reading. Just having an open book in your hand and moving your eyes across a page doesn't mean you are reading effectively. Reading textbooks takes energy, even if you do it sitting down. There's a saying about corporation presidents— that they usually wear out the front of their chairs first. Approach your reading assignment like a company president. Sit up. Keep your spine straight. Use the edge of your chair. And avoid reading in bed—except for fun.

READ

Step 5   **Underline**   Deface your books. Use them up. Have fun writing in them. Indulge yourself as you never could with your grade-school books.

The purpose of making marks in a text is to call out important concepts or information that you will need to review later. Underlining can save lots of time when you are studying for tests.

Underlining offers a secondary benefit. When you read with a pen or pencil in your hand, you involve your kinesthetic senses of touch and motion. Being physical with your books can help build strong neural pathways in your memory.

Avoid underlining too soon. Wait until you complete a chapter or section to make sure you know the key points. Then mark up the text. Sometimes, underlining after you read each paragraph works best.

Underline sparingly, usually less than 10 percent of the text. If you mark up too much on a page, you defeat the purpose—to flag the most important material for review.

In addition to underlining, you can mark up a text in the following ways:

- Place an asterisk (*) or an exclamation point (!) in the margin next to an especially important sentence or term.

- Circle key terms and words to look up later in a dictionary.

→ Five smart ways to highlight a text

Underlining a text with a pen can make underlined sections—the important parts—harder to read. As an alternative, many students use colored highlighters to flag key words and sentences.

Highlighting can be a powerful tool. It also presents a danger—the ever-present temptation to highlight too much text. Excessive highlighting leads to wasted time during reviews and can also spoil the appearance of your books. Get the most out of all that money you pay for books. Highlight in an efficient way that leaves texts readable for years to come.

Read carefully first. Read an entire chapter or section at least once before you begin highlighting. Don't be in a hurry to mark up your book. Get to know the text first. Make two or three passes through difficult sections before you highlight.

Make choices up front about what to highlight.
Perhaps you can accomplish your purposes by highlighting only certain chapters or sections of a text. When you highlight, remember to look for passages that directly answer the questions you posed during step 3 of Muscle Reading. Within these passages, highlight individual words, phrases, or sentences rather than whole paragraphs. The important thing is to choose an overall strategy before you put highlighter to paper.

Recite first. You might want to apply step 7 of Muscle Reading before you highlight. Talking about what you read—to yourself or with other people—can help you grasp the essence of a text. Recite first, then go back and highlight. You'll probably highlight more selectively.

Underline, then highlight. Underline key passages lightly in pencil. Then close your text and come back to it later. Assess your underlining. Perhaps you can highlight less than you underlined and still capture the key points.

Use highlighting to monitor your comprehension.
Critical thinking plays a role in underlining and highlighting. When highlighting, you're making moment-by-moment decisions about what you want to remember from a text. You're also making inferences about what material might be included on a test.

Take your critical thinking a step further by using highlighting to check your comprehension. Stop reading periodically and look back over the sentences you've highlighted. See if you are making accurate distinctions between main points and supporting material. Highlighting too much—more than 10 percent of the text—can be a sign that you're not making this distinction and that you don't fully understand what you're reading. See the article "When reading is tough" later in this chapter for suggestions that can help.

- Write short definitions of key terms in the margin.

- Write a "Q" in the margin to highlight possible test questions, passages you don't understand, and questions to ask in class.

- Write personal comments in the margin—points of agreement or disagreement with the author.

- Write mini-indexes in the margin, that is, the numbers of other pages in the book where the same topic is discussed.

- Write summaries by listing the main points or key events covered in a chapter.

- Rewrite chapter titles, headings, and subheadings so that they're more meaningful to you.

- Draw diagrams, pictures, tables, or maps that translate text into visual terms.

- Number each step in a list or series of related points.

Step 6   Answer

Answer   As you read, seek out the answers to your questions and write them down. Fill in your outline. Jot down new questions and note when you don't find the answers you are looking for. Use these notes to ask questions in class, or see your instructor personally.

When you read, create an image of yourself as a person in search of the answers. You are a detective, watching for every clue, sitting erect in your straight-back chair, demanding that your textbook give you what you want—the answers.

PHASE THREE

After you read

Step 7   Recite

Recite   Talk to yourself about what you've read. Or talk to someone else. When you're finished with a reading assignment, make a speech about it. A classic study

suggests that you can profitably devote up to 80 percent of your study time to active reciting.[1] When you recite, you practice an important aspect of metacognition—synthesis, or combining individual ideas and facts into a meaningful whole.

One way to get yourself to recite is to look at each underlined point. Note what you marked, then put the book down and start talking out loud. Explain as much as you can about that particular point.

To make this technique more effective, do it in front of a mirror. It might seem silly, but the benefits can be enormous. Reap them at exam time.

Classmates are even better than mirrors. Form a group and practice teaching each other what you have read. One of the best ways to learn anything is to teach it to someone else.

In addition, talk about your reading whenever you can. Tell friends and family members what you're learning from your textbooks.

Talking about your reading reinforces a valuable skill—the ability to summarize. To practice this skill, pick one chapter (or one section of one chapter) from any of your textbooks. State the main topic covered in this chapter. Then state the main points that the author makes about this topic.

For example, the main topic up to this point in this chapter is Muscle Reading. The main point about this topic is that Muscle Reading includes three phases—steps to take before you read, while you read, and after you read. For a more detailed summary, you could name each of the nine steps.

Note: This "topic-point" method does not work so well when you want to summarize short stories, novels, plays, and other works of fiction. Instead, focus on action. In most stories, the main character confronts a major problem and takes a series of actions to solve it.

Describe that problem and talk about the character's key actions—the turning points in the story.

Step 8 Review

Plan to do your first complete review within 24 hours of reading the material. Sound the trumpets! This point is critical: A review within 24 hours moves information from your short-term memory to your long-term memory.

Review within one day. If you read it on Wednesday, review it on Thursday. During this review, look over your notes and clear up anything you don't understand. Recite some of the main points again.

This review can be short. You might spend as little as 15 minutes reviewing a difficult two-hour reading assignment. Investing that time now can save you hours later when studying for exams.

Step 9 Review again

The final step in Muscle Reading is the weekly or monthly review. This step can be very short—perhaps only four or five minutes per assignment. Simply go over your notes. Read the highlighted parts of your text. Recite one or two of the more complicated points.

> ## Muscle Reading—a leaner approach
>
> Keep in mind that Muscle Reading is an overall approach, not a rigid, step-by-step procedure. Here's a shorter variation that students have found helpful. Practice it with any chapter in this book:
>
> - *Preview and question.* Flip through the pages, looking at anything that catches your eye—headings, subheadings, illustrations, photographs. Turn the title of each article into a question. For example, "How Muscle Reading works" can become "How does Muscle Reading work?" List your questions on a separate sheet of paper, or write each question on a 3x5 card.
>
> - *Read to answer your questions.* Read each article, then go back over the text and underline or highlight answers to the appropriate questions on your list.
>
> - *Recite and review.* When you're done with the chapter, close the book. Recite by reading each question—and answering it—out loud. Review the chapter by looking up the answers to your questions. (It's easy—they're already highlighted.) Review again by quizzing yourself one more time with your list of questions.

The purpose of these reviews is to keep the neural pathways to the information open and to make them more distinct. That way, the information can be easier to recall. You can accomplish these short reviews anytime, anywhere, if you are prepared.

Conduct a five-minute review while you are waiting for a bus, for your socks to dry, or for the water to boil. Three-by-five cards are a handy review tool. Write ideas, formulas, concepts, and facts on cards and carry them with you.

These short review periods can be effortless and fun.

Sometimes longer review periods are appropriate. For example, if you found an assignment difficult, consider rereading it. Start over, as if you had never seen the material before. Sometimes a second reading will provide you with surprising insights.

Decades ago, psychologists identified the primacy-recency effect, which suggests that we most easily remember the first and last items in any presentation.[2] Previewing and reviewing your reading can put this theory to work for you. ✖

REVIEW

BUT

ONCE AGAIN

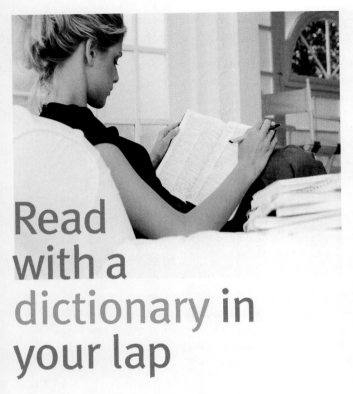

Read with a dictionary in your lap

A large vocabulary makes reading more enjoyable and increases the range of materials you can explore. In addition, building your vocabulary gives you more options for self-expression when speaking or writing. When you can choose from a larger pool of words, you increase the precision and power of your thinking.

Strengthen your vocabulary by taking delight in words. Look up unfamiliar words. Pay special attention to words that arouse your curiosity.

Students regularly use two kinds of dictionaries: the desk dictionary and the unabridged dictionary. A desk dictionary is an easy-to-handle abridged dictionary that you normally use several times in the course of a day. Keep this book within easy reach (maybe in your lap) so you can look up unfamiliar words while reading. You can find a large, unabridged dictionary in a library or bookstore. It provides more complete information about words and definitions not included in your desk dictionary, as well as synonyms, usage notes, and word histories. Both kinds of dictionaries are available on CDs for personal computers.

Construct a word stack. When you come across an unfamiliar word, write it down on a 3x5 card. Below the word, copy the sentence in which it was used. You can look up each word immediately, or you can accumulate a stack of these cards and look up the words later. Write the definition of each word on the back of the 3x5 card, adding the diacritical marks that tell you how to pronounce it.

To expand your vocabulary and learn the history behind the words, take your stack of cards to an unabridged dictionary. As you find related words in the dictionary, add them to your stack. These cards become a portable study aid that you can review in your spare moments.

Learn—even when your dictionary is across town. When you are listening to a lecture and hear an unusual word or when you are reading on the bus and encounter a word you don't know, you can still build your word stack. Pull out a 3x5 card and write down the word and its sentence. Later, you can look up the definition and write it on the back of the card.

Divide words into parts. Another suggestion is to divide an unfamiliar word into syllables and look for familiar parts. This works well if you make it a point to learn common prefixes (beginning syllables) and suffixes (ending syllables). For example, the suffix -*tude* usually refers to a condition or state of being. Knowing this makes it easier to conclude that *habitude* refers to a usual way of doing something and that *similitude* means being similar or having a quality of resemblance. See an unabridged dictionary for more examples of word parts.

Infer the meaning of words from their context. You can often deduce the meaning of an unfamiliar word simply by paying attention to its context—the surrounding words, phrases, sentences, paragraphs, or images. Later you can confirm your deduction by consulting a dictionary.

Practice looking for context clues such as:

- *Definitions.* A key word might be defined right in the text. Look for phrases such as *defined as* or *in other words.* These often introduce definitions.

- *Examples.* Authors often provide examples to clarify a word meaning. If the word is not explicitly defined, then study the examples. They're often preceded by the phrases *for example, for instance,* or *such as.*

- *Lists.* When a word is listed in a series, pay attention to the other items in the series. They might define the unfamiliar word through association.

- *Comparisons.* You might find a new word surrounded by synonyms—words with a similar meaning. Look for synonyms after words such as *like* and *as.*

- *Contrasts.* A writer might juxtapose a word with its antonym—a word or phrase with the opposite meaning. Look for phrases such as *on the contrary* and *on the other hand.*

One way to read faster is to read faster. This might sound like double talk, but it is a serious suggestion. The fact is, you can probably read faster—without any loss in comprehension—simply by making a conscious effort to do so. Your comprehension might even improve.

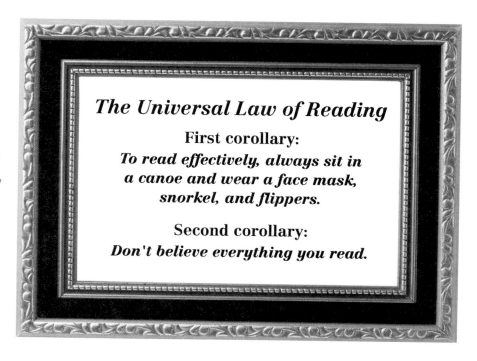

The Universal Law of Reading

First corollary:
To read effectively, always sit in a canoe and wear a face mask, snorkel, and flippers.

Second corollary:
Don't believe everything you read.

Reading fast

Experiment with the "just do it" method right now. Read the rest of this article as fast as you can. After you finish, come back and reread the same paragraphs at your usual rate. Note how much you remember from your first sprint through the text. You might be surprised to find out how well you comprehend material even at dramatically increased speeds. Build on that success by experimenting with the following guidelines.

Get your body ready. Gear up for reading faster. Get off the couch. Sit up straight at a desk or table, on the edge of your chair, with your feet flat on the floor. If you're feeling adventurous, read standing up.

Set a time limit. When you read, use a clock or a digital watch with a built-in stopwatch to time yourself. You are not aiming to set speed records, so be realistic. For example, set a goal to read two or three sections of a chapter in an hour, using all of the Muscle Reading steps. If that works, set a goal of 50 minutes for reading the same number of sections. Test your limits. The idea is to give yourself a gentle push, increasing your reading speed without sacrificing comprehension.

The idea is to give yourself a gentle push, increasing your reading speed without sacrificing comprehension.

Relax. It's not only possible to read fast when you're relaxed, it's easier. Relaxation promotes concentration. And remember, relaxation is not the same as sleep. You can be relaxed *and* alert at the same time.

Move your eyes faster. When we read, our eyes leap across the page in short bursts called *saccades* (pronounced *saˇ- käds´*). A saccade is also a sharp jerk on the reins of a horse—a violent pull to stop the animal quickly. Our eyes stop like that, too, in pauses called *fixations*.

Although we experience the illusion of continuously scanning each line, our eyes actually take in groups of words, usually about three at a time. For more than 90 percent of reading time, our eyes are at a dead stop, in those fixations.

One way to decrease saccades is to follow your finger as you read. The faster your finger moves, the faster your eyes move. You can also use a pen, pencil, or 3x5 card as a guide.

Your eyes can move faster if they take in more words with each burst—for example, six instead of three. To practice taking in more words between fixations, find a newspaper with narrow columns. Then read down one column at a time and fixate only once per line.

In addition to using the above techniques, simply make a conscious effort to fixate less. You might feel a little uncomfortable at first. That's normal. Just practice often, for short periods of time.

Notice and release ineffective habits. Our eyes make regressions, that is, they back up and reread words. You can reduce regressions by paying attention to them. Use the handy 3x5 card to cover words and lines that you have just read. You can then note how often you stop and move the card back to reread the text. Don't be discouraged if you stop often at first. Being aware of it helps you regress less frequently.

Also notice vocalizing. You are more likely to read faster if you don't read out loud or move your lips. You can also increase your speed if you don't subvocalize— that is, if you don't mentally "hear" the words as you read them. To stop doing it, just be aware of it.

Another habit to release is reading letter by letter. When we first learn to read, we do it one letter at a time. By now you have memorized many words by their shape, so you don't have to focus on the letters at all. Read this example: "Rasrhcers at Cbmrigae Uivnretisy funod taht eprxert raeedrs dno't eevn look at the lteters." You get the point. Skilled readers recognize many words and phrases in this way, taking them in at a single glance.

When you first attempt to release these habits, choose simpler reading material. That way, you can pay closer attention to your reading technique. Gradually work your way up to more complex material.

If you're pressed for time, skim. When you're in a hurry, experiment by skimming the assignment instead of reading the whole thing. Read the headings, subheadings, lists, charts, graphs, and summary paragraphs. Summaries are especially important. They are usually found at the beginning or end of a chapter or section.

Stay flexible. Remember that speed isn't everything. Skillful readers vary their reading rate according to their purpose and the nature of the material. An advanced text in analytic geometry usually calls for a different reading rate than the Sunday comics.

You also can use different reading rates on the same material. For example, you might first sprint through an assignment for the key words and ideas, then return to the difficult parts for a slower and more thorough reading.

Explore more resources. You can find many books about speed-reading. Ask a librarian to help you find a few. Using them can be a lot of fun. For more possibilities, including courses and workshops, go to your favorite search engine on the Internet and key in the word *speed-reading.*

In your research, you might discover people who offer to take you beyond speed-reading. According to some teachers, you can learn to flip through a book and "mentally photograph" each page—hundreds or even thousands of words at once. To prepare for this feat, you first do relaxation exercises to release tension while remaining alert. In this state, you can theoretically process vast quantities of information at a level other than your conscious mind.

You might find these ideas controversial. Approach them in the spirit of the Power Process: "Ideas are tools." Also remember that you can use more conventional reading techniques at any time.

One word of caution: Courses and workshops range from free to expensive. Before you lay out any money, check the instructor's credentials and talk to people who've taken the course. Also find out whether the instructor offers free "sampler sessions" and whether you can cancel at some point in the course for a full refund.

Finally, remember the first rule of reading fast: Just do it! ⬙

exercise 15

RELAX

Eye strain can be the result of continuous stress. Take a break from your reading and use this exercise to release tension.

1. Sit on a chair or lie down and take a few moments to breathe deeply.

2. Close your eyes, place your palms over your eyes, and visualize a perfect field of black.

3. Continue to be aware of the blackness for two or three minutes while you breathe deeply.

4. Now remove your hands from your eyes and open your eyes slowly.

5. Relax for a minute more, then continue reading.

When reading is tough

Sometimes ordinary reading methods are not enough. Many students get bogged down in a murky reading assignment. If you are ever up to your neck in textbook alligators, you can use the following techniques to drain the swamp.

Read it again. Difficult material—such as the technical writing in science texts—is often easier the second time around. If you read an assignment and are completely lost, do not despair. Admit your confusion. Sleep on it. When you return to the assignment, regard it with fresh eyes.

Look for essential words. If you are stuck on a paragraph, mentally cross out all of the adjectives and adverbs and read the sentence without them. Find the important words. These will usually be verbs and nouns.

Hold a minireview. Pause briefly to summarize—either verbally or in writing—what you've read so far. Stop at the end of a paragraph and recite, in your own words,

what you have just read. Jot down some notes or create a short outline or summary.

Read it out loud. Make noise. Read a passage out loud several times, each time using a different inflection and emphasizing a different part of the sentence. Be creative. Imagine that you are the author talking.

Talk to your instructor. Admit when you are stuck and make an appointment with your instructor. Most teachers welcome the opportunity to work individually with students. Be specific about your confusion. Point out the paragraph that you found toughest to understand.

Stand up. Changing positions periodically can combat fatigue. Experiment with standing as you read, especially if you get stuck on a tough passage and decide to read it out loud.

Skip around. Jump immediately to the end of the article or chapter. You might have lost the big picture, and sometimes simply seeing the conclusion or summary is all you need to put the details in context. Retrace the steps in a chain of ideas and look for examples. Absorb facts and ideas in whatever order works for you—which may be different than the author's presentation.

Find a tutor. Many schools provide free tutoring services. If tutoring services are not provided by your school, other students who have completed the course can assist you.

Use another text. Find a similar text in the library. Sometimes a concept is easier to understand if it is expressed another way. Children's books, especially children's encyclopedias, can provide useful overviews of baffling subjects.

Pretend you understand, then explain it. We often understand more than we think we do. Pretend that the material is clear as a bell and explain it to another person, or even yourself. Write down your explanation. You might be amazed by what you know.

Ask: "What's going on here?" When you feel stuck, stop reading for a moment and diagnose what's happening. At these stop points, mark your place in the margin of the page with a penciled "S" for "Stuck." A pattern to your marks over several pages might indicate a question you want to answer before going further. Or you might discover a reading habit you'd like to change.

Stop reading. When none of the above suggestions work, do not despair. Admit your confusion and then take a break. Catch a movie, go for a walk, study another subject, or sleep on it. The concepts you've already absorbed might come together at a subconscious level as you move on to other activities. Allow some time for that process. When you return to the reading material, see it with fresh eyes. ⊠

voices

I never understood how valuable a dictionary was until I found out that I could access one on the Web. I made a file in my word processing program to store the words I looked up and reviewed them prior to my tests. Reading this book taught me the value of looking up words I didn't understand.

—YAHJA MAHMOUD

journal entry 11

Discovery Statement

Now that you've read about Muscle Reading, review your assessment of your reading skills in the Discovery Wheel on page 31. Do you still think your evaluation was accurate? What new insights do you have about the way you read? Are you a more effective reader than you thought you were? Less effective? Record your observations below.

_____

_____

_____

_____

_____

_____

_____

_____

_____

_____

_____

_____

_____

_____

_____

_____

_____

_____

_____

_____

_____

_____

_____

_____

_____

_____

English as a second language

If you grew up speaking a language other than English, you're probably called a student of English as a Second Language (ESL). This term might not do full justice to your experience. Your cultural background as a whole might differ greatly from many of your fellow students. You might also speak *several* languages in addition to English.

Knowing a language other than English offers advantages. You can think thoughts that are not possible in English and see the world in ways that are unique to people who speak your native language.

If you are having difficulties mastering English, experiment with the following suggestions to learn English with more success.

Celebrate mistakes

English is a complex language. Whenever you extend your vocabulary and range of expression, the likelihood of making mistakes increases. The person who wants to master English yet seldom makes mistakes is probably being too careful. Do not look upon mistakes as a sign of weakness. Mistakes can be your best teachers—if you are willing to learn from them.

Analyze mistakes

To learn from your mistakes, first make a list of them. Ask an instructor or an English-speaking friend to help you.

Analyze the list and note your most common errors in English vocabulary, grammar, and usage. Write down several examples of these mistakes. For each example, write a corresponding sentence in your native language. Then write the examples correctly in English. Comparing the sets of examples will help you understand how the languages differ and can help you discover the source of your errors.

Learn by speaking and listening

You probably started your English studies by using textbooks. Writing and reading in English are important. To gain greater fluency, also make it your goal to hear and speak English.

For example, listen to radio talk shows. Imitate the speaker's pronunciation by repeating phrases and sentences that you hear. During conversations, also notice the facial expressions and gestures that accompany certain English words and phrases.

If you speak English with an accent, do not be concerned. Many people speak clear, accented English. Work on your accent only if you can't be easily understood.

When in doubt, use expressions you understand

Native speakers of English use many informal expressions that are called *slang*. You are more likely to find slang in conversations than in written English.

Native speakers also use *idioms*—colorful expressions with meanings that are not always obvious. Idioms can often be misunderstood. For instance, a "fork in the road" does not refer to an eating utensil discarded on a street.

Learning how to use slang and idioms is part of gaining fluency in English. However, these elements of the language are tricky. If you mispronounce a key word or leave one out, you can create a misunderstanding. In important situations—such as applying for a job or meeting with a teacher—use expressions you fully understand.

Create a community of English learners

Learning as part of a community can increase your mastery. For example, when completing a writing assignment in English, get together with other people who are learning the language. Read each other's papers and suggest revisions. Plan on revising your paper a number of times based on feedback from your peers.

You might feel awkward about sharing your writing with other people. Accept that feeling—and then remind yourself of everything you have to gain by learning from a group. In addition to learning English more quickly, you can raise your grades and make new friends.

Native speakers of English might be willing to assist your group. Ask your instructors to suggest someone. This person can benefit from the exchange of ideas and the chance to learn about other cultures.

Celebrate your gains

Every time you analyze and correct an error in English, you make a small gain. Celebrate those gains. Taken together over time, they add up to major progress in mastering English as a second language. ▨

Reading with children underfoot

It is possible to combine effective study time and quality time with children. The following suggestions come mostly from students who are also parents. The specific strategies you use will depend on your schedule and the ages of your children.

Attend to your children first. When you first come home from school, keep your books out of sight. Spend 10 minutes with your children before you settle in to study. Give them hugs and ask about their day. Then explain that you have some work to do. Your children might reward you with 30 minutes of quiet time. A short time of full, focused attention from a parent can be more satisfying than longer periods of partial attention.

Of course, this suggestion won't work with the youngest children. If your children are infants or toddlers, schedule sessions of concentrated study for when they are asleep.

Use "pockets" of time. See if you can arrange study time at school before you come home. If you arrive at school 15 minutes earlier and stay 15 minutes later, you can squeeze in an extra half-hour of study time that day. Also look for opportunities to study in between classes.

Before you shuttle children to soccer games or dance classes, throw a book in the car. While your children are warming up for the game or changing clothes, steal another 15 minutes to read.

Plan special activities for your child. Find a regular playmate for your child. Some children can pair off with close friends and safely retreat to their rooms for hours of private play. You can check on them occasionally and still get lots of reading done.

Another option is to take your children to a public playground. While they swing, slide, and dig in the sand, you can dig into your textbooks. Lots of physical activity will tire out your children in constructive ways. If they go to bed a little early, that's extra time for you to read.

After you set up appropriate activities for your children, don't attend to them every second, even if you're nearby as they play. Obviously, you want to break up fights, stop unsafe activity, and handle emergencies. Short of such incidents, you're free to read.

Use television responsibly. Another option is to use television as a babysitter—when you can control the programming. Rent a videotape for your child to watch as you study. If you're concerned about your child becoming a "couch potato," select educational programs that keep his mind active and engaged.

See if your child can use headphones while watching television. That way, the house stays quiet while you study.

Allow for interruptions. It's possible that you'll be interrupted even if you set up special activities for your child in advance. If so, schedule the kind of studying that can be interrupted. For instance, you could write out or review flash cards with key terms and definitions. Save the tasks that require sustained attention for other times.

Plan study breaks with children. Another option is to spend 10 minutes with your children for every 50 minutes that you study. View this not as an interruption but as a study break.

Or schedule time to be with your children when you've finished studying. Let your children in on the plan: "I'll be done reading at 7:30. That gives us a whole hour to play before you go to bed."

Many children love visible reminders that "their time" is approaching. An oven timer works well for this purpose. Set it for 15 minutes of quiet time. Follow that with five minutes of show-and-tell, storybooks, or another activity with your child. Then set the timer for another 15 minutes of studying, another break, and so on.

Develop a routine. Many young children love routines. They often feel more comfortable and secure when they know what to expect. You can use this to your benefit. One option is to develop a regular time for studying and let your child know this schedule: "I have to do my homework between 4 p.m. and 5 p.m. every day." Then enforce it.

Bargain with children. Reward them for respecting your schedule. In return for quiet time, give your child an extra allowance or a special treat. Children might enjoy gaining "credits" for this purpose. Each time they give you an hour of quiet time for studying, make an entry on a chart, put a star on their bulletin board, or give them a "coupon." After they've accumulated a certain number of entries, stars, or coupons, they can cash them in for a big reward—a movie or a trip to the zoo.

Ask other adults for help. This suggestion for studying with children is a message repeated throughout the book: Enlist other people to help support your success.

Getting help can be as simple as asking your spouse, partner, neighbor, or a fellow student to take care of the children while you study. Offer to trade childcare with a neighbor: You will take his kids and yours for two hours on Thursday night if he'll take them for two hours on Saturday morning. Some parents start blockwide baby-sitting co-ops based on the same idea.

A short time of full, focused attention from a parent can be more satisfying than longer periods of partial attention.

Find community activities and services. Ask if your school provides a day care service. In some cases, these services are available to students at a reduced cost. Community agencies such as the YMCA might offer similar programs.

You can also find special events that appeal to children. Storytelling hours at the library are one example. While your child is being entertained or supervised, you can stay close by. Use the time in this quiet setting to read a chapter or review class notes.

Make it a game. Reading a chemistry textbook with a 3-year-old in the same room is not as preposterous as it sounds. The secret is to involve your child. For instance, use this time to recite. Make funny faces as you say the properties of the transition elements in the periodic table. Talk in a weird voice as you repeat Faraday's laws. Draw pictures and make up an exciting story about the process of titration.

Read out loud to your children, or use them as an audience for a speech. If you invent rhymes, poems, or songs to help you remember formulas or dates, teach them to your children. Be playful. Kids are attracted to energy and enthusiasm.

Whenever possible, involve family members in tasks related to reading. Older children can help you with research tasks—finding books at the library, looking up news articles, even helping with typing.

When you can't read everything, just read something. One objection to reading with children nearby is "I just can't concentrate. There's no way I can get it all done while children are around."

That's OK. Even if you can't absorb an entire chapter while the kids are running past your desk, you can skim the chapter. Or you could just read the introduction and summary. When you can't get it *all* done, just get *something* done.

Caution: If you always read this way, your education might be compromised. Supplement this strategy with others so that you can get all of your reading done. ◪

Discover more ways to study with children underfoot at | masterstudent.college.hmco.com

Read an editorial in a newspaper or magazine. Analyze this editorial by taking notes in the three-column format below. Use the first column for listing major points, the second for supporting points, and the third for key facts or statistics that support the major or minor points. For example:

Major point

The "female condom" has not yet been proved effective as a method of birth control.

Supporting point

Few studies exist on this method.

Key fact

One of the few studies showed a 26 percent failure rate for the female condom.

Major point	Supporting point	Key fact

Ask another student to do this exercise with you. Then compare and discuss your notes. See if you identified the same main points.

power process

Notice your pictures and let them go

One of the brain's primary jobs is to manufacture images. We use mental pictures to make predictions about the world, and we base much of our behavior on those predictions.

When a cook adds chopped onions, mushrooms, and garlic to a spaghetti sauce, he has a picture of how the sauce will taste and measures each ingredient according to that picture. When an artist is creating a painting or sculpture, he has a mental picture of the finished piece. Novelists often have mental images of the characters that they're about to bring to life. Many parents have a picture about what they want their children to become.

These kinds of pictures and many more have a profound influence on us. Our pictures direct our thinking, our conversations, and our actions—all of which help create our immediate circumstances. That's amazing, considering that we often operate with little, if any, conscious knowledge of our pictures.

Just about any time we feel a need, we conjure up a picture of what will satisfy that need. A baby feels hunger pangs and starts to cry. Within seconds, his mother appears and he is satisfied. The baby stores a mental picture of his mother feeding him. He connects that picture with stopping the hunger pangs. Voilà! Now he knows how to solve the hunger problem. The picture goes on file.

According to psychologist William Glasser, our minds function like a huge photo album.[3] Its pages include pictures of all the ways we've satisfied needs in the past. Whenever we feel dissatisfied, we mentally search the album for a picture of how to make the dissatisfaction go away. With that picture firmly in mind, we act in ways to make the world outside our heads match the pictures inside.

Remember that pictures are not strictly visual images. They can involve any of the senses. When you buy a CD, you have a picture of how it will sound. When you buy a sweater, you have a picture of how it will feel.

A problem with pictures

The pictures we make in our heads are survival mechanisms. Without them, we couldn't get from one end of town to the other. We couldn't feed or clothe ourselves. Without a picture of a socket, we couldn't screw in a light bulb.

Pictures can also get in our way. Take the case of a student who plans to attend a school he hasn't visited. He chose this school for its strong curriculum and good academic standing, but his brain didn't stop there. In his mind, the campus has historic buildings with ivy-covered walls and tree-lined avenues. The professors, he imagines, will be as articulate as Bill Moyers and as entertaining as Oprah Winfrey. His roommate will be his best friend. The cafeteria will be a cozy nook serving delicate quiche and fragrant teas. He will gather there with fellow students for hours of stimulating, intellectual conversation. The library will have every book, while the computer lab will boast the newest technology.

The school turns out to be four gray buildings downtown, next to the bus station. The first class he attends is taught by an overweight, balding professor, who is wearing a purple-and-orange bird of paradise tie and has a bad case of the sniffles. The cafeteria is a nondescript hall with machine-dispensed food, and the student's apartment is barely large enough to accommodate his roommate's tuba. This hypothetical student gets depressed. He begins to think about dropping out of school.

The problem with pictures is that they can prevent us from seeing what is really there. That happened to the student in this story. His pictures prevented him from noticing that his school is in the heart of a culturally vital city—close to theaters, museums, government offices, clubs, and all kinds of stores. The professor with the weird tie is not only an expert in his field, but is also a superior teacher. The school cafeteria is skimpy because it can't compete with the variety of inexpensive restaurants in the area. There might even be hope for a tuba-playing roommate.

Anger and disappointment are often the results of our pictures. We set up expectations of events before they occur, which can lead to disappointment. Sometimes we don't even realize that we have these expectations. The next time you discover you are angry, disappointed, or frustrated, look to see which of your pictures aren't being fulfilled.

Take charge of your pictures

Having pictures is unavoidable. Letting these pictures control our lives *is* avoidable. Some techniques for dealing with pictures are so simple and effortless, they might seem silly.

One way to deal with pictures is to be aware of them. Open up your mental photo album and notice how the pictures there influence your thoughts, feelings, and actions. Just becoming aware of your pictures—and how they affect you—can help you take a huge step toward dealing with them effectively.

Our pictures direct our thinking, our conversations, and our actions—all of which help create our immediate circumstances.

When you notice that pictures are getting in your way, then, in the most gentle manner possible, let your pictures go. Let them drift away like wisps of smoke picked up by a gentle wind.

Pictures are persistent. They come back over and over. Notice them again and let them go again. At first, a picture might return repeatedly and insistently. Pictures are like independent beings. They want to live. If you can see the picture as a thought independent from you, you will likely find it easier to let it go.

You are more than your pictures. Many images and words will pop into your head in the course of a lifetime. You do not have to identify with these pictures. You can let pictures go without giving up yourself.

If your pictures are interfering with your education, visualize them scurrying around inside your head. See yourself tying them to a brightly colored helium balloon and letting them go. Let them float away again and again.

Sometimes we can let go of old pictures and replace them with new ones. We stored all of those pictures in the first place. We can replace them. Our student's new picture of a great education can include the skimpy cafeteria, the professor with the weird tie, and the roommate with the tuba.

We can take charge of the images that float through our minds. We don't have to be ruled by an album of outdated pictures. We can stay aware of our pictures and keep looking for new ones. And when *those* new pictures no longer serve us, we can also let them go. ⬧

put it to work

In the year 2000, researchers from the University of California, Berkeley, estimated that the world produces between one and two exabytes of information each year.[4] To put this figure in perspective, consider that one exabyte equals 250 megabytes for each individual on earth. (The complete works of Shakespeare would take up only five megabytes of space on your computer's hard drive.)

Much of your personal 250 megabytes might come in the form of work-related reading: technical manuals, sales manuals, policies and procedures, memos, e-mail, Web pages, newsletters, invoices, application forms, meeting minutes, brochures, annual reports, job descriptions, and more.

The techniques of Muscle Reading will help you plow through all that material and extract what you want to know. Also keep the following suggestions in mind.

Read with a purpose. At work, you're probably reading in order to produce an outcome. Determine your purpose in reading each document and extract only what you need to effect that outcome.

Print out online documents to read later. Research indicates that people can read faster on paper than on the computer screen.[5] Be kind to your eyes. Print out long attachments and e-mails and read them afterwards.

Make several passes through reading material. You don't have to "get it all" the first time you read a document. Make your first pass a quick preview. Then go for a second pass, reading the first sentence of each paragraph or the first and last paragraphs in each section. If you want more detail, then make a third pass, reading the material paragraph by paragraph, sentence by sentence.

Read only the relevant sections of documents. Don't feel obligated to read every document completely. Many business documents include executive summaries. Look for them. Everything you want to know might be there, all in a page or two.

Schedule regular reading time at work. Read during times of the day when your energy peaks.

Discuss what you read with coworkers. Make time for one-on-one, face-to-face conversations. Talking about what you read is a powerful way to transform data into insight.

Create "read anytime" files. Much of the papers and online documents that cross your desk will probably consist of basic background material—items that are important to read but not urgent. Place these documents in a folder and save them for a Friday afternoon or a plane trip.

Name _____ Date _____/_____/_____

1. Name the acrostic that can help you remember the steps of Muscle Reading.

2. You must complete all nine steps of Muscle Reading to get the most out of any reading assignment. True or False? Explain your answer.

3. Describe at least three strategies you can use to preview a reading assignment.

4. What is one benefit of outlining a reading assignment?

5. Define the terms *prefix* and *suffix,* and explain how they can assist you in learning the meanings of new words.

6. To get the most benefit from marking a book, underline at least 25 percent of the text. True or False? Explain your answer.

7. Explain at least three techniques you can use when reading is tough.

8. According to the Power Process in this chapter, mental pictures are strictly visual images. True or False? Explain your answer.

9. Define the "topic-point" method of summarizing.

10. List at least three techniques for increasing your reading speed.

learning styles application

The questions below will "cycle" you through four styles, or modes, of learning as explained in the article "Learning Styles: Discover how you learn" in Chapter One. Each question will help you explore a different mode. You can answer the questions in any order.

what if *Consider how you might adapt or modify Muscle Reading to make it more useful. List any steps that you would add, subtract, or change.*

why *List current reading assignments that you could use to practice Muscle Reading.*

how *Briefly describe how you will approach reading assignments differently after studying this chapter.*

what *List the three most useful suggestions for reading that you gained from this chapter.*

master student profile

HELEN KELLER

(1880–1968) Author and lecturer. Illness left her blind, deaf, and mute at the age of 19 months.

The morning after my teacher came she led me into her room and gave me a doll. The little blind children at the Perkins Institution had sent it and Laura Bridgman had dressed it; but I did not know this until afterward. When I had played with it a little while, Miss Sullivan slowly spelled into my hand the word "d-o-l-l." I was at once interested in this finger play and tried to imitate it. When I finally succeeded in making the letters correctly I was flushed with childish pleasure and pride. Running downstairs to my mother I held up my hand and made the letters for doll. I did not know that I was spelling a word or even that words existed; I was simply making my fingers go in monkey-like imitation. In the days that followed I learned to spell in this uncomprehending way a great many words, among them *pin*, *hat*, *cup*, and a few verbs like *sit*, *stand*, and *walk*. But my teacher had been with me several weeks before I understood that everything has a name.

One day, while I was playing with my new doll, Miss Sullivan put my big rag doll into my lap also, spelled "d-o-l-l" and tried to make me understand that "d-o-l-l" applied to both. Earlier in the day we had had a tussle over the words "m-u-g" and "w-a-t-e-r." Miss Sullivan had tried to impress it upon me that "m-u-g" is mug and that "w-a-t-e-r" is water, but I persisted in confounding the two. In despair she had dropped the subject for the time, only to renew it at the first opportunity. I became impatient at her repeated attempts and, seizing the new doll, I dashed it upon the floor. I was keenly delighted when I felt the fragments of the broken doll at my feet. Neither sorrow nor regret followed my passionate outburst. I had not loved the doll. In the still, dark world in which I lived there was no strong sentiment or tenderness. I felt my teacher sweep the fragments to one side of the hearth, and I had a sense of satisfaction that the cause of my discomfort was removed. She brought me my hat, and I knew I was going out into the warm sunshine. This thought, if a wordless sensation may be called a thought, made me hop and skip with pleasure.

We walked down the path to the well house, attracted by the fragrance of honeysuckle with which it was covered. Someone was drawing water and my teacher placed my hand under the spout. As the cool stream gushed over one hand she spelled into the other the word *water*, first slowly, then rapidly. I stood still, my whole attention fixed upon the motions of her fingers. Suddenly I felt a misty consciousness as of something forgotten—a thrill of returning to thought; and somehow the mystery of language was revealed to me. I knew then that "w-a-t-e-r" meant the wonderful cool something that was flowing over my hand. That living word awakened my soul, it gave it light, hope, joy, set it free! There were barriers still, it is true, but barriers that could in time be swept away.

I left the well house eager to learn. Everything had a name, and each name gave birth to a new thought. As we returned to the house, every object which I touched seemed to quiver with life. That was because I saw everything with the strange, new sight that had come to me. ✄

From Helen Keller, *The Story of My Life* (New York: Doubleday, Page & Company, 1905), 22–24.

For more biographical information on Helen Keller, visit the Master Student Hall of Fame on the *Becoming a Master Student* Web site at

masterstudent.college.hmco.com

5

Notes

why
this chapter matters . . .

Note taking helps you remember information and influences how well you do on tests

what
is included . . .

The note-taking process flows
Observe
Record
Review
Improving your handwriting
Create your instructor
When your instructor talks fast
Taking notes on your journey: The art of journal writing
Taking notes while reading
Power Process: "I create it all"
Master Student Profile: Craig Kielburger

how
you can use this chapter . . .

Experiment with several formats for note taking.
Create a note-taking format that works especially well for you.
Take effective notes in special situations—while reading, when instructors talk fast, and to chronicle your life.

As you read, ask yourself
what if . . .

I could take notes that remain informative and useful for weeks, months, or even years to come?

Rather than try to gauge your note-taking skill by quantity, think in this way: am I simply doing clerk's work or am I assimilating new knowledge and putting down my own thoughts? To put down your own thoughts you must put down your own words.... If the note taken shows signs of having passed through a mind, it is a good test of its relevance and adequacy.

JACQUES BARZUN AND HENRY GRAFF

The note-taking process flows

One way to understand note taking is to realize that taking notes is just one part of the process. Effective note taking consists of three parts: observing, recording, and reviewing. First, you observe an "event"—a statement by an instructor, a lab experiment, a slide show of an artist's works, or a chapter of required reading. Then you record your observations of that event, that is, you "take notes." Finally, you review what you have recorded.

Each part of the process is essential, and each depends on the others. Your observations determine what you record. What you record determines what you review. And the quality of your review can determine how effective your next observations will be. For example, if you review your notes on the Sino-Japanese War of 1894, the next day's lecture on the Boxer Rebellion of 1900 will make more sense.

Legible and speedy handwriting is also useful in taking notes. A knowledge of outlining is handy, too. A nifty pen, a new notebook, and a laptop computer are all great note-taking devices. And they're all worthless—unless you participate as an energetic observer *in* class and regularly review your notes *after* class. If you take those two steps, you can turn even the most disorganized chicken scratches into a powerful tool. Sometimes note taking looks like a passive affair, especially in large lecture classes. One person at the front of the room does most of the talking. Everyone else is seated and silent, taking notes. The lecturer seems to be doing all of the work.

Don't be deceived. Observe more closely, and you'll see some students taking notes in a way that radiates energy. They're awake and alert, poised on the edge of their seats. They're writing, a physical activity that expresses mental engagement. These students listen for levels of ideas and information, make choices about what to record, and compile materials to review. In higher education, you might spend hundreds of hours taking notes. Making them more effective is a direct investment in your success. Think of your notes as a textbook that *you* create—one that's more current and more in tune with your learning preferences than any textbook you could buy.

journal entry 12

Discovery/Intention Statement

Think about the possible benefits of improving your skills at note taking. Recall a recent incident in which you had difficulty taking notes. Perhaps you were listening to an instructor who talked fast, or you got confused and stopped taking notes altogether. Describe the incident in the space below.

_____

_____

_____

_____

Now preview this chapter to find at least five strategies that you can use right away to help you take better notes. Sum up each of those strategies in a few words and note page numbers where you can find out more about each suggestion.

Strategy   *Page number*

_____

_____

_____

_____

_____

Reflect on your intention to experiment actively with this chapter. Describe a specific situation in which you might apply the strategies you listed above. If possible, choose a situation that will occur within the next 24 hours.

I intend to . . .

_____

_____

_____

_____

OBSERVE

The note-taking process flows

Sherlock Holmes, a fictional master detective and student of the obvious, could track down a villain by observing the fold of his scarf and the mud on his shoes. In real life, a doctor can save a life by observing a mole—one a patient has always had—that undergoes a rapid change.

An accountant can save a client thousands of dollars by observing the details of a spreadsheet. A student can save hours of study time by observing that she gets twice as much done at a particular time of day.

Keen observers see facts and relationships. They know ways to focus their attention on the details, then tap their creative energy to discover patterns. To sharpen your classroom observation skills, experiment with the following techniques and continue to use those that you find most valuable.

Set the stage

Complete outside assignments. Nothing is more discouraging (or boring) than sitting through a lecture about the relationship of Le Chatelier's principle to the principle of kinetics if you've never heard of Henri Louis Le Chatelier or kinetics. Instructors usually assume that students complete assignments, and they construct their lectures accordingly. The more familiar you are with a subject, the more easily you can absorb important information during class lectures.

Bring the right materials. A good pen does not make you a good observer, but the lack of a pen or a notebook can be distracting enough to take the fine edge off your concentration. Make sure you have a pen, pencil, notebook, and any other materials you will need. Bring your textbook to class, especially if the lectures relate closely to the text.

If you are consistently unprepared for a class, that might be a message about your intentions concerning the course. Find out if it is. The next time you're in a frantic scramble to borrow pen and paper 37 seconds before the class begins, notice the cost. Use the borrowed pen and paper to write a Discovery Statement about your lack of preparation. Consider whether you intend to be successful in the course.

Sit front and center. Students who get as close as possible to the front and center of the classroom often do better on tests for several reasons. The closer you sit to the lecturer, the harder it is to fall asleep. The closer you sit to the front, the fewer interesting, or distracting, classmates are situated between you and the instructor. Material on the board is easier to read from up front. Also, the instructor can see you more easily when you have a question.

Instructors are usually not trained to perform. While some can project their energy to a large audience, some cannot. A professor who sounds boring from the back of the room might sound more interesting up close.

Sitting up front enables you to become a constructive force in the classroom. By returning the positive energy that an engaged teacher gives out, you can reinforce the teacher's enthusiasm and enhance your experience of the class.

In addition, sound waves from the human voice begin to degrade at a distance of eight to 12 feet. If you sit more than 15 feet from the speaker, your ability to hear and take effective notes might be compromised. Get close to the source of the sound. Get close to the energy.

Sitting close to the front is a way to commit yourself to getting what you want out of school. One reason students gravitate to the back of the classroom is that they think the instructor is less likely to call on them. Sitting in back can signal a lack of commitment. When you sit up front, you are declaring your willingness to take a risk and participate.

Conduct a short preclass review. Arrive early, then put your brain in gear by reviewing your notes from the previous class. Scan your reading assignment. Look at the sections you have underlined. Review assigned problems and exercises. Note questions you intend to ask.

Clarify your intentions. Take a 3x5 card to class with you. On that card, write a short Intention Statement about what you plan to get from the class. Describe your intended level of participation or the quality of attention you will bring to the subject. Be specific. If you found your previous class notes to be inadequate, write down what you intend to do to make your notes from this class session more useful.

"Be here now" In class

Accept your wandering mind. The techniques in the Power Process: "Be here now" can be especially useful when your head soars into the clouds. Don't fight daydreaming. When you notice your mind wandering during class, look at this as an opportunity to refocus your attention. If thermodynamics is losing out to beach parties, let go of the beach.

Notice your writing. When you discover yourself slipping into a fantasyland, feel the weight of your pen in your hand. Notice how your notes look. Paying attention to the act of writing can bring you back to the here and now.

You also can use writing in a more direct way to clear your mind of distracting thoughts. Pause for a few seconds and write those thoughts down. If you're distracted by thoughts of errands you need to run after class, list them on a 3x5 card and stick it in your pocket. Or simply put a symbol, such as an arrow or asterisk, in your notes to mark the places where your mind started to wander. Once your distractions are out of your mind and safely stored on paper, you can gently return your attention to taking notes.

Be with the instructor. In your mind, put yourself right up front with the instructor. Imagine that you and the instructor are the only ones in the room and that the lecture is a personal conversation between the two of you. Pay attention to the instructor's body language and

facial expressions. Look the instructor in the eye.

Notice your environment. When you become aware of yourself daydreaming, bring yourself back to class by paying attention to the temperature in the room, the feel of your chair, or the quality of light coming through the window. Run your hand along the surface of your desk. Listen to the chalk on the blackboard or the sound of the teacher's voice. Be in that environment. Once your attention is back in the room, you can focus on what's happening in class.

Postpone debate. When you hear something you disagree with, note your disagreement and let it go. Don't allow your internal dialogue to drown out subsequent material. If your disagreement is persistent and strong, make note of this and then move on. Internal debate can prevent you from absorbing new information. It is OK to absorb information you don't agree with. Just absorb it with the mental tag "My instructor says ..., and I don't agree with this."

Let go of judgments about lecture styles. Human beings are judgment machines. We evaluate everything, especially other people. If another person's eyebrows are too close together (or too far apart), if she walks a certain way or speaks with an unusual accent, we instantly make up a story about her. We do this so quickly that the process is usually not a conscious one.

Don't let your attitude about an instructor's lecture style, habits, or appearance get in the way of your education. You can decrease the power of your judgments if you pay attention to them and let them go.

You can even let go of judgments about rambling, unorganized lectures. Turn them to your advantage. Take the initiative and organize the material yourself. While taking notes, separate the key points from the examples and supporting evidence. Note the places where you got confused and make a list of questions to ask.

Participate in class activities. Ask questions. Volunteer for demonstrations. Join in class discussions. Be willing to take a risk or look foolish, if that's what it takes for you to learn. Chances are, the question you think is "dumb" is also on the minds of several of your classmates.

Relate the class to your goals. If you have trouble staying awake in a particular class, write at the top of your notes how that class relates to a specific goal. Identify the reward or payoff for reaching that goal.

Think critically about what you hear. This might seem contrary to the previously mentioned technique "Postpone debate." It's not. You might choose not to think critically about the instructor's ideas during the lecture. That's fine. Do it later, as you review and edit your notes. This is a time to list questions or write down your agreements and disagreements.

Watch for clues

Be alert to repetition. When an instructor repeats a phrase or an idea, make a note of it. Repetition is a signal that the instructor thinks the information is important.

Listen for introductory, concluding, and transition words and phrases. These include phrases such as "the following three factors," "in conclusion," "the most important consideration," "in addition to," and "on the other hand." These phrases and others signal relationships, definitions, new subjects, conclusions, cause and effect, and examples. They reveal the structure of the lecture. You can use these phrases to organize your notes.

Watch the board or overhead projector. If an instructor takes the time to write something down, consider the material to be important. Copy all diagrams and drawings, equations, names, places, dates, statistics, and definitions.

Watch the instructor's eyes. If an instructor glances at her notes and then makes a point, it is probably a signal that the information is especially important. Anything she reads from her notes is a potential test question.

Highlight the obvious clues. Instructors will often tell students point-blank that certain information is likely to appear on an exam. Make stars or other special marks in your notes next to this information. Instructors are not trying to hide what's important.

Notice the instructor's interest level. If the instructor is excited about a topic, it is more likely to appear on an exam. Pay attention when she seems more animated than usual. ▧

journal entry 13

Discovery/Intention Statement

Think back on the last few lectures you have attended. How do you currently observe (listen to) lectures? What specific behaviors do you have as you sit and listen? Briefly describe your responses in the space below.

I discovered that I . . .

_____

_____

_____

Now write an Intention Statement about any changes you want to make in the way you respond to lectures.

I intend to . . .

_____

_____

_____

_____

→ What to do when you miss a class

For most courses, you'll benefit by attending every class session. If you miss a class, try to catch up as quickly as possible.

Clarify policies on missed classes. On the first day of classes, find out about your instructors' policies on absences. See if you can make up assignments, quizzes, and tests. Also inquire about doing extra-credit assignments.

Contact a classmate. Early in the semester, identify a student in each class who seems responsible and dependable. Exchange e-mail addresses and phone numbers. If you know you won't be in class, contact this student ahead of time. When you notice that your classmate is absent, pick up extra copies of handouts, make assignments lists, and offer copies of your notes.

Contact your instructor. If you miss a class, e-mail, phone, or fax your instructor, or put a note in her mailbox. Ask if she has another section of the same course that you could attend so you won't miss the lecture information. Also ask about getting handouts you might need before the next class meeting.

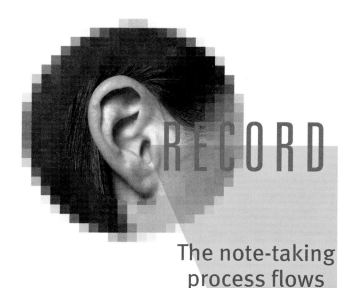

RECORD

The note-taking process flows

The format and structure of your notes are more important than how fast you write or how elegant your handwriting is. The following techniques can improve the effectiveness of your notes.

General techniques for note taking

Use key words. An easy way to sort the extraneous material from the important points is to take notes using key words. Key words or phrases contain the essence of communication. They include technical terms, names, numbers, equations, and words of degree: *most, least, faster,* etc. Key words evoke images and associations with other words and ideas. They trigger your memory. That makes them powerful review tools.

One key word can initiate the recall of a whole cluster of ideas. A few key words can form a chain from which you can reconstruct an entire lecture.

To see how key words work, take yourself to an imaginary classroom. You are now in the middle of an anatomy lecture. Picture what the room looks like, what it feels like, how it smells. You hear the instructor say:

OK, what happens when we look directly over our heads and see a piano falling out of the sky? How do we take that signal and translate it into the action of getting out of the way? The first thing that happens is that a stimulus is generated in the neurons—receptor neurons—of the eye. Light reflected from the piano reaches our eyes. In other words, we see the piano. The receptor neurons in the eye transmit that sensory signal, the sight of the piano, to the body's nervous system. That's all they can do, pass on information. So we've got a sensory signal coming into the nervous

system. But the neurons that initiate movement in our legs are effector neurons. The information from the sensory neurons must be transmitted to effector neurons or we will get squashed by the piano. There must be some kind of interconnection between receptor and effector neurons. What happens between the two? What is the connection?

Key words you might note in this example include *stimulus, generated, receptor neurons, transmit, sensory signals, nervous system, effector neurons,* and *connection.* You could reduce the instructor's 163 words to these 12 key words. With a few transitional words, your notes might look like this:

> Stimulus (piano) generated in receptor neurons (eye). Sensory signals transmitted by nervous system to effector neurons (legs). What connects receptor to effector?

Note the last key word of the lecture above—*connection.* This word is part of the instructor's question and leads to the next point in the lecture. Be on the lookout for questions like this. They can help you organize your notes and are often clues for test questions.

Use pictures and diagrams. Make relationships visual. Copy all diagrams from the board and invent your own.

A drawing of a piano falling on someone who is looking up, for example, might be used to demonstrate the relationship of receptor neurons to effector neurons. Label the eyes "receptor" and the feet "effector." This picture implies that the sight of the piano must be translated into a motor response. By connecting the explanation of the process with the unusual picture of the piano falling, you can link the elements of the process together.

Write notes in paragraphs. When it is difficult to follow the organization of a lecture or to put information into outline form, create a series of informal paragraphs. These paragraphs will contain few complete sentences. Reserve complete sentences for precise definitions, direct quotations, and important points that the instructor emphasizes by repetition or other signals—such as the phrase "This is an important point." For other material, apply the suggestions in this article for using key words.

Copy material from the board. Record all formulas, diagrams, and problems that the teacher rights down. Copy dates, numbers, names, places, and other facts. If it's on the board, put it in your notes. You can even use your own signal or code to flag that material. If it appears on the board, it can appear on a test.

Use a three-ring binder. Three-ring binders have several advantages over other kinds of notebooks. First, pages can be removed and spread out when you review. This way, you can get the whole picture of a lecture. Second, the three-ring binder format allows you to insert handouts right into your notes. Third, you can insert your own out-of-class notes in the correct order. Fourth, you can easily make additions, corrections, and revisions.

Use only one side of a piece of paper. When you use one side of a page, you can review and organize all your notes by spreading them out side by side. Most students find the benefit well worth the cost of the paper. Perhaps you're concerned about the environmental impact of consuming more paper. If so, you can use the blank side of old notes and use recycled paper.

Use 3x5 cards. As an alternative to using notebook paper, use 3x5 cards to take lecture notes. Copy each new concept onto a separate 3x5 card. Later, you can organize these cards in an outline form and use them as pocket flash cards.

Keep your own thoughts separate. For the most part, avoid making editorial comments in your lecture notes. The danger is that when you return to your notes, you might mistake your own idea for that of the instructor. If you want to make a comment—either a question to ask later or a strong disagreement—clearly label it as your own. Pick a symbol or code and use it in every class.

Use an "I'm lost" signal. No matter how attentive and alert you are, you might get lost and confused in a lecture. If it is inappropriate to ask a question, record in your notes that you were lost. Invent your own signal— for example, a circled question mark. When you write down your code for "I'm lost," leave space for the explanation or clarification that you will get later. The space will also be a signal that you missed something. Later, you can speak to your instructor or ask to see a fellow student's notes. As long as you are honest with yourself when you don't understand, you can stay on top of the course.

Label, number, and date all notes. Develop the habit of labeling and dating your notes at the beginning of each class. Number the page, too. Sometimes the sequence of material in a lecture is important. Write your name and phone number in each notebook in case you lose it. Class notes become more and more valuable as a term or semester progresses.

Use standard abbreviations. Be consistent with your abbreviations. If you make up your own abbreviations or symbols, write a key explaining them in your notes. Avoid vague abbreviations. When you use an abbreviation such as *comm.* for *committee*, you run the risk of not being able to remember whether you meant *committee, commission, common, commit, community, communicate,* or *communist.*

One way to abbreviate is to leave out vowels. For example, *talk* becomes *tlk, said* becomes *sd, American* becomes *Amrcn.*

Leave blank space. Notes tightly crammed into every corner of the page are hard to read and difficult to use for review. Give your eyes a break by leaving plenty of space.

Later, when you review, you can use the blank spaces in your notes to clarify points, write questions, or add other material. Instructors often return to material covered earlier in the lecture.

Take notes in different colors. You can use colors as highly visible organizers. For example, you can signal important points with red. Or use one color of ink for notes about the text and another color for lecture notes. Notes that are visually pleasing can be easier to review.

Use graphic signals. The following ideas can be used with any note-taking format.

- Use brackets, parentheses, circles, and squares to group information that belongs together.

- Use stars, arrows, and underlining to indicate important points. Flag the most important points with double stars, double arrows, or double underlines.

- Use arrows and connecting lines to link related groups and to replace words such as *leads to, becomes,* and *produces.*

- Use equal signs and greater- and less-than signs to indicate compared quantities.

- Use question marks for their obvious purpose. Double question marks can signal tough questions or especially confusing points.

To avoid creating confusion with graphic symbols, use them carefully and consistently. Write a "dictionary" of your symbols in the front of your notebooks, such as the one shown below.

Use recorders effectively. There are persuasive arguments for not using a tape recorder or digital recorder. Here are the main ones.

When you tape a lecture, there is a strong temptation to daydream. After all, you can always listen to the lecture again later on. Unfortunately, if you let the recorder do all of the work, you are skipping a valuable part of the learning process. Actively participating in class can turn a lecture into a valuable study session.

There are more potential problems. Listening to recorded lectures can take a lot of time—more time than reviewing written notes. Recorders can't answer the questions you didn't ask in class. Also, recording devices malfunction. In fact, the unscientific Hypothesis of Recording Glitches states that the tendency of recorders to malfunction is directly proportional to the importance of the material. With those warnings in mind, some students use a recorder effectively. For example, you can use recordings as backups to written notes. (Check with your instructor first. Some prefer not to be recorded.) Turn the recorder on, then take notes as if it weren't there. Recordings can be especially useful if an instructor speaks fast.

You could also record yourself after class, reading your written notes. Teaching the class to yourself is a powerful review tool. Instead of taping all of your notes, for example, you might record only the key facts or concepts.

The Cornell format

A note-taking system that has worked for students around the world is the *Cornell format*.[1] Originally developed by Walter Pauk at Cornell University during the 1950s, this approach continues to be taught across the United States and in other countries as well.

The cornerstone of this system is what Pauk calls the *cue column*—a wide margin on the left-hand side of the paper. The cue column is the key to the Cornell format's many benefits. Here's how to use the Cornell format.

Format your paper. On each sheet of your note paper, draw a vertical line, top to bottom, about two inches from the left edge of the paper. This line creates the cue column—the space to the left of the line.

Take notes, leaving the cue column blank. As you read an assignment or listen to a lecture, take notes on the right-hand side of the paper. Fill up this column with sentences, paragraphs, outlines, charts, or drawings. Do not write in the cue column. You'll use this space later, as you do the next steps.

Condense your notes in the cue column. Think of the notes you took on the right-hand side of the paper as a set of answers. In the cue column, list potential test questions that correspond to your notes. Write one question for each major term or point.

As an alternative to questions, you can list key words from your notes. Yet another option is to pretend that your notes are a series of articles on different topics. In the cue column, write a newspaper-style headline for each "article." In any case, be brief. If you cram the cue column full of words, you defeat its purpose—to reduce the number and length of your notes.

Write a summary. Pauk recommends that you reduce your notes even more by writing a brief summary at the bottom of each page. This step offers you another way to engage actively with the material. It can also make your notes easier to review for tests.

Cue column	Notes
What are some key changes in U.S. health over the last 50 years?	Over the past 50 years in the U.S.: — The number of smokers decreased. — Infant mortality dropped to a record low. — Life expectancy hit a record high—about 77 years.
Who announced these changes?	Source: Health, United States 2002, Centers for Disease Control. Health and Human Services Secretary Tommy Thompson announced this report.

Summary
Changes in American health over the last 50 years include fewer smokers, lower infant mortality, and record life expectancy.

Use the cue column to recite. Cover the right-hand side of your notes with a blank sheet of paper. Leave only the cue column showing. Then look at each item you wrote in the cue column and talk about it. If you wrote questions, answer each question. If you wrote key words, define each word and talk about why it's important. If you wrote headlines in the cue column, explain what each one means and offer supporting details. After reciting, uncover your notes and look for any important points you missed. Repeat this cycle of reciting and checking until you've mastered the material.

Mind mapping

This system, developed by Tony Buzan,[2] can be used in conjunction with the Cornell format. In some circumstances, you might want to use mind maps exclusively.

To understand mind maps, first review the features of traditional note taking. Outlines (explained in the next section) divide major topics into minor topics, which, in turn, are subdivided further. They organize information in a sequential, linear way.

This kind of organization doesn't reflect certain aspects of brain function, a point that has been made in discussions about "left brain" and "right brain" activities. People often use the term *right brain* when referring to creative, pattern-making, visual, intuitive brain activity. They use the term *left brain* when talking about orderly, logical, step-by-step characteristics of thought. Writing teacher Gabrielle Rico uses another metaphor. She refers to the left-brain mode as our "sign mind" (concerned with words) and the right-brain mode as our "design mind" (concerned with visuals).[3]

A mind map uses both kinds of brain functions. Mind maps can contain lists and sequences and show relationships. They can also provide a picture of a subject. Mind maps are visual patterns that can serve as a framework for recalling information. They work on both verbal and nonverbal levels.

One benefit of mind maps is that they quickly, vividly, and accurately show the relationships between ideas. Also, mind mapping helps you think from general to specific. By choosing a main topic, you focus first on the big picture, then zero in on subordinate details. And by using only key words, you can condense a large subject into a small area on a mind map. You can review more quickly by looking at the key words on a mind map than by reading notes word for word.

Give yourself plenty of room. Use blank paper that measures at least 11 by 17 inches. If that's not available, turn regular notebook paper on its side so that you can take notes in a horizontal (instead of vertical) format. Another option is to find software that allows you to draw flow charts or diagrams. Then you can generate mind maps on a computer.

Determine the main concept of the lecture. Write that concept in the center of the paper and circle it, underline it, or highlight it with color. You can also write the concept in large letters. Record concepts related to the main concept on lines that radiate outward from the center. An alternative is to circle these concepts.

Use key words only. Whenever possible, reduce each concept to a single word per line or circle in your mind map. Though this might seem awkward at first, it prompts you to summarize and to condense ideas to their essence. That means fewer words for you to write now and fewer to review when it's time to prepare for tests. (Using shorthand symbols and abbreviations can help.) Key words are usually nouns and verbs that communicate the bulk of the speaker's ideas. Choose words that are rich in associations and that can help you re-create the lecture.

Jazz it up. Use color to organize your mind map. If there are three main subjects covered in the lecture, you can record each subject in a different color. Add symbols and other images as well.

Create links. One mind map doesn't have to include all of the ideas in a book or an article. Instead, you can link mind maps. For example, draw a mind map that sums up the five key points in a chapter, and then make a separate, more detailed mind map for each of those key points. Within each mind map, include references to the other mind maps. This helps explain and reinforce the relationships among many ideas. Some students pin several mind maps next to each other on a bulletin board

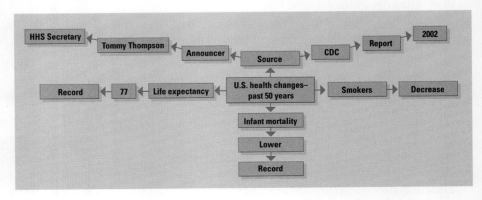

or tape them to a wall. This allows for a dramatic—and effective—look at the big picture.

Outlining

An outline shows the relationship between major points and supporting ideas. One benefit of taking notes in the outline format is that doing so can totally occupy your attention. You are recording ideas and also organizing them. This can be an advantage if the material has been presented in a disorganized way. Perhaps you've had negative experiences with outlining in the past. Teachers might have required you to use complex, rigid outlining formats based exclusively on Roman numerals or on some unfamiliar system. By playing with variations, you can discover the power of outlining to reveal relationships between ideas. Technically, each word, phrase, or sentence that appears in an outline is called a *heading*. These are arranged in different levels:

- In the first or "top" level of headings, note the major topics that are presented in a lecture or reading assignment.

- In the second level of headings, record the key points that relate to each topic in the first-level headings.

- In the third level of headings, record specific facts and details that support or explain each of your second-level headings. Each additional level of subordinate heading supports the ideas in the previous level of heading.

Roman numerals offer one way to illustrate the difference between levels of headings. See the following example.

First-level heading

I. Health and Human Services Secretary Tommy G. Thompson reports that Americans' health changed over the past 50 years.

Second-level heading

   A. Thompson: "When you take the long view, you see clearly how far we've come in combating diseases, making workplaces safer, and avoiding risks such as smoking."
   B. Thompson referred to *Health, United States, 2002,* a report from the Centers for Disease Control and Prevention (CDC).

II. By 2000, infant morality dropped to a record low and life expectancy hit a record high.
   A. Death rates among children up to age 24 were cut in half.
   B. Americans enjoyed the longest life expectancy in U.S. history.

III. Among working-age adults, fewer are dying from unintentional injuries, heart disease, stroke, and AIDS.

Third-level heading

   A. After 1995, deaths from AIDS dropped.
     1. Powerful new drugs contributed to this result.
     2. Other drugs are now in development.
   B. A decline in smoking contributed to the decline in heart disease.
     1. More than 40 percent of adults were smokers in 1965.
     2. In 2000, just 23 percent smoked.

You can also use other heading styles, as illustrated at right.

Combining formats

Feel free to use different note-taking systems for different subjects and to combine formats. Do what works for you.

Distinguish levels with indentations only:

First-level heading
   Second-level heading
      Third-level heading
         Fourth-level heading

Distinguish levels with bullets and dashes:

FIRST–LEVEL HEADING
   • Second-level heading
     – Third-level heading

Distinguish headings by size:

FIRST–LEVEL HEADING
Second-level heading
Third-level heading

For example, combine mind maps along with the Cornell format. You can modify the Cornell format by dividing your note paper in half, reserving one half for mind maps and the other for linear information, such as lists, graphs, and outlines, as well as equations, long explanations, and word-for-word definitions. You can incorporate a mind map into your paragraph-style notes whenever you feel one is appropriate. Mind maps are also useful for summarizing notes taken in the Cornell format.

John Sperry, a teacher at Utah Valley State College, developed a note-taking system that can include all of the formats discussed in this article:

- Fill up a three-ring binder with fresh paper. Open your notebook so that you see two blank pages—one on the left and one on the right. Plan to take notes across this entire two-page spread.

- During class or while reading, write your notes only on the left-hand page. Place a large dash next to each main topic or point. If your instructor skips a step or switches topics unexpectedly, just keep writing.

- Later, use the right-hand page to review and elaborate on the notes that you took earlier. This page is for anything you want. For example, add visuals such as mind maps. Write review questions, headlines, possible test questions, summaries, outlines, mnemonics, or analogies that link new concepts to your current knowledge.

- To keep ideas in sequence, place appropriate numbers on top of the dashes in your notes on the left-hand page. Even if concepts are presented out of order during class, they'll still be numbered correctly in your notes. ⊠

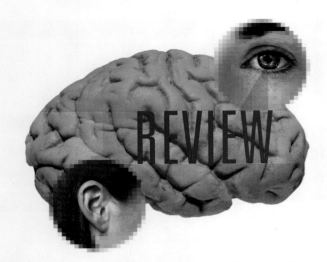

The note-taking process flows

Think of reviewing as an integral part of note taking rather than as an added task. To make new information useful, encode it in a way that connects to your long-term memory. The key is reviewing.

Review within 24 hours. In the last chapter, when you read the suggestion to review what you've read within 24 hours, you were asked to sound the trumpet. Well, if you have one, get it out and sound it again. This might be the most powerful note-taking technique you can use. It can save you hours of review time later in the term.

Many students are surprised that they can remember the content of a lecture in the minutes and hours after class. They are even more surprised by how well they can read the sloppiest of notes. Unfortunately, short-term memory deteriorates quickly. The good news is that if you review your notes soon enough, you can move that information from short-term to long-term memory. And you can do it in just a few minutes—often 10 minutes or less.

The sooner you review your notes, the better, especially if the class was difficult. In fact, you can start reviewing during class. When your instructor pauses to set up the overhead projector or erase the board, scan your notes. Dot the i's, cross the t's, and write out unclear abbreviations. Another way to use this technique is to get to your next class as quickly as you can. Then use the four or five minutes before the lecture begins to review the notes you just took in the previous class. If you do not get to your notes immediately after class, you can still benefit by reviewing later in the day. A review right before you go to sleep can also be valuable.

Think of the day's unreviewed notes as leaky faucets, constantly dripping, losing precious information until you shut them off with a quick review. Remember, it's possible to forget up to 80 percent of the material within 24 hours—unless you review.

Edit notes. During your first review, fix words that are illegible. Write out abbreviated words that might be unclear to you later. Make sure you can read everything. If you can't read something or don't understand something you *can* read, mark it, and make a note to ask your instructor or another student. Check to see that your notes are labeled with the date and class and that the pages are numbered. You can edit with a different colored pen or pencil if you want to distinguish between what you wrote in class and what you filled in later.

Fill in key words in the left-hand column. This task is important if you are to get the full benefit of using the Cornell format. Using the key word principles described earlier in this chapter, go through your notes and write key words or phrases in the left-hand column.

These key words will speed up the review process later. As you read your notes and focus on extracting important concepts, your understanding of the lecture is further reinforced.

Use your key words as cues to recite. With a blank sheet of paper, cover your notes, leaving only the key words in the left-hand margin showing. Take each key word in order and recite as much as you can about the point. Then uncover your notes and look for any important points you missed.

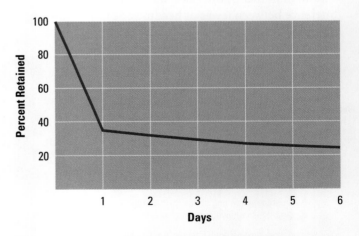

To study the process of memory and forgetting, Hermann Ebbinghaus devised a method for testing memory. The results, shown here in what has come to be known as the Ebbinghaus forgetting curve, demonstrate that forgetting occurs most rapidly shortly after learning and then gradually declines over time.

Conduct short weekly review periods. Once a week, review all of your notes again. The review sessions don't need to take a lot of time. Even a 20-minute weekly review period is valuable. Some students find that a weekend review, say on Sunday afternoon, helps them stay in continuous touch with the material. Scheduling regular review sessions on your calendar helps develop the habit.

As you review, step back to see the larger picture. In addition to reciting or repeating the material to yourself, ask questions about it: "Does this relate to my goals? How does this compare to information I already know, in this field or another? Will I be tested on this material? What will I do with this material? How can I associate it with something that deeply interests me? Am I unclear on any points? If so, what exactly is the question I want to ask?"

Consider typing up your notes. Some students type up their handwritten notes using a computer. The argument for doing so is threefold. First, typed notes are easier to read. Second, they take up less space. Third, the process of typing them forces you to review the material.

Another alternative is to bypass handwriting altogether and take notes in class on a laptop computer. This solution has drawbacks: laptops are more expensive than PCs, and computer errors can wipe out your notes, leaving you with no handwritten backup.

Experiment with typing notes and see what works for you. For example, you might type up only key portions of notes, such as summaries or outlines.

Create mind map summaries. Mind mapping is an excellent way to make summary sheets. After drawing your map, look at your original notes and fill in anything you missed. This system is fun to use. It's quick, and it gives your brain a hook on which to fasten the material. ◪

journal entry 14

Discovery Statement

Think about the way you have conducted reviews of your notes in the past. Respond to the following statements by checking "Always," "Often," "Sometimes," "Seldom," or "Never" after each.

I review my notes immediately after class.
___Always ___Often ___Sometimes
___Seldom ___Never

I conduct weekly reviews of my notes.
___Always ___Often ___Sometimes
___Seldom ___Never

I make summary sheets of my notes.
___Always ___Often ___Sometimes
___Seldom ___Never

I edit my notes within 24 hours.
___Always ___Often ___Sometimes
___Seldom ___Never

Before class, I conduct a brief review of the notes I took in the previous class.
___Always ___Often ___Sometimes
___Seldom ___Never

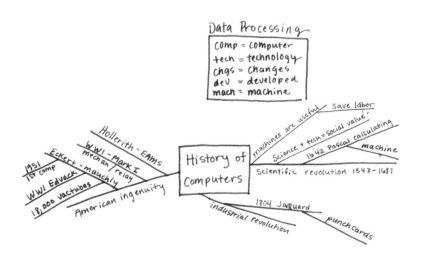

Improving your handwriting

Many people are resigned to writing illegibly for the rest of their lives. They feel that they have no control over their handwriting. Yet everyone's handwriting does change.

When you're on top of the world, your handwriting is not the same as when you are down in the dumps. Handwriting also changes as you mature. Since handwriting undergoes change unconsciously, you can make a conscious effort to change it. The prerequisite for improving your handwriting is simply the desire to do so.

If you want to write more legibly, here are some possibilities.

Use the First Step technique. Take a First Step by telling the truth about the problem. Admit its existence, then acknowledge your desire to improve.

The problem, by the way, is not bad handwriting; it's the impact of the handwriting. The problem is usually expressed as "I can't read my notes and therefore I have difficulty studying" or "The people I work with are getting upset because they can't read what I write."

Use creative visualizations. Find a quiet spot to sit, then relax your whole body, close your eyes, and see yourself writing clearly. Feel the pen as it moves over the page and visualize neat, legible letters as you write them.

Notice the shape of individual letters. Your handwriting might get sloppy due to the simple fact that you think in words, not in letters. However, writing is formed from individual letters of the alphabet. A simple shift in your attention—noticing letter shapes—can have a positive impact on the neatness and consistency of your handwriting.

Keep your eye on the ballpoint. Watch the way you write. Don't "try" to change. Focus all of your attention on the tip of the pen, right where it meets the paper. When you do this, let go of judgments or evaluations about how you write. By concentrating on the tip of your pen, you are giving your brain something to do, thereby allowing your body do the writing.

Demonstrate your excellence. At least once a day, write something down as clearly as you can. Write it as if it were going to appear on the front page of the *New York Times*. You can program your body to write clearly.

Revise sloppy writing immediately. Use an erasable pen or pencil. When you write something sloppily, fix it immediately. At first, you might find yourself rewriting almost everything. This technique can help you learn to write legibly.

Practice with the best materials. When you put a quality pen to fancy paper, there is incentive to produce clean, crisp, pleasing lines. Practice with these fine materials by writing notes to people you care about.

Take a calligraphy course. Improve your hand-eye coordination with calligraphy. The practice you get working with a calligraphy pen might improve your overall writing.

Dot all i's and cross all t's. The time you spend dotting and crossing will eliminate time spent scratching your head.

Ensure that holes exist. Leave holes in your a's, e's, and o's. If you don't, they can easily be mistaken for i's.

Notice problem letters. Go through your notes and circle letters that you have difficulty deciphering. Practice writing these letters.

When understanding is critical, print. When an important idea must be letter perfect, print it. Printing will stand out from your other notes. And you can read printing faster when you review.

Be willing to slow down—some. Weigh the costs and benefits of writing more slowly as a way to improve your handwriting. If you cannot read what you write, speed is of little use. On the other hand, writing too slowly and carefully when taking notes can result in missing the main points of a lecture. One possible solution is to write less. Take fewer notes; write down only what's essential. Learning to take notes efficiently could allow you to improve your handwriting and spend less time writing and more time learning.

Appreciate the value of legible writing. Notice how you feel when your own handwriting works well for you. Write a Discovery Statement when you become aware that you have improved your handwriting and list the benefits of the improvement. ⬕

CONSIDER THE IMPACT OF HANDWRITING

Step 1

Imagine for a moment that you are the teacher of this course. Following is a Discovery Statement submitted by one of your students.

I discovered that I prefer the Cornell system when taking Notes in my psychology class.

I also discovered that creating a mind map works better for notes in my philosophy course.

Describe below your first impressions of this student's handwriting. List any assumptions you have made about:

- The student's level of interest in the class.

- The amount of time the student put into the assignment.

- The student's feelings about you as a teacher.

Also note any feelings you have about the student, based on this piece of writing.

Step 2

Bring yourself back to your current role as a student in this course. Copy the above Discovery Statement in your own handwriting. Use the following space to do your writing.

Step 3

Now consider your handwriting. In the space below, list the assumptions your instructor might make about you and your commitment to this class. Follow up with an Intention Statement about any changes you want to make in your handwriting.

Create your instructor

Research the instructor. There are formal and informal sources of information you can turn to before you register for class. One is the school catalog. Alumni magazines or newsletters or the school newspaper might run articles on teachers. In some schools, students circulate informal evaluations of instructors. Also talk to students who have taken courses from the instructor.

Or introduce yourself to the instructor. Set up a visit during office hours and ask about the course. This can help you get the flavor of the class, as well as clues to the instructor's teaching style.

Show interest in class. Students give teachers moment-by-moment feedback in class. That feedback comes through posture, eye contact, responses to questions, and participation in class discussions. If you find a class boring, re-create the instructor through a massive display of interest. Ask lots of questions. Show enthusiasm through nonverbal language—sit up straight, make eye contact, take detailed notes. Your enthusiasm might enliven your instructor. If not, you are still creating a more enjoyable class for yourself.

Take responsibility for your attitude. Maybe your instructor reminds you of someone you don't like—your annoying Aunt Edna, a rude store clerk, or the fifth-grade teacher who kept you after school. Your attitudes are in your own head and beyond the instructor's control.

An instructor's beliefs about politics, religion, or feminism are not related to teaching ability. Likewise, using a formal or informal lecture style does not indicate knowledge of subject matter. Being aware of such things can help you let go of negative judgments.

Get to know the instructor better. You might be missing the strong points of an instructor you don't like. Meet with your instructor during office hours. Ask questions that weren't answered in class. Teachers who seem boring in class can be fascinating in person. Send follow-up notes via e-mail. Prepare to notice your pictures and let them go.

Open up to diversity. Sometimes students can create their instructors by letting go of pictures about different races and ethnic groups. According to one picture, a Hispanic person cannot teach English literature. According to other pictures, a white teacher cannot have anything valid to say about African music; a teacher in a wheelchair cannot command the attention of 100 people in a lecture hall; and a male instructor cannot speak credibly about feminism. All of those pictures can clash with reality. Releasing them can open up new opportunities for understanding and appreciation.

There are as many definitions of a "poor" instructor as there are students. For some students, "poor" means "boring," "rude," or "insensitive." Or maybe it's an instructor who never remembers what day it is, blows her nose every five minutes, and wears a cologne that could kill a hamster at 30 paces.

Faced with such facts, you have some choices. One is to label the instructor a "dud," "dweeb," "geek," or "airhead," and let it go at that. When you choose this solution, you get to endure class, complain to other students, and wait for a miracle. This choice puts you at the mercy of circumstance. It gives your instructor responsibility for the quality of your education, not to mention responsibility for giving you value for your money.

There is another option. You do not have to give away your power. Instead, you can take responsibility for your education. Use any of the following techniques to change the way you experience your instructors. In effect, you can "create your instructor."

Separate liking from learning. If you're dissatisfied with your instructor, your assessment is probably valid. Don't assume that you are wrong for disliking her. Instructors who know a lot about their specialty might not be skilled teachers.

Even in this situation, you can still create value. The idea is to accept your feelings and take responsibility for what you learn. Remember, you don't have to like an instructor to learn from one.

One strategy is to focus on content instead of form. Form is the way something is organized or presented. If you are irritated at the sound of an instructor's voice, you're focusing on the form of her presentation. When you put aside your concern about her voice and turn your attention to the points she's making, you're focusing on content.

Personal preferences regarding an instructor's clothes, hairstyle, political views, or mannerisms can get in the way, too. When this happens, notice your response without judgment. Then gently return your attention to the class content.

Form your own opinion about each instructor. You might hear conflicting reports about teachers from other students. The same instructor could be described as a riveting speaker or as completely lacking in charisma. Decide for yourself.

Seek alternatives. You might feel more comfortable with another teacher's style or method of organizing course materials. Consider changing teachers, asking another teacher for help outside of class, or attending an additional section taught by a different instructor. You can also learn from other students, courses, tutors, study groups, books, DVDs, and tapes. You can be a master student, even when you have teachers you don't like. Your education is your own creation.

Avoid excuses. Instructors know them all. Most teachers can see a snow job coming before the first flake hits the ground. Accept responsibility for your own mistakes, and avoid thinking that you can fool the teacher. When you treat instructors honestly, you are more likely to be treated as a responsible adult in return.

Submit professional work. Prepare papers and projects as if you were submitting them to an employer. Pay attention to form. Imagine that a promotion and raise will be determined by your work. Instructors often grade hundreds of papers during a term. Your neat, orderly, well-organized paper can lift a teacher's spirits after a long night of deciphering gibberish.

Arrive early for class. You can visit with your instructor and get to know her better. You can review notes and prepare for class. Being on time demonstrates your commitment and interest.

Accept criticism. Learn from your teachers' comments about your work. It is a teacher's job to give feedback. Don't take it personally.

Use conference time effectively. Instructors are usually happy to answer questions about class content. To get the most out of conference time, be prepared to ask those questions. Bring your notes, text, and any other materials you might need. During this session you can also address more difficult subjects, such as grades, attendance policies, lecture styles, term papers, or personality conflicts.

Instead of trying to solve a serious problem in the few minutes before or after class, set up a separate meeting. The instructor might feel uncomfortable discussing the problem in front of the other students. The communication techniques suggested in this chapter can help make your conference time more effective.

Use course evaluations. In many classes you'll have an opportunity to evaluate the instructor. When you're asked to do so, respond honestly. Write about the aspects of the class that did not work well for you. Offer specific ideas for improvement. Also note what *did* work well. Formal evaluations often come late in the course, after final tests and assignments. This might lead students to gloss over evaluations or give only vague feedback. If you want your feedback to make a difference, treat this evaluation as you would an assignment.

Take further steps, if appropriate. Sometimes severe conflict develops between students and instructors. Feedback from students might not be enough to reach a resolution. In such cases, you might decide to file a complaint or ask for help from a third party, such as an administrator.

If you do, be prepared to document your case in writing. When talking about the instructor, offer details. Describe specific actions that created problems for the class. Stick to the facts—events that other class members can verify. Your school might have a set of established grievance procedures to use in these cases. Before you act, understand what the policies are. You are a consumer of education. You have a right and a responsibility to complain if you think you have been treated unfairly. ✖

When your instructor *talks fast*

Take more time to prepare for class. Familiarity with a subject increases your ability to pick up on key points. If an instructor lectures quickly or is difficult to understand, conduct a thorough preview of the material to be covered.

Be willing to make choices. When an instructor talks fast, focus your attention on key points. Instead of trying to write everything down, choose what you think is important. Occasionally, you will make a wrong choice and neglect an important point. Worse things could happen. Stay with the lecture, write down key words, and revise your notes immediately after class.

Exchange photocopies of notes with classmates. Your fellow students might write down something you missed. At the same time, your notes might help them. Exchanging photocopies can fill in the gaps.

Leave large empty spaces in your notes. Leave plenty of room for filling in information you missed. Use a symbol that signals you've missed something, so you can remember to come back to it.

See the instructor after class. Take your class notes with you and show the instructor what you missed.

Use a tape recorder. Taping a lecture gives you a chance to hear it again whenever you choose. Some recorders allow you to vary the speed of the tape. With this feature, you can perform magic and actually slow down the instructor's speech.

Before class, take notes on your reading assignment. You can take detailed notes on the text before class. Leave plenty of blank space. Take these notes with you to class and simply add your lecture notes to them.

Go to the lecture again. Many classes are taught in multiple sections. That gives you the chance to hear a lecture at least twice—once in your regular class and again in another section of the class.

Learn shorthand. Some note-taking systems, known as shorthand, are specifically designed for getting ideas down fast. Books and courses are available to help you learn these systems. You can also devise your own shorthand method by inventing one- or two-letter symbols for common words and phrases.

Ask questions—even if you're totally lost. Many instructors allow a question session. This is the time to ask about the points you missed.

There might be times when you feel so lost that you can't even formulate a question. That's OK. One option is to report this fact to the instructor. She can often guide you to a clear question. Another option is to ask a related question. This might lead you to the question you really wanted to ask.

Ask the instructor to slow down. This is the most obvious solution. If asking the instructor to slow down doesn't work, ask her to repeat what you missed. ◼

voices

student

Joining a study group has helped me to improve my note taking skills. My group members rely on me to take neat notes in class, especially to help the other group members to fill in places that they've missed. Now when my Psychology professor talks fast, I don't panic. Sharing the notes after class helps my whole group get the important information.

—MARCO JUAREZ

Taking notes on your journey

The art of journal writing

If you've been creating Discovery and Intention Statements as you use *Becoming a Master Student*, you've already practiced the art of writing to enhance your success. You can continue this practice well beyond this course—for a lifetime, in fact.

Journal writing provides many benefits. To begin with, it offers a chance to hone writing skills and reflect on course work. In addition, journals promote self-awareness by helping us discover patterns in our lives. Our experiences take on the form of a story, with a beginning, middle, and end. Through journal writing we learn to step back from the daily hustle, spot recurring problems, and invent solutions.

Journal writing can enhance any strategy explained in this book and can help you in any course. Here is a chance for you to stretch out mentally: Reflect on the significance of your courses. Mine your own experiences for examples of the ideas you're learning about. Speculate about how you might apply what you're learning in class. Writing prompts you to think both creatively and critically.

In addition, writing is a multisensory activity, one that involves touching, seeing, and even hearing (the sound of a pencil scratching across paper or fingers tapping a keyboard). Each sensory mode opens up a channel to your brain, offering ways to make your learning more vivid and to transfer the content of your writing from short-term to long-term memory. The things you write about with the most interest and passion are the things you'll remember after you graduate.

Keeping a journal is a low-cost activity with a high return on investment. Begin with a pencil and a ream of the cheapest paper you can find. As your budget allows, you might wish to work with fancy pens and high-quality paper. You can also key in journal entries on a computer.

Just jump in and start. One thing that stops people from keeping a journal is writer's block. To get past this problem, do a free writing exercise. Set a timer and write for five minutes without stopping to revise. Just keep your hand moving and write anything that pops into your head. Put yourself on automatic pilot until the words start happening on their own.

There are many other ways to get started. Write letters—including those you don't plan to send. The person you're writing to can be famous or obscure, near or far, dead or alive. This can be a useful way to deal with anger or grief.

Also use leading sentences to jump-start your writing. For example, many Journal Entries in this book start with "I discovered that I ..." or "I intend to...." Invent your own lead-ins.

Feel free to dream wildly. Create a compelling future. Include the details—what you want to have, do, and be 5, 10, or 50 years from now. Write as if you've already attained your long-term goals. After this kind of brainstorm, focus on one goal and write an action plan to achieve it.

Make lists. For example, write down the five most influential people in your life and what they've taught you. If you're a parent, list the three most important skills you want to teach your children.

Keep a list of your favorite quotations. Record notable things that you and your friends say. In addition, list new words and their definitions. Writing them down helps these words become part of your working vocabulary.

You can make lists of any persons you've harmed and note how you plan to make amends. Listing resentments can rob them of their power and move you toward forgiveness.

Also make a list of what you've received from others. Record your thanks to people from whom you have benefited. You could end up with "an attitude of gratitude."

You know what's going on in your life better than anyone else. Create lists that serve your own purposes.

Use a journal for critical thinking. There's a saying about note taking: Words that go directly from the instructor's mouth to the student's paper—without ever entering the student's mind.

You can avoid this fate by writing in a journal. Here is a chance for you to expand your horizons. Reflect on the significance of your courses. Draw on your own experiences for examples of the ideas you're studying. Speculate about how you might apply what you're learning in class.

One technique recommended by writing teachers Richard Solly and Roseann Lloyd is to imagine that you're sitting face to face with the author of your textbook.[4] Write down what you would say to this person. Argue. Debate. Note questions you'd want to ask this person and then pose them in class.

Play with learning styles. Use a journal to take risks and explore new learning styles. Journals don't have to be limited to note paper. Dictate your journal entries into a recorder. Draw. Paint. Create a collage or sculpture. Write a piece of music. Visualizing through art is a powerful way to remember your experiences.

If you're shy about doing any of this, remember that no one else has to see the results. Your journal is in safe hands—your own.

Reread your journal. Use journals to get in touch periodically with an old friend—yourself. Rereading a journal entry can transport you across the years and alter your emotional state in seconds. Reading about times when you made a commitment to excel at work, school, or relationships can rekindle your zest for life.

To aid in locating important entries, create an index or a table of contents for your journal notebook. If you use a computer for journal writing, see if your word processing software can do this automatically.

Use a journal to manage stress. Much stress has its source in negative self-talk—nagging voices in our heads that make dire predictions for the future and undermine our abilities: "This is the worst thing that could ever happen to me" or "I never finish what I start."

Getting these disempowering ideas out of your head and onto paper is one way to defuse them. Begin by listing any irrational, self-defeating beliefs you have. Then write down more reasonable, empowering beliefs and Intention Statements.

Use a journal to increase writing skills. Writing in a journal can sharpen your powers of observation. To begin with, list as many details as you can about a person or an object in your environment. Make your description as complete, vivid, and detailed as you can.

Try your hand at fiction, too. Create characters for plays or novels. Write poems, short stories, or articles that you might submit for publication.

Review your journal for writing topics. Perhaps you've already written down something that could become the basis for a research paper.

Use a journal for personal growth. Visualizations and affirmations can begin on the pages of your journal. Also write about your fears, hopes, dreams, and ambitions. In this way, a journal becomes a trusted confidant who always respects your safety and privacy. Here is a counselor who's available anyplace, anytime—for free. ◪

exercise 17

TELEVISION NOTE TAKING

You can use evening news broadcasts to practice listening for key words, writing quickly, focusing your attention, and reviewing. As with other skills, the more you practice note taking, the better you become.

The next time you watch the news, use pen and paper to jot down key words and information. During the commercials, review and revise your notes. At the end of the broadcast, spend five minutes reviewing all of your notes. Create a mind map of a few news stories, then sum up the news of the day for a friend.

This exercise will help you develop an ear for key words. Since you can't ask questions or request that the speaker slow down, you train yourself to stay totally in the moment. If you get behind, relax, leave a space, and return your attention to the broadcast.

Don't be discouraged if you miss a lot the first time around. Do this exercise several times and observe how your mind works.

If you find it too difficult to take notes during a fast-paced television news show, check your local broadcast schedule for a news documentary. These are often slower paced. Another option is to tape a program and then take notes. You can stop the tape at any point to review your notes.

You can also ask a classmate to do the same exercise, and then compare notes the next day.

Taking notes while reading

Taking notes while reading requires the same skills that apply to class notes: observing, recording, and reviewing. Just remember that there are two kinds of notes that apply to reading: review notes and research notes.

Review notes. These will look like the notes you take in class. Sometimes you will want more extensive notes than writing in the margin of your text allows. You can't underline or make notes in library books, so these sources will require separate notes, too.

Mind map summaries of textbook materials are particularly useful for review. You can also use outlining or take notes in paragraph form. Single out a particularly difficult section of a text and make separate notes. Or make mind map summaries of overlapping lecture and textbook materials. Use the left-hand column for key words and questions, just as you do in your class notes.

When you read scientific or other technical materials, copy important formulas or equations and write down data that might appear on an exam. Re-create important diagrams and draw your own visual representations of concepts.

Research notes. Writing papers and speeches is a special challenge, and the way you take notes can help you face that challenge.

Use the mighty 3x5 card. There are two kinds of research cards: source cards and information cards. Source cards identify where you found the information contained in your paper or speech. For example, a source card for a book will show the author, title, date and place of publication, and publisher. Source cards are also written for magazine articles, interviews, dissertations, tapes, or any other research materials.

When you write source cards, give each source a code—the initials of the author, a number, or a combination of numbers and letters. A key advantage of using source cards is that you are creating your bibliography as you do the research. When you are done, simply alphabetize the cards by author and—voilà!—instant bibliography.

Write the actual research notes on information cards. At the top of each information card, write the code for the source from which you got the information. Also include the page numbers your notes are based on.

Most important, write only one piece of information on each information card. You can then sort the cards and use them to construct an outline of your paper or speech.

Another option is to take notes using a computer. This offers the same advantage as 3x5 cards—ease of rearranging text and pictures—while enabling you to print out copies to exchange with other students.

Online material. You can print out anything that appears on a computer screen. This includes online course materials, articles, books, manuscripts, e-mail messages, chat room sessions, and more.

One potential problem: Students might skip taking notes on this material altogether. ("I can just print out everything!") These students miss the chance to internalize a new idea by restating it in their own words—a principal benefit of note taking. Result: Material passes from computer to printer without ever intersecting a student's brain.

To prevent this problem, find ways to engage actively with online materials. Take review notes in Cornell, mind map, concept map, or outline format. Write Discovery and Intention Statements to capture key insights from the materials and to state ways you intend to apply them. Also talk about what you're learning. Recite key points out loud and discuss what you read online with other students.

Of course, it's fine to print out online material. If you do, treat your printouts like a textbook and apply the steps of Muscle Reading explained in Chapter Four.

Thinking about notes. Whenever you take notes, use your own words as much as possible. When you do so, you are thinking about what you are reading. If you do quote your source word for word, put that material within quotation marks.

Close the book after reading an assignment and quickly jot down a summary of the material. This writing can be loose, without any structure or format. The important thing is to do it right away, while the material is still fresh in your mind. Restating concepts in this way helps you remember them.

Special cases. The style of your notes can vary according to the nature of the material. If you are assigned a short story or poem, read the entire work once without taking any notes. On your first reading, simply enjoy the piece. When you finish, write down your immediate impressions. Then go over the piece and make brief notes on characters, images, symbols, settings, plot, point of view, or other aspects of the work.

Normally, you would ask yourself questions *before* you read an assignment. When you read fiction or poetry, however, ask yourself questions *after* you have read the piece. Then reread it (or skim it, if it's long) to get answers. Your notes can reflect this question-and-answer process.

REVISIT YOUR GOALS

One powerful way to achieve any goal is to assess periodically your progress in meeting it. This is especially important with long-term goals—those that can take years to achieve.

When you did Exercise #7: "Get real with your goals" on page 69, you focused on one long-term goal and planned a detailed way to achieve it. This involved setting mid-term and short-term goals that will lead to achieving your long-term goal. Take a minute to review that exercise and revisit the goals you set. Then complete the following steps.

1. Take your long-term goal from Exercise #7 and rewrite it in the space below. If you can think of a more precise way to state it, feel free to change the wording.

_____

_____

_____

_____

2. Next, check in with yourself. How do you feel about this goal? Does it still excite your interest and enthusiasm? On a scale of one to ten, how committed are you to achieving this goal? Write down your level of commitment in the space below.

_____

_____

_____

3. If your level of commitment is five or less, you might want to drop the goal and replace it with a new one. To set a new goal, just turn back to Exercise #7 and do it again. And release any self-judgment about dropping your original long-term goal. Letting go of one goal creates space in your life to set and achieve a new one.

4. If you're committed to the goal you listed in step 1 of this exercise, consider whether you're still on track to achieve it. Have you met any of the short-term goals related to this long-term goal? If so, list your completed goals in the space below.

_____

_____

_____

Before going on to the next step, take a minute to congratulate yourself and celebrate your success.

5. Finally, consider any adjustments you'd like to make to your plan. For example, write additional short-term or mid-term goals that will take you closer to your long-term goal. Or cross out any goals that you no longer deem necessary. Make a copy of your current plan in the space below.

Long-term goal (to achieve within your lifetime):

_____

_____

_____

_____

_____

Supporting mid-term goals (to achieve in one to five years):

_____

_____

_____

_____

Supporting short-term goals (to achieve within the coming year):

_____

_____

_____

_____

_____

Get to the bones of your book with concept maps

Concept mapping, pioneered by Joseph Novak and D. Bob Gowin, is a tool to make the main ideas in a book leap off the page.[5] In creating a concept map, you reduce an author's message to its essence—its bare bones. Concept maps can also be used to display the organization underlying lectures, discussions, and other reading materials.

To develop the technique of concept mapping, Novak and Gowin drew on ideas from David Ausubel, an educational psychologist.[6] Ausubel stated that human knowledge consists of a series of propositions. A proposition states a relationship between two or more concepts. A subject that you study in school might include dozens or even hundreds of concepts and propositions. However, learning the subject relies on a simple, underlying process: You take one new concept at a time and link it to a concept that you already understand, creating a new proposition.

Concept maps take this process out of your head and put in on paper in a visual format. You list concepts and arrange them in a meaningful order. Then you explicitly state the relationships between concepts, forming meaningful propositions.

Concept maps also promote critical thinking. Creating a concept map can alert you to gaps in your understanding—missing concepts or concepts with illogical links.

To create a concept map, use the following four steps:

1. List the key concepts in the text. Aim to express each concept in three words or less. Most concept words are nouns, including terms and proper names. At this point, you can list the concepts in any order. For ease in ranking the concepts later, write each one on a single 3x5 card.

2. Rank the concepts so that they flow from general to specific. On a large sheet of paper, write the main concept at the top of the

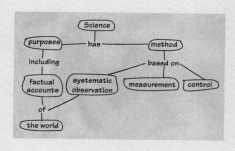

page. Place the most specific concepts near the bottom. Arrange the rest of the concepts in appropriate positions throughout the middle of the page. Circle each concept.

3. Draw lines that connect the concepts. On these connecting lines, add words that describe the relationship between the concepts. Again, limit yourself to the fewest words needed to make an accurate link—three words or less. Linking words are often verbs, verb phrases, or prepositions.

4. Finally, review your map. Look for any concepts that are repeated in several places on the map. You can avoid these repetitions by adding more links between concepts. Also look for accurate linking words and missing concepts.

As you gain facility with concept maps, you might wish to create them on a computer. Use any software with drawing capabilities. For example, the software program Inspiration, a visual thinking and learning tool, is specifically designed to create concept maps.

Sample concept maps based on selected articles in this book are available online at masterstudent.college.hmco.com

PRACTICING CRITICAL THINKING

6

Use a concept map as a tool to interpret and evaluate a piece of writing. First, list the key concepts from a chapter (or section of a chapter) in a textbook you're reading. Then connect these concepts with linking words, using the format described in the article "Get to the bones of your book with concept maps." Create your concept map on a separate sheet of paper. Then take a few minutes to assess the author's presentation as reflected in your concept map. Pay special attention to the links between concepts. Are they accurate? Do they reveal false assumptions or lack of evidence? Write your evaluation of your concept map on a separate sheet of paper.

power process

I create it all

This is a powerful tool in times of trouble. In a crisis, "I create it all" can lead the way to solutions. "I create it all" means treating experiences, events, and circumstances in your life as if you created them.

When your dog tracks fresh tar on the white carpet, when your political science teacher is a crushing bore, when your spouse dents the car, when your test on Latin American literature focuses on an author you've never read—it's time for a Power Process. Tell yourself, "I created it all."

"Baloney!" you shout. "I didn't let the dog in, that teacher really is a bore, I wasn't even in the car, and nobody told me to read Gabriel García Márquez. I didn't create these disasters."

Good points. Obviously, "I create it all" is one of the most unusual and bizarre suggestions in this book. It certainly is not an idea that is easily believed. In fact, believing it can get you into trouble. "I create it all" is strictly a practical idea. Use it when it works. Don't when it doesn't.

Keeping that caution in mind, consider how powerful this Power Process can be. It is really about the difference between two distinct positions in life: being a victim or being self-responsible. A victim of circumstances is controlled by outside forces. We've all felt like victims at one time or another. When tar-footed dogs tromped on the white carpets of our lives, we felt helpless. In contrast, we can take responsibility. *Responsibility* is the important word. It does not mean "blame." Far from it. Responsibility is "response-ability"—the ability to choose a response.

Practicing resignation

By not taking responsibility, we are acknowledging that the power to determine what happens in our lives is beyond our grasp. When we feel as if we don't have control over our lives, we feel resigned. The opposite of practicing "I create it all" is practicing resignation.

There is a phenomenon called *learned resignation*. An interesting experiment with dogs demonstrates how learned resignation works. A dog is put in a caged pen with a metal floor that can be electrified. When the cage door is left open and the dog is given a mild shock, she runs out of the cage to escape the discomfort. Then the dog is put back into the cage, the door is shut and locked, and a mild shock is given again. The dog runs around, looking for an escape. When she doesn't find one, she just lies down, sits, or stands there, and quits trying to find a way out. She has no control over her circumstances and is learning to be resigned.

Now, here comes the interesting part. After the dog has consistently stopped trying to escape the shock, the door is opened and the dog is led in and out several times. Then the dog is left in the cage, the door is left open, and the shock is administered once again. Amazingly, the dog doesn't even try to escape, even though the open door is right there in front of her. Instead, the dog continues to endure the shock. She has learned to be resigned.

A variety of this phenomenon can occur in human beings as well. When we consistently give control of our lives over to other people and to circumstances, we run the risk of learning to give up. We might develop the habit of being resigned, even though there is abundant opportunity all around us.

Applying this process

Many students approach grades from the position of being victims. When the student who sees the world this way gets an F, she reacts something like this:

"Oh, no!" (Slaps forehead)

"Rats!" (Slaps forehead again) (Students who get lots of F's often have flat foreheads.)

"Another F! That teacher couldn't teach her way out of a wet paper bag. She can't teach English for anything.

And that textbook—what a bore! How could I read it with a houseful of kids making noise all the time? And then friends came over and wanted to party, and...."

The problem with this viewpoint is that in looking for excuses, the student is robbing herself of the power to get any grade other than an F. She's giving all of her power to a bad teacher, a boring textbook, noisy children, and friends.

There is another way, called *taking responsibility*. You can recognize that you choose your grades by choosing your actions. Then you are the source, rather than the result, of the grades you get. The student who got an F could react like this:

"Another F! Oh, shoot! Well, hmmm.... How did I choose this F? What did I do to create it?"

Now, that's power. By asking "How did I contribute to this outcome?" you give yourself a measure of control. You are no longer the victim. This student might continue by saying, "Well, let's see. I didn't review my notes after class. That might have done it." Or "I studied in the same room with my children while they watched TV. Then I went out with my friends the night before the test. Well, that probably helped me fulfill some of the requirements for getting an F."

The point is this: When the F is the result of your kids, your friends, the book, or the teacher, you probably can't do anything about it. However, if you *chose* the F, you can choose a different grade next time. You are in charge.

Choosing our thoughts

There are times when we don't create it all. We do not create earthquakes, floods, avalanches, or monsoons. Yet if we look closely, we discover that we *do* create a larger part of our circumstances than most of us are willing to admit.

For example, we can choose our thoughts. And thoughts can control our perceptions by screening information from our senses. We can never be aware of every single thing in our environment. If we could, we'd go crazy from sensory overload. Instead, our brains filter out most sensory inputs. This filtering colors the way we think about the world.

Choosing our behaviors

Moment by moment we make choices about what we will do and where we will go. The results of these choices

are where we are in life. A whole school of psychology called *control theory* is based on this idea, and psychiatrist William Glasser has written extensively about it.[7]

All of those choices help create our current circumstances—even those circumstances that are not "our fault." After a car accident, we tell ourselves, "It just happened. That car came out of nowhere and hit me." We forget that driving five miles per hour slower and paying closer attention might have allowed us to miss the driver who was "to blame."

Some cautions

The presence of blame is a warning that this Power Process is being misused. "I create it all" is not about blaming yourself or others.

Feeling guilty is another warning signal. Guilt actually involves the same dynamic as blame. If you are feeling guilty, you have just shifted the blame from another person to yourself.

Another caution is that this Power Process is not a religion. Saying that you "create it all" does not mean that you have divine powers. It is simply a way to expand the choices you already have. This Power Process is easy to deny. Tell your friends about it, and they're likely to say, "What about world hunger? I didn't cause that. What about people who get cancer? Did they create that?"

These are good arguments—and they miss the point. Victims of rape, abuse, incest, and other forms of violence can still use "I create it all" to choose their response to the people and events that violated them.

Some people approach world hunger, imprisonment, and even cancer with this attitude: "Pretend for a moment that I am responsible for this. What will I do about it?" These people see problems in a new way, and they discover choices that other people miss.

"I create it all" is not always about disaster. It also works when life is going great. We often give credit to others for our good fortune when it's actually time to pat ourselves on the back. By choosing our behavior and thoughts, we can create A's, interesting classes, enjoyable relationships, material wealth, and ways to contribute to a better world.

Whenever tar-footed dogs are getting in the way of your education, remember this Power Process. When you use it, you instantly open up a world of choices. You give yourself power. 🔀

put it to work

You can adapt any of the suggestions in this chapter for use in the workplace. For example:

- Before meetings, complete background reading on the topics to be discussed. You'll be better prepared to take notes.

- During meetings, experiment with taking notes in several formats: Cornell, mind mapping, outlining, concept mapping, or some combination.

- After meetings, review the notes you took. Edit or rewrite your notes for clarity. If you took handwritten notes, you might want to key the important points into a computer file.

- No matter what format you choose for note taking, include key items of information about any meeting: the time and place, the people present, a list of agreements reached, and any items that require follow-up action.

- During a presentation or training session, let go of any judgments about the presenter's speaking style or appearance. Focus on the content of this person's message and look for ideas to remember and use. Capture those ideas fully and accurately in your notes.

- When taking notes during fast-paced meetings and conference calls, use suggestions from the article "When your instructor talks fast." Immediately after the call or meeting, review and edit your notes. Flag items that require follow-up action.

- Notice the times that colleagues read your handwriting, for example, on expense reports, time sheets, or drafts of a proposal or report. If your penmanship creates communication problems or does not convey a positive image, turn to the article "Improving your handwriting" in this chapter for help.

- In your personal journal, write about ways to be more effective at work. State a work-related problem and brainstorm to come up with possible solutions. List career goals and write Intention Statements about how you plan to achieve them.

- Apply the Power Process: "I create it all" to people and situations at work. If you feel tempted to blame a problem on a coworker, look for any ways that you might have contributed to the problem. Consider what you will think, say, and do differently to create a better work environment. ⊠

Name _____ Date _____/_____/_____

1. What are the three major steps of effective note taking as explained in this chapter? Summarize each step in one sentence.

2. Techniques you can use to "set the stage" for note taking do not include:
   (a) Complete outside assignments.
   (b) Bring the right materials.
   (c) Set aside questions in order to concentrate.
   (d) Conduct a short preclass review.
   (e) Sit front and center.

3. What is an advantage of sitting in the front and center of the classroom?

4. By the way they behave, instructors sometimes give clues that the material they are presenting is important. Describe at least three of these behaviors.

5. An effective method to postpone debate during a lecture is to ignore your own opinions and passively record the instructor's words. True or False? Explain your answer.

6. When using the Cornell system of note taking:
   (a) Write the main point on a line or in a box, circle, or any other shape.
   (b) Use only Roman numerals in an outline form.
   (c) Copy each new concept on a separate 3x5 card.
   (d) Remember never to combine it with mind mapping.
   (e) Draw a vertical line about two inches from the left edge of the paper.

7. Explain how key words can be used when taking notes. Then select and write down at least five key words from this chapter.

8. Reviewing within 24 hours assists short-term memory only. Long-term memory requires reviews over a longer period of time. True or False? Explain your answer.

9. Compare and contrast source cards and information cards. How are they alike? How are they different?

10. Briefly explain one of the cautions given regarding the use of the Power Process: "I create it all."

learning styles application

The questions below will "cycle" you through four styles, or modes, of learning as explained in the article "Learning styles: Discovering how you learn" in Chapter One. Each question will help you explore a different mode. You can answer the questions in any order.

what if *Create an original format for taking notes. Think about how you could modify or combine the note-taking systems discussed in this chapter. Describe your format here.*

why *Describe a situation in school or at work in which you could benefit by taking more effective notes.*

how *Of the note-taking techniques in this chapter that you like and intend to apply, choose one and describe when and where you will use it.*

what *Think back to the major note-taking systems discussed in this chapter: the Cornell format, mind mapping, outlining, concept mapping, or some combination. Choose one system that you intend to apply and briefly summarize its key features.*

master student profile

CRAIG KIELBURGER

In 1995, at age 12, Craig Kielburger founded Free the Children International, an organization of children helping children who are the victims of poverty and exploitation. He has also served as an ambassador to the Children's Embassy in Sarajevo and was named a Global Leader of Tomorrow at the 1998 World Economic Forum.

picked up the Toronto Star **and** put it on the table. But I didn't make it past the front page. Staring back at me was the headline, "BATTLED CHILD LABOUR, BOY, 12, MURDERED." It was a jolt. Twelve, the same age as I was. My eyes fixed on the picture of a boy in a bright-red vest. He had a broad smile, his arm raised straight in the air, a fist clenched....

Riding the bus to school later that morning, I could think of nothing but the article I had read on the front page. What kind of parents would sell their children into slavery at four years of age? And who would ever chain a child to a carpet loom?

Throughout the day I was consumed by Iqbal's story. In my Grade Seven class we had studied the American Civil War, and Abraham Lincoln, and how some of the slaves in the United States had escaped into Canada. But that was history from centuries ago. Surely slavery had been abolished throughout the world by now. If it wasn't, why had I never heard about it?

The school library was no help. After a thorough search I still hadn't found a scrap of information. After school, I decided to make the trek to the public library.

The librarian knew me from my previous visits. Luckily, she had read the same article that morning and was just as intrigued. Together, we searched out more information on child labour. We found a few newspaper and magazine articles, and made copies.

By the time I returned home, images of child labour had imbedded themselves in my mind: children younger than me forced to make carpets for endless hours in dimly lit rooms; others toiling in underground pits, struggling to get coal to the surface; others maimed or killed by explosions raging through fireworks factories. I was angry at the world for letting these things happen to children. Why was nothing being done to stop such cruelty?...

At lunchtime that day, some of us got together and talked about what we could do. I was amazed at how enthusiastic they all were. I told them about the youth fair on Friday.

"Do you think we could put together a display?" I asked. "We haven't got much time."

"Sure. Let's do it."

"We can all meet at my house," I said.

That night, twelve of us got together. It was a very tight deadline, with just two days to prepare. We found an old science fair board, and we covered it with coloured paper, pasting on all the information I had found on child labour in the library, then drawing pictures to illustrate it.

We had determined that our first objective should be to inform people of the plight of child labourers. Armed with such knowledge, they might be willing to help. We decided to draw up a petition to present to the government, and called on the expertise of a couple of human rights groups to refine the wording for us.

But we were still without a name for our group. For more than an hour we struggled to come up with something suitable. We flipped through the newspaper clippings for inspiration. One of them reported on a demonstration in Delhi, India, where 250 children had marched through the streets with placards, chanting, "We want an education," "We want freedom," "Free the children!"

"That's it!" someone shouted. "Free the Children." ⬚

From *Free the Children* by Craig Kielburger with Kevin Major. Copyright © 1998 by Craig Kielburger. Reprinted by permission of HarperCollins Publishers, Inc.

For more biographical information on Craig Kielburger, visit the Master Student Hall of Fame on the *Becoming a Master Student* **Web site at**

masterstudent.college.hmco.com

6

Tests

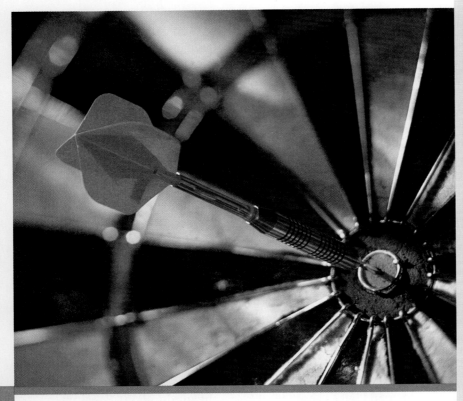

Learn from the mistakes of others—you can never live long enough to make them all yourself.

JOHN LUTHER

Keep in mind that neither success nor failure is ever final.

ROGER BABSON

why
this chapter matters . . .

Adopting a few simple techniques can make a major difference in how you feel about tests—and how you perform on them.

what
is included . . .

how
you can use this chapter . . .

Predict test questions and use your study time more effectively.
Harness the power of cooperative learning by studying with other people.
Learn to look on an F as *feedback* rather than *failure*.

As you read, ask yourself
what if . . .

I could let go of anxiety about tests—or anything else?

Disarm tests

On the surface, tests don't look dangerous, yet sometimes we treat them as if they were land mines. Suppose a stranger walks up to you on the street and asks, "Does a finite abelian P-group have a basis?" Will you break out in a cold sweat? Will your muscles tense up? Will your breathing become shallow?

Probably not. Even if you have never heard of a finite abelian P-group, you are likely to remain coolly detached. However, if you find the same question on a test and if you have never heard of a finite abelian P-group, your hands might get clammy.

Grades (A to F) are what we use to give power to tests. And there are lots of misconceptions about what grades are. Grades are not a measure of intelligence or creativity. They are not an indication of our ability to contribute to society. Grades are simply a measure of how well we do on tests. Some people think that a test score measures what a student has accomplished in a course. This is false. A test score is a measure of what a student scored on a test. If you are anxious about a test and blank out, the grade cannot measure what you've learned. The reverse is also true: If you are good at taking tests and a lucky guesser, the score won't be an accurate reflection of what you know.

Grades are not a measure of self-worth. Yet we tend to give test scores the power to determine how we feel about ourselves. Common thoughts include "If I fail a test, I am a failure" or "If I do badly on a test, I am a bad person." The truth is that if you do badly on a test, you are a person who did badly on a test. That's all.

Carrying around misconceptions about tests and grades can put undue pressure on your performance. It's like balancing on a railroad track. Many people can walk along the rail and stay balanced for long periods. Yet the task seems entirely different if the rail is placed between two buildings, 52 stories up.

It is easier to do well on exams if you don't put too much pressure on yourself. Don't give the test some magical power over your own worth as a human being. Academic tests are not a matter of life and death. Scoring low on important tests—entrance tests for college or medical school, bar exams, CPA exams—usually means only a delay.

Whether the chance of doing poorly is real or exaggerated, worrying about it can become paralyzing. The way to deal with tests is to keep them in perspective. Keep the railroad track on the ground. ⬥

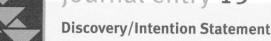

journal entry 15

Discovery/Intention Statement

Mentally re-create a time when you had difficulty taking a test. Do anything that helps you re-experience this event. You could draw a picture of yourself in this situation, list some of the questions you had difficulty answering, or tell how you felt after finding out your score on the test. Briefly describe that experience in the space below.

I discovered that I . . .

_____

_____

_____

Now wipe your mental slate clean and declare your intention to replace it with a new scenario. Describe how you want your experience of test taking to change. For example, you might write: "I intend to walk into every test I take feeling well rested and thoroughly prepared."

I intend to . . .

_____

_____

_____

Preview this chapter, looking for at least five strategies that can help you accomplish your goal. List those strategies below and note the page numbers where you can find out more about them.

Strategy   *Page number*

_____

_____

_____

_____

_____

What to do before the test

One way to save hours of wasted study time is to look on each test as a performance. From this point of view, preparing for a test means rehearsing. Study for a test in the way that a musician rehearses for a concert or an actor prepares for opening night—by simulating the physical and psychological conditions you'll encounter when you actually enter the exam room.

Rehearsing means doing the kind of tasks that you'll perform during a test—answering questions, solving problems, composing essays. Start this process with regular reviews of course content. Test preparation comes down to answering questions about your self-awareness (What do I know?), task awareness (What do I have to learn?), and strategy awareness (How can I close the gap between what I know and what I don't know?). Answering these questions means managing your review time, creating review tools, and planning your test-taking strategy.

Manage review time

A key to successful test preparation is managing review time. The biggest benefit of early review is that facts have time to roam around in your head. A lot of learning takes place when you are not consciously studying. Your brain has time to create relationships that can show up when you need them—like during a test. Use short daily review sessions to prepare the way for major review sessions. Reviewing with a group often generates new insights and questions.

Daily reviews. Daily reviews include the short pre- and post-class reviews of lecture notes. Research indicates that this is an effective tool for moving ideas from short-term to long-term memory (see Chapter Three: Memory). Also conduct brief daily reviews when you read. Before reading a new assignment, scan your notes and the sections you underlined in the previous assignment. Use the time you spend waiting for the bus or doing the laundry to conduct short reviews. Concentrate daily reviews on two kinds of material: material you have just learned, either in class or in your reading, and material that involves simple memorization (equations, formulas, dates, definitions).

Conduct short daily reviews several times through-out the day. To make sure you do, include them on your daily to-do list. Write down reminders, such as "5 min. review of biology" or "10 min. review of economics," and give yourself the satisfaction of crossing them off your list.

Begin to review on the first day of class. Most instructors outline the whole course at that time. You can start reviewing within seconds after learning. During a lull in class, go over the notes you just took. Then immediately after class, review your notes again.

Weekly reviews. Weekly reviews are longer—about an hour per subject. They are also more structured than short daily reviews. When a subject is complex, the brain requires time to dig into the material. Avoid skipping from subject to subject too quickly. Review each subject at least once a week. Weekly sessions include reviews of assigned reading and lecture notes. Look over any mind map summaries or flash cards you have created. You can also practice working on sample problems.

Major reviews. Major reviews are usually conducted the week before finals or other critical exams. They help integrate concepts and deepen understanding of the material presented throughout the term. These are longer review periods—two to five hours at a stretch, punctuated by sufficient breaks. Remember that the effectiveness of your review begins to drop after an hour or so unless you give yourself a short rest.

After a certain point, short breaks every hour might not be enough to refresh you. That's when it's time to quit. Learn your limits by being conscious of the quality of your concentration. During long sessions, study the most difficult subjects when you are the most alert: at the beginning of the session.

Your commitment to review is your most powerful ally. Create a system of rewards for time spent reviewing. Use the Intention Statements in this chapter or invent your own to draw detailed plans for review time.

Scheduling reviews. If you have a monthly or weekly planner, use it to schedule specific review periods. Plan on at least two major review sessions, lasting two to five hours each, for every course. If you think you'll need extra time for review, consider rearranging tasks or changing their priority in order to free up more study time. Start reviewing key topics at least five days before you'll be tested on them. This allows plenty of time to find the answers to questions and close any gaps in your understanding.

Staying positive. As you review, start every session with affirmations such as "I study with energy and efficiency" or "I am smart and prepared to do well on this test." Keep these statements simple and to the point. This powerful technique can help you stay positive.

Create review tools

Study checklists. Study checklists are used the way a pilot uses a preflight checklist. Pilots go through a standard routine before they take off. They physically mark off each item: test flaps, check magnetos, check fuel tanks, adjust instruments, check rudder. They use a written list to be absolutely certain they don't miss anything. Once they are in the air, it's too late, and the consequences of failing to check the fuel tanks could be drastic. Taking an exam is like flying a plane. Once the test begins, it's too late to memorize that one equation you forgot to include in your review.

Make a list for each subject. List reading assignments by chapters or page numbers. List dates of lecture notes. Write down various types of problems you will need to solve. Write down other skills you must master. Include major ideas, definitions, theories, formulas, and equations. For math and science tests, choose some problems and do them over again as a way to review for the test.

A study checklist is not a review sheet; it is a to-do list. Checklists contain the briefest possible description of each item to study.

Mind map summary sheets. There are several ways to make a mind map as you study for tests. Start by creating a map totally from memory. You might be surprised by how much you already know. Mind maps release floods of information from the brain because the mind works by association. Each idea is linked to many other ideas. You think of one and other associations come to mind.

Let the associations flow. If one seems to go someplace else, simply start another branch on your map. After you have gone as far as you can using recall alone, go over your notes and text and fill in the rest of the map.

Another way to create a mind map summary is to go through your notes and pick out key words. Then, without looking at your notes, create a mind map of everything you can recall about each key word. Finally, go back to your notes and fill in material you left out. You can also start a mind map with underlined sections from your text.

Flash cards. Three-by-five flash cards are like portable test questions. Take them with you everywhere and use them anytime. On one side of the cards, write the questions. On the other, write the answers. It's that simple.

Use flash cards for formulas, definitions, theories, key

words from your notes, axioms, dates, foreign language phrases, hypotheses, and sample problems. Create flash cards regularly as the term progresses. Buy an inexpensive card file to keep your flash cards arranged by subject.

Always carry a pack of flash cards with you, and review them whenever you have a minute to spare.

Monitoring your reviews. Each day that you prepare for a test, assess what you have learned and what you still need to learn. See how many items you've covered from your study checklist. Look at the tables of contents in your textbooks and write an X next to the sections that you've summarized. Using a monitoring system can help you gauge the thoroughness of your reviews and alert you to areas that still need attention.

Plan a test-taking strategy

Knowing what is going to be on a test doesn't require highly sophisticated technology or code breaking. With some practice, you can learn to predict the types of questions and their level of difficulty.

Do a dry run. Write up your own questions and take this "test" several times before the actual exam. Say that the exam will include mainly true/false or short-answer questions. Brainstorm a list of such questions—a mock test—and do a dry run. You might type up this "test" so that it looks like the real thing. Meet with your teacher to go over your mock test. Ask whether your questions focus on appropriate topics and represent the kind of items you can expect to see on the actual test.

Ask the instructor what to expect. One great source of information about the test is your instructor. Ask him what to expect. What topics will be emphasized? What kinds of questions will be included? How can you best allocate your review time? The instructor might decline to give you any of this information. More often, instructors will answer some or all of your questions about the test.

Get copies of old exams. Copies of previous exams for the class might be available from the instructor, the instructor's department, the library, or the counseling office. Old tests can help you plan a review strategy. One caution: If you rely on old tests exclusively, you might gloss over material the instructor has added since the last test. Check your school's policy about making past tests available to students. Some might not allow it. ✖

Ways to predict test questions

Predicting test questions can do more than get you a better grade. It can also keep you focused on the purpose of a course and help you design your learning strategies. Making predictions can be fun, too—especially when they turn out to be accurate.

Ask about the nature of the test. Tests are written from a plan, based on what a teacher considers important. This is not a random or mysterious process. See if you can discover the plan.

Eliminate as much guesswork about tests as possible. Ask your instructor to describe upcoming tests. Do this early in the term so you can be alert for possible test questions throughout the course. Many instructors are happy to answer such questions directly.

Some possible questions to ask are:

- What course material will the test cover—readings, lectures, lab sessions, or a combination?

- Will the test be cumulative, or will it cover just the most recent material you've studied?

- Will the test focus on facts and details or major themes and relationships?

- Will the test call on you to solve problems or apply concepts?

- What types of questions will be on the test—true/false, multiple choice, short-answer, essay?

- Will you have choices about which questions to answer?

- Will your teacher write and score the test—or will a teaching assistant perform those tasks?

Note: In order to study appropriately for essay tests, find out how much detail the instructor wants in your answers. Ask how much time you'll be allowed for the test and how long the essay answers should be (number of pages, blue books, or word limit). Having that information before you begin studying will help you gauge the depth to which you must know the material.

Put yourself in your instructor's shoes. If you were teaching the course, what information would you want students to take away? What kinds of questions would you put on an exam? Make up practice test questions and then answer them. You can also brainstorm test questions with other students—a great activity for study groups.

Look for possible test questions in your notes. Have a separate section in your notebook labeled "Test questions." Add several questions to this section after every lecture and assignment. You can also create your own code or graphic signal—such as a *T!* in a circle—to flag possible test questions in your notes.

See the article "Words to watch for in essay questions" in this chapter. Use it as a guide to turn the key words in your notes into questions.

Look for clues to possible questions during class. During lectures you can predict test questions by observing what an instructor says and how he says it. Instructors often give clues. For example, they might repeat important points several times, write them on the board, or return to them in subsequent classes.

Certain gestures can indicate critical points. For example, your instructor might pause, look at notes, or read passages word for word.

Notice whether your teacher has any strong points of view on certain issues. Questions on those issues are likely to appear on a test. Also pay attention to questions the instructor poses to students, and note questions that other students ask.

When material from reading assignments is covered extensively in class, it is likely to be on a test. For science courses and other courses involving problem solving, work on sample problems using different variables.

Save all quizzes, papers, lab sheets, and graded materials of any kind. Quiz questions have a way of reappearing, in slightly altered form, on final exams. If copies of previous exams and other graded materials are available, use them to predict test questions.

Remember the obvious. Be on the lookout for these words: *This material will be on the test.*

Apply your predictions. To get the most value from your predictions, use them to guide your review sessions.[1]

For suggestions on ways to predict a variety of test questions, go to

masterstudent.college.hmco.com

Cooperative learning
Studying with people

Education often seems like a never-ending competition. We compete for entrance to school, for scholarships and grades while we're in school, and for jobs when we leave school. In that climate, it's easy to overlook the power of cooperation.

Consider the idea that you can achieve success in school without competing. Sometimes competitiveness actually works against success. It is often stressful and can strain relationships. We can often get more done by sharing our skills and resources than by working alone.

As social animals, humans draw strength from groups. Study groups can be a source of this strength, while supplying you with energy. In addition to offering camaraderie, study groups can elevate your spirits and firm your resolve on days when you just don't feel like working at your education. If you skip a solo study session, no one else will know. If you declare your intention to study with others who are depending on you, your intention gains strength. In addition to drawing strength from the group, you can help others when they are in need of support.

Study groups are especially important if going to school has thrown you into a new culture. Joining a study group with people you already know can help ease the transition. Promote your success in school by refusing to go it alone. To multiply the benefits of working with study groups, seek out people of other cultures, races, and ethnic groups. You can get a whole new perspective on the world, along with some valued new friends. And you can experience what it's like to be part of a diverse team—an important asset in today's job market.

Form a study group

Choose a focus for your group. Many students assume that the purpose of a study group is to help its members prepare for a test. That's one valid purpose—and there are others.

Through his research on cooperative learning, psychologist Joe Cuseo has identified several kinds of study groups.[2] For instance, some study groups meet after tests to compare answers and help each other discover sources of errors. Note-taking groups focus on comparing and editing notes, often meeting directly after the day's class. Research groups meet to help each other find, evaluate, and take notes on background materials for papers and presentations. Reading groups can be useful for courses in which test questions are based largely on textbooks. Meet with classmates to compare the passages you highlighted and the notes you made in the margins of your books.

Look for dedicated students. Find people you are comfortable with and who share some of your academic goals. Look for students who pay attention, ask questions, and take notes during class, and invite them to join your group.

Another way to form a study group is to post a note on a bulletin board asking interested students to contact you. Or pass around a sign-up sheet before class. While these methods can reach many people, they take more time to achieve results. And you have less control over who applies to join the group.

Balance common interests with diversity. Include in your group people who face academic or personal challenges similar to your own. For example, if you are divorced and have two toddlers at home, you might look for other single parents who have returned to school.

Studying with friends is fine, but if your common interests are beer and jokes, beware of getting together for schoolwork.

To get the benefit of other perspectives, include people who face challenges that are different from your own. Choose people with similar educational goals who have different backgrounds and methods of learning. Each of you can gain by seeing the material from a new perspective.

Limit groups to four people. Research on cooperative learning indicates that four people is an ideal group size.[3] Larger ones can be unwieldy.

Hold a planning session. Ask two or three people to get together for a snack and talk about group goals, meeting times, and other logistics. You don't have to make an immediate commitment.

Do a trial run. Test the group first by planning a one-time session. If that session works, plan another. After a few successful sessions, you can schedule regular meetings.

Conduct your study group

There are many ways to conduct a study group. Begin with the following suggestions and see what works.

Test each other by asking questions. Group members can agree to bring five to ten sample test questions to each meeting. Then you can all take the test made up from these questions.

Practice teaching each other. Teaching is a great way to learn something. Turn the material you're studying into a list of topics and assign a specific topic to each person, who will then teach it to the group. When you teach something, you naturally assume a teacher's attitude ("I know this"), as opposed to a student's attitude ("I still have to learn this"). The vocalization involved in teaching further reinforces the concepts.

Compare notes. Make sure that you all heard the same thing in class and that you all recorded the important information. Ask others to help explain material in your notes that is confusing to you.

Brainstorm test questions. Set aside five to 10 minutes of each study session to use brainstorming techniques (described in detail in Chapter Seven) to create test questions. You can add these to the "Test questions" section of your notebook.

Set an agenda for each meeting. Select activities from this article, or create other activities to do as a group. Set approximate time limits for each agenda item and determine a quitting time. Finally, end each meeting with assignments for all members.

Keep the group on task. If the discussion wanders off-topic, remind members of the time limits and agenda for the meeting.

Ask each member to contribute. Recognize signs that group members are not contributing in equal ways. For instance, someone in your group might consistently fail to prepare for meetings or feel that he has nothing to contribute. Other members might dominate the group discussions.

As a group, brainstorm ways to get unprepared members involved. Reel in a dominating member by reminding him of the importance that everyone's voice be heard.

Work in groups of two at a computer to review a course. One person can operate the keyboard while the other person dictates summaries of lectures and assigned readings. Together, both group members can check facts by consulting textbooks, lecture notes, and class handouts.

Create wall-sized mind maps or concept maps to summarize a textbook or series of lectures. Work on large sheets of butcher paper, or tape together pieces of construction paper. When doing a mind map, assign one branch of the mind map to each member of the study group. Use a different colored pen or marker for each branch. (For more information on concept maps and mind maps, see Chapter Five: Notes.)

Pair off to do "book reports." One person can summarize a reading assignment. The other person can act as an interviewer on a talk show, posing questions and asking for further clarification.

Ask members of your group to prepare and deliver full-length lectures on different topics of a course. Volunteer to lecture on the topic that you know least about, and come prepared to answer questions from other group members.

Ask for group support in personal areas. Other people might have insight into problems such as transportation, childcare, finances, and time scheduling. Study groups can provide personal support for getting what you want from school.

journal entry 16

Intention Statement

In the space below, outline a plan to form a study group. Explain the steps you will take to get the group organized and set a first meeting date.

I intend to . . .

_____

_____

_____

_____

Now describe the reward you anticipate for fulfilling this intention.

_____

_____

_____

_____

What to do during the test

Prepare yourself for the test by arriving early. That often leaves time to do a relaxation exercise. While you're waiting for the test to begin and talking with classmates, avoid the question "How much did you study for the test?" This question might fuel anxious thoughts that you didn't study enough.

As you begin

Ask the teacher or test administrator if you can use scratch paper during the test. If you use a separate sheet of paper without permission, you might appear to be cheating. If you get permission, use this paper to jot down memory aids, formulas, equations, facts, or other material you know you'll need and might forget. An alternative is to make quick notes in the margins of the test sheet.

Pay attention to verbal directions given as a test is distributed. Then scan the whole test immediately. Evaluate the importance of each section. Notice how many points each part of the test is worth and estimate how much time you'll need for each section, using its point value as your guide. For example, don't budget 20 percent of your time for a section that is worth only 10 percent of the points.

Read the directions slowly. Then reread them. It can be agonizing to discover that you lost points on a test merely because you failed to follow the directions. When the directions are confusing, ask to have them clarified.

Now you are ready to begin the test. If necessary, allow yourself a minute or two of "panic" time. Notice any tension you feel, and apply one of the techniques explained in the article "Let go of test anxiety" later in this chapter.

Answer the easiest, shortest questions first. This gives you the experience of success. It also stimulates associations and prepares you for more difficult questions. Pace yourself and watch the time. If you can't think of an answer, move on. Follow your time plan.

If you are unable to determine the answer to a test question, keep an eye out throughout the text for context clues that may remind you of the correct answer, or provide you with evidence to eliminate wrong answers.

Multiple choice questions

- *Answer each question in your head first.* Do this before you look at the possible answers. If you come up with an answer that you're confident is right, look for that answer in the list of choices.

- *Read all possible answers before selecting one.* Sometimes two answers will be similar and only one will be correct.

- *Test each possible answer.* Remember that multiple choice questions consist of two parts: the stem (an incomplete statement at the beginning) and a list of possible answers. Each answer, when combined with the stem, makes a complete statement that is either true or false. When you combine the stem with each possible answer, you are turning each multiple choice question into a small series of true/false questions. Choose the answer that makes a true statement.

- *Eliminate incorrect answers.* Cross off the answers that are clearly not correct. The answer you cannot eliminate is probably the best choice.

True/false questions

- *Read the entire question.* Separate the statement into its grammatical parts—individual clauses and phrases—and then test each one. If any part is false, the entire statement is false.

- *Look for qualifiers.* These include words such as *all, most, sometimes,* or *rarely.* Absolute qualifiers such as *always* or *never* generally indicate a false statement.

- *Find the devil in the details.* Double-check each number, fact, and date in a true/false statement. Look for numbers that have been transposed or facts that have been slightly altered. These are signals of a false statement.

- *Watch for negatives.* Look for words such as *not* and *cannot.* Read the sentence without these words and see if you come up with a true or false statement. Then reinsert the negative words and see if the statement makes more sense. Watch especially for sentences with two negative words. As in math operations, two negatives cancel each other out: *We cannot say that Chekov never succeeded at short story writing* means the same as *Chekov succeeded at short story writing.*

Computer-graded tests

- Make sure that the answer you mark corresponds to the question you are answering.

- Check the test booklet against the answer sheet whenever you switch sections and whenever you come to the top of a column.

- Watch for stray marks; they can look like answers.

- If you change an answer, be sure to erase the wrong answer completely, removing all pencil marking completely.

Open-book tests

- Carefully organize your notes, readings, and any other materials you plan to consult when writing answers.

- Write down any formulas you will need on a separate sheet of paper.

- Bookmark the table of contents and index in each of your textbooks. Place Post-it Notes and Index Flags or paper clips on other important pages of books (pages with tables, for instance).

- Create an informal table of contents or index for the notes you took in class.

- Predict which material will be covered on the test and highlight relevant sections in your readings and notes.

Short-answer/fill-in-the-blank tests

- Concentrate on key words and facts. Be brief.

- Overlearning material can really pay off. When you know a subject backward and forward, you can

answer this type of question almost as fast as you can write.

Matching tests

- Begin by reading through each column, starting with the one with fewer items. Check the number of items in each column to see if they're equal. If they're not, look for an item in one column that you can match with two or more items in the other column.

- Look for any items with similar wording and make special note of the differences between these items.

- Match words that are similar grammatically. For example, match verbs with verbs and nouns with nouns.

- When matching individual words with phrases, first read a phrase. Then look for the word that logically completes the phrase.

- Cross out items in each column when you are through with them.

Essay questions

Managing your time is crucial to answering essay questions. Note how many questions you have to answer and monitor your progress during the test period. Writing shorter answers and completing all of the questions on an essay test will probably yield a better score than leaving some questions blank.

Find out what an essay question is asking—precisely. If a question asks you to *compare* the ideas of Sigmund Freud and Karl Marx, no matter how eloquently you *explain* them, you are on a one-way trip to No Credit City.

Before you write, make a quick outline. An outline can help speed up the writing of your detailed answer, you're less likely to leave out important facts, and if you don't have time to finish your answer, your outline could win you some points. To use test time efficiently, keep your outline brief. Focus on key words to use in your answer.

Introduce your answer by getting to the point. General statements such as "There are many interesting facets to this difficult question" can cause acute irritation for teachers grading dozens of tests.

One way to get to the point is to begin your answer with part of the question. Suppose the question is "Discuss how increasing the city police budget might or might not contribute to a decrease in street crime." Your first sentence might be "An increase in police expenditures will not have a significant effect on street crime for the following reasons." Your position is clear. You are on your way to an answer.

When you expand your answer with supporting ideas and facts, start out with the most solid points. Be brief and avoid filler sentences.

Write legibly. Grading essay questions is in large part a subjective process. Sloppy, difficult-to-read handwriting might actually lower your grade.

Write on one side of the paper only. If you write on both sides of the paper, writing will show through and obscure the writing on the other side. If necessary, use the blank side to add points you missed. Leave a generous left-hand margin and plenty of space between your answers, in case you want to add to them later.

Finally, if you have time, review your answers for grammar and spelling errors, clarity, and legibility. ⊠

Words to watch for in essay questions

The following words are commonly found in essay test questions. If you want to do well on essay tests, study this page thoroughly. Know these words backward and forward. To heighten your awareness of them, underline the words when you see them in a test question.

Analyze: Break into separate parts and discuss, examine, or interpret each part. Then give your opinion.

Compare: Examine two or more items. Identify similarities and differences.

Contrast: Show differences. Set in opposition.

Criticize: Make judgments. Evaluate comparative worth. Criticism often involves analysis.

Define: Explain the exact meaning—usually, a meaning specific to the course or subject. Definitions are usually short.

Describe: Give a detailed account. Make a picture with words. List characteristics, qualities, and parts.

Discuss: Consider and debate or argue the pros and cons of an issue. Write about any conflict. Compare and contrast.

Explain: Make an idea clear. Show logically how a concept is developed. Give the reasons for an event.

Prove: Support with facts (especially facts presented in class or in the text).

Relate: Show the connections between ideas or events. Provide a larger context for seeing the big picture.

State: Explain precisely.

Summarize: Give a brief, condensed account. Include conclusions. Avoid unnecessary details.

Trace: Show the order of events or the progress of a subject or event.

If any of these terms are still unclear to you, consult your unabridged dictionary. A thorough knowledge of these words helps you answer essay questions in a way that best demonstrates your understanding of the course content.

Review these key words and other helpful vocabulary terms by using the online flash cards at

masterstudent.college.hmco.com

The test isn't over until ...

Many students believe that a test is over as soon as they turn in the answer sheet. Consider another point of view: You're not done with a test until you know the answer to any question that you missed—and why you missed it.

This point of view offers major benefits. Tests in many courses are cumulative. In other words, the content included on the first test is assumed to be working knowledge for the second test, mid-term, or final exam. When you discover what questions you missed and understand the reasons for lost points, you learn something—and you greatly increase your odds of achieving better scores later in the course.

To get the most value from any test, take control of what you do at two critical points: the time immediately following the test, and the time when the test is returned to you.

Immediately following the test. After finishing a test, your first thought might be to nap, snack, rent a DVD, or go out with friends to celebrate. Restrain those impulses for a short while so that you can reflect on the test. The time you invest now carries the potential to raise your grades in the future.

To begin with, sit down in a quiet place and take a few minutes to write some Discovery Statements related to your experience of taking the test. Doing this while the test is still fresh in your mind increases the value of this technique. Describe how you felt about taking the test, how effective your review strategies were, and whether you accurately predicted the questions that appeared on the test.

Follow up with an Intention Statement or two. State what, if anything, you will do differently to prepare for the next test. The more specific you are, the better. If the test revealed any gaps in your knowledge, list follow-up questions to ask in class.

When the test is returned. When a returned test includes a teacher's comments, view this document as a treasure-trove of intellectual gold.

First, make sure that the point totals add up correctly and double-check for any other errors in grading. Even the best teachers make an occasional mistake.

Next, ask these questions:

- On what material did the teacher base test questions—readings, lectures, discussions, or other class activities?

- What types of questions appeared in the test— objective (such as matching items, true/false questions, or multiple choice), short-answer, or essay?

- What types of questions did you miss?

- Can you learn anything from the instructor's comments that will help you prepare for the next test?

Also see if you can correct any answers that lost points. To do this, carefully analyze the source of your errors and find a solution. Consult the following chart for help. ⊠

Source of test error	Possible solutions
Study errors–studying material that was not included on the test, or spending too little time on material that *did* appear on the test	• Ask your teacher about specific topics that will be included on a test. • Practice predicting test questions. • Form a study group with class members to create mock tests.
Careless errors, such as skipping or misreading directions	• Read and follow directions more carefully–especially when tests are divided into several sections with different directions. • Set aside time during the next test to proofread your answers.
Concept errors–mistakes made when you do not understand the underlying principles needed to answer a question or solve a problem	• Look for patterns in the questions you missed. • Make sure that you complete all assigned readings, attend all lectures, and show up for laboratory sessions. • Ask your teacher for help with specific questions.
Application errors–mistakes made when you understand underlying principles but fail to apply them correctly	• Rewrite your answers correctly. • When studying, spend more time on solving sample problems. • Predict application questions that will appear in future tests and practice answering them.
Test mechanics errors–missing more questions in certain parts of the test than others, changing correct answers to incorrect ones at the last minute, leaving items blank, miscopying answers from scratch paper to the answer sheet	• Set time limits for taking each section of a test and stick to them. • Proofread your test answers carefully. • Look for patterns in the kind of answers you change at the last minute. • Change answers only if you can state a clear and compelling reason to do so.

Integrity in test taking
The costs of cheating

Cheating on tests can be a tempting choice. One benefit is that we might get a good grade without having to study.

Instead of studying, we could spend more time watching TV, partying, sleeping, or doing anything that seems like more fun. Another benefit is that we could avoid the risk of doing poorly on a test—which could happen even if we *do* study.

But before you rush out to make cheating a habit, remember that it also carries costs. Here are some to consider.

We learn less. While we might think that some courses offer little or no value, it is more likely that we can create value from any course. If we look deeply enough, we can discover some idea or acquire some skill to prepare us for future courses or a career after graduation.

We lose money. Getting an education costs a lot of money. Cheating sabotages our purchase. We pay full tuition without getting full value for it.

Fear of getting caught promotes stress. When we're fully aware of our emotions about cheating, we might discover intense stress. Even if we're not fully aware of our emotions, we're likely to feel some level of discomfort about getting caught.

Violating our values promotes stress. Even if we don't get caught cheating, we can feel stress about violating our own ethical standards. Stress can compromise our physical health and overall quality of life.

Cheating on tests can make it easier to violate our integrity again. Human beings become comfortable with behaviors that they repeat. Cheating is no exception.

Think about the first time you drove a car. You might have felt excited—even a little frightened. Now driving is probably second nature, and you don't give it much thought. Repeated experience with driving creates familiarity, which lessens the intense feelings you had during your first time at the wheel.

We can experience the same process with almost any behavior. Cheating once will make it easier to cheat again. And if we become comfortable with compromising our integrity in one area of life, we might find it easier to compromise in other areas.

Cheating lowers our self-concept. Whether or not we are fully aware of it, cheating sends us the message that we are not smart enough or responsible enough to make it on our own. We deny ourselves the celebration and satisfaction of authentic success.

An effective alternative to cheating is to become a master student. Ways to do this are described on every page of this book.

→ Have some FUN!

Contrary to popular belief, finals week does not have to be a drag.

In fact, if you have used techniques in this chapter, exam week can be fun. By planning ahead, you will have done most of your studying long before finals arrive. You can feel confident and relaxed.

When you are well prepared for tests, you can even use fun as a technique to enhance your performance. The day before a final, go for a run or play a game of basketball. Take in a movie or a concert. Watch TV. A relaxed brain is a more effective brain. If you have studied for a test, your mind will continue to prepare itself even while you're at the movies.

Get plenty of rest, too. There's no need to cram until 3 a.m. when you have used the techniques in this chapter.

On the first day of finals, you can wake up refreshed, have a good breakfast, and walk into the exam room with a smile on your face. You can also leave with a smile on your face, knowing that you are going to have a fun week. It's your reward for studying regularly throughout the term.

If this kind of exam week sounds inviting, you can begin preparing for it right now.

Let go of test anxiety

If you freeze during tests and flub questions when you know the answers, you might be suffering from test anxiety.

A little tension before a test is good. That tingly, butterflies-in-the-stomach feeling you get from extra adrenaline can sharpen your awareness and keep you alert. You can enjoy the benefits of a little tension while you stay confident and relaxed. Sometimes, however, tension is persistent and extreme. It causes loss of sleep, appetite, and sometimes even hair. That kind of tension is damaging. It is a symptom of test anxiety, and it can prevent you from doing your best on exams.

Other symptoms include nervousness, fear, dread, irritability, and a sense of hopelessness. Boredom also can be a symptom of test anxiety. Frequent yawning immediately before a test is a common reaction. Though it suggests boredom, yawning is often a sign of tension. It means that oxygen is not getting to the brain because the body is tense. A yawn is one way the body increases its supply of oxygen.

You might experience headaches, an inability to concentrate, or a craving for food. For some people, test anxiety makes asthma or high blood pressure worse. During an exam, symptoms can include confusion, panic, mental blocks, fainting, sweaty palms, and nausea. Symptoms after a test include the following.

Mock indifference: "I answered all the multiple choice questions as 'none of the above' because I was bored."
Guilt: "Why didn't I study more?"
Anger: "The teacher never wanted me to pass this stupid course anyway."
Blame: "If only the textbook weren't so dull."
Depression: "After that test, I don't see any point in staying in school."

Test anxiety can be serious—students have committed suicide over test scores. This anxiety can also be managed.

Test anxiety has two components: mental and physical. The mental component of stress includes all of your thoughts and worries about tests. The physical component includes bodily sensations and tension.

The following techniques can help you deal with the mental and physical components of stress in any situation, from test anxiety to stage fright.

Dealing with thoughts

Yell "Stop!" When you notice that your mind is consumed with worries and fears, that your thoughts are spinning out of control, mentally yell "Stop!" If you're in a situation that allows it, yell it out loud.

This action is likely to bring your focus back to the present moment and allow you to redirect your thoughts. Once you've broken the cycle of worry or panic, you can use any of the following techniques.

Daydream. When you fill your mind with pleasant thoughts, there is no room left for anxiety. If you notice yourself worrying about an upcoming test, replace visions of doom with images of something you like to do. Daydream about being with a special friend or walking alone in a favorite place.

Visualize success. Most of us live up—or down—to our own expectations. If we spend a lot of time mentally rehearsing what it will be like to fail a test, our chances of doing so increase. Instead, you can take time to rehearse what it will be like to succeed. Be specific. Create detailed pictures, actions, and even sounds as part of your visualization. If you are able to visit the room where you will take the test, mentally rehearse while you are actually in this room.

Focus. Focus your attention on a specific object. Examine details of a painting, study the branches on a tree, or observe the face of your watch (right down to the tiny scratches in the glass). During an exam, take a few seconds to listen to the sounds of concentration—the squeaking of chairs, the scratching of pencils, the muted coughs. Touch the surface of your desk and notice the texture.

Concentrate all of your attention on one point. Don't leave room in your mind for anxiety-related thoughts.

Praise yourself. Talk to yourself in a positive way. Many of us take the first opportunity to belittle ourselves: "Way to go, dummy! You don't even know the answer to the first question on the test." We wouldn't dream of treating a friend this way, yet we do it to ourselves.

An alternative is to give yourself some encouragement. Treat yourself as if you were your own best friend. Consider telling yourself, "I am very relaxed. I am doing a great job on this test."

Consider the worst. Rather than trying to put a stop to your worrying, consider the very worst thing that could happen. Take your fear to the limit of absurdity.

Imagine the catastrophic problems that might occur if you were to fail the test. You might say to yourself, "Well, if I fail this test, I might fail the course, lose my financial aid, and get kicked out of school. Then I won't be able to get a job, so the bank will repossess my car, and I'll start drinking." Keep going until you see the absurdity of your predictions.

After you stop chuckling, you can backtrack to discover a reasonable level of concern. Your worry about failing the entire course if you fail the test might be justified. At that point ask yourself, "Can I live with that?" Unless you are taking a test in parachute packing and the final question involves jumping out of a plane, the answer will almost always be yes. (If the answer is no, use another technique. In fact, use several other techniques.)

The cold facts are hardly ever as bad as our worst fears. Shine a light on your fears, and they become more manageable.

Zoom out. When you're in the middle of a test or another situation in which you feel distressed, zoom out. Think the way film directors do when they dolly a camera out and away from an action scene. In your mind, imagine that you're floating away and viewing the situation as a detached outside observer.

If you're extremely distressed, let your imagination take you even farther. See yourself rising above the scene so that your whole community, city, nation, or planet is within view.

From this larger viewpoint, ask yourself whether this situation is worth worrying about. A negative response is not a license to belittle or avoid problems; it is permission to gain some perspective.

Another option is to zoom out in time. Imagine yourself one week, one month, one year, one decade, or one century from today. Assess how much the current situation will matter when that time comes.

Dealing with the physical sensations of anxiety

Breathe. You can calm physical sensations within your body by focusing your attention on your breathing. Concentrate on the air going in and out of your lungs. Experience it as it passes through your nose and mouth.

Do this for two to five minutes. If you notice that you are taking short, shallow breaths, begin to take longer and deeper breaths. Imagine your lungs to be a pair of bagpipes. Expand your chest to bring in as much air as possible. Then listen to the plaintive chords as you slowly release the air.

Scan your body. Simple awareness is an effective technique to reduce the tension in your body.

Sit comfortably and close your eyes. Focus your attention on the muscles in your feet and notice if they are relaxed. Tell the muscles in your feet that they can relax.

Move up to your ankles and repeat the procedure. Next go to your calves and thighs and buttocks, telling each group of muscles to relax.

Do the same for your lower back, diaphragm, chest, upper back, neck, shoulders, jaw, face, upper arms, lower arms, fingers, and scalp.

Tense and relax. If you are aware of a particularly tense part of your body or if you discover tension when you're scanning your body, you can release this tension with the tense-relax method.

To do this, find a muscle that is tense and make it even more tense. If your shoulders are tense, pull them back, arch your back, and tense your shoulder muscles even more tightly. Then relax. The net result is that you can be aware of the relaxation and allow yourself to relax even more.

You can use the same procedure with your legs, arms, abdomen, chest, face, and neck. Clench your fists, tighten your jaw, straighten your legs, and tense your abdomen all at once. Then relax and pay close attention to the sensations of relaxation. By paying attention, you can learn to re-create these sensations whenever you choose.

Use guided imagery. Relax completely and take a quick fantasy trip. Close your eyes, free your body of tension, and imagine yourself in a beautiful, peaceful, natural setting. Create as much of the scene as you can. Be specific. Use all of your senses.

For example, you might imagine yourself at a beach. Hear the surf rolling in and the sea gulls calling to each other. Feel the sun on your face and the hot sand between your toes. Smell the sea breeze. Taste the salty mist from the surf. Notice the ships on the horizon and the rolling sand dunes. Use all of your senses to create a vivid imaginary trip.

Some people find that a mountain scene or a lush meadow scene works well. You can take yourself to a place you've never been or re-create an experience out of your past. Find a place that works for you and practice getting there. When you become proficient, you can return to it quickly for trips that might last only a few seconds.

With practice, you can use this technique even while you are taking a test.

Describe it. Focus your attention on your anxiety. If you are feeling nauseated or if you have a headache, concentrate on that feeling. Describe it to yourself. Tell yourself how large it is, where it is located in your body, what color it is, what shape it is, what texture it is, how much water it might hold if it had volume, and how heavy it is.

Be with it. As you describe your anxiety in detail, don't resist it. When you completely experience a physical sensation, it will often disappear. People suffering from severe and chronic pain have used this technique successfully.

Exercise aerobically. This is one technique that won't work in the classroom or while you're taking a test. Yet it is an excellent way to reduce body tension. Exercise regularly during the days that you review for a test. See what effect this has on your ability to focus and relax during the test.

Do some kind of exercise that will get your heart beating at twice your normal rate and keep it beating at that rate for 15 or 20 minutes. Aerobic exercises include rapid walking, jogging, swimming, bicycling, basketball, and anything else that elevates your heart rate and keeps it elevated.

Get help. When these techniques don't work, when anxiety is serious, get help. If you become withdrawn, have frequent thoughts about death or suicide, get depressed and stay depressed for more than a few days, or have prolonged feelings of hopelessness, see a counselor.

Depression and anxiety are common among students. Suicide is the second leading cause of death among young adults between the ages of 15 and 25. This is tragic and unnecessary. Many schools have counselors available. If not, the student health service or another office can refer you to community agencies that provide free or inexpensive counseling. You can also get emergency assistance over the phone. Most phone books contain listings for suicide prevention hot lines and other emergency services. ◪

exercise 19

TWENTY THINGS I LIKE TO DO

One way to relieve tension is to mentally yell "Stop!" and substitute a pleasant daydream for the stressful thoughts and emotions you are experiencing.

In order to create a supply of pleasant images to recall during times of stress, conduct an eight-minute brainstorm about things you like to do. Your goal is to generate at least 20 ideas. Time yourself and write as fast as you can in the space below.

_____

_____

_____

_____

_____

_____

_____

_____

_____

_____

_____

_____

_____

_____

_____

_____

_____

_____

_____

When you have completed your list, study it. Pick out two activities that seem especially pleasant and elaborate on them by creating a mind map. Write down all of the memories you have about that activity.

You can use these images to calm yourself in stressful situations.

journal entry 17

Discovery/Intention Statement

Do a timed, four-minute brainstorm of all the reasons, rationalizations, justifications, and excuses you have used to avoid studying. Be creative. List your thoughts in the space below by completing the following Discovery Statement.

I discovered that I . . .

_____

_____

_____

_____

_____

_____

_____

_____

_____

_____

_____

_____

Next, review your list, pick the excuse that you use the most, and circle it. In the space below, write an Intention Statement about what you will do to begin eliminating your favorite excuse. Make this Intention Statement one that you can keep, with a timeline and a reward.

I intend to . . .

_____

_____

_____

_____

journal entry 18

Discovery Statement

Explore your feelings about tests. Complete the following sentences.

As exam time gets closer, one thing I notice that I do is . . .

_____

_____

When it comes to taking tests, I have trouble . . .

_____

_____

The night before a test, I usually feel . . .

_____

_____

The morning of a test, I usually feel . . .

_____

_____

During a test, I usually feel . . .

_____

_____

After a test, I usually feel . . .

_____

_____

When I get a test score, I usually feel . . .

_____

_____

_____

An online version of this exercise is available at   masterstudent.college.hmco.com

Overcoming math and science anxiety

$$\sum_{n=1}^{\infty}(-1)^n\frac{|\sin(n)|}{n}$$

$$) = \begin{cases} \frac{x\cos x}{\sin x} \\ 1 \end{cases}$$

When they open books about math or science, some capable students break out in a cold sweat. This is a symptom of two conditions that can undermine students' confidence—math anxiety and science anxiety.

If you want to improve your math or science skills, you're in distinguished company. Albert Einstein felt he needed to learn more math to work out his general theory of relativity, so he asked a friend, mathematician Marcel Grossman, to teach him. It took several years. You won't need that long.

Think of the benefits of overcoming math and science anxiety. Many more courses, majors, jobs, and careers could open up for you. Knowing these subjects can also put you at ease in everyday situations: calculating the tip for a waiter, balancing your checkbook, working with a spreadsheet on a computer. Speaking the languages of math and science can help you feel at home in a world driven by technology.

Many schools offer courses in overcoming math and science anxiety. It can pay to check them out. The following suggestions just might start you on the road to enjoying science and mathematics.

Notice your pictures about math and science.
Sometimes what keeps people from succeeding at math and science is their mental picture of scientists and mathematicians. Often that picture includes a man dressed in a faded plaid shirt, baggy pants, and wingtip shoes. He's got a calculator on his belt and six pencils jammed in his shirt pocket.

Such pictures are far from the truth. Succeeding in math and science won't turn you into a nerd. Not only can you enjoy school more, you'll find that your friends and family will still like you.

Our mental pictures about math and science can be funny. At the same time, they can have serious effects. For

many years, science and math were viewed especially as fields for white males. This picture excluded women and people of color. Promoting success in these subjects for all students is a key step in overcoming racism and sexism.

Look out for shaky assumptions. Sheila Tobias, author of several books on overcoming math anxiety, points out that people often make faulty assumptions about how math and science are learned.[4] These assumptions can include the following:

- Math calls only for logic, not imagination.

- There's only one right way to do a science experiment or solve a math problem.

- There is a secret to doing well in math and science, and only a few, select people know it.

These ideas can be easily refuted. To begin with, mathematicians and scientists regularly talk about the importance of creativity and imagination in their work. They sometimes find it hard to explain how they arrive at a particular hypothesis or conclusion. And as far as we know, the only secret they count on is hard work—something that any determined person is capable of.

Get your self-talk out in the open and change it.
When students fear math and science, they often say negative things to themselves about their abilities in these subjects. Many times this self-talk includes statements such as the following:

- "I'll never be fast enough at solving math problems."

- "I'm one of those people who can't function in a science lab."

- "I'm good with words, so I can't be good with numbers."

Faced with this kind of self-talk, you can take three steps.

First, get a clear picture of such statements. When negative thoughts come to mind, speak them out loud or write them down. Getting self-doubt out into the open makes it easier to refute.

Next, do some critical thinking about these statements. Look for the hidden assumptions they contain. Acknowledge what is accurate about them and also what's false.

Negative self-statements are usually based on scant evidence. They can often be reduced to two simple ideas: "Everybody else is better at math and science than I am" and "Since I don't understand it right now, I'll never understand it." Both of these statements are illogical. Many people lack confidence in their math and science skills. To verify this, just ask other students. Also ask about ways they deal with the confusion. Remember that you can overcome negative self-statements when they trouble you in other courses. If you can learn a rap song or sketch the outline of a tree, you can do mathematics and science.

Finally, start some new self-talk. Use self-statements that affirm your ability to succeed in math and science such as:

- "When learning about math or science, I proceed with patience and confidence."

- "Any confusion I feel now will be resolved."

- "I learn math and science without comparing myself to others."

- "I ask whatever questions are needed to aid my understanding."

- "I am fundamentally OK as a person, even if I make errors in math and science."

- "I can succeed in math and science."

Notice your body sensations. Math or science anxiety is seldom just "in your head." It registers in our bodies, too. Examples can include a tight feeling in the chest, sweaty palms, drowsiness, or a mild headache.

Let those sensations come to the surface. Instead of repressing them, open up to them. Doing so often decreases their urgency.

Take a First Step about your current level of knowledge. In terms of acquiring knowledge, math and science are cumulative. Concepts tend to build upon each other in sequential order. If you struggled with algebra, for example, you will probably have trouble with trigonometry or calculus.

To ensure that you have an adequate base of knowledge, tell the truth about your current level of knowledge and skill. Before you register for a math or science course, seek out the assigned texts for the class. Look at the kind of material that's covered in early chapters. If that material seems new or difficult for you, see the instructor and express any concerns you have. Ask for suggestions on ways to prepare for the course.

Remember that it's OK to continue your study of math and science from your current level of ability—whatever that level might be.

Choose teachers with care. Whenever possible, find a math teacher whose approach to math matches key aspects of your learning style. One way to do this is trial and error. Simply try several teachers until you find one whom you enjoy. However, this approach takes time and could lead to needless frustration. An alternative is to ask around and discover which teachers have a gift for making math understandable. To do this:

- Look for math courses that tend to fill up early and find out who teaches them.

- Notice the office hours posted for math teachers; some might be more available to answer questions than others.

- Ask your academic advisor to recommend math teachers.

- Ask classmates to name their favorite math teachers—and to explain *why* they view these teachers as favorites.

Of course, you might not always have a choice. Perhaps only one teacher is offering the course you need during a given term. If so, there's still plenty you learn from this teacher, regardless of his teaching style. Consider the possibility that the teacher could open up a whole new way of learning math for you. Also form a study group early in the course and ask for help at the first sign that you're failing to understand an assignment.

Take math courses "back to back." You might find it tempting to take a break between required math classes. That's understandable, and this choice can make it harder for you to succeed. Think about math in the same way that you think about learning a foreign language. If you take a year off in between Spanish I and Spanish II, you won't expect to gain much fluency. To master a language, you take courses back to back. It works the same way with math—a kind of foreign language in itself.

Beware of short courses. Courses that you take during summer school or another shortened term are—by necessity—condensed. You can find yourself doing far more reading and homework each week that you do in longer courses. If you enjoy math, the extra intensity can provide a stimulus to learn. If math is not your favorite subject, give yourself the gift of extra course time. Enroll in courses with more calendar days.

Make your text an A priority. In a history, an English, or an economics class, the teacher might refer to some of the required readings only in passing. In contrast, math and science courses are often text-driven—that is, class activities closely follow the format and content of the book. This makes it doubly important to complete your reading assignments. Master one concept before going on to the next, and stay current with your reading.

Read slowly when appropriate. It's ineffective to breeze through a math or science book as you would the newspaper. To get the most out of your text, be willing to read each sentence slowly and reread it as needed. A single paragraph might merit 15 or 20 minutes of sustained attention.

Read chapters and sections in order, as they're laid out in the text. To strengthen your understanding of the main concepts, study all tables, charts, graphs, case studies, and sample problems. From time to time, stop, close your book, and mentally reconstruct the steps of an experiment or a mathematical proof.

Read actively. Science is not only a body of knowledge, it is an activity. To get the most out of your math and science texts, read with paper and pencil in hand. Work out examples and copy diagrams, formulas, and equations. Understand each step used in solving a problem or testing a hypothesis. *Study diagrams, charts, and other illustrations carefully.* They are important learning tools and are often a source for test questions.

Examples are particularly important. When reading texts in other courses, you might skim over examples to focus on major concepts. Math and science call for close attention to detail. In some cases, the examples included in the text *are* the main points.

Participate actively in class. Success in math and science depends on your active involvement. Attending class regularly, completing homework assignments, speaking up when you have a question, and seeking extra help can be crucial. Some students bemoan that they'll never be any good in math and science and then behave in a way that confirms that belief. Get around this mental trap by giving to math and science at least

the same amount of time that you give to other courses. If you want to succeed, make daily contact with these subjects.

Learn from specific to general. A powerful way to learn material in some courses is to get an overview of the main topic before focusing on the details. You might want to use the opposite strategy when studying math and science. Learning these subjects often means comprehending one limited concept before going on to the next one. Through an orderly process of cumulative knowledge, the big picture gradually comes into view. Jumping to general conclusions too soon might be confusing or inaccurate.

Remind yourself of the big picture. Pause occasionally to get an overview of the branch of science or math that you're studying. What's it all about? What basic problems is the discipline trying to solve? How is this knowledge applied in daily life?

For example, much of calculus has to do with finding the areas of "funny shapes"—shapes other than circles that have curves. Physics examines how matter and energy interact. Many professionals, including architects, engineers, and space scientists, use physics and calculus on a daily basis.

Ask questions fearlessly. In any subject, learning is enhanced when we ask questions. And there are no dumb questions. To master math and science, ask whatever questions will aid your understanding. Students come to higher education with widely varying backgrounds in these subjects. Your questions might not be the same as those of other people in your class. Go ahead and ask.

One barrier to asking questions is the thought "Will the teacher and other students think I'm stupid or ill-prepared? What if they laugh or roll their eyes?" This will usually not happen. If it does, remember your reasons for going to school. Your purpose is not to impress the teacher or the other students—it is to learn. And sometimes learning means admitting ignorance.

Part of an instructor's responsibility is to offer help to students who seek it. If the jump to the big picture looks like you are crossing a void, remember that teachers and tutors are there to help you reach the other side.

Apply what you've learned. Applying strategies that you've already learned in this book will help you in math and science. Use chapter summaries and introductory outlines to organize your learning. Review your notes frequently to transfer information into your long-term memory. Develop a strategy and schedule that works best for you, and make a date with yourself to study.

Instead of going it alone, harness the power of cooperative learning.

Use lab sessions to your advantage. Laboratory work is crucial to many science classes. To get the most out of these sessions, prepare. Know in advance what procedures you'll be doing and what materials you'll need. If possible, visit the lab before your assigned time and get to know the territory. Find out where materials are stored and where to dispose of chemicals or specimens. Bring your lab notebook and worksheets to class to record and summarize your findings.

If you're not planning to become a scientist, the main point is to understand the process of science—how scientists observe, collect data, and arrive at conclusions.

This is more important than the result of any one experiment.

Use cooperative learning. Math and science are often seen as solitary endeavors in which students either sink or swim on their own. This does not have to be your experience. Instead of going it alone, harness the power of cooperative learning. Study math and science with others. That way you can learn about different approaches to reaching solutions. By studying with others and creating an environment in which it's OK to make mistakes, you can overcome a variety of fears. ▧

journal entry 19

Discovery/Intention Statement

Most of us can recall a time when learning became associated with anxiety. For many of us, this happened early with math and science.

One step toward getting past this anxiety is to write a math or science autobiography. Recall specific experiences in which you first felt stress over these subjects. Where were you? How old were you? What were you doing, thinking, and feeling? Who else was with you? What did those people say or do?

Describe one of these experiences in the space below.

_____

_____

_____

_____

Now recall any incidents in your life that gave you positive feelings about math or science. Describe one of these incidents in detail in the space below.

_____

_____

_____

_____

Now sum up the significant discoveries you made while describing these two sets of experiences.

I discovered that my biggest barrier in math or science is . . .

_____

_____

_____

I discovered that the most satisfying aspect of doing math and science is . . .

_____

_____

_____

Now prepare to take positive action. List three things you can do to overcome any anxiety you feel about math or science. Include a specific time frame for taking each action.

Action 1: I intend to . . .

_____

_____

Action 2: I intend to . . .

_____

_____

Action 3: I intend to . . .

_____

_____

Taking Math & Science Tests

Use time drills. To prepare for math and science tests, practice working problems fast. Time yourself. Exchange problems with a friend and time each other. You can also do this in a study group.

Review formulas. Right before the test, review any formulas you'll need to use. Then write them down in the margins of the test or on the back of the test paper. Check with your instructor before the day of the test to make sure he will allow you to write formulas or prompts on the test form or your answer sheet or on scratch paper.

Read the problem at least twice. Read slowly. Be sure to understand what is being asked. Let go of the expectation that you'll find the answer right away. You might make several attempts at solving the problem before you find a solution that works.

Translate problems into English. Putting problems into words aids your understanding. When you study equations and formulas, put those into words, too. Using words can help you see a variety of applications for each formula. For example, $c^2 = a^2 + b^2$ can be translated as "the square of the hypotenuse of a right triangle is equal to the sum of the squares of the other two sides."

Analyze before you compute. Set up the problem before you begin to solve it. When a problem is worth a lot of points, read it twice, slowly. Examine it carefully.

When you take the time to analyze a problem, you can often discover computational shortcuts.

List what you already know and what you want to find out. Survey each problem for all of the givens. Look for what is to be proved or what is to be discovered. Consider using three columns labeled "What I already know," "What I want to find out," and "What relates the two." This last column is the place to record a formula that can help you solve the problem.

For clarity in problem solving, reduce the number of unknowns as much as you can. You might need to create a separate equation to solve each unknown.

Decide how you will solve the problem. Before you start crunching numbers or punching a calculator, take a moment to plan your approach. Choose which arithmetic operations (addition, subtraction, multiplication, division) or formulas you will use.

Estimate first. Estimating is a good way to double-check your work. Doing this first can help you notice when your computations go awry, allowing you to correct the error quickly.

Perform opposite operations. If a problem involves multiplication, check your work by division; add, then subtract; factor, then multiply; find the square root, then the square; differentiate, then integrate.

Make a picture. When you are stuck, draw a picture or a diagram. Sometimes a visual representation will clear a blocked mind. Making pictures is also an excellent study and review tool in math and science.

Play with possible solutions. There's usually not one "right" way to solve a problem. Several approaches or formulas might work, though one might be more efficient than another. Be willing to think about the problem from several angles or to proceed by trial and error. Remember that solving a math or science problem is like putting together a puzzle. You might work around the edges for a while and try many pieces before finding one that fits.

How to cram (even though you shouldn't)

First, know the limitations of cramming and be aware of its costs. Cramming won't work if you've neglected all of the reading assignments, or if you've skipped most of the lectures and daydreamed through the rest.

The more courses you have to cram for, the less effective cramming will be. Cramming is not the same as learning. When you rely on cramming, you cheat yourself out of a true education for one basic reason: You won't remember what you cram.

This point is especially important to recognize if you cram for mid-term exams. Some students think they are actually learning the material that they cram into their heads. They will be unpleasantly surprised during finals.

Cramming is also more work. It takes longer to learn material when you do it under pressure. You can't learn the same quantity of material in less time when you cram. You can learn some of the material, though with less comprehension and little or no long-term retention.

The purpose of cramming, therefore, is only to make the best of the situation. Cram to get by in a course so that you can do better next time. Cramming might help raise a grade, if you have been reasonably attentive in class, have taken fair notes, and have read or skimmed most of the material for the course.

Keep these limitations and costs of cramming in mind as you read the following suggestions to help with last-minute studying.

Make choices. Don't try to learn it all when you cram. You can't. Instead, pick out a few of the most important elements of the course and learn those backwards, forwards, and upside down.

For example, you can devote most of your attention to the topic sentences, tables, and charts in a long reading assignment instead of reading the whole assignment. A useful guideline is to spend 25 percent of cramming time learning new material and 75 percent of cramming time drilling yourself on that material.

Make a plan. Cramming is always done when time is short. It's easy to panic and jump right in. Taking a few minutes to create a plan first can actually save you time and allow you to work faster. After you've chosen what you want to study, determine how much time you have and set timelines for yourself.

Use mind map review sheets and flash cards. Condense the material you have chosen to learn onto mind maps. Choose several elements of the mind maps to put on 3x5 flash cards. Practice re-creating the mind maps, complete with illustrations. Drill yourself with the flash cards.

Recite and recite again. The key to cramming is repetitive recitation. Recitation can burn facts into your brain like no other study method. Go over your material again and again and again. One option is to tape-record yourself while you recite. Then play the tape as you fall asleep and as you get up in the morning.

Relax. Because you do not learn material well when you cram, you are more likely to freeze and forget it under the pressure of an exam. Relaxation techniques can be used to reduce test anxiety, both before and during the test.

Don't "should" yourself. One word to avoid during the cramming process is *should*. For example, you could start your cramming session by telling yourself you should have studied earlier, you should have read the assignments, and you should have been more conscientious. By the time you open your book, you might feel too guilty and depressed to continue.

Consider this approach. Tell yourself it would have been more effective to study earlier and more often. Remind yourself that you will have an opportunity to do so next time and write an Intention Statement detailing how you plan to change your study habits.

Finally, lighten up. Our brains work better when we aren't criticizing ourselves. Give yourself permission to be the fallible human being you are.

Check your work for precision and accuracy. Use common sense. Step back and ask if the solution seems reasonable at first glance. Reread the problem and remind yourself of the key question it asks. For example, if you're asked to apply a discount to an item, that item should cost less in your solution.

Keep units of measurement clear. Say that you're calculating the velocity of an object. If you're measuring distance in meters and time in seconds, the final velocity should be in meters per second.

Put your answers to the test. Plug your answer back into the original equation or problem and see if it works out correctly. ▨

8 reasons to celebrate mistakes

Most of us are haunted by the fear of failure. We dread the thought of making mistakes or being held responsible for a major breakdown. We shudder at the missteps that could cost us grades, careers, money, or even relationships.

It's possible to take an entirely different attitude toward mistakes. Rather than fearing them, we could actually celebrate them. We could revel in our redundancies, frolic in our failures, and glory in our goof-ups. We could marvel at our mistakes and bark with loud laughter when we "blow it."

A creative environment is one in which failure is not fatal. Businesses, striving to be on the cutting edge of competition, desperately seek innovative changes. They know that innovation requires risk taking, despite the chance of failure.

This is not idle talk. There are places where people actually celebrate mistakes. Management consultant Tom Peters gives the following examples in an issue of the *Executive Excellence* newsletter:

- One marketing director at Pizza Hut ended up with $5 million in unused sunglasses when a sales promotion scheme backfired. (The sunglasses were specifically designed for viewing the movie *Back to the Future, Part*

II.) He was promoted soon afterward, and the company's profits still increased 36 percent that year.

- The chief executive officer of Temps & Co., a temporary services firm, opens some meetings by asking managers to describe their biggest mistakes. The person with the "best" mistake gets a $100 prize. One of the winning mistakes was typing a social security number in the place of the dollar amount and cutting a multimillion-dollar paycheck.

- At its First Annual Doobie Awards, the Public Broadcasting System honored prominent mistakes made by its members. Nominees included an executive whose "improved" time sheets required three sign-offs instead of one. "It's a way of not taking ourselves too seriously," said one recipient of the award. "It gets a message across.... That it's okay to try and fail."

Note: Nothing in this article amounts to an argument in favor of *making* mistakes in the first place. Rather, the intention is to encourage shining a light on mistakes so that we can examine them and fix them. Mistakes that are hidden cannot be corrected.

Eight solid reasons for celebrating mistakes

1 Celebration allows us to notice the mistake. Celebrating mistakes gets them out into the open. This is the opposite of covering up mistakes or blaming others for them. Hiding mistakes takes a lot of energy— energy that could be channeled into correcting errors.

2 Mistakes are valuable feedback. A manager of a major corporation once made a mistake that cost his company $100,000. He predicted that he would be fired when his boss found out. Instead, his boss responded, "Fire you? I can't afford to do that. I just spent $100,000 training you." Mistakes are part of the learning process. Not only are mistakes usually more interesting than most successes—they're often more instructive.

3 Mistakes demonstrate that we're taking risks. People who play it safe make few

I learned from my mistake

mistakes. Making mistakes is evidence that we're stretching to the limit of our abilities—growing, risking, and learning. Fear of making mistakes can paralyze us into inaction. Celebrating mistakes helps us move into gear and get things done.

4 Celebrating mistakes reminds us that it's OK to make them. When we celebrate, we remind ourselves that the person who made the mistake is not bad—just human. This is not a recommendation that you purposely set out to make mistakes. Mistakes are not an end in themselves. Rather, their value lies in what we learn from them. When we make a mistake, we can admit it and correct it.

5 Celebrating mistakes includes everyone. It reminds us that the exclusive club named the Perfect Performance Society has no members. All of us make mistakes. When we notice them, we can work together. Blaming others or the system prevents the cooperative efforts that can improve our circumstances.

6 Mistakes occur only when we aim at a clear goal. We can express concern about missing a target only if the target is there in the first place. If there's no target or purpose, there's no concern about missing it. Making a mistake affirms something of great value—that we have a plan.

7 Mistakes happen only when we're committed to making things work. Systems work when people are willing to be held accountable. Openly admitting mistakes promotes accountability. Imagine a school where there's no concern about quality and effectiveness. Teachers usually come to class late. Residence halls are never cleaned, and scholarship checks are always late. The administration is in chronic debt, students seldom pay tuition on time, and no one cares. In this school, the word *mistake* would have little meaning. Mistakes become apparent only when people are committed to improving the quality of an institution. Mistakes go hand in hand with a commitment to quality.

8 Celebrating mistakes cuts the problem down to size. On top of the mistake itself, there is often a layer of regret, worry, and desperation about having made the mistake in the first place. Not only do people have a problem with the consequences of the mistake, they have a problem with themselves for making a mistake in the first place. When we celebrate mistakes, we eliminate that layer of concern. When our anxiety about making a mistake is behind us, we can get down to the business of correcting the mistake. ▨

PRACTICING CRITICAL THINKING 7

Create a short multiple choice test on a topic in a course you're taking right now. Ask several people from the class to take this exam.

Then, as a group, discuss the answer you chose for each question. Also talk about *why* and *how* you chose each answer. The purpose is to identify the strategies that different people use when answering a multiple choice question—especially when they are unsure of the correct answer.

You might discover some test-taking strategies that you would use in the future. List those strategies in the space below.

_____

_____

_____

_____

_____

_____

_____

_____

_____

_____

_____

_____

_____

_____

_____

Repeat this exercise by creating and discussing tests in other formats: short-answer, true/false, and essay.

power process

Detach

This Power Process helps you release the powerful, natural student within you. It is especially useful whenever negative emotions are getting in the way of your education.

Attachments are addictions. When we are attached to something, we think we cannot live without it, just as a drug addict feels he cannot live without drugs. We believe our well-being depends on maintaining our attachments.

We can be attached to just about anything—expectations, ideas, objects, self-perceptions, people, results, rewards. The list is endless.

One person, for example, might be so attached to his car that he takes an accident as a personal attack. Pity the poor unfortunate who backs into this person's car. He might as well back into the owner himself.

Another person might be attached to his job. His identity and sense of well-being depend on it. He could become suicidally depressed if he gets fired.

We can be addicted to our emotions as well as to our thoughts. We can identify with our anger so strongly that we are unwilling to let it go. We can also be addicted to our pessimism and reluctant to give it up. Rather than perceive these emotions as liabilities, we can see them as indications that it's time to practice detachment.

Most of us are addicted, to some extent, to our identities: We are Americans, veterans, high achievers, bowlers, loyal friends, business owners, humanitarians, devoted parents, dancers, hockey fans, or birdwatchers. If we are attached to these roles, they can dictate who we think we are.

When these identities are threatened, we might fight for

them as if we were defending our lives. The more addicted we are to an identity, the harder we fight to keep it.

Ways to recognize an attachment

When we are attached and things don't go our way, we might feel irritated, angry, jealous, confused, fatigued, bored, frightened, or resentful.

Suppose you are attached to getting an A on your physics test. You feel as though your success in life depends on getting an A. It's not just that you want an A. You *need* an A. During the exam, the thought "I must get an A" is in the back of your mind as you begin to work a problem. And the problem is difficult. The first time you read it, you have no idea how to solve it. The second time around, you aren't even sure what it's asking. The more you struggle to understand it, the more confused you get. To top it all off, this problem is worth 40 percent of your score.

As the clock ticks away, you work harder, getting more stuck, while that voice in your head gets louder: "I must get an A. I MUST get an A. I MUST GET AN A!"

At this point, your hands begin to sweat and shake. Your heart is pounding. You feel nauseated. You can't concentrate. You flail about for the answer as if you were drowning. You look up at the clock, sickened by the inexorable sweep of the second hand. You are doomed.

Now is a time to detach.

Ways to use this process

Detachment can be challenging. In times of stress, it might seem like the most difficult thing in the world to do. You can practice a variety of strategies to help you move toward detachment.

Practice observer consciousness. This is the quiet

state above and beyond your usual thoughts, the place where you can be aware of being aware. It's a tranquil spot, apart from your emotions. From here, you can observe yourself objectively, as if you were someone else. Pay attention to your emotions and physical sensations. If you are confused and feeling stuck, tell yourself, "Here I am, confused and stuck." If your palms are sweaty and your stomach is one big knot, admit it.

Practice perspective. Put current circumstances into a broader perspective. View personal issues within the larger context of your community, your nation, or your planet. You will likely see them from a different point of view. Imagine the impact your present problems will have 20 or even 100 years from now.

Take a moment to consider the worst that could happen. During that physics exam, notice your attachment to getting an A. Realize that even flunking the test will not ruin your life. Seeing this helps you put the test in perspective.

Practice breathing. Calm your mind and body with breathing or relaxation techniques.

Note: It might be easier to practice these techniques when you're not feeling strong emotions. Notice your thoughts, behaviors, and feelings during neutral activities such as watching television or taking a walk.

Practice detaching. The key is to let go of automatic emotional reactions when you don't get what you want.

Rewrite the equation

To further understand this notion of detaching, we can borrow an idea from mathematics. An equation is a set of symbols joined by an equals sign (=) that forms a true statement. Examples are $2 + 2 = 4$ and $a + b = c$.

Equations also work with words. In fact, our self-image can be thought of as a collection of equations. For example, the thought "I am capable" can be written as the equation "I = capable." "My happiness depends on my car" can be written as "happiness = car." The statement "My well-being depends on my job" becomes "well-being = job." Each equation is a tip-off to an attachment. When we're upset, a closer look often reveals that one of our attachments is threatened. The person who believes that his happiness is equal to his current job will probably be devastated if his company downsizes and he's laid off.

Once we discover a hidden equation, we can rewrite it. In the process, we can watch our upsets disappear. The person who gets laid off can change his equation to "my happiness = my happiness." In other words, his happiness does not have to depend on any particular job.

People can rewrite equations under the most extreme circumstances. A man dying from lung cancer spent his last days celebrating his long life. One day his son asked him how he was feeling.

"Oh, I'm great," said the man with cancer. "Your mom and I have been having a wonderful time just rejoicing in the life that we have had together."

"Oh, I'm glad you're doing well," said the man's son. "The prednisone you have been taking must have kicked in again and helped your breathing."

"Well, not exactly. Actually, my body is in terrible shape, and my breathing has been a struggle these last few days. I guess what I'm saying is that my body is not working well at all, but I'm still great."

The dying man rewrote the equation "I = my body." He knew that he had a body and that he was more than his body. This man lived this Power Process and gave his son—the author of this book—an unforgettable lesson about detachment.

Some cautions

Giving up an addiction to being an A student does not mean giving up being an A student. And giving up an addiction to a job doesn't mean getting rid of the job. It means not investing your entire well-being in the grade or the job. Keep your desires and goals alive and healthy while detaching from the compulsion to reach them.

Notice also that detachment is different from denial. Denial implies running away from whatever you find unpleasant. In contrast, detachment includes accepting your emotions and knowing the details of them—down to every last thought and physical sensation involved. It's OK to be angry or sad. Once you accept and fully experience your emotions, you can more easily move beyond them.

Being detached is not the same as being apathetic. We can be 100 percent detached and 100 percent involved at the same time. In fact, our commitment toward achieving a particular result is usually enhanced by being detached from it.

Detach and succeed

When we are detached, we perform better. When we think everything is at stake, the results might suffer. Without anxiety and the need to get an A on the physics test, we are more likely to recognize the problem and remember the solution.

This Power Process is useful when you notice that attachments are keeping you from accomplishing your goals. Behind your attachments is a master student. By detaching, you release that master student. Detach. ◙

put it to work

You can apply many of the techniques discussed in this chapter directly to common situations in the workplace. For example, use the test-taking strategies when you take licensing exams, certification exams, and other tests in your career field. In addition, consider the following suggestions.

Seize opportunities to learn cooperatively. Forming study groups or committees helps you develop important workplace skills. Almost every job is accomplished by the combined efforts of many people. For example, manufacturing a single car calls for the contribution of designers, welders, painters, electricians, marketing executives, computer programmers, and many others.

Perhaps you prefer to complete your assignments by working independently. However, teamwork is often required in the workplace. Joining study groups now, while you are in school, can help you expand your learning styles and succeed in the workplace.

Apply your cooperative learning skills to working on project teams. To create a successful project team at work, combine the individual skills of team members in complementary ways. Major tasks in any project include:

- *Planning*—defining the desired outcomes, setting due dates for each task, and generating commitment to action.

- *Doing*—carrying out assigned tasks.

- *Reflecting*—meeting regularly to discuss what's working well and ways to improve the next phase of the project.

- *Interpreting*—discussing what the team has learned from the project and ways to apply that learning to the whole organization.

Many people are drawn to one of these tasks more than the others. Assign tasks to people based on their strengths and preferences.

One potential trap of working in teams is that one person ends up doing most of the work. This person might feel resentful and complain. If you find yourself in this situation, transform your complaint into a request. Instead of scolding team members for being lazy, request help. Ask team members to take over tasks that you've been doing. Delegate specific jobs.

Manage job stress. The same techniques that help you manage test anxiety can help you manage stress at work. Apply techniques for managing the mental and physical aspects of stress while interviewing for a job, making a presentation, doing a performance review, or carrying out any task that raises your anxiety level.

Celebrate mistakes. Recall a mistake you made at work and then write about it. In a Discovery Statement, describe what you did to create a result you didn't want ("I discovered that I tend to underestimate the number of hours projects take"). Then write an Intention Statement describing something you can do differently in the future ("I intend to keep track of my actual hours on each project so that I can give more accurate estimates").

Go for fun. Finally, see if you can adapt suggestions from "Have some FUN!" to cultivate enjoyment at work. One benefit of career planning (see Chapter Twelve) is finding a job that allows you to follow your interests—in other words, to have fun. Successful people often eliminate the distinction between work and play in their lives. You're more likely to excel professionally when you're having a blast at your job. ⊠

Name _____ Date _____/_____/_____

quiz

1. Preparing for tests can include creating review tools. Name at least two of these tools.

2. When answering multiple choice questions, it is better to read all of the possible answers before answering the question in your head. True or False? Explain your answer.

3. The presence of absolute qualifiers, such as *always* or *never*, generally indicates a false statement. True or False? Explain your answer.

4. When answering an essay question, which of the following techniques is least effective?
   (a) Make a quick outline before answering the question.
   (b) Save the best points for last.
   (c) Know standard essay question words.
   (d) Include part of the question in your answer.
   (e) Avoid filler sentences.

5. Grades are:
   (a) A measure of creativity.
   (b) An indication of your ability to contribute to society.
   (c) A measure of intelligence.
   (d) A measure of test performance.
   (e) C and D.

6. Describe how *detachment* differs from *denial*.

7. Choose one technique for taking math and science tests and explain how it, or some variation of it, could apply to taking a test in another subject.

8. Name at least three benefits of participating in a study group.

9. Describe at least three techniques for dealing with the thoughts connected to test anxiety.

10. Describe at least three techniques for dealing with the physical feelings connected to test anxiety.

learning styles application

The questions below will "cycle" you through four styles, or modes, of learning as explained in the article "Learning styles: Discovering how you learn" in Chapter One. Each question will help you explore a different mode. You can answer the questions in any order.

what if
Explain how a suggestion for managing test anxiety could help you manage stress in a situation that you face outside of school.

why
Name at least one benefit you could experience—in addition to better grades—by taking tests more effectively.

how
Of the techniques that you gained from this chapter, choose one that you will use on your next test. Describe exactly how you intend to apply the technique.

what
List three new techniques for reviewing course material or taking tests that you gained from reading this chapter.

master student
profile

BARBARA JORDAN

(1936–1996) the first African American to become a state senator in Texas and the first African American to enter Congress since the Reconstruction.

So I was at Boston University in this new and strange and different world, and it occurred to me that if I was going to succeed at this strange new adventure, I would have to read longer and more thoroughly than my colleagues at law school had to read. I felt that in order to compensate for what I had missed in earlier years, I would have to work harder, and study longer, than anybody else.... I did my reading not in the law library, but in a library at my graduate dorm, upstairs where it was very quiet, because apparently nobody else studied there. So I would go there at night after dinner. I would load my books under my arm and go to the library, and I would read until the wee hours of the morning and then go to bed....

I was always delighted when I would get called upon to recite in class. But the professors did not call on the "ladies" very much. There were certain favored people who always got called on, and then on some rare occasions a professor would come in and would announce: "We're going to have Ladies Day today." And he would call on the ladies. We were just tolerated. We weren't considered really top drawer when it came to the study of law.

At some time in the spring, Bill Gibson, who was dating my new roommate, Norma Walker, organized a black study group, as we blacks had to form our own. This was because we were not invited into any of the other study groups. There were six or seven in our group—Bill, and Issie, and I think Maynard Jackson—and we would just gather and talk it out and hear ourselves do that. One thing I learned was that you had to talk out the issues, the facts, the cases, the decisions, the process. You couldn't just read the cases and study alone in your library as I had been doing; and you couldn't get it all in the classroom. But once you had talked it out in the study group, it flowed more easily and made a lot more sense....

Finally I felt I was really learning things, really going to school. I felt that I was getting educated, whatever that was. I became familiar with the process of thinking. I learned to think things out and reach conclusions and defend what I had said.

In the past I had got along by spouting off. Whether you talked about debates or oratory, you dealt with speechifying. But I could no longer orate and let that pass for reasoning because there was not any demand for an orator in Boston University Law School. You had to think and read and understand and reason. I had learned at twenty-one that you couldn't just say a thing is so because it might not be so, and somebody brighter, smarter, and more thoughtful would come out and tell you it wasn't so. Then, if you still thought it was, you had to prove it. Well, that was a new thing for me. I cannot, I really cannot describe what that did to my insides and to my head. I thought: I'm being educated finally. ✖

From *Barbara Jordan, a Self-Portrait* by Barbara Jordan and Shelby Hearon. Reprinted by permission of The Wendy Weil Agency, Inc. Copyright © 1978, 1979 by Barbara Jordan and Shelby Hearon.

For more biographical information on Barbara Jordan, visit the Master Student Hall of Fame on the *Becoming a Master Student* Web site at

masterstudent.college.hmco.com

7

Thinking

I always wanted to be somebody, but I should've been more specific.

LILY TOMLIN

Creativity was in each one of us as a small child. In children it is universal. Among adults it is almost nonexistent. The great question is: What has happened to this enormous and universal human capacity?

TILLIE OLSEN

why
this chapter matters . . .

The ability to think creatively and critically helps you succeed in any course.

what
is included . . .

Critical thinking: A survival skill
Becoming a critical thinker
Finding "aha!": Creativity fuels critical thinking
Ways to create ideas
Ways to fool yourself: Six common mistakes in logic
Uncovering assumptions
Gaining skill at decision making
Four ways to solve problems
"But I don't know what I want to do": Choosing a major
Majors for the taking
Solving math and science problems
Asking questions
Power Process: "Find a bigger problem"
Master Student Profile: Paul Farmer

how
you can use this chapter . . .

Read, write, speak, and listen more effectively.
Learn strategies to enhance your success in problem solving. Apply thinking skills to practical decisions such as choosing a major.

As you read, ask yourself
what if . . .

I could solve problems more creatively and make decisions in every area of life with more confidence?

Critical thinking: A survival skill

Society depends on persuasion. Advertisers want us to spend money on their products. Political candidates want us to "buy" their stands on the issues. Teachers want us to agree that their classes are vital to our success. Parents want us to accept their values. Authors want us to read their books. Broadcasters want us to spend our time in front of the radio or television, consuming their programs and not those of the competition. The business of persuasion has an impact on all of us.

A typical American sees thousands of television commercials each year. And that's just one medium of communication. Add to that the writers and speakers who enter our lives through radio shows, magazines, books, billboards, brochures, Internet sites, and fundraising appeals—all with a product, service, cause, or opinion for us to embrace.

This leaves us with hundreds of choices about what to buy, where to go, and who to be. It's easy to lose our heads in the crosscurrent of competing ideas—unless we develop skills in critical thinking. When we think critically, we can make choices with open eyes.

Uses of critical thinking

Critical thinking underlies reading, writing, speaking, and listening. These are the basic elements of comm-unication—a process that occupies most of our waking hours.

Critical thinking also plays an important part in social change. Consider that the institutions in any society—courts, governments, schools, businesses—are the products of a certain way of thinking. Any organization draws its life from certain assumptions about the way things should be done. Before the institution can change, those assumptions need to be loosened up or reinvented. In many ways, the real location of an institution is inside our heads.

Critical thinking also helps us uncover bias and prejudice. This is a first step toward communicating with people of other races, ethnic backgrounds, and cultures.

Crises occur when our thinking fails to keep pace with reality. An example is the world's ecological crisis, which arose when people polluted the earth, air, and water without considering the long-term consequences. Imagine how different our world would be if our leaders had thought like the first female chief of the Cherokees.

journal entry 20

Discovery/Intention Statement

Think back to a time when you felt unable to choose among several different solutions to a problem or several stands on a key issue in your life. In the space below, describe this experience.

I discovered that . . .

_____

_____

_____

Now scan this chapter to find useful suggestions for decision making, problem solving, and critical thinking. Note below at least four techniques that look especially promising to you.

Strategy   *Page number*

_____

_____

_____

_____

_____

Finally, declare a time that you intend to explore these techniques in more detail, along with a situation coming up during this term in which you could apply them.

I intend to improve my thinking skills by . . .

_____

_____

_____

_____

_____

_____

Asked about the best advice her elders had given her, she replied, "Look forward. Turn what has been done into a better path. If you are a leader, think about the impact of your decision on seven generations into the future."

Novelist Ernest Hemingway once said that anyone who wants to be a great writer must have a built-in, shockproof "crap" detector.[1] That inelegant comment points to a basic truth: As critical thinkers, we are constantly on the lookout for thinking that's inaccurate, sloppy, or misleading.

Critical thinking is a skill that will never go out of style. Throughout history, half-truths, faulty assumptions, and other nonsense have at one time been commonly accepted as true. Examples include:

- Illness results from an imbalance in the four vital fluids: blood, phlegm, water, and bile.

- Caucasians are inherently more intelligent than people of other races.

- Women are incapable of voting intelligently.

- We will never invent anything smaller than a transistor. (That was before the computer chip.)

- Computer technology will usher in the age of the paperless office.

The critical thinkers of history courageously challenged such ideas. These men and women pointed out that—metaphorically speaking—the emperor had no clothes.

Critical thinking is a path to freedom from half-truths and deception. You have the right to question what you see, hear, and read. Acquiring this ability is one of the major goals of a liberal arts education.

Critical thinking as thorough thinking

For some people, the term *critical thinking* has negative connotations. If you prefer, use *thorough thinking* instead. Both terms point to the same array of activities: sorting out conflicting claims, weighing the evidence, letting go of personal biases, and arriving at reasonable conclusions. This adds up to an ongoing conversation—a constant process, not a final product.

We live in a society that seems to value quick answers and certainty. This is often at odds with effective thinking. Thorough thinking is the ability to examine and re-examine ideas that might seem obvious. Such thinking takes time and the willingness to say three subversive words: "I don't know."

Thorough thinking is also the willingness to change our opinion as we continue to examine a problem. This calls for courage and detachment. Just ask anyone who has given up a cherished point of view in light of new evidence.

Skilled students are thorough thinkers. They distinguish between opinion and fact. They ask probing questions and make detailed observations. They uncover assumptions and define their terms. They make assertions carefully, basing them on sound logic and solid evidence. Almost everything that we call *knowledge* is a result of these activities. This means that critical thinking and learning are intimately linked.

It's been said that human beings are rational creatures. Yet no one is born a thorough thinker. This is a learned skill. Use the suggestions in this chapter to claim the thinking powers that are your birthright. The critical thinker is one aspect of the master student who lives inside you. ⊠

voices

student

The first time I tried to apply creative thinking to my schoolwork was for a term paper. It was very hard because it was something that I was not used to. But the more that I worked at it— brainstorming, focusing, questioning my conclusions—the easier it became. Now I automatically go through this process, whether I'm writing a report or choosing the best brand of peanut butter.

—SCOOTER WILLIAMS

Becoming a Critical Thinker

Critical thinking is a path to intellectual adventure. Though there are dozens of possible approaches, the process can be boiled down to concrete steps.

Stripped to its essence, critical thinking means asking and answering questions. The four basic questions in the Learning Styles Applications in this book—*Why? What? How?* and *What if?*—are a powerful tool for thinking. As they take you through the cycle of learning, they can also guide you in becoming a critical thinker. This article offers a variety of tools for answering those questions. For more handy implements, see *Becoming a Critical Thinker* by Vincent Ryan Ruggiero.

1 *Why* am I considering this issue? Critical thinking and personal passion go together. Begin critical thinking with a question that matters to you. Seek a rationale for your learning. Understand why it is important for you to think about a specific topic. You might want to arrive at a new conclusion, make a prediction, or solve a problem. By finding a personal connection with an issue, your interest in acquiring and retaining new information increases.

One path to critical thinking is tolerance for a wide range of opinions.

2 *What* are various points of view on this issue? Imagine Karl Marx, Cesar Chavez, and Donald Trump assembled in one room to choose the most desirable economic system. Picture Mahatma Gandhi, Winnie Mandela, and General George Patton lecturing at a United Nations conference on conflict resolution. Visualize Fidel Castro, George W. Bush, and Mother Teresa in a discussion about distributing the world's resources equitably. When seeking out alternative points of view, let such events unfold in your mind.

Dozens of viewpoints exist on every important issue—reducing crime, ending world hunger, preventing war, educating our children, and countless other concerns. In fact, few problems allow for any single, permanent solution. Each generation produces its own answers to critical questions, based on current conditions. Our search for answers is a conversation that spans centuries. On each question, many voices are waiting to be heard.

You can take advantage of this diversity by seeking out alternative views with an open mind. When talking to another person, be willing to walk away with a new point of view—even if it's the one you brought to the table, supported with new evidence. After thinking thoroughly, you can adopt new perspectives or hold your current viewpoints in a different way.

Examining different points of view is an exercise in analysis, which you can do with the suggestions that follow.

Define terms. Imagine two people arguing about whether an employer should limit health care benefits to members of a family. To one person, the word *family* means a mother, father, and children; to the other person, the word *family* applies to any long-term, supportive relationship between people who live together. Chances are, the debate will go nowhere until these people realize that they're defining the same word in different ways.

Conflicts of opinion can often be resolved—or at least clarified—when we define our key terms up front. This is especially true with abstract, emotion-laden terms such as *freedom, peace, progress,* or *justice.* Blood has been shed over the meaning of these words. Define them with care.

Look for assertions. A speaker's or writer's key terms occur in a larger context called an assertion. An *assertion* is a complete sentence that directly answers a key question. For example, consider this sentence from the article "The Master Student" in Chapter One: "A master is a person who has attained a level of skill that goes beyond technique." This sentence is an assertion that answers an important question: How do we recognize a master?

Look for at least three viewpoints. When asking questions, let go of the temptation to settle for just a single answer. Once you have come up with an answer, say to yourself, "Yes, that is one answer. Now what's another?" Using this approach can sustain honest inquiry, fuel creativity, and lead to conceptual break-throughs. Be prepared: The world is complicated, and critical thinking is a complex business. Some of your ans-wers might contradict others. Resist the temptation to have all of your ideas in a neat, orderly bundle.

Practice tolerance. One path to critical thinking is tolerance for a wide range of opinions. Taking a position on important issues is natural. When we stop having an opinion on things, we've probably stopped breathing.

The problem occurs when we become so attached to our current viewpoints that we refuse to consider alternatives. Many ideas that are widely accepted in Western cultures—for example, civil liberties for people of color and the right of women to vote—were once

Effective understanding calls for listening without judgment.

considered dangerous. Viewpoints that seem outlandish today might become widely accepted a century, a decade, or even a year from now. Remembering this can help us practice tolerance for differing beliefs and, in doing so, make room for new ideas that might alter our lives.

3 *How* well is each point of view supported? Uncritical thinkers shield themselves from new information and ideas. As an alternative, you can follow the example of scientists, who constantly search for evidence that contradicts their theories. The following suggestions can help.

Look for logic and evidence. The aim of using logic is to make statements that are clear, consistent, and coherent. As you examine a speaker's or writer's assert-ions, you might find errors in logic—assertions that contradict each other or assumptions that are unfounded.

Also assess the evidence used to support points of view. Evidence comes in several forms, including facts, expert testimony, and examples. To think critically about evidence, ask questions such as:

- Are all or most of the relevant facts presented?

- Are the facts consistent with each other?

- Are facts presented accurately—or in a misleading way?

- Are enough examples included to make a solid case for the viewpoint?

- Do the examples truly support the viewpoint?

- Are the examples typical? That is, could the author or speaker support the assertion with other examples that are similar?

- Is the expert credible—truly knowledgeable about the topic?

Consider the source. Look again at that article on the problems of manufacturing cars powered by natural gas. It might have been written by an executive from an oil company. Check out the expert who disputes the connection between smoking and lung cancer. That "expert" might be the president of a tobacco company.

This is not to say that we should dismiss the ideas of people who have a vested interest in stating their opinions. Rather, we can take

their self-interest into account as we consider their ideas.

Understand before criticizing. Polished debaters can sum up their opponents' viewpoints—often better than the people who support those viewpoints themselves. Likewise, critical thinkers take the time to understand a statement of opinion before agreeing or disagreeing with it.

Effective understanding calls for listening without judgment. Enter another person's world by expressing her viewpoint in your own words. If you're conversing with that person, keep revising your summary until she agrees that you've stated her position accurately. If you're reading an article, write a short summary of it. Then scan the article again, checking to see if your synopsis is on target.

Watch for hot spots. Many people have mental "hot spots"— topics that provoke strong opinions and feelings. Examples are abortion, homosexuality, gun control, and the death penalty.

To become more skilled at examining various points of view, notice your own particular hot spots. Make a clear intention to accept your feelings about these topics and to continue using critical thinking techniques.

One way to cool down our hot spots is to remember that we can change or even give up our current opinions without giving up ourselves. That's a key message behind the articles "Ideas are tools" and "Detach." These Power Processes remind us that human beings are much more than the sum of their current opinions.

Be willing to be uncertain. Some of the most profound thinkers have practiced the art of thinking by using a magic sentence: "I'm not sure yet."

Those are words that many people do not like to hear. Our society rewards quick answers and quotable sound bites. We're under considerable pressure to utter the truth in 10 seconds or less.

In such a society, it is courageous and unusual to take the time to pause, to look, to examine, to be thoughtful, to consider many points of view—and to be unsure. When a society adopts half-truths in a blind rush for certainty, a willingness to embrace uncertainty can move us forward.

4 *What if* **I could combine various points of view or create a new one?** Finding the truth is like painting a barn door by tossing an open can of paint at it. Few people who throw at the door miss it entirely. Yet no one can cover the whole door in a single toss.

People who express a viewpoint are seeking the truth. And no reasonable person claims to cover the whole barn door—to understand the whole truth about anything. Instead, each viewpoint can be seen as one approach among many possible alternatives. If you don't think that any one opinion is complete, combine different perspectives on the issue.

Create a critical thinking "spreadsheet." When you consult authorities with different stands on an issue, you might feel confused about how to sort out, evaluate, and combine their points of view. To overcome confusion, create a critical thinking "spreadsheet." List the authorities across the top of a page and key questions down the left side. Then indicate each authority's answer to each question, along with your own answers.

For example, the following spreadsheet clarifies different points of view on the issue of whether to outlaw boxing.

	Medical doctor	Former boxer	Sports journalist	Me
Is boxing a sport?	No	Yes	Yes	Yes
Is boxing dangerous?	Yes	Yes	Yes	Yes
Is boxing more dangerous than other sports?	Yes	No	Yes	No
Can the risk of injury be overcome by proper training?	No	No	No	Yes

Source: Vincent Ryan Ruggiero, *Becoming a Critical Thinker,* Fourth Edition. Copyright © 2002 by Houghton Mifflin Company. Reprinted with permission.

You could state your own viewpoint by combining your answers to the questions in the above spreadsheet: "I favor legalized boxing. While boxing poses dangers, so do other sports. And as with other sports, the risk of injury can be reduced when boxers get proper training."

Write about it. Thoughts can move at blinding speed. Writing slows down that process. Gaps in logic that slip by us in thought or speech are often exposed when we

commit the same ideas to paper. Writing down our thoughts allows us to compare, contrast, and combine points of view more clearly—and therefore to think more thoroughly.

Accept your changing perspectives.

Researcher William Perry found that students in higher education move through stages of intellectual development.[2] Students in earlier stages tend to think there is only one correct viewpoint on each issue, and they look to their instructors to reveal that truth. Later, students acknowledge a variety of opinions on issues and construct their own viewpoints.

Monitor changes in your thinking processes as you combine viewpoints. Distinguish between opinions that you accept from authorities and opinions that are based on your own use of logic and your search for evidence. Also look for opinions that result from objective procedures (such as using the *Why? What? How?* and *What if?* questions in this article) and personal sources (using intuition or "gut feelings").

Remember that the process of becoming a critical thinker will take you through a variety of stages. Give yourself time, and celebrate your growing mastery. ◩

→ Attitudes of a critical thinker

The American Philosophical Association invited a panel of 46 scholars from the United States and Canada to come up with answers to the following two questions: "What is college-level critical thinking?" and "What leads us to conclude that a person is an effective critical thinker?"[3] After two years of work, this panel concluded that critical thinkers share the attitudes summarized in the following chart.

Attitude	Sample statement
Truth-seeking	"Let's follow this idea and see where it leads, even if we feel uncomfortable with what we find out."
Open-minded	"I have a point of view on this subject, and I'm anxious to hear yours as well."
Analytical	"Taking a stand on the issue commits me to take some new action."
Systematic	"The speaker made several interesting points, and I'd like to hear some more evidence to support each one."
Self-confident	"After reading the book for the first time, I was confused. I'll be able to understand it after studying the book some more."
Inquisitive	"When I first saw that painting, I wanted to know what was going on in the artist's life when she painted it."
Mature	"I'll wait until I gather some more facts before reaching a conclusion on this issue."

Finding "aha!"
Creativity fuels critical thinking

This chapter offers you a chance to practice two types of critical thinking: convergent thinking and divergent thinking. One focuses on finding a single solution to a problem, while the other asks you to consider as many viewpoints as possible.

Convergent thinking involves a narrowing-down process. Out of all the possible viewpoints on an issue or alternative solutions to a problem, you choose the one that is the most reasonable or that provides the most logical basis for action.

Some people see convergent thinking and critical thinking as the same thing. However, there's more to critical thinking. Before you choose among viewpoints, generate as many of them as possible. Open up alternatives and consider all of your options. Define problems in different ways. Keep asking questions and looking for answers. This opening-up process is called *divergent* or *creative thinking*. Creative thinking provides the basis for convergent thinking. In other words, one path toward having good ideas is to have *lots* of ideas. Then you can pick and choose from among them, combining and refining them as you see fit.

Choose when to think creatively. The key is to make conscious choices about what kind of thinking to do in any given moment. Generally speaking, creative thinking is more appropriate in the early stages of planning and problem solving. Feel free to dwell in this domain for a while. If you narrow down your options too soon, you run the risk of missing an exciting solution or of neglecting a novel viewpoint. Convergent thinking is essential, and you should save it until you have plenty of options on the table.

Remember that creative thinking and convergent thinking take place in a continuous cycle. After you've used convergent thinking to narrow down your options, you can return to creative thinking at any time to generate new ones.

Cultivate "aha!" Central to creative thinking is something called the "aha!" experience. Nineteenth-century poet Emily Dickinson described aha! this way: "If I feel physically as if the top of my head were taken off, I know that is poetry." Aha! is the burst of creative energy heralded by the arrival of a new, original idea. It is the sudden emergence of an unfamiliar pattern, a previously undetected relationship, or an unusual combination of familiar elements. It is an exhilarating experience.

Aha! does not always result in a timeless poem or a Nobel Prize. It can be inspired by anything from playing a new riff on a guitar to figuring out why your car's fuel pump doesn't work. A nurse might notice a patient's symptom that everyone else missed. That's an aha! An accountant might discover a tax break for a client. That's an aha! A teacher might devise a way to reach a difficult student. Aha!

Follow through. The flip side of aha! is following through. Thinking is both fun and work. It is effortless and uncomfortable. It's the result of luck and persistence. It involves spontaneity and step-by-step procedures, planning and action, convergent and creative thinking.

Employers in all fields are desperately seeking those rare people who can find aha! and do something with it. The necessary skills include the ability to spot assumptions, weigh evidence, separate fact from opinion, organize thoughts, and avoid errors in logic. All of this can be demanding work. Just as often, it can be energizing and fun.

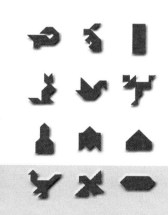

Tangram

A tangram is an ancient Chinese puzzle game that stimulates the "play instinct" so critical to creative thinking. The cat figure above was created by rearranging seven sections of a square. Hundreds of images can be devised in this manner. Playing with tangrams allows us to see relationships we didn't notice before.

The rules of the game are simple: Use these seven pieces to create something that wasn't there before. Be sure to use all seven. You might start by mixing up the pieces and seeing whether you can put them back together to form a square.

Make your own tangram by cutting pieces like those above out of poster board. When you come up with a pattern you like, trace around the outside edges of it and see if a friend can discover how you did it.

Ways to create ideas

Use the following techniques to generate ideas about everything, whether you're studying math problems, remodeling a house, or writing a bestseller. With practice, you can set the stage for creative leaps, jump with style, and land on your feet with brand-new ideas in hand.

Conduct a brainstorm.
Brainstorming is a technique for finding solutions, creating plans, and discovering new ideas. When you are stuck on a problem, brainstorming can break the logjam.

For example, if you run out of money two days before payday every week, you can brainstorm ways to make your money last longer. You can brainstorm ways to pay for your education. You can brainstorm ways to find a job.

The purpose of brainstorming is to generate as many solutions as possible. Sometimes the craziest, most outlandish ideas, while unworkable in themselves, can lead to new ways to solve problems. Use the following steps to try out the brainstorming process.

First, state the issue or problem precisely by writing it down. For example, you might write, "Methods and techniques I can use to get more information about multinational trade organizations in Central Africa."

Next, set a time limit for your brainstorming session. Use a clock to time it to the minute. Digital sports watches with built-in stopwatches work well. Experiment with various lengths of time. Both short and long brainstorms can produce powerful results.

Before you begin, sit quietly for a few seconds to collect your thoughts. Then start timing and write as fast as you can.

Write down everything. Accept every idea. If it pops into your head, put it down on paper. Quantity, not quality, is the goal. Avoid making judgments and evaluations during the brainstorming session.

After the session, review, evaluate, and edit. Toss out any truly nutty ideas, but not before you give them a chance.

For example, during your brainstorm on Central African trade organizations, you might have written "Go to Central Africa and ask someone about them." Impossible? Perhaps your school would allow you to schedule a semester of independent study to research the subject. A trade organization might offer you a scholarship to pay for the trip. You could also "visit" Central Africa via a Web site, or communicate directly with a trade organization by e-mail.

Brainstorms often produce solutions that look wacky at first and can later bring about surprising, life-changing results. Stay open to possibilities.

Here are some other tips for brainstorming sessions:

- *Let go of the need for a particular solution.* Brainstorming sessions can reveal new ways of thinking about old problems.

- *Relax.* Creativity is enhanced by a state of relaxed

alertness. If you are tense or anxious, use some of the relaxation techniques described in this text. (Start with the article "Let go of test anxiety" in Chapter Six: Tests.)

- *Set a quota or goal for the number of solutions you want to generate.* Goals give your subconscious mind something to aim for.

- *Use 3x5 cards or a computer to record each solution.* When you review your session, you can arrange solutions in patterns to look for relationships. Or you can arrange them in order of priority.

- *Brainstorm with others.* This is a powerful technique. Group brainstorms can take on a life of their own. Ask one member of the group to write down solutions. Feed off the ideas of others, and remember to avoid evaluating or judging anyone's idea during the brainstorm.

- *Multiply brainstorms.* Pick one item from your first brainstorm and conduct another brainstorm about that idea.

- *Be wild and crazy.* If you get stuck, think of an outlandish idea and write it down. One crazy idea can unleash a flood of other, more workable solutions.

 **Focus and let go.** Focusing and letting go are alternating parts of the same process. Intense focus taps the resources of your conscious mind. Letting go gives your subconscious mind time to work. When you focus for intense periods and then let go for a while, the conscious and subconscious parts of your brain work in harmony. In doing so, they can produce the highest-quality results.

Focusing attention means being in the here and now. To focus your attention on a project, notice when you pay attention and when your mind starts to wander. And involve all of your senses.

For example, if you are having difficulty writing a paper at a computer, practice focusing by listening to the sounds as you type. Notice the feel of the keys as you strike them. When you know the sights, sounds, and sensations you associate with being truly in focus, you'll be able to repeat the experience and return to your paper more easily.

You can use your body to focus your concentration. Some people concentrate better lying down. Others focus more easily if they stand or pace back and forth. Still others need to have something in their hands.

Experiment. Notice what works for you and use it.

Be willing to recognize conflict, tension, and discomfort. Notice them and fully accept them, rather than fighting against them. Look for the specific thoughts and body sensations that make up the discomfort. Allow them to come fully into your awareness, and then let them pass.

You might not be focused all of the time. Periods of inspiration might last only seconds. Be gentle with yourself when you notice that your concentration has lapsed.

In fact, that might be a time to let go. "Letting go" means not forcing yourself to be creative.

Practice focusing for short periods at first, then give yourself a break. Phone a friend. Get up and take a walk around the room or around your block. Take a few minutes to look out your window. Listen to some music or, better yet, sing a few songs to yourself.

You also can break up periods of focused concentration with stretches, sit-ups, or pushups. Use relaxation and breathing exercises. Muscle tension and the lack of oxygen can inhibit self-expression.

Movies, music, walks in the park, and other pleasant activities stir the creative soup that's simmering in your brain.

Take a nap when you are tired. Thomas Edison took frequent naps. Then the light bulb clicked on.

 **Cultivate creative serendipity.** The word *serendipity* was coined by the English author Horace Walpole from the title of an ancient Persian fairy tale, "The Three Princes of Serendip." The princes had a knack for making lucky discoveries. Serendipity is that knack, and it involves more than luck. It is the ability to see something valuable that you weren't looking for. History is full of serendipitous people. Country doctor Edward Jenner noticed "by accident" that milkmaids seldom got smallpox. The result was his discovery that mild cases of cowpox immunized them. Penicillin was also discovered "by accident." Scottish scientist Alexander Fleming was growing bacteria in a laboratory petri dish. A spore of *Penicillium notatum,* a kind of mold, blew in the window and landed in the dish, killing the bacteria. Fleming isolated the active ingredient. A few years later, during World War II, it saved thousands of lives. Had Fleming not been alert to the possibility, the discovery might never have been made.

You can train yourself in the art of serendipity. First, keep your eyes open. You might find a solution to an accounting problem in a Saturday morning cartoon. You might discover a topic for your term paper at the corner convenience store. Multiply your contacts with the world. Resolve to meet new people. Join a study or discussion group. Read. Go to plays, concerts, art shows, lectures, and movies. Watch television programs you normally wouldn't watch. Use idea files and play with data, as described below.

Finally, expect discoveries. One secret for success is being prepared to recognize "luck" when you see it.

Keep idea files. We all have ideas. People who are viewed as creative are those who treat their ideas with care. That means not only recognizing ideas, but also recording them and following up on them.

One way to keep track of ideas is to write them down on 3x5 cards. Invent your own categories and number the cards so you can cross-reference them. For example, if you have an idea about making a new kind of bookshelf, you might file a card under "Remodeling." A second card might also be filed under "Marketable Ideas." On the first card, you can write down your ideas, and on the second, you can write "See card #321—Remodeling." Include in your files powerful quotations, random insights, notes on your reading, and useful ideas that you encounter in class. Collect jokes, too.

Keep a journal. Journals don't have to be exclusively about your own thoughts and feelings. You can record observations about the world around you, conversations with friends, important or offbeat ideas—anything.

To fuel your creativity, read voraciously, including newspapers and magazines. Keep a clip file of interesting articles. Explore beyond mainstream journalism. There are hundreds of low-circulation specialty magazines and online news journals that cover almost any subject you can imagine.

Keep letter-sized file folders of important correspondence, magazine and news articles, and other material. You can also create idea files on a computer using word processing, outlining, or database software.

Safeguard your ideas, even if you're pressed for time. Jotting down four or five words is enough to capture the essence of an idea. You can write down one quotation in a minute or two. And if you carry 3x5 cards in a pocket or purse, you can record ideas while standing in line or sitting in a waiting room.

Review your files regularly. Some amusing thought that came to you in November might be the perfect solution to a problem in March.

Collect and play with data. Look from all sides at the data you collect. Switch your attention from one aspect to another. Examine each fact, and avoid getting stuck on one particular part of a problem.

Turn a problem upside down by picking a solution first and then working backward. Ask other people to look at the data. Solicit opinions.

Living with the problem invites a solution. Write down data, possible solutions, or a formulation of the problem on 3x5 cards and carry them with you. Look at them before you go to bed at night. Review them when you are waiting for the bus. Make them part of your life and think about them frequently.

Look for the obvious solutions or the obvious "truths" about the problem—then toss them out. Ask yourself: "Well, I know X is true, but if X were *not* true, what would happen?" Or ask the reverse: "If that *were* true, what would follow next?"

Put unrelated facts next to each other and invent a relationship between them, even if it seems absurd at first. In *The Act of Creation,* novelist Arthur Koestler says that finding a context in which to combine opposites is the essence of creativity.[4]

Make imaginary pictures with the data. Condense it. Categorize it. Put it in chronological order. Put it in alphabetical order. Put it in random order. Order it from most to least complex. Reverse all of those orders. Look for opposites.

It has been said that there are no new ideas—only new ways to combine old ideas. Creativity is the ability to discover those new combinations.

Create while you sleep. A part of our mind works as we sleep. You've experienced this directly if you've ever fallen asleep with a problem on your mind and awakened the next morning with a solution. For some of us, the solution appears in a dream or just before falling asleep or waking up.

You can experiment with this process. Ask yourself a question as you fall asleep. Keep pencil and paper or a recorder near your bed. The moment you wake up, begin writing or speaking and see if an answer to your question emerges.

Many of us have awakened from a dream with a great idea, only to fall asleep and lose it forever. To capture your ideas, keep a notebook by your bed at all times. Put the notebook where you can find it easily.

There is a story about how Benjamin Franklin used

this suggestion. Late in the evenings, as he was becoming drowsy, he would sit in his rocking chair with a rock in his right hand and a metal bucket on the floor beneath the rock. The moment he fell asleep, the rock would fall from his grip into the bottom of the bucket, making a loud noise that awakened him. Having placed a pen and paper nearby, he immediately wrote down what he was thinking. Experience taught him that his thoughts at this moment were often insightful and creative.

Refine ideas and follow through.

Many of us ignore this part of the creative process. How many great moneymaking schemes have we had that we never pursued? How many good ideas have we had for short stories that we never wrote? How many times have we said to ourselves, "You know, what they ought to do is attach two handles to one of those things, paint it orange, and sell it to police departments. They'd make a fortune." And we never realize that we are "they."

Genius resides in the follow-through—the application of perspiration to inspiration. One powerful tool you can use to follow through is the Discovery and Intention Journal Entry system. First write down your idea in a Discovery Statement, and then write what you intend to do about it in an Intention Statement. You also can explore the writing techniques discussed in Chapter Eight: Communicating as a guide for refining your ideas.

Another way to refine an idea is to simplify it. And if that doesn't work, mess it up. Make it more complex.

Finally, keep a separate file in your ideas folder for your own inspirations. Return to it regularly to see if there is anything you can use. Today's defunct term paper idea could be next year's A in speech class.

Create success strategies.

Use creative thinking techniques to go beyond the pages of this book and create your own ways to succeed in school. Read other books on success. Interview successful people. Reflect on any of your current behaviors that help you do well in school. Change any habits that fail to serve you.

If you have created a study group with people from one of your classes, set aside time to talk about ways to succeed in any class. Challenge each other to practice your powers of invention. Test any new strategies you create and report to the group on how well they're working for you.

Trust the process.

Learn to trust the creative process—even when no answers are in sight. We are often reluctant to look at problems if no immediate solution is at hand. We grow impatient and tend to avoid frustration by giving up altogether.

Most of us do this to some degree with personal problems as well. If we are having difficulty with a relationship and don't see a quick resolution, we deny that the problem exists rather than facing up to it.

Trust that a solution will show up. Frustration and a feeling of being stuck are often signals that a solution is imminent.

Sometimes solutions break through in a giant AHA! More often they come in a series of little aha!s. Be aware of what your aha!s look, feel, and sound like. That sets the stage for even more flights of creative thinking. ▨

→ Create on your feet

A popular trend in executive offices is the "stand-up" desk—a raised working surface at which you stand rather than sit.

Standing has advantages over sitting for long periods. You can stay more alert and creative when you're on your feet. One theory is that our problem-solving ability improves when we stand, due to increased heart rate and blood flow to the brain.

Standing is great for easing lower-back pain, too. Sitting aggravates the spine and its supporting muscles.

This is a technique with tradition. If you search the Web for stand-up desks, you'll find models based on desks used by Thomas Jefferson, Winston Churchill, and writer Virginia Woolf. Consider setting your desk up on blocks or putting a box on top of your desk so that you can stand while writing, preparing speeches, or studying. Discover whether this approach works for you.

Ways to fool yourself

Six common mistakes in logic

Logic is a branch of philosophy that seeks to distinguish between effective and ineffective reasoning.

Students of logic look for valid steps in an argument, or a series of assertions. The opening assertions of the argument are the premises, and the final assertion is the conclusion.

Over the last 2,500 years, specialists in logic have listed some classic land mines in the field of logic—common mistakes that are called *fallacies*. These fallacies are included in just about every logic textbook. Following are six examples. Knowing about them before you string together a bunch of assertions can help you avoid getting fooled.

1 Jump to conclusions. Jumping to conclusions is the only exercise that some lazy thinkers get. This fallacy involves drawing conclusions without sufficient evidence. Take the bank officer who hears about a student failing to pay back an education loan. After that, the officer turns down all loan applications from students. This person has formed a rigid opinion on the basis of hearsay. Jumping to conclusions—also called *hasty generalization*—is at work here.

2 Attack the person. This mistake in logic is common at election time. An example is the candidate who claims that her opponent has failed to attend church regularly during the campaign. People who indulge in personal attacks are attempting an intellectual sleight of hand to divert our attention from the truly relevant issues.

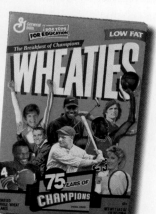

3 Appeal to authority. A professional athlete endorses a brand of breakfast cereal. A famous musician features a soft drink company's product in a rock video. The promotional brochure for an advertising agency lists all of the large companies that have used its services.

In each case, the people involved are trying to win your confidence—and your dollars—by citing authorities. The underlying assumption is usually this: *Famous people and organizations buy our product. Therefore, you should buy it too.* Or: *You should accept this idea merely because someone who's well known says it's true.*

Appealing to authority is usually a substitute for producing real evidence. It invites sloppy thinking. When our only evidence for a viewpoint is an appeal to authority, it's time to think more thoroughly.

4 Point to a false cause. The fact that one event follows another does not necessarily mean that the two events have a cause-and-effect relationship. All we can actually say is that the events might be correlated. For example, as children's vocabularies improve, they can get more cavities. This does not mean that cavities are the result of an improved vocabulary. Instead, the increase in cavities is due to other factors, such as physical maturation and changes in diet or personal care.

5 Think in all-or-nothing terms. Consider these statements: *Doctors are greedy.... You can't trust politicians.... Students these days are in school just to get high-paying jobs; they lack idealism.... Homeless people don't want to work.*

These opinions imply the word *all.* They gloss over individual differences, claiming that all members of a group are exactly alike. They also ignore key facts, for instance, that some doctors volunteer their time at free medical clinics and that many homeless people are children who are too young to work. All-or-nothing thinking is one of the most common errors in logic.

6 Base arguments on emotion. The politician who ends every campaign speech with flag waving and slides of her mother eating apple pie is staking her future on appeals to emotion. So is the candidate who paints a grim scenario of the disaster and ruination that will transpire unless she is elected. Get past the fluff and histrionics to see if you can uncover any worthwhile ideas. ✖

voices

student

Successful choices are a result of solving a problem, looking at pros and cons, making the decision or choice, and checking how you feel about (and how others will be affected by) this conclusion. This takes concerted effort, but a master student uses this inquisitive, analytical, and open-minded process to gain self-confidence and maturity.

—KRISTINE RUGGLES

Consider the following argument:

Orca whales mate for life.
Orca whales travel in family groups.
Science has revealed that Orca whales are intelligent.
Therefore, Orca whales should be saved from
    extinction.

One idea underlies this line of thought:

Any animal that displays significant human
    characteristics deserves special protection.

Whether or not you agree with this argument, consider for a moment the process of making assumptions. Assumptions are assertions that guide our thinking and behavior. Often these assertions are unconscious. People can remain unaware of their most basic and far-reaching assumptions—the very ideas that shape their lives.

Spotting assumptions can be tricky, since they are usually unstated and offered without evidence. And scores of assumptions can be held at the same time. Those assumptions might even contradict each other, resulting in muddled thinking and confused behavior. This makes uncovering assumptions a feat worthy of the greatest detective.

Letting assumptions remain in our subconscious can erect barriers to our success. Take the person who says, "I don't worry about saving money for the future. I think life is meant to be enjoyed today—not later." This statement rests on at least two assumptions: *saving money is not enjoyable*, and *we can enjoy ourselves only when we're spending money.*

It would be no surprise to find out that this person runs out of money near the end of each month and depends on cash advances from high-interest credit cards. She is shielding herself from some ideas that could erase her debt: Saving money can be a source of satisfaction, and many enjoyable activities cost nothing.

The stakes in uncovering assumptions are high. Prejudice thrives on the beliefs that certain people are inferior or dangerous due to their skin color, ethnic background, or sexual orientation. Those beliefs have led to flawed assumptions such as *mixing the blood of the races will lead to genetically inferior offspring* and *racial integration of the armed forces will lead to the destruction of morale.*

When we remain ignorant of our assumptions, we also make it easier for people with hidden agendas to do our thinking for us. Demagogues and unethical advertisers know that unchallenged assumptions are potent tools for influencing our attitudes and behavior.

Take this claim from an advertisement: "Successful students have large vocabularies, so sign up today for our

Uncovering assumptions

seminar on word power!" Embedded in this sentence are several assumptions. One is that a cause-and-effect relationship exists between a large vocabulary and success in school. Another is that a large vocabulary is the single or most important factor in that success. This claim also assumes that the advertiser's seminar is the best way to develop your vocabulary. In reality, none of these assumptions is necessarily true.

Assertions and opinions flow from our assumptions. Heated conflict and hard feelings often result when people argue on the level of opinions—forgetting that the real conflict lies at the level of their assumptions.

An example is the question about whether the government should fund public works programs that create jobs during a recession. People who advocate such programs might assume that creating such jobs is an appropriate task for the federal government. On the other hand, people who argue against such programs might assume that the government has no business interfering with the free workings of the economy. There's little hope of resolving this conflict of opinion unless we deal with something more basic: our assumptions about the proper role of government.

You can follow a three-step method for testing the validity of any viewpoint. First, look for the assumptions—the assertions implied by that viewpoint. Second, write down these assumptions. Third, see if you can find any exceptions to them. This technique helps detect many errors in logic. ◪

Gaining skill at decision making

When people refuse to make decisions, they leave their lives to chance. Philosopher Walter Kaufman calls this decidophobia—the fear of making decisions. He defines the alternative—autonomy—as "making with open eyes the decisions that give shape to one's life."[5]

We make decisions all of the time, whether we realize it or not. Even avoiding decisions is a form of decision making. The student who puts off studying for a test until the last minute might really be saying, "I've decided this course is not important" or "I've decided not to give this course much time."

Decide right now to apply some of the following suggestions, and you can take your overall decision making to new heights of effectiveness.

Recognize decisions. Decisions are more than wishes or desires. There's a world of difference between "I wish I could be a better student" and "I will take more powerful notes, read with greater retention, and review my class notes daily." Decisions are specific and lead to focused action. When we decide, we narrow down. We give up actions that are inconsistent with our decision. Deciding to eat fruit for dessert instead of ice cream rules out the next trip to the ice cream store.

Establish priorities. Some decisions are trivial. No matter what the outcome, your life is not affected much. Other decisions can shape your circumstances for years. Devote more time and energy to the decisions with big outcomes. Base your decisions on a life plan. The value of having a long-term plan for our lives is that it provides a basis for many of our year-to-year and week-to-week decisions. Being certain about what we want to accomplish this year and this month makes today's choices more clear.

Clarify your values. When you know specifically what you want from life, making decisions becomes easier. This is especially true when you define your values precisely and put them in writing. Saying that you value education is fine. Now give that declaration some teeth. Note that you value continuous learning as a chance to upgrade your career skills, for instance. That can make registering for next term's classes much easier.

Choose an overall strategy. Every time you make a decision, you choose a strategy—even when you're not aware of it. Effective decision makers can articulate and choose from among several strategies.

- *Find all of the available options and choose one deliberately.* Save this strategy for times when you have a relatively small number of options, each of which leads to noticeably different results.

- *Find all of the available options and choose one randomly.* This strategy can be risky. Save it for times when your options are basically similar and fairness is the main issue.

- *Limit the options, then choose.* When deciding which search engine to use on the World Wide Web, visit many sites and then narrow the list down to two or three that you choose.

- *Choose the first acceptable option that you find.* This strategy can work well when you have many options, and when thoroughly researching each option will take too much time or create too little benefit. For instance, when you're writing a paper and are pressed for time, write down the first five facts you find that directly support your thesis. You could look for more facts, but the extra investment of time might not produce enough usable results.

- *Choose to act on someone else's decision.* You use this strategy, for example, when you buy a CD based on a friend's recommendation. A more sophisticated version of this strategy is arbitration—people who are in conflict agree to act on the decision made by a third party, such as a judge, who listens to each person's case.

Use time as an ally. Sometimes we face dilemmas—situations in which any course of action leads to undesirable consequences. In such cases, consider putting a decision on hold. Wait it out. Do nothing until the circumstances change, making one alternative clearly preferable to another.

Use intuition. Some decisions seem to make themselves. A solution pops into our mind and we gain newfound clarity. Using intuition is not the same as forgetting about the decision or refusing to make it. Intuitive decisions usually arrive after we've gathered the relevant facts and faced a problem for some time.

Act on your decision. There comes a time to move from the realm of discovery and intention to the arena of action. Action is a hallmark of a true decision.

Evaluate your decision. Hindsight can be a valuable source of insight. After you act on a decision, observe the consequences over time. Reflect on how well your decision worked and what you might have done differently. ✖

Four ways to solve problems

There is a vast literature on problem-solving techniques. Much of it can be traced to American philosopher John Dewey, who devised these steps of effective problem solving:

- Perceive a "felt difficulty" and state it clearly and concisely.

- Invent possible solutions.

- Rationally test each solution by anticipating its possible consequences.

- Act on the preferred solution, evaluate the consequences, and determine whether a new solution is needed.[6]

Much of what you'll read about problem solving amounts to variations on Dewey's steps. Think of problem solving as a process with four P's: Define the *problem*, generate *possibilities*, create a *plan*, and *perform* your plan.

1 **Define the problem.** To define a problem effectively, understand what a problem is—a mismatch between what you want and what you have. Problem solving is all about reducing the gap between these two factors.

Start with what you have. Tell the truth about what's present in your life right now, without shame or blame. For example: "I often get sleepy while reading my physics assignments, and after closing the book I cannot remember what I just read."

Next, describe in detail what you want. Go for specifics: "I want to remain alert as I read about physics. I also want to accurately summarize each chapter I read."

Remember that when we define a problem in limiting ways, our solutions merely generate new problems. As Einstein said, "The world we have made is a result of the level of thinking we have done thus far. We cannot solve problems at the same level at which we created them."[7]

This idea has many applications for success in school. An example is the student who struggles with note taking. The problem, she thinks, is that her notes are too sketchy. The logical solution, she decides, is to take more notes, and her new goal is to write down almost everything her instructors say. No matter how fast and furiously she writes, she cannot capture all of the instructors' comments.

Consider what happens when this student defines the problem in a new way. After more thought, she decides that her dilemma is not the *quantity* of her notes but their *quality*. She adopts a new format for taking notes, dividing her note paper into two columns. In the right-hand column she writes down only the main points of each lecture. And in the left-hand column she notes two or three supporting details for each point.

Over time, this student makes the joyous discovery that there are usually just three or four core ideas to remember from each lecture. She originally thought the solution was to take more notes. What really worked was taking notes in a new way.

2 **Generate possibilities.** Now put on your creative thinking hat. Open up. Brainstorm as many possible solutions to the problem as you can. At this stage, quantity counts. As you generate possibilities, gather relevant facts. For example, when you're faced with a dilemma about what courses to take next term, get information on class times, locations, and instructors. If you haven't decided which summer job offer to accept, gather information on salary, benefits, and working conditions.

3 **Create a plan.** After rereading your problem definition and list of possible solutions, choose the solution that seems most workable. Think about specific actions that will reduce the gap between what you have and what you want. Visualize the steps you will take to make this solution a reality and arrange them in chronological order. To make your plan even more powerful, put it in writing.

4 **Perform your plan.** This step gets you off your chair and out into the world. Now you actually *do* what you have planned. Ultimately, your skill in solving problems lies in how well you perform your plan. Through the quality of your actions, you become the architect of your own success.

Note that the four P's of this problem-solving process closely parallel the four key questions listed in the article "Becoming a critical thinker":

Define the **problem**	**What** is the problem?
Generate **possibilities**	**What if** there are several possible solutions?
Create a **plan**	**How** would this possible solution work?
Perform your plan	**Why** is one solution more workable than another?

When facing problems, experiment with these four P's, and remember that the order of steps is not absolute. Also remember that any solution has the potential to create new problems. If that happens, cycle through the four P's of problem solving again.

"But I don't know what I want to do"
Choosing a major

One decision that troubles many students in higher education is the choice of an academic major. Here is an opportunity to apply your skills at critical thinking, decision making, and problem solving. The following suggestions can guide you through this process.

Link your major to your goals. Your choice of a major can fall into place once you determine what you want in life. Before you choose a major, back up to a bigger picture. List your core values, such as contributing to society, achieving financial security and professional recognition, enjoying good health, or making time for fun. Also write down specific goals that you want to accomplish in 5 years, 10 years, or even 50 years from today.

Many students find that the prospect of getting what they want in life justifies all of the time, money, and day-to-day effort invested in going to school. Having a major gives you a powerful incentive for attending classes, taking part in discussions, reading textbooks, writing papers, and completing other assignments. When you see a clear connection between finishing school and creating the life of your dreams, the daily tasks of higher education become charged with meaning.

Studies indicate that the biggest factor associated with completing a degree in higher education is commitment to personal goals.[8] A choice of major is one of those goals, and selecting the appropriate courses to complete your major is a form of planning that directly promotes your success.

Your career goals can have a significant impact on your choice of major. For an overview of this topic and an immediate chance to put ideas down on paper, see the article "Career planning: Begin the process now" in Chapter Twelve.

Just choose—now. Don't delay the benefits of choosing a major. Even if you're undecided right now, you probably have an idea about what your major will be.

To verify this, do a short experiment. Search your school's catalog for a list of available majors. Read through the list two or three times. Then pretend that you have to choose a major today. Write down the first three ideas that come to mind.

Hold onto this list, which reflects your intuition or "gut feelings," as you perform the more arduous task of researching various majors and careers in detail. Your research might lead to a new choice of major—or it might simply confirm one of the majors on your original list.

Test your trial choice. When you've made a trial choice of major, take on the role of a scientist. Treat your choice as a hypothesis and then design a series of experiments to test it. For example:

- Study your school's list of required courses for this major, looking for a fit with your interests and long-term goals.

- Visit with instructors who teach courses in the major, asking about required course work and career options in the field.

- Discuss your trial choice with an academic advisor or career counselor.

- Enroll in a course related to your possible major.

- Find a volunteer experience, internship, part-time job, or service learning experience related to the major.

- Meet informally with students who have declared the same major.

- Interview someone who works in a field related to the major.

If these experiences confirm your choice of major, celebrate that fact. If they result in choosing a new major, celebrate that outcome as well.

Ask other people.

Key people in your life might have valuable suggestions about your choice of major or career goals. Ask for their ideas and listen with an open mind.

At the same time, distance yourself from any pressure to choose a major or career that fails to interest you. If you make a choice based solely on the expectations of other people, you could end up with a job you don't enjoy—and a major barrier to your life satisfaction.

Learn more about yourself.

Choosing a major can be more effective when you begin from a basis of self-knowledge. As you learn about your passions and potentials, let your choice of a major reflect that ongoing discovery. The exercises and Journal Entries in this book are a starting place. After reviewing what you have written, do any of them again and look for insights that bear on your choice of major.

Another path to self-knowledge includes questionnaires or inventories that are designed to correlate your interests with specific career choices. Your academic advisor or someone at your school's career planning and job placement office can give you more details about these inventories. You might wish to take several of them and meet with an advisor to interpret the results.

Keep in mind that there is no questionnaire, inventory, test, or other tool that can tell you exactly which career to choose or what goals to set for the rest of your life. Likewise, there is no expert who can make these choices for you. Inventories can help you gain self-knowledge, and other people can offer valuable perspectives. However, what you do with that knowledge and advice is entirely up to you. The only expert on your life choices is you.

Invent a major.

When choosing a major, you might not need to limit yourself to those listed in your course catalog. Many schools now have flexible programs that allow for independent study. Through such programs you might be able to combine two existing majors, or invent an entirely new one of your own.

Choose a complementary minor.

You can add flexibility to your academic program by choosing a minor to complement or contrast with your major. The student who wants to be a minister could opt for a minor in English; all of those courses in composition can help in writing sermons. Or the student with a major in psychology might choose a minor in business administration, with the idea of managing a counseling service some day. An effective choice of a minor can expand your skills and career options.

Choose again.

Keep your choice of a major in perspective. There is probably no single "correct" choice. Rather, your unique collection of skills is likely to provide the basis for majoring in several fields.

Odds are that you'll change your major at least once—and that you'll change careers several times during your life. You might even pursue a career that's unrelated to your major.

Students often find that their choice of a major does not bind them to a certain job or career. Many of the majors offered in higher education can help you prepare for several different careers, or for further study in graduate school. One benefit of higher education is mobility—gaining transferable skills that can help you move into a new career field at any time.

Viewing a major as a one-time choice that determines your entire future can raise your stress levels. Instead, look at choosing a major as the start of a continuing path of discovery, intention, and action. ✖

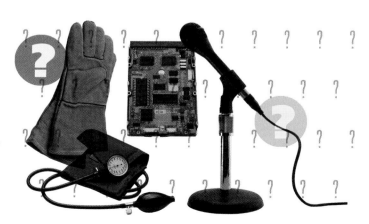

The variety of majors available in higher education is staggering. Below, for example, is a list of 100 majors culled from the catalogs of several colleges.

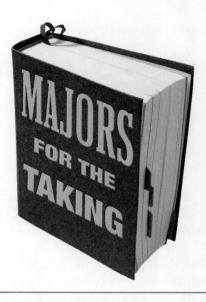

Accounting
Actuarial Science
Advertising
Aerospace Engineering
African American Studies
Agronomy
American Indian Studies
American Studies
Anthropology
Architecture
Art
Astronomy
Biochemistry
Biology
Botany
Broadcast Engineering
Building Construction
Chemical Engineering
Chemistry
Chicano Studies
Child Psychology
Civil Engineering
Clothing Design
Computer Engineering
Construction Management
Corrections Management
Criminal Justice
Dance
Dental Hygiene
Dentistry
Dietetics
Economics
Education
Electrical Engineering
English
Environmental Sciences
Equestrian Studies
Exercise and Sport Science
Family Social Science
Fashion Design and Merchandising
Film Studies
Finance
Fisheries and Wildlife
Food Science
Forestry
Geography
Geological Engineering

Geology
Geophysics
Global Studies
Graphic Arts
History
Hospital Administration
Hospitality and Tourism Services
Human Resource Development
Industrial Psychology
Industrial Technology
Interior Design
International Relations
Jewish Studies
Journalism
Kinesiology
Labor Relations
Latin
Liberal Studies
Library Science
Linguistics
Management Information Systems
Marketing
Mass Communication
Mathematics
Mechanical Engineering
Medical Records Services
Medical Technology
Merchandising
Meteorology
Microbiology
Music
Nursing
Personnel Management
Pharmacy
Philosophy
Physical Therapy
Physics
Physiology
Political Science
Psychology
Public Relations
Religious Studies
Retail Merchandising
Scientific and Technical Communication

Sociology
Speech and Hearing Science
Statistics
Substance Abuse Counseling
Theatre Arts
Theology
Urban Studies
Women's Studies
Zoological Sciences

This is not an exhaustive list. You'll find additional examples in your own school catalog.

Many schools also allow for double majors, individually designed majors, interdepartmental majors, and minors in many areas. You have plenty of options for creating a course of study that matches your skills, interests, and passions.

exercise 20

MAKE A TRIAL CHOICE OF MAJOR

Read the list of majors in the article "Majors for the taking." Expand this list by adding majors listed in your own school's catalog.

Next, take your expanded list and cross out all of the majors that you already know are not right for you. You will probably eliminate well over half the list.

Now scan the remaining majors. Next to the ones that definitely interest you, write "yes." Next to majors that you're willing to consider and are still unsure about, write "maybe."

Focus on your "yes" choices. See if you can narrow them down to three majors. List those here.

_____

_____

_____

Finally, write an asterisk next to the major that interests you most right now. This is your trial choice of major.

Solving math and science problems

Solving problems is a key part of reading textbooks about math and science. You can approach math and science problems the way rock climbers approach mountains. The first part of the process is devoted to preparations you make before you get to the rock. The second part is devoted to techniques used on the rock (or problem) itself.

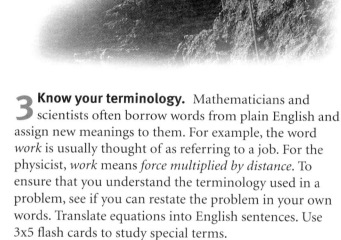

To the uninitiated, rock climbing looks dangerous. For the unprepared, it is. A novice might come to a difficult place in a climb and panic. When a climber freezes, she is truly stuck. Experienced rock climbers figure out strategies in advance for as many situations as possible. With preparation and training, the sport takes on a different cast.

Sometimes students get stuck, panic, and freeze when working on problems. Use the following suggestions to avoid that. Experiment with these techniques as you work your way through textbooks in math and science. You can also use them on tests.

Before you get to the rock

1 Review. Review problems you've solved before. Look over assigned problems and more. Come up with your own variations on these problems. Work with a classmate and make up problems for each other to solve. The more problems you review, the more comfortable you're likely to feel solving new ones. Set clear goals for practice and write Intention Statements about meeting those goals. Find out if practice problems or previous tests are on file in the library.

2 Classify problems by type. Make a list of the different kinds of problems and note the elements of each. After classifying problems by type or category, you can isolate those that you find the most difficult. Practice them more often and get help if you need it.

3 Know your terminology. Mathematicians and scientists often borrow words from plain English and assign new meanings to them. For example, the word *work* is usually thought of as referring to a job. For the physicist, *work* means *force multiplied by distance*. To ensure that you understand the terminology used in a problem, see if you can restate the problem in your own words. Translate equations into English sentences. Use 3x5 flash cards to study special terms.

4 Understand formulas. Some students memorize the problems and answers discussed in class without learning the formulas or general principles behind the problems. This kind of rote learning doesn't allow for the application of principles and formulas to new problems. One approach is to practice a variety of problems to understand ways to arrive at the correct solutions.

You might be asked to memorize some formulas for convenience. If you understand the basic concepts behind these formulas, it is easier to recall them accurately. More importantly, you will probably be able to re-create the formulas if your recall falters. Understanding is preferable to memorization.

5 Learn the metric system. Developed in France during the 1790s, this decimal system of weights and measures is based on the meter as a unit of length and the gram as a unit of mass or weight. Long used universally in science, and now in trade and commerce as well, the metric system forms units by powers of ten. For instance, the U.S. dollar, the world's first decimal currency, consists of 100 cents. Known today as the International System of Units, the metric system is easy to learn—and it's a great example of applying a logical thought process to a problem.

6 Use summary sheets. Groups of terms and formulas can be easier to recall if you list them on a sheet of paper or put them on 3x5 cards. Mind map summary sheets allow you to see how various kinds of problems relate to one another. Creating a structure on which you can hang data helps your recall.

7 Time yourself. Sometimes speed counts. When practicing problems, notice how fast you can work them. This gives you an idea of how much time to allot for different types of problems. Remember that it is always important to practice before taking tests.

8 Use creative visualizations. Before you begin a problem-solving session, take a minute to relax, breathe deeply, and prepare yourself for the task ahead. See yourself solving problems successfully. A calm attitude is important. Visualize preparing for a test, taking the test, and solving the problems with ease.

On the rock

1 Survey the territory thoroughly. Read the problem at least twice before you begin. Read slowly. Be sure you understand what is being asked.

Let go of the expectation that you'll find the solution right away. You might make several attempts at solving the problem before you find a solution that works.

2 Sort the facts. Survey the problem for all of the givens. Determine the principles and relationships involved. Look for what is to be proved or what is to be discovered. Write these down.

3 Set up the problem. Before you begin to compute, determine the strategies you will use to arrive at solutions. When solving equations, carry out the algebra as far as you can before plugging in the actual numbers.

Remember that solving a math or science problem is like putting together a puzzle. You might work around the edges for a while and try many pieces before finding one that fits.

4 Cancel and combine. When you set up a problem logically, you can take shortcuts. For example, if the same term appears in both dividend and divisor, they will cancel each other out.

5 Draw a picture. Or make a diagram. A visual approach to math and science problems might work best for you. Pictures and diagrams help keep the facts straight. They can show relationships more effectively than words.

To keep on track, record your facts in tables. Consider using three columns labeled "What I already know," "What I want to find out," and "What connects the two." This third column is the place to record a formula that can help you solve the problem.

6 Read the problem out loud. Sometimes the sound of your voice will jar loose the solution to a problem. Talk yourself through the solution. Read equations out loud.

7 Play with possibilities. There's usually not one "right" way to solve a problem. Several approaches or formulas might work, though one might be more efficient than another. Be willing to think about the problem from several angles or to proceed by trial and error.

8 Notice when you're in deep water. It's tempting to shy away from difficult problems. Unfortunately, the more you do this, the more difficult the problems become.

Math and science courses present wonderful opportunities to use the First Step technique explained in Chapter One. When you feel that you're beginning to get into trouble, write a precise Discovery Statement about the problem. Then write an Intention Statement about what you will do to solve the problem.

9 Check results. Work problems backwards, then forwards. Start at both ends and work toward the middle to check your work.

Take a minute to make sure you've kept the units of measurement clear. Say that you're calculating the velocity of an object. If you're measuring distance in meters and time in seconds, the final velocity should be in meters per second.

Another way to check your work is to estimate the answer before you compute it. Then ask yourself if your answer to the problem seems likely when compared to the estimate.

10 Savor the solution. Savor the times when you're getting correct answers to most of the problems in the textbook. Relish the times when you feel relaxed and confident as you work, or when the problems seem easy. Then remember these times if you feel math or science anxiety.

Asking questions

Thinking is born of questions. Questions open up options that might otherwise remain unexplored. Questions wake up people and lead them to investigate more closely issues and assumptions that had previously gone unchallenged. Questions promote curiosity, create new distinctions, and multiply possibilities. Besides, teachers love them. One of the best ways to develop your relationship with a teacher is to ask a question.

Asking questions is also a great way to improve relationships with friends and coworkers. When you ask a question, you offer a huge gift to people—an opportunity for them to speak their brilliance and for you to listen to their answers.

Students often say, "I don't know what to ask." If you have ever been at a loss for what to ask, here are some ways to construct powerful questions about any subject you study in school, or about any area of your life that you choose to examine.

Let your pen start moving. Sometimes you can access a deeper level of knowledge by taking out your pen, putting it on a piece of paper, and writing down questions—even before you know what to write. Don't think. Just watch the paper and notice what appears. The results might be surprising.

Ask about what's missing. Another way to invent useful questions is to notice what's missing from your life and then ask how to supply it. For example, if you want to take better notes, you can write, "What's missing is skill in note taking. How can I gain more skill in taking notes?" Or "What's missing is time. How do I create enough time in my day to actually do the things that I say I want to do?"

Pretend to be someone else. Another way to invent questions is first to think of someone you greatly respect. Then pretend you're that person and ask the questions you think she would ask.

Begin a general question, then brainstorm endings. By starting with a general question and then brainstorming a long list of endings, you can invent a question that you've never asked before. For example:

What can I do when ...? What can I do when an instructor calls on me in class and I have no idea what to say? What can I do when a teacher doesn't show up for class on time? What can I do when I feel overwhelmed with assignments?

How can I ...? How can I get just the kind of courses that I want? How can I expand my career options? How can I become much more effective as a student, starting today?

When do I ...? When do I decide on a major? When do I transfer to another school? When do I meet with an instructor to discuss an upcoming term paper?

Ask what else you want to know. Many times you can quickly generate questions by simply asking yourself, "What else do I want to know?" Ask this question immediately after you read a paragraph in a book or listen to someone speak.

Start from the assumption that you are brilliant, and begin asking questions that can help you unlock your brilliance. ✍

When you ask a question, you offer a huge gift to people—an opportunity for them to speak their brilliance and for you to listen to their answers.

PRACTICING CRITICAL THINKING

8

Statement #2:

_____
_____
_____
_____
_____
_____
_____

The art of asking questions is just as important to critical thinking as answering them. One eye-opening way to create questions is to write something you're sure of and simply put a question mark after it. (You might need to rephrase the question for grammatical sense.) The question you create can lead to others.

For example, someone might say, "I would never take a philosophy course." This person can write "I would never take a philosophy course?" That suggests other questions: "In what ways would taking a philosophy course serve my success in school?" "Could taking a philosophy course help me become a better writer?"

In the space below, write three statements that you accept with certainty. Then rephrase each statement as a question.

Question #2:

_____
_____
_____
_____
_____
_____
_____
_____

Statement #1:

_____
_____
_____
_____
_____

Statement #3:

_____
_____
_____
_____
_____

Question #1:

_____
_____
_____
_____
_____
_____

Question #3:

_____
_____
_____
_____
_____
_____

exercise 21

EXPLORE EMOTIONAL REACTIONS

Each of us has certain "hot spots"—issues that trigger strong emotional reactions. For some people, these topics include abortion, gay and lesbian rights, capital punishment, and funding for welfare programs. There are many other examples, varying from person to person. Examine your own hot spots by writing a word or short phrase summarizing each issue. Then, describe what you typically say or do when each issue comes up in conversation.

After you have completed your list, think about what you can do to become a more effective thinker when you encounter one of these issues. For example, you could breathe deeply and count to five before you offer your own point of view. Or you might preface your opinion with an objective statement, such as "There are many valid points of view on this issue. Here's the way I see it, and I'm open to your ideas."

exercise 22

TRANSLATING GOALS INTO ACTION

Goal setting is an exercise in decision making and problem solving. Choose one long-range goal such as a personal project or a social change you'd like to help bring about. Examples include learning to scuba dive, eating a more healthful diet, studying to be an astronaut, improving health care for chronically ill children, inventing energy-saving technology, increasing the effectiveness of American schools, and becoming a better parent. List your goal here.

_____

Next, ask yourself: "What specific actions are needed in the short term to meet my long-range goal?" List those actions, focusing on those you could complete in less than one hour or could start in the next 24 hours.

_____
_____
_____
_____

journal entry 21

Discovery/Intention Statement

Reflect for a moment on your experience with Exercise #20: "Make a trial choice of major." If you had already chosen a major, did it confirm that choice? Did you uncover any new or surprising possibilities for declaring a major?

I discovered that I . . .

_____
_____
_____
_____

Now consider the major that is your current top choice. Think of publications you expect to find, resources you plan to investigate, and people you intend to consult in order to gather more information about this major.

I intend to . . .

_____
_____
_____
_____

Plan to repeat this Journal Entry and the preceding exercise several times. You might find yourself researching several majors and changing your mind. That's fine. The aim is to start thinking about your major now.

power process

Find a bigger problem

Most of the time we view problems as barriers. They are a source of inconvenience and annoyance. They get in our way and prevent us from having happy and productive lives. When we see problems in this way, our goal becomes to eliminate problems.

This point of view might be flawed. For one thing, it is impossible to live a life without problems. Besides, they serve a purpose. They are opportunities to participate in life. Problems stimulate us and pull us forward.

Seen from this perspective, the goal becomes not to eliminate problems, but to find problems that are worthy of us. Worthy problems are those that draw on our talents, move us toward our purpose, and increase our skills. The challenge is to tackle those problems that provide the greatest benefits for others and ourselves. Viewed in this way, problems give meaning to our lives.

Problems fill the available space

Problems seem to follow the same law of physics that gases do: They expand to fill whatever space is available. If your only problem is to write a follow-up letter to a job interview, you can spend the entire day thinking about what you're going to say, writing the letter, finding a stamp, going to the post office—and then thinking about all of the things you forgot to say. If, on that same day, you also need to go food shopping, the problem of the letter shrinks to make room for a trip to the grocery store. If you want to buy a car, too, it's amazing how quickly and easily the letter and the grocery shopping tasks are finished. One way to handle little problems is to find bigger ones. Remember that the smaller problems still need to be solved. The goal is to do it with less time and energy.

Bigger problems are plentiful

Bigger problems are not in short supply. Consider world hunger. Every minute of every day, people die because they don't have enough to eat. Also consider nuclear war, which threatens to end life on the planet. Child abuse, environmental pollution, terrorism, human rights violations, drug abuse, street crime, energy shortages, poverty, and wars throughout the world await your attention and involvement. You can make a contribution.

Worthy problems are those that draw on our talents, move us toward our purpose, and increase our skills.

can experience efficiency and enthusiasm as natural parts of our daily routines. Energy and vitality can accompany most of our activities.

When we take on a bigger problem, we play full out. We do justice to our potentials. We then love what we do and do what we love. We're awake, alert, and engaged. Playing full out means living our lives as if our lives depended on it.

You can make a difference

Perhaps a little voice in your mind is saying, "That's crazy. I can't do anything about global problems" or "Everyone knows that hunger has always been around and always will be, and there is nothing anyone can do about it." These thoughts might prevent you from taking on bigger problems.

Realize that you *can* make a difference. Your thoughts and actions can change the quality of life on the planet.

This is your life. It's your school, your city, your country, and your world. Own it. Inhabit it. Treat it with the same care that you would a prized possession.

One way to find problems that are worthy of your talents and energies is to take on bigger ones. Take responsibility for problems that are bigger than you are sure you can handle. Then notice how your other problems dwindle in importance—or even vanish. 🗷

Playing full out means living our lives as if our lives depended on it.

Play full out

Considering bigger problems does not have to be depressing. In fact, it can be energizing—a reason for getting up in the morning. Taking on a huge project can provide a means to channel your passion and purpose.

Some people spend vast amounts of time in activities they consider boring: their jobs, their hobbies, their relationships. They find themselves going through the motions, doing the same walk-on part day after day without passion or intensity. American author Henry David Thoreau described this kind of existence as "lives of quiet desperation."

Playing full out suggests another possibility: We can spend much of our time fully focused and involved. We

exercise 23

FIX-THE-WORLD BRAINSTORM

This exercise works well with four to six people. Pick a major world problem such as hunger, nuclear proliferation, poverty, terrorism, overpopulation, or pollution. Then conduct a 10-minute brainstorm about the steps an individual could take to contribute to solving the problem.

Use the brainstorming techniques explained earlier in this chapter. Remember not to evaluate or judge the solutions during the process. The purpose of a brainstorm is to generate a flow of ideas and record them all.

After the brainstorming session, discuss the process and the solutions that it generated. Did you feel any energy from the group? Was a long list of ideas generated? Are several of them worth pursuing?

put it to work

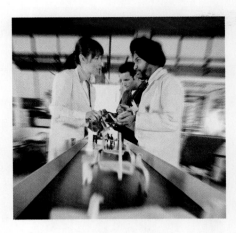

Strategies for creative and critical thinking can assist you in developing new products and services in the workplace. Some examples follow.

State the obvious and go for the opposite. One way to generate a burst of creativity followed by critical thinking is to take an idea that seems obvious and state its opposite. Then see if you can find evidence to support the opposite idea.

This principle has been used with great success in business. An example comes from Jan Carlzon, former president of the Scandinavian Airline SAS. Carlzon questioned an "obvious" truth—that upper management in any company should make most of the decisions. He went for the opposite idea and allowed rank-and-file employees to make daily decisions that directly affected customers. If a customer got bumped from a flight, an SAS counter clerk could decide on the spot whether to pay the customer's hotel bill for the night or find the customer an alternative flight on a competitor's airline. After implementing this policy, SAS's business grew dramatically.[9]

Find a smaller problem. After reading the Power Process: "Find a bigger problem," consider the merits of the opposite strategy. For example, you might feel overwhelmed with managing a complex, year-long project at work. One response is to give up—to quit. Another is to resign yourself to drudgery and dive into the project with a deep sigh.

"Find a smaller problem" offers an alternative: Just divide a huge project into many small jobs. Rather than worry about the project as a whole, turn your full attention to a small, specific task until it is complete. Do the same with the next small task, and the next. Just handle the details, one after another, until the project is finished.

The role of planning is critical. "Find a smaller problem" is not a suggestion to fill your days with busywork. When you plan effectively, the small jobs you do are critical to the success of the bigger project.

Experiment with the decreasing options technique. The decreasing options technique (DOT) is a

decision-making strategy. It allows you to rank a large pool of ideas created by groups of people in meetings. Before you put DOT in action, go to an office supply store and get a package of several hundred adhesive dots—small stickers that can be attached to a sheet of paper. Then follow these steps:

- *Ask meeting participants to brainstorm solutions to a problem*. Permit all ideas to be expressed. Don't edit them yet. To save time, ask participants to submit ideas before the meeting takes place. That way you can summarize and post ideas ahead of time.

- *Summarize each idea in a single word or phrase on a large sheet of paper*. Write letters that are big enough to be seen across the meeting room. Place only one idea on each sheet of paper.

- *Post the sheets where all meeting participants can see them.*

- *Do an initial review of the ideas*. Ask participants if they can eliminate some ideas as obviously unworkable. Also group similar ideas together and eliminate duplications.

- *"Dot" ideas*. Give each participant a handful of sticker dots. Then ask participants to go around the room and place an adhesive dot next to the ideas that they consider most important.

- *Discuss the most important ideas*. Stand back and review the ideas. The high-priority concerns of the group will stand out clearly as the sheets with the most dots. Now you can bring these important ideas to the discussion table.

You can also use the DOT method online with bulletin boards or "virtual" meetings. Participants can use e-mail or networking software to post their ideas and manipulate computer graphics that look like sticker dots. ⊠

Name _____ Date _____/_____/_____

1. List four questions that can guide you on your path to becoming a critical thinker.

2. Explain what is meant in this chapter by *aha*!

3. Define *serendipity* and give an example.

4. List and briefly describe three ways to create ideas.

5. Most students choose their major during their first year in higher education. True or False? Explain your answer.

6. According to the text, *critical thinking* and *thorough thinking* are two distinct and different activities. True or False? Explain your answer.

7. Define *all-or-nothing thinking* and give an example.

8. Explain the suggestion "watch for hot spots" and describe its connection to critical thinking.

9. Name at least one fallacy involved in this statement: "Everyone who's ever visited this school has agreed that it's the best in the state."

10. List the four suggested steps for problem solving and give an example of each step.

learning styles application

The questions below will "cycle" you through four styles, or modes, of learning as explained in the article "Learning styles: Discovering how you learn" in Chapter One. Each question will help you explore a different mode. You can answer the questions in any order.

what if *Explain how you would modify a technique from this chapter to make it a more effective tool for decision making—or describe an original technique of your own.*

why *Think of a major decision you face right now and put it into the form of a question. Possible examples are: "What major will I declare?" or "What is my top priority goal for this year?"*

how *Briefly describe how you will use a technique from this chapter to make a major decision.*

what *List a technique from this chapter that could help you make a major decision you face right now (such as the decision you list under Why?).*

master student

profile

PAUL FARMER

a Harvard professor, renowned infectious-disease specialist, and the recipient of a MacArthur Foundation "genius" award. In medical school, found his life's calling—to diagnose and cure infectious diseases and to bring the lifesaving tools of modern medicine to those who need them most.

Dr. Farmer does not have anywhere near the name recognition of, say, Albert Schweitzer or Mother Teresa. But if any one person can be given credit for transforming the medical establishment's thinking about health care for the destitute, it is Paul Farmer.

Through the charity that Dr. Farmer helped found, Partners in Health, the health system, Zanmi Lasante (Creole for Partners in Health), not only cares for hundreds of thousands of peasants, but has also built schools and sanitation and water systems, vaccinated all the children, reduced the rate of H.I.V. transmission from mothers to babies, and successfully treated patients suffering from complicated drug-resistant strains of tuberculosis.

How has he done it? Dr. Farmer simply refuses to accept any excuse— no matter how reasonable—for not treating the poor. No doctors? We'll train them. High drug prices? We'll get the pharmaceutical companies to lower them. Misguided policies? We'll change them.

Working locally and globally simultaneously means pushing himself to extremes. He has a punishing schedule and rarely sees his Haitian-born wife, Didi, and daughter.

"The problem is, if I don't work this hard, someone will die who doesn't have to," he confesses in a rare moment of frustration. Dr. Farmer [was] pushed to branch out from Haiti after his colleague and kindred spirit, Jim Yong Kim, discover[ed] puzzling cases of lethal and drug-resistant strains of TB in the slums of Peru. Peru had an excellent TB control program. But in one of the horribly twisted ironies that tend to afflict the poor, the very medicine that was saving lives was also—through repeated treatments—breeding mutant strains resistant to conventional drugs.

Getting the medical establishment in Peru and at W.H.O., [World Health Organization] a United Nations agency, to change the prescribed regimen for TB drugs was formidable. Health experts dismissed the idea that complex diseases like drug-resistant TB or AIDS could even be treated in poor areas. In the end, Dr. Farmer and Dr. Kim prevailed, helping to lower the price of drugs and changing W.H.O.'s treatment guidelines. What's more, they had challenged the philosophy and the accuracy of cost-effectiveness analysis that ruled public health-care decisions at the highest level.

Near the end of [*Mountains Beyond Mountains*, author Tracy] Kidder details the wrenching efforts of some Partners in Health workers to help a 12-year-old Haitian boy suffering from a rare cancer. They hire a medevac helicopter for nearly $19,000 to bring the deathly ill boy to Boston for treatment. When he arrives the doctors learn the cancer has infiltrated his wasted body. He [died] three weeks later. To some it was an exercise in futility and excessive heroics. After all, how many other children could have been fed with that money?

But as Mr. Kidder explains, that kind of cost-benefit analysis is what Dr. Farmer has been fighting his whole life. If it were you, if it were your child and there was a chance to save him, would you think it was too much? Why, Dr. Farmer wants to know, don't people question why a young American doctor earns "five times what it cost to try to save a boy's life?" ⊠

For more biographical information on Paul Farmer, visit the Master Student Hall of Fame on the *Becoming a Master Student* Web site at

masterstudent.college.hmco.com

8

Communicating

Listening means trying to see the problem the way the speaker sees it—which means not sympathy, which is feeling for him, but empathy, which is feeling with him.

S. I. HAYAKAWA

You have two ears and one mouth. Remember to use them in more or less that proportion.

PAULA BERN

why

this chapter matters . . .

Your communication abilities—
    including your skills at listening,
    speaking, and writing—are as
    important to your success as your
    technical skills.

what

is included . . .

how

you can use this chapter . . .

Listen, speak, and write more
    effectively.
Prevent and resolve conflict with other
    people.
Experience more satisfying
    relationships in all areas of your life.

As you read, ask yourself

What if . . .

I could use my capacity to make and
    keep agreements as a tool for
    creating my future?

Communicating creates our world

Certain things are real for us because we can see them, touch them, hear them, smell them, or taste them. Books, pencils, tables, chairs, and food all are real in this sense. They enter our world in a straightforward, uncomplicated way.

Many other aspects of our lives, however, do not have this kind of reality. None of us can point to a *purpose*, for example. Nor would a purpose step up and introduce itself or buy us lunch. The same is true about other abstract concepts, such as *quality, intelligence, love, trust, human rights*, or *student success*.

Concepts such as these shape our experience of life. Yet they don't really exist until we talk about them. These concepts come alive for us only to the degree that we define and discuss them. Communicating brings our world into being.

According to communication theorist Lee Thayer, there are two basic life processes. One is acquiring and processing energy. The other is acquiring and processing information, also known as communication.[1] From this point of view, communicating is just as fundamental to life as eating.

Through communication, we take raw impressions and organize them into meaningful patterns. With our senses, we perceive sights, sounds, and other sensations. However, none of our sense organs is capable of perceiving *meaning*. We create meaning by finding patterns in our sensations and communicating them.

In our daily contact with other people and mass media, we are exposed to hundreds of messages. Yet the obstacles to receiving those messages accurately are numerous. For one thing, only a small percentage of communication is verbal. We also send messages with our bodies and with the tone of our voice. Throw in a few other factors, such as a hot room or background noise, and it's a wonder we communicate at all.

Another problem is that the message sent is often not the message received. Even the simplest message can get muddled. For some, the word *chair* conjures up the image of an overstuffed rocking recliner. Others visualize a metal folding chair. And some people think of the person who "chairs" a meeting. If things like this can be misunderstood, it's easy to see how complex ideas can wreak havoc.

Written communication adds a whole other set of variables. When you speak, you supplement the meaning of your words with the power of body language and voice inflection. When you write, those nonverbal elements are absent. Instead, you depend on your skills at word choice, sentence construction, and punctuation to get your message across. The choices that you make in these areas can serve as an aid—or a hindrance—to communication. ⊠

journal entry 22

Discovery/Intention Statement

Think of a time when you experienced an emotionally charged conflict with another person. Were you able to resolve this dispute effectively? If so, list below the strategies you used. If not, describe what you could have done differently.

I discovered that I . . .

_____

_____

Now scan this chapter for ideas that can help you get your feelings across more skillfully in similar situations. List at least four ideas here, along with the page numbers where you can read more about them.

Strategy	*Page number*

Describe an upcoming situation in which you intend to apply these techniques. If possible, choose a situation that will occur within the next week.

I intend to . . .

_____

_____

_____

_____

The communication loop

Communication is often garbled when we try to send and receive messages at the same time.

One effective way to improve your ability to communicate is to be aware of when you are the receiver and when you are the sender. If you are receiving (listening), just receive. Avoid switching into the sending (talking) mode. When you are sending, stick with it until you are finished.

If the other person is trying to send a message when you want to be the sender, you have at least three choices: Stop sending and be the receiver, stop sending and leave, or ask the other person to stop sending so that you can send. It is ineffective to try to send and receive at the same time.

This becomes clear when we look at what happens in a conversation. When we talk, we put thoughts into words. Words are a code for what we experience. This is called *encoding*. The person who receives the message takes our words and translates them into his own experience. This is called *decoding*.

A conversation between two people is like a communication between two telegraph operators. One encodes a message and sends it over the wire. The operator at the other end receives the coded signal, decodes it, evaluates it, and sends back another coded message. The first operator decodes this message and sends another. The cycle continues. The messages look like this:

1 ..—..—.-.-   3 —.—..— OPERATOR 1

2 —.-..-..   4 -..- —...-. OPERATOR 2

This encoding-decoding loop is most effective when we continually switch roles. One minute we send, the next we receive. If both operators send at the same time, neither knows what the other one sent. Neither can reply. Communication works best when each of us has plenty of time to receive what others send—that is, to *listen*—and the opportunity to send a complete message when it's our turn.

THE COMMUNICATION LOOP
Listening

You observe a person in a conversation who is not talking. Is he listening? Maybe. Maybe not. He might be preparing his response or daydreaming.

Listening is not easy. Doing it effectively requires concentration and energy.

It's worth it. Listening well promotes success in school: more powerful notes, more productive study groups, and better relationships with students and instructors. A skilled listener is appreciated by friends, family, and business associates. The best salespeople and managers are the best listeners. People love a good listener. Through skilled listening, you gain more than respect. You gain insight into other people. You learn about the world and about yourself.

To be a good listener, choose to listen. Once you've made this choice, you can use the following techniques to be a more effective listener. These ideas are especially useful in times of high emotional tension.

Through skilled listening, you gain more than respect. You gain insight into other people. You learn about the world and about yourself.

Nonverbal listening

Much of listening is nonverbal. Here are five guidelines for effective nonverbal listening.

Be quiet. Silence is more than staying quiet while someone is speaking. Allowing several seconds to pass before you begin to talk gives the speaker time to catch his breath and gather his thoughts. He might want to continue. Someone who talks nonstop might fear he will lose the floor if he pauses.

If the message being sent is complete, this short break gives you time to form your response and helps you avoid the biggest barrier to listening—listening with your answer running. If you make up a response before the person is finished, you might miss the end of the message—which is often the main point.

In some circumstances, pausing for several seconds might be inappropriate. Ignore this suggestion completely when someone asks in a panic where to find the nearest phone to call the fire department.

Maintain eye contact. Look at the other person while he speaks. Doing so demonstrates your attentiveness and helps keep your mind from wandering. Your eyes also let you "listen" to body language and behavior. When some of us avoid eye contact, not only do we fail to see—we fail to listen.

This idea is not an absolute. While maintaining eye contact is important in some cultures, people from other cultures are uncomfortable with sustained eye contact. Some individuals learn primarily by hearing; they can listen more effectively by turning off the visual input once in a while. Keep in mind the differences among people.

Display openness. You can communicate openness by means of your facial expression and body position. Uncross your arms and legs. Sit up straight. Face the other person and remove any physical barriers between you, such as a pile of books.

Listen without response. This doesn't mean that you should never respond. It means that you should wait for an appropriate moment to respond. When listening to another person, we often interrupt with our own stories, opinions, suggestions, and comments, as in the following dialogue:

"Oh, I'm so excited. I just found out that I've been nominated to be in *Who's Who in American Musicians*."

"Yeah, that's neat. My Uncle Elmer got into *Who's Who in American Veterinarians*. He sure has an interesting job. One time I went along when he was treating a cow."

Watch your nonverbal responses, too. A look of "Good grief!" from you can deter the other person from finishing his message.

Send acknowledgments. It is important to let the speaker know periodically that you are still there. Words and nonverbal gestures of acknowledgment convey to the speaker that you are interested and that you are receiving his message. These include "Umhum," "OK," "Yes," and head nods.

These acknowledgments do not imply your agreement. When people tell you what they don't like about you, your head nod doesn't mean that you agree. It just indicates that you are listening.

Verbal listening

Sometimes speaking promotes listening. Below are suggestions for effective verbal listening.

Feed back meaning. Paraphrase the communication. This does not mean parroting what another person says. Instead, briefly summarize. Feed back what you see as the essence of that person's message: "Let me see if I understood what you said . . ." or "What I'm hearing you say is. . . ." (Psychotherapist Carl Rogers referred to this technique as *reflection*.)[2] Often, the other person will say, "No, that's not what I meant. What I said was. . . ."

There will be no doubt when you get it right. The sender will say, "Yeah, that's it," and either continue with another message or stop sending when he knows you understand.

If you don't understand the message, be persistent. Be concise. This is not a time to stop the other person by talking on and on about what you think you heard.

Listen beyond words. Be aware of nonverbal messages and behavior. You might point out that the speaker's body language seems to be the exact opposite of his words. For example: "I noticed you said you are excited, but you look bored."

Keep in mind that the same nonverbal behavior can have different meanings, depending on the listener's cultural background. Someone who looks bored might simply be listening in a different way.

The idea is to listen not only to the words but also to the emotion behind the words. Sometimes that emotional message is more important than the verbal content.

Take care of yourself. People seek good listeners, and there are times when you don't want to listen. You might be distracted with your own concerns. Be honest. Don't pretend to listen. You can say, "What you're telling me is important, and I'm pressed for time right now. Can we set aside another time to talk about this?" It's OK not to listen.

Listen for requests and intentions. "This class is a waste of my time." "Our instructor talks too fast." An effective way to listen to such complaints is to look for the request hidden in them.

"This class is a waste of my time" can be heard as "Please tell me what I'll gain if I participate actively in class." "The instructor talks too fast" might be asking "What strategies can I use to take notes when the instructor covers material rapidly?" We can even

transform complaints into intentions. Take this complaint: "The parking lot by the dorms is so dark at night that I'm afraid to go to my car." This complaint can result in having a light installed in the parking lot.

Viewing complaints as requests gives us more choices. Rather than responding with defensiveness ("What does he know anyway?"), resignation ("It's always been this way and always will be"), or indifference ("It's not my job"), we can decide whether to grant the request (do what will alleviate the other's difficulty) or help the person translate his own complaint into an action plan.

THE COMMUNICATION LOOP
Sending

We have been talking with people for years, and we usually manage to get our messages across. There are times, though, when we don't. Often, these times are emotionally charged.

Sometimes we feel wonderful or rotten or sad or scared, and we want to express it. Emotions can get in the way of the message. Described below are four techniques for delivering a message through tears, laughter, fist pounding, or hugging. They are: Replace "You" messages with "I" messages, avoid questions that aren't really questions, notice nonverbal messages, and notice barriers to communication.

Replace "You" messages with "I" messages. It can be difficult to disagree with someone without his becoming angry or your becoming upset. When conflict occurs, we often make statements about the other person, or "You" messages:

"You are rude."
"You make me mad."
"You must be crazy."
"You don't love me anymore."

This kind of communication results in defensiveness. The responses might be:

"I am not rude."
"I don't care."

"No, *you* are crazy."
"No, *you* don't love *me*!"

"You" messages are hard to listen to. They label, judge, blame, and assume things that might or might not be true. They demand rebuttal. Even praise can sometimes be an ineffective "You" message. "You" messages don't work.

When communication is emotionally charged, psychologist Thomas Gordon suggests that you consider limiting your statements to descriptions about yourself.[3] Replace "You" messages with "I" messages.

> "You are rude" might become
>   "I feel upset."
> "You make me mad" could be
>   "I feel angry."
> "You must be crazy" can be
>   "I don't understand."
> "You don't love me anymore"
>   could become "I'm afraid we're
>   drifting apart."

Suppose a friend asks you to pick him up at the airport. You drive 20 miles and wait for the plane. No friend. You decide your friend missed his plane, so you wait three hours for the next flight. No friend. Perplexed and worried, you drive home. The next day, you see your friend downtown.

Most nonverbal behavior is unconscious. We can learn to be aware of it and choose our nonverbal messages.

"What happened?" you ask.
"Oh, I caught an earlier flight."
"You are a rude person," you reply.

Look for the facts, the observable behavior. Everyone will agree that your friend asked you to pick him up, that he did take an earlier flight, and that you did not receive a call from him. But the idea that he is rude is not a fact—it's a judgment.

He might go on to say, "I called your home and no one answered. My mom had a stroke and was rushed to Valley View. I caught the earliest flight I could get." Your judgment no longer fits.

When you saw your friend, you might have said, "I waited and waited at the airport. I was worried about you. I didn't get a call. I feel angry and hurt. I don't want to waste my time. Next time, you can call me when your flight arrives, and I'll be happy to pick you up."

"I" messages don't judge, blame, criticize, or insult. They don't invite the other person to counterattack with more of the same. "I" messages are also more accurate. They report our own thoughts and feelings.

At first, "I" messages might feel uncomfortable or seem forced. That's OK. Use the five ways to say "I" explained above.

→ Five ways to say "I"

An "I" message can include any or all of the following five elements. Be careful when including the last two, since they can contain hidden judgments or threats.

Observations. Describe the facts—the indisputable, observable realities. Talk about what you—or anyone else—can see, hear, smell, taste, or touch. Avoid judgments, interpretations, or opinions. Instead of saying, "You're a slob," say, "Last night's lasagna pan was still on the stove this morning."

Feelings. Describe your own feelings. It is easier to listen to "I feel frustrated" than to "You never help me." Stating how you feel about another's actions can be valuable feedback for that person.

Wants. You are far more likely to get what you want if you say what you want. If someone doesn't know what you

want, he doesn't have a chance to help you get it. Ask clearly. Avoid demanding or using the word *need*. Most people like to feel helpful, not obligated. Instead of saying, "Do the dishes when it's your turn, or else!" say, "I want to divide the housework fairly."

Thoughts. Communicate your thoughts, and use caution. Beginning your statement with the word "I" doesn't make it an "I" message. "I think you are a slob" is a "You" judgment in disguise. Instead, say, "I'd have more time to study if I didn't have to clean up so often."

Intentions. The last part of an "I" message is a statement about what you intend to do. Have a plan that doesn't depend on the other person. For example, instead of "From now on we're going to split the dishwashing evenly," you could say, "I intend to do my share of the housework and leave the rest."

Remember that questions are not always questions. You've heard these "questions" before. A parent asks, "Don't you want to look nice?" Translation: "I wish you'd cut your hair, lose the blue jeans, and put on a tie." Or how about this question from a spouse: "Honey, wouldn't you love to go to an exciting hockey game tonight?" Translation: "I've already bought tickets."

We use questions that aren't questions to sneak our opinions and requests into conversations. "Doesn't it upset you?" means "It upsets me," and "Shouldn't we hang the picture over here?" means "I want to hang the picture over here."

Communication improves when we say, "I'm upset" and "Let's hang the picture over here."

Choose nonverbal messages. How you say something can be more important than what you say. Your tone of

doesn't mean being insensitive to the impact that our messages have on others. Tact is a virtue; letting fear prevent communication is not.

Assumptions can also be used as excuses for not sending messages. "He already knows this," we tell ourselves.

Predictions of failure can be barriers to sending, too. "He won't listen," we assure ourselves. That statement might be inaccurate. Perhaps the other person senses that we're angry and listens in a guarded way. Or perhaps he is listening and sending nonverbal messages we don't understand.

Or we might predict, "He'll never do anything about it, even if I tell him." Again, making assumptions can defeat your message before you send it.

It's easy to make excuses for not communicating. If you have fear or some other concern about sending a

voice and gestures add up to a silent message that you send. This message can support, modify, or contradict your words. Your posture, the way you dress, how often you shower, and even the poster hanging on your wall can negate your words before you say them. Most nonverbal behavior is unconscious. We can learn to be aware of it and choose our nonverbal messages. The key is to be clear about our intention and purpose. When we know what we want to say and are committed to getting it across, our inflections, gestures, and words work together and send a unified message.

Notice barriers to sending messages. Sometimes fear stops us from sending messages. We are afraid of other people's reactions, sometimes justifiably. Being truthful

message, be aware of it. Don't expect the concern to go away. Realize that you can communicate even with your concerns. You can choose to make them a part of the message: "I am going to tell you how I feel, and I'm afraid that you will think it's stupid."

Talking to someone when you don't want to could be a matter of educational survival. A short talk with an advisor, a teacher, a friend, or a family member might solve a problem that could jeopardize your education. ◩

journal entry 23

Discovery/Intention Statement

Think about one of your relationships for a few minutes. It can involve a parent, sibling, spouse, child, friend, hairdresser, or anyone else. In the space below, write down some things that are not working in the relationship. What bugs you? What do you find irritating or unsatisfying?

I discovered that . . .

_____

_____

_____

_____

_____

_____

_____

Now think for a moment about what you want from this relationship. More attention? Less nagging? More openness, trust, financial security, or freedom? Choose a suggestion from this chapter and describe how you could use it to make the relationship work.

I intend to . . .

_____

_____

_____

_____

_____

_____

_____

_____

_____

The fine art of conflict management

Conflict management is one of the most practical skills you'll ever learn. Following are several strategies that can help. To bring these ideas to life, think of ways to apply them to a current conflict in your life.

State the problem openly. Using "I" messages as explained earlier in this chapter, state the problem. Tell people what you observe, feel, think, want, and intend to do. Allow the other person in a particular conflict to do the same. You might have different perceptions. This is the time to define the conflict clearly. It's hard to fix something unless everyone agrees on what's broken.

We can move toward agreement more quickly by laying all of our cards on the table. People are often reluctant to communicate all of their concerns. This very reluctance holds some problems in place.

Focus on solutions. After stating the problem, dream up as many solutions as you can. Be outrageous. Don't hold back. Quantity, not quality, is the key. If you get stuck, restate the problem and continue brainstorming.

Next, evaluate the solutions you brainstormed. Discard the unacceptable ones. Talk about which solutions will work and how difficult they will be to implement. You might hit upon a totally new solution.

Choose one solution that is most acceptable to everyone involved and implement it. Agree on who is going to do what by when. Then keep your agreements.

Finally, evaluate the effectiveness of your solution. If it works, pat yourselves on the back. If not, make changes or implement a new solution.

Understand all points of view. If you want to defuse tension or defensiveness, set aside your opinions for a moment. Take the time to understand the other points of view. Sum up those viewpoints in words that the other parties can accept. When people feel that they've been heard, they're often more willing to listen.

Step back from the conflict. Instead of trading personal attacks during a conflict, step back. Defuse the situation by approaching it in a neutral way. Define the conflict as a problem to be solved, not as a contest to be won. Detach. Let go of being "right" and aim for being effective instead.

Let it get worse before it gets better. Sometimes a conflict needs to escalate so that everyone is truly aware of it. Many of us are reluctant to allow this to happen. That's understandable—and it can prevent us from getting to the bottom of the problem.

Often it is not necessary for a conflict to get worse. Yet being willing to allow this possibility gives us freedom to clear the air.

Speak your mind. When we're locked in combat with someone, it's tempting to hold back—to say only a fraction of what we're thinking or feeling. This can be one more way to keep the conflict alive. An alternative is to "empty our buckets"—to let the words and the feelings flow spontaneously. In this case, we don't worry about making a perfect "I" statement. We just say the first things that come to mind. This is one way to get all of our cards on the table.

Commit to the relationship. The thorniest conflicts usually arise between people who genuinely care for each other. We're less likely to be in conflict when the relationship doesn't matter to us.

Begin by affirming your commitment to the other person: "I care about you, and I want this relationship to last. So I'm willing to do whatever it takes to resolve this problem." Also ask the other person for a similar commitment.

You might be unsure of your commitment to the relationship. If so, postpone any further communication for now. Take some time to be alone and consider the value of this relationship to you. People engaged in conflict often stop seeing each other. Many times we increase the odds of solving the problem when we stay in a relationship.

Back up to common ground. Conflict heightens the differences between people. When this happens, it's easy to forget how much we still agree with each other.

As a first step in managing conflict, back up to common ground. List all of the points on which you are *not* in conflict: "I know that we disagree about how much to spend on a new car, but we do agree that the old one needs to be replaced." Often, such comments put the problem in perspective and pave the way for a solution.

Listen for the request behind the complaint. People complain to us when they want something different from us. And when we take the complaint at face value, we might feel blamed or put down. Go deeper. Listen for the request that's behind the complaint. If a friend complains that you always interrupt him, take it as a request: "Please let me finish what I'm saying before you speak." It's easier to respond to the request than to the accusation or the anger.

Slow down the communication. In times of great conflict, people often talk all at once. Words fly like speeding bullets and no one is really listening. Such discussions generate a lot of heat and little light. Chances for resolving the conflict take a nosedive.

When this happens, choose either to listen or to talk—not both at the same time. Just send your message. Or just receive the other person's message. Usually, this slows down the pace, clears the smoke, and allows everyone to become more levelheaded.

To slow down the communication even more, take a break. Depending upon the level of conflict, that might mean anything from a few minutes to a few days.

A related suggestion is to do something non-threatening together. Share an activity with others that's not a source of conflict.

Be a complete listener. In times of conflict, we often say one thing and mean another. So before responding to what the other person says, use active listening. Check to see if you have correctly received that person's message: "What I'm hearing you say is. . . . Did I get it correctly?"

Listening completely can also include asking for more discussion. People will often stop short of their true

message. Encourage them to continue by asking for it: "Anything else that you want to say about that? Is something more on your mind right now?"

Get to the point—then elaborate. Sometimes people in conflict shore up their argument by painstakingly laying the groundwork for their main point. This technique works well for actors on a stage who want to add drama to a scene. It doesn't work so well for the rest of us, especially when we're in conflict.

Making your listener wait in suspense while you build your case can lead to problems. During the interval, the listener might become impatient and more irritable. Or he could imagine something far worse than what you actually intend to say. As an alternative, get to your point right away. When that's done, there is usually the opportunity to provide supporting details.

Recap your message. As we send messages in times of conflict, we might talk for a long time. Sometimes people under emotional stress can't take it all in. And even if they get our whole message, they might not understand which of our points is most important.

You can follow that homespun advice given to professional speakers: First, tell 'em what you're going to say. Then tell 'em. Then tell 'em what you've told 'em.

Before you yield the floor to someone else, review your main messages and repeat your key requests.

Use a mediator. Even an untrained mediator—someone who's not a party to the conflict—can do much to decrease tension. Mediators can help all those involved get their points of view across. In this case, the mediator's role is not to give advice but to keep the discussion on track and moving toward a solution.

Allow for cultural differences. People respond to conflict in different ways, depending on their cultural background. Some stand close, speak loudly, and make direct eye contact. Other people avert their eyes, mute their voices, and increase physical distance.

Even small gestures carry different meanings across cultures. For example, people in the United States sometimes make an "OK" sign by curling the thumb and index finger of one hand into a circular shape. In other countries, this gesture is considered obscene.

When it seems to you that other people are sidestepping or escalating a conflict, consider whether your reaction is based on cultural bias.

Apologize or ask for forgiveness. Conflict often arises from our own errors. We usually don't do these things on purpose. They're just mistakes.

Others might move quickly to end the conflict when

we acknowledge this fact, apologize, and ask for forgiveness. This is "spending face"—an alternative to the age-old habit of "saving face." We can simply admit that we are less than perfect by owning up to our mistakes.

Write a letter and send it. What can be difficult to say to another person face to face might be effectively communicated in writing. When people in conflict write letters to each other, they automatically apply many of the suggestions in this article. Letter writing is a way to slow down the communication and ensure that only one person at a time is sending a message.

There is a drawback: It's possible for people to misunderstand what you say in a letter. To avoid further problems, make clear what you are *not* saying: "I am saying that I want to be alone for a few days. I am *not* saying that I want you to stay away forever." Saying what you are *not* saying is often useful in face-to-face communication as well. Before you send your letter, put yourself in the shoes of the person who will receive it. Imagine how your comments could be misinterpreted. Then rewrite your letter, correcting any wording that is open to misinterpretation.

Write a letter and don't send it. Sometimes we feel compelled to blame other people or speak to them angrily. This is likely to fan the flames instead of resolve the conflict.

If this happens, consider a way to get the problem off your chest and the upset out of your system without beating up the other person:

> *We can peacefully coexist with other people—and respect them—even though we don't agree on fundamental issues.*

Write the nastiest, meanest letter you can imagine. Let all of your frustration, anger, and venom flow onto the page. Be as mean and blaming as possible. When your pen has cooled off, see if there is anything else you want to add.

Then take the letter and destroy it. Your writing has served its purpose. Chances are that you've calmed down and are ready to engage in skillful conflict management.

Note: If you're composing the letter while using e-mail software, do not insert the complete address of the recipient. This will prevent you from accidentally sending the letter.

Permit the emotion. Crying is OK. Being upset is all right. Feeling angry is often appropriate. Allowing other people to see the strength of our feelings can go a long way toward clearing up the conflict. Emotion is part of life and an important part of any communication.

Just allow the full range of your feelings. Often what's on the far side of anger is love. When we clear out the resentment and hostility, we might find genuine compassion in its place.

Tape the disagreement. This is an option for the brave—those who really want feedback on their conflict management skills. With the agreement of all parties involved, set up a camera and record your conversation. Later, play back the recording and review your side of the conversation. Look for any ways that you perpetuated the upset. Spot anything you did or said to move the problem toward a solution.

In the midst of a raging argument, when emotions run high, it's almost impossible to see ourselves objectively. Let the camera be your unbiased observer.

Agree to disagree. Sometimes we say all we have to say. We do all of the problem solving we can do. We get all points of view across. And the conflict still remains, staring us right in the face.

What's left is to recognize that honest disagreement is a fact of life. We can peacefully coexist with other people—and respect them—even though we don't agree on fundamental issues. Conflict can be accepted even when it is not resolved.

Do nothing. Sometimes we worsen a conflict by insisting that it be solved immediately. An alternative is to sit tight and wait things out. Some conflicts resolve themselves with the passage of time.

See the conflict within you. Sometimes the turmoil we see in the outside world has its source in our own inner world. A cofounder of Alcoholics Anonymous put it this way: "It is a spiritual axiom that every time we are disturbed, no matter what the cause, there is something awry with us."

It's been said that our own thoughts can do more damage than anything anybody else has to say. When we're angry or upset, we can take a minute to look inside. Perhaps we were ready to take offense, waiting to pounce on something the other person said. Perhaps, without realizing it, we did something to create the conflict. Or maybe the other person is simply saying what we don't want to admit is true.

When these things happen, we can shine a light on our own thinking. A simple spot check might help the conflict disappear—right before our eyes. ▧

→ You deserve compliments

For some people, compliments are more difficult to accept than criticisms. Here are some hints for handling compliments.

Accept the compliment. People sometimes respond to praise with "Oh, it's really nothing" or "This old thing? I've had it for years." This type of response undermines both you and the person who sent the compliment.

Choose another time to deliver your own compliments. Automatically returning a compliment can appear suspiciously polite and insincere.

Let the compliment stand. "Do you really think so?" questions the integrity of the message. It can also sound as if you're fishing for more compliments.

Accepting compliments is not the same as being conceited. If you're in doubt about how to respond, just smile and say "Thank you!" This simple response affirms the compliment along with the person who delivered it.

You are worthy and capable. Allow people to acknowledge that.

exercise 24

WRITE AN "I" MESSAGE

First, pick something about school that irritates you. Then pretend that you are talking to the person who is associated with this irritation. In the space below, write down what you would say to this person as a "You" message.

_____

_____

_____

_____

_____

_____

Now write the same complaint as an "I" message. Include at least the first three elements suggested in "Five ways to say 'I.'"

_____

_____

_____

_____

_____

_____

_____

_____

voices

student

I used to be a very shy person who didn't communicate or participate in class or out of class; after I read this chapter and started to use some of the techniques this book offers, I have accomplished my goal of becoming more communicative.

—BRITTANY SCHULTZ

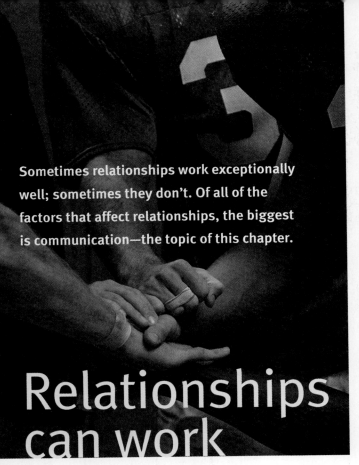

Sometimes relationships work exceptionally well; sometimes they don't. Of all of the factors that affect relationships, the biggest is communication—the topic of this chapter.

Relationships can work

Here's a list of other actions that can benefit your relationships.

Do tell the truth. Life is complicated when you don't. For example, if you think a friend is addicted to drugs, telling him so in a supportive, nonjudgmental way is a sign of friendship. Psychotherapist Sidney Jourard referred to such openness and honesty as *transparency* and wrote eloquently about how it can heal and deepen relationships.[4]

Do support others. Encourage fellow students to reach their goals and be successful. Respect their study time. Helping them stay focused can help you as well.

Don't pry. Being a good listener is invitation enough for classmates to share their problems, feelings, and personal goals.

Don't borrow—too much. Borrowing a book or a tennis racket might seem like a small thing. Yet these requests can become a sore point in a relationship. Some people have difficulty saying no and resent lending things. Consider keeping borrowing to a minimum.

Do divide chores. Whether it's a class project or a household chore, do your part. Frustrations result when

people can't come to an agreement on a fair division of work—or fail to live up to such an agreement.

Don't gripe. There is a difference between griping and sharing problems. Gripers usually don't seek solutions. They just want everyone to know how unhappy they are. Sharing a problem is an appropriate way to start the search for a solution.

Do write a letter. When it's not easy to express viewpoints face to face, write a letter. Even if you never send it, you've rehearsed what you want to say.

Do get involved. Being involved in extracurricular activities is a great way to meet people with common interests. If you commute and have little time for these activities, you can study at the library, eat at the cafeteria, or relax at the student union. You might be surprised at how many friends you can make.

Don't brag. Other students are turned off by constant references to how much money you have, how great your girlfriend is, how numerous your social successes are, or how much status your family enjoys. There is a difference between sharing excitement and being obnoxious.

Do detach. Allow others to accept responsibility for their problems. Pitying them, getting upset along with them, or assuming responsibility for solving their problems is not helpful.

Do allow people to be upset. Trying to joke people out of their upset by discounting their frustration or minimizing their disappointment invalidates their feelings. You can best support them by allowing them to express their emotions.

Do ask for help. One of the central messages of this book is that you are not alone. You can draw on the talent, strength, and wisdom of others. People often respond to a genuine request for help.

Do share yourself. When we brood on negative thoughts and refuse to speak them out loud, we lose perspective. And when we keep joys to ourselves, we diminish our satisfaction. A solution is to share regularly what we think and feel. Imagine a community in which people freely and lovingly speak their minds—without fear or defensiveness. That can be your community.

Don't preach. This piece of advice might seem funny at the end of a list of do's and don't's. Sometimes people ask for advice. It's OK to share your values and opinions. It's not OK to pretend that you know what's best for someone else. Respect the differences between people and don't try to reform the world. ⊠

Relationships change

Relationships change, and the changes can be painful. Be prepared. Forget about buying broken heart insurance. We are at too high a risk. In fact, any time we choose to care about another person, we risk a painful, but rarely fatal, broken heart.

Relationships grow and die. Friends transfer schools and graduate. Lovers and spouses leave. Children grow up and move away. Parents die. We might even surpass the people we once looked up to as role models; that's a kind of loss, too. All of these events can lead to pain. And sometimes the pain is intense.

Pain is a part of living. You can learn how to deal with it in several ways.

Feel the feeling—and stay active. One way to work through pain is to do something. When an important relationship ends and you feel bad, allow yourself to experience that feeling. It is appropriate to be miserable when you are. It's normal to cry and express your feelings. It is also possible to go to class, study, work, eat, and feel miserable at the same time.

Do anything. Exercise. Mop the kitchen floor. Clean out your dresser drawers. Iron your shirts. This sounds ridiculous, and it works.

Remember that your purpose is not to avoid pain, but to see it from a more balanced viewpoint. Japanese psychiatrist Morita Masatake, a contemporary of Sigmund Freud, based his whole approach toward treatment on this insight: We can face our emotional pain directly and still take constructive action. One of Masatake's favorite suggestions for people who felt depressed was that they tend a garden.[5]

Exaggerate the feeling. This suggestion—when applied with care—can sometimes help. If you feel absolutely useless, ugly, and unlovable, look in the mirror and tell yourself over and over again how useless, ugly, and unlovable you are. It might be hard to berate yourself for very long and keep a straight face. Another option is to throw a pity party and talk about how rotten things have been going for you. Be prepared for your depressed mood to change quickly.

If you are determined to feel sorry for yourself, go all the way. Increase your misery by studying a few extra hours. It could go like this: You get some extra studying done and start feeling like a good student. Maybe you are more worthwhile than you thought. You fight it, but you can't help feeling pleased with yourself. The misery subsides. Feeling good about yourself has an interesting side effect—usually, others start feeling good about you, too.

Use the Power Processes. Experience a barrier and "be here now" with it. Surrender to your emotions, and then detach. Notice your pictures and let them go—then find a bigger problem. Yes, it can be difficult to practice the Power Processes at times like this. And when your practice becomes this intense, it can yield the most learning.

Writing about your feelings and what you're learning through the pain can also bring perspective. Your journal is one friend who is on call 24 hours each day, every day of the year. You can approach this friend in any mood and say anything at all. Now that's unconditional acceptance.

Connect with people. If you feel severely depressed and stay that way, talk to someone. Talking to people is a way of healing. Do things with other people. Include old friends. Make new friends.

If friends and family members can't help, remember that most schools and communities have counselors available. Take action. Depression can affect your health, and it can be alleviated.

Remember that pain passes. Emotional pain does not last forever. Often it ends in a matter of weeks. One case disappeared in 4 hours and 12 minutes.

There's no need to let a broken heart stop your life. Though you can find abundant advice on the subject, just remember a simple and powerful idea: "This, too, shall pass." ⊠

> *Remember that your purpose is not to avoid pain, but to see it from a more balanced viewpoint.*

7 steps to effective complaints

Sometimes relationship building involves making a complaint. Whining, blaming, pouting, kicking, and spitting usually don't get results. Here are some guidelines for complaining effectively.

1 Go to the source. Start with the person who is most directly involved with the problem.

2 Present the facts without blaming anyone. Your complaint will carry more weight if you document the facts. Keep track of names and dates. Note what actions were promised and what results actually occurred.

3 Go up the ladder to people with more responsibility. If you don't get satisfaction at the first level, go to that person's direct supervisor.

Requesting a supervisor's name will often get results. Write a letter to the company president.

4 Ask for commitments. When you find someone who is willing to solve your problem, get him to say exactly what he is going to do and when.

5 Use available support. There are dozens of groups, as well as government agencies, willing to get involved in resolving complaints. Contact consumer groups of the Better Business Bureau. Trade associations can sometimes help. Ask city council members, county commissioners, state legislators, and senators and representatives. All of them want your vote, so they are usually eager to help.

6 Take legal action, if necessary. Small-claims court is relatively inexpensive, and you don't have to hire a lawyer. These courts can handle cases involving small amounts of money (usually up to a few thousand dollars). Legal aid offices can sometimes answer questions.

7 Don't give up. Assume that others are on your team. Many people are out there to help you. State what you intend to do and ask for their partnership. ⊠

Criticism really can be constructive

Although receiving criticism is rarely fun, it is often educational. Here are some ways to get the most value from it.

Avoid finding fault. When your mind is occupied with finding fault in others, you aren't open to hearing constructive comments about yourself.

Take it seriously. Some people laugh or joke in order to cover up their anger or embarrassment at being criticized. A humorous reaction on your part can be mistaken for a lack of concern.

React to criticism with acceptance. Most people don't enjoy pointing out another's faults. Denial, argument, or joking makes it more difficult for them to give honest feedback. You can disagree with criticism and still accept it calmly.

Keep it in perspective. Avoid blowing the criticism out of proportion. The purpose of criticism is to generate positive change and self-improvement. There's no need to overreact to it.

Listen without defensiveness. You can't hear the criticism if you're busy framing your rebuttal.

V.I.P.'S (VERY IMPORTANT PERSONS)

Step 1 Under the column below titled "Name," write the names of at least seven people who have positively influenced your life. They might be relatives, friends, teachers, or perhaps persons you have never met. (Complete each step before moving on.)

Step 2 In the next column, rate your gratitude for this person's influence (from 1 to 5, with 1 being a little grateful and 5 being extremely grateful).

Step 3 In the third column, rate how fully you have communicated your appreciation to this person (again, 1 to 5, with 1 being not communicated and 5 being fully communicated).

Step 4 In the final column, put a U to indicate the persons with whom you have unfinished business (such as an important communication that you have not yet sent).

	Name	Grateful (1–5)	Communicated (1–5)	U
1.				
2.				
3.				
4.				
5.				
6.				
7.				

Step 5 Now select two persons with U's beside their names and write them a letter. Express the love, tenderness, and joy you feel toward them. Tell them exactly how they have helped change your life and how glad you are that they did.

Step 6 You also have an impact on others. Make a list of people whose lives you have influenced. Consider sharing with these people why you enjoy being a part of their lives.

Three phases
of effective writing

Writing is a way to learn. Professional writers report that one of the joys of their craft is the opportunity to explore new fields. They constantly learn new subjects by researching and writing about them. They know that you can literally write your way into a subject.

Through writing, you can get a much clearer picture of what you know, what you don't know, and where to look for the missing pieces. Through writing, you can turn raw data into useful insight.

This chapter outlines a three-phase process for writing any paper or speech:

1. Getting ready to write
2. Writing a first draft
3. Revising your draft

Even though the following articles lay out a step-by-step process, remember that writing is highly personal. You might go through the steps in a different order or find yourself working on several at once.

Note: For specific suggestions on ways to write more efficiently with word processing software, see Chapter Ten: Technology.

PHASE ONE
Getting ready to write

Schedule and list writing tasks

You can divide the ultimate goal—a finished paper—into smaller steps that you can tackle right away. Estimate how long it will take to complete each step. Start with the date your paper is due and work backward to the present. Say that the due date is December 1 and you have about three months to write the paper. Schedule November 20 as your targeted completion date, plan what you want to get done by November 1, then list what you want to get done by October 1.

Generate ideas for a topic

Brainstorm with a group. There's no need to create in isolation. Forget the myth of the lonely, frustrated artist hashing out his ideas alone in a dimly lit Paris cafe. You can harness the energy and the natural creative power of a group to assist you. For ideas about ways to brainstorm, see Chapter Seven: Thinking.

Speak it. To get ideas flowing, start talking. Admit your confusion or lack of a clear idea. Then just speak. By putting your thoughts into words, you'll start thinking more clearly. Novelist E. M. Forster said, "'Speak before you think' is creation's motto."[6]

Use free writing. Free writing, a technique championed by writing teacher Peter Elbow, sends a depth probe into your creative mind.[7] This is one way to bypass your internal censors, those little voices in your head that constantly say, "That sentence wasn't very good. Why don't you stop this before you get hurt?"

There's only one rule in free writing: Write without stopping. Set a time limit—say, 10 minutes—and keep your pencil in motion or your fingers dancing across the keyboard the whole time.

Give yourself permission to keep writing. Ignore the urge to stop and rewrite, even if you think what you've written isn't very good. There's no need to worry about spelling, punctuation, or grammar. It's OK if you stray from the initial subject. Just keep writing and let the ideas flow. Experiment with free writing as soon as your instructor assigns a paper.

Refine initial ideas

Select a topic and working title. It's easy to put off writing if you have a hard time choosing a topic. However, it is almost impossible to make a wrong choice at this stage. Just choose any subject. You can choose again later.

Using your instructor's guidelines for the paper or speech, write down a list of topics that interest you. Write as many of these as you can think of in two minutes. Then choose one. If you can't decide, use scissors to cut your list into single items, put them in a box, and pull one out. To avoid getting stuck on this step, set a precise timeline: "I will choose a topic by 4 p.m. on Wednesday."

The most common pitfall is selecting a topic that's too broad. "Harriet Tubman" is not a useful topic for your American history paper. Instead, consider "Harriet Tubman's activities as a Union spy during the Civil War." Your topic statement can function as a working title.

Write a thesis statement. Clarify what you want to say by summarizing it in one concise sentence. This sentence, called a thesis statement, refines your working title. It also helps in making a preliminary outline.

You might write a thesis statement such as "Harriet Tubman's activities with the Underground Railroad led to a relationship with the Union army during the Civil War." A statement that's clear and to the point can make your paper easier to write. Remember, you can always rewrite your thesis statement as you learn more about your topic.

A thesis statement is different from a topic statement. Like newspaper headlines, a thesis statement makes an assertion or describes an action. It is expressed in a complete sentence, including a verb. "Diversity" is a topic. "Cultural diversity is valuable" is a thesis statement.

Consider your purpose

Effective writing flows from a purpose. Discuss the purpose of your assignment with your instructor. Also think about how you'd like your reader or listener to respond after considering your ideas. Do you want him to think differently, to feel differently, or to take a certain action?

Your writing strategy is greatly affected by how you answer these questions. If you want someone to think differently, make your writing clear and logical. Support your assertions with evidence. If you want someone to feel differently, consider crafting a story. Write about a character your audience can empathize with, and tell how he resolves a problem that they can relate to. And if your purpose is to move the reader into action, explain exactly what steps to take and offer solid benefits for doing so.

To clarify your purpose, state it in one sentence. For example, "The purpose of this paper is to define the term *success* in such a clear and convincing way that I win a scholarship from Houghton Mifflin."

Do initial research

At this stage, the objective of your research is not to uncover specific facts about your topic. That comes later. First, you want to gain an overview of the subject. Discover the structure of your topic—its major divisions and branches. Say that you want to persuade the reader to vote for a certain candidate. You must first learn enough about this person to summarize his background and state his stands on key issues.

Outline

An outline is a kind of map. When you follow a map, you avoid getting lost. Likewise, an outline keeps you from wandering off the topic.

To start an outline, gather a stack of 3x5 cards and brainstorm ideas you want to include in your paper. Write one phrase or sentence per card.

Then experiment with the cards. Group them into separate stacks, each stack representing one major category. After that, arrange the stacks in order. Finally, arrange the cards within each stack in a logical order. Rearrange them until you discover an organization that you like.

If you write on a computer, consider using outlining software. These programs allow you to record and rearrange ideas on the screen, much like the way you'd create and shuffle 3x5 cards.

After you write the first draft of your outline, test it. Make sure that each word relates directly to your statement of purpose.

Do in-depth research

You can find information about research skills in Chapter Four: Reading and in Chapter Five: Notes. Following are added suggestions.

Use 3x5 cards. If 3x5 cards haven't found their way into your life by now, joy awaits you. These cards work wonders when conducting research. Just write down one idea per card. This makes it easy to organize—and reorganize—your ideas.

Organizing research cards as you create them saves time. Use rubber bands to keep source cards separate from information cards and to maintain general categories.

You can also save time in two other ways. First, copy all of the information correctly. Always include the source code and page number on information cards. Second, write legibly, using the same format for all of your cards.

In addition to source cards and information cards, generate idea cards. If you have a thought while you are researching, write it down on a card. Label these cards clearly as your own ideas.

An alternative to 3x5 cards is a computer outlining or database program. Some word processing packages also include features that can be used for note taking.

Sense the time to begin writing. A common mistake that beginning writers make is to hold their noses, close their eyes, and jump into the writing process with both feet first—and few facts. Avoid this temptation by gathering more information than you think you can use.

You can begin writing even before your research is complete. The act of writing creates ideas and reveals areas where more research is needed.

Finding a natural place to begin is one signal to start writing. This is not to say that the skies will suddenly open up and your completed paper, flanked by trumpeting angels, will appear before your eyes. You might instead get a strong sense of how to write just one small section of your paper or speech. When this happens, write.

PHASE TWO
Writing a first draft

If you've planned your writing project and completed your research, you've already done much of the hard work. Now you can relax into writing your first draft.

To create your draft, gather your notes and arrange them to follow your outline. Then write about the ideas in your notes. Write in paragraphs, one idea per paragraph. If you have organized your notes logically, related facts will appear close to each other. As you complete this task, keep the following suggestions in mind.

Remember that the first draft is not for keeps. You can save quality for later, when you revise. Your goal at this point is simply to generate lots of material.

Don't worry about grammar, punctuation, or spelling as you write your first draft. Write as if you were explaining the subject to a friend. Let the words flow. The very act of writing will release creative energy. It's perfectly all right to crank out a draft that you heavily rewrite or even throw away. The purpose of a first draft is merely to have something to work with—period. For most of us, that's a heck of a lot better than facing a blank page. You will revise this rough draft several times, so don't be concerned if it seems rough or choppy.

Write freely. Many writers prefer to get their first draft down quickly. Their advice is just to keep writing, much as in free writing. You can pause occasionally to glance at your notes and outline. The idea is to avoid stopping to edit your work. You can save that for the next step.

Another option is to write a first draft without referring back to your notes and outline. If you've immersed yourself in the topic, chances are that much of the information is already bubbling up near the surface of your mind anyway. Later, when you edit, you can go back to your notes and correct any errors.

Keep in mind that you don't have to follow your outline from beginning to end. Some professional writers prefer to write the last chapter of a novel or the last scene of a play first. With the ending firmly in mind, they can then guide the reader through all of the incidents that lead up to it. You might feel more comfortable with certain aspects of your topic than with others. Dive in where you feel most comfortable.

Be yourself. Let go of the urge to sound "official" or "scholarly," and write in a natural voice instead. Address your thoughts not to the teacher but to an intelligent student or someone you care about. Visualize this person and choose the three or four most important things you'd say to him about the topic. This helps you avoid

the temptation to write merely to impress.

The flip side of this point is that we can't really write the way we speak. The spoken word is accompanied by facial expressions and gestures, as well as changes in voice tone, pitch, and volume. Slang expressions used in everyday speech are not appropriate in academic writing. Compensate for elements peculiar to the spoken language by being clear and concise in your writing and by providing smooth, logical transitions from subject to subject.

Let your inner writer take over. There might be times when ideas come to you spontaneously— when thoughts flow from your head to your hand without conscious effort. This is a "natural high," similar to states that accomplished athletes, musicians, and artists have described. Writer Natalie Goldberg says that during such moments you are in touch with your "inner writer."[8] Such "peak experiences" can yield moments of pure joy. Often, those moments come just after a period of feeling stuck. Welcome getting stuck. A breakthrough is not far behind.

Ease into it. Some people find that it works well to forget the word *writing*. Instead, they ease into the task with activities that help generate ideas. You can free-associate, cluster, meditate, daydream, doodle, draw diagrams, visualize the event you want to describe, talk into a voice recorder— anything that gets you started.

Make writing a habit. The word *inspiration* is not in the working vocabulary for many professional writers. Instead of waiting for inspiration to strike, they simply make a habit of writing at a certain time each day. You can use the same strategy. Schedule a block of time to write your first draft. The very act of writing can breed inspiration.

Respect your deep mind. Part of the process of writing takes place outside our awareness. There's nothing mysterious about this. Many people report that ideas come to them while they're doing something totally unrelated to writing. Often this happens after they've been grappling with a question and have reached a point where they feel stuck. It's like the composer who said, "There I was, sitting and eating a sandwich, and all of a sudden this darn tune pops into my head." You can trust your deep mind. It's writing while you eat, sleep, and brush your teeth.

Get physical. Writing is physical, like jogging or playing tennis. You can move your body in ways that are in tune with the flow of your ideas. While working on the first draft, take breaks. Go for a walk. Speak or sing your ideas out loud. From time to time, practice relaxation techniques and breathe deeply.

Use affirmations and visualizations. Write with the idea that the finished paper or speech is inside you, waiting to be released. Affirmations and visualizations can help you with this. Imagine what your finished paper will look like. Construct a detailed mental picture of the title page and major sections of the paper. See a clean, typed copy, and speculate how it will feel to hold the paper and flip through the pages. Visualize the reaction of audience members after you've given your speech.

Then support your writing by sprinkling your self-talk with statements that affirm your abilities. For example: "I express myself clearly and persuasively." "I am using an effective process to write my paper." "I will be pleased with the results."

Hide it in your drawer for a while. Schedule time for rewrites before you begin, and schedule at least one day in between revisions so that you can let the material sit. On Tuesday night, you might think your writing sings the song of beautiful language. On Wednesday, you will see that those same words, such as the phrase "sings the song of beautiful language," belong in the trash basket.

Ideally, a student will revise a paper two or three times, make a clean copy of those revisions, then let the last revised draft sit for at least three or four days. The brain needs that much time to disengage itself from the project. Obvious grammatical mistakes, awkward constructions, and lapses in logic are hidden from us when we are in the middle of the creative process. Give yourself time to step back, and then go over the paper one last time before starting the third phase of the writing process.

PHASE THREE
Revising your draft

One definition of a writer is simply anyone who rewrites. Some people who write for a living will rewrite a piece seven, eight, or even more times. Ernest Hemingway rewrote the last page of _A Farewell to Arms_ 39 times before he was satisfied with it. When asked what the most difficult part of this process was, he simply said, "Getting the words right."[9]

People who rewrite care. They care about the reader. They care about precise language and careful thinking. And they care about themselves. They know that the act of rewriting teaches them more about the topic than almost any other step in the process.

There's a difference in pace between writing a first draft and revising it. Keep in mind the saying "Write in haste, revise at leisure." When you edit and revise, slow down and take a microscope to your work. One guideline is to allow 50 percent of writing time for planning, research, and writing the first draft. Then give the remaining 50 percent to revising.

An effective way to revise your paper is to read it out loud. The eyes tend to fill in the blanks in our own writing. The combination of voice and ears forces us to pay attention to the details.

Another technique is to have a friend look over your

paper. This is never a substitute for your own review, but a friend can often see mistakes you miss. Remember, when other people criticize or review your work, they're not attacking you. They're just commenting on your paper. With a little practice, you can actually learn to welcome feedback.

Reading aloud and having a friend comment on your paper are techniques that can help you in each step of rewriting explained below.

Cut

Writer Theodore Cheney suggests that an efficient way to begin revising is to cut the passages that don't contribute to your purpose.[10] It might not pay to polish individual words, phrases, and sentences right now—especially if you end up deleting them later. To save time, focus instead on deciding which words you want to keep and which ones you want to let go.

Look for excess baggage. Avoid at all costs and at all times the really, really terrible mistake of using way too many unnecessary words, a mistake that some student writers often make when they sit down to write papers for the various courses in which they participate at the fine institutions of higher learning that they are fortunate enough to attend. (Example: The previous sentence could be edited to "Avoid unnecessary words.")

Approach your rough draft as if it were a chunk of granite from which you will chisel the final product. In the end, much of your first draft will be lying on the floor. What is left will be the clean, clear, polished product. Sometimes the revisions are painful. Sooner or later, every writer invents a phrase that is truly clever but makes no contribution to the purpose of the paper. Grit your teeth and let it go.

Note: For maximum efficiency, make the larger cuts first—sections, chapters, pages. Then go for the smaller cuts—paragraphs, sentences, phrases, words.

Keep in mind that cutting a passage means just for now, for this paper, for this assignment. You might want to keep a file of deleted writings to save for future use.

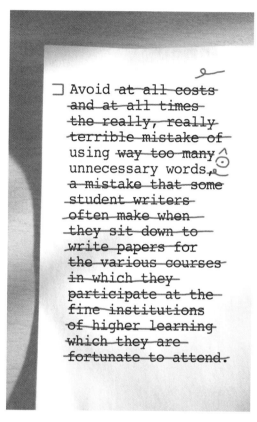

Avoid ~~at all costs and at all times~~ the really, really terrible mistake of using ~~way too many~~ unnecessary words, ~~a mistake that some student writers often make when they sit down to write papers for the various courses in which they participate at the fine institutions of higher learning which they are fortunate to attend.~~

Paste

In deleting passages, you've probably removed some of the original transitions and connecting ideas from your draft. The next task is to rearrange what's left of your paper or speech so that it flows logically. Look for consistency within paragraphs and for transitions from paragraph to paragraph and section to section.

If your draft doesn't hang together, reorder your ideas. Imagine yourself with scissors and glue, cutting the paper into scraps—one scrap for each point. Then paste these points down in a new, more logical order.

Fix

Now it's time to look at individual words and phrases.

In general, rely on nouns and verbs. Using too many adjectives and adverbs weakens your message and adds unnecessary bulk to your writing. Write about the details and be specific. Also, use the active rather than the passive voice.

Instead of writing in the passive voice:
A project was initiated.

You can use the active voice:
The research team began a project.

Instead of writing verbosely:
After making a timely arrival and perspicaciously observing the unfolding events, I emerged totally and gloriously victorious.

You can write to the point, as Julius Caesar did:
I came, I saw, I conquered.

Instead of writing vaguely:
The speaker made effective use of the television medium, asking in no uncertain terms that we change our belief systems.

You can write specifically:
The reformed criminal stared straight into the television camera and shouted, "Take a good look at what you're doing! Will it get you what you really want?"

Also, define any terms that the reader might not know, putting them in plain English whenever you can.

Prepare

In a sense, any paper is a sales effort. If you hand in a paper with wrinkled jeans, its hair tangled and unwashed and its shoes untied, your instructor is less likely to buy it. To avoid this situation, format your paper following accepted standards for margin widths, endnotes, title pages, and other details.

Ask your instructor for specific instructions on how to cite the sources used in writing your paper. You can find useful guidelines in the *MLA Handbook for Writers of Research Papers,* a book from the Modern Language Association. Also visit the MLA Web site at **http://www.mla.org/style_faq.**

If you "cut and paste" material from a Web page directly into your paper, be sure to place that material in quotation marks and cite the source. And before referencing an e-mail message, verify the sender's identity. Remember that anyone sending e-mail can pretend to be someone else.

Use quality paper for your final version. For an even more professional appearance, bind your paper with a paper or plastic cover.

Proof

As you ease down the homestretch, read your revised paper one more time. This time, go for the big picture and look for

- A clear thesis statement.

- Sentences that introduce your topic, guide the reader through the major sections of your paper, and summarize your conclusions.

- Details—such as quotations, examples, and statistics—that support your conclusions.

- Lean sentences that have been purged of needless words.

- Plenty of action verbs and concrete, specific nouns.

Finally, look over your paper with an eye for spelling and grammar mistakes.

When you're through proofreading, take a minute to savor the result. You've just witnessed something of a miracle—the mind attaining clarity and resolution. That's the aha! in writing. ▧

journal entry 24

Discovery Statement

This Journal Entry is for people who avoid writing. As with any anxiety, you can approach writing anxiety by accepting it fully. Realize that it's OK to feel anxious about writing. Others have shared this feeling, and many people have worked with it successfully.

Begin by telling the truth. Describe exactly what happens when you start to write. What thoughts or images run through your mind? Do you feel any tension or discomfort in your body? Where? Let the thoughts and images come to the surface without resistance. Complete the following statement.

When I begin to write, I discover that I . . .

_____

_____

_____

_____

_____

_____

_____

_____

_____

_____

Giving credit where credit is due

Avoiding the high cost of PLAGIARISM

There's a branch of law known as intellectual property. This field is based on the idea that original works—such as speeches, publications, and works of art—are not free for the taking. Anyone who borrows from these works is obligated to acknowledge the work's creator. This is the purpose behind copyrights, patents, and trademarks.

Using another person's words or pictures without giving proper credit is called *plagiarism*. This is a real concern for anyone who writes, including students. Plagiarism amounts to stealing someone else's work and claiming it as your own—the equivalent of cheating on a test.

Higher education consists of a community of scholars who trust each other to speak and write with integrity. Plagiarism undermines this trust. The consequences can range from a failing grade to expulsion from school.

There are several ways to avoid plagiarism when writing.

If your writing includes a passage, identifiable phrase, sequence of ideas, or visual image created by another person, be sure to acknowledge this fact.

Also be careful as you take notes. Clearly distinguish your own ideas from the ideas of others. If you use a direct quote from another writer or speaker, put that person's words in quotation marks. Also note details about the source of the quotation: author, publication title, publisher, date, and page number. Many instructors will require you to add endnotes to your paper with this information, so include it with each quotation in your notes. Ask your instructor for examples of the format to use for endnotes.

If you do research online, you might find yourself copying sentences or paragraphs from a Web page and pasting them directly into your notes. This is the same as taking direct quotes from your source. To avoid plagiarism, identify such passages in an obvious way. Besides enclosing them in quotation marks, you could format them in a different font or color. Also capture relevant information about the Web page where the passages originally appeared: author, title, sponsoring organization, URL, publication date, revision date, and date that you accessed that page. For more information crediting Internet sources, go online to the Modern Language Association's Web site at **http://www.mla.org/publications/style/style_faq/ style_faq4.**

Instead of using a direct quote, you might choose to paraphrase an author's words. Paraphrasing means restating the original passage in different words, usually making it shorter and simpler. Paraphrase with care. Students who copy a passage word for word and then just rearrange or delete a few phrases are running a serious risk of plagiarism. Consider this paragraph:

Higher education also offers you the chance to learn how to learn. In fact, that's the subject of this book. Employers value the person who is a "quick study" when it comes to learning a new job. That makes your ability to learn a marketable skill.

Following is an improper paraphrase of that passage:

With higher education comes the chance to learn how to learn. Employers value the person who is a "quick study" when it comes to learning a new job. Your ability to learn is a marketable skill.

A better paraphrase of the same passage would be:

The author notes that when we learn how to learn, we gain a skill that is valued by employers.

Be sure to credit paraphrases in the same way that you credit direct quotes.

When you use the same sequence of ideas as one of your sources—even if you haven't summarized, paraphrased, or quoted—cite that source.

Finally, submit only your own original work, not materials that have been written or revised by someone else.

Out of a concern for avoiding plagiarism, some students go overboard in crediting their sources. You do not need to credit wording that's wholly your own. Nor do you need to credit general ideas. For example, the suggestion that people use a to-do list to plan their time is a general idea. When you use your own words to describe to-do lists, there's no need to credit a source. But if you borrow someone else's words or images to explain this idea, do give credit. ▨

Writing and delivering speeches

Organize your presentation

Writing a speech is similar to writing a paper. Speeches are usually organized in three main parts: the introduction, the main body, and the conclusion.

To make an effective speech, be precise about your purpose and main point, or thesis. Speeches can inform, persuade, motivate, or entertain. Choose what you want to do, let your audience know what your intention is, and state your thesis early on.

Consider the length of your presentation. Plan on delivering about 100 words per minute. This is only a general guideline, however, so time yourself as you practice your presentation. Aim for a lean presentation—enough words to make your point but not so many as to make your audience restless. Be brief, be seated, and leave your listeners wanting more.

Write the introduction. Rambling speeches with no clear point or organization put audiences to sleep. Solve this problem with your introduction. The following introduction, for example, reveals the thesis and exactly what's coming. The speech will have three distinct parts, each in logical order:

> *Dog fighting is a cruel sport. I intend to describe exactly what happens to the animals, tell you who is doing this, and show you how you can stop this inhumane practice.*

Whenever possible, talk about things that hold your interest. Include your personal experiences and start with a bang! Consider this introduction to a speech on the subject of world hunger:

> *I'm very honored to be here with you today. I intend to talk about malnutrition and starvation. First, I want to outline the extent of these problems, then I will discuss some basic assumptions concerning world hunger, and finally I will propose some solutions.*

Some people tune out during a speech. Just think of all the times you have listened to instructors, lecturers, politicians, and others. Remember all the wonderful daydreams you have had during their speeches.

Your audiences are like you. The way you plan and present your speech can determine the number of audience members who will stay with you until the end. Polishing your speaking and presentation skills can also help you think on your feet and communicate clearly. These are skills that you can use in any course and in any career you choose.

You can learn a lot about effective speaking simply by observing other speakers. Besides hearing *what* they say, notice *how* they present themselves. Also experiment with the suggestions that follow.

You can almost hear the snores from the audience. Following is a rewrite:

More people have died from hunger in the past five years than have been killed in all of the wars, revolutions, and murders in the past 150 years. Yet there is enough food to go around. I'm honored to be here with you today to discuss solutions to this problem.

Though some members of an audience begin to drift during any speech, most people pay attention for at least the first few seconds. Your main points should be highlighted in the beginning sentences of your speech. Draft your introduction and then come back to it after you've written the rest of your speech. In the process of creating the main body and conclusion, your thoughts about the purpose and main points of your speech might change. You might even want to write the introduction last.

Write the main body. The main body of your speech is the content, which accounts for 70 to 90 percent of most speeches. In the main body, you develop your ideas in much the same way that you develop a written paper.

In speeches, transitions are especially important. Give your audience a signal when you change points, using meaningful pauses and verbal emphasis as well as transitional phrases: "On the other hand, until the public realizes what is happening to children in these countries . . ." or "The second reason hunger persists is. . . ."

In long speeches, recap from time to time and preview what's to come. Use facts, descriptions, expert opinions, and statistics to hold your audience's attention.

Write the conclusion. At the end of the speech, summarize your points and draw your conclusion. You started with a bang; now finish with drama. The first and last parts of a speech are the most important. Make it clear to your audience when you've reached the end. Avoid endings such as "This is the end of my speech." A simple standby is "So in conclusion, I want to reiterate three points: First. . . ." When you are finished, stop talking.

Create speaking notes. Some professional speakers recommend writing out your speech in full, then putting key words or main points on a few 3x5 cards. Number the cards so that if you drop them, you can quickly put them in order again. As you finish the information on each card, move it to the back of the pile. Write information clearly and in letters large enough to be seen from a distance.

The disadvantage of the 3x5 card system is that it involves card shuffling. Some speakers prefer to use standard outlined notes. Another option is mind mapping. Even an hour-long speech can be mapped on one sheet of paper. You can also use memory techniques to memorize the outline of your speech.

Start with a process speech. One way to start building your speaking skills is to explain a way to do or make something. Examples are changing a tire, planting asparagus, or preparing a healthy meal in 15 minutes. Choose a short, step-by-step process with a concrete outcome. This makes it easier to organize, practice, and deliver your first presentation.

In the introduction to your speech, get the audience's attention and establish rapport. State the topic and purpose of your speech. Relate the topic to something that audience members care about. During the body of your speech, explain each step in the process, following a logical order. To conclude, quickly summarize the process and remind your audience of its usefulness.

Practice your presentation

The key to successful public speaking is practice.

Use your "speaker's voice." When you practice, do so in a loud voice. Your voice sounds different when you talk loudly, and this can be unnerving. Get used to it early on.

Practice in the room in which you will deliver your speech. Hear what your voice sounds like over a sound system. If you can't practice your speech in the actual room, at least visit the site ahead of time. Also make sure that the materials you will need for your speech, such as an overhead projector and screen, will be available when you want them.

Make a recording. Many schools have recording equipment available for student use. Use it while you practice, then view the finished recording to evaluate your presentation.

Listen for repeated phrases. Examples include *you know, kind of, really*, plus any little *uh*'s, *umm*'s, and *ah*'s. To get rid of these, tell yourself that you intend to notice every time they pop up in your daily speech. When you hear them, remind yourself that you don't use those words anymore.

Keep practicing until you know your material inside and out. Avoid speaking word for word, as if you were reading a script. When you know your material well, you can deliver it in a natural way. Practice your presentation until you could deliver it in your sleep, then run through it a few more times.

→ Making the grade in group presentations

When preparing group presentations, you can use three strategies for making a memorable impression.

Get organized. As soon as you get the assignment, select a group leader and exchange contact information. Schedule specific times and places for planning, researching, writing, and practicing your presentation.

At your first meeting, write a to-do list including all of the tasks involved in completing the assignment. Distribute tasks fairly, paying attention to the strengths of individuals in your group. For example, some people excel at brainstorming while others prefer researching.

As you get organized, remember how your presentation will be evaluated. If the instructor doesn't give grading criteria, create your own.

One powerful way to get started is to define clearly the topic and thesis, or main point, of your presentation. Then support your thesis by looking for the most powerful facts, quotations, and anecdotes you can find.

Get coordinated. Coordinate your presentation so that you have transitions between individual speakers. Practice making those transitions smooth.

Also practice using visuals such as flipboards, posters, DVDs, videotapes, or slides. To give visuals their full impact, make them appropriate for the room where you will present. Make sure that text is large enough to be seen from the back of the room. For bigger rooms, consider using presentation software or making overhead transparencies.

Get cooperation. Presentations that get top scores take teamwork and planning—not egos. Communicate with group members in an open and sensitive way. Contribute your ideas and be responsive to the viewpoints of other members. When you do, your group is on the way to scoring well.

For more strategies on overcoming communication apprehension, visit

masterstudent.college.hmco.com

Deliver your presentation

Before you begin, get the audience's attention. If people are still filing into the room or adjusting their seats, they're not ready to listen. When all eyes are on you, then begin.

Deal with stage fright by noticing it. Use the Power Process: "Love your problems." Tell yourself, "Yes, my hands are clammy. I notice that my stomach is slightly upset. My face feels numb." Allow these symptoms to exist. Experience them fully. When you do, they often become less persistent. Notice all of your thoughts and feelings, then gently release them.

Project your voice. When you speak, talk loudly enough to be heard. Avoid leaning over your notes or the podium.

Maintain eye contact. When you look at people, they become less frightening. Remember, too, that it is easier for the audience to listen to someone when that person is looking at them. Find a few friendly faces around the room and imagine that you are talking to each person individually.

Notice your nonverbal communication. Only a fraction of our communication is verbal. Be aware of what your body is telling your audience. Contrived or staged gestures will look dishonest. Be natural. If you don't know what to do with your hands, notice that. Then don't do anything with them.

Notice the time. You can increase the impact of your words by keeping track of the time during your speech. Better to end early than run late. The conclusion of your speech is what is likely to be remembered, and you might lose this opportunity if people are looking at the clock.

Pause when appropriate. Beginners sometimes feel that they have to fill every moment with the sound of their voice. Release that expectation. Give your listeners a chance to make notes and absorb what you say.

Have fun. One way to feel at ease while speaking is to look at your audience and imagine everyone dressed as clowns. Chances are that if you lighten up and enjoy your presentation, so will they.

Reflect on your presentation

Review and reflect upon your performance. Did you finish on time? Did you cover all of the points you intended to cover? Was the audience attentive? Did you handle any nervousness effectively?

Welcome evaluation from others. Most of us find it difficult to hear criticism about our speaking. Be aware of resisting such criticism and then let go of your resistance. Listening to feedback will increase your skill. ⊠

PRACTICING CRITICAL THINKING

9

Discuss a controversial issue of your choosing with a small group of classmates. At several points in your discussion, stop to evaluate your group's critical thinking. Answer the following questions in writing.

Are we staying open to opposing ideas, even if we initially disagree with them?

_____

_____

_____

_____

_____

Are we asking for evidence for each key assertion?

_____

_____

_____

_____

_____

Are we adequately summarizing one another's point of view before analyzing it?

_____

_____

_____

_____

_____

Are we foreseeing the possible consequences of taking a particular stand on any issue?

_____

_____

_____

_____

_____

Are we considering more than one solution to problems?

_____

_____

_____

_____

_____

Are we willing to change our stands on issues or suspend judgment when appropriate?

_____

_____

_____

_____

Are we being systematic as we consider the issues?

_____

_____

_____

_____

power process

Employ your word

When you speak and give your word, you are creating—literally. Your speaking brings life to your values. In large part, others know who you are by the words you speak and the agreements you make. You can learn who you are by observing which commitments you choose to make and which ones you choose to avoid.

Your word makes things happen. Circumstances, events, and attitudes fall into place. The resources needed to accomplish whatever was promised become available. When you give your word, all this comes about.

The person you are right now is, for the most part, a result of the choices and agreements you've made in your life up to this point. Your future is determined largely by the choices and agreements you will make from this point on. By making and keeping agreements, you employ your word to create your future.

The world works by agreement

There are over six billion people on planet Earth. We live on different continents and in different nations, and communicate in different languages. We have diverse political ideologies and subscribe to various social and moral codes.

This complex planetary network is held together by people keeping their word. Agreements minimize confusion, prevent social turmoil, and keep order. Projects are finished, goods are exchanged, and treaties are made. People, organizations, and nations know what to expect when agreements are kept. When people keep their word, the world works. Agreements are the foundation of many things that we often take for granted. Language, our basic tool of communication, works only because we agree about the meanings of words. A pencil is a pencil only because everyone agrees to call a thin, wood-covered column of graphite a pencil. We could just as easily call them ziddles. Then you might hear someone say, "Do you have an extra ziddle? I forgot mine."

Money exists only by agreement. If we leave a $100 Monopoly bill (play money) on a park bench next to a real $100 bill (backed by the United States Treasury), one is more likely to disappear than the other. The only important difference between the two pieces of paper is that everyone agrees that one can be exchanged for goods and services and the other cannot. Shopkeepers will sell merchandise for the "real" $100 bill because they trust a continuing agreement.

Relationships work by agreement

Relationships are built on agreements. They begin with our most intimate personal contacts and move through all levels of families, organizations, communities, and nations.

When we break a promise to be faithful to a spouse, to help a friend move to a new apartment, or to pay a bill on time, relationships are strained and the consequences can be painful. When we keep our word, relationships are more likely to be satisfying and harmonious. Expectations of trust and accountability develop. Others are more likely to keep their promises to us.

Perhaps our most important relationship is the one we have with ourselves. Trusting ourselves to keep our word is enlivening. As we experience success, our self-confidence increases.

When we commit to complete a class assignment and then keep our word, our understanding of the subject improves. So does our grade. We experience satisfaction and success. If we break our word, we create a gap in our learning, a lower grade, and possibly negative feelings.

Ways to make and keep agreements

Being cautious about making agreements can improve the quality of our lives. Making only those promises that we fully intend to keep improves the likelihood of reaching our goals. We can ask ourselves what level of commitment we have to a particular promise.

At the same time, if we are willing to take risks, we can open new doors and increase our possibilities for success. The only way to ensure that we keep all of our agreements is either to make none or to make only those that are absolutely guaranteed. In either case, we are probably cheating ourselves. Some of the most powerful promises we can make are those that we have no idea how to keep. We can stretch ourselves and set goals that are both high and realistic.

If we break an agreement, we can choose to be gentle with ourselves. We can be courageous, quickly admit our mistake to the people involved, and consider ways to deal with the consequences.

Examining our agreements can improve our effectiveness. Perhaps we took on too much—or too little. Perhaps we did not use all the resources that were available to us—or we used too many. Perhaps we did not fully understand what we were promising. When we learn from both our mistakes and our successes, we can become more effective at employing our word.

Move up the ladder of powerful speaking

The words used to talk about whether or not something will happen fall into several different levels. We can think of each level as one rung on a ladder—the ladder of powerful speaking. As we move up the ladder, our speaking becomes more effective.

Obligation. The lowest rung on the ladder is *obligation*. Words used at this level include *I should, he ought to,*

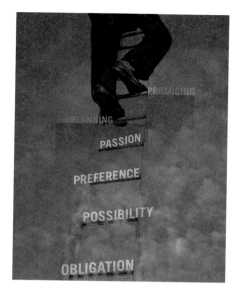

By making and keeping agreements, you employ your word to create your future.

someone better, they need to, I must, and *I had to.* Speaking this way implies that people and circumstances other than ourselves are in control of our lives. When we live at the level of obligation, we often feel passive and helpless to change anything.

Note: When we move to the next rung, we leave behind obligation and advance to self-responsibility. All of the rungs work together to reinforce this characteristic.

Possibility. The next rung up is *possibility*. At this level, we examine new options. We play with new ideas, possible solutions, and alternative courses of action. As we do, we learn that we can make choices that dramatically affect the quality of our lives. We are not the victims of circumstance. Phrases that signal this level include *I might, I could, I'll consider, I hope to,* and *maybe.*

Preference. From possibility we can move up to *preference*. Here we begin the process of choice. The words *I prefer* signal that we're moving toward one set of possibilities over another, perhaps setting the stage for eventual action.

Passion. Above preference is a rung called *passion*. Again, certain words signal this level: *I want to, I'm really excited to do that, I can't wait.* Possibility and passion are both exciting places to be. Even at these levels, though, we're still far from action. Many of us want to achieve lots of things and have no specific plan for doing so.

Planning. Action comes with the next rung—*planning*. When people use phrases such as *I intend to, my goal is to, I plan to,* and *I'll try like mad to*, they're at the level of planning. The Intention Statements you write in this book are examples of planning.

Promising. The highest rung on the ladder is *promising*. This is where the power of your word really comes into play. At this level, it's common to use phrases such as these: *I will, I promise to, I am committed, you can count on it.* This is where we bridge from possibility and planning to action. Promising brings with it all of the rewards of employing your word. ✖

put it to work

According to the National Association of Colleges and Employers, verbal and written communication tops the list of skills that companies look for in college graduates.[11] The techniques described in this chapter have many direct applications in the workplace.

Reread specific articles with the workplace in mind.
Simply by remembering to separate the processes of sending and receiving, you can immediately improve your relationships with both supervisors and employees.

Use ideas from "Writing and delivering speeches" to craft presentations that persuade your supervisor to increase your department budget—or give you a raise.

If you get into a personal conflict with a coworker, reread the article "The fine art of conflict management" and choose a suggestion to apply. As you read, visualize the suggestion working for you.

Use ideas from "Relationships can work" to stay in contact with coworkers as they change jobs or move to new companies. These people could be in a position to hire you some day.

Make effective presentations with visuals.
Presentations often include visuals such as overhead transparencies, flip charts, or "slides" created with presentation software. These can reinforce your main points and help your audience understand how your presentation is organized. In addition, visuals can serve as your speaking notes.

Use visuals to *complement* rather than *replace* your speaking. If you use too many visuals—or visuals that are too complex—your audience might focus on them and forget about you. To avoid this fate:

- Limit the amount of text on each visual. Stick to key words presented in short sentences and bulleted or numbered lists. Use a consistent set of plain fonts that are large enough for all audience members to see.

- Stick with a simple, coherent color scheme. Use light-colored text on a dark background, or dark text on a light background.

- Use consistent terminology in your speaking, your handouts, and your visuals. Inconsistency can lead people to feel lost or to question your credibility.

- Proofread your visuals for spelling and other mechanical errors.

Write for workplace audiences.
Good writing is a marketable skill. To verify this, flip through the help wanted section in a large Sunday newspaper. Note how many job descriptions call for good writing skills. Writing techniques can assist you in preparing memos, reports, e-mail messages, and Web sites.

Jakob Nielsen, author of *Designing Web Usability: The Practice of Simplicity*, suggests that effectively written Web pages are:

- *Concise*—free of needless words and organized so that the main point of each section and paragraph comes at the beginning.

- *Scannable*—prepared with subheadings and visuals that allow readers to skim and quickly find what they need.

- *Objective*—packed with credible facts and free of "hype," that is, vague claims presented without evidence.[12]

These three guidelines can assist you in *all* forms of business writing.

Work effectively in teams.
In their book *When Teams Work Best*, Frank LaFasto and Carl Larson summarize the lessons learned from studying 600 teams in both public and private organizations. These ranged from the Mount Everest climbing team to the workers who produced the Boeing 747 airplane—the world's largest aircraft and a product of 75,000 blueprints.

According to these authors, the most common barrier to effective teamwork is an atmosphere of defensiveness. Team members can solve this problem by: creating an environment in which all opinions are valued; resolving personal conflicts actively rather than ignoring them; staying focused on relevant problems rather than side issues; choosing leaders who allow all opinions to be expressed and keep the team focused; using a simple and clear process for decision-making, allowing people to take immediate action without excess paperwork or time-wasting procedures; defining the team's outcome clearly and how individual team members can contribute directly to that outcome.[13]

Name _____ Date _____/_____/_____

1. What is the difference between encoding and decoding as explained in this chapter?

2. One suggested guideline for nonverbal listening is to respond frequently to the speaker. True or False? Explain your answer.

3. The suggested techniques for verbal listening include which of the following?
   (a) Parrot exactly what another person says.
   (b) Pay attention to the speaker's words and not the emotions behind the words.
   (c) Always put your own concerns aside in order to listen attentively.
   (d) Look for the requests hidden in complaints.

4. Reword the following complaint as a request: "You always interrupt when I talk!"

5. List the five parts of an "I" message (the five ways to say "I").

6. The fact that a disagreement is getting worse means that there's little hope for conflict resolution. True or False? Explain your answer.

7. Which of the following is an effective thesis statement? Explain your answer.
   (a) Two types of thinking.
   (b) Critical thinking and creative thinking go hand in hand.
   (c) The relationship between critical thinking and creative thinking.

8. Define *plagiarism* and explain ways to avoid it.

9. Describe at least three techniques for practicing and delivering a speech.

10. What characteristic distinguishes the top five rungs of the ladder of powerful speaking from the bottom rung?

learning styles application

The questions below will "cycle" you through four styles, or modes, of learning as explained in the article "Learning styles: Discovering how you learn" in Chapter One. Each question will help you explore a different mode. You can answer the questions in any order.

what if *After reading this chapter, will you generally approach conflict management in a different way? Briefly explain your answer.*

why *Think of a conflict you are experiencing right now with an important person in your life. (If you cannot think of one, recall a conflict you've experienced in the past.) Do you think that any of the suggestions in this chapter could help you resolve this conflict? Briefly explain your answer.*

how *Describe when and where you plan to use a suggestion from this chapter to resolve a conflict with another person.*

what *Choose a specific suggestion from this chapter that could help you resolve a conflict you are experiencing right now with another person.*

master student

profile

RON BROWN

(1941–1996) first African American secretary of commerce and first African American chairman of the Democratic National Committee. Died in a plane crash in Bosnia while on a diplomatic mission.

Ron Brown was born in Washington, D.C., to William and Gloria Brown, both graduates of Howard University. The family moved to New York City when he was relatively young. His father managed the legendary Hotel Theresa in Harlem. Here, Ron encountered the social, artistic, political, and powerful elite of the African-American community. He encountered people who ran the race of life brilliantly, daring to be first in what they did. They were people like Jackie Robinson, the first African American to play professional baseball; W. E. B. Du Bois, one of the first African Americans to receive a Ph.D. from Harvard; Duke Ellington, one of the first African Americans to own and lead an internationally acclaimed big band; Ralph Ellison, one of the first widely successful African-American writers; Adam Clayton Powell, the first African-American congressman from Harlem. . . . Often as he peered out of the twelfth floor window of the Hotel Theresa, and observed the hustle and bustle of 125th St. below, he realized how easy it was to get lost in the superficial crowd of everyday life. He realized that the view from the top was a little better than the view from the bottom and that the Hotel Theresa with its legendary reputation and world famous clientele was simply his personal tutoring ground, training him to see above and beyond the crowded streets of New York City.

From the many heated discussions that Ron was involved in at the Hotel Theresa, Ron developed an agile mind and a disciplined tongue. He became almost invincible in his ability to present sound and convincing arguments. In this black cultural Mecca, he studied how creative, artistic, and powerful African-American people behaved. He learned early that hard work, commitment, and perseverance characterized people of position and power. He learned the importance of appearance, preparation, and personal influence in the race called life as he listened intensely to guests' lively stories and daring escapades of world travel.

With this strong sense of self and the willingness to seek different academic and cultural experiences, he got himself accepted by Middlebury College in rural Vermont. This was significant, in that Middlebury was the first college known to have graduated an African American (Alexander L. Twight, in 1823). At Middlebury, far from the blacktop boulevards and the high-rise tenements of Harlem, Ron really began to excel. He was the first black initiated into the Middlebury chapter of the national, all-white fraternity Sigma Phi Epsilon, which eventually lost its national charter because of his induction. . . .

Paramount in Ronald Harmon Brown's strategies for success was knowing how to solicit trust from himself. He learned early to accept himself for who he was and what he could or couldn't do. Knowing his own strengths and weaknesses, he never shortchanged himself. He learned self-reliance by preparing for every area of his life. He was confident in his ability to lead, orchestrate, mediate, and guide. He knew the importance of building lasting relationships. . . .

Ron Brown's life shouts to each of us, "Be your own best cheerleader. Root for a winner. Be that winner yourself." ✉

Osborne Robinson, Jr., *African American Master Student Profiles.* Copyright © 1998 by Houghton Mifflin Company. Reprinted with permission.

For more biographical information on Ron Brown, visit the Master Student Hall of Fame on the *Becoming a Master Student* Web site at

masterstudent.college.hmco.com

9

Diversity

why
this chapter matters . . .

You're likely to learn and work with people from many different cultures.

what
is included . . .

Living with diversity
Diversity is real—and valuable
Communicating across cultures
Overcome stereotypes with critical thinking
Students with disabilities: Ask for what you want
Dealing with sexism and sexual harassment
Seven steps to nonsexist writing
We are all leaders
Power Process: "Choose your conversations and your community"
Master Student Profile: Bayard Rustin

how
you can use this chapter . . .

Study effectively with people of different racial and ethnic groups.
Gain skills to succeed in a multicultural work force.
Choose conversations that promote your success.

As you read, ask yourself
what if . . .

. . . I could create positive relationships with people of any race, ethnic group, or culture?

Candor is a compliment; it implies equality. It's how true friends talk.

PEGGY NOONAN

We don't see things as they are, we see things as we are.

ANAÏS NIN

Living with diversity

Those of us who can study, work, and live with people from other cultures, economic classes, and races can enjoy more success at school, on the job, and in our neighborhoods. Sharing in this success means learning new ways to think, speak, and act. Learning about diversity opens up a myriad of possibilities—an education in itself. At first, this can seem frightening, frustrating, or even painful. It can also be exciting, enriching, and affirming.

The people called "minorities" in this country are already a numerical majority across the world. According to the world population profile from the U.S. Census Bureau, China and India account for almost two of every five people on earth. The more developed countries make up only 20 percent of the world's population, and the population of the United States makes up less than 5 percent of our global village. In the United States, white people of non-Hispanic origin could make up just 53 percent of the population by 2050—down from the current level of 69 percent.[1] The cultures of the world meet daily. Several forces are shrinking our globe. One is the growth of a world economy. Another is the "electronic village" forged across nations by newspapers, radios, televisions, telephones, fax machines, and computers.

We have an opportunity to benefit from this change instead of merely reacting to it. At one time, only sociologists and futurists talked about the meeting of cultures. Now all of us can enter this conversation. We can value cultural diversity and learn how to thrive with it.

There are no quick, easy answers to overcoming the long history of prejudice and the need to embrace diversity. Each suggestion in this chapter is merely a starting point. Continue to experiment and see what works for you. As you read, constantly ask yourself: "How can I use this material to live and work more effectively in a multicultural world?" The answers could change your life. ✕

journal entry 25

Discovery/Intention Statement

Briefly describe an incident in which you were discriminated against because you differed in some way from the other people involved. This could be any kind of difference, such as hair length, style of clothing, political affiliation, religion, skin color, sexual orientation, age, gender, economic status, or accent.

I discovered that I . . .

_____

_____

_____

Scan this chapter for ideas that could help you respond more effectively to discrimination, whether it occurs to you or someone else. List at least five ideas that you intend to explore in more detail, along with their associated page numbers.

Strategy   *Page number*

_____

_____

_____

_____

_____

Schedule a time to explore these techniques in more detail. Also describe a situation coming up this term in which you could apply them.

I intend to . . .

_____

_____

_____

_____

_____

Diversity is real— and valuable

We have always lived with people of different races and cultures. Many of us come from families who immigrated to the United States or Canada just two or three generations ago. The things we eat, the tools we use, and the words we speak are a cultural tapestry woven by many different peoples.

Think about a common daily routine. A typical American citizen awakens in a bed (an invention from the Near East). After dressing in clothes (often designed in Italy), she slices a banana (grown in Honduras) on her bowl (made in China) of cereal, and brews coffee (shipped from Nicaragua). After breakfast, she reads the morning newspaper (printed by a process invented in Germany on paper, which was first made in China). Then she flips on a CD player (made in Japan) and listens to music (possibly performed by a band from Cuba). Multiculturalism refers to racial and ethnic diversity—and many other kinds of diversity as well. As anthropologist Dorothy Lee reminds us, culture is simply one society's solutions to perennial human problems, such as how to worship, celebrate, resolve conflict, work, think, and learn.[2] Culture is a set of learned behaviors—a broader concept than race, which refers to the biological makeup of people. From this standpoint, we can speak of the culture of large corporations or the culture of the fine arts.

Multiculturalism refers to racial and ethnic diversity—and many other kinds of diversity as well.

There are the cultures of men and women; heterosexual, homosexual, and bisexual people; and older and younger people. There are differences between urban and rural dwellers, between able-bodied people and those with disabilities, and between people from two-parent families and people from single-parent families. There are social classes based on differences in standards of living. And diversity in religion is a factor, too. This can be especially difficult to accept, since many people identify strongly with their religious faith. In some respects, culture can be compared to an iceberg. Only parts of any given culture—such as language patterns or distinctive apparel—exist on a visible level. Just as most of an iceberg lies under water and out of sight, many aspects of culture lie beneath our conscious awareness. This invisible realm includes assumptions about the meanings of beauty and friendship, the concepts of sin and justice, approaches to problem solving, interpretations of eye contact and body language, and patterns of supervisor and employee relationships.

People can differ in countless ways—race, gender, ethnic group, sexual orientation, and more. The suggestions offered in this chapter can help you respond effectively to the many kinds of diversity you'll encounter. Higher education can help reinforce an attitude of tolerance, open-mindedness, and respect for individual differences.

Discrimination is also real. The ability to live with diversity is now more critical than ever. Racism, homophobia, and other forms of discrimination still exist, even in higher education. According to the FBI, a total of 7,462 hate crimes took place in the United States during 2002. About 49 percent of those crimes were based on race, and nearly 17 percent were based on sexual orientation. Almost 11 percent of all hate crimes took place in college and other school settings.[3]

Of course, discrimination can be far more subtle than hate crimes. Consider how you would respond to the following situations:

- Members of a sociology class are debating the merits of reforming the state's welfare system. The instructor calls on a student from a reservation and says, "Tell us. What's the Native American perspective on this issue anyway?" Here the student is being typecast as a spokesperson for her entire ethnic group.

- Students in a mass media communications class are learning to think critically about television programs. They're talking about a situation comedy set in an urban high-rise apartment building with mostly African American residents. "Man, they really whitewashed that show," says one student. "It's mostly about inner-city black people, but they didn't show anybody on welfare, doing drugs, or joining gangs." The student's comment perpetuates common racial stereotypes.

- On the first day of the term, students taking English composition enter a class taught by a professor from Puerto Rico. One of the students asks the professor, "Am I in the right class? Maybe there's been a mistake. I thought this was supposed to be an English class, not a Spanish class." The student assumed that only Caucasian people are qualified to teach English courses.

Higher education can help reinforce an attitude of tolerance, open-mindedness, and respect for individual differences.

Forrest Toms of Training Research and Development defines racism as "prejudice plus power"—the power to define reality, to enshrine one set of biases. The operating assumption behind racism is that differences mean deficits.

When racism lives, we all lose—even those groups with social and political power. We lose the ability to make friends and to function effectively on teams. We crush human potential. People without the skills to bridge cultures are already at a disadvantage.

Higher education offers a chance to change this. Academic environments can become cultural laboratories—places where people of diverse races and cultures can meet in an atmosphere of tolerance. Students who create alliances outside their immediate group are preparing to succeed in both school and work.

Diversity is valuable. Synergy is the idea that the whole is more than the sum of its parts. Consider some examples: A symphony orchestra consists of many different instruments; when played together, their effect is multiplied many times. A football team has members with different specialties; when their talents are combined, they can win a league championship.

Diversity in a society offers another example of synergy. It takes no more energy to believe that differences enrich us than it does to believe that differences endanger us. Embracing diversity adds value to any organization and can be far more exciting than just meeting the minimum requirements for affirmative action.

Today we are waking up not only to the *fact* of diversity but also to the *value* of diversity. Biologists tell us that diversity of animal species benefits our ecology. The same idea applies to the human species. Through education our goal can be to see that we are all part of a complex world—that our own culture is different from, not better than, others. Knowing this, we can stop saying, "This is the way to work, learn, relate to others, and view the world." Instead, we can say, "Here is the way I have been doing it. I would also like to see your way."

The fact of diversity also represents opportunity in the workplace. Understanding cultural differences—internationally and domestically—will help you to embrace others' viewpoints that lead to profitable solutions. Organizations that are attuned to diversity are more likely to prosper in the global marketplace.

Accepting diversity does not mean ignoring the differences among cultures so that we all become part of a faceless "melting pot." Instead, we can become more like a mosaic—a piece of art in which each element maintains its individuality and blends with others to form a harmonious whole.

Learning to live with diversity is a process of returning to "beginner's mind"—a place where we question our biases and assumptions. This is a magical place, a place of new beginnings and options. It takes courage to dwell in beginner's mind—courage to go outside the confines of our own culture and world-view. It can feel uncomfortable at first. Yet there are lasting rewards to gain.

As you read the following articles, look to yourself. This chapter aims to help you examine your own biases. With self-awareness, you can go beyond them. ◈

voices

student

A master student tries on other people's skin, and it is not judgmental. We are all different and a master student accepts that diversity.

—LYNN LINEBERGER

Communicating across cultures

Communicating with people of other cultures is a learned skill—a habit. According to Stephen R. Covey, author of *The Seven Habits of Highly Effective People*, a habit is the point at which desire, knowledge, and skill meet.[4] Desire is about wanting to do something. Knowledge is understanding what to do. And skill is the ability to do it.

Desire, knowledge, and skill are equally important for bridging gaps in cultural understanding. This article speaks to the first two factors—*desire* and *knowledge*—and also provides suggestions for gaining *skill*.

Desire to communicate. When our actions are grounded in a sincere desire to understand others, we can be much more effective. Knowing techniques for communicating across cultures is valuable. At the same time, this cannot take the place of the sincere desire and commitment to create understanding. If you truly value cultural diversity, you can discover and create ways to build bridges between people.

Know about other cultures. Back up your desire with knowledge. People from different cultures read differently, write differently, think differently, eat differently, and learn differently than you. Knowing this, you can be more effective with your classmates, coworkers, and neighbors.

Cultures also differ in a variety of dimensions. One of the most important dimensions is *style*. We can also speak of learning styles, communication styles, relationship styles, and other styles.

James Anderson, Dean of the Division of Undergraduate Studies at North Carolina State University, speaks of the relationship between analytical and relational styles.[5] Most of our schools favor students with an analytical style. These students learn abstract concepts easily and are adept at reading, writing, and discussing ideas. They can learn parts of a subject even if they don't have a view of the whole. Often these students are self-directed, and their performance is not affected by the opinions of others.

A bias toward the analytical style tends to exclude students with a relational style—students who learn by getting the big picture of a subject before the details. They learn better initially by speaking, listening, and doing rather than by reading or writing. These students prefer to learn about subjects that relate to their concerns or are presented in a lively, humorous way. In addition, they are influenced by the opinions of people they value and respect. All of these things point to a unique learning style.

Differing styles exist in every aspect of life—family structure, religion, relationships with authority, and more. Native Americans might avoid conflict and seek mediators. People from certain Asian cultures might feel that it's rude to ask questions. Knowing about such differences can help avoid misunderstandings.

Today there is a wealth of material about cultural diversity. The greater our knowledge of other cultures, the easier it is for us to be tolerant. The more we explore our differences, the more we can discover our similarities.

Begin with an intention to increase your sensitivity toward other cultures. Be willing to ask questions and share ideas with all kinds of people. Just get the conversation started. You can learn something valuable from anyone when you reach out.

Develop skills. With the desire to communicate and gain knowledge of other cultures, you can develop specific skills on three levels. The first is personal—becoming aware of your own biases. The second is interpersonal—forming alliances with people of other races and cultures. The third is institutional— pointing out the discrimination and racism that you observe in organizations. Be an advocate for change.

Be active. Learning implies activity. Learning ways to communicate across cultures is no exception. It's ineffective to assume that this skill will come to you merely by sharing the same classroom with people from other races and ethnic groups. It's not the responsibility of others to raise your cultural awareness. That job is yours, and it calls for energy.

Look for common ground. Some goals cross culture lines. Most people want health, physical safety, economic security, and education.

Most students want to succeed in school and prepare for a career. They often share the same teachers. They have access to many of the same resources at school. They meet in the classroom, on the athletic field, and at cultural events. To promote cultural understanding, we can become aware of and celebrate our differences. We

The greater our knowledge of other cultures, the easier it is for us to be tolerant.

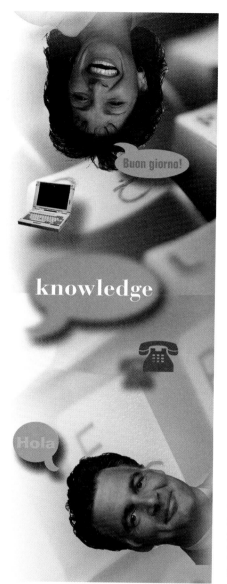

can also return to our common ground.

Practice looking for common ground. You can cultivate friends from other cultures. Do this through volunteering, serving on committees, or joining study groups—any activity in which people from other cultures are also involved. Then your understanding of other people unfolds in a natural, spontaneous way.

The key is to honor the differences among people while remembering what we have in common.

Assume differences in meaning. Each day we can make an intention to act and speak with the awareness that cultures differ. One option is to look for several possible meanings of our words and actions.

Assume that differences in meaning exist, even if you don't know what they are. After first speaking to someone from another culture, don't assume that you've been understood or that you fully understand the other person. The same action can have different meanings at different times, even for members of the same culture. Check it out. Verify what you think you have heard. Listen to see if what you spoke is what the other person received.

If you're speaking to someone who doesn't understand English well, keep the following ideas in mind:

- Speak slowly and distinctly.

- To clarify your statement, don't repeat individual words over and over again. Restate your entire message in simple, direct language. Avoid slang.

- Use gestures to accompany your words.

- Since English courses for non-native speakers often emphasize written English, write down what you're saying. Print your message in capitalized block letters.

- Stay calm and avoid sending nonverbal messages that you're frustrated.

Look for individuals, not group representatives.
Sometimes the way we speak glosses over differences among individuals and reinforces stereotypes. For example, a student worried about her grade in math expresses concern over "all those Asian students who are skewing the class curve." Or a Caucasian music major assumes that her African American classmate knows a lot about jazz. We can avoid such errors by seeing people as individuals—not spokespersons for an entire group.

Get inside another culture. You might find yourself fascinated by one particular culture. Consider learning as much about it as possible. Immerse yourself in that culture. Read novels, see plays, go to concerts, listen to music, look at art, take courses, learn the language. Find opportunities to speak with members of that culture. Your quest for knowledge will be an opening to new conversations.

Celebrate your own culture.
Learning about other cultures does not mean abandoning your own. You could gain new appreciation for it. You might even find out that members of your ethnic group have suffered discrimination. In the process of celebrating your own culture, you can gain valuable insights into the experiences of other people.

Find a translator, mediator, or model. People who move with ease in two or more cultures can help us greatly. Diane de Anda, a professor at the University of California, Los Angeles, speaks of three kinds of people who can communicate across cultures. She calls them *translators, mediators,* and *models.*[6]

A *translator* is someone who is truly bicultural—a person who relates skillfully to people in a mainstream culture and people from a contrasting culture. This person can share her own experiences in overcoming

discrimination, learning another language or dialect, and coping with stress. She can point out differences in meaning between cultures and help resolve conflict.

Mediators are people who belong to the dominant or mainstream culture. Unlike translators, they might not be bicultural. However, mediators value diversity and are committed to cultural understanding. Often they are teachers, counselors, tutors, mentors, or social workers.

Models are members of a culture who are positive examples. Models include students from any racial or cultural group who participate in class and demonstrate effective study habits. Models can also include entertainers, athletes, and community leaders.

Your school might have people who serve these functions, even if they're not labeled translators, mediators, or models. Some schools have mentor or "bridge" programs that pair new students with teachers of the same race or culture. Students in these programs get coaching in study skills and life skills; they also develop friendships with possible role models. Ask your student counseling service about such programs.

Develop support systems. Many students find that their social adjustment affects their academic performance. Students with strong support systems—such as families, friends, churches, self-help groups, and mentors—are using a powerful strategy for success in school. As an exercise, list the support systems that you rely on right now. Also list new support systems you could develop.

Support systems can help you bridge culture gaps. With a strong base of support in your own group, you can feel more confident in meeting people outside that group.

Ask for help. If you're unsure about how well you're communicating, ask questions: "I don't know how to make this idea clear for you. How might I communicate better?" "When you look away from me during our

The key is to honor the differences among people while remembering what we have in common.

conversation, I feel uneasy. Is there something else we need to talk about?" "When you don't ask questions, I wonder if I am being clear. Do you want any more explanation?" Questions such as these can get cultural differences out in the open in a constructive way.

Remember diversity when managing conflict. While in school or on the job, you might come into conflict with a person from another culture. Conflict is challenging enough to manage when it occurs between members of the same culture. When conflict gets enmeshed with cultural differences, the situation can become even more difficult.

Fortunately, many of the guidelines for managing conflict offered in Chapter Eight: Communicating apply across cultures. Also keep the following suggestions in mind:

- *Keep your temper in check.* People from other cultures might shrink from displays of sudden, negative emotion—for example, shouting or pointing.

- *Deliver your criticisms in private.* People in many Asian and Middle Eastern cultures place value on "saving face" in public.

- *Give the other person space.* Standing too close can be seen as a gesture of intimidation.

- *Address people as equals.* For example, don't offer the other person a chair so that she can sit while you stand and talk.

- *Stick to the point.* When feeling angry or afraid, you might talk more than usual. A person from another culture—especially one who's learning your language—might find it hard to take in everything you're saying. Pause from time to time so that others can ask clarifying questions.

- *Focus on actions, not personalities.* People are less likely to feel personally attacked when you request

specific changes in behavior. "Please show up for work right at 9 a.m." is often more effective than "You're irresponsible."

- *Be patient.* This guideline applies especially when you're a manager or supervisor. People from other cultures might find it difficult to speak candidly with someone they view as an authority figure. Encourage others to speak. Allowing periods of silence might help.

- *Take time to comment when others do well.* However, avoid excessive compliments. People from other cultures might be uncomfortable with public praise and even question your sincerity.

Change the institution. None of us are individuals living in isolation. We live in systems that can be racist. As a student, you might see people of color ignored in class. You might see people of a certain ethnic group passed over in job hiring or underrepresented in school organizations. And you might see gay and lesbian students ridiculed or even threatened with violence. One way to stop these actions is to point them out.

Federal civil rights laws, as well as the written policies of most schools, ban racial and ethnic discrimination. If your school receives federal aid, it must set up procedures that protect students against such discrimination. Find out what those procedures are and use them, if necessary.

Throughout recent history, much social change has been fueled by students. When it comes to ending discrimination, you are in an environment where you can make a difference. Run for student government. Write for school publications. Speak at rallies. Express your viewpoint. This is training for citizenship in a multicultural world.

Reap the rewards. The price we pay for failing to understand other cultures is fear and bigotry—the assumption that one group has the right to define all others. Attitudes such as these cannot withstand the light of knowledge, compassion, and common values.

Overcome stereotypes with critical thinking

Consider assertions such as "College students like to drink heavily," "People who speak English as a second language are hard to understand," and "Americans who criticize the President are unpatriotic."

These are examples of stereotyping—generalizing about a group of people based on the behavior of isolated group members. Stereotypes are a potent source of intellectual error. They are signals to shift our thinking skills into high gear—to demand evidence, examine logic, and insist on accurate information.

The word *stereotype* originally referred to a method used by printers to produce duplicate pages of text. This usage still rings true. When we stereotype, we gloss over individual differences and assume that every member of a group is the same.

Stereotypes infiltrate every dimension of human individuality. People are stereotyped on the basis of their race, ethnic group, religion, political affiliation, geographic location, job, age, gender, IQ, height, or hobby. We stereotype people based on everything from the color of their hair to the year of their car.

Stereotypes have many possible sources: fear of the unknown, uncritical thinking, and negative encounters between individual members of different groups. Whatever their cause, stereotypes abound.

In themselves, generalizations are neither good nor bad. In fact, they are essential. Mentally sorting people, events, and objects into groups allows us to make sense of the world. But when we consciously or unconsciously make generalizations that rigidly divide the people of the world into "us" versus "them," we create stereotypes and put on the blinders of prejudice.

You can take several steps to free yourself from stereotypes.

Look for errors in thinking. Some of the most common errors are:

- *Selective perception.* Stereotypes can literally change the way we see the world. If we assume that homeless people are lazy, for instance, we tend to notice only the examples that support our opinion. Stories about homeless people who are too young or too ill to work will probably escape our attention.

- *Self-fulfilling prophecy.* When we interact with people based on stereotypes, we set them up in ways that confirm our thinking. For example, when people of color were denied access to higher education based on stereotypes about their intelligence, they were deprived of opportunities to demonstrate their intellectual gifts.

- *Self-justification.* Stereotypes can allow people to assume the role of a victim and to avoid taking responsibility for their own lives. An unemployed white male might believe that affirmative action programs are making it impossible for him to get a job—even as he overlooks his own lack of experience or qualifications.

Create categories in a more flexible way. Stereotyping has been described as a case of "hardening of the categories." Avoid this problem by making your categories broader. Instead of seeing people based on their skin color, you could look at them on the basis of their heredity. (People of all races share most of the same genes.) Or you could make your categories narrower. Instead of talking about "religious extremists," look for subgroups among the people who adopt a certain religion. Distinguish between groups that advocate violence and those that shun it.

Test your generalizations about people through action. You can do this by actually meeting people of other cultures. It's easy to believe almost anything about certain groups of people as long as we never deal directly with individuals. Inaccurate pictures tend to die when people from different cultures study together, work together, and live together. Consider joining a school or community organization that will put you in contact with people of other cultures. Your rewards will include a more global perspective and an ability to thrive in a multicultural world.

Be willing to see your own stereotypes. The Power Process: "Notice your pictures and let them go" can help. One belief about ourselves that many of us can shed is *I have no pictures about people from other cultures.* Even people with the best of intentions can harbor subtle biases. Admitting this possibility allows us to look inward even more deeply for stereotypes. Every time that we notice an inaccurate picture buried in our mind and let it go, we take a personal step toward embracing diversity.

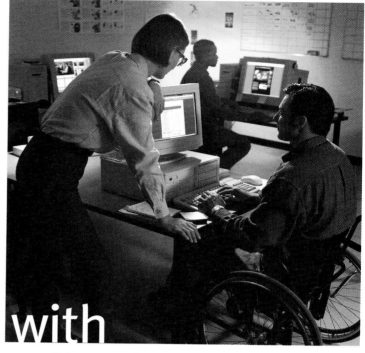

Equal opportunity for people with disabilities is the law. In the United States, both the Civil Rights Act of 1964 and the Rehabilitation Act of 1973 offer legal protection. The Americans with Disabilities Act of 1990 extends earlier legislation.

Students with disabilities

Ask for what you want

It used to be that students with disabilities faced a restricted set of choices in school. For instance, many had trouble majoring in subjects—engineering, science, or medicine—that call for using technical equipment. New technology, such as computers and calculators operated with voice commands, can change that. Students with disabilities can now choose from any course or major offered in higher education.

Even the most well-intentioned instructors can forget about promoting learning for people with disabilities. To protect your rights, speak up. Ask for what you want. Begin with the suggestions in Chapter Eight: Communicating about being assertive, using "I" messages, and listening actively. All of them can help you succeed in school. So can the following.

Use available resources

A wealth of resources already exists to support your success in school. To begin with, check into services offered by your state. Departments of rehabilitation often provide funds for education or can help you find that money. State commissions on disabilities can guide you to services. In addition, the Job Accommodation Network (1-800-526-7234) offers help in placing employees with learning or physical disabilities.

Also find out about services at your school. Libraries might furnish books in Braille or on audiotapes for the visually impaired. Many counseling and student health centers target certain services to people with disabilities, including learning disabilities. Some schools offer disability resource centers. Other services to ask about include:

- Permits that allow you to park a car closer to classrooms.

- Note-taking services.

- Lecture transcriptions.

- Textbook-reading services and textbooks on tape.

- Sign language interpreters.

- Help in selecting courses and registering for classes.

- Assistants for laboratory courses in science.

- Shuttle buses for transportation between classes.

- Closed captioning for instructional television programs.
- TTY/TDD devices for students with hearing impairments.
- Assistance with taking tests.

Speak assertively

Tell instructors when it's appropriate to consider your disability. If you use a wheelchair, for example, ask for appropriate transportation on field trips. If you have a visual disability, request that instructors speak as they write on the chalkboard. Also ask them to use high-contrast colors and to write legibly.

Plan ahead

Meet with your counselor or advisor to design an educational plan—one that takes your disability into account. A key part of this plan is choosing instructors. Ask for recommendations before registering for classes. Interview prospective instructors and sit in on their classes. Express an interest in the class, ask to see a course outline, and discuss any adjustments that could help you complete the course. Some of the services you request might take extra time to deliver. Allow for possible delays as you plan your schedule.

Use empowering words

Changing just a few words can make the difference between asking for what you want and apologizing for it. When people refer to disabilities, you might hear words such as *special treatment, accommodation,* and *adaptation.* Experiment with using *adjustment* and *alternative* instead. The difference between these terms is equality. Asking for an adjustment in an assignment is asking for the right to produce equal work—not for special treatment that "waters down" the assignment.

Ask for appropriate treatment

Many instructors will be eager to help you. At times they might go overboard. For example, a student who has trouble writing by hand might ask to complete in-class writing assignments on a computer. "OK," the teacher might reply, "and take a little extra time. For you, there's no rush."

For some students this is a welcome response. For others, there is no need for an extended timeline. They can reply, "Thank you for thinking of me. I'd prefer to finish the assignment in the time frame allotted for the rest of the class."

Take care of yourself

Many students with chronic illnesses or disabilities find that rest breaks are essential. If this is true for you, write such breaks into your daily or weekly plan. A related suggestion is to treat yourself with respect. If your health changes in a way that you don't like, avoid berating yourself. Even when you do not choose the conditions in your life, you can choose your attitude toward those conditions.

It's important to accept compliments and periodically review your accomplishments in school. Fill yourself with affirmation. As you educate yourself, you are attaining mastery.

voices

student

Before I was diagnosed with dyslexia, I was constantly frustrated whenever I had to take a test. I was never able to complete my exams because I didn't read or write as quickly as the other students in my class. When I discussed this problem with my advisor, he recommended I talk to a counselor in the learning assistance center. Now, I take my tests at the learning center and have additional time to accommodate for my disability.

—IRENE CHO

Dealing with sexism and sexual harassment

Sexism and sexual harassment are real. These are events that occur throughout the year at schools and workplaces. Nearly all of these incidents are illegal or violate organizational policies.

Until the early nineteenth century, women in the United States were banned from attending colleges and universities. Today they make up the majority of first-year students in higher education, yet they still encounter bias based on gender.

This bias can take many forms. For example, instructors might gloss over the contributions of women. Students in philosophy class might never hear of a woman named Hypatia, an ancient Greek philosopher and mathematician. Those majoring in computer science might never learn about Rear Admiral Grace Murray Hopper, who pioneered the development of a computer language named COBOL. And your art history textbook might not mention the Mexican painter Frida Kahlo or the American painter Georgia O'Keeffe.

Though men can be subjects of sexism and sexual harassment, women are more likely to experience this form of discrimination. Even the most well-intentioned people might behave in ways that hurt or discount women. Sexism is a factor when:

- Instructors use only masculine pronouns—*he, his,* and *him*—to refer to both men and women.

- Career counselors hint that careers in mathematics and science are not appropriate for women.

- Students pay more attention to feedback from a male teacher than from a female teacher.

- Women are not called on in class, their comments are ignored, or they are overly praised for answering the simplest questions.

- Examples given in a textbook or lecture assign women only to traditionally "female" roles, such as wife, mother, day care provider, elementary school teacher, or nurse.

- People assume that middle-aged women who return to school have too many family commitments to study adequately or do well in their classes.

Many kinds of behavior—both verbal and physical—can be categorized as sexual harassment. This kind of discrimination involves unwelcome sexual conduct. Examples of such conduct in a school setting are:

- Sexual touching or advances.

- Any other unwanted touch.

- Unwanted verbal intimacy.

- Sexual graffiti.

- Displaying or distributing sexually explicit materials.

- Sexual gestures or jokes.

- Pressure for sexual favors.

- Talking about personal sexual activity.

- Spreading rumors about someone's sexual activity or rating someone's sexual performance.

Sexual Harassment: It's Not Academic, a pamphlet from the U.S. Department of Education, quotes a woman who experienced sexual harassment in higher education: "The financial officer made it clear that I could get the money I needed if I slept with him."

That's an example of *quid pro quo harassment.* This legal term applies when students believe that an educational decision depends on submitting to unwelcome sexual conduct. *Hostile environment harassment* takes place when such incidents are severe, persistent, or pervasive.

The feminist movement has raised awareness about discrimination against women. We can now respond to sexism and sexual harassment in the places we live, work, and go to school. Specific strategies follow.

Point out sexist language and behavior. When you see examples of sexism, point them out. Your message can be more effective if you use "I" messages instead of personal attacks, as explained in Chapter Eight: Communicating. Indicate the specific statements and behaviors that you consider sexist.

For example, you could rephrase a sexist comment so that it targets another group, such as Jews or African Americans. People might spot anti-Semitism or racism more readily than sexism.

Keep in mind that men can also be subjected to sexism, ranging from antagonistic humor to exclusion from jobs that have traditionally been done by women.

Observe your own language and behavior. Looking for sexist behavior in others is effective. Detecting it in yourself can be just as powerful. Write a Discovery Statement about specific comments that could be interpreted as sexist. Then notice if you say any of these things. Also ask people you know to point out occasions when you use similar statements. Follow up with an Intention Statement that describes how you plan to change your speaking or behavior.

You can also write Discovery Statements about the current level of intimacy (physical and verbal) in any of your relationships at home, work, or school. Be sure that any increase in the level of intimacy is mutually agreed upon.

Encourage support for women. Through networks, women can work to overcome the effects of sexism. Strategies include study groups for women, women's job networks, and professional organizations, such as Women in Communications. Other examples are counseling services and health centers for women, family planning agencies, and rape prevention centers. Check your school catalog and library to see if any of these services are available at your school.

If your school does not have the women's networks you want, you can help form them. Sponsor a one-day or one-week conference on women's issues. Create a discussion or reading group for the women in your class, department, residence hall, union, or neighborhood.

Set limits. Women, value yourselves. Recognize your right to an education without the distraction of inappropriate and invasive behavior. Trust your judgment about when your privacy or your rights are being violated. Decide now what kind of sexual comments and actions you're uncomfortable with—and refuse to put up with them.

Take action. If you are sexually harassed, take action. Some key federal legislation protects the rights of women. One is Title VII of the Civil Rights Act of 1964. Guidelines for interpreting this law offer the following definition of harassment. *Unwelcome sexual advances, requests for sexual favors, and other verbal or physical conduct of a sexual nature constitute sexual harassment when:*

1. Submission to this conduct becomes a condition of employment.

2. Women's response to such conduct is used as a basis for employment decisions.

3. This conduct interferes with work performance or creates an offensive work environment.

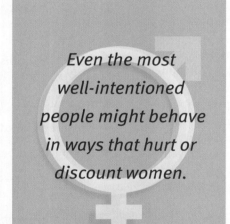

Even the most well-intentioned people might behave in ways that hurt or discount women.

The law also states that schools must take action to prevent sexual harassment.

Another relevant law is Title IX of the Education Amendments of 1972. This act bans discrimination against students and employees on the basis of gender. It applies to any educational program receiving federal funds.

If you believe that you've been sexually harassed, report the incident to a school official. This person can be a teacher, administrator, or campus security officer. Check to see if your school has someone specially designated to handle your complaint, such as an affirmative action officer or Title IX coordinator.

You can also file a complaint with the Office for Civil Rights (OCR), a federal agency that makes sure schools and workplaces comply with Title IX. In your complaint, include your name, address, and daytime phone number, along with the date of the incident and a description of it. Do this within 180 days of the incident. You can contact the OCR at 1-800-421-3481 or go to the agency's Web site at **http://bcol01.ed.gov/CFAPPS/OCR/ contactus.cfm**. Your community might also offer resources to protect against sexual discrimination. Examples are public interest law firms, legal aid societies, and unions that employ lawyers to represent students. ◪

Seven steps to nonsexist writing

Picture a country that is dominated by women. The vast majority of people in positions of power are female.

This includes executives, administrators, managers, police officers, judges, physicians, and lawyers. Ninety-nine percent of this country's elected officials are women. In fact, the country has never had a male president. In the country's 200-year history, only two men have sat on the Supreme Court. Most of the announcers on radio and television are female. And during marriage ceremonies, it's the custom for a minister (almost always a woman) to say, "I now pronounce you woman and husband."

Now imagine that you're reading a popular book about the history of this society. You might find a passage like this one: "The story of this country is a tale of uncommon courage. We can remember the women who fought to free our country from colonial domination and the women who drafted its constitution. Our proud foremothers guided the country from infancy into the splendor of full-fledged womanhood. And the spirit of this country is still unshakable, thanks to the women who guide it now."

Men reading these words might feel excluded—and for good reason. Judging from the way this passage was written, it's hard to imagine that men even exist.

Now return to our world. You're likely to find examples of a similar problem—only this time, it's women who are being left out.

The lesson is clear: Use language that includes both women and men. Carrying out this suggestion can be challenging, even when the best intentions are involved. Following are some tools you can use to create writing that's gender fair—without twisting yourself into verbal knots.

1 Use gender-neutral terms. Instead of writing *policeman* or *chairman*, for example, use *police officer* or *chairperson*. In many cases there's no need to identify the gender or marital status of a person. This allows us to dispose of expressions such as *female driver, little woman,* and *lady doctor.*

2 Use examples that include both men and women. Good writing thrives on examples and illustrations. As you search for details to support the main points in your paper, include the stories and accomplishments of women as well as men.

3 Alternate pronoun gender. In an attempt to be gender fair, some writers make a point of mentioning both sexes whenever they refer to gender. Another method is to alternate the gender of pronouns throughout a text. Still another option is to alternate male and female pronouns in even- and odd-numbered chapters—the strategy used in this book.

4 Switch to plural. With this approach, a sentence such as *The writer has many tools at her disposal* becomes *Writers have many tools at their disposal.*

5 Avoid words that imply sexist stereotypes. Included here are terms such as *tomboy, sissy, office boy, advertising man, man-eater, mama's boy, old lady,* and *powder puff.*

6 Use parallel names. When referring to men and women, use first and last names consistently. Within the same paper, for instance, avoid the phrase *President George W. Bush and his wife.* An alternative is to mention the First Lady's full name: *Laura Welch Bush.*

7 Visualize a world of gender equality. Our writing is a direct reflection of the way we perceive the world. As we make a habit of recognizing women in roles of leadership, our writing can reflect this shift in viewpoint. That's a powerful step toward gender-fair writing. ✖

We are all leaders

No matter our station in life, at some point most of us become leaders.

Many people mistakenly think that leaders are only those with formal titles such as *supervisor* or *manager*. In fact, some leaders have no such titles. Some have never supervised others. Like Mahatma Gandhi, some people change the face of the world without ever reaching a formal leadership position.

While many of us will never become so well known, we all have the capacity to make significant changes in the world around us. Through our actions and words we constantly influence what happens in our classrooms, offices, communities, and families. We are all conscious leaders, even if sometimes we are unconscious of that fact.

To become more effective leaders, we can better understand the many ways we influence others. The following strategies can have a positive impact on our relationships with our children, parents, friends, teachers, employers, and employees. They can help us relate to our politicians, our places of worship, our cities, our states, and our planet.

Own your leadership

Let go of the reluctance that many of us feel toward assuming leadership. It's impossible to escape leadership. Every time you speak, you lead others in some small or large way. Every time you take action, you lead others through your example. Every time you ask someone to do something, you are in essence leading that person. Leadership becomes more effective when it is consciously applied.

Be willing to be uncomfortable

Leadership is a courageous act. Leaders often are not appreciated or even liked. They can feel isolated, cut off from their colleagues. This can sometimes lead to self-doubt and even fear.

Before you take on a leadership role, be aware that you might experience such feelings. Also remember that none of them needs to stop you from leading.

Allow huge mistakes

The more important and influential you are, the more likely it is that your mistakes will have huge consequences. The chief financial officer for a large company can make a mistake that costs thousands or even millions of dollars. A physician's error could cost a life. As commander in chief of the armed forces, the president of a country can make a decision that costs thousands of lives.

At the same time, these people are in a position to make huge changes for the better—to save thousands of dollars or lives through their power, skill, and influence.

People in leadership positions can become paralyzed and ineffective if they fear making a mistake. It's necessary for them to act even when information is incomplete or when they know a catastrophic mistake is a possible outcome.

Take on big projects

Leaders make promises. And effective leaders make big promises. These words—"I will do it. You can count on me"—distinguish a leader.

Look around your world to see what needs to be done and then take it on. Consider taking on the biggest project you can think of—ending world hunger, eliminating nuclear weapons, wiping out poverty, promoting universal literacy. Think about how you'd spend your life if you knew that you could make a difference regarding these overwhelming problems. Then take the actions you considered. See what a difference they can make for you and for others.

Tackle projects that stretch you to your limits—projects that are worthy of your time and talents.

Tackle projects that stretch you to your limits— projects that are worthy of your time and talents.

Provide feedback

An effective leader is a mirror to others. Share what you see. Talk with others about what they are doing effectively—*and* what they are doing ineffectively.

Keep in mind that people might not enjoy your feedback. Some would probably rather not hear it at all.

Two things can help. One is to let people know up front that if they sign on to work with you, they can expect feedback. Also give your feedback with skill. Use "I" messages as explained in Chapter Eight: Communicating. Back up any criticisms with specific observations and facts. And when people complete a task with exceptional skill, point that out, too.

Paint a vision

Help others see the big picture, the ultimate purpose of a project. Speak a lot about the end result and the potential value of what you're doing.

There's a biblical saying: "Without vision, the people perish." Long-term goals usually involve many intermediate steps. Unless we're reminded of the purpose for those day-to-day actions, our work can feel like a grind. Leadership is the art of helping others lift their eyes to the horizon—keeping them in touch with the ultimate value and purpose of a project. Keeping the vision alive helps spirits soar again.

Model your values

"Be the change you want to see" is a useful motto for leaders. Perhaps you want to see integrity, focused attention, and productivity in the people around you. Begin by modeling these qualities yourself.

It's easy to excite others about a goal when you are enthusiastic about it yourself. Having fun while being productive is contagious. If you bring these qualities to a project, others might follow suit.

Make requests—lots of them

An effective leader is a request machine. Making requests—both large and small—is an act of respect. When we ask a lot from others, we demonstrate our respect for them and our confidence in their abilities.

At first, some people might get angry when we make requests of them. Over time, many will see that requests are compliments, opportunities to expand their skills. Ask a lot from others, and they might appreciate you for it.

Follow up

What we don't inspect, people don't respect. When other people agree to do a job for you, follow up to see how it is going. This can be done in a way that communicates your respect and interest—not your fear that the project might flounder. When you display a genuine interest in other people and their work, they are more likely to view you as a partner in achieving a shared goal.

Focus on the problem, not the person

Sometimes projects do not go as planned. Big mistakes occur. If this happens, focus on the project and the mistakes—not the personal faults of your colleagues. People do not make mistakes on purpose. If they did, we would call them "on-purposes," not mistakes. Most people will join you in solving a problem if your focus is on the problem, not on what they did wrong.

Acknowledge others

Express genuine appreciation for the energy and creativity that others have put into their work. Take the time to be interested in what they have done and to care about the results they have accomplished. Thank and acknowledge them with your eyes, your words, and the tone of your voice.

Share credit

As a leader, constantly give away the praise and acknowledgment that you receive. When you're congratulated for your performance, pass it on to others. Share the credit with the group.

When you're a leader, the results you achieve depend on the efforts of many others. Acknowledging that fact often is more than telling the truth—it's essential if you want to continue to count on their support in the future.

Delegate

Ask a coworker or classmate to take on a job that you'd like to see done. Ask the same of your family or friends.

Delegate tasks to the mayor of your town, the governor of your state, and the leaders of your country.

Take on projects that are important to you. Then find people who can lead the effort. You can do this even when you have no formal role as a leader.

We often see delegation as a tool that's available only to those above us in the chain of command. Actually, delegating up or across an organization can be just as effective. Consider delegating a project to your boss. That is, ask her to take on a job that you'd like to see accomplished. This might be a job that you cannot do, given your position in the company.

Communicate assertively—not aggressively

Aggressive behavior is generally ineffective. People who act aggressively are domineering. They often get what they want by putting down other people or using strong-arm methods. When they win, other people lose.

Assertive behavior is a sign of a healthy, strong leader. Assertive people are confident and respectful of others as well as themselves. They ask directly for what they want without feeling embarrassed or inadequate. When they fail to get what they want, their self-esteem does not suffer.

Many of us don't act assertively out of fear that we will appear aggressive. However, *passive behavior*—neither assertive nor aggressive—can get us nowhere. By remaining quiet and submissive, we allow others to infringe on our rights. When others run our lives, we fail to have the lives we want. The alternative is to ask for what we want, appropriately and assertively.

Listen

Sometimes it seems that effective leaders talk a lot. Chances are, they also listen a lot. As a leader, be aware of what other people are thinking, feeling, and wanting. Listen fully to their concerns and joys. Before you criticize their views or make personal judgments, take the time to understand what's going on inside them.

This is not merely a personal favor to the people you work with. The more you know about your coworkers or classmates, the more effectively you can lead them.

Practice

Leadership is an acquired skill. No one is born knowing how to make requests, give feedback, create budgets, do long-range planning, or delegate tasks. We learn these things over time, with practice, by seeing what works and what doesn't.

At times, leadership is a matter of trial and error and flying by the seat of your pants. As a leader, you might sometimes feel that you don't know what you're doing. That's OK. A powerful course of action can be discovered in midstream. You can *act* as a leader even when you don't *feel* like a leader. As a process of constant learning, leadership calls for all of the skills of master students. Look for areas in which you can make a difference and experiment with these strategies. Right now there's something worth doing that calls for your leadership. Take action and others will join you. ⊠

voices

student

As a parent, returning to college has been a positive experience for my entire family. I have had a chance to model being a good student for my children. They are eager to finish high school and continue on to college just like their dad.

—LAMONT JACKSON

→ The world you live in

As you have read, diversity is not just about desire: it's also about knowledge. In order for you to communicate effectively, it is important to know about the people and cultures around you. Here are just a few websites that you can look to for information on the changing landscape of your state, country, and the world. Understanding all the circumstances, trends, and changes affecting the different populations and cultures of the world can give you a better understanding of who you are.

http://www.fedstats.gov/
Statistics by state or subject from hundreds of US Federal agencies.

http://www.census.gov/
Access to statistics from the US Census Bureau.

http://uscis.gov/graphics/index.htm
Information on immigration in the US.

http://stats.bls.gov/
Employment and occupational outlook information from the Department of Labor.

http://fisher.lib.virginia.edu/collections/stats/histcensus/
Population and economic statistics from 1790 to 1960, provided by the University of Virginia Library.

http://www.prb.org/
Information on population trends, national and international, from the Population Reference Bureau.

http://www.cia.gov/cia/publications/factbook/index.html
Information on population, technology, economy, agriculture, and other data on over 260 nations throughout the world from the CIA World Factbook.

http://www.worldbank.org
Statistics on poverty in developing countries across the world.

http://www.who.int/en/
Information related to healthcare worldwide from the World Health Organization.

For further research suggestions, visit the *Becoming a Master Student* Web site at

m>
masterstudent.college.hmco.com

journal entry 26

Discovery/Intention Statement

There are things we think about telling people, but don't. Examine your relationships and complete the following statements.

I discovered that I am not communicating about . . .

_____

_____

with . . .

_____

_____

I discovered that I am not communicating about . . .

_____

_____

with . . .

_____

_____

I discovered that I am not communicating about . . .

_____

_____

with . . .

_____

_____

Now choose one idea from this chapter that can open communication with these people in these areas. Describe below how you will use this idea.

I intend to . . .

_____

_____

_____

_____

journal entry 27

Discovery Statement

In the space below, describe the circumstances of a conversation you had today and summarize its content.

_____

_____

_____

_____

_____

Now reflect on this conversation. Determine whether it aligned with your values and goals.

I discovered that . . .

_____

_____

_____

_____

_____

_____

voices

student

The whole concept of choosing your conversations to be successful was probably the most useful for me in the book. I discovered that the people and conversations I chose to surround myself were getting me nowhere, fast! As soon as I made the change to choose my conversations around everyone, I noticed a difference in myself and my motivation to succeed in school.

—MARIA MARTINEZ

Write down the first words that come to mind when you hear the terms listed below. Do this now.

musician

_____

_____

homeless people

_____

_____

_____

football players

_____

_____

computer programmers

_____

_____

disabled person

_____

_____

_____

retired person

_____

_____

_____

adult learner

_____

_____

Next, exchange your responses to this exercise with a friend. Did you discover stereotypes or other examples of bias? What counts as evidence of bias? Summarize your answers here.

_____

_____

_____

_____

_____

_____

_____

_____

_____

power process

Choose your conversations and your community

Conversations can exist in many forms. One involves people talking out loud to each other. At other times, the conversation takes place inside our own heads, and we call it thinking. We are even having a conversation when we read a magazine or a book, watch television or a movie, or write a letter or a report. These observations have three implications that wind their way through every aspect of our lives.

Conversations shape our lives

One is that conversations exercise incredible power over what we think, feel, and do. We become our conversations. They shape our attitudes, our decisions, our opinions, our emotions, and our actions. Each of these is primarily the result of what we say over and over again, to ourselves and to others. If you want clues as to what a person will be like tomorrow, listen to what she's talking about today.

Conversation is constant

This leads to a second discovery. Given that conversations are so powerful, it's amazing that few people act on this fact. Most of us swim in a constant sea of conversations, almost none of which we carefully and thoughtfully choose.

Consider how this works. It begins when we pick up the morning paper. The articles on the front page invite us to a conversation about current events. Often the headlines speak of war, famine, unemployment figures, and other species of disaster. The advertisements start up a conversation about fantastic products for us to buy.

They talk about hundreds of ways for us to part with our money.

That's not all. If we flip on the radio or television, or if we surf the Web, millions of other conversations await us. Thanks to modern digital technology, many of these conversations take place in CD-quality sound, high-resolution images, and living color 24 hours each day.

Something happens when we tune in to conversation in any of its forms. We give someone else permission to dramatically influence our thoughts—the conversation in our heads. When we watch a movie, scenes from that movie become the images in our minds. When we read a book, passages from that book become the voice in our heads. It's possible to let this happen dozens of times each day without realizing it.

You have a choice

The real power of this process lies in a third discovery: We can choose our conversations. Certain conversations create real value for us. They give us fuel for reaching our goals. Others distract us from what we want. They might even create lasting unhappiness and frustration.

We can choose more of the conversations that exhilarate and sustain us. Sometimes we can't control the outward

circumstances of our lives. Yet no matter what happens, we can retain the right to choose our conversations.

Suppose that you meet with an instructor to ask about some guidelines for writing a term paper. She launches into a tirade about your writing skills and lack of preparation for higher education. This presents you with several options. One is to talk about what a jerk the instructor is and give up on the idea of learning to write well. Another option is to refocus the conversation on what you can do to improve your writing skills, such as working with a writing tutor or taking a basic composition class. These two sets of conversations will have vastly different consequences for your success in school.

The conversations you have are dramatically influenced by the people you associate with. If you want to change your attitudes about almost anything—prejudice, politics, religion, humor—choose your conversations by choosing your community. Spend time with people who speak about and live consistently with the attitudes you value. Use conversations to change habits. Use conversations to create new options in your life.

A big part of this Power Process is choosing *not* to participate in certain conversations. Sometimes we find ourselves in conversations that are not empowering— gripe sessions, gossip, and the like. That's a time for us to switch the conversation channel. It can be as simple as changing the topic, politely offering a new point of view, or excusing ourselves and walking away.

Some conversations are about antagonism. Instead of resolving conflict, they fan the flames of prejudice, half-truths, and misunderstanding. We can begin taking charge of these conversations by noticing where they start and choosing ways to change them.

Go for balance

One immediate way to take charge of any conversation is to notice its *time frame*—whether the conversation dwells on the past, the present, or the future.

Conversations about the past can be fun and valuable. When we focus exclusively on the past, however, we can end up rehashing the same incidents over and over again. Our future could become little more than a minor variation of what has already occurred in our lives.

Conversations with a focus on the future can also be empowering. A problem arises if these conversations focus on worst-case scenarios about what could go wrong next week, next month, or next year. Having too many of these conversations can add a baseline of worry and fear to our lives.

As an alternative, we can choose to have constructive conversations about the present as well as the past and

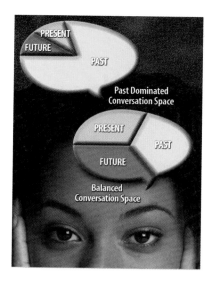

future. Conversations about the past can dwell on what we learn from our experiences. Conversations about the present can focus on what we currently love about our lives and on ways to solve problems. Instead of worrying about the future, we can use our planning skills to set goals that we feel passionately about and consider ways to prevent potential problems.

In looking for ways to balance our conversations, we can also select among four categories of *topics:* things, other people, ourselves, and relationships. Most conversations fall into one of these categories.

Many people talk about things (cars, houses, trips, football games, weather) or gossip about others (politicians, actors, neighbors, kids, coworkers) far more than they talk about anything else. To create more balance in your conversations, remember the other two categories of topics. Talk about yourself—your heartfelt desires, fears, and joys—and about ways to create more loving relationships as well.

Conversations promote success

Excelling in higher education means allowing plenty of time for conversations that start in class and continue in your reading and your notes. Extend those conversations by visiting with your instructors during their office hours, talking to classmates, and forming study groups.

Right now you're holding a conversation about student success. This conversation has a big red cover that features the words *Becoming a Master Student*. Its chapters invite you to 12 subconversations that can make a real difference in what you get in exchange for your hard-earned tuition money.

When we choose our conversations, we discover a tool of unsurpassed power. This tool has the capacity to remake our thoughts—and thus our lives. It's as simple as choosing the next article you read or the next topic you discuss with a friend.

Begin applying this Power Process today. Start choosing your conversations and watch what happens. ◈

put it to work

By 2008, the U.S. Department of Labor predicts that 27 percent of the total U.S. civilian work force will be either African American, Hispanic, or Asian. Your next boss or coworker could be a person whose life experience and view of the world differs radically from yours.

Geert Hofstede, a Dutch psychologist and author of *Culture's Consequences: Comparing Values, Behaviors, Institutions and Organizations Across Nations*, identifies several core dimensions of cultural difference. Keeping them in mind can help you prevent and resolve conflict with coworkers on project teams.

Power-distance. If you observe teams from cultures based on high power-distance, you will see clear differences in status and power between team members. Some people will clearly function as leaders and others as followers. Compare such teams to those from low power-distance cultures, in which people function basically as equals and decisions are based on consensus. To cope with these differences, ask your team leader to clarify roles. Explain how members are expected to participate in decision making and how their performance will be evaluated.

Supervision. Some of your coworkers might do what they can to avoid uncertainty. They focus on details, expect close supervision, and prefer clearly defined tasks with specific due dates. In contrast, other team members might want less supervision rather than more, preferring to work independently. Your team can function more effectively when you look for such differences and tailor assignments to individual preferences.

Individual and collective orientations. People from many Western cultures value individual achievement, competition, and personal recognition. These workers might clash with people from Latin American and Asian cultures that emphasize group cohesion and cooperation.

If you lead a team marked by this cultural difference, take action to balance these differences. When

supervising workers who are motivated by competition, acknowledge their achievements—and remind them that they are members of a group with a shared goal.

Long-term and short-term orientations. Some workers like to lift their eyes to the horizon and set goals to meet over several years or decades. Their orientation leads them to value patience, and they might be willing to make sacrifices now for long-term gains later. On the other hand, workers with a short-term orientation value immediate results and might quickly tire of long-range planning.

By recognizing this difference in orientation up front, you can make it work for you. Ask workers with a long-term orientation to craft a mission statement, list of core values, and five-year plan for your organization. Leave the details of implementing the plan to team members with a short-term orientation. These workers can focus on the month-by-month and week-by-week tasks that lead to achieving long-range goals. ▨

Name _____ Date _____/_____/_____

1. Racial, ethnic, and other kinds of diversity have become key factors in our lives only in the last decade or two. True or False? Explain your answer.

2. Define the term *culture* and give three examples of different cultures.

3. List three strategies for communicating across cultures.

4. Give two examples of sexist behavior that could take place in higher education.

5. Define the terms *translator, mediator,* and *model* as explained in this chapter.

6. Describe at least one way to overcome stereotypes with critical thinking.

7. Explain a strategy for taking charge of the conversations in your life.

8. Describe three ways to create "gender-fair" writing.

9. Rewrite the following sentence so that it is gender neutral: "Any writer can benefit from honing his skill at observing people."

10. Few of us get the chance to be leaders. True or False? Explain your answer.

learning styles application

The questions below will "cycle" you through four styles, or modes, of learning as explained in the article "Learning styles: Discovering how you learn" in Chapter One. Each question will help you explore a different mode. You can answer the questions in any order.

what if *Describe one action you could take to reduce racism in your community.*

why *Describe an example of discrimination or sexual harassment you've personally experienced or witnessed.*

how *Briefly describe how you will respond differently to incidents of discrimination or sexual harassment after reading this chapter.*

what *List two or three of the most valuable suggestions you gained from this chapter for overcoming discrimination or sexual harassment.*

master student profile

BAYARD RUSTIN

(1912–1987) best remembered as the organizer of the 1963 March on Washington, he brought Gandhi's protest techniques to the American civil rights movement and helped mold Martin Luther King, Jr., into an international symbol of peace and nonviolence.

He wished more than anything else to remake the world around him. He wanted to shift the balance between white supremacy and racial justice, between violence and cooperation in the conduct of nations, between the wealth and power of the few and the poverty and powerlessness of the many. He believed that the most antagonistic human relationships— between a white sheriff and a black sharecropper, between the European colonizer and the Africans he lorded over, between the filthy rich and the struggling poor—could be transformed. He believed that ordinary individuals could make a vast difference in the world, and he communicated this conviction widely.

His strategy rested on a bedrock of optimism that the American political system was flexible and responsive enough to embrace change of revolutionary dimensions. He believed that peaceful democratic means were adequate to the task of remaking relations of power. Rustin also had faith that individual human beings themselves were just as flexible and that, over time, they could be moved to

recognize the worth of every one of their fellows and act accordingly.

In [Martin Luther King, Jr.], Rustin found the person who might take his own deepest aspirations and broadcast them to the nation and the world.

Rustin became teacher to a pupil whose fame would soon outstrip his mentor's. "We hit it off immediately," Rustin recalled, "particularly in terms of the whole concept of nonviolence." Through his theological education, King had a passing acquaintance with the philosophy and career of Gandhi, but it was hardly a resource to draw on in the midst of the pressures of the boycott. Rustin initiated the process that transformed King into the most illustrious American proponent of nonviolence in the twentieth century.

Rustin's Gandhian credentials were impeccable. He had what [King] most immediately needed: extensive experience in nonviolent protest. But Rustin also had something more—years of serious meditation about how the philosophy, strategy, and tactics of nonviolence were of a piece and how together they might fashion a transformative revolutionary movement.

By the 1990's, the fax machine, the laptop computer, e-mail, the World Wide Web, and the mobile phone had dramatically simplified the tasks of communicating and organizing, yet the fact that dates of marches are typically chosen more than a year in ad-

vance suggests that they are detached from immediate events, timely goals, or explosive political situations. Marching on Washington has evolved into public spectacle, weekend entertainment posing as politics.

This was not the case in 1963. Then the idea was bold, fresh, and untried. No one had ever witnessed a mass descent on the nation's capital, unless one counts the Bonus Expeditionary March of veterans at the height of the Great Depression, an undertaking disastrous in every way. Now the civil rights leadership was proclaiming its intention to bring 100,000 protesters to Washington.

[At the march] Rustin led the crowd in a recitation of a pledge to continue the struggle: "I affirm my complete personal commitment for the struggle for jobs and freedom . . . I will pledge my heart and my mind and my body unequivocally and without regard to personal sacrifice, to the achievement of social peace through social justice." ▨

For more biographical information on Bayard Rustin, visit the Master Student Hall of Fame on the *Becoming a Master Student* Web site at

masterstudent.college.hmco.com

10

Technology

Technology, like art, is a soaring exercise of the human imagination.

DANIEL BELL

The test of the machine is the satisfaction it gives you. There isn't any other test.

ROBERT PIRSIG

why

this chapter matters . . .

Your skill with information technology might be as critical to your success as the ability to read, write, listen, and speak well.

what

is included . . .

Technology, satisfaction, and success
Connect to cyberspace
Finding what you want on the Internet
Thinking critically about information on the Internet
Using technology to manage time and money
Write e-mail that gets results
"Netiquette": Being kind while you're online
Joining online communities
Becoming an online learner
Library—the buried treasure
Power Process: "Risk being a fool"
Master Student Profile: Fred Smith

how

you can use this chapter . . .

Become an effective learner when you go online.
Find useful, accurate information on the Internet—and filter out irrelevant content.
Take part in online communities that promote your success.

As you read, ask yourself

what if . . .

I could stay up-to-date with information technology and use it with confidence to achieve my goals?

Technology, satisfaction, and success

Information technology pervades our lives. Computers are not only found on our desktops, in our libraries, and on our laps. They are embedded in cars, appliances, automatic teller machines, grocery checkout lanes, and sometimes—given the latest advances in medical technology—the human body.

Several years ago, the Massachusetts Institute of Technology made headlines by making the content for all of its courses available on the Internet. At the time, this event seemed exotic. Today it is not far from the norm on many campuses.

Courses in higher education are no longer divided into separate categories—distance learning (delivered exclusively over the Internet) versus traditional courses (delivered by human beings standing in front of a classroom). A new model has emerged: the hybrid course that combines online instruction with class meetings and textbooks. Course management software such as WebCT and Blackboard creates virtual classrooms—sites on the World Wide Web where a teacher can post a syllabus, readings, announcements, tests, grades, and a digital "drop box" for student assignments. Digital discussions and debates can also take place via computer bulletin boards, chat rooms, and two-way audio and visual connections. In this chapter, the term *online learning* refers to all of these tools. You can use information technology to succeed in school, advance in your career, and achieve many other goals. Besides helping you complete your course work, computer applications can assist you in creating calendars, setting goals, and managing to-do lists. You can crunch numbers, maintain mailing lists, send and receive faxes, manage your finances, stay abreast of the news, and connect you to people and organizations across the world. In addition, you can edit photos, create videos, produce audio files, and launch a personal Web site that introduces you to the worldwide online community.

There's more to technology savvy than just showing up on campus with your own computer or locating your school's computer labs. Knowing which hardware to use is an essential starting point. Mastering software applications such as word processing, databases, and spreadsheets will also help you succeed with technology in the classroom and in the workplace.

At the same time, succeeding with technology is not about becoming a "hacker" or an expert on the latest digital gadgets. Even students who major in computer science can fumble when it comes to online learning.

The bigger picture is that higher education offers you the chance to integrate technology with your own method of processing information. ▨

journal entry 28

Discovery/Intention Statement

Recall an incident when you felt frustrated during an attempt to use computer-based technology to complete a course assignment. Briefly describe what happened.

I discovered that I . . .

_____

_____

_____

_____

Now skim this chapter for at least five ideas that you intend to explore in more detail—suggestions that could help you become a powerful online learner. Summarize each suggestion in a short phrase and list the page where you found it.

Strategy	Page number

Finally, describe a situation coming up this term—preferably within the next week—in which you could apply several of the suggestions you just listed.

I intend to . . .

_____

_____

_____

_____

Connect to cyberspace

You can take two paths to accessing information technology in higher education. One is through the resources offered by your school. The other is through your own technology resources, including a personal computer.

Your school's resources. Pose the following questions to advisors, librarians, and the staff of your campus computer center. These are especially useful questions to ask when applying to a college or university, or when transferring to a new school.

- Does the school require a level of computer competency for graduation or for completing specific majors?

- How many public access computers are available on campus?

- Are discounts available for students who want to buy a computer through the school?

- Does the school loan or lease computers to students?

- What computer support and troubleshooting services are available on campus?

- What library resources are available online, and are they accessible from remote locations?

- Can students receive credit for courses taken online from other schools?

- Is the school catalogue available online?

- Can students access grades and other personal information online?

- Can students register for classes, drop classes, and add classes online?

- Can students handle financial transactions online—for example, tuition payments, financial aid, and bookstore purchases?

- Are students allowed to create personal Web pages and online portfolios?

- Do faculty members distribute course materials online and accept assignments submitted via e-mail?

- Does tuition include a technology fee? If so, what services does it cover?

- Does the campus provide high-speed Internet connections in residence halls and class buildings?

Your personal resources.
Many campuses have computer labs with equipment that's available for students for free. These labs can get crowded, especially during finals week or when other major assignments are due in large courses. To maintain your access to computers, find several sources of public computers on campus and check their availability.

With some creative thinking, you might find even more possibilities. A library on campus or in your community might offer public access. Some students get permission to use computers at their workplace after hours. Perhaps a friend or family member would be willing to loan you a computer or offer you computer time at his home. If you choose one of these options, be realistic about the number of hours that the computer will be available to you.

You might find that it's more convenient to buy your own computer and peripheral equipment. Find out whether your campus bookstore or another outlet on campus sells computer hardware at a student discount. Also ask about getting an extended warranty with technical support. Other options include leasing a computer or buying a used one.

To make an informed purchase, take your time. Start by contacting an admissions counselor or academic advisor at your school and asking the following questions.

Should I get a laptop computer or a desktop computer? Laptop computers have the obvious advantage of portability. They also take up less space—a key consideration if you live in a dorm room. Yet laptops tend to be more fragile and more expensive than desktop computers.

Also, the portability of laptop computers makes them easy targets for thieves. If you get one, keep it in a secure place or always carry it with you in public. Don't leave your computer unattended, even for a few seconds. Treat your laptop the same way that you treat your wallet or purse. Your computer dealer can give you information about security devices for laptops. These include locks and software that identifies the Internet addresses of stolen computers when thieves use them to go online.

What platform will work better for me—Windows or Macintosh? The majority of personal computers used in higher education and business settings are Windows-based. However, most campuses accommodate Macintoshes. You might also find that students with certain majors—such as art, music, or video production—favor Macintoshes. Ask your academic advisor for guidance in this area. If you use a Macintosh, look for software that freely exchanges files with Windows.

What hardware specifications should my computer meet? To find a personal computer that supports your academic success, think about technical specifications. These are the requirements that computers must meet in order to connect to the campus network and run software applications commonly used by students. In particular ask about requirements for your computer's:

- *Operating system*, the built-in software that keeps track of computer files and allows you to run software applications.

- *Processor*, the piece of hardware that actually carries out the operating system's commands. Processor speed is measured in megahertz (MHz) or gigahertz (GHz). One GHz is about the same as 1,000 MHz. The higher this rating, the faster your computer will run.

- *Random Access Memory (RAM)*, a temporary storage area for data that you're actively using, such as word processing or database files. RAM is measured in megabytes (MB). Get as much RAM as you can afford. The extra memory helps your computer run faster and allows you to open up more software applications at once.

- *Hard drive*, which stores the operating system along with all of the other files you save and use. Space on a hard drive is measured in gigabytes (GB). One gigabyte equals about one 1,000 megabytes.

- *Ethernet card*, sometimes called a network adapter or network interface card (NIC). This allows you to connect your computer to campus networks and the Internet. The speed of an Ethernet card is measured in megabits per second (Mbps). Find out what speed is recommended for your campus.

- *Optical drive*, a piece of equipment built into newer computers, though you can buy it separately. An optical drive allows you to read and write data to compact discs (CDs), digital video discs (DVDs), or both. Use optical drives to make backup copies of all your working files. Another option is to use an Iomega Zip drive and Zip disks to create backups.

What software do I need to successfully complete coursework? Many students find that a package—including a word processor as well as spreadsheet, database, and presentation software—meets their needs. Find out what's recommended for your campus. Again, check with your campus bookstore to see if student discounts are offered on software packages. Also ask whether your school provides software to access the Internet (e-mail and Web browsers) and to protect your computer from viruses.

→ Overcoming technophobia

If you are experiencing technophobia (fear of technology, including computers), this is a wonderful time to overcome it. You can start with these strategies:

- Get in touch with the benefits of technology. Being comfortable with computers can give you an edge in almost every aspect of being a student, from doing library research to planning your career. In the eyes of many employers, experience with computers is sometimes a necessity and almost always a plus.

- Sign up for a computer class for beginners.

- Ask questions. When it comes to computers, there truly aren't any "dumb" questions.

- Find a competent teacher—someone who remembers what it was like to know nothing about computers.

- Just experiment. Sit down, do something, and see what happens. Short of dropping a computer or hitting it with a hammer, you can't hurt the thing.

- Remember that computers are not always user-friendly—at least not yet. Learning how to use them takes patience and time. Knowing this up front can put you at ease and prepare you for the cyberspace adventures ahead.

- Also remind yourself of past successes in making transitions. As far as technology is concerned, this includes everything from writing with a pen to driving a car. You're already mastering a major life change—the transition to higher education. In doing so, you've shown that you have what it takes to tame any technology that enters your life.

Finding what you want on the Internet

Imagine a library with millions of books—a place where anyone can bring in materials and place them on any shelf or even toss them randomly on the floor. That's something like the way information accumulates on the Internet. Finding your way through this maze can be a challenge. But it's worth it.

Experiment with different search sites. Before you go to a computer, think for a moment about how you find information in printed form. When searching a nonfiction book for a specific idea or fact, you can use some basic tools. One is the table of contents, a brief ordered list of the major topics in each chapter. Another tool is the index, a detailed, alphabetized list of topics and subtopics and their associated page numbers.

When searching the Internet—especially the World Wide Web—you can use similar tools:

- *Directories* such as Yahoo.com offer extensive lists of Web pages, all grouped by topic. Think of directories as a table of contents for the Web. Human beings create and maintain these directories, just as writers and editors create a table of contents for a book.

  You might find it helpful to use directories when starting your research. Since these sites are organized by subject, you can often get results that are relevant to your purpose. Go to a search engine later in your research, when you've narrowed down your topic.

- *Search engines* are more like indexes. These tools send out "spiders"—computer programs that "crawl" the Web and other parts of the Internet to find sites that relate to a specific topic. These programs scan millions of Web pages in the same way that a human indexer reviews hundreds of book pages.

- *Meta search engines* draw on the capabilities of several search engines at once—similar to scanning several book indexes at the same time. Examples of meta search engines include Dogpile.com and Metacrawler.com. These tools can be useful when directories and conventional search engines come up with disappointing results.

Each search site has different features. Some, such as Google.com, combine aspects of directories and search engines.

Look for links on each search site that explain how to use advanced search capabilities.

In any case, find a few search sites you like and use them consistently. That way you get to know each one well and capitalize on its strengths.

Treat searches as dialogues with your computer. Even though you're dealing with a machine, you can treat computer-based searches as a series of questions and answers. When doing research, start with a question you want to answer, such as "What mutual funds invest in bonds issued by the U.S. Treasury?" Write the question out as precisely as you can.

Next, identify the key words in this question—for example, *mutual funds, bonds,* and *U.S. Treasury*. Type these words into the blank box that appears on your search site's main page. Be sure you spell your key words correctly. Hit the return key or "Search" button on the screen and wait for your computer to answer with a "hit list" of relevant Web pages.

Check three to five of these pages to see if they include answers to your original question. If not, rephrase your question and search again with different key words.

> *Look for links on each search site that explain how to use advanced search capabilities.*

Use Boolean operators. Boolean operators include the words *AND, OR,* and *NOT.* For example, if you type *portfolios AND résumés,* you'll get a list of Web sites that refer to both portfolios and résumés. *Portfolios OR résumés* will give you sites that refer to either topic. *Portfolios NOT résumés* will give you sites that relate only to portfolios. With some search tools, a plus sign (+) functions like the term *AND.* A minus sign (−) functions in the same way as the term *NOT.*

Use more searching tricks. Knowing some other nifty shortcuts can help you save research time:

- Bookmark Web sites that you visit frequently.

- Restrict your search to specific types of files, such as audio or video files, images, or newsgroup postings.

- Put quotation marks around key words that you want to appear all together and in a specific order on Web pages. For example, using the key words *online learning skills* might return a list of sites about general learning skills as well as sites devoted specifically to online learning. Enclosing those words in quotation marks *("online learning skills")* will yield only the pages where all three of them appear together—an exact match for your key words.

- After performing one key word search, open up a new window and search again using different key words. Compare the search results listed in the two windows.

Scrutinize search results. The Web pages listed at the top of your search results might not be the most suitable ones for your purpose. Many search engines generate revenue by prominently displaying the Web sites of their advertisers. The most useful search tools clearly separate these listings from the rest of their results.

Dig into the "invisible Web." As you use the Web for research, remember that some pages elude conventional search engines. Examples are pages that are searchable only *within* a particular Web site—for example, databases that you can access exclusively from the U.S. Census Bureau site. A popular name for this group of "hidden" pages is the *invisible Web.*

Over time, the size of the invisible Web will shrink as more sophisticated search engines appear. For now, check out search sites that mine all of those hard-to-find pages—for example, *Invisible-Web.net* (**www.invisibleweb.net**) and *The Invisible Web* (**www.invisibleweb.com**). ⊠

exercise 26

EVALUATE SEARCH SITES

Use a computer to access several popular search sites on the Web. Possibilities include:

Alta Vista	www.altavista.com
Ask Jeeves	www.ask.com
Dogpile	www.dogpile.com
Excite	www.excite.com
Google	www.google.com
HotBot	www.hotbot.com
Yahoo	www.yahoo.com

Choose a specific topic that you'd like to research—preferably one related to a paper or other assignment that you will complete this term. Identify key words for this topic and enter them in several search sites. (Open up a different window in your browser for each site.) Be sure to use the same key words each time that you search.

Next, evaluate the search sites by comparing the results that you got and the following factors:

- Simplicity of the site's design and use.

- Number of results you got.

- Presence of duplicate results.

- Quality of results—that is, their relevance to your topic.

- Number of sponsored results (links to the search site's advertisers or paid sponsors) and how clearly these results are identified.

- Number of results that are "dead" links (leading you to inactive Web sites).

- Options for doing advanced searches and the ease of using those options.

Based on your evaluation, list your favorite search sites here:

_____

_____

_____

_____

_____

_____

Chapter Ten **TECHNOLOGY** **311**

Thinking critically
about information on the Internet

Sources of information on the Internet range from the reputable (such as the Library of Congress) to the flamboyant (such as the *National Enquirer*). This fact underscores the need for thinking critically about everything you see online.

Long before the Internet, critical thinking created value in every form of communication. Typos, mistakes, rumors, and downright lies can easily creep into print publications and television programs. Newspaper, magazine, and book publishers often employ fact checkers, editors, and lawyers to screen out errors and scrutinize questionable material before publication.

However, authors of Web pages and other Internet sources might not have these resources or choose to use them. People are free to post anything on the Internet, and this can include outdated facts as well as intentional misinformation. Do not assume that Internet content is more accurate or current than what you find in print.

Taking a few simple precautions when you surf the Internet can keep you from crashing onto the rocky shore of misinformation.

Distinguish between ideas and information. To think more powerfully about what you find on the Internet, remember the difference between information and ideas. For example, consider the following sentence: *Nelson Mandela became president of South Africa in 1994.* That statement provides information about South Africa. In contrast, the following sentence states an idea: *Nelson Mandela's presidency means that apartheid has no future in South Africa.*

Information refers to facts that can be verified by independent observers. *Ideas* are interpretations or opinions based on facts. These include statements of opinion and value judgments. Several people with the same information might adopt different ideas based on that information.

People who speak of the Internet as the "information superhighway" often forget to make the distinction between information and ideas. Don't assume that an idea is more current, reasonable, or accurate just because you find it on the Internet. Apply your critical thinking skills to all published material—print and online.

Look for overall quality. To begin thinking critically about a Web site, step back and examine the features of that site in general. Notice the effectiveness of the text and visuals as a whole. Also note how well the site is organized and whether you can navigate the site's features with ease. Look for the date that crucial information was posted, and determine how often the site is updated.

Next, take a more detailed look at the site's content. Link between several of the site's pages and look for consistency of facts, quality of information, and competency with grammar and spelling.

Also evaluate the site's links to related Web pages. Look for links to pages of reputable organizations. Click on a few of those links. If they lead you to dead ends, this might indicate a site that's not updated often—one that's not a reliable source for late-breaking information.

Look at the source. Think about the credibility of the person or organization that posts a Web site. Look for a list of author credentials and publications.

Notice evidence of bias or special interest. Perhaps the site's sponsoring organization wants you to buy a service, a product, or a point of view. If so, determine whether this fact colors the ideas and information posted on the Web site.

The domain in the Uniform Resource Locator (URL) for a Web site can give you clues about sources of information and possible bias. For example, distinguish between information from a for-profit commercial enterprise (URL ending in .com), a nonprofit organization (.org), a government agency (.gov), and a school, college, or university (.edu). In addition, reputable sites usually include a way for you to contact the author or sponsoring organization outside of the Internet, including a mailing address and phone number.

Look for documentation. When you encounter an assertion on a Web page or some other Internet resource, note the types and quality of the evidence offered. Look for credible examples, quotations from authorities in the field, documented statistics, or summaries of scientific studies. Also look for source notes, bibliographies, or another way to find the original sources of information on your own.

Set an example. In the midst of the Internet's chaotic growth, you can light a path of rationality. Whether you're sending a short e-mail message or building a massive Web site, bring your own critical thinking skills into play. Every word and image that you send down the wires to the Web can display the hallmarks of critical thinking—sound logic, credible evidence, and respect for your audience. ⊠

Using technology to manage time and money

When it comes to managing your time and financial resources, your computer can become as valuable as your calendar and your checkbook.

In addition, gaining experience with time management, project planning, and financial software now—while you are in school—can give you additional skills to list on your résumé. Get started with the following options.

Set and meet goals. Review your responses to the goal-setting exercises in Chapter Two of this book. Take your written goals—long-term, mid-term, and short-term—and key them into a word processing file or database file. Open up this file every day to review your goals and track your progress toward meeting them.

Since success hinges on keeping goals fresh in your memory, print out a copy of your goals file each time you update it. You might wish to post your printout in a visible place, such as in your study area, on your refrigerator, or even next to a bathroom mirror.

In addition to lists of goals, keep files of inspirational quotes, stories, articles, and images.

Another key to goal achievement is asking other people to hold you accountable. Consider sending e-mail messages to friends and family members about your goals. Ask these people to check in with you periodically as key due dates approach, inquire about your progress, and send notes of encouragement.

Save yourself a trip or phone call. The Web offers sites that allow you to manage your bank account, get stock quotes, place classified ads for items you want to sell, book airline reservations, and buy almost anything. Use these sites to reduce shopping time, eliminate errands, and get discounts on purchases.

Also employ technology to decrease phone time and avoid long-distance charges. Use e-mail and real time on-line chatting software to stay in contact with friends, family members, classmates, and teachers.

Manage calendars, contacts, and projects. Software can help you create and edit calendars and to-do lists on your computer. Typically, these applications also allow you to store contact information—mailing addresses, phone numbers, and e-mail addresses—for the key people in your life. To find such products, search the Web using the key words *contact management, project management, time management,* and *software.*

Also use your computer to prevent the snafus that can result when you want to coordinate your calendar with those of several other people. This is often a necessity in completing group projects. Consider creating an area on the Web where group members can post messages, share files, and access an online calendar that shows scheduled events. One option is the *calendar* link at **www.yahoo.com**. You can search the Web for more sites of this type.

Project planning software offers a way to coordinate the work of many people working in teams. Look for features that allow you to create sophisticated timelines such as Gantt, PERT (Program Evaluation Review Technique), and CPM (Critical Path Method) charts. These display a list of tasks, the estimated duration of each task, and the person responsible for completing it.

Crunch numbers and manage money. Many students can benefit from crunching numbers on a computer with spreadsheets such as Excel. This type of computer soft-ware allows you to create and alter budgets of any size. By plugging in numbers based on assumptions about the future, you can quickly create many scenarios for future income and expenses. Quicken and similar products include spreadsheets and other features that can help you manage personal and organizational finances.

Employ a personal digital assistant (PDA). These devices—also called *palmtops* or *pocket PCs*—are handheld computers designed to replace paper-based calendars and planning systems. Many PDAs are small enough to fit in a pocket or purse. You can use them to list appointments and view your schedule in a daily, weekly, or monthly format. If you have a recurring event, such as a meeting that takes place at the same time every week, you can just enter it once and watch it show up automatically on your PDA.

Using a PDA, you can also take notes, create contact lists, manage to-do lists, and keep track of personal expenses. Capabilities for connecting to the Internet and sending e-mail are becoming standard features as well. In addition, PDAs come with software for exchanging files with a personal computer. This allows you to store essential information—such as appointments, to-do lists, and contacts—in a form that's even more portable than a laptop computer.

Some Web sites allow you to download content that is formatted specifically for PDAs. Perhaps some of your online course material will be available in this way.

Before you invest in a PDA, consider its price and potential value. Talk to people who use PDAs and ask about their experience with these devices. You might find a PDA's capabilities to be nice but not essential for the way you work. And after seeing a PDA's small screen size, you might prefer a paper calendar printed in a larger format.

To enter information in a PDA, you'll need to use a tiny onscreen keyboard or a stylus that requires you to form handwritten letters and numbers in a special way. An alternative available with many PDAs is a portable keyboard that you can fold up and store in a briefcase or backpack.

If you do decide to use a PDA, allow for a learning curve. It takes some time to master these time-management devices. ✖

Ways to waste time with your computer

Stay alert for the following computer-based time-wasters.

Trial-and-error learning. Flying by the seat of your pants as you learn the computer sometimes works well. In other cases, you can save critical hours by spending a few minutes reading the instructions or by taking a computer class.

Hours that evaporate while you play. When cruising the Internet or playing computer games, you might find that a whole morning, afternoon, or evening has disappeared into the digital void. If you start losing too much time to computer play, set a specific time to end the fun before you start. Or consider playing a computer game for 20 minutes as a reward for completing your homework.

Endless revising. Computers make it easy to revise your writing, and you might feel tempted to keep fiddling with a paper to the point that you miss your deadline. Experiment with dictating your revisions or marking them on hard copy with a red pencil.

Losing data. It's been said that the two most important words about using a computer are *save* and *backup*. This refers to the fact that power surges and loss of electricity can destroy data. Most computer users can tell stories about losing many hours of work in a millisecond. To prevent this fate, take three simple but powerful steps. First, while you're creating or editing a computer file, save your work every few minutes. Your computer manual will explain how. (Some software does this automatically.)

Second, make backup copies of your files on separate storage media, such as Zip disks or CDs. Having backups promotes peace of mind. Should your computer files ever be lost or damaged, you'll avoid the countless hours of recreating your work from scratch.

Finally, make sure that the computer you're working on has software to detect viruses and repair the damage they can do. Update this software regularly.

Crashing and freezing. Your computer might *crash* or *freeze*—that is, suddenly quit or refuse to respond to anything that you type. Find out how to shut down and restart the computer if this happens.

Getting "spammed." *Spam* is the Internet equivalent of junk mail—unwanted messages that show up in your e-mail inbox. To reduce spam, be selective in giving out your e-mail address. Also check with your Internet service provider for help in minimizing spam.

One more caution. Don't expect your life to slow down or your grades to soar right after you start using a time management application or other new software. Becoming more productive can take several weeks. And there's always more to learn.

Computers can perform many tasks with dizzying speed. What they *don't* do is write papers, create ideas, read textbooks, or attend classes. For those tasks, human beings are irreplaceable.

Write e-mail that gets results

Using e-mail can save paper, time, and postage. By sending e-mail messages, you can avoid playing "phone tag." Used ineffectively, however, e-mail can waste time and cause a host of other frustrations. To get the most from this medium of communication, consider the suggestions that follow.

Target your audience. Be conscious of the amount of e-mail that busy people receive. Send e-mail messages only to the people who need them, and only when necessary.

Write an informative subject line. Along with your name, the subject line is what a recipient sees when your message shows up in his e-mail box. Rather than writing a generic description, include a capsule summary of your message. "Biology 100 Report due next Tuesday" packs more information than "Report." If your message is urgent, include that word in the subject line as well. Your teachers might require a specific format for the subject line of e-mail messages you send to them. Follow those instructions.

Think short. Keep your subject line short, your paragraphs short, and your message as a whole short. Most people don't want to read long documents on a computer screen.

Put the point first. People who use the Internet are often pressed for time. They tend to skim rather than read in detail. To make sure your point gets across, put it at the top of the first paragraph. If your message will take up more than one screen's worth of text, break it up into short sections and add a heading for each section. Then pack those headlines with the important ideas.

Consider how long your message might be stored. Your message could dwell in a recipient's in-basket for weeks or months. Think carefully about the impact of your message, both in the short term and the long term. When composing e-mail, ask for what you want; at the same time, be courteous. Edit sentences written in the heat of a strong emotion—sentences that you might regret later. Also remember that it's easy to send a message to the wrong person. Don't include a statement in any e-mail that would embarrass you if this should happen.

Review your message. Every message you send—even the shortest, most informal message—says something about your attention to detail. Put your best electronic foot forward. If you plan to send a long message, draft it in a word processing program first so that you can take advantage of spelling checkers and other editing devices. Then copy the text and paste it into the body of an e-mail message. Before you hit the "send" button, ask someone else to review the message for clarity.

Use text formatting carefully. Boldface, italics, underlining, smart quotes, and other formatting options might not transfer well across e-mail programs. If your message will be widely circulated, use generic characters that any computer can read.

For example, use asterisks to *emphasize* words. Place titles within plain quotation marks. Don't indent the first line of a paragraph. Instead, insert a "hard return"—a blank line—between paragraphs. Use two hyphens (--) in place of a dash (—). Avoid using special symbols such as ©; instead, use an alternative such as (c).

Test attachments. If you plan to send an attachment, do a dry run first. You might find that it takes a couple of tries to send attachments in a format that your recipient can read. For instructions on how to prepare files as attachments, see the help feature in your e-mail program.

Note: Attachments sometimes come with computer viruses that can damage your hard disk. Open attachments only from people you know, and use antivirus software. Forward attachments with extreme care.

Reply promptly and consciously. Provide context. If you're responding to a question from a previous e-mail, include that question in your response.

Be aware of everyone who will receive your reply. If you hit the "reply to all" button, your response will go to all of the people who received the original message—including those on the "cc" (carbon copy) line. Instead, you might want to reply to just one or two of these people.

Forward messages selectively. Think twice before forwarding generic messages from other sources—cartoons, joke files, political diatribes, and "inspirational" readings. Your recipients might already have an in-basket overflowing with e-mail. Such forwarded messages might be viewed as irritating clutter.

Protect your privacy. Any competent hacker can intercept a private message. Treat all online communication as public communication. Include only content that you're willing to circulate widely, and share personal data with caution. Before sending, ask yourself: "What would be the costs if this information were made public?"

Stay on top of your in-box. Read and respond to new messages promptly. Identify messages that you might refer to again. Sort these by date received, subject, or sender—whatever will help you retrieve them later. Consider printing out essential messages, such as schedules and lists of assignments. Most e-mail programs provide an option to save messages into folders for future reference. Use this option to organize messages that you send and receive. However, if there's little chance that you will refer to a message in the future, delete it now. Tame the e-mail tiger. ✉

"Netiquette"

Being kind while you're online

Certain kinds of exchanges can send the tone of online communications into the gutter. To promote a cordial online community, abide by the following guidelines.

Respect others' time. People often turn to the Internet with the hope of saving time—not wasting it. You can accommodate their desires by typing concise messages. Adopt the habit of getting to your point, sticking to it, and getting to the end.

Fine-tune the mechanics. Proofread your message for spelling and grammar—just as you would a printed message. Some email programs have built-in spelling checkers as an optional tool. Give your readers the gift of clarity and precision. Use electronic communications as a chance to hone your writing skills.

Avoid typing passages in ALL UPPERCASE LETTERS. This is the online equivalent of shouting.

Design your messages for fast retrieval. Avoid graphics and attachments that take a long time to download, tying up your recipient's computer.

Respect copyrights. If you want to quote at length from another person's work, get that person's permission. If you do quote, credit the original source and tell readers where to find it.

Don't dish out spam. *Spam* refers to unsolicited messages, often meant to advertise a product or service, that are sent indiscriminately to large numbers of computer users.

Can the sarcasm. Use humor—especially sarcasm—with caution. A joke that's funny when you tell it in person might fall flat or even offend someone when you put it in writing and send it down the computer wires.

Put out flames. *Flaming* takes place when someone sends an online message tinged with sarcasm or outright hostility. To create positive relationships when you're online, avoid sending such messages. If you get one, do not respond in kind.

Remember that the message is missing the emotion. When you communicate online, the people who receive your e-mail will miss out on voice inflection and nonverbal cues that are present in face-to-face communication. Without these cues, words can be easily misinterpreted.

Reread your message before sending it to be sure you have clarified what you want to say and how you feel.

Some people use *emoticons*—combinations of keyboard characters that represent an emotion. An example is :>) (turn the book sideways to see a smiling face). Keep in mind, though, that emoticons might not be appropriate for some Internet-based communications, such as exchanges with a prospective employer.

Add your signature. End messages with your name and e-mail address. Most e-mail software allows you to create a "signature file" with this information that will appear automatically at the end of every message you send.

Remember common courtesy. The idea of Netiquette extends to the way that you use any piece of technology. For instance, a cell phone that rings in class offends teachers and irritates almost everyone else in the room. Turn off your cell phone and check voice mail messages after class. The cornerstone of Netiquette is to remember that the recipient on the other end is a human being. Whenever you're at the keyboard typing up messages, ask yourself one question: "Would I say this to the person's face?" ✉

Joining online communities

Online communities come in many varieties. You can find them in three basic formats: e-mail lists, newsgroups, and chat rooms.

Listservs

Listservs consist of e-mail addresses for groups of people who want to automatically receive messages on a certain topic. To get the messages, you have to subscribe to the list.

Your instructors might use listservs to communicate with members of a class, especially when large numbers of students are involved.

When you subscribe to a listserv, you can send a message to a posting address at any time. Everyone who subscribes to the list will receive your message. Likewise, you will receive e-mails that other subscribers send to the posting address. Some lists are highly active, generating dozens of messages daily.

Newsgroups

Newsgroups—also called *Usenet groups, Web forums, bulletin boards*, and *discussion boards*—allow members to post and read e-mail messages. Usually, there is some type of subscribing process, which is often free. Once you subscribe to a group, you can choose whether you want to receive new e-mail messages as they appear, daily summaries of messages, or no e-mail messages at all. In the last case, you just view messages at the group's Web site at your convenience.

Newsgroups usually focus on a particular topic—anything from astronomy to Zen Buddhism. Some groups are moderated by a person or group that screens messages. Other groups are a free-for-all, open to any message from any person. Again, instructors might set up newsgroups for members of a class.

To access a newsgroup, you'll need special software. Today that software is often bundled into a Web browser such as Internet Explorer or an e-mail program.

Chat rooms

Chat rooms—sometimes called MUDs (multi-user domains) or MOOs (multi-user domains, object oriented)—allow you to send and receive messages live, in real time. This is as close to a live conversation as most computer users get while they're online. To join in, you'll need to download instant messaging software or use a similar application bundled with your Web browser.

Some chat rooms are set up for specific audiences and special purposes. Rooms might be ongoing or planned to last only for a limited time. For example, newspapers and magazines might create chat rooms that allow readers to discuss feature articles. Your teachers might also set up chat rooms where you and your classmates can take part in digital exchanges for the duration of a course. You might even do group exercises and role playing via chat rooms.

Consider the following suggestions for mastering online communities.

Learn the ground rules. Online communities have written policies about what kinds of messages are permitted. Often you'll receive these rules when you join. Look for a frequently asked questions (FAQ) file that explains the policies.

Stick to the topic. To make an effective contribution to the discussion, write courteous messages that are brief, informative, and relevant to the topic.

Review before you post. By observing what people write and what they don't, you'll learn the unwritten rules for that group. If you include statistics or quote material from someone else, cite the source. Avoid slang, jargon, and sarcasm, especially in class-related discussions.

For more information on mastering online communities, visit

masterstudent.college.hmco.com

Becoming an online learner

Online learning presents an opportunity to practice critical thinking, especially when you hear statements such as these:

- *You have to know a lot about computers in order to take online courses.*

- *If you don't like lecture classes, online courses are the way to go.*

- *Online courses take a lot less time than other courses.*

- *The great thing about online coursework is that you can communicate with instructors any time, and course materials are always available.*

- *Online courses can be fun, but they don't allow you to make any friends.*

- *Turning in online assignments is convenient, but you won't get any feedback on them.*

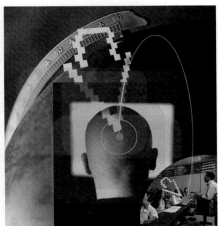

There's compelling evidence against all of these assertions. Get past the misconceptions and set yourself up for successful online learning by using specific strategies before courses begin. Also consider new ways to complete your online coursework, and expand your learning strategies as a whole to include technology.

Before courses begin

Take a First Step about technology. Before you begin your next experience with online learning, practice telling the truth about your current skills in this area. Taking a First Step can uncover hidden strengths and help you make concrete plans to develop new technology skills. The *Becoming a Master Student* Web site has a special tool for this purpose. Go online to **masterstudent. college.hmco.com** and select the link to the E-Learning Readiness Self-Assessment.

Check out the technology requirements for your courses. You can begin to prepare for online learning even before you register for a course. Contact the instructor to see if you can get a course syllabus. Ask about the specifications your computer will need to meet and the applications you'll be expected to use. Your instructor might also assume that students have a certain of amount of experience with online learning, so ask about that as well.

If you're planning to use a computer lab on campus, find one with hardware and software that meets course requirements.

Keep in mind that on-campus computer labs may not allow you to install software you own or software that comes loaded on a CD included with a textbook.

Set up your computer for comfort. If you own a personal computer, you don't have to live with the way it feels and looks when it first comes out of the box. Explore the options for changing onscreen fonts, font sizes, color, brightness, contrast, icon size, keyboard sensitivity, speed of the pointer as it moves across the screen, and screensavers. You can adjust many of these functions via control panels that are part of your computer's system software. For more details, consult the manuals and help programs that come with your computer.

Many computers allow you to add a trail to the pointer so that it becomes easier to find on the screen. Also explore the possibilities for speech-to-text translation. This allow you to use your voice instead of the keyboard to carry out certain commands. Your computer might be able to "read" large sections of text out loud to you. Making such adjustments can be a real help for students with visual impairments—or anyone who faces the prospect of long hours at a computer.

Do a trial run with course technology. Most online courses have been created using course-management software like WebCT or Blackboard. You do not need to install this software to access the online course, but you will need to know the procedure, access code, and password to get into the online course site. Get the details and then verify your access to course Web sites, including online tutorials, presentations, readings, quizzes, tests, assignments, and links to other sites. Also see if you can log on to course-based bulletin boards and chat rooms. Work out any bugs well before the first assignment is due.

Locate support services. If you feel intimidated by technology, remember that there are living, breathing human beings who can help. Possibilities include instructors, people who staff computer labs, librarians, and on-campus technical support services. Computer dealers or manufacturers might offer similar resources, including online help and toll-free numbers for customer service. Locate helpful people and services *before* courses begin. Post their phone numbers next to your computer or in another place you can easily find them when hardware or software breaks down.

Develop a contingency plan. Murphy's Law of Computer Crashes states that technology tends to break down at the moment of greatest inconvenience. You might not find this piece of folklore to be true, but it's still wise to prepare for it in advance:

- Identify several on-campus computer labs with the technology you need.

- Find a technology buddy in each of your classes—someone who can update you on assignments and contact the instructor if you lose Internet access.

- Set up a backup e-mail account in case your Internet service provider goes offline. Many Web sites offer this service for free.

- Get complete contact information—address and office phone and fax numbers—for your instructors.

- Keep extra printer supplies—paper and toner or ink cartridges—always on hand. Don't run out of either on the day that a paper is due.

Set up files. Before classes meet, create a separate folder for each class on your computer's hard disk. Give each folder a meaningful name, such as *biology-spring2007*. Place all files related to a course in the appropriate folder. Doing this can save you from one of the main technology-related time-wasters—searching for lost files.

Also name individual files with care. Avoid changing extensions that identify different types of files, such as .ppt for PowerPoint presentations or .pdf for files in the Adobe Reader portable document format. If you change extensions, you could have problems finding files later or sharing them with other users.

During your online courses

Take responsibility. All learning, especially online learning, depends on your initiative. Don't rely on an instructor to motivate you, particularly in courses that depend heavily on technology. Instead, manufacture your own motivation. Be clear about what you'll gain by doing well in the course. Relate course content to your personal goals. Don't wait to be contacted by your classmates and instructor. Initiate that contact on your own—right at the beginning of the course.

Manage your time. Some students act as if they have all the time in the world to complete their online assign-

ments. The temptation to procrastinate can be strongest with courses that take place mostly or totally online. Such courses can become invisible in your weekly academic schedule, creating the possibility of late-semester all-nighters for completing last-minute work.

Early in the term, create a detailed timeline with a due date for each assignment. Break big assignments into smaller steps and schedule a due date for each step. If possible, submit online assignments early. Staying ahead of the game will help you avoid an all-nighter at the computer during finals week.

The earlier you clarify expectations for online coursework, the greater your opportunities to succeed. When you receive an online assignment, e-mail questions immediately. If you want to meet with an instructor in person, request an appointment several days in advance. In

exercise 27

MAYBE IT'S YOUR BREATH

The way you breathe affects the way you think, and the way you think affects the way you breathe. A good supply of oxygen to the brain is essential for focused concentration.

The next time you find your mind wandering, take a short break and do the following exercise. Read all of the directions; then take a moment to practice this technique. It's especially useful when you've been sitting at a computer for hours and feel fatigued—an example of "techno-stress."

1. Sit up in your chair in a relaxed position. Keep your spine, neck, and head straight. Place your hands uncrossed in your lap.

2. Close your eyes and take 20 or 30 seconds to relax. Let go of any tension in your face, neck, and shoulders.

3. Inhale slowly, breathing deeply. Your chest will expand as your lungs fill with air.

4. When your lungs are full, pause; purse your lips as if you were about to whistle; then exhale evenly and with force through the small hole between your lips.

5. At the end of your exhalation, pause; then push out the last bit of remaining air in three short, forceful puffs.

6. Repeat this process three to five times.

7. When you have finished, sit quietly for a while, observing the rise and fall of your abdomen as you breathe normally.

addition, download or print out online course materials as soon as they're posted on the class Web site. These materials might not be available later in the term.

Consider scheduling times in your daily or weekly calendar to complete online coursework. Give these scheduled sessions the same priority as regular classroom meetings. At these times, check for announcements relating to assignments, tests, and other course events.

Focus your attention. Some students are used to visiting Web sites while watching television, listening to loud music, or using instant messaging software. When applied to online learning, these habits can reduce your learning and imperil your grades. To succeed with technology, turn off the television, quit online chat sessions, and turn down the music. Stay in charge of your attention whenever you learn online.

Ask for feedback. To get the most from online learning, request feedback from your instructor via e-mail. When appropriate, ask for conferences by phone or in person. Be sure to check with your instructor to see how he wants e-mail messages from online course students to be addressed. Many teachers use a standard subject area format so that e-mails from online students can be quickly and easily recognized.

One powerful feature of technology is ease of file sharing. This feature makes it possible to share ideas and collaborate on projects with people who are located across campus—or around the world. Find out how to attach word processing files and other types of documents to your e-mail messages. Software such as Microsoft Word has a "tracking" feature that allows other people to insert comments into your files and even make suggested revisions. These alterations are highlighted on the screen, on a printout, or both. Use such tools to get feedback from both and instructors and peers on your online assignments.

Contact other students. Make personal contact with at least one other student in each of your classes—especially those that involve lots of online coursework. Meet with this person to share notes, quiz each other, critique papers, and do other cooperative learning tasks. This source of support can help you keep current with online work and promote your success.

Merging technology and learning strategies

You can integrate information technology with daily study tasks in a variety of ways. Experiment with the following and invent more of your own.

Create course glossaries. One way to review for tests is to create and maintain a glossary of key terms for each of your courses. Every time you encounter a key word or technical term in your course notes or textbooks, key that word into a word processing or database file. Create a separate file for each of your courses. For each term, write a definition and a sentence using the word in context. Sort the terms in alphabetical order.

Update your glossary files once weekly, based on that week's class work and assigned readings. Each time you update a glossary file, print it out. Keep a current printout in your backpack or briefcase to study on the go.

Capture your notes on disk. Software offers many possibilities for organizing and reviewing the notes you take when listening to lectures or studying textbooks. For example, take lecture notes directly on a laptop, or take handwritten notes and key them into your computer after class. Divide your notes into sections, then write a heading to capture the main point of each section. For greater depth of detail, use several levels of headings ranging from major to minor. To save time when you review, display the headings and scan them as you would scan the headlines in a newspaper. Also use drawing and painting tools to create maps, charts, diagrams, and other visuals that enhance your notes. Look for personal digital assistants that can convert your handwritten notes into text that can be uploaded to your personal computer.

Use computers for cooperative learning. You can turn any study group into an active online community. Experiment with e-mail, bulletin boards, chat rooms, and instant messaging software. These technologies can be lifesavers when your group finds it too difficult to meet in person.

Reflect on your learning. Classroom discussion often provides the opportunity to make connections between theory and practice. Teachers can give examples that relate concepts presented in class to your daily experience.

You can delve into this dimension whenever you learn online. Take the time to reflect on facts and ideas. Write Discovery and Intention Statements to record your personal insights and state how you'll apply what you've learned.

After completing online courses, take time to evaluate the experience. Write about what you liked, what you didn't like, and what you can do to become a more effective online learner. Go beyond the technology and focus on the outcomes—the knowledge and skills you gained. When you create ways to make online education work, you gain another option for lifelong learning. ✖

STAYING MOTIVATED WITH TECHNOLOGY

This exercise demonstrates one way that you can use technology to transform data into useful information and strategies for action. There are six steps. Allow about one hour to complete the exercise.

1. Use a Web browser such as Netscape Navigator or Microsoft Internet Explorer to access the Web site for one of your courses. (Ask your instructor whether you need a password and user ID to do this.)

2. Once you've accessed the site, find the course syllabus or another document that lists assignments, topics to be covered in class, and information about upcoming tests.

3. Copy the syllabus information and paste it into a blank word processing file. Then make this document your own by adding notes. Highlight key information and include any ideas that can help you succeed in the course. For example, you could put due dates for assignments and test dates in boldface. You could also list questions that you want to ask the instructor or specific steps that you plan to take in completing an assignment.

4. Next, write a goal that describes a lasting benefit you want to gain from this course. Focus on a specific body of information you'd like to remember after the course is over, or on a job skill you'd like to acquire. Add your goal to the file you've created and highlight it in boldface or a bright color. Refer to this goal if you ever feel stuck or discouraged while taking the course.

5. List specifically what you will do to meet your course goal. Examples include forming a study group or searching for Web sites that are relevant to the course.

6. Finally, identify specific people who can help you succeed in the course and meet the goal you just created. For instance, highlight contact information (e-mail address, phone number, and office hours and location) for your instructor. Also add contact information for other students in the class—people who can share notes with you, take part in a study group, or assist you in any other way to meet your course goal. Consider adding their e-mail addresses to the address book in your e-mail software.

Staying up-to-date with technology

Computer technology is so dynamic that statements made about it can become outdated almost instantaneously. What once seemed like remote possibilities—such as Web-based television and Internet connection via cable television lines—quickly became realities.

To get the most value from emerging technology, adopt the following habits that can help you to stay up-to-date.

Read. Much of the hottest information about new technology still appears in print. Several magazines and periodicals are devoted to emerging technology. For example, the *Chronicle of Higher Education* regularly includes articles about new technology and its implications for vocational schools, colleges, and universities. *Wired* magazine covers digital technology and popular culture. Many such magazines have related Web sites.

Go to the Internet. Search engines and directories often highlight Web sites that cover the latest technology developments. To find basic information, do a search using the key words *Internet tutorial* or *technology tutorial*.

Hang out with those who know. Seek out people who seem technologically savvy. Go to computer stores and browse among the displays and new products. Talk with the salespeople and ask about what's new. Investigate computer clubs at your school or in your community. Talk to knowledgeable people at on-campus computer labs. Look for a student-friendly help desk or links to technical support on your school's Web site.

Look beyond personal computers. Watch for continuing innovation in other forms of digital technology. These include new capabilities for DVDs, PDAs, cellular phones with an Internet connection, and watches and other small devices with computing and communication capabilities.

Go back to your purpose. Technology can add value to your life—and can also complicate it. Laptops and PDAs make it possible for you to work all of the time, anywhere. Cell phones and text messaging create the risk of interruption at any moment. That might not be what you want. Consider the purposes and values served by the technology in your life. Machines exist to serve you—not the other way around.

Library
the buried treasure

Knowing ways to unearth a library's treasures can enhance your writing, boost your presentation skills, help you plan your career, and enable you to continue learning for the rest of your life. In the early days of the Internet, researchers used to distinguish between sources published in print and sources published online. Today that distinction no longer holds so tightly. There are still benefits to actually going to a library to start your research. In addition to housing print and audiovisual materials, many libraries give you access to online sources—including special databases that are not available on the Web. Also remember that much published material is available only in print, not on the Internet. Books—a form of information technology that's been with us for centuries—still have something to offer.

Remember the best library resource. Libraries give you access to one resource that goes beyond the pages of a book or a site on the Web. That resource is a living person called a librarian.

Librarians have different specialties. Start with a reference librarian, who can usually tell you whether the library has the material that you want or direct you to another source, such as a business, community agency, or government office.

Librarians are trained explorers who can guide you on your expedition into the information jungle. Asking them for help can save you hours.

Take a tour. Libraries—from the smallest one in your hometown to the Smithsonian in Washington, D.C.— consist of just three basic elements:

- *Catalogs*—Online databases that list all of the library's accessible sources.

- *Collections*—Materials, such as periodicals (magazines and newspapers), books, audiovisual materials, and materials available from other collections via interlibrary loans.

- *Computer resources*—Internet access; connections to campus-wide computer networks; and databases stored on CD-ROMs, CDs, DVDs, or online. Through your library, you might have access to databases that are available only by subscription. Ask a librarian for a list of these and about how to access them.

Before you start your next research project, take some time to investigate all three elements of your campus or community library. Start with a library orientation session or tour. Step into each room and ask about what's available there. Find out whether the library houses any special collections or provides access to primary sources that are related to your major.

Search the catalog. A library's catalog lists the materials available in its collections. These listings used to be kept on index cards. Today, libraries catalog their materials on computers; some even include listings for several libraries. To find materials in a library's collections, do a key word search—much like using a search engine on the Internet. The catalog is an alphabetical listing that is cross-referenced by subject, author, and title. Each listing carries the author's name, the title, the publisher, the date of publication, the number of pages and illustrations, the Library of Congress or Dewey decimal system number (for locating materials), and sometimes a brief description of the material. Some catalogs let you see if a book or periodical is on the shelf or checked out—and even allow you to put a hold on the materials you want.

Inspect the collection. When inspecting a library's collections, look for materials such as the following:

- *Encyclopedias*—Use leading print encyclopedias like *Encyclopaedia Britannica*. Specialized encyclopedias cover many fields and include, for example, *Encyclopedia of Psychology, Encyclopedia of the Biological Sciences, Encyclopedia of Asian History,* and *McGraw-Hill Encyclopedia of Science and Technology.*

- *Biographies*—Read accounts of people's lives in biographical works such as *Who's Who, Dictionary of American Biography,* and *Biography Index: A Cumulative Index to Biographical Material in Books and Magazines.*

- *Critical works*—Read what scholars have to say about works of art and literature in *Oxford Companion* volumes (such as *Oxford Companion to Art* and *Oxford Companion to African American Literature*).

- *Statistics and government documents*—Among many useful sources are *Statistical Abstract of the United*

States, Handbook of Labor Statistics, Occupational Outlook Handbook, and U.S. Census publications.

- *Almanacs, atlases, and gazetteers*—For population statistics and boundary changes, see *The World Almanac, Countries of the World,* or *Information Please.*

- *Dictionaries*—Consult *American Heritage Dictionary of the English Language, Oxford English Dictionary*, and other specialized dictionaries such as *Dictionary of Literary Terms and Literary Theory* and *Dictionary of the Social Sciences.*

- *Indexes and databases*—Databases contain publication information and an abstract, or sometimes the full text, of an article, available for downloading or printing from your computer. Your library houses print and CD-ROM databases and subscribes to some online databases; others are accessible through online library catalogs or Web links.

- *Reference works in specific subject areas*—These cover a vast range. Examples include the *Oxford Companion to Art, Encyclopedia of the Biological Sciences,* and *Concise Oxford Companion to Classical Literature.* Ask a librarian for more.

- *Periodical articles*—Find articles in periodicals (works issued periodically, such as scholarly journals, magazines, and newspapers) by using a periodical index. Use electronic indexes for recent works, print indexes for earlier works—especially for works written before 1980. Check to see which services your library subscribes to and the dates the indexes cover. Indexes might provide abstracts; some, such as Lexis-Nexis Academic Universe, Infotrac, OCLC FirstSearch, and New York Times Ondisc, provide the full text of articles. You might be able to access such indexes from a computer in your dorm room or apartment.

Access computer resources. Many libraries offer computers with Internet access. These computers are often available on a first-come, first-served basis, for free or for a nominal cost. Also remember that the Web gives you access to the online resources of many libraries. Some useful sites are: Library of Congress (**http://lcweb.loc.gov**), Smithsonian Institution Libraries (**http://www.sil.si.edu/**), New York Public Library (**http://www.nypl.org/**), Internet Public Library (**http://www.ipl.org**), and WWW Virtual Library (**http://www.vlib.org**).[1]

Gain information literacy. *Information literacy* is the ability to locate, evaluate, use, and document sources of ideas and facts. Considering the variety of materials available at modern, fully equipped libraries, improving your ability to access information efficiently will help promote your success in school.

Start with the distinction between primary and secondary sources. *Primary sources* are often the researcher's dream. These are firsthand materials such as personal journals, letters, speeches, reports of scientific research, scholarly articles, field observations, archeological digs, and original works of art.

Secondary sources explain and comment on primary sources. Examples are nationally circulated newspapers such as the *Washington Post, New York Times*, and *Los Angeles Times.* Magazines with wide circulation but substantial treatment of current issues—such as the *Atlantic Monthly* and *Scientific American*—are secondary sources. So are general reference works such as the *Encyclopedia Britannica.*

Secondary sources are useful places to start your research by getting an overview of your topic. They might even be all you need for informal research. Other research projects in higher education—major papers, presentations, theses, or manuscripts you want to publish—will call on you to find primary sources.

Once you find the sources you want, inspect each one. With print sources, look at the preface, publication data, table of contents, bibliography, glossary, endnotes, and index. (Nonprint materials, including online documents, often include similar types of information.) Also scan any headings, subheadings, and summaries. If you have time, read a chapter or section. Then evaluate sources according to their:

- *Relevance*—Look for sources that deal directly with your research questions. If you're in doubt about the relevance of a particular source, ask yourself: "Will this material help me achieve the purpose of my research and support my thesis?"

- *Currentness*—Notice the published date of your source material (usually found in the front matter on the copyright page). If your topic is time-sensitive, set some guidelines about how current you want your sources to be.

- *Credibility*—Scan the source for biographical information about the author. Look for education, training, and work experience that qualifies this person to publish on the topic. Also notice any possible sources of bias, such as political affiliations or funding sources that might color the author's point of view.

Keen researchers see facts and relationships. They focus their attention on the details, then discover unifying patterns. Far from being a mere academic exercise, library research can evolve into a path of continual discovery.

REVISIT YOUR GOALS, TAKE TWO

One powerful way to achieve any goal is periodically to step back from your day-to-day activities and assess your progress in meeting that goal. This is especially important with goals that can take years to achieve.

Exercise #7: "Get real with your goals" (on page 69) asked you to focus on one long-term goal and create a detailed plan to achieve it—including short-term and mid-term goals related to the long-term goal. Exercise #18: "Revisit your goals" (on page 178) asked you to revisit the same long-term goal and determine its continuing relevance to your life.

You can now take another opportunity to sustain this process. Before you begin, take a few minutes to read your responses to those previous exercises. Then complete the following steps.

1. Rewrite your long-term goal in the space below. If you would like to reword it, feel free to do so.

_____

_____

_____

2. Next, ask yourself how you feel about this goal. Is your enthusiasm still high? On a scale of one to ten (with ten as the highest level of commitment), rate your current interest in achieving this goal.

_____

_____

3. If your level of commitment is five or less, you might want to drop the goal and replace it with a new one. To set a new goal, just turn back to Exercise #7 and do it again. Also release any self-judgment about dropping your original long-term goal. Letting go of one long-term goal creates space in your life to set and achieve a new one.

4. If you're committed to the goal you listed in step 1, consider whether you're still on track to achieve it. Have you met any of the short-term goals you'll need in order to achieve this long-term goal? If so, list your completed goals here:

_____

_____

_____

_____

Before going on to the next step, take a minute to congratulate yourself. Celebrate your success in achieving the goals you just listed.

5. Finally, consider any adjustments you'd like to make to your plan. For example, write additional short-term or mid-term goals that will take you closer to your long-term goal. Or cross out any goals that you no longer see as necessary. Make a clean copy of your current plan in the space below.

Long-term goal from step 1 above (to achieve within your lifetime):

_____

_____

_____

_____

Supporting mid-term goals (to achieve in one to five years):

_____

_____

_____

_____

_____

Supporting short-term goals (to achieve within the coming year):

_____

_____

_____

_____

_____

_____

_____

Read the following two passages. Each makes a prediction about how computer technology could change our society over the next two decades.

Passage #1

Today's technology could evolve into a source of increasing tranquility. Software will search Web sites specifically for news and other information that interests you, screening out hordes of irrelevant data. Cell phones will give way to portable personal communicators that are completely voice-activated and small enough to wear on a necklace or wrist band. Desktop and laptop computers will disappear from most homes as separate pieces of technology. Instead, computer chips will be embedded into most home appliances. Large, flat-panel screens—also voice-activated—will serve as a combination television, movie screen, and monitor for viewing Internet content. Rather than commuting to offices or schools, most people will work and educate themselves at home, leading to a slower, more relaxed pace of life.

Passage #2

We are on the verge of social disruption caused by technology. Advances in robotics will lead to machines that replace factory workers. White-collar workers of every variety will experience the same fate. Sophisticated automatic teller machines (ATMs) will completely replace human bank tellers. Most of the services now offered by travel agents, lawyers, accountants, tax preparers, investment advisors, and teachers will be automated in similar ways. Currently, people in these jobs stake their careers on access to special bodies of knowledge. In the future, thanks to easy-to-use software and vast digital libraries, this knowledge will be freely available to almost anyone. Many jobs will simply disappear, and it's not certain what will replace them. Massive unemployment could result in higher crime rates and urban decay along with record levels of suicide, alcoholism, and other drug addiction.

Assess the claims and evidence presented in the above passages. Then, in the space below, write a one-paragraph response—a prediction of your own about the future impact of technology. Be sure to include evidence to back up your prediction.

_____

_____

_____

_____

_____

_____

_____

_____

_____

_____

_____

_____

_____

_____

_____

Share your responses to this exercise on the Web and see what other students predict. Go online to

masterstudent.college.hmco.com

power process

Risk being a fool

A powerful person has the courage to take risks. And taking risks means being willing to fail sometimes—even to be a fool. This idea can work for you because you already are a fool.

Don't be upset. All of us are fools at one time or another. There are no exceptions. If you doubt it, think back to that stupid thing you did just a few days ago. You know the one. Yes . . . *that* one. It was embarrassing and you tried to hide it. You pretended you weren't a fool. This happens to everyone.

People who insist that they have never been fools are perhaps the biggest fools of all. We are all fallible human beings. Most of us, however, spend too much time and energy trying to hide our fool-hood. No one is really tricked by this—not even ourselves. And whenever we pretend to be something we're not, we miss part of life.

For example, many of us never dance because we don't want to risk looking ridiculous. We're not wrong. We probably would look ridiculous. That's the secret of risking being a fool.

It's OK to look ridiculous while dancing. It's all right to sound silly when singing to your kids. Sometimes it's OK to be absurd. It comes with taking risks.

Taking risks is not being foolhardy

Sometimes it's not OK to be absurd. This Power Process comes with a warning label: Taking risks does *not* mean escaping responsibility for our actions. "Risk being a fool" is not a suggestion to get drunk at a party and make a fool of yourself. It is not a suggestion to act the fool by

disrupting class. It is not a suggestion to be foolhardy or to "fool around."

"Risk being a fool" means recognizing that foolishness—along with dignity, courage, cowardice, grace, clumsiness, and other qualities—is a human characteristic. We all share it. You might as well risk being a fool because you already are one, and nothing in the world can change that. Why not enjoy it once in a while? Consider the case of the person who won't dance because he's afraid he'll look foolish. This same person will spend an afternoon tripping over his feet on a basketball court. If you say that his jump shot from the top of the key looks like a circus accident, he might even agree.

"So what?" he might say. "I'm no Michael Jordan." He's right. On the basketball court, he is willing to risk looking like a fool in order to enjoy the game.

He is no Fred Astaire, either. For some reason, that bothers him. The result is that he misses the fun of dancing. (Dancing badly is as much fun as shooting baskets badly—and maybe a lot more fun.)

There's one sure-fire way to avoid any risk of being a fool, and that's to avoid life. The writer who never finishes a book will never have to worry about getting negative reviews. The center fielder who sits out every game is safe from making any errors. And the comedian who never performs in front of an audience is certain to avoid telling jokes that fall flat. The possibility of succeeding at any venture increases when we're comfortable with making mistakes—that is, with the risk of being a fool.

Look at courage in a new way

Again, remember the warning label. This Power Process does not suggest that the way to be happy in life is to do

The possibility of succeeding at any venture increases when we're comfortable with making mistakes—that is, with the risk of being a fool.

things badly. Courage involves the willingness to face danger and risk failure. Mediocrity is not the goal. The point is that mastery in most activities calls for the willingness to do something new, to fail, to make corrections, to fail again, and so on. On the way to becoming a good writer, be willing to be a bad writer.

Consider these revised clichés: Anything worth doing is worth doing badly at first. Practice makes improvement. If at first you don't fail, try again.

Most artists and athletes have learned the secret of being foolish. Comedians are especially well versed in this art. All of us know how it feels to tell a joke and get complete silence. We truly look and feel like fools. Professional comedians risk feeling that way for a living. Being funny is not enough for success in the comedy business. A comedian must have the courage to face failure.

Courage is an old-fashioned word for an old-fashioned virtue. Traditionally, people have reserved that word for illustrious acts of exceptional people—the campaigns of generals and the missions of heroes.

This concept of courage is fine. At the same time, it can be limiting and can prevent us from seeing courage in everyday actions. Courage is the kindergartner who, with heart pounding, waves good-bye to his parents and boards the bus for his first day of school. Courage is the 40-year-old who registers for college courses after being away from the classroom for 20 years.

For a student, the willingness to take risks means the willingness to experiment with new skills, to achieve personal growth, and sometimes to fail. The rewards of risk taking include expanded creativity, more satisfying self-expression, and more joy.

An experiment for you

Here's an experiment you can conduct to experience the joys of risk taking. The next time you take a risk and end up doing something silly or stupid, allow yourself to be totally aware of your reaction. Don't deny it. Don't cover it up. Notice everything about the feeling, including the physical sensations and thoughts that come with it. Acknowledge the foolishness. Be exactly who you are. Explore all of the emotions, images, and sensations surrounding your experience.

Also remember that we can act independently of our feelings. Courage is not the absence of fear but the willingness to take risks even when we feel fear. We can be keenly homesick and still register for classes. We can tremble at the thought of speaking in public yet still walk up to the microphone.

When we fully experience it, the fear of taking risks loses its power. Then we have the freedom to expand and grow. ⊠

put it to work

Having a working knowledge of information technology will be an asset as you enter the workplace or change jobs.

The phrase *working knowledge* can have many different definitions over time, depending on the current state of technology and your personal goals.

You can use the cycle of discovery, intention, and action explained in this book to integrate technology continuously with your interests and career path. The idea is to continuously keep your technology skills updated for the workplace.

Step 1: Discover what you know about technology.
Consider the following levels of knowledge and skill related to personal computers:

Discussing technology. People with this level of knowledge can walk into a computer store and describe what kind of hardware and software they want for home or professional use.

Performing basic functions. Examples are turning the computer off and on, opening and closing windows on a computer desktop, managing files and folders, installing software, and making backup copies of working files.

Finding information. This cluster of skills enables you to search the Internet or a library catalog to locate sources that can help you answer a specific question.

Creating and editing documents and presentations. With these types of skills, you can:

- Use a word processor to write a memo, letter, report, or research paper.

- Use a database program to organize bodies of data such as a mailing list.

- Use a spreadsheet to manage your household finances, track business expenses for your job, or run your own business.

- Use presentation software to create supporting visuals for a speech or a class you plan to teach.

Functioning in online communities. Included at this stage is the ability to use e-mail with attachments, listservs, newsgroups, chat rooms, and instant messaging software.

After reviewing the above list, write in a personal journal about your current skill with technology. Describe your strengths, along with any significant gaps in your knowledge or ability.

Step 2: Clarify your intentions for learning about technology.
Next, describe what you'd like to be able to do with computer technology that you can't do now. Consider the skills you'll want to gain in order to meet your current career goals. Talk to people working in your chosen field and ask them how they use technology in their day-to-day work. Follow up by writing specifically about what you intend to learn.

Step 3: Act on your intentions.
Find sources of information, ideas, and personal support as you act on your intentions to learn about technology. Options include:

- Books, periodicals, and Web sites about technology. These are available for people at all levels of technological savvy—from first-time computer users to management information specialists.

- Help screens and tutorials included with personal computer software.

- Courses offered through your school, workplace, library, or another community organization.

- A technology mentor—someone who can clearly answer your technology questions, demonstrate the skills you want to gain, and coach you as you sit at the keyboard.

Note: Plan to cycle through the above three suggestions many times in your career. Consider doing them every year to review your knowledge and update your technology skills for the workplace. ✕

Name _____ Date _____/_____/_____

1. List three strategies that you can use before courses begin to promote your success as an online learner.

2. Define the term *Boolean operators* and explain how they can help you conduct Internet searches.

3. In general, you can assume that information you find on the Internet is more current and accurate than information you find in print materials. True or False? Explain your answer.

4. The Power Process in this chapter distinguishes between "being a fool" and "being foolhardy." Explain this distinction by giving an example.

5. Define the term *information literacy*.

6. List four strategies for writing effective e-mail messages.

7. The term *invisible Web* refers to Web sites that cannot be accessed due to temporary technical problems. True or False? Explain your answer.

8. State the distinction between *ideas* and *information* given in this chapter and explain how it relates to thinking critically about Internet content.

9. Newsgroups are online communities that are also referred to as:
    (a) Usenet groups
    (b) Web forums
    (c) bulletin boards
    (d) discussion boards
    (e) all of the above

10. List one strategy for mastering online communities.

learning styles application

The questions below will "cycle" you through four styles, or modes, of learning as explained in the article "Learning styles: Discovering how you learn" in Chapter One. Each question will help you explore a different mode. You can answer the questions in any order.

what if *Explain how a technique from this chapter could help you succeed as a user of technology in the workplace.*

why *Name at least one benefit you could experience in school by gaining more skills with information technology. Examples of these skills include conducting Internet searches, studying online course material, accessing library materials, and joining online communities.*

how *Of the techniques you gained from this chapter, choose one that you will use. Describe exactly how you intend to apply the technique.*

what *List three techniques from this chapter that could significantly improve your skills as an online learner.*

master student

profile

FRED SMITH

a graduate of Yale and the founder and CEO of Federal Express Corporation.

Frederick W. Smith may have a common last name, but he is a most uncommon man. What other American business leader of today had a revolutionary idea and converted it into a company that, starting from scratch and with heavy early losses, passed the $500 million revenue mark and had a 10 percent net profit margin in a few years?

What other American business leader with so brilliant an idea first wrote it out in a college paper that was graded C? Or says that the people with the greatest impact on him have been a poorly educated sergeant whom he led in combat and a science professor who liked to buzz a university stadium in a fighter plane?

Fred Smith is chairman and chief executive officer of Memphis-based Federal Express Corporation, an air cargo firm that specializes in overnight delivery door-to-door, using its own planes.

To put it another way, Fred Smith is Federal Express.

Smith got his revolutionary idea in the 60's while majoring in economics and political science at Yale. Technological change had opened a radically new transportation market, he decided. . . .

"Steamboats and trains were the logistics arm of the Industrial Revolution's first stage," he says. "Trucks became a good logistics arm later— and still are because of their flexibility. But moving the parts and pieces to support the Electronics Age requires very fast transportation over long distances. I became convinced that a different type of system was going to be a major part of the national economy. . . ."

Smith spelled it out in an overdue economics paper. To cut cost and time, packages from all over the country would be flown to a central point, there to be distributed and flown out again to their destinations—a hub-and-spokes pattern, his company calls it today. The flying would be late at night when air lanes were empty. Equipment and documents from anywhere in the U.S. could be delivered anywhere in the U.S. the next day. . . .

For the benefit of business history, it would be nice to have that college paper today. But who saves college papers, particularly those done in one night and branded mediocre?

He says one reason he was no scholastic superstar was that many courses he had to take didn't interest him. Other things did. He and two faculty members resurrected a long-dormant flying club at Yale. One of his cohorts was Professor Norwood Russell Hansen.

"Russ taught the psychology of science—how science was developed," Smith says. "I was a friend of his, not one of his students. He had a big impact on me because of his outlook on life. He was a great singer and a pianist of virtual concert talent. He rode a motorcycle, and he had a World War II fighter plane that he flew all over the place. He buzzed Yale Bowl from time to time. He marched to the beat of a different drummer. . . ."

Will Smith be successful in future undertakings? Says Arthur C. Bass, vice chairman: "A few years ago, some of us used to let off steam in the afternoon playing basketball on a court behind an apartment house. It was amazing—no matter who had the ball and no matter where Fred was on the court, if Fred's side needed to score to win, he would get the ball and make the winning basket. That's the way he is in the business world." ⬙

"A Business Visionary Who Really Delivered" by Henry Altman, from *Nation's Business,* November 1981. Reprinted by permission of *Nation's Business,* November 1981. Copyright ©1981, U.S. Chamber of Commerce.

For more biographical information on Fred Smith, visit the Master Student Hall of Fame on the *Becoming a Master Student* Web site at:

masterstudent.college.hmco.com

11

Health

To be somebody you must last.

RUTH GORDON

Emotion, which is suffering, ceases to be suffering as soon as we have a clear picture of it.

BARUCH SPINOZA

why

this chapter matters . . .

Preserving your health is one way to maintain the personal resources needed to succeed in higher education.

what

is included . . .

how

you can use this chapter . . .

Maintain physical and mental energy by treating your body as an incredible machine.
Choose ways to fuel, move, rest, observe, and protect your machine.
Develop self-esteem while considering a new way of thinking about alcohol and other drugs.

As you read, ask yourself

what if . . .

I could meet the demands of daily life with energy and optimism to spare?

Thinking about health

If you want to experience greater health, start by exercising some tissue that lies between your ears—the organ called your brain. Often the path to greater health starts not with new food or aerobic activity but with a change in thinking.

Consider the power of beliefs. Some of them erect barriers to higher levels of health: "Your health is programmed by your heredity." "Some people are just low on energy." "Healthful food doesn't taste very good." "Over the long run, people just don't change their habits."

Add to this some basic confusion about what the word *health* means. Ask 20 different people for a definition. You'll probably get 20 different answers—10 of them variations on "I don't know." That's amazing, given the fact that bookstores stock hundreds of titles about health and popular magazines feature the topic every month.

To think clearly about health, start with language. The word *health* is similar in origin to *whole, hale, hardy,* and even *holy*. Implied in this list are qualities that most of us associate with healthy people: alertness, vitality, and vigor. Healthy people meet the demands of daily life with energy to spare. Illness or stress might slow them down for a while, and then they bounce back. They are complete, sound in body, mind, and spirit.

To open up your inquiry into health—and to open up new possibilities for your life—consider two ideas.

First, health is a continuum. On one end of that continuum is a death that comes too early. On the other end is a long life filled with satisfying work and fulfilling relationships. Many of us exist between those extremes at a point we might call average. Most of the time we're not sick. And most of the time we're not truly thriving, either.

Second, health changes. Health is not a fixed state. In fact, health fluctuates from year to year, day to day, and moment to moment. Those changes can occur by chance. Or they can occur by choice, as we take conscious control of our thinking and behavior.

Perhaps *health* is one of those rich, multilayered concepts that we can never define completely. That's okay. We can still clear our mental decks of beliefs that undermine us. We can also adopt habits that lengthen life and sustain our well-being.

You don't have to accept these two ideas just because they're printed here. Test them as you would any other idea in this book. Ultimately, your definition of health comes from your own experience. The proof lies not on the page but in your life—in the level of health that you create, starting now.

journal entry 29

Discovery/Intention Statement

In the space below, make a quick list of your activities during the last 48 hours, including exercise sessions and the foods you ate at each meal. Circle any activities on your list that promoted your health. Underline any activities that could detract from your health.

I discovered that I . . .

_____

_____

_____

_____

Next, scan this chapter for at least five strategies you can use immediately to sustain any behaviors you just circled—or to change any behavior you underlined. List the strategies you want to read about in more detail and their associated page numbers.

Strategy   *Page number*

_____

_____

_____

_____

_____

_____

Finally, describe how you can use these strategies to achieve a health-related goal that matters to you. Choose a goal—such as sleeping better, losing weight, or having more energy—that will significantly raise the quality of your life.

I intend to . . .

_____

_____

_____

Some people are offended by the notion that the human body is a machine.

Take care of your machine

This analogy is made with great respect for our bodies and with the understanding that we are more than our bodies. We have a mind and a soul that are certainly separate from our bodies, even though they are connected. And in order to house our mind and soul, we have a body—a fantastic machine.

Our machines are truly incredible. They often continue to operate despite abuse. We pollute them, dent them, run them too hard, let them sit idle for years, even wreck them. At times we try to fuel our machines with junk food. We pollute them with empty calories and expose them to unnecessary risks of illnesses or accidents. And still our incredible machines continue to run—most of the time. Ironically, we can also take excellent care of our machines, only to have them quit on us just when we need them most.

To an extent greater than most of us imagine, we choose our level of health. We can promote our health by taking definite steps.

When we buy a car or a new appliance, we generally look at the owner's manual. We study it to find out just how this new machine works. We make sure we under-

To an extent greater than most of us imagine, we choose our level of health.

stand all of its features and what is needed to properly maintain it. For example, we know that people can prevent damage to their cars by performing simple maintenance procedures, such as regular oil changes and tune-ups.

It's amazing that many of us take better care of our cars, dishwashers, air conditioners, and furnaces than we do of our bodies. We can change this. We can spend at least as much time learning about our own health as we do reading the owner's manual for a new car.

It would be easier if each of us received an owner's manual for our bodies at the moment of birth. Unfortunately, no such manual exists. Our challenge is to create a personal guidebook to health based on our own observations, studies, and experiences.

The suggestions in this chapter are accepted by many experts on health. Study them as if they were an owner's manual for a priceless machine—one that can't be replaced, one that your life depends on. That machine is your body.

YOUR MACHINE
Fuel it

It's a cliché, and it's true: You are what you eat. What you eat can have immediate and long-term effects on your performance as a student. That giant jelly donut can make you drowsy within minutes. A steady diet of them can affect the amount of energy you have available to meet and juggle the demands of classes, family members, jobs, extracurricular activities, and other commitments.

Start with widely accepted guidelines. There have been hundreds of books written about nutrition. One says don't drink milk. Another says buy a cow. This debate can be confusing. There is, however, wide agreement among nutritional scientists. A list of dietary guidelines was developed by the U.S. government and is updated every five years (see "The experts recommend—seven dietary guidelines" on page 344 in this chapter). Though you might find a more healthful diet, you can do well by following these guidelines.

Avoid fad diets. If you are overweight, avoid people who make claims about a quick fix. Even if that "Lose 20 pounds in 20 days!" diet works at first, you're likely to gain the weight back.

For example, think critically about low-carbohydrate plans such as the Atkins diet. These plans can lead to significant weight loss in the short term. However, research undercuts claims for long-term benefits. The "drop-out" rate for the Atkins diet is comparable to that of other diets.[1] Many people simply find these plans too difficult to sustain. In addition, low-carbohydrate diets focus on meat and dairy products with high levels of saturated fat, which can increase the risk of heart disease and several forms of cancer. The formula for weight loss is simple, though not always easy: Eat better food, eat less food, and exercise regularly. To find safe weight-loss and nutrition programs, visit your doctor or campus health service. Look for a program that provides peer support.

Limit fast foods. Fast foods can be tempting, especially if you're pressed for time. When eaten consistently, these foods can also expand your waistline and drain your budget. A medium soda, large order of fries, and double cheeseburger can pack over 1,500 calories and 60 grams of fat.

About 30 percent of U.S. adults are obese. Our love affair with fast food contributes to that figure.[2]

To save money and promote health, prepare meals at home and center them on whole grains, legumes, fruits, and vegetables. When you eat out, reduce portions.

➔ Prevent and treat eating disorders

Eating disorders affect many students. These disorders involve serious disturbances in eating behavior. Examples are overeating or extreme reduction of food intake, as well as irrational concern about body shape or weight. Women are much more likely to develop these disorders than men.

Bulimia involves cycles of excessive eating and forced purges. A person with this disorder might gorge on a pizza, donuts, and ice cream and then force herself to vomit. Or she might compensate for overeating with excessive use of laxatives, enemas, or diuretics. *Anorexia nervosa* is a potentially fatal illness marked by self-starvation, either through extended fasts or by eating only one food for weeks at a time.

Eating disorders are not due to a failure of willpower. Instead, these are real illnesses in which harmful patterns of eating take on a life of their own.

Eating disorders can lead to many complications, including life-threatening heart conditions and kidney failure. Many people with eating disorders also struggle with depression, substance abuse, and anxiety.

These disorders require immediate treatment to stabilize health. This is usually followed by continuing medical care, counseling, and medication to promote a full recovery.

If you're worried about having an eating disorder, visit a doctor, campus health service, or local public health clinic. If you see signs of an eating disorder in someone else, express your concern with "I" messages as explained in Chapter Eight: Communicating. For more information, contact the National Eating Disorders Association at 1-800-931-2237 and online at **http://www.nationaleatingdisorders.org**.

Splitting a meal with someone reduces both cost and calories.

Take time to enjoy your food. Eating can be one of life's greatest pleasures. If you eat slowly and savor each bite, you can be satisfied with smaller portions. Use meal times as a chance to relax, reduce stress, and connect with people.

YOUR MACHINE
Move it

Our bodies need to be exercised. The world ran on muscle power back in the era when we had to hunt down a woolly mammoth every few weeks and drag it back to the cave. Now we can grab a burger at a drive-up window. It's convenient, but it doesn't do much for our deltoids or quadriceps.

The heart is a muscle that can get fat, too. A fat belly might be unattractive. A fat heart can be lethal.

Getting in shape can do more than improve how you look in designer jeans. Exercise offers a way to perform better at whatever you do, whether it's mammoth hunting or boning up on math. Your brain usually functions best when the rest of your body is in shape. Physical activity is also an effective way to dissipate the tension that builds up when you are hunched over a keyboard, hammering out a term paper.

In addition to weight control, physical activity helps to prevent heart disease, control cholesterol levels and diabetes, and slow the bone loss that comes with aging.

Exercise also lowers the risk of certain cancers and helps to reduce anxiety and depression.

Sometimes people who are out of shape or overweight think that they cannot change. The human body *can* change. Inside even the most dilapidated body there is a trim, healthy, energized body that is waiting to emerge.

Your brain usually functions best when the rest of your body is in shape.

You can make real progress in a matter of weeks. Remember, dieting alone doesn't create lean muscles and a strong heart. The only way to get leaner is by moving.

You don't have to train for the Boston Marathon, however. It's not even smart, unless you're already in great shape. Do something you enjoy. Start by walking briskly for at least 15 minutes every day. Increase that time gradually and add a little running.

Once you're in reasonable shape, you can stay there by doing aerobic activity on most days of the week. An hour of daily activity is ideal, but do whatever you can. Some activity is better than none.

According to a report from the U.S. Surgeon General, all of the following activities will burn an average of 150 calories per day, which translates into losing 10 pounds per year:[3]

- Climb stairs for 15 minutes.
- Dance for 30 minutes.
- Rake leaves for 30 minutes.
- Run 1.5 miles in 15 minutes.
- Swim laps for 20 minutes.

voices

student

Staying in shape has always been important to me, so including time in my schedule for exercise is something I always try to do. It started to be the one thing I wasn't accomplishing because I had let reading or studying to prepare for class take precedence. Then I signed up for a water aerobics course that met once a week. Having a fixed time when I knew I had to be at the specific class helped me keep it a priority.

—LUPE SANTIAGO

- Walk 2 miles in 30 minutes.
- Bicycle 5 miles in 30 minutes.
- Garden for 30 to 45 minutes.
- Jump rope for 15 minutes.

These figures are based on the assumption that the number of calories you eat remains constant. To double your potential weight loss, consume 150 calories less each day. As a point of reference, remember that a small chocolate chip cookie contains about 50 calories. A jelly-filled doughnut weighs in at 300 calories.

Look for exercise facilities on campus. Classes might also be offered in aerobics, swimming, volleyball, basketball, golf, tennis, and other sports. School can be a great place to get in shape.

Before beginning any vigorous exercise program, consult a health care professional. This is critical if you are overweight, over age 60, in poor condition, or a heavy smoker, or if you have a history of health problems.

YOUR MACHINE
Rest it

In addition to requiring activity, human bodies need sufficient periods of rest. A lack of rest can decrease your immunity to illness and impair your performance in school.

As a student, you might be tempted to cut back drastically on your sleep once in a while. All-nighters to study for exams or catch up on a lengthy reading assignment are common for some students. If you find you are indulging in them often, read Chapter Two: Planning for some time-management ideas. Depriving yourself of sleep is a choice you can avoid.

Promote sound sleep. Sometimes, getting to sleep isn't easy, even when you feel tired. If you have trouble falling asleep, experiment with the following suggestions:

- Exercise daily. For many people, this promotes sounder sleep. However, finish exercising several hours before you want to go to sleep.
- Avoid naps during the daytime.
- Monitor your caffeine intake, especially in the afternoon and evening.
- Take a warm bath, not a shower, just before bed.
- Keep your sleeping room cool.

- Sleep in the same place each night. When you're there, your body gets the message "It's time to go to sleep."
- Practice relaxation techniques while lying in bed. A simple one is to count your breaths and release distracting thoughts as they arise.
- Get up and study or do something else until you're tired.
- See a doctor if sleeplessness persists.

How much sleep is enough? Your body knows when it's tired. Also look for signs of depression, irritability, and other emotional problems. Lack of sleep can interfere with your memory, your concentration, and your ability to stay awake in class. The solution is a good night's sleep.

Manage stress. With high stress levels, you can sleep 12 hours a day and still not get enough rest. School environments can be especially stressful, so it is important that you know ways to relax.

Stress is not always harmful. It can result from pleasant experiences as well as unpleasant ones. The excitement of a new term—new classes, new instructors, new classmates—can be fun and stressful at the same time.

Oddly enough, your body perceives excitement in almost the same way that it perceives fear. Both emotions produce rapid heart rates, increased adrenaline flow, and muscle contractions. Both emotions produce stress.

Stress, at appropriate times and at manageable levels, is normal and useful. It can sharpen our awareness and boost our energy just when we need it the most. When stress persists or becomes excessive, it is harmful.

Chances are, your stress level is too high if you consistently experience any of the following symptoms: irritability; depression; low productivity; strained relationships at work or home; health problems such as an upset stomach, frequent colds, and a low energy level; a pattern of avoiding tasks; difficulty falling asleep or staying asleep; feeling burned out at home or at work; feeling tense, nervous, or fearful.

Stress has both mental and physical components. The mental components include thoughts that promote fear and anxiety; the physical components include illnesses and muscle tension.

The fact that stress has these elements points to several broad strategies for managing it:

- *Deal with stressful thoughts by releasing irrational beliefs.* According to Martin Seligman and other cognitive psychologists, stress results not from events in our lives but from the way we *think* about those events.[4] If we believe that people should always behave in exactly the way we expect them to, for instance, we set ourselves up for stress. Noticing these beliefs and replacing them with more rational ones (such as *I can control my own behavior but not the behavior of others*) can reduce stress significantly.

- *Deal with stressful thoughts by releasing them altogether.* Meditation offers a way to release distressing thoughts. While meditating, you simply notice your thoughts as they arise and pass—without reacting to them. Eventually, your stream of thinking slows down. You might even find that it comes to a complete stop while at the same time you remain alert and aware. This is a state of deep relaxation that might also yield life-changing insights. Many religious organizations offer meditation classes. You can also find meditation instruction through health maintenance organizations, YMCAs or YWCAs, and community education programs.

- *Counter the physical element of stress.* Options include breathing exercises, relaxation techniques, yoga, and therapeutic bodywork such as massage. Some schools offer classes in these subjects.

- *Use this book.* It includes relaxation and breathing exercises. Many of the Power Processes and the techniques for letting go of test anxiety can also help you manage stress.

Know when to get professional help. If your stress levels are too high and the above techniques don't work within a few weeks, get help. See your doctor or a counselor at your student health service. Stress management is a well-researched field. There is no need to continue to have a pain in your neck, a knot in your stomach, cold feet, or other symptoms of tension. Relax.

YOUR MACHINE
Observe it

Like a skilled mechanic, you are an expert on your body. You are more likely to notice changes before anyone else does. Pay attention to these changes. They are often your first clue about the need for medical treatment or intervention.

Watch for the following signs:

- Weight loss of more than 10 pounds in 10 weeks with no apparent cause.

- A sore, scab, or ulcer that does not heal in three weeks.

- A skin blemish or mole that bleeds, itches, or changes size, shape, or color.

- Persistent or severe headaches.

- Sudden vomiting that is not preceded by nausea.

- Fainting spells.

- Double vision.

- Difficulty swallowing.

- Persistent hoarseness or a nagging cough.

- Blood that is coughed up or vomited.

- Shortness of breath for no apparent reason.

- Persistent indigestion or abdominal pain.

- A big change in normal bowel habits, such as alternating diarrhea and constipation.

- Black and tarry bowel movements.

- Rectal bleeding.
- Pink, red, or unusually cloudy urine.
- Discomfort or difficulty when urinating or during sexual intercourse.
- Lumps or thickening in a breast.
- Vaginal bleeding between menstrual periods or after menopause.

If you are experiencing any of these symptoms, get help. Even if you think it might not be serious, check it out. Without timely and proper treatment, a minor illness or injury can lead to serious problems. Begin with your medical health care professional or school health service.

journal entry 30

Discovery/Intention Statement

For three minutes, brainstorm things you can do during the next month to improve the ways that you fuel, move, rest, and observe your body. Write your ideas in the space below. Use additional paper if needed.

I discovered that I . . .

_____

_____

_____

_____

_____

Next, pick three of your ideas that you can begin to use or practice this week. Write an Intention Statement below about how and when you intend to use these ideas.

I intend to . . .

_____

_____

_____

_____

_____

YOUR MACHINE
Protect it

Protect against sexually transmitted diseases.
Choices about sex can be life altering. Sex is a basic human drive, and it can be wonderful. In certain conditions, sex can also be hazardous to your health. It pays to be clear about the pitfalls, including sexually transmitted diseases and unwanted pregnancies.

Technically, anyone who has sex is at risk of getting a sexually transmitted disease (STD). Without treatment, some of these diseases can lead to blindness, infertility, cancer, heart disease, or even death. Sometimes there are no signs or symptoms of an STD; the only way to tell if you're infected is to be tested by a health care professional.

STDs are often spread through body fluids that are exchanged during sex—semen, vaginal secretions, and blood. Some STDs, such as herpes and genital warts, are spread by direct contact with infected skin. Human immunodeficiency virus (HIV) can be spread in other ways as well.

There are more than 25 kinds of STDs, including chlamydia, gonorrhea ("clap"), syphilis, genital warts, genital herpes, and trichomoniasis. Hepatitis can also be spread through sexual contact. STDs are the most common contagious diseases in the United States.

HIV is one of the most serious STDs, and it is different from the others in several respects. HIV is the virus that causes acquired immune deficiency syndrome (AIDS). AIDS is the last stage of HIV infection. A person with AIDS has an immune system that is weakened to the point of having difficulty in fighting off many kinds of infections and cancers.

Someone infected with HIV might feel no symptoms for months—sometimes years. Many times, those who are spreading HIV don't even know that they have it.

HIV/AIDS is not transmitted just through unprotected sexual contact. It can be transmitted by shared needles or equipment used to inject drugs. The virus can also be passed from an infected pregnant woman to her fetus during pregnancy or delivery, or through breast-feeding after delivery. Before 1985, HIV was sometimes spread through contaminated blood transfusions. Since March 1985, blood supplies have been screened for HIV, and blood transfusion is no longer considered a means of HIV infection.

Although the disease was initially prevalent in this country among male homosexuals, HIV/AIDS is becoming

increasingly common among heterosexuals. HIV/AIDS cases among women have been rising steadily, and it is predicted to become one of the five leading causes of death among women.

Public hysteria and misinformation about HIV/AIDS still flourish. You cannot get HIV/AIDS from touching, kissing, hugging, food, coughs, mosquitoes, toilet seats, hot tubs, or swimming pools.

Being infected with HIV is not a death sentence. There are medical treatments that can slow down the rate at which HIV weakens the immune system. Some of the illnesses associated with AIDS can be prevented or treated, although AIDS itself is not curable. Some people live with HIV for years without developing AIDS, and people with AIDS might live for years after developing the condition. As with other chronic illnesses, early detection and early entry into medical care offers more options for treatment and a longer life.

STDs other than AIDS and herpes can be cured, if treated early. Prevention is better. Remember these guidelines:

- *Abstain from sex, or have sex exclusively with one person who is free of infection and has no other sex partners.* This is the only way to be absolutely safe from STDs.

- *Talk about STDs.* Ask sex partners if they have an STD. Tell your partner if you have one.

- *Recognize the symptoms of STDs in yourself and others.* Symptoms include swollen glands with fever and aching; itching around the vagina; vaginal discharge; pain during sex or when urinating; sore throat following oral sex; anal pain after anal sex; sores, blisters, scabs, or warts on the genitals, anus,

tongue, or throat; rashes on the palms of your hands or soles of your feet; dark urine; loose and light-colored stools; and unexplained fatigue, weight loss, and night sweats.

- *Avoid injecting illegal drugs.* Sharing needles or other paraphernalia with other drug users is a behavior that can spread STDs.

- *Take action soon after you have sex.* Urinate soon after you have sex and wash your genitals with soap and water.

- *See a doctor to get checked for STDs twice each year.* If you have sex with several different people, get checked for STDs even if you have no symptoms. The more people you have sex with, the greater your risk. You are at risk even if you have sex only once with one person who is infected.

- *Use condoms.* Male condoms are thin latex membranes stretched over the penis prior to intercourse. (Female condoms are an option, but they are not as effective as male condoms.) Condoms prevent semen from entering the vagina. Both women and men can carry them and insist that they be used. Use a condom every time you have sex, and for any type of sex—oral, vaginal, or anal. Use latex condoms—not lambskin.

Note: Do not use spermicides containing nonoxynol-9. Also avoid lubricants, condoms, and other sex products with nonoxynol-9. At one time, researchers thought that this ingredient could help prevent STDs. New studies indicates that nonoxynol-9 can irritate the vagina and cervix, which actually increases the risk of STDs.

Remember that having multiple sex partners puts you at risk for STDs, even if you use condoms. While condoms can be effective, they are not guaranteed to work all of the time. Condoms can break, leak, or slip off. In addition, condoms cannot protect you from STDs that are spread by contact with herpes sores or warts.

If you think you have an STD, call your medical health care professional, campus health service, or local public health clinic. Seek counseling and further testing to find out if you are really infected. Early entry into treatment might prevent serious health problems. To avoid infecting other people, abstain from sex until you are treated and cured.

Protect against unwanted pregnancy. Following is some information that can help you and your partner avoid unwanted pregnancy. This is not a complete list of options, so be sure to supplement it with information from your medical health care professional.

Total abstinence and sterilization are the most effective methods of birth control. Other methods can fail. Also, many forms of birth control do not protect against STDs, including AIDS.

Abstinence is choosing not to have intercourse. You might feel pressured to change your mind about this choice. Keep in mind that, contrary to popular belief, many people exist happily without sexual intercourse. In addition, remember that abstinence as a means of birth control is guaranteed only when it is practiced without exception.

The *"pill"* is a synthetic hormone that "tells" a woman's body not to produce eggs. To be effective, it must be taken every day for 21 days a month. Birth control pills must be prescribed by a medical health care professional; the type of pill and the dose needed vary from one woman to the next. Side effects sometimes include slight nausea, breast tenderness, weight gain from water retention, and moodiness.

Some women choose not to take the pill due to increased risks of heart disease, including high blood pressure, blood clots, and breast or endometrial cancer. If you have a history of any of these conditions, see a doctor before taking the pill. If you are over age 35 and smoke, also see your doctor before using this form of birth control.

A *contraceptive injection* (Depo-Provera) into the buttocks or arm muscle is administered by a doctor or nurse every three months. This hormone prevents pregnancy by decreasing ovulation, preventing sperm from reaching the egg, and preventing a fertilized egg from implanting in the uterus. Unlike the pill, this method requires little effort: Women simply need an injection every three months. Side effects can include irregular periods, weight gain, and breast tenderness.

The *contraceptive implant device* (Norplant) is a small contraceptive inserted under the skin of a woman's upper arm. This device releases a steady stream of the hormone progestin (one of the hormones in the pill). Side effects can include inflammation or infection at the site of the implant, menstrual cycle changes, weight gain, and breast tenderness. **Note:** This device was taken off the market in July 2002. If you are using this form of birth control, see your doctor to talk about other options.

An *intrauterine device* (IUD) is a small metal or plastic device that is inserted in the uterus and left there for one to 10 years. It prevents fertilized eggs from developing. Side effects might include heavier menstrual flow, anemia, pelvic infection, perforation of the cervix or uterus, or septic abortion.

One brand of IUD—the Dalkon Shield—was taken off the market in 1975 after it was associated with pelvic infection, infertility, and some deaths. Today, IUDs rarely lead to serious complications. Possible side effects include increased risk of pelvic inflammatory disease, perforation of the uterus, abnormal bleeding, and cramps. A *diaphragm* is a shallow rubber dome that is covered with a spermicide (sperm-killing cream) and inserted in the vagina. It fits over the cervix, which is the opening of the uterus, and prevents sperm from getting to the egg. A trained medical health care professional must measure and fit the diaphragm. It must be inserted before intercourse and left in place for six to eight hours after intercourse. It is more than 80 percent effective.

The *cervical cap* is a soft rubber cup that fits snugly around the cervix. Available by prescription only, it is also used with spermicide. Wearing it for more than 48 hours is not recommended due to a low risk of toxic shock syndrome.

A *sponge* works something like a diaphragm. It is effective for 24 hours. The sponge has been unavailable since 1995 when its only producer stopped making it. However, the sponge still has federal approval and might be marketed in the future.

The *hormonal vaginal contraceptive ring* (NuvaRing) releases the hormones progestin and estrogen from a ring placed inside the vagina and around the cervix. A woman removes the ring during her period and then puts in a new ring. This form of birth control is available only by prescription.

Foams, creams, tablets, suppositories, and *jellies* are chemicals that are placed in the vagina before intercourse and prevent sperm from getting to the egg.

When used carefully and consistently, *male condoms* offer a safe method of birth control. Latex condoms work the best for reducing the risk of STDs. Do not use male

→ Stay up-to-date on STDs

Our knowledge of HIV/AIDS and other STDs is changing constantly. For the latest statistics and information on prevention, check these resources from the Centers for Disease Control:

- National STD and AIDS Hot Line, 1-800-342-2437; Spanish, 1-800-344-7432; TTY, 1-800-243-7889
- Division of HIV/AIDS Prevention, **http://www.cdc.gov/hiv/dhap.htm**
- Division of STD Prevention, **http://www.cdc.gov/nchstp/dstd/dstdp.html**

You can also call your state health department.

condoms with oil-based lubricants such as petroleum jelly, lotions, or baby oil, all of which can lead to breakage.

The *female condom* is a sheath of lubricated polyurethane with a ring on each end that is inserted into the vagina. This is a relatively new form of contraception, and not many studies exist to document its effectiveness. Ask your doctor for the latest information.

The *rhythm method* involves avoiding intercourse during ovulation. The problem with this method is that it is difficult to know for sure when a woman is ovulating.

Natural family planning is based on looking for specific signs of fertility in a woman. (This is not to be confused with the rhythm method.) There are no side effects with natural family planning, and this method is gaining acceptance. Before you consider it, however, talk to a qualified instructor.

Douching is flushing the vagina with water or another liquid after intercourse. Do not use it for birth control. Even if a woman douches immediately after intercourse, this method is ineffective. Sperm are quicker than humans.

Withdrawal is the act of removing the penis before ejaculation occurs. This is also ineffective, since sperm can be present in pre-ejaculation fluid.

Sterilization is a permanent form of birth control, and one to avoid if you still want to have children.

All of these methods vary in effectiveness. Of course, abstinence is 100 percent effective in preventing preg-nancy when practiced faithfully, and sterilization is nearly 100 percent effective. Methods that deliver extra hormones to a woman—through pills, injections, or implants—are typically rated 95 to 99 percent effective, as is the IUD. Condoms for both women and men are less effective—around 80 percent.

However, effectiveness rates can only be estimated. The actual effectiveness of most contraceptive methods depends on many factors—for example, the health of the people using them, the number of sex partners, and the frequency of sexual activity. Effectiveness also depends on how carefully and consistently the methods are used.

Protect against rape. Rape and other forms of sexual assault are all too common at vocational schools, colleges, and universities. People often hesitate to report rape for many reasons, such as fear, embarrassment, and concerns about credibility. Both women and men can take steps to prevent rape from occurring in the first place. For example:

- Get together with a group of people and take a tour of the school grounds. Make a special note of danger spots, such as unlighted paths and unguarded buildings. Keep in mind that rape can occur during daylight and in well-lit places.

- Ask if your school has escort services for people taking evening classes. These might include personal escorts, car escorts, or both. If you do take an evening class, ask if there are security officers on duty before and after the class.

- Take a course or seminar on self-defense and rape prevention. To find out where these courses are being held, check with your student counseling service, community education center, or local library.

- If you are raped, get to the nearest rape crisis center, hospital, student health service, or police station. Report the crime as soon as you can, and also arrange for follow-up counseling.

Date rape—the act of forcing sex on a date—is the most common form of rape among college students. Date rape is rape. It is a crime. It is particularly danger-ous when neither the victim nor the perpetrator realizes that a crime has taken place. A person who has been raped by a date might become depressed, feel guilty, have difficulty in school, lose a sense of trust, have sexual problems, or experience self-blame.

Drugs such as rohypnol and GHB (gamma hydroxybu-tyrate) have been used to facilitate date rape. These drugs, often given to people without their knowledge, reduce resistance to sexual advances and produce an amnesia-like effect. People who have taken these drugs might not remember the circumstances that led to their being raped.

You can take steps to protect yourself by communicat-ing clearly what you want and don't want. That means being assertive. It also pays to be cautious about using al-cohol or drugs, and to be wary of dates who get drunk or high. You can also provide your own transportation on dates and avoid going to secluded places with people you don't know well.

Forcing someone to have sex is *never* acceptable—under any circumstances. You have the right to refuse to have sex with anyone, including dates. You also have the right to refuse sex with your partner, fiancé(e), or spouse.

Protect against accidents. In North America, millions of disabling injuries occur every year in the haven called the home, and thousands of people die in home acci-dents. Even more die in their cars. Following are ways you can greatly reduce the odds of such accidents:

- Don't drive after drinking alcohol or using psychoactive drugs.

- Drive with the realization that other drivers are possibly preoccupied, intoxicated, or careless.

- Put poisons out of reach of children, and label poisons clearly. Poisoning takes a larger toll on

people aged 15 to 45 than on children.

- Keep stairs, halls, doorways, and other pathways clear of shoes, toys, newspapers, and other clutter.

- Don't smoke in bed.

- Don't let candles burn unattended.

- Keep children away from hot stoves, and turn pot handles inward.

- Check electrical cords for fraying, loose connections, or breaks in insulation. Don't over-load extension cords.

- Keep a fire extinguisher handy.

- Watch for ways that an infant or a toddler could suffocate or choke: small objects that can be swallowed, old refrigerators or freezers that can act as air-tight prisons, unattended or unfenced swimming pools, kerosene heaters in tightly closed rooms, and plastic kitchen or clothing bags.

- Install smoke detectors where you live and work. Most of these run on batteries that need occasional replacement. Follow the manufacturer's guidelines. ◪

journal entry 31

Intention Statement

Choose one habit related to protecting your body that you would like to change immediately. Below write an Intention Statement about changing this habit so that your body can begin experiencing greater health today.

I intend to . . .

_____

_____

_____

_____

_____

_____

The experts recommend— seven dietary guidelines

4 **Choose beverages and foods to moderate your intake of sugars.** Get most of your calories from whole grains, fruits, and vegetables; low-fat or non-fat dairy products; and lean meats or meat substitutes. Don't let soft drinks or sweets crowd out other foods you need to maintain health. Drink water often.

5 **Choose and prepare foods with less salt.** Many people can reduce their chance of developing high blood pressure by consuming less salt. Read labels to find foods lower in sodium—especially prepared foods.

6 **If you drink alcoholic beverages, do so in moderation.** Alcoholic beverages supply calories but few nutrients. Excessive alcohol consumption affects judgment and can lead to dependency. It also increases the risk of motor vehicle crashes and other injuries, violence, suicide, high blood pressure, stroke, and certain types of cancer. If you choose to drink alcoholic beverages, consume them only in moderation—up to one drink per day for women or two drinks per day for men. Drink with meals to slow alcohol absorption.

7 **Aim for a healthy weight.** In addition to following the above guidelines, get at least 30 minutes of moderate physical activity each day. Such activity requires about as much energy as walking two miles in 30 minutes. ▧

Adapted from *Dietary Guidelines for Americans 2000*, 5th ed., U.S. Department of Agriculture and U.S. Department of Health and Human Services.

1 **Choose a variety of fruits, vegetables, and grains daily, especially whole grains.** Eating plenty of fruits, vegetables, and grains of different kinds might help protect you against many chronic diseases. Remember that whole grains provide more fiber and other nutrients than processed grains. For those who eat little meat, combining whole grains with legumes (dried beans and soy products) will provide important nutrients.

2 **Keep food safe to eat.** Wash hands and cooking surfaces often. Separate raw, cooked, and ready-to-eat foods while shopping, preparing, or storing. Read labels for instructions on preparing foods, and refrigerate perishable foods promptly. When serving, keep hot foods hot and cold foods cold. If you're in doubt about the safety of a food, throw it out.

3 **Choose a diet that is low in saturated fat and cholesterol and moderate in total fat.** Limit solid fats, such as butter, hard margarines, lard, and partially hydrogenated shortenings. Use canola or olive oils and a heart-healthy spread as a substitute.

journal entry 32

Discovery Statement

If you look and feel healthy, a greater understanding of your body can help you be aware of what you're doing right. If you are not content with your present physical or emotional health, you might discover some ways to adjust your personal habits and increase your sense of well-being.

This exercise is a structured Discovery Statement that allows you to look closely at your health. As with the Discovery Wheel exercise in Chapter One, the usefulness of this exercise will be determined by your honesty and courage.

To begin, draw a simple outline of your body on a separate sheet of paper. You might have positive and negative feelings about various internal and external parts of your body. Label the parts and include a short description of the attributes you like or dislike, for example, straight teeth, fat thighs, clear lungs, double chin, straight posture, etc.

The body you drew substantially reflects your past health practices. To discover how well you take care of your body, complete the following sentences on a separate sheet of paper.

Eating

1. What I know about the way I eat is . . .

2. What I would most like to change about my diet is . . .

3. My eating habits lead me to be . . .

Exercise

1. The way I usually exercise is . . .

2. The last time I did 20 minutes or more of heart/lung (aerobic) exercise was . . .

3. As a result of my physical conditioning I feel . . .

4. And I look . . .

5. It would be easier for me to work out regularly if I . . .

6. The most important benefit for me in exercising more is . . .

Substances

1. My history of cigarette smoking is . . .

2. An objective observer would say my use of alcohol is . . .

3. In the last 10 days the number of alcoholic drinks I have had is . . .

4. I would describe my use of coffee, colas, and other caffeinated drinks as . . .

5. I have used the following illegal drugs in the past week:

6. When it comes to drugs, what I am sometimes concerned about is . . .

7. I take the following prescription drugs:

Relationships

1. Someone who knows me fairly well would say I am emotionally . . .

2. The way I look and feel has affected my relationships by . . .

3. My use of drugs or alcohol has been an issue with . . .

4. The best thing I could do for myself and my relationships would be to . . .

Sleep

1. The number of hours I sleep each night is . . .

2. On weekends I normally sleep . . .

3. I have trouble sleeping when . . .

4. Last night I . . .

5. The quality of my sleep is usually . . .

In general

What concerns me more than anything else about my health is . . .

Crazed
glazed donut
runs amok

Editor's note: For those of you who think this article might be a bit cutesy, please understand the theoretical and pedagogical rationale for its inclusion, which incorporated the purpose of puncturing the pretentiousness of pundits' puritanical prattle. This article is here to lighten up a subject that is so often approached with guilt and the solemnity of a final exam.

By Bill Harlan

PANCREAS CITY, IOWA— A glazed donut, apparently out of control, caused a multisugar pileup here early yesterday.

The entire state is reeling in lethargy, and the governor has called in extra fatty tissue.

The pileup occurred shortly after 9 a.m., when assistant brain cells in Hypothalamusville noticed an energy shortage. They telephoned the state procurement office in Right Hand with a request for a glazed donut.

Procurement officers delivered the donut to Mouth, two miles north of Throat, at 9:04 a.m. "We were only following orders," one said.

When the donut reached Stomach, the town was nearly deserted. "No one had been here since dinner the night before," a witness said. The donut raced straight through Duodenum Gap and into Intestine County.

Records indicate that the energy level throughout the state did rise for more than a half-hour. However, about 45 minutes after the donut was delivered, residents in Eyelid noticed what one witness described as "a sort of drooping effect." Within 90 minutes the whole state was in a frenzy. Energy levels dropped. Tremors were reported in Hand. A suspicious "growl" was heard near Stomach.

By that time, confusion reigned in Pancreas.

Officials there later claimed the donut was pure glucose, the kind of sugar that causes an immediate but short-lived energy boost. The glazed perpetrator apparently burned itself out in a metabolic rampage. Soon, only the smoking traces of burned glucose remained.

Minutes later, terror-stricken cells near Stomach began screaming, "Send down a candy bar." The cry was taken up throughout the state, as cells everywhere begged for more sugar.

For the rest of the day, the state reeled under an assault of caffeine and sugar. Three candy bars. Four soft drinks. Pie and coffee.

By evening, the governor's office had called up the Alcohol Reserves. "We've been recommending complex carbohydrates and small amounts of protein since Tuesday," said a highly placed source, who was reached on vacation at the Isle of Langerhans in Lake Pancreas. "Carbohydrates and proteins burn energy gradually, all day. An egg, some cereal, a piece of fruit, and this tragedy could have been avoided. Heck, a burger would have been better. This donut thing has got to stop."

This morning, a saddened state lies under a layer of fat. "I'm guessing it will take a hard 10-mile run to get this mess cleaned up," an administrative assistant in Cerebellum said.

Officials in Legs could not be reached. ⊠

Developing self-esteem

The challenge of higher education often puts self-esteem at risk. The rigors of class work, financial pressures, and new social settings can test our ability to adapt and change.

Our self-esteem can erode in ways that are imperceptible to us. Over time, we can gradually buy into a reduced sense of our own possibilities in life. This orientation makes it less likely that we'll take risks, create a vision for the future, and accomplish our goals.

During the past 30 years, psychologists have produced several key studies about *self-efficacy*. This term refers to your belief in your ability to determine the outcomes of events—especially outcomes that are strongly influenced by your own behavior. A strong sense of self-efficacy allows you to tackle problems with confidence, set long-term goals, and see difficult tasks as creative challenges rather than potential disasters.

The field of self-efficacy research is closely associated with psychologist Albert Bandura of Stanford University.[7] While self-esteem refers to an overall impression of your abilities, self-efficacy is more exact, pointing to specific factors that influence the ways you think, feel, and act. According to Bandura, self-efficacy has several sources. You can use specific strategies to strengthen them.

Set up situations in which you can win

Start by planning scenarios in which you can succeed. Bandura calls these "mastery situations." For example, set yourself up for success by breaking a big project down into small, doable tasks. Then tackle and complete the first task. This accomplishment can help you move on to the next task with higher self-efficacy. Success breeds more success.

Set goals with care

If you want to boost self-efficacy, also be picky about your goals. According to the research, goals that you find easy to meet will not boost your self-efficacy. Instead, set goals that call on you to overcome obstacles, make persistent effort, and even fail occasionally.

At the same time, it's important to avoid situations in which you are *often* likely to fail. Setting goals that you have little chance to meet can undermine your self-efficacy. Ideal goals are both challenging *and* achievable.

Adopt a model

In self-efficacy research, the word *model* has a special definition. This term refers to someone who is similar to you in key ways, and who succeeds in the kinds of situations in which you want to succeed. To find a model, gather with people who share your interests. Look for people with whom you have a lot in common— and who have mastered the skills that you want to acquire. Besides demonstrating strategies and techniques for you to use, these people hold out a real possibility of success for you.

Change the conversation about yourself

Monitor what you say and think about yourself. Remember that this self-talk might be so habitual that you don't even notice it. Whether

A strong sense of self-efficacy allows you to tackle problems with confidence, set long-term goals, and see difficult tasks as creative challenges rather than potential disasters.

you are fully aware of them or not, your thoughts can make or break your sense of self-efficacy.

Pay close attention and notice when you speak or think negatively about yourself. Telling the truth about your weaknesses is one thing. Consistently underrating yourself is another. In the conversation about yourself, go for balance. Tell the truth about the times you set a goal and miss it. Also take the time to write and speak about the goals you meet and what works well in your life.

People with a strong sense of self-efficacy attribute their failures to skills that they currently lack—and that they can acquire in the future. This approach chooses not to look on failures as permanent, personal defects. Rather than saying "I just don't have what it takes to become a skilled test taker," say "I can adopt techniques to help me remember key facts even when I feel stressed."

Interpret stress in a new way

Achieving your goals might place you right in the middle of situations in which you feel stress. You might find yourself meeting new people, leading a meeting, speaking in public, or doing something else that you've never done before. That can feel scary.

Remember that stress comes in two forms—thoughts and physical sensations. Thoughts can include mental pictures of yourself making mistakes or being publicly humiliated, and statements such as "This is the worst possible thing that could happen to me." Sensations can include shortness of breath, dry mouth, knots in the stomach, tingling feelings, headaches, and other forms of discomfort.

The way you interpret stress as you become aware of it can make a big difference in your sense of self-efficacy. During moments when you want to do well, you might rely on a stream of personal impressions to judge your performance. In those moments, see if you can focus your attention. Rather than attaching negative interpretations to your experience of stress, simply notice your thoughts and sensations. Release them instead of

dwelling on them or trying to resist them. As you observe yourself over time, you might find that the physical sensations associated with your sense of stress and your sense of excitement are largely the same. Instead of viewing these sensations as signs of impending doom, see them as a boost of energy and enthusiasm that you can channel into performing well.

Compare yourself to yourself

Our own failures are often more dramatic to us than the failures of others, and our own successes are often more invisible. When we're unsure of ourselves, we can look in any direction and see people who seem more competent and more confident than we do. When we start the comparison game, we open the door to self-doubt.

There is a way to play the comparison game and win: Instead of comparing yourself to others, compare yourself to yourself. Measure success in terms of self-improvement rather than of triumphs over others. Take time to note any progress you've made toward your goals over time. Write Discovery Statements about that progress. Celebrate your success in any area of life, no matter how small that success might seem.

There is a way to play the comparison game and win: Instead of comparing yourself to others, compare yourself to yourself.

Soak in the acknowledgments of others

Instead of deflecting compliments ("It was nothing"), fully receive the positive things that others say about you ("Thank you"). Also take public credit for your successes. "Well, I was just lucky" can change to "I worked hard to achieve that goal." ⬧

Emotional pain is not a sickness

Emotional pain has gotten a bad name. This type of slander is undeserved. There is nothing wrong with feeling bad. It's OK to feel miserable, depressed, sad, upset, angry, dejected, gloomy, or unhappy.

It might not be pleasant to feel bad, but it can be good for you. Often, the appropriate way to feel is bad. When you leave a place you love, sadness is natural. When you lose a friend or lover, misery might be in order. When someone treats you badly, it is probably appropriate to feel angry.

Unless you are suicidally depressed, it is almost impossible to feel too bad. Feeling bad for too long can be a problem. If depression, sadness, or anger persists, get help. Otherwise, allow yourself to experience these emotions. They're usually appropriate and necessary for personal growth.

When a loved one dies, it is necessary to grieve. The grief might appear in the form of depression, sadness, or anger. There is nothing wrong with extreme emotional pain. It is natural, and it doesn't have to be fixed.

When feeling bad becomes a problem, it is usually because you didn't allow yourself to feel bad at the outset. So the next time you feel rotten, go ahead and feel rotten. It will pass—and probably more quickly if you don't fight it or try to ignore it.

Allowing yourself to feel bad might even help you get smart. Harvey Jackins, a psychotherapist, bases his work on this premise.[8] Jackins believes that when people fully experience and release their emotions, they also remove blocks to their thinking and clear a path for profound personal insights. And Daniel Goleman, author of *Emotional Intelligence,* asserts that being attuned to feelings can lead to sounder personal decisions.[9]

Following are some good ways to feel bad.

Don't worry about reasons. Sometimes we allow ourselves to feel bad if we have a good reason. For example: "Well, I feel very sad, but that is because I just found out my best friend is moving to Europe." It's all right to know the reason why you are sad, and it is fine *not* to know. You can feel bad for no apparent reason. The reason doesn't matter.

Set a time limit. If you are concerned about feeling bad, if you are worried that you need to "fix it," give yourself a little time. Before you force yourself not to feel the way you feel, set a time limit. Say to yourself, "I am going to give myself until Monday at noon, and if I don't feel better by then, I am going to try to fix myself." Sometimes it is appropriate to fix a bad feeling. There might be a problem that needs a solution. You can use feeling bad as your motivation to solve the problem. And sometimes it helps just to feel bad for a while.

Reassure others. Sometimes other people—friends or family members, for example—have a hard time letting you feel bad. They might be worried that they did something wrong and want to make it better. They want you to quit feeling bad. Tell them you will. Assure them that you will feel good again, but that for right now, you just want to feel bad.

This is no joke. Sometimes students think that this whole idea of allowing yourself to feel bad is a joke, reverse psychology, or something else. It isn't. This suggestion is based on the notion that good mental health is possible only if you allow yourself to feel the full range of your emotions. ✉

Suicide

Suicide is one of the leading causes of death among students.

While preparing for and entering higher education, people typically face major changes. The stress that they feel can lead to an increase in depression, anxiety, and attempted suicide.

Recognize danger signals

Talking about suicide. People who attempt suicide often talk about it. They might say, "I just don't want to live anymore." Or "I want you to know that no matter what happens, I've always loved you." Or "Tomorrow night at 7:30 I'm going to end it all with a gun."

Planning for it. People planning suicide will sometimes put their affairs in order. They might close bank accounts, give away or sell precious possessions, or make or update a will. They might even develop specific plans on how to kill themselves.

Having a history of previous attempts. Some estimates suggest that up to 50 percent of the people who kill themselves have attempted suicide at least once before.

Dwelling on problems. Expressing extreme helplessness or hopelessness about solving problems can indicate that someone might be considering suicide.

Feeling depressed. Although not everyone who is depressed attempts suicide, almost everyone who attempts suicide feels depressed.

Take prompt action

Most often, suicide can be prevented. If you suspect that someone you know is considering suicide, do whatever it takes to ensure the person's safety. Let this person know that you will persist until you are certain that she's safe. Any of the following actions can help.

Take it seriously. Taking suicidal comments seriously is especially important when you hear them from young adults. Suicide threats are more common in this age group and might be dismissed as "normal." Err on the side of being too careful rather than on the side of being negligent.

Listen fully. Encourage the person at risk to express thoughts and feelings appropriately. If she claims that she doesn't want to talk, be inviting, be assertive, and be persistent. Be totally committed to listening.

Speak powerfully. Let the person at risk know that you care. Trying to talk someone out of suicide or minimizing problems is generally useless. Acknowledge that problems are serious *and* that they can be solved. Point out that suicide is a permanent solution to a temporary problem—and that help is available.

Get professional help. Suggest that the person see a mental health professional. If she resists help, offer to schedule the appointment for her and to take her to it. If this fails, get others involved, including the depressed person's family or school personnel.

Remove access to firearms. Most suicides are attempted with guns. Get rid of any that might be around. Also remove dangerous drugs and razors.

Ask the person to sign a "no-suicide contract." Get a promise, in writing, that the person will not hurt herself before speaking to you. A written promise can provide the "excuse" she needs not to take action.

Handle an emergency. If a situation becomes a crisis, do not leave the person alone. Call a crisis hot line, 911, or a social service agency. If necessary, take the person to the nearest hospital emergency room, clinic, or police station.

Follow up. Someone in danger of attempting suicide might resist further help even if your first intervention succeeds. Ask this person if she's keeping counseling appointments and taking prescribed medication. Help this person apply strategies for solving problems. Stay in touch.

Take care of yourself

If you ever begin to think about committing suicide, remember that you can apply any of the above suggestions to yourself. For example, look for warning signs and take them seriously. Seek out someone you trust and tell this person how you feel. If necessary, make an appointment to see a counselor and ask someone to accompany you. When you're at risk, you deserve the same compassion that you'd willingly extend to another person.

Find out more on this topic from the American Foundation for Suicide Prevention at 1-888-333-AFSP or **http://www.afsp.org**.

The truth is that getting high can be fun.

In our culture, and especially in our media, getting high has become synonymous with having a good time. Even if you don't smoke, drink, or use other drugs, you are certain to come in contact with people who do.

For centuries, human beings have devised ways to change their feelings and thoughts by altering their body chemistry. The Chinese were using marijuana five thousand years ago. Herodotus, the ancient Greek historian, wrote about a group of people in Eastern Europe who threw marijuana on hot stones and inhaled the vapors. More recently, during the American Civil War, customers could buy opium and morphine across the counter of their neighborhood store. A few decades later, Americans were able to buy soft drinks that contained coca—the plant from which cocaine is derived.

Today we are still a drug-using society. Of course, some of those uses are therapeutic and lawful, including drugs that are taken as prescribed by a doctor or psychologist. The problem comes when we turn to drugs as *the* solution to any problem, even before seeking professional guidance. Are you uncomfortable? Often the first response is "Take something."

We live in times when reaching for instant comfort via chemicals is not only condoned—it is approved. If you're bored, tense, or anxious, you can drink a can of beer, down a glass of wine, or light up a cigarette. And these are only the legal options. If you're willing to take risks, you can pick from a large selection of illegal drugs on the street.

There is a big payoff in using alcohol, tobacco, caffeine, cocaine, heroin, or other drugs—or people wouldn't do it. The payoff can be direct, such as relaxation, self-confidence, comfort, excitement, or other forms of pleasure. At times, the payoff is not so obvious, as when people seek to avoid rejection, mask emotional pain, win peer group acceptance, or reject authority.

Perhaps drugs have a timeless appeal because human beings face two perennial problems: how to cope with unpleasant moods, and how to deal with difficult circumstances such as poverty, loneliness, or the prospect of

Alcohol, tobacco, and drugs: The truth

We might take care of ourselves when we see that the costs of using a substance outweigh the benefits.

death. When faced with either problem, people are often tempted to ignore potential solutions and go directly to the chemical fix.

In addition to the payoffs, there are costs. For some people, the cost is much greater than the payoff. That cost goes beyond money. Even if illegal drug use doesn't make you broke, it can make you crazy. This is not necessarily the kind of crazy where you dress up like Napoleon. Rather, it is the kind where you care about little else except finding more drugs—friends, school, work, and family be damned.

Substance abuse—the compulsive use of a chemical in alcohol or drugs resulting in negative consequences—is only part of the picture. People can also relate to food, gambling, money, sex, and even work in compulsive ways.

Some people will stop abusing a substance or activity when the consequences get serious enough. Other people don't stop. They continue their self-defeating behaviors, no matter the consequences for themselves, their friends, or their families. At that point the problem goes beyond abuse. It's addiction.

With substance addiction, the costs can include overdose, infection, and lowered immunity to disease—all of which can be fatal. Long-term excessive drinking damages every organ system in the human body. Each year, almost 400,000 people die from the effects of cigarette smoking.

Lectures about why to avoid alcohol and drug abuse and addiction can be pointless. Ultimately, we don't take care of our bodies because someone says we should. We might take care of ourselves when we see that the costs of using a substance outweigh the benefits. You choose. It's your body.

Acknowledging that alcohol, tobacco, and other drugs can be fun infuriates a lot of people who might assume that this is the same as condoning their use. The point is this: People are more likely to abstain when they're convinced that using these substances leads to more pain than pleasure over the long run. ⌧

Some facts . . .

In the United States, substance abuse and addiction take a heavy toll on students in higher education, especially those aged 18 to 24. In this group:

- 31 percent met criteria for a diagnosis of alcohol abuse and 6 percent for a diagnosis of alcohol dependence in the past 12 months, according to questionnaire-based self-reports about their drinking.

- About 25 percent report academic consequences of their drinking, including missing class, falling behind, doing poorly on exams or papers, and receiving lower grades overall.

- 1,400 die each year from alcohol-related unintentional injuries, including motor vehicle crashes.

- 500,000 are unintentionally injured under the influence of alcohol.

- 400,000 had unprotected sex, and more than 100,000 students report having been too intoxicated to know if they consented to having sex.

- 70,000 are victims of alcohol-related sexual assault or date rape.

For related information from the National Institute for Alcohol Abuse and Alcoholism, go online to **http://www. collegedrinkingprevention.gov.**

Sources: R. W. Hingson, T. Heeren, R. C. Zakocs, A. Kopstein, and H. Wechsler, "Magnitude of Alcohol-Related Mortality and Morbidity among U.S. College Students Ages 18–24," *Journal of Studies on Alcohol* 63, no. 2 (2002): 136–144.

H. Wechsler, J. E. Lee, M. Kuo, M. Seibring, T. F. Nelson, and H. P. Lee, "Trends in College Binge Drinking during a Period of Increased Prevention Efforts: Findings from Four Harvard School of Public Health Study Surveys, 1993–2001," *Journal of American College Health* 50, no. 5 (2002): 203–217.

J. R. Knight, H. Wechsler, M. Kuo, M. Seibring, E. R. Weitzman, and M. Schuckit, "Alcohol Abuse and Dependence among U.S. College Students," *Journal of Studies on Alcohol* 63, no. 3 (2002): 263–270.

ADDICTION: HOW DO I KNOW . . . ?

People who have problems with drugs and alcohol are great at hiding that fact from themselves and from others. It is also hard to admit that a friend or loved one might have a problem.

The purpose of this exercise is to give you an objective way to look at your relationship with drugs or alcohol. There are signals that indicate when drug or alcohol use has become abusive or even addictive. This exercise can also help you determine if a friend might be addicted.

Answer the following questions quickly and honestly with "yes," "no," or "n/a" (not applicable). If you are concerned about someone else, rephrase each question using that person's name.

_____ Are you uncomfortable discussing drug abuse or addiction?

_____ Are you worried about your own drug or alcohol use?

_____ Are any of your friends worried about your drug or alcohol use?

_____ Have you ever hidden from a friend, spouse, employer, or coworker the fact that you were drinking? (Pretended you were sober? Covered up alcohol breath?)

_____ Do you sometimes use alcohol or drugs to escape lows rather than to produce highs?

_____ Have you ever gotten angry when confronted about your use?

_____ Do you brag about how much you consume? ("I drank her under the table.")

_____ Do you think about or do drugs when you are alone?

_____ Do you store up alcohol, drugs, cigarettes, or caffeine (in coffee or soft drinks) to be sure you won't run out?

_____ Does having a party almost always include alcohol or drugs?

_____ Do you try to control your drinking so that it won't be a problem? ("I drink only on weekends now." "I never drink before 5 p.m." "I drink only beer.")

_____ Do you often explain to other people why you are drinking? ("It's my birthday." "It's my friend's birthday." "It's Veterans Day." "It sure is a hot day.")

_____ Have you changed friends to accommodate your drinking? ("She's OK, but she isn't excited about getting high.")

_____ Has your behavior changed in the last several months? (Grades down? Lack of interest in a hobby? Change of values or of what you think is moral?)

_____ Do you drink to relieve tension? ("What a day! I need a drink.")

_____ Do you have medical problems (stomach trouble, malnutrition, liver problems, anemia) that could be related to drinking?

_____ Have you ever decided to quit drugs or alcohol and then changed your mind?

_____ Have you had any fights, accidents, or similar incidents related to drinking or drugs in the last year?

_____ Has your drinking or drug use ever caused a problem at home?

_____ Do you envy people who go overboard with alcohol or drugs?

_____ Have you ever told yourself you can quit at any time?

_____ Have you ever been in trouble with the police after or while you were drinking?

_____ Have you ever missed school or work because you had a hangover?

_____ Have you ever had a blackout (a period you can't remember) after drinking?

_____ Do you wish that people would mind their own business when it comes to your use of alcohol or drugs?

_____ Is the cost of alcohol or other drugs taxing your budget or resulting in financial stress?

_____ Do you need increasing amounts of the drug to produce the desired effect?

_____ When you stop taking the drug, do you experience withdrawal?

_____ Do you spend a great deal of time obtaining and using alcohol or other drugs?

_____ Have you used alcohol or another drug when it was physically dangerous to do so (such as when driving a car or working with machines)?

_____ Have you been arrested or had other legal problems resulting from the use of a substance?

Now count the number of questions you answered "yes." If you answered "yes" five or more times, talk with a professional. Five "yes" answers does not necessarily mean that you are addicted. It does point out that alcohol or other drugs are adversely affecting your life. Talk to someone with training in recovery from chemical dependency. Do not rely on the opinion of anyone who lacks such training.

If you filled out this questionnaire about another person and you answered "yes" five or more times, your friend might need help. You probably can't provide that help alone. Seek out a counselor or a support group such as Al-Anon. Call the local Alcoholics Anonymous chapter to find out about an Al-Anon meeting near you.

Seeing the full scope of addiction

Here are some guidelines that can help you decide if addiction is a barrier for you right now. Most addictions share some key features, such as the following:

- *Loss of control*—continued substance use or activity in spite of adverse consequences.

- *Pattern of relapse*—vowing to quit or limit the activity or substance use and continually failing to do so.

- *Tolerance*—the need to take increasing amounts of a substance to produce the desired effect.

- *Withdrawal*—signs and symptoms of physical and mental discomfort or illness when the substance is taken away.[10]

The same basic features can be present in anything from cocaine use to compulsive gambling. All of this can add up to a continuous cycle of abuse or addiction. These common features prompt many people to call some forms of addiction a disease. The American Medical Association formally recognized alcoholism as a disease in 1956. Some people do not agree that alcoholism is a disease or that all addictions can be labeled with that term. You don't have to wait until this question is settled before examining your own life.

If you have a problem with addiction, consider getting help. The problem might be your own addiction or perhaps the behavior of someone you love. In any case, consider acting on several of the following suggestions.

Admit the problem. People with active addictions are a varied group—rich and poor, young and old, successful and unsuccessful. Often these people do have one thing in common: They are masters of denial. They deny that they are unhappy. They deny that they have hurt anyone. They are convinced that they can quit any time they want. They sometimes become so adept at hiding the problem from themselves that they die.

Pay attention. If you do use a substance compulsively or behave in compulsive ways, do so with awareness. Then pay attention to the consequences. Act with deliberate decision rather than out of habit or under pressure from others.

Look at the costs. There is always a tradeoff. Drinking 10 beers might result in a temporary high, and you will probably remember that feeling. No one feels great the morning after consuming 10 beers, but it seems easier to forget pain. Often people don't notice how bad alcoholism, drug addiction, or other forms of substance abuse make them feel.

Take responsibility. Nobody plans to become an addict. If you have pneumonia, you can recover without guilt or shame. Approach an addiction in yourself or others in the same way. You can take responsibility for your recovery without blame, shame, or guilt.

Get help. Many people find that they cannot treat addiction on their own. Addictive behaviors are often symptoms of an illness that needs treatment.

Two broad options exist for getting help with addiction. One is the growing self-help movement. The other is formal treatment. People recovering from addiction often combine the two.

Many self-help groups are modeled after Alcoholics Anonymous. AA is made up of recovering alcoholics and addicts. These people understand the problems of abuse firsthand, and they follow a systematic, 12-step approach to living without it. This is one of the oldest and most successful self-help programs in the world. Chapters of AA welcome people from all walks of life, and you don't have to be an alcoholic to attend most meetings. Programs based on AA principles exist for many other forms of addiction as well.

Some people feel uncomfortable with the AA approach. Other resources exist for these people, including private therapy and group therapy. Also investigate

You can take responsibility for your recovery without blame, shame, or guilt.

organizations such as Women for Sobriety, the Secular Organizations for Sobriety, and Rational Recovery Systems. Use whatever works for you.

Treatment programs are available in almost every community. They might be residential (you live there for weeks or months at a time) or outpatient (you visit several hours a day). Find out where these treatment centers are located by calling a doctor, a mental health professional, or a local hospital.

Alcohol and drug treatments are now covered by many health insurance programs. If you don't have insurance, it is usually possible to arrange some other payment program. Cost is no reason to avoid treatment.

Get help for a friend or family member. You might know someone who uses alcohol or other drugs in a way that can lead to serious and sustained negative consequences. If so, you have every right to express your concern to that person. Wait until the person is clear-headed and then mention specific incidents. For example: "Last night you drank five beers when we were at my apartment, and then you wanted to drive home. When I offered to call a cab for you instead, you refused." Also be prepared to offer a source of help, such as the phone number of a local treatment center.

→ Where to turn for more information on recovery

Begin with your doctor or campus health care center. You can also contact:

Alcoholics Anonymous World Services
1-212-870-3400
www.alcoholics-anonymous.org

Center for Substance Abuse Treatment
1-800-662-4357
www.samhsa.gov/centers/csat2002/csat_frame.html

National Black Alcoholism and Addictions Council
www.nbacinc.org/

National Alliance for Hispanic Health
1-202-387-5000
www.hispanichealth.org/

Rational Recovery
1-800-303-2873
www.rational.org/recovery

Women for Sobriety
1-215-536-8026
www.womenforsobriety.org

Warning
Advertising can be dangerous to your health

The average American is exposed to hundreds of advertising messages per day. Unless you are stranded on a desert island, you are affected by commercial messages.

Advertising serves a useful function. It helps us make choices about how we spend our money. We can choose among cars, kitchen appliances, health clubs, books, plants, groceries, home builders, dog groomers, piano tuners, vacation spots, locksmiths, movies, amusement parks—the list is endless. Advertising makes us aware of the options.

Advertising space is also expensive, and the messages are carefully crafted to get the most value for the cost. Advertisements can play on our emotions and be dangerously manipulative. For example, consider the messages that ads convey about your health. Advertising alcohol, tobacco, and pain relievers is a big business. Much of the revenue earned by newspapers, magazines, radio, television, and Web sites comes from advertisements for these products.

Ads for alcohol glorify drinking. One of the aims of these ads is to convince heavy drinkers that the amount they drink is normal. Advertisers imply that daily drinking is the norm, pleasant experiences are enhanced by drinking, holidays naturally include alcohol, parties are a flop without it, relationships are more romantic over cocktails, and everybody drinks. Each of these implications is questionable.

Advertising can affect our self-image. A typical advertising message is "You are not OK unless you buy our product." These messages are painstakingly programmed to get us to buy clothes, makeup, and hair products to make us look OK; drugs, alcohol, and food to make us feel OK; perfumes, toothpaste, and deodorants to make us smell OK. Advertising also promotes the idea that buying the right product is essential to having valuable relationships in our lives.

Advertising affects what we eat. Multimedia advertisers portray the primary staples of our diets as sugary breakfast cereals, candy bars, and soft drinks. The least nutritious foods receive the most advertising money.

Another problem with advertising is the image of women that is commonly portrayed. The basic message is that women love to spend hours discussing floor wax, deodorants, tampons, and laundry detergent—and that they think constantly about losing weight and looking sexy. In some ads, women handle everything from kitchen to bedroom to boardroom—these women are Superwomen.

Images such as these are demeaning to women and damaging to men. Women lose when they allow their self-image to be influenced by ads. Men lose when they expect real-life women to look and act like the women on television and in magazines. Advertising photography creates illusions. The next time you're in a crowd, notice how few people look like those in the media.

Though advertising is making progress in representing racial diversity, it still frequently excludes people of color. If our perceptions were based solely on advertising, we would be hard pressed to know that our society is racially and ethnically diverse. See how many examples of cultural stereotypes you can find in the ads you encounter this week.

Use advertising as a continual opportunity to develop the qualities of a critical thinker. Be aware of how a multibillion-dollar industry threatens your health and well-being. ◪

journal entry 33

Discovery/Intention Statement

Think of a time when—after seeing an advertisement or a commercial—you craved a certain food or drink or you really wanted to buy something. Describe how the advertising influenced you.

I discovered that I . . .

_____

_____

_____

Now describe anything you'd like to do differently in the future when you notice that advertising affects you in the way you just described.

I intend to . . .

_____

_____

_____

This exercise is about clarifying the differences between behaviors and interpretations. A behavior is factual and observable, while an interpretation is subjective and often based on observed behaviors. Understanding this distinction can help you think clearly about your behaviors—including those that affect your emotional health by influencing your key relationships.

For instance, arriving 10 minutes after a lecture starts or pulling a dog's tail are both observable behaviors. In contrast, an interpretation is a conclusion we draw on the basis of the observed behavior: "She's either too rude or too irresponsible to get to a lecture on time." "She hates animals. Just look at how she pulled that dog's tail!" Keep in mind that other interpretations are possible. Perhaps the person's car broke down on the way to the lecture. And maybe the owner of the dog is playing a game that her pet enjoys.

Consider another example. "She shouted at me, left the room, and slammed the door" is a statement that describes behaviors. "She was angry" is one interpretation of the social significance or meaning of the observed behavior.

With this distinction in mind, brainstorm a list of behaviors you have seen in others when they were in conflict with you. Use the space below to record your brainstorm. Afterward, review your list to see if some of the behaviors you noted are actually interpretations.

CHAPTER 11

Power Process | Put It to Work | Quiz | Learning Styles Application | Master Student Profile

power process

Surrender

Life can be magnificent and satisfying. It can also be devastating.

Sometimes there is too much pain or confusion. Problems can be too big and too numerous. Life can bring us to our knees in a pitiful, helpless, and hopeless state. A broken relationship with a loved one, a sudden diagnosis of cancer, total frustration with a child's behavior problem, or even the prospect of several long years of school are situations that can leave us feeling overwhelmed—powerless.

In these troubling situations, the first thing we can do is to admit that we don't have the resources to handle the problem. No matter how hard we try and no matter what skills we bring to bear, some problems remain out of our control. When this is the case, we can tell the truth: "It's too big and too mean. I can't handle it."

Releasing control, receiving help

Desperately struggling to control a problem can easily result in the problem's controlling you. Surrender is letting go of being the master in order to avoid becoming the slave.

Once you have acknowledged your lack of control, all that remains is to surrender. Many traditions make note of this. Western religions speak of surrendering to God. Hindus say surrender to the Self. Members of Alcoholics Anonymous talk about turning their lives over to a Higher Power. Agnostics might suggest surrendering to the ultimate source of power. Others might speak of following their intuition, their inner guide, or their con-

science. William James wrote about surrender as a part of the conversion experience.[11]

In any case, surrender means being receptive to help. Once we admit that we're at the end of our rope, we open ourselves up to receiving help. We learn that we don't have to go it alone. We find out that other people have faced similar problems and survived. We give up our old habits of thinking and behaving as if we have to be in control of everything. We stop acting as general manager of the universe. We surrender. And that creates a space for something new in our lives.

Surrender works

Surrender works for life's major barriers as well as for its insignificant hassles.

You might say, as you struggle to remember someone's name, "It's on the tip of my tongue." Then you surrender. You give up trying and say, "Oh well, it will come to me later." Then the name pops into your mind.

An alcoholic admits that he just can't control his drinking. This becomes the key that allows him to seek treatment.

A person with multiple sclerosis admits that she's gradually losing the ability to walk. She tells others about this fact. Now the people around her can understand, be supportive, and explore ways to help.

A man is devastated when his girlfriend abandons him. He is a "basket case," unable to work for days. Instead of struggling against this fact, he simply admits the full extent of his pain. In that moment, he is able to trust. He trusts that help will come and that one day he will be OK again. He trusts in his ability to learn and to create a new life. He trusts that new opportunities for love will come his way.

After trying unsuccessfully for years to have a baby, a couple finally surrenders and considers adoption. The woman then conceives in a few months.

After finding out she has terminal cancer, a woman shifts between panic and depression. Nothing seems to console her. Finally, she accepts the truth and stops fighting her tragedy. She surrenders. Now at peace, she invests her remaining years in meaningful moments with the people she loves.

A writer is tackling the first chapter of his novel, feeling totally in control. He has painstakingly outlined the whole plot, recording each character's actions on individual 3x5 cards. Three sentences into his first draft, he finds that he's spending most of his time shuffling cards instead of putting words on paper. Finally, he puts the cards aside, forgets about the outline, and just tells the story. The words start to flow effortlessly, and he loses himself in the act of writing.

In each of these cases, the people involved learned the power of surrendering.

Once we admit that we're at the end of our rope, we open ourselves up to receiving help.

What surrender is not

Surrender is not resignation. It is not a suggestion to quit and do nothing about your problems. You have many skills and resources. Use them. You can apply all of your energy to handling a situation and surrender at the same time. Surrender includes doing whatever you can in a positive, trusting spirit. Giving up is fatalistic and accomplishes nothing. So let go, keep going, and know that the true source of control lies beyond you.

This Power Process says, in effect, don't fight the current. Imagine a person rafting down a flowing river with a rapid current. She's likely to do fine if she surrenders control and lets the raft flow with the current. After all, the current always goes around the rocks. If she tries to fight the current, she could end up in an argument with a rock about where the current is going—and lose.

Detachment helps us surrender

Watching yourself with detachment can help your ability to surrender. Pretend that you are floating away from your body, and then watch what's going on from a distance.

Objectively witness the drama of your life unfolding as if you were watching a play. When you see yourself as part of a much broader perspective, surrender seems obvious and natural.

"Surrender" might seem inconsistent with the Power Process: "I create it all." An old parable says that the Garden of Truth, the grand place everyone wants to enter, is guarded by two monsters—Fear and Paradox. Most of us can see how fear keeps us from getting what we want. The role of paradox might not be as clear.

The word *paradox* refers to a seemingly contradictory statement that might nonetheless be true. It is our difficulty in holding seemingly contradictory thoughts that sometimes keeps us out of the Garden of Truth. If we suspend the sovereignty of logic, we might discover that ideas that seem contradictory can actually coexist. With application, we can see that both "Surrender" and "I create it all" are valuable tools. ✖

put it to work

Suggestions for managing your health can help you achieve the mental and physical energy needed to work to your full capacity. Following are ways to transfer two key topics of this chapter—physical health and substance abuse—to the workplace.

Apply insights from ergonomics. The field of study called *ergonomics* focuses on ways to prevent health problems due to human behavior and workplace conditions. Recently, specialists in ergonomics have developed many suggestions for people who work continually at computers. These people can experience health problems that range from eyestrain and lower back pain to numbness in the arms and wrists.

You can hire specialists in ergonomics to redesign your workspace. That costs money. The following suggestions are free:

■ *Rest your eyes.* To prevent eyestrain caused by staring too long at a computer screen, give your eyes rest from time to time. Looking out a window or at another object that is closer or farther away can help by forcing your eyes to readjust their focus. Also, set up your computer away from windows so that you can avoid squinting as you look at the screen.

■ *Take breaks.* Get away from the computer. Stretch. Move. Walk, jog, or run.

■ *Pay attention to your posture.* To avoid lower back problems, pay attention to your posture as you sit at the computer. Adjust your chair so that you can sit comfortably, with your back relaxed and your spine erect. Placing a pillow or small cushion behind your lower back might help.

■ *Type with the keyboard in your lap.* This allows your hands to be lower than your elbows and minimizes the tension in your shoulders.

The idea behind each of the above suggestions is to position yourself so that you remain alert *and* relaxed while you're at the computer. Taking some simple precautions now can help you avoid feeling like a pretzel in a few years.

Remember the toll that addiction to alcohol and other drugs can take on your workplace. Employees who show up to work hung over or "under the influence" are, at the very least, unproductive. If they drive or operate machinery, they are downright dangerous. Use your skill with "I" statements (see Chapter Eight: Communicating) to speak candidly with a colleague about her drinking or drug use problem and offer help. ⊠

Name _____ Date _____/_____/_____

1. Explain three ways you can respond effectively if someone you know threatens to commit suicide.

2. The strategies suggested for dealing with stress do *not* include:
   (a) Release irrational beliefs.
   (b) Use breathing and relaxation exercises included in this book.
   (c) Cut back on exercising.
   (d) Consider therapeutic bodywork such as massage.
   (e) Check with your student health service.

3. How is the Power Process: "Surrender" different from giving up?

4. A person infected with HIV might have no symptoms for months—sometimes years. True or False? Explain your answer.

5. Define *date rape* and describe at least two ways to protect yourself against it.

6. List at least three dietary guidelines that can contribute to your health.

7. One of the suggestions for dealing with addiction is "Pay attention." This implies that it's OK to use drugs, as long as you do so with full awareness. True or False? Explain your answer.

8. Name at least three methods for preventing unwanted pregnancy.

9. The article "Emotional pain is not a sickness" suggests that sometimes it helps to allow yourself to feel bad for a while. What is the point behind this idea?

10. Explain two ways that an uncritical response to advertising can undermine your health.

learning styles application

The questions below will "cycle" you through four styles, or modes, of learning as explained in the article "Learning styles: Discovering how you learn" in Chapter One. Each question will help you explore a different mode. You can answer the questions in any order.

what if *After using a plan to improve your health based on the suggestions in this chapter, consider how well the plan worked for you. Which actions do you intend to continue on a regular basis? Are there any new actions you intend to take?*

why *Name one specific health benefit you'd like to gain from this chapter. Possibilities include stress reduction, weight loss, or a higher energy level.*

how *Using suggestions from this chapter, create an action plan for meeting an important goal relating to your health. List the actions you will take and set a date for taking each action or beginning a new health habit. (Continue writing on additional paper, if necessary.)*

what *List three suggestions from this chapter that can help you meet an important goal relating to your health.*

master student profile

CHRISTOPHER REEVE

(1952–2004) left paralyzed after a horseback riding accident in 1995, this on-screen Superman and real-life hero was a tireless activist who helped raise millions of dollars for spinal cord research before his death in 2004.

Soon I realized that I'd have to leave Kessler [hospital] at some point. A tentative date was set for sometime between Thanksgiving and mid-December. I thought: God, I've totally given up on breathing. So what am I going to do, stay on a ventilator for the rest of my life?. . .

I announced that on the first Monday of November, I was going to try again to breathe on my own. At 3:30 in the afternoon of November 2, Bill Carroll, Dr. Kirshblum, Dr. Finley, and Erica met me in the PT room. And I remember thinking: This is it. I've got to do something, I have simply got to. I don't know where it's going to come from, but I've got to produce some air from someplace.

Dr. Finley said, "We're going to take you off the ventilator. I want you to try to take ten breaths. If you can only do three, then that's the way it is, but I want you to try for ten. And I'm going to measure how much air you move with each breath, and let's just see where you are. Okay?"

And I took ten breaths. I was lying on my back on the mat. My head moved as I struggled to draw in air; I wasn't able to move my diaphragm at all, just my chest, neck, and shoulder muscles in an intense effort to bring some air into my lungs. I was only able to draw in an average of 50 cc's with each attempt. But at least it was something. I had moved the dial.

We came back the next day, and now I was really motivated. I prepared myself mentally by imagining my chest as a huge bellows that I could open and close at will. I told myself over and over again that I was going home soon and that I couldn't leave without making some real progress. Dr. Finley asked me to take another ten breaths for a comparison with yesterday's numbers. I took the ten breaths, and my average for each one was 450 cc's.

They couldn't believe it. I thought to myself: All right. Now we're getting somewhere.

At 3:30 the next day I was in place and ready to begin. . . . Finally I was really taking charge. When Dr. Finley arrived once again he asked me to take ten breaths. This time the average was 560 cc's per breath. A cheer broke out in the room. . . .

After that Erica and I worked alone. Every day we would breathe. I went from seven minutes to twelve to fifteen. Just before I left Kessler on the thirteenth of December, I gave it

everything I had, and I breathed for thirty minutes. . . . The previous summer, still adjusting to my new circumstances, I had given up. But by November I had the motivation to go forward. . . .

Juice had often told me, "You've been to the grave two times this year, brother. You're not going there again. You are here for a reason." He thought my injury had meaning, had a purpose. I believed, and still do, that my injury was simply an accident. But maybe Juice and I are both right, because I have the opportunity now to make sense of this accident. I believe that it's what you do after an accident that can give it meaning.

I began to face my new life. On Thanksgiving in 1995, I went home to Bedford to spend the day with my family. In the driveway, when I saw our home again, I wept. Dana held me. At the dinner table, when each of us in turn spoke a few words about what we were thankful for, Will said, "Dad." ✖

From *Still Me* by Christopher Reeve. Copyright © 1998 by Cambria Productions, Inc. Used by permission of Random House, Inc.

For more biographical information on Christopher Reeve, visit the Master Student Hall of Fame on the *Becoming a Master Student* Web site at

masterstudent.college.hmco.com

12

What's Next?

Live as if you were to die tomorrow. Learn as if you were to live forever.

GANDHI

Learning is not a task or a problem—it is a way to be in the world. Man learns as he pursues goals and projects that have meaning for him.

SIDNEY JOURARD

why
this chapter matters . . .

You can use the techniques introduced in this book to set and achieve goals for the rest of your life.

what
is included . . .

Now that you're done—begin
". . . use the following suggestions to continue . . ."
Transferring to another school
Career planning: Begin the process now
Use the SCANS reports to discover your skills
Jumpstart your education with transferable skills
Use résumés and interviews to "hire" an employer
Cruising for jobs on the Internet
Creating and using portfolios
Contributing: The art of selfishness
Service learning: The art of learning by contributing
Define your values, align your actions
One set of values
Power Process: "Be it"
Master Student Profile: Golda Meir

how
you can use this chapter . . .

Choose the next steps in your education and career.
Document your continuing success with a portfolio.
Experience the joys of contributing.
Use a Power Process that enhances every technique in this book.

As you read, ask yourself
what if . . .

I could begin creating the life of my dreams—starting today?

Now that you're done—begin

If you used this book fully—if you actively participated in reading the contents, writing the journals, doing the exercises, practicing critical thinking, completing the learning styles applications, and applying the suggestions—you have had quite a journey.

Recall some high points of that journey. The first half of this book is about the nuts and bolts of education—the business of acquiring knowledge. It helps prepare you for making the transition to higher education and suggests that you take a First Step by telling the truth about your skills and setting goals to expand them. Also included are guidelines for planning your time, making your memory more effective, improving your reading skills, taking useful notes, and succeeding at tests. All of this activity prepares you for another aim of education—generating new knowledge and creating a unique place for yourself in the world. Meeting this aim leads you to the topics in the second half of this book: thinking for yourself, enhancing your communication skills, embracing diversity, mastering technology, and living with vibrant health. All are steps on the path of becoming a master student. Now what? What's the next step?

As you ponder this question, consider the possibility that you can create the life of your dreams. Your responses to the ideas, exercises, and Journal Entries in this book can lead you to think new thoughts, say new things, and do what you never believed you could do. If you're willing to master new ways to learn, the possibilities are endless. This message is more fundamental than any individual tool or technique you'll ever read about.

There are people who scoff at the suggestion that they can create the life of their dreams. These people have a perspective that is widely shared. Please release it.

You are on the edge of a universe so miraculous and full of wonder that your imagination at its most creative moment cannot encompass it. Paths are open to lead you to worlds beyond your wildest dreams.

If this sounds like a pitch for the latest recreational drug, it might be. That drug is adrenaline, and it is automatically generated by your body when you are learning, growing, taking risks, and discovering new worlds inside and outside your skin. The world is packed with possibilities for master students. If you excel in adventure, exploration, discovery, and creativity, you will never lack for opportunities.

One of the first articles in this book is about transitions. You are about to make another transition—not just to another chapter of this book but to the next chapter of your life. Remember the process of discovery, intention, and action. This tool can help you master any change and achieve any goal. In the following pages, look for ways to reinforce this process. Use it to choose what's next for you. ⊠

journal entry 34

Discovery/Intention Statement

Complete the following sentences with the first thoughts that come to mind.

From my life, I have discovered that I want . . .

_____

_____

_____

_____

_____

To get what I want from my life, I intend to . . .

_____

_____

_____

_____

_____

voices

In reviewing the table of contents, I discovered that almost every skill could be turned into an applicable career tool. I intend to discuss these master student qualities in an upcoming job interview.

—SEAN CUDDY

"... use the following suggestions to continue ..."

Keep a journal. Psychotherapist Ira Progoff based his Intensive Journal System on the idea that regular journaling can be a path to life-changing insights.[1] To begin journaling, consider buying a bound notebook in which to record your private reflections and dreams for the future. Get one that will be worthy of your personal discoveries and intentions. Write in this journal daily. Record what you are learning about yourself and the world.

Write about your hopes, wishes, and goals. Keep a record of significant events. Consider using the format of Discovery Statements and Intention Statements that you learned in this book. For more ideas, see "Taking notes on your journey: The art of journal writing" in Chapter Five.

Take a workshop. Schooling doesn't have to stop at graduation, and it doesn't have to take place on a campus. In most cities, there are a variety of organizations that sponsor ongoing workshops, covering topics from cosmetology to cosmology. Use workshops to learn skills, understand the world, and discover yourself. You can be trained in cardiopulmonary resuscitation (CPR), attend a lecture on developing nations, or take a course on assertiveness training.

Read, watch, and listen. Publications related to the topic of becoming a master student are recommended in the additional reading at the end of this book. Ask friends and instructors what they are reading. Sample a variety of newspapers and magazines. None of them has all of the truth; most of them have a piece of it. In addition to books, many bookstores and publishing houses offer audio- and videotapes on personal growth topics. Record your most exciting discoveries in an idea file.

Take an unrelated class. Sign up for a class that is totally unrelated to your major. If you are studying to be a secretary, take a physics course. If you are going to be a doctor, take a bookkeeping course. Take a course that will help you develop new computer skills and expand your possibilities for online learning.

You can discover a lot about yourself and your intended future when you step out of old patterns. In addition to formal courses offered at your school, check into local community education courses. These offer a low-cost alternative that poses no threat to your grade point average.

Travel. See the world. Visit new neighborhoods. Travel to other countries. Explore. Find out what it looks like inside buildings that you normally have no reason to enter, museums that you never found interesting before, cities that are out of the way, forests and mountains that lie beyond your old boundaries, and far-off places that require planning and saving to reach.

Get counseling. Solving emotional problems is not the only reason to visit a counselor, therapist, or psychologist. These people are excellent resources for personal growth. You can use counseling to look at and talk about yourself in ways that might be uncomfortable for anyone except a trained professional. Counseling offers a chance to focus exclusively on yourself, something that is usually not possible in normal social settings.

Form a support group. Just as a well-organized study group can promote your success in school, an organized support group can help you reach goals in other areas of your life.

Today, people in support groups help one another lose weight, stay sober, cope with chronic illness, recover from emotional trauma, and overcome drug addiction.

Groups can also brainstorm possibilities for job hunting, career planning, parenting, solving problems in relationships, promoting spiritual growth—for reaching almost any goal you choose.

Find a mentor—or become one. Seek the counsel of experienced people you respect and admire. Use them as role models. If they are willing, ask them to be sounding boards for your plans and ideas. Many people are flattered to be asked.

You can also become a mentor. If you want to perfect your skills as a master student, teach them to someone else. Offer to coach another student in study skills in exchange for childcare, free lunches, or something else you value. A mentor relationship can bridge the boundaries of age, race, and culture.

Redo this book. Start by redoing one chapter or maybe just one exercise. If you didn't get everything you wanted from this book, it's not too late.

You can also reread and redo portions that you found valuable. As you plan your career and hunt for jobs, you might find that the Put It to Work articles in each chapter acquire new meaning. Redo the quizzes to test your ability to recall certain information. Redo the exercises that were particularly effective for you. They can work again. Many of the exercises in this book can produce a different result after a few months. You are changing, and your responses change, too.

The Discovery Wheel can be useful in revealing techniques you have actually put into practice. This exercise is available online at **masterstudent.college. hmco.com,** and you can redo it as many times as you like. You can also redo the Journal Entries. If you keep your own journal, refer to it as you rewrite the Journal Entries in this book.

As you redo this book or any part of it, reconsider techniques that you skimmed over or skipped before. They might work for you now. Modify the suggestions or add new ones. Redoing this book can refresh and fine-tune your study habits.

Another way to redo this book is to retake your student success course. People who do this often say that the second time is much different from the first. They pick up ideas and techniques that they missed the first time around and gain deeper insight into things they already know. ◪

DO SOMETHING YOU CAN'T

Few significant accomplishments result when people stick to the familiar. You can accomplish much more than you think you can. Doing something you can't involves taking risks.

This exercise has three parts.

Part 1 Select something that you have never done before, that you don't know how to do, that you are fearful of doing, or that you think you probably can't do. Use the space below to describe the thing you have chosen.

Be smart. Don't pick something that will hurt you physically, such as flying from a third-floor window.

_____

_____

_____

_____

_____

Part 2 Do it. Of course, this is easier to say than to do. This exercise is not about easy. It is about discovering capabilities that stretch your self-image.

In order to accomplish something that is bigger than your self-perceived abilities, use any of the tools you have gained from this book. Develop a plan. Divide and conquer. Stay focused. Use outside resources. Let go of self-destructive thoughts.

Summarize the tools you will use.

_____

_____

_____

Part 3 In the space below, write about the results of this exercise.

_____

_____

_____

_____

Transferring
to another school

Transferring to a different school involves making a decision that will have a major impact on your education. This is true at many points in higher education—such as when you're transferring from a two-year to a four-year school, or when you're choosing a graduate school.

Selecting a school for the next step in your higher education is much like choosing a career. First, you define the profile of an ideal prospective school, much as you would that of an ideal job. Next, you create a profile of yourself—your skills, background, experience, learning style, and other preferences. Then you seek a reasonable fit between yourself and your ideal school, just as you seek a fit between yourself and your ideal job.

Know key terms

As you begin researching schools, take a few minutes to review some key terms.

Articulation agreements are official documents that spell out the course equivalents a school accepts.

An *Associate of Arts (A.A.)* or *Associate of Science (A.S.)* is the degree title conferred by many two-year colleges. Having a degree from a two-year college might save you time and money when transferring to another school.

Course equivalents are courses you've already taken that another school will accept as meeting its requirements. Since no two schools offer the same curriculum, determining course equivalents is often a matter of interpretation. In some cases, you might be able to persuade a registrar or an admissions office to accept some of your previous courses.

Prerequisites are courses or skills that a school requires students to complete or have before they enter or graduate.

Learn about the different types of schools

Start digging up key facts in the following areas about each school you're considering.

Number of students. The largest state universities can have a student body numbering 50,000 or more. Small private schools and vocational schools might have fewer than 1,000 students. The student bodies of many schools lie between these extremes.

Class sizes. Large schools might enroll 1,000 in a general education course. At smaller schools, your largest class might number between 20 and 30 people. You might enroll in seminars with a handful of students or take an individualized, guided reading course. Even within a single school, class sizes can vary between course levels and departments.

Contact with instructors. Some schools employ faculty members who are dedicated to teaching. You could take most of your classes from associate or full professors. In other schools, graduate assistants teach lower-level courses, and professors focus mainly on graduate students, publishing, or research. If you value close contact with your instructors, this is a crucial factor to investigate.

Admissions criteria. Some schools are highly competitive, admitting only a small percentage of the students who apply each year. Other schools are relatively open, admitting most students with high school diplomas.

Availability of degrees. Community colleges and vocational-technical schools commonly offer Associate of Arts (A.A.) and Associate of Science (A.S.) degrees, also called two-year degrees. Public and private colleges and universities generally offer four-year degrees, such as the Bachelor of Arts (B.A.) or Bachelor of Science (B.S.). Because their schedules vary so greatly, students might find that these degrees take longer than two or four years to complete. Many larger schools also offer graduate programs, leading to master's and doctoral degrees or specialized degrees in law, medicine, dentistry, or the ministry. If you want to make only one transfer, the availability of such degrees can have an impact on your decision.

Costs. Schools that receive public funding generally have lower tuition rates than private schools. Also, residents of a state might pay lower tuition fees to attend schools in that state. The requirements to be considered a resident vary among schools. Remember that tuition is only one of the costs of attending school. Others include books, materials, residence hall fees, health insurance, and laboratory fees. If you plan to live off campus, factor in the cost of living in the surrounding community.

Mission. Schools that emphasize liberal education could have fewer courses that prepare students for specific careers. In contrast, many community colleges and vocational schools offer degrees geared toward a specific job field, such as dental assistance, real estate, or auto mechanics. Some schools have a reputation for their teacher education programs, while others excel in research or offer outstanding graduate programs.

Location. The school you choose might be nestled in an idyllic rural setting or thrive in the heart of a large city. The differences can greatly color your experience of higher education. Also consider the school's distance from your current home.

Religious affiliation. You might value contact with students who share your sense of spirituality. Or perhaps you want a school attended by people of many spiritual perspectives. Schools differ greatly along this continuum.

Diversity. This term can apply to faculty members as well as students. Some schools primarily serve women or people of color, while others enroll a highly diverse student body. Also consider the mix between full-time and part-time students, students who live at the school and those who commute, and graduate and undergraduate students.

Dig up other key facts

Gather the facts about your current academic profile. This includes grades, courses completed, degrees attained, and grade point average (GPA). Standardized test scores are important, such as those for the Scholastic Aptitude Test (SAT), the American College Test (ACT), the Graduate Record Exam (GRE), and any advanced placement tests you've taken. Keep a folder of syllabuses from your courses; they can be useful when transferring credits.

List each school's course requirements. Note all prerequisites, including those required for general education or your proposed major, and any other courses required for graduation. Check the availability of courses in your major, including any graduate courses and advanced degrees, if you're planning on graduate work.

With your requirements in hand, begin creating a list of course equivalents. Most schools will have specific worksheets for this purpose. The school's registrar or admissions office can answer your questions about how to complete these forms.

After totaling the costs of attending a school, check on the financial aid that would be available at this school.

Turn to three basic sources

So far, this article has suggested what to ask about when you research a school. How to find this information is a separate question. Basically, you can turn to three sources: materials, people, and your own experience.

Materials include print sources, such as school catalogs. Also check more general guides, such as *Barron's Profiles of American Colleges, Peterson's National College Data Bank,* or *The Big Book of Minority Opportunities: The Directory of Special Programs for Minority Group Members.* In addition, many schools have Web sites that you can find using a search engine.

People include instructors, academic advisors, counselors, and other school staff members. Also seek out current students at the schools you are considering, as well as former students who are now working in your chosen field.

Your own experience includes a visit to the two or three schools on the top of your list. Take a thorough tour of the campus—the classrooms, laboratories, residence halls, bookstores, cafeterias, library, sports facilities, and student center. Also ask about sources of entertainment, such as restaurants, theaters, galleries, and concert halls. When you're done with the "official" tour, just walk around and observe the school grounds. Your direct experience of a school can be more intensive if you work in the surrounding community for a summer or take a course at the school before you transfer.

Put this choice in context

Consider the needs and wishes of your family members. Ask for their guidance and support. If you involve them in the decision, they can have more stake in your success.

Consider the purposes, values, and long-term goals you've generated through exercises such as the "Create a lifeline" exercise in Chapter Two and the Journal Entries in this book.

Your experience of a school goes well beyond the facts listed in the catalog. Pay attention to your instincts and intuition—your attraction to one school or feelings of hesitation about another.

Finally, just choose. There is no one "right" school for you, and you could probably thrive at many schools (perhaps even your current one). Use the suggestions in this book to practice self-responsibility and take charge of your education—no matter what school you attend. ◪

Career planning

Begin the process now

A satisfying and lucrative career is often the goal of education. It pays to define clearly both your career goal and your strategy for reaching that goal. Then you can plan your education effectively.

Career planning is an adventure that involves continuous exploration. There are dozens of effective paths to planning your career. You can begin your career-planning adventure now by remembering the following ideas.

Acknowledge what you already know

When people learn study skills and life skills, they usually start with finding out things they don't know. That means discovering new strategies for taking notes, reading, writing, managing time, and the other subjects covered in this book.

Career planning is different. You can begin by realizing how much you know right now. You've already made many decisions about your career. This is true for young people who say, "I don't have any idea what I want to be when I grow up." It's also true for midlife career changers.

Consider the student who can't decide if he wants to be a cost accountant or a tax accountant and then jumps to the conclusion that he is totally lost when it comes to career planning. It's the same with the student who doesn't know if he wants to be a veterinary assistant or a nurse.

These people forget that they already know a lot about their career choices. The person who couldn't decide between veterinary assistance and nursing had already ruled out becoming a lawyer, computer programmer, or teacher. He just didn't know yet whether he had the right bedside manner for horses or for people. The person who was debating tax accounting versus cost accounting already knew he didn't want to be a doctor, playwright, or taxicab driver. He did know he liked working with numbers and balancing books.

In each case, these people have already narrowed their list of career choices to a number of jobs in the same field—jobs that draw on the same core skills. In general, they already know what they want to be when they grow up.

Demonstrate this for yourself. Find a long list of occupations. (One source is *The Dictionary of Occupational Titles,* a government publication available at many libraries.) Using a stack of 3x5 cards, write down about 100 randomly selected job titles, one title per card. Sort through the cards and divide them into two piles. Label one pile "Careers I've Definitely Ruled Out for Now." Label the other pile "Possibilities I'm Willing to Consider."

It's common for people to go through a stack of 100 such cards and end up with 95 in the "definitely ruled out" pile and five in the "possibilities" pile. This demonstrates that they already have a career in mind.

See your career as your creation

Many people approach career planning as if they were panning for gold. They keep sifting through the dirt, clearing the dust, and throwing out the rocks. They are hoping to strike it rich and discover the perfect career.

Other people believe that they'll wake up one morning, see the heavens part, and suddenly know what they're supposed to do. Many of them are still waiting for that magical day to dawn.

We can approach career planning in a different way. Career planning can be the bridge between our dreams and the reality of our future. Instead of seeing a career as something we discover, we can see it as something we choose. We don't find the right career. We create it.

There's a big difference between these two approaches. Thinking that there's only one "correct" choice for your career can lead to a lot of anxiety: "Did I choose the right one?" "What if I made a mistake?"

Viewing your career as your creation helps you relax. Instead of anguishing over finding the right career, you can stay open to possibilities. You can choose one career today, knowing that you can choose again later.

Suppose that you've narrowed your list of possible careers to five, and you still can't decide. Then just choose one. Any one. Many people will have five careers in a lifetime anyway. You might be able to do all of your careers, and you can do any one of them first. The important thing is to choose.

One caution is in order. Choosing your career is not something to do in an information vacuum. Rather, choose after you've done a lot of research. That includes research into yourself—your skills and interests—and a thorough knowledge of what careers are available.

After all of the data has been gathered, there's only one person who can choose your career: you. This choice does not have to be a weighty one. In fact, it can be like going into your favorite restaurant and choosing from a menu that includes all of your favorite dishes. At this point, it's difficult to make a mistake. Whatever your choice, you know you'll enjoy it.

Discover your skills

The word *job* brings to mind many other terms. Among them are *task, role, duty, chore, responsibility,* and *function*. But one word comes closest to the heart of what we do in our jobs. That word is *skill*.

Skills are the core content—the "skeleton"—of any job. A career consists of the skills you use across several jobs in a related field. Talking the language of skills provides a key to planning your career, which in turn can help you choose your major.

Begin from the perspective that you have many skills. The Encarta World English dictionary defines *skill* as "the ability to do something well, usually gained through experience and training."

You can gain skills by taking advanced degrees or spending years in the work force. But there are ways to gains skills other than formal education or professional experience. In fact, *any* activity that you improve with practice can be called a skill. Just by going to school,

Career planning can be the bridge between our dreams and the reality of our future.

managing a household, relating to people, and pursuing your interests, you're constantly developing skills. If you can run a meeting, organize your study area, plant a garden, comfort a troubled friend, or draw interesting doodles, you've got skills that are worth money.

Keep in mind that there are at least two types of skills: content skills and transferable skills. Recognizing all of your skills—content and transferable—can help you assess the full range of your current abilities and choose new skills to develop.

Content skills reflect how much you know about a specific subject or how well you can perform a particular procedure. The ability to speak Spanish is a content skill. So are the abilities to program a computer, repair a car transmission, fix a broken television, or play the piano in a jazz band. In each case, these activities call for specialized knowledge and activity.

Transferable skills are general abilities that apply across many different content areas. For example, if you do well at writing term papers in history, you could probably write well about English literature, computers, or just about anything else. You might need to acquire some new content knowledge, but you already have the ability to write—that is, to compare, analyze, and combine ideas and express them in words.

Following are more examples of transferable skills:

- Attending to detail
- Budgeting
- Calculating
- Coaching
- Consulting
- Counseling
- Drawing
- Editing
- Estimating costs

This is only a partial list. You can learn to recognize more. In fact, most of the topics covered in this book are examples of transferable skills.

Plan by naming names

One key to making your career plan real and to ensuring that you can act on it is naming. Go back over your plan to see that you include specific names whenever they're called for:

- *Name your job.* Take the skills you enjoy using and find out which jobs use them. What are those jobs called? List them. Note that the same job might have different names.

- *Name your company—the agency or organization you want to work for.* If you want to be self-employed or start your own business, name the product or service you'd sell. Also list some possible names for your business. If you plan to work for others, name the organizations or agencies that are high on your list.

- *Name your contacts.* Take the list of organizations you just compiled. What people in these organizations are responsible for hiring? List those people and contact them directly. If you choose self-employment, list the names of possible customers or clients. All of these people are job contacts.

  Expand your list of contacts by brainstorming with your family and friends. Come up with a list of names—anyone who can help you with career planning and job hunting. Write each of these names on a 3x5 card or Rolodex card. You can also use a spiral-bound notebook or a computer.

  Next, call the key people on your list. After you speak with them, make brief notes about what you discussed. Also jot down any actions you agreed to take, such as a follow-up call.

  Consider everyone you meet a potential member of your job network, and be prepared to talk about what you do. Develop a "pitch"—a short statement of your career goal that you can easily share with your contacts. For example: "After I graduate, I plan to work in the travel business. I'm looking for an internship in a travel agency for next summer. Do you know of any agencies that take interns?"

- *Name your location.* Ask if your career choices are consistent with your preferences about where to live and work. For example, someone who wants to make a living as a studio musician might consider living in a large city such as New York or Toronto. This contrasts with the freelance graphic artist who conducts his business mainly by phone, fax, and e-mail. He might be able to live anywhere and still pursue his career.

> *Your life purpose is like the guidance system for a rocket. It keeps the plan on target while revealing a path for soaring to the heights.*

Remember your purpose

While digging deep into the details of career planning, take some time to back up to the big picture. Listing skills, researching jobs, writing résumés—all of this is necessary and useful. At the same time, attending to these tasks can obscure our broadest goals. To get perspective, we can go back to the basics—a life purpose.

Your deepest desire might be to see that hungry children are fed, to make sure that beautiful music keeps getting heard, or to help alcoholics become sober. When such a large purpose is clear, smaller decisions about what to do are often easier.

A life purpose makes a career plan simpler and more powerful. It cuts through the stacks of job data and employment figures. Your life purpose is like the guidance system for a rocket. It keeps the plan on target while revealing a path for soaring to the heights.

Test your career choice—and be willing to change

Career-planning materials and counselors can help you on both counts. Read books about careers and search for

---

> ### Twenty-five transferable skills
>
> Use the following list of transferable skills as a starting point for making an inventory of your abilities. There are literally hundreds of transferable skills, so expand this list based on your own lifetime of experiences.
>
> | | |
> |---|---|
> | Analyzing | Planning |
> | Budgeting | Reading |
> | Coaching | Researching |
> | Consulting | Problem solving |
> | Decision making | Selling |
> | Editing | Serving customers |
> | Evaluating | Speaking |
> | Interviewing | Supervising |
> | Learning | Thinking critically |
> | Listening | Training |
> | Managing time | Writing |
> | Negotiating | Working on teams |
> | Organizing | |

career-planning Web sites. Ask career counselors about skills assessments that can help you discover more about your skills and identify jobs that call for those skills. Take career-planning courses and workshops sponsored by your school. Visit the career-planning and job placement offices on campus.

Once you have a possible career choice in mind, run some informal tests to see if it will work for you. For example:

- Contact people who are actually doing the job you're researching and ask them what it's like (an *information interview*).

- Choose an internship or volunteer position in a field that interests you.

- Get a part-time or summer job in your career field.

The people you meet through these experiences are possible sources of recommendations, referrals, and employment in the future.

Career planning is not a once-and-for-all proposition. Rather, career plans are made to be changed and refined as you gain new information about yourself and the world. Career planning never ends. If your present career no longer feels right, you can choose again—no matter what stage of life you're in. The process is the same, whether you're choosing your first career or your fifth.

From Dave Ellis, Stan Lankowitz, Ed Stupka, and Doug Toft, *Career Planning*, Third Edition. Copyright © 2003 by Houghton Mifflin Company. Reprinted by permission.

RECOGNIZE YOUR SKILLS

This exercise about discovering your skills includes three steps. Before you begin, gather at least 100 3x5 cards and a pen or pencil. Allow about one hour to complete the exercise.

Step 1

Recall your activities during the past week or month. To refresh your memory, review your responses to the Time Monitor/Time Plan in Chapter Two. (You might even benefit from doing that exercise again.)

Write down as many activities as you can, listing each one on a separate 3x5 card. Include work-related activities, school activities, and hobbies. Some of your cards might read "washed dishes," "tuned up my car," or "tutored a French class."

In addition to daily activities, recall any rewards you've received or recognition of your achievements during the past year. Examples include scholarship awards, athletic awards, or recognitions for volunteer work. Again, list the activities that were involved.

Spend 20 minutes on this step, listing all of the activities you can recall.

Step 2

Next, look over your activity cards. Then take another 20 minutes to list any specialized knowledge or procedures needed to complete those activities. These are your *content skills*. For example, tutoring a French class requires a working knowledge of that language. Tuning a car requires knowing how to adjust a car's timing and replace spark plugs. You could list several content skills for any one activity. Write each skill on a separate card and label it "Content."

Step 3

Go over your activity cards one more time. Look for examples of *transferable skills*. For instance, giving a speech or working as a salesperson in a computer store requires the ability to persuade people. That's a transferable skill. Tuning a car means that you can attend to details and troubleshoot. Tutoring in French requires teaching, listening, and speaking skills.

Write each of your transferable skills on a separate card.

Congratulations—you now have a detailed picture of your skills. Keep your lists of content and transferable skills on hand when writing your résumé, preparing for job interviews, and other career-planning tasks. As you think of new skills, add them to the lists.

Use the SCANS reports to discover your skills

The U.S. Department of Labor has issued a series of reports created by the Secretary's Commission on Achieving Necessary Skills (SCANS). This influential series of documents lists essential skills for workers in the twenty-first century. You might find this list helpful in assessing your current skills and planning to develop new ones.

Basic skills

- Reading to locate, understand, and interpret written information.
- Writing to communicate ideas and information.
- Using arithmetic to perform basic computations and solve problems.
- Listening to interpret and respond to verbal messages and other cues.

Thinking skills

- Speaking to inform and persuade others.
- Creative thinking to generate new ideas.
- Decision making to set and meet goals.
- Problem solving to identify challenges and implement action plans.
- Seeing things in the mind's eye to interpret and create symbols, pictures, graphs, and other visual tools.
- Knowing how to learn.

Personal qualities

- Responsibility to exert high effort and persist in meeting goals.
- Self-esteem to maintain a positive view of your abilities.
- Social skills that demonstrate adaptability and empathy.
- Self-management to assess yourself accurately, set personal goals, and monitor personal progress.

Skills in using resources

- Allocating time for goal-relevant activities.
- Allocating money to prepare budgets and meet them.
- Allocating materials and facilities.
- Allocating human resources to assign tasks effectively and provide others with feedback.

Interpersonal skills

- Participating as a member of a team.
- Teaching others.
- Serving clients and customers.
- Exercising leadership.
- Negotiating to reach agreements.
- Working with diversity.

Skills in working with information

- Acquiring and evaluating information.
- Organizing and maintaining information.
- Interpreting and communicating information in oral, written, and visual forms.
- Using computers to process information.

Skills in working with systems

- Understanding how social and technological systems operate.
- Monitoring and correcting performance.
- Improving or designing systems.

Skills in working with technology

- Selecting appropriate technology.
- Applying technology to tasks.
- Maintaining and troubleshooting technology.

Adapted from U.S. Department of Labor, *Skills and Tasks for Jobs: A SCANS Report for America 2000*. Access it online at http://wdr.doleta.gov/SCANS/whatwork/whatwork.html.

Jumpstart your education with transferable skills

When meeting with an academic advisor, some students say, "I've just been taking general education and liberal arts courses. I haven't got any marketable skills."

Think again.

Few words are as widely misunderstood as *skill*. Defining it carefully can have an immediate and positive impact on your career planning.

Two kinds of skills

One dictionary defines *skill* as "the ability to do something well, usually gained by training or experience." Some skills—such as the ability to repair fiber-optic cables or do brain surgery—are acquired through formal schooling, on-the-job training, or both. These abilities are called *work-content skills*. People with such skills have mastered a specialized body of knowledge needed to do a specific kind of work.

However, there is another category of skills that we develop through experiences both inside and outside the classroom. We may never receive formal training to develop these abilities. Yet they are key to success in the workplace. These are *transferable skills*. Transferable skills are the kind of abilities that help people thrive in any job—no matter what work-content skills they have.

Perhaps you've heard someone described this way: "She's really smart and knows what she's doing, but she's got lousy people skills." People skills—such as *listening* and *negotiating*—are prime examples of transferable skills. Other examples are listed on page 372.

Succeeding in many situations

Transferable skills are often invisible to us. The problem begins when we assume that a given skill can only be used in one context, such as being in school or working at a particular job. Thinking in this way places an artificial limit on our possibilities. As an alternative, think about the things you routinely do to succeed in school. Analyze your activities to isolate specific skills. Then brainstorm a list of jobs where you could use the same skills.

Consider the task of writing a research paper. This calls for skills such as:

- *Planning*—setting goals for completing your outline, first draft, second draft, and final draft.

- *Managing time* to meet your writing goals.

- *Interviewing* people who know a lot about the topic of your paper.

- *Researching* using the Internet and campus library to discover key facts and ideas to include in your paper.

- *Writing* to present those facts and ideas in an original way.

- *Editing* your drafts for clarity and correctness.

Now consider the kinds of jobs that draw on these skills.

For example, you could transfer your skill at writing papers to a possible career in journalism, technical writing, or advertising copywriting.

You could use your editing skills to work in the field of publishing as a magazine or book editor.

Interviewing and research skills could help you enter the field of market research. And, the abilities to plan, manage time, and meet deadlines will help you succeed in all the jobs mentioned so far.

Use the same kind of analysis to think about transferring skills from one job to another job. Say that you work part-time as an administrative assistant at a computer dealer that sells a variety of hardware and software. You take phone calls from potential customers, help current customers solve problems using their computers, and attend meetings where your coworkers plan ways to market new products. You are developing skills at *selling, serving customers,* and *working on teams* that could help you land a job as a sales representative for a computer manufacturer or software developer.

The basic idea is to take a cue from the word *transferable*. Almost any skill you use to succeed in one situation can *transfer* to success in another situation.

The concept of transferable skills creates a powerful link between higher education and the work world. Skills are the core elements of any job. While taking any course, list the specific skills you are developing and how you can transfer them to the work world. Almost everything you do in school can be applied to your career—if you consistently pursue this line of thought.

Ask four questions

To experiment further with this concept of transferable skills, ask and answer four questions derived from the Master Student Map.

***Why* identify my transferable skills?** Getting past the "I-don't-have-any-skills" syndrome means that you can approach job hunting with more confidence. As you uncover these hidden assets, your list of qualifications will grow as if by magic. You won't be padding your résumé. You'll simply be using action words to tell the full truth about what you can do.

Identifying your transferable skills takes a little time. And the payoffs are numerous. A complete and accurate list of transferable skills can help you land jobs that involve more responsibility, more variety, more freedom to structure your time, and more money.

Transferable skills also help you thrive in the midst of constant change. Technology will continue to upgrade. Ongoing discoveries in many fields could render current knowledge obsolete. Jobs that exist today may disappear in a few years, only to be replaced by entirely new ones. Your keys to prospering in this environment are transferable skills—those that you can carry from one career to another.

***What* are my transferable skills?** Discover your transferable skills by reflecting on key experiences. Recall a time when you performed at the peak of your ability, overcame obstacles, won an award, gained a high grade, or met a significant goal. List the skills you used to create those successes.

In each case, remember that the word *skill* points to something that you *do*. In your list of transferable skills, start each item with an action verb such as *budget* or *coach* or *consult*. Or use a closely related part of speech—*budgeting* or *coaching*.

For a more complete picture of your transferable skills, describe the object of your action. Say that one of the skills on your list is *organizing*. This could refer to organizing ideas, organizing people, or organizing objects in a room. Specify the kind of organizing that you like to do.

***How* do I perform these skills?** You can bring your transferable skills into even sharper focus by adding adverbs—words that describe *how* you take action. You might say that you edit *accurately* or learn *quickly*.

In summary, you can use a three-column chart to list your transferable skills. For example:

Verb	Object	Adverb
Organizing	Records	Effectively
Serving	Customers	Courteously
Coordinating	Special events	Efficiently

Add a specific example of each skill to your list, and you're well on the way to an engaging résumé and a winning job interview.

As you list your transferable skills, focus on the skills that you most enjoy using. Then look for careers and jobs that directly involve those skills.

***What* if I could expand my transferable skills?** In addition to thinking about the skills you already have, consider the skills you'd like to acquire. Describe them in detail and list experiences that can help you develop them. Possibilities include extracurricular activities, group memberships, internships, volunteer positions, work-study assignments, and other part-time jobs. Throughout this book, *Put It to Work* articles highlighted transferable skills you can continue to develop in the classroom that can be transferred to the workplace. Let your list of transferable skills grow and develop as you do. ⬥

Job hunting is like prospecting for gold. You dig a lot of holes and sift through a lot of possibilities. Eventually, you will strike it rich—and find a job.

Use résumés and interviews to "hire" an employer

Before you start your search, set a quota. Tell yourself you will continue the search until you have spoken to at least 100 people, or some other number you can live with.

After two or three interviews you might get tired of hearing people say, "We don't have an opening" or "We've already filled that job." At this point, consider your quota. If you ask enough people, someone will say, "Yes!" Each time you hear "No," silently thank the person for putting you one "no" closer to a "yes."

Consider creating your own job or becoming self-employed. You could offer any service from lawn mowing to computer consulting. Self-created jobs can blossom into amazing careers. For example, David Filo and Jerry Yang started making lists of their favorite sites on the World Wide Web while they were graduate students. They went on to create Yahoo!—an Internet search directory and one of today's most influential Web sites.

Rethink typical job-hunting strategies

The logical outcome of your career plan is a focused job hunt. Mention the phrase *job hunting,* and many people envision someone poring through the help wanted sections in newspapers or on Web sites, sending out hundreds of résumés, or enlisting the services of employment agencies to find job openings and set up interviews.

Richard Bolles—author of *What Color Is Your Parachute?*—points out a fatal shortcoming of these job-hunting strategies: Most job openings are never advertised. Many employers turn to help wanted listings, résumés, and employment agencies only as a last resort. When jobs open up, they prefer instead to hire people they know—friends and colleagues—or people who walk through the door and prove that they're excellent candidates for available jobs. Your best source of information about new jobs

is people—friends, relatives, coworkers, and fellow students. Ask around. Tell everyone you want a job. In particular, tell people who might be able to create a job for you. Some jobs are created on the spot when a person with potential simply shows up and asks.

In summary, Bolles recommends the following steps in career planning and job hunting:[2]

- Discover which skills you want to use in your career.
- Discover which jobs draw on the skills you want to use.
- Interview people who are doing the kind of jobs you'd want to do.
- Research companies you'd like to work for and find out what kinds of problems they face on a daily basis.
- Identify your contacts—a person at each one of these companies who has the power to hire you.
- Arrange an interview with that person, even if the company has no job openings at the moment.
- Stay in contact with the people who interviewed you, knowing that a job opening can occur at any time.

Use résumés to get interviews

A résumé is a piece of persuasive writing, not a dry recitation of facts or a laundry list of previous jobs. It has a basic purpose—to get you to the next step in the hiring process, usually an interview.

Begin your résumé with your name, address, phone number, and e-mail address. Then name your desired job, often called an "objective" or "goal." Follow with the body of your résumé—your skills, work experience, and education. In fact, you can use those last three topics as major headings printed in bold in a larger font.

Write your résumé so that the facts leap off the page. Describe your work experiences in short phrases that start with active verbs: "*Supervised* three people." "*Wrote* two annual reports." "*Set up* sales calls." Also leave reasonable margins and space between paragraphs. The person who scans your résumé will sigh with relief when he sees a piece of paper that's not crammed full of ink.

As you draft your résumé, remember that every organization has problems to solve. Factories grapple with employee turnover. Software developers struggle to get their products out faster than the competition. Publishers seek ways to make their books, periodicals, and Web sites capture consumer attention.

Show in your résumé that you know about those problems and can offer your skills as solutions. Whenever you can, give evidence that you used those skills to get measurable results.

Use interviews to screen employers

You might think of job interviews as a time when a potential employer sizes you up and possibly screens you out. Consider another viewpoint—that interviews offer you a chance to size up potential employers and possibly screen *them* out.

This attitude is easier to take on when you've already done your homework by completing the previous steps mentioned in this article. Those steps can lead you to a strong list of contacts, along with specific ideas about *what* job skills you want to use and *where* you want to use them. By the time you get to a job interview, you'll be able to see if the job is something that you really want. By interviewing, you're "hiring" yourself an employer.

To get the most from your interviews, learn everything you can about each organization that interests you. Get a feel for its strong points and know about its successes in the marketplace. Also find out what challenges the organization faces. As in a résumé, use interviews to present your skills as unique solutions for those challenges.

Job interviewers have many standard questions. Most of them boil down to a few major concerns:

- How did you find out about us?
- Would we be comfortable working with you?
- How can you help us?
- Will you learn this job quickly?
- What makes you different from other applicants?

Before your interview, prepare some answers to these questions.

If you get turned down for the job after your interview, don't take it personally. Every interview is a source of feedback about what works—and what doesn't work—in contacting employers. Use that feedback to interview more effectively next time.

Counter bias and discrimination

During your job hunt, you might worry about discrimination based on your race, ethnic background, gender, or sexual orientation. Protect yourself by keeping records, including copies of all correspondence from perspective employers. Remember that Title VII of the Civil Rights Act bans discrimination in virtually all aspects of the workplace, from hiring to firing. Congress set up the Equal Employment Opportunity Commission (EEOC) to enforce this act. You can contact this agency at 1-800-669-4000 and get more information through its Web site at **http:// www.eeoc.gov**.

Be prepared to act like a free agent

International competition, corporate downsizing, and new technology could make the typical job as we know it a thing of the past. The workplace of the future might be organized around projects done by flexible teams of free agents instead of employees who spend years with a single company.

If this happens, you can prosper by seeing yourself as self-employed—even if you have a "regular" job. Think like a freelance or contract employee who's hired to complete a specific project. Demonstrate your value in each project, continually revise your job goals, expand your contacts, and constantly update your skills. ⬙

This article includes material from *Career Planning*, Third Edition, by Dave Ellis, Stan Lankowitz, Ed Stupka, and Doug Toft, Copyright © 2003 by Houghton Mifflin Company. Reprinted by permission.

Modern technology is creating new ways for you to plan your career and find jobs in the future. On the World Wide Web, you can research companies you'd like to work for, read lists of job openings, and post your résumé and a digital recording of yourself. Through faxes, overnight deliveries, mobile phones, and e-mail, you can stay in continual contact with potential employers. Widespread availability of high-speed Internet access has increased the number of long-distance job interviews being conducted via video conference or in a real time chatroom, and has increased the possibility of sending an electronic portfolio attachment with a résumé.

According to one estimate, about two million people go online every month to hunt for jobs. That's a testament to the potential power of the digital medium and to some of its pitfalls as well. When you're looking for a job, the strength of the Internet—the sheer density of data—can also lead to frustration:

- The haphazard organization of the Internet makes it hard for potential employers to find your résumé when you post it online. The organizations you most want to work for might avoid using the Internet to find job applicants.

- Job openings listed on the Internet can be heavily skewed to certain fields, such as jobs for computer professionals or people in other technical fields.

- Across all fields, the majority of job openings are not listed on the Internet (or in newspaper want ads, for that matter).

This is not meant to disparage the Internet as a tool for job hunters and career planners. The point is that posting a résumé on a Web site will not automatically lead to an e-mail in-basket that's bursting to its digital seams with job offers. For an effective job search, view the Internet as just one resource.

With this caveat in mind, you might choose to post your résumé online and scan Internet job ads. If you do, begin with sites such as that for JobBank USA (**http://www.jobbankusa.com**), which links to over 20 search engines for finding job openings. Also check CareerBuilder.com (**http://www.CareerBuilder.com**) for want ads, updated weekly, from major U.S. newspapers. When responding to ads and posting résumés online, avoid some common mistakes. One is to use word processing software to create lots of fancy formatting for your résumé and then attach it to an e-mail message. Many Web sites are not powerful enough to handle such formatting and will garble your attachments. Instead, skip the word processing and paste your résumé right

Cruising for jobs on the Internet

into an e-mail message. Proofread it one more time before you hit the "send" button.

Some people create personal Web pages to highlight their accomplishments and entice employers. If you go this route, keep your page simple and easy to download. Some Web hosts will want to run banner ads on your page. These ads are widely seen as tacky. Avoid them.

Even if you don't choose to post a digital résumé or Web page, you can access career-planning resources on the Internet. Begin with "gateway" sites that offer organized links to many career-related pages on the World Wide Web. For instance, the Riley Guide (**http://www. rileyguide.com**) gives an overview of job hunting on the Internet.

Also check JobHuntersBible.com (**http://www. jobhuntersbible.com**), a site maintained by Richard Bolles, author of *What Color Is Your Parachute?* This site focuses on effective ways to use the Internet. And for some revealing figures, visit sites such as Salary.com to find out the current pay scales of typical jobs in your field. One way in which the Internet can really help you is in researching organizations before you contact them. Chances are that the company you're interested in has a Web site. Go to the site to gather information, discover the names of key players, and view financial data. Doing so will show potential employers that you've done your homework. That can make a favorable impression and even land you a job.

Intention Statement

Even if you are not sure of your career preference, write a career plan right now. Include three elements: a career goal, a list of steps you can take to prepare for that career, and a timeline for reaching that career goal.

Your plan might be incomplete or tentative. No problem. You can change this plan later—even throw it out and start all over. Career planning is a continual cycle of discovery, intention, and feedback.

The point is to dive into the process and make career planning a lifelong habit. This habit can radically affect the quality of your life.

You can plan now, with no further research. Go ahead. There's nothing to lose and lots of space to write in. Make an outline, do a mind map—use any format you like. Discover what you already know.

Mind map, outline, or write down your career plan now. Begin using the following space and continue as needed on a sheet of separate paper. You can also use a computer for this purpose.

Creating and using portfolios

In medieval times, artisans who wished to join a guild presented samples of their work. Furniture makers showed cabinets and chairs to their potential mentors. Painters presented samples of their sketches and portraits. Centuries later, people still value a purposeful collection of work samples. It is called a portfolio.

The word *portfolio* derives from two Latin terms: *port,* which means "to move," and *folio,* which means "papers" or "artifacts."[3] True to these ancient meanings, portfolios are movable collections of papers and artifacts.

Portfolios differ from résumés. A résumé lists facts, including your interests, skills, work history, and accomplishments. Although a portfolio might include these facts, it also includes tangible objects to verify the facts—anything from transcripts of your grades to a videotape that you produced. Résumés offer facts; portfolios provide artifacts.

Photographers, contractors, and designers regularly show portfolios filled with samples of their work. Today,

employers and educators increasingly see the portfolio as a tool that's useful for everyone. Some schools require students to create them, and some employers expect to see a portfolio before they'll hire a job applicant.

Enjoy the benefits—academic, professional, and personal

A well-done portfolio benefits its intended audience. To an instructor, your portfolio gives a rich, detailed picture of what you did to create value from a class. To a potential employer, your portfolio gives observable evidence of your skills and achievements. In both cases, a portfolio also documents something more intangible—your levels of energy, passion, and creativity.

Portfolios benefit you in specific ways. When you create a portfolio to document what you learned during a class, you review the content of the entire course. When you're creating a portfolio related to your career, you think about the skills you want to develop and ways to showcase those skills. And when you're applying for work, creating a portfolio prepares you for job interviews. Your portfolio can stand out from stacks of letters and résumés and distinguish you from other applicants.

By creating and using portfolios, you also position yourself for the workplace of the future. People such as William Bridges, author of *Jobshift,* have predicted a "jobless economy."[4] In such an economy, work will be done by teams assembled for specific projects instead of by employees in permanent positions. Workers will move from team to team, company to company, and career to career far more often than they do today. If these changes take place on a wide scale, listing your job titles on a résumé will be less useful than documenting your skills in a vivid, detailed way. Creating and using portfolios is a wonderful way to provide that documentation.

In a more general sense, creating a portfolio helps you reflect on your life as a whole. When selecting artifacts to include in your portfolio, you celebrate your accomplishments. You discover key themes in your experience. You clarify what's important to you and create goals for the future. Portfolios promote the cycle of discovery, intention, and action presented in Journal Entries and exercises throughout this text. To create a portfolio, experiment with a four-step process:

1. Collect and catalog artifacts.

2. Plan your portfolio.

3. Assemble your portfolio.

4. Present your portfolio.

⤷ Artifacts for your portfolio

When looking for items to include in a portfolio, start with the following checklist. Then brainstorm your own list of added possibilities.

❏ Brochures describing a product or service you've created, or workshops you've attended

❏ Certificates, licenses, and awards

❏ Computer disks with sample publications, databases, or computer programs you've created

❏ Course descriptions and syllabuses of classes you've taken or taught

❏ Formal evaluations of your work

❏ Job descriptions of positions you've held

❏ Letters of recommendation

❏ Lists of grants, scholarships, clients, customers, and organizations you've joined

❏ Newspaper and magazine articles about projects you've participated in

❏ Objects you've created or received—anything from badges to jewelry

❏ Plans—lists of personal and professional values, goals, action plans, completed tasks, project timelines, and lifelines

❏ Printouts of e-mail and Web pages (including your personal Web page)

❏ Programs from artistic performances or exhibitions

❏ Recordings (digital or voice), compact discs, or CD-ROMs

❏ Résumés or a curriculum vitae

❏ Sheet music or scores

❏ Transcripts of grades, test scores, vocational aptitude tests, or learning style inventories

❏ Visual art, including drawings, photographs, collages, and computer graphics

❏ Writing samples, such as class reports, workplace memos, proposals, policy and mission statements, bids, manuscripts for articles and books, and published pieces or bibliographies of published writing

Collect and catalog artifacts

An artifact is any object that's important to you and that reveals something about yourself. Examples include photographs, awards, recommendation letters, job descriptions for positions you've held, newspaper articles about projects you've done, lists of grants or scholarships you've received, programs from performances you've given, transcripts of your grades, or models you've constructed.

Taken together, your artifacts form a large and visible "database" that gives a picture of you—what you value, what you've done, and what skills you have. You can add to this database during every year of your life. From this constantly evolving collection of artifacts, you can create many portfolios for different purposes and different audiences.

Start collecting now. Write down the kinds of artifacts you'd like to save. Think about what will be most useful to you in creating portfolios for your courses and your job search. In some cases, collecting artifacts requires follow-up. You might call former instructors or employers to request letters of recommendation. Or you might track down newspaper articles about a service-learning project you did. Your responses to the Journal Entries and exercises in this book can also become part of your portfolio. To save hours when you create your next portfolio, start documenting your artifacts. On a 3x5 card, record the "five W's" about each artifact: *who* was involved with it, *what* you did with it, *when* it was created, *where* it was created, and *why* the artifact is important to you. File these cards and update them as you collect new artifacts. Another option is to manage this information with a computer, using word processing or database software.

Plan your portfolio

When you're ready to create a portfolio for a specific audience, allow some time for planning. Begin with your purpose for creating the portfolio—for example, to demonstrate your learning or to document your work experience as you prepare for a job interview.

Also list some specifics about your audience. Write a description of anyone who will see your portfolio. List what each person already knows about you and predict what else these people will want to know. Answer their questions in your portfolio.

Being aware of your purpose and audience will serve you at every step of creating a portfolio. Screen artifacts with these two factors in mind. If a beautiful artifact fails to meet your purpose or fit your audience, leave it out for now. Save the artifact for a future portfolio.

When you plan your portfolio, also think about how to order and arrange your artifacts. One basic option is a chronological organization. For example, start with work samples from your earliest jobs and work up to the present.

Another option is to structure your portfolio around key themes, such as your values or work skills. When preparing this type of portfolio, you can define *work* to include any time you used a job-related skill, whether or not you got paid.

Assemble your portfolio

With a collection of artifacts and a written plan, you're ready to assemble your portfolio. Arranging artifacts according to your design is a big part of this process. Also include elements to orient your audience members and guide them through your portfolio. Such elements can include:

- A table of contents.
- An overview or summary of the portfolio.
- Titles and captions for each artifact.
- An index to your artifacts.

Although many portfolios take their final form as a collection of papers, remember that this is just one possibility. You can also create a bulletin board, a display, or a case that contains your artifacts. You could even create a recording or a digital portfolio in the form of a personal Web site.

You might find it useful to combine your résumé and portfolio into one document. In other cases, you can mention in your résumé that a separate portfolio is available on request.

Present your portfolio

Your audience might ask you to present your portfolio as part of an interview or oral exam. If that's the case, rehearse your portfolio presentation the way you would rehearse a speech. Write down questions that people might ask about your portfolio. Prepare some answers, then do a dry run. Present your portfolio to friends and people in your career field, and request their feedback.

That feedback will give you plenty of ideas about ways to revise your portfolio. A portfolio is a living document. Update it as you acquire new perspectives and skills. ◪

For more ideas on portfolios, go online to

mastersstudent.college.hmco.com

Contributing:
The art of selfishness

This book is about contributing to yourself—about taking care of yourself, being selfish, and fulfilling your own needs. The techniques and suggestions in these pages focus on ways to get what you want out of school and out of life.

One of the results of all this successful selfishness is the capacity for contributing, for giving to others. Contributing is what's left to do when you're satisfied, when your needs are fulfilled—and it completes the process.

People who are satisfied with life can share that satisfaction with others. It is not easy to contribute to another person's joy until you experience joy yourself. The same is true for love. When people are filled with love, they can more easily contribute love to others.

Our interdependence calls for contributing.
Every day we depend on contributing. We stake our lives on the compassion of other people.

When we drive, we depend on others for our lives. If a driver in an oncoming lane should cross into our own lane, we might die. We also depend upon the sensibilities of world leaders for our safety. People everywhere are growing more interdependent. A plunge in the U.S. stock market reverberates in markets across the planet. A decrease in oil prices gives businesses everywhere a shot in the arm. A nuclear war would ignore national boundaries and devastate life on the planet. Successful arms negotiations allow all people to sleep a little easier.

In this interdependent world, there is no such thing as win/lose. If others lose, their loss directly affects us. If we lose, it is more difficult to contribute to others.

The only way to win and to get what we want in life is for others to win, also.

A caution. The idea of contributing is not the same as knowing what is best for other people. We can't know. There are people, of course, who go around "fixing" others: "I know what you need. Here, do it my way." That is not contributing. It often causes more harm than good and can result in dependence on the part of the person we are "helping."

True contributing occurs only after you find out what another person wants or needs and then determine that you can lovingly support his having it.

How you can begin contributing. The world will welcome your gifts of time, money, and talent. The advantages of contributing are clear. When we contribute, the whole human family benefits in a tangible way. Close to home, contributing often means getting involved with other people. This is one way to "break the ice" in a new community and meet people with interests similar to your own.

When you've made the decision to contribute, the next step is knowing how. There are ways to contribute in your immediate surroundings. Visit a neighbor, take a family member to a movie, or offer to tutor a roommate. Look for ways you can contribute by volunteering. An additional benefit of volunteer work is that it offers a way to explore possible career choices. Consider the following organizations, for starters.

Sierra Club, Greenpeace, Audubon Society, World Wildlife Fund, and similar organizations are dedicated to protecting the environment and endangered species.

Amnesty International investigates human rights violations. It assists people who are imprisoned or tortured for peacefully expressing their points of view. You can participate in letter-writing campaigns.

Museums and art galleries need interested people to conduct tours and provide supervision. Performing arts organizations, such as local theater groups or ballet companies, are always in need of volunteers for everything from set decoration to ticket sales.

Hospitals and hospice programs often depend on volunteer help to supplement patient care provided by the professional staff. Nursing homes welcome visitors who are willing to spend time listening to and talking with residents. Most communities have volunteer-based programs for people living with HIV infection or AIDS that provide daily hot meals to men, women, and children too ill to cook for themselves. Political parties, candidates,

It is not easy to contribute to another person's joy until you experience joy yourself.

and special interest groups need volunteers to stuff envelopes, gather petition signatures, and distribute literature. The American Red Cross provides disaster relief. Local community care centers use volunteers to help feed homeless people.

Service organizations such as Jaycees, Kiwanis, Lions, American Association of University Women, Business and Professional Women, and Rotary want members who are willing to serve others.

Tutoring centers offer opportunities for competent students to help non-English-speaking people, grade school and high school students, and illiterate adults. Churches of all denominations want volunteers to assist with projects for the community and beyond. World hunger groups want you to help feed starving people and to inform all of us about the problems of malnutrition, food spoilage, and starvation. These groups include Oxfam America, CARE, and The Hunger Project.

Considering the full scope of our international problems reminds us that there are plenty of opportunities for contributing. For instance, there are still enough nuclear warheads on the planet to end human life. And, according to the *Human Development Report 2003*, commissioned by the United Nations, 1,242 million people in the world live on less than one dollar per day.[5]

If they remain unused, the techniques and strategies in this book make no difference in all this. However, *you* can make a difference. By using these techniques to work with others, you can choose a new future for our planet. ⊠

Service learning
The art of learning by contributing

As part of a service-learning project for a sociology course, students volunteer at a community center for older adults. For another service-learning project, history students interview people in veterans' hospitals about their war experiences. These students plan to share their interview results with a psychiatrist on the hospital staff.

Meanwhile, business students provide free tax-preparation help at a center for low-income people. Students in graphic arts classes create free promotional materials for charities. Other students staff a food cooperative and community credit union.

These examples of actual projects from the National Service-Learning Clearinghouse demonstrate the working premise of service learning—that volunteer work and other forms of contributing can become a vehicle for higher education.

Service learning generally includes three elements: meaningful community service, a formal academic curriculum, and time for students to reflect on what they learn from service. That reflection can include speeches, journal writing, and research papers.

Service learning creates a win/win scenario. For one thing, students gain the satisfaction of contributing. They also gain experiences that can guide their career choices and help them develop job skills.

At the same time, service learning adds a valuable resource to the community with a handsome return on investment. For example, participants in the Learn and Serve program (administered by the Corporation for National and Community Service) provided community services valued at four times the program cost. When you design a service-learning project, consider these suggestions:

- Work with a community agency that has experience with students. Make sure that the agency has liability insurance to cover volunteers.

- Handle logistics. Integrating service learning into your schedule can call for detailed planning. If your volunteer work takes place off campus, arrange for transportation and allow for travel time.

- Reflect on your service-learning project with a tool you've used throughout this book—the Discovery and Intention Journal Entry system explained in the Introduction. Write Discovery Statements about what you want to gain from service learning and how you feel about what you're doing. Follow up with Intention Statements about what you'll do differently for your next volunteer experience.

- Include ways to evaluate your project. From your Intention Statements, create action goals and outcome goals. *Action goals* state what you plan to do and how many people you intend to serve, for instance, "We plan to provide 100 hours of literacy tutoring to 10 people in the community." *Outcome goals* describe the actual impact that your project will have: "At the end of our project, 60 percent of the people we tutor will be able to write a résumé and fill out a job application." Build numbers into your goals whenever possible. That makes it easier to evaluate the success of your project.

- Create a way to build long-term impact into your project. One potential pitfall of service learning is that the programs are often short-lived. After students pack up and return to campus, programs can die. To avoid this outcome, make sure that other students or community members are willing to step in and take over for you when the semester ends.

- Celebrate mistakes. If your project fails to meet its goals, have a party. State—in writing—the obstacles you encountered and ways to overcome them. The solutions you offer will be worth gold to the people who follow in your footsteps. Sharing the lessons learned from your mistakes is an act of service in itself. ⊠

voices

I first began working with a local environmental organization in our community during my freshman year. It was intended partly as a way to be more social in a strange, new town, but after a year of service, we now have a university-supported recycling program that services both the students and the local residents.

—MANDY WISCONSIN

PRACTICING CRITICAL THINKING

13

Imagine that you are about to teach a student success course. Analyze the topic of student success and then create a brief outline or syllabus for the course. Choose the main subtopics you will cover, any texts or other materials you will use, and any guest speakers you will invite. Write down your ideas in the space below.

_____

_____

_____

_____

_____

_____

_____

_____

_____

_____

_____

_____

_____

_____

_____

_____

_____

_____

_____

_____

Now reflect on what you just wrote. What results do you want students to achieve in this course? For each result you list, include ways that you as a teacher could help students achieve these results.

_____

_____

_____

_____

_____

_____

_____

_____

_____

_____

_____

_____

_____

_____

_____

_____

Finally, look over the lists you just wrote. Circle any ideas that you can use right now to enhance the value that you take away from this student success course.

Define your values
align your actions

One key way to choose what's next in your life is to define your values. Values are the things in life that you want for their own sake. Values influence and guide your choices, including your moment-by-moment choices of what to do and what to have. Your values define who you are and who you want to be.

Some people are guided by values that they automatically adopt from others or by values that remain largely unconscious. These people could be missing the opportunity to live a life that's truly of their own choosing.

Investing time and energy to define your values is a pivotal suggestion in this book. In fact, *Becoming a Master Student* is based on a particular value system that underlies suggestions given throughout the book. This system includes the values of:

- Focused attention
- Self-responsibility
- Integrity
- Risk-taking
- Contributing

You'll find these values and related ones directly stated in the Power Processes throughout the text. For instance:

Discover what you want is about the importance of living a purpose-based life.

Ideas are tools points to the benefits of being willing to experiment with new ideas.

Be here now expresses the value of focused attention.

Love your problems (and experience your barriers) is about seeing difficulties as opportunities to develop new skills.

Notice your pictures and let them go is about adopting an attitude of open-mindedness.

I create it all is about taking responsibility for our beliefs and behaviors.

Detach reminds us that our core identity and value as a person does not depend on our possessions, our circumstances, or even our accomplishments.

Find a bigger problem is about offering our lives by contributing to others.

Employ your word expresses the value of making and keeping agreements.

Choose your conversations and your community reminds us of the power of language, and that we can reshape our lives by taking charge of our thoughts.

Risk being a fool is about courage—the willingness to take risks for the sake of learning something new.

Surrender points to the value of human community and the power of asking for help.

Be it is specifically about the power of attitudes—the idea that change proceeds from the inside out as we learn to see ourselves in new ways.

In addition, most of the study skills and life skills you read about in these pages have their source in values. The Time Monitor/Time Plan exercise, for example, calls for focused attention. Even the simple act of sharing your notes with a student who missed a class is an example of contributing.

As you begin to define your values, consider those who have gone before you. In creeds, scriptures, philosophies, myths, and sacred stories, the human race has left a vast and varied record of values. Be willing to look everywhere, including sources that are close to home. The creed of your local church or temple might eloquently describe some of your values—so might the mission statement of your school, company, or club. Another way to define your values is to describe the qualities of people you admire.

Also translate your values into behavior. Though defining your values is powerful, it doesn't guarantee any results. To achieve your goals, take actions that align with your values. ◪

One set of values

Following is a sample list of values. Don't read it with the idea that it is the "right" set of values for you. Instead, use this list as a point of departure in creating your own list.

Value: **Be accountable**

This means being:

- Honest
- Reliable
- Trustworthy
- Dependable
- Responsible

Being accountable includes making and keeping agreements—operating with integrity.

Value: **Be loving**

This means being:

- Affectionate
- Dedicated
- Devoted
- Equitable
- Accepting

Being loving includes appreciating ourselves and others—being gentle, considerate, forgiving, respectful, friendly, and courteous. It also includes being nonantagonistic, nonresistant, inclusive, understanding, compassionate, fair, and ethical.

Value: **Be self-generating**

This means being:

- Self-responsible
- The creator of our internal experiences—regardless of our external circumstances

Being self-generating includes not being a victim and not blaming others. Instead, we choose how to interpret and respond to all stimuli.

Value: **Be promotive**

This means being:

- Nurturing
- Contributing
- Frugal
- Helpful
- Encouraging
- Reasonable
- Judicious
- Cooperative
- Appreciative

Value: **Be candid**

This means being:

- Honest
- Authentic
- Genuine
- Self-expressed
- Frank
- Outspoken
- Spontaneous
- Sincere
- Free of deceit
- Able to avoid false modesty without arrogance
- Self-disclosing
- Open about strengths and weaknesses

Value: **Be detached**

This means being:

- Impartial
- Unbiased
- Experimental
- Satisfied
- Patient (not resigned)
- Open-minded
- Without distress
- Adaptable
- Trusting
- Tolerant
- Willing to surrender
- Joyful—fun-loving, humorous, light-hearted, and happy

Detachment includes being separate from but aware of thoughts, emotions, body, health, accomplishments, relationships, desires, commitments, possessions, values, opinions, roles, and expectations. The opposite of detachment is being addicted (physically or emotionally), dogmatic, bigoted, absolutely certain, prejudiced, anxious, grave, or somber.

Value: **Be aware of the possible**

This means being:

- Creative
- Imaginative
- Resourceful
- Inventive
- Foresighted
- Holistic
- Visionary
- Inquisitive
- Audacious
- Exploring

Being aware of the possible means expecting great things of ourselves and others.

Value: **Be involved**

This means being:

- Committed
- Participative
- Focused
- Enthusiastic
- Enduring
- Courageous
- Energetic
- Productive

THE DISCOVERY WHEEL—COMING FULL CIRCLE

Do this exercise online at (masterstudent.college.hmco.com)

This book doesn't work. It is worthless. Only you can work. Only you can make a difference and use this book to become a more effective student.

The purpose of this book is to give you the opportunity to change your behavior. The fact that something seems like a good idea doesn't necessarily mean that you will put it into practice. This exercise gives

you a chance to see what behaviors you have changed on your journey toward becoming a master student.

Answer each question quickly and honestly. Record your results on the Discovery Wheel on this page and then compare it with the one you completed in Chapter One.

The scores on this Discovery Wheel indicate your current strengths and weaknesses on your path toward becoming a master student. The last Journal Entry in this chapter provides an opportunity to write

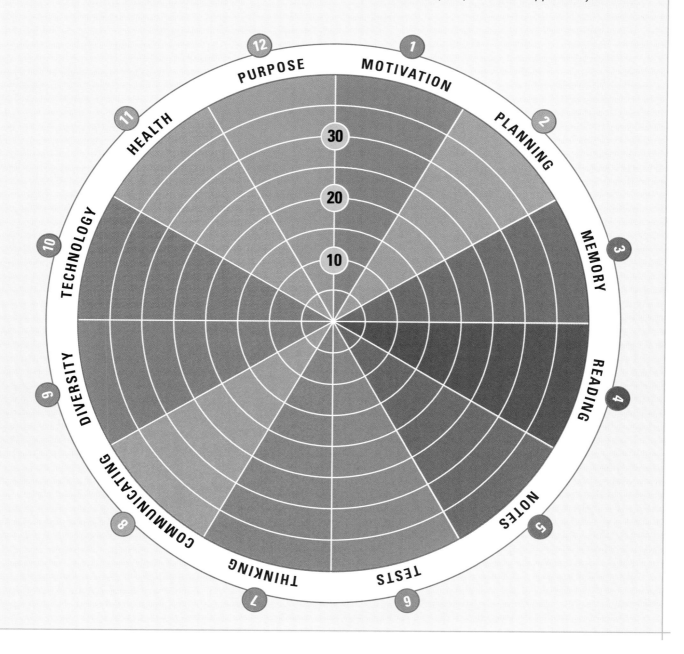

about how you intend to change. As you complete this self-evaluation, keep in mind that your commitment to change allows you to become a master student. *Your scores might be lower here than on your earlier Discovery Wheel.* That's OK. Lower scores might result from increased self-awareness and honesty, and other valuable assets.

Note: The online version of this exercise does not include number ratings, so the results will be formatted differently than described here. If you did your previous Discovery Wheel online, do it online again. This will help you compare your two sets of responses more accurately.

5 points
This statement is always or almost always true of me.

4 points
This statement is often true of me.

3 points
This statement is true of me about half the time.

2 points
This statement is seldom true of me.

1 point
This statement is never or almost never true of me.

1. _____ I enjoy learning.
2. _____ I understand and apply the concept of multiple intelligences.
3. _____ I connect my courses to my purpose for being in school.
4. _____ I make a habit of assessing my personal strengths and areas for improvement.
5. _____ I am satisfied with how I am progressing toward achieving my goals.
6. _____ I use my knowledge of learning styles to support my success in school.
7. _____ I am willing to consider any idea that can help me succeed in school—even if I initially disagree with that idea.
8. _____ I regularly remind myself of the benefits I intend to get from my education.

_____ Total score (1) *Motivation*

1. _____ I set long-term goals and periodically review them.
2. _____ I set short-term goals to support my long-term goals.
3. _____ I write a plan for each day and each week.
4. _____ I assign priorities to what I choose to do each day.
5. _____ I plan regular recreation time.
6. _____ I adjust my study time to meet the demands of individual courses.
7. _____ I have adequate time each day to accomplish what I plan.
8. _____ I am confident that I will find the resources to finance my education.

_____ Total score (2) *Planning*

1. _____ I am confident of my ability to remember.
2. _____ I can remember people's names.
3. _____ At the end of a lecture, I can summarize what was presented.
4. _____ I apply techniques that enhance my memory skills.
5. _____ I can recall information when I'm under pressure.
6. _____ I remember important information clearly and easily.
7. _____ I can jog my memory when I have difficulty recalling.
8. _____ I can relate new information to what I've already learned.

_____ Total score (3) *Memory*

1. _____ I preview and review reading assignments.
2. _____ When reading, I ask myself questions about the material.
3. _____ I underline or highlight important passages when reading.
4. _____ When I read textbooks, I am alert and awake.
5. _____ I relate what I read to my life.
6. _____ I select a reading strategy to fit the type of material I'm reading.
7. _____ I take effective notes when I read.

8. _____ When I don't understand what I'm reading, I note my questions and find answers.

_____ Total score (4) *Reading*

1. _____ When I am in class, I focus my attention.
2. _____ I take notes in class.
3. _____ I am aware of various methods for taking notes and choose those that work best for me.
4. _____ I distinguish important material and note key phrases in a lecture.
5. _____ I copy down material that the instructor writes on the chalkboard or overhead projector.
6. _____ I can put important concepts into my own words.
7. _____ My notes are valuable for review.
8. _____ I review class notes within 24 hours.

_____ Total score (5) *Notes*

1. _____ I feel confident and calm during an exam.
2. _____ I manage my time during exams and am able to complete them.
3. _____ I am able to predict test questions.
4. _____ I adapt my test-taking strategy to the kind of test I'm taking.
5. _____ I understand what essay questions ask and can answer them completely and accurately.
6. _____ I start reviewing for tests at the beginning of the term.
7. _____ I continue reviewing for tests throughout the term.
8. _____ My sense of personal worth is independent of my test scores.

_____ Total score (6) *Tests*

1. _____ I have flashes of insight and often think of solutions to problems at unusual times.
2. _____ I use brainstorming to generate solutions to a variety of problems.
3. _____ When I get stuck on a creative project, I use specific methods to get unstuck.

4. _____ I see problems and tough decisions as opportunities for learning and personal growth.
5. _____ I am willing to consider different points of view and alternative solutions.
6. _____ I can detect common errors in logic.
7. _____ I construct viewpoints by drawing on information and ideas from many sources.
8. _____ As I share my viewpoints with others, I am open to their feedback.

_____ Total score (7) *Thinking*

1. _____ I am candid with others about who I am, what I feel, and what I want.
2. _____ Other people tell me that I am a good listener.
3. _____ I can communicate my upset and anger without blaming others.
4. _____ I can make friends and create valuable relationships in a new setting.
5. _____ I am open to being with people I don't especially like in order to learn from them.
6. _____ I can effectively plan and research a large writing assignment.
7. _____ I create first drafts without criticizing my writing, then edit later for clarity, accuracy, and coherence.
8. _____ I know ways to prepare and deliver effective speeches.

_____ Total score (8) *Communicating*

1. _____ I am aware of my biases and am open to understanding people from other cultures, races, and ethnic groups.
2. _____ I build rewarding relationships with people from other backgrounds.
3. _____ I can point out examples of discrimination and sexual harassment and effectively respond to them.
4. _____ I am learning ways to thrive with diversity—attitudes and behaviors that will support my career success.
5. _____ I can effectively resolve conflict with people from other cultures.

6. _____ My writing and speaking are free of sexist expressions.

7. _____ I can recognize bias and discrimination in the media.

8. _____ I am aware of the changing demographics in my country and community.

_____ Total score (9) *Diversity*

1. _____ I learn effectively from course materials and activities that are posted online.

2. _____ I can efficiently find information on the Internet.

3. _____ I think critically about information and ideas that I access online.

4. _____ I write clear and concise e-mail messages that generate the results I want.

5. _____ My online communication is fair and respectful to other people.

6. _____ I monitor new technology that can support my success in school.

7. _____ I monitor new technology that can support my success in my career.

8. _____ I effectively use libraries to find the resources and information I want.

_____ Total score (10) *Technology*

1. _____ I have enough energy to study and still fully enjoy other areas of my life.

2. _____ If the situation calls for it, I have enough reserve energy to put in a long day.

3. _____ The food I eat supports my long-term health.

4. _____ The way I eat is independent of my feelings of self-worth.

5. _____ I exercise regularly to maintain a healthful weight.

6. _____ My emotional health supports my ability to learn.

7. _____ I notice changes in my physical condition and respond effectively.

8. _____ I am in control of any alcohol or other drugs I put into my body.

_____ Total score (11) *Health*

1. _____ I see learning as a lifelong process.

2. _____ I relate school to what I plan to do for the rest of my life.

3. _____ I learn by contributing to others.

4. _____ I revise my plans as I learn, change, and grow.

5. _____ I am clear about my purpose in life.

6. _____ I know that I am responsible for my own education.

7. _____ I take responsibility for the quality of my life.

8. _____ I am willing to accept challenges even when I'm not sure how to meet them.

_____ Total score (12) *Purpose*

Filling in your Discovery Wheel

Using the total score from each category, shade in each section of the Discovery Wheel on page 389. Use different colors, if you want. For example, you could use green to denote areas you want to work on. When you have finished, complete the following Journal Entry.

journal entry 36

Discovery/Intention Statement

The purpose of this Journal Entry is to (1) review both of the Discovery Wheels you completed in this book, (2) summarize your insights from doing them, and (3) declare how you will use these insights to promote your continued success in school.

Again, a lower score on the second Discovery Wheel does not necessarily indicate decreased personal effectiveness. Instead, the lower score could result from increased honesty and greater self-awareness.

	Chapter 1	Chapter 12
Motivation		
Time		
Memory		
Reading		
Notes		
Tests		
Thinking		
Communicating		
Diversity		
Technology		
Health		
Purpose		

Comparing the Discovery Wheel in this chapter with the Discovery Wheel in Chapter One, I discovered that I . . .

_____
_____
_____
_____
_____
_____
_____

In the next six months, I intend to review the following articles from this book for additional suggestions I could use:

_____
_____
_____
_____
_____
_____
_____
_____

exercise 34

THIS BOOK SHOUTS, "USE ME!"

Becoming a Master Student is designed to be used for years. The success strategies presented here are not likely to become habits overnight. There are more suggestions than can be put into action immediately. Some of what is discussed might not apply to your life right now, but might be just what you could use in a few months.

Plan to keep this book and use it again. Imagine that your book has a mouth. (Visualize the mouth.) Also imagine that it has arms and legs. (Visualize them.)

Now picture your book sitting on a shelf or table that you see every day. Imagine a time when you are having trouble in school and struggling to be successful as a student. Visualize your book jumping up and down, shouting, "Use me! Read me! I might have the solution to your problem, and I know I can help you solve it."

This is a memory technique to remind you to use a resource. Sometimes when you are stuck, all you need is a small push or a list of possible actions. At those times, hear your book shout, "Use me!"

power process

Be it

All of the techniques in this book are enhanced by this Power Process.

To tap into its full benefits, consider that most of our choices in life fall into three categories. We can:

- Increase our material wealth (what we have).
- Improve our skills (what we do).
- Develop our "being" (who we are).

Many people devote their entire lifetime to the first two categories. They act as if they are "human havings" instead of human beings. For them, the quality of life hinges on what they have. They devote most of their waking hours to getting more—more clothes, more cars, more relationships, more degrees, more trophies. "Human havings" define themselves by looking at the circumstances in their lives—what they have.

Some people escape this materialist trap by adding another dimension to their identities. In addition to living as "human havings," they also live as "human doings." They thrive on working hard and doing everything well. They define themselves by how efficiently they do their jobs, how effectively they raise their children, and how actively they participate in clubs and organizations. Their thoughts are constantly about methods, techniques, and skills.

Look beyond doing and having

In addition to focusing on what we have and what we do, we can also focus on our being. While it is impossible to live our lives without having things and doing things, this Power Process suggests that we balance our experience by giving lots of attention to who we are—an aspect of our lives that goes beyond having and doing. Call it soul, passion, purpose, or values. Call it being. This word describes how we see ourselves—our deepest commitments, the ground from which our actions spring.

The realm of being is profound and subtle. It is also difficult to capture in words, though philosophers have tried for centuries. Christian theologian Paul Tillich described this realm when he defined faith as "ultimate commitment" and the "ground of being." In the New Testament, Jesus talked about being when he asked his followers to love God with all of their heart, soul, and mind. An ancient Hindu text also touches on being: "You are what your deep, driving desire is."

If all this seems far removed from taking notes or answering test questions, read on. Consider an example of how "Be it" can assist in career choices. In a letter to his father, a young man wrote:

We just went to see the Dance Theatre of Harlem. It was great! After the last number, I decided that I want to dance more than anything. I have a great passion to do it, more than anything else I can think or dream of. Dancing is what will make me happy and feel like I can leave this earth when my time comes. It is what I must do. I think that if I never fulfill this passion, I will never feel complete or satisfied with what I have done with my life.

In his heart, this man *is* a dancer now, even before his formal training is complete. From his passion, desire, commitment, and self-image (his *being*) comes his willingness to take classes and rehearse (*doing*). And from his doing he might eventually *have* a job with a professional dance company.

Picture the result as you begin

The example of the dancer illustrates that once you have a clear picture of what you want to *be,* the things you *do* and *have* fall more naturally into place.

The idea is this: Getting where you want to be by what you do or by what you have is like swimming against the current. Have → do → be is a tough journey. It's much easier to go in the other direction: be → do → have.

Usually, we work against nature by trying to have something or do something before being it. That's hard. All of your deeds (what you do) might not get you where you want to be. Getting all of the right things (what you have) might not get you there either.

Take the person who values athletics and wants to master tennis. He buys an expensive racket and a stylish tennis wardrobe. Yet he still can't return a serve. Merely having the right things doesn't deliver what he values.

Suppose that this person takes a year's worth of tennis lessons. Week after week, he practices doing everything "right." Still, his game doesn't quite make it.

What goes wrong is hard to detect. "He lost the match even though he played a good game," people say. "Something seemed to be wrong. His technique was fine, but each swing was just a little off." Perhaps the source of his problem is that he cannot see himself as ever mastering the game. What he has and what he does are at war with his mental picture of himself.

You can see this happen in other areas of life. Two people tell the same joke in what seems to be the same way. Yet one person brings a smile, while the other person has you laughing so hard your muscles hurt. The difference in how they do the joke is imperceptible. When the successful comedian tells a joke, he does it from his experience of already being funny.

Change the way you see yourself, and watch your actions and results shift as if by magic.

To have and do what you want, be it. Picture the result as you begin. If you can first visualize where you want to be, if you can go there in your imagination, if you can be it today, you set yourself up to succeed.

Be a master student now

Now relate this Power Process to succeeding in school. All of the techniques in this book can be worthless if you operate with the idea that you are an ineffective student. You might do almost everything this book suggests and still never achieve the success in school that you desire.

For example, if you believe that you are stupid in math, you are likely to fail at math. If you believe that you are not skilled at remembering, all of the memory techniques in the world might not improve your recall. Generally, we don't outperform our self-concept.

If you value success in school, picture yourself as a master student right now. Through higher education you are gaining knowledge and skills that reflect and reinforce this view of yourself.

This principle works in other areas of life. For example, if you value a fulfilling career, picture yourself as already being on a path to a job you love. Use affirmations and visualizations to plant this idea firmly in your mind. Change the way you see yourself, and watch your actions and results shift as if by magic.

While you're at it, remember that "Be it" is not positive thinking or mental cheerleading. This Power Process works well when you take a First Step—when you tell the truth about your current abilities. The very act of accepting who you are and what you can do right now unleashes a powerful force for personal change.

Flow with the natural current of be → do → have. Then watch your circumstances change.

If you want it, be it. ⊠

put it to work

Plan for change. Even the most brilliant people can fall flat when predicting trends in business and the workplace. Case in point: Thomas Watson, founder of IBM, said, "I think there's a world market for about five computers."[6]

Still, you can benefit from making predictions about changes in the workplace that affect your own employment opportunities. Keep up-to-date with breaking changes as you decide what's next in your career. This is easier to do than ever before, thanks to resources mentioned throughout this book:

- *The Internet.* Use your skills in searching the Internet to find Web sites devoted to your field. Start by keying your job title into a search engine such as Google or Yahoo! Also search for career-related listservs—programs that distribute e-mail messages to groups of people with similar interests.

- *Periodicals.* Read the business sections of the *New York Times* and the *Wall Street Journal*, for example. Most newspapers also have online editions, as do general-interest magazines such as *Time* and *Business Week.*

- *Professional associations.* People in similar jobs like to band together and give each other a heads up on emerging trends—one reason for professional associations. These range from the American Medical Association to the Society of Actuaries. There's bound to be one for people in your field. Ask colleagues and search the Internet. **Note:** Many associations post Web sites and publish newsletters or trade magazines.

- *Conferences and conventions.* Many professional associations sponsor annual meetings. Here's where you can meet people face-to-face and use your networking skills. Print and online publications are powerful sources of news, but sometimes nothing beats plain old schmoozing.

Consider coaching. Consider receiving life coaching as a way to continue the cycle of discovery, intention, and action you started in this book. A life coach is someone with training in counseling or a related field who meets with clients several times per month in person or over the phone. Life coaches can help you define your personal values, align your daily life with those values, write goals and action plans, and create projects that allow you to contribute to others. With the support of a life coach, you can start now to envision the jobs you want to have in 5 years, 10 years, and 20 or more years into the future. You can set comprehensive, long-term goals in every other area of your life as well. Like other professionals, life coaches charge for their services. Fees vary widely. Consider life coaching even if you can afford only a few hours of this service a year.

You can also meet with friends to offer each other free coaching. Start by redoing the exercises and Journal Entries in this book, sharing the results, and inventing new exercises of your own. The results can be dramatic.

Continue the conversation about success. As you begin your life beyond this student success course, continue to engage in a conversation about what you want from your life and how you intend to get it. You can experience success as you define it and live the life of your dreams. ⬧

Name _____ Date _____/_____/_____

1. Briefly discuss the meaning of "Now that you're done—begin."

2. Explain how *content skills* and *transferable skills* differ. Give one example of each kind of skill.

3. Explain how career planning can be a process of choosing instead of a process of discovery.

4. List three suggestions for designing an effective service-learning project.

5. Describe the three main types of life choices explained in the Power Process: "Be it."

6. Using the Power Process: "Be it" eliminates the need to take action. True or False? Explain your answer.

7. If your scores are lower on the Discovery Wheel the second time you complete it, that means your study skills have not improved. True or False? Explain your answer.

8. Contributing to others does *not* involve:
   (a) Telling people what is best for them.
   (b) Finding out what people want or need.
   (c) Determining if you can help people get what they want.
   (d) Giving your time, talent, or money.
   (e) Making sure that you experience satisfaction, also.

9. Describe a flaw associated with the typical job-hunting strategy of looking through help wanted advertisements. Suggest an alternative approach to job hunting.

10. List at least four ways that you can continue on your path of becoming a master student after completing this book.

learning styles application

The questions below will "cycle" you through four styles, or modes, of learning as explained in the article "Learning styles: Discovering how you learn" in Chapter One. Each question will help you explore a different mode. You can answer the questions in any order.

what if Consider this statement from the first article in this chapter: "You are on the edge of a universe so miraculous and full of wonder that your imagination at its most creative moment cannot encompass it. Paths are open to lead you to worlds beyond your wildest dreams." If you adopted this statement as a working principle, what would you do differently on a daily basis?

why Consider your experience with this book and your student success class. Which of your attitudes or actions changed as a result of this experience?

how List one suggestion from this book that you would like to apply but have not yet acted upon. Describe exactly how you will implement this suggestion.

what List five suggestions from this book that you've already applied. Rate each suggestion for its effectiveness on a scale of 1 to 5 (1 is most effective, 5 is least effective).

master student profile

GOLDA MEIR

(1898–1978) a pioneer in the creation of Israel, was elected its fourth prime minister.

started school in a huge, fortress like building on Fourth Street near Milwaukee's famous Schlitz beer factory, and I loved it. I can't remember how long it took me to learn English (at home, of course, we spoke Yiddish, and luckily, so did almost everyone else on Walnut Street), but I have no recollection of the language ever being a real problem for me, so I must have picked it up quickly. I made friends quickly, too. Two of those early first- or second-grade friends remained friends all my life, and both live in Israel now. One was Regina Hamburger (today Medzini), who lived on our street and who was to leave America when I did; the other was Sarah Feder, who became one of the leaders of Labor Zionism in the United States.. . .

More than fifty years later—when I was seventy-one and a prime minister—I went back to that school for a few hours. It had not changed very much in all those years except that the vast majority of its pupils were now black, not Jewish, as in

1906. They welcomed me as though I were a queen. Standing in rows on the creaky old stage I remembered so well, freshly scrubbed and neat as pins, they serenaded me with Yiddish and Hebrew songs and raised their voices to peal out the Israeli anthem "Hatikvah" which made my eyes fill with tears. Each one of the classrooms had been beautifully decorated with posters about Israel and signs reading SHALOM (one of the children thought it was my family name), and when I entered the school, two little girls wearing headbands with Stars of David on them solemnly presented me with an enormous white rose made of tissue paper and pipe cleaners, which I wore all day and carefully carried back to Israel with me.

Another of the gifts I got that day in 1971 from the Fourth Street School was a record of my grades for one of the years I had spent there: 95 in reading, 90 in spelling, 95 in arithmetic, 85 in music, and a mysterious 90 in something called manual arts, which I cannot remember at all. But when the children asked me to talk to them for a few minutes, it was not about book learning that I chose to speak. I had learned a lot more than fractions or how to spell at Fourth Street, and I decided to tell those eager, attentive children—born, as I myself had

been, into a minority and living, as I myself had lived, without much extravagance (to put it mildly)— what the gist of that learning had been. "It isn't really important to decide when you are very young just exactly what you want to become when you grow up," I told them. "It is much more important to decide on the way you want to live. If you are going to get involved with causes which are good for others, not only for yourselves, then it seems to me that that is sufficient, and maybe what you will be is only a matter of chance." I had a feeling that they understood me. ▨

From *My Life* by Golda Meir. Reprinted with permission of Weidenfeld & Nicholson.

For more biographical information on Golda Meir, visit the Master Student Hall of Fame on the *Becoming a Master Student* Web site at

masterstudent.college.hmco.com

photo and Illustration credits

Introduction   p. xiv: (swimmer) Image100/Wonderfile, (girl eating apple) RubberBall/Picturequest, (woman at computer) PhotoDisc/Picturequest, (woman with paper) Photomondo/PhotoDisc Red/Getty, (graduate) Ryan McVay/PhotoDisc Green/Getty, (sitting man with book) PNC/PhotoDisc Red/Getty, (mortarboard) Thinkstock/Getty, (collage) Walter Kopec; p. 6: Catherine Hawkes/Cat & Mouse Design; pp. 7–8: Catherine Hawkes/Cat & Mouse Design; pp. 9–10: © David H. Wells/Corbis; pp. 11–12: (books) Comstock Images/Alamy, (woman/child) Scott T. Barker/PhotoDisc Green/Getty, (woman at desk) Stockbyte, (illustration) Brian Reardon; p. 13: PhotoDisc; p. 14: PhotoDisc; p. 15: courtesy of Habitat for Humanity; p. 16: Walter Kopec; p. 17: Stockbyte; Don Farrall/PhotoDisc Green/Getty Images; © Franco Vogt/Corbis; (monitor/keyboard) PhotoDisc, (illustration) Walter Kopec; PhotoDisc Royalty Free/Fotosearch; Digital Vision Royalty Free/Fotosearch; Big Cheese Photo LLC/Alamy; PhotoDisc/Fotosearch; Digital Vision/Wonderfile; Digital Vision/Fotosearch; pp. 18–19: (all) PhotoDisc; p. 22: (faces) PhotoDisc, (inset background) Photomondo/PhotoDisc Red/Getty, (collage) Walter Kopec.

Chapter 1   p. 24: ©Elektra Vision: AG/PictureQuest; p. 26: (refresh button) © Royalty Free/Corbis, (illustration) Walter Kopec; pp. 28, 31: Walter Kopec; pp. 33, 35: Catherine Hawkes/Cat & Mouse Design; p. 41: (demonstration) © Michael Newman/Photo Edit, (girl practicing CPR) Stockbyte Royalty Free/Fotosearch; p. 43: (collage) Walter Kopec; p. 55: (man) PhotoDisc, (lightbulbs) ComstockKLIPS, (collage) Walter Kopec; p. 56: Stockbyte; p. 59: courtesy of Suny Urritia Moore.

Chapter 2   p. 60: Matheisl/Getty; p. 70: Deborah Jaffe/The Image Bank/Getty Images; p. 72: (wings, boy) PhotoDisc, (collage) Walter Kopec; p. 73: (collage) Walter Kopec; p. 77: (monitor with notes) Janis Christie/PhotoDisc Green/Getty, (illustration) Walter Kopec; p. 80: C Squared Studios/PhotoDisc Green/Getty Images; p. 85: (woman's face, clock, trash can) PhotoDisc, (gears, eight ball, "Rush" stamp) ComstockKLIPS, (collage) Walter Kopec; p. 86: (woman's face, clock, folders) PhotoDisc, (gears, "Stop" sign) ComstockKlips, (hammock) Artville, (collage) Walter Kopec; p. 95: Ryan McVay/PhotoDisc Green/Getty Images; p. 96: Ryan McVay/PhotoDisc Green/Getty Images; p. 99: (piggy bank) Duncan Smith/PhotoDisc Green/Getty, (burning bill) Don Farrall/PhotoDisc Green/Getty, (illustration) Walter Kopec; p. 103: Comstock; p. 107: © Bettman/Corbis; p. 104: Don Farrall/PhotoDisc Green/Getty Images.

Chapter 3   p. 108: Digital Vision/Getty; p. 110: PhotoDisc; p. 111: (all) PhotoDisc; p. 112: (all) Walter Kopec; p. 114: Brand X Pictures/Alamy; p. 116: Walter Kopec; p. 118: (shark) Digital Vision/Getty, (windmill) Digital Vision/Getty, (illustration) Walter Kopec; p. 119: (phone) Index Stock/Alamy, (door) Ryan McVay/PhotoDisc Green/Getty, (illustration) Walter Kopec; p. 122: (door) Photospin, (illustration) Walter Kopec; p. 124: (door) Photospin, (Bill of Rights) public domain, (illustration) Walter Kopec; p. 129: (both women) PhotoDisc Blue, (illustration) Walter Kopec; p. 130: © Franco Vogt/Corbis; p. 133: © Bettman/Corbis.

Chapter 4   p. 134: Corbis/Royalty Free; p. 136: (images) PhotoDisc, (collage) Walter Kopec; pp. 137, 138, 139, 140, 141: (images) PhotoDisc, (collage) Walter Kopec; p. 142: Stockbyte; p. 143: (frame) PhotoDisc; p. 145: PhotoDisc Green/Getty; p. 148: Digital Vision/PictureQuest; p. 154: (monitor/keyboard) PhotoDisc, (illustration) Walter Kopec; p. 157: © Hulton-Deutsch Collection/Corbis.

Chapter 5   p. 159: Brand X Pictures/Alamy; p. 160: (eye) PhotoDisc; p. 163: (ear) PhotoDisc; p. 168: (brain) Brand X Pictures/Alamy, (eye, ear) PhotoDisc; p. 172: (people) PhotoDisc, (collage) Brian Reardon; p. 175: Comstock Royalty Free/Fotosearch; p. 181: Corbis/Royalty Free;

p. 182: PhotoDisc Royalty Free/Fotosearch; p. 185: courtesy Craig Keilburger.

Chapter 6   p. 186: © Comstock IMAGES; p. 188: Gaetano Images Inc./Alamy; p. 193: Image Source Royalty Free/Fotosearch; p. 194: Image Source Royalty Free/Fotosearch; p. 198: PhotoDisc; p. 206: (board, molecule, beaker) PhotoDisc; p. 208: PhotoDisc; p. 210: ©Elektra Vision/AG/PictureQuest; p. 212: Corbis Royalty Free/Fotosearch; p. 215: © Bettman/Corbis.

Chapter 7   pp. 216, 219, 220, 221, 222: PhotoDisc; p. 223: (all) Catherine Hawkes/Cat & Mouse Design; p. 224: (chess pieces) PhotoDisc, (illustration) Brian Reardon; p. 228: AP Photo/Jim Mone; p. 232: (images) PhotoDisc, (collage) Walter Kopec; p. 233: (images) PhotoDisc, (collage) Walter Kopec; p. 241: © Digital Vision; p. 242: Image100 Royalty Free/Fotosearch; p. 245: Copyright 2003 President and Fellows of Harvard College on behalf of HMS Media Services, photo by Liza Green, HMS Media Services, all rights reserved.

Chapter 8   p. 246: EyeWire (PhotoDisc)/Fotosearch; p. 248: (images) Eyewire, Corbis, PhotoDisc, (collage) Walter Kopec; p. 252: (images) Eyewire, Corbis, PhotoDisc, (collage) Walter Kopec; p. 254: ImageState/Fotosearch; p. 256: Comstock/Fotosearch; p. 258: Comstock/Fotosearch; p. 260: PhotoDisc/Fotosearch; p. 262: PhotoDisc/Fotosearch; p. 270: Digital Vision/Fotosearch; p. 275: (clouds) Brand X (X Collection)/Wonderfile, (illustration) Walter Kopec; p. 276: Digital Vision Royalty Free/Fotosearch; p. 279: © Leif Skoogfors/Corbis.

Chapter 9   p. 280: Corbis/Royalty Free; p. 282: (flags) Stockbyte, (collage) Walter Kopec; pp. 284, 285, 286: (images) PhotoDisc, (collage) Walter Kopec; p. 289: © Keith Brofsky/PhotoDisc/PictureQuest; p. 294: (Mrs. Eleanor Roosevelt), (Maria Tallchief, "Firebird") New York City Ballet, (Roberto Clemente), (Fredrick Douglass) Charles Phelps Cushing, (Nelson Mandela) © Paul Velasco/Gallo Images/Corbis, (Copernicus), (Thomas A. Edison), (Aung San Suu Kyi) Emmanuel Dunand/Getty, (Winston Churchill), (Queen Elizabeth 1), (Albert Einstein) Alan W. Richards/Princeton, (Jesse Owens) ©Bettman, (Marian Anderson) New York Public Library, (Golda Meir) ©Reuters/Corbis; pp. 300, 301: PhotoDisc; p. 302: Big Cheese Photo LLC/Alamy; p. 305: © Bettman/Corbis.

Chapter 10   p. 306: Wonderfile; p. 308: PhotoDisc; p. 313: Brand X Pictures/Fotosearch; p. 318: (man) Jonnie Miles/Getty, (globe) PhotoDisc/Getty, (classroom) PhotoDisc, (collage) Walter Kopec; p. 322: (trunk) Comstock/Fotosearch, (illustration) Walter Kopec; p. 327: Corbis/Royalty Free; p. 328: PhotoDisc/Fotosearch; p. 331: © Hekimian Julien/Corbis Sygma.

Chapter 11   p. 331: © Ron Chapple/Thinkstock/PictureQuest; p. 334: (man) PhotoDisc, (gears) PhotoDisc, (collage) Walter Kopec; p. 335: Iconotec/Wonderfile; p. 336: Brand X (X Collection)/Wonderfile; p. 337: Image Source/Wonderfile; p. 338: PhotoDisc/Fotosearch; p. 340: Brand X Pictures/Alamy; p. 344: PhotoDisc; p. 346: (donut) Medio Images/Fotosearch, (illustration) Walter Kopec; pp. 347, 348: Walter Kopec; p. 354: PhotoDisc/Fotosearch; p. 359: © Ron Chapple/Thinkstock/PictureQuest; p. 360: Digital Vision/Wonderfile; p. 363: © Reuters/Corbis.

Chapter 12   p. 364: (collage) Walter Kopec; pp. 366, 368, 370: PhotoDisc; p. 377: Thinkstock/Alamy; p. 378: Image Source/Alamy; p. 379: Dynamic Graphics Group/IT Stock Free/Alamy; p. 384: © Corbis Images/PictureQuest; p. 395: (thinking man) Digital Vision/Wonderfile, (graduate) Digital Vision/Wonderfile, (collage) Walter Kopec; p. 396: Digital Vision/Fotosearch; p. 399: © Reuters/Corbis.

endnotes

introduction

1. U.S. Department of Labor, Bureau of Labor Statistics, "Education pays . . . ," August 7, 2003, http://www.bls.gov/emp/emptab7.htm (accessed May 3, 2004). National Center for Education Statistics, "Annual Earnings of Young Adults," http://www.nces.ed.gov/programs/coe/2002/section2/indicator16.asp, 2002 (accessed January 13, 2004).
2. Robert Mager, *Preparing Instructional Objectives* (Belmont, CA: Fearon, 1975).
3. Malcolm Knowles, *Andragogy in Action* (San Francisco: Jossey-Bass, 1984).
4. Abraham H. Maslow, *The Farther Reaches of Human Nature* (New York: Viking, 1971)
5. Richard Saul Wurman, Loring Leifer, and David Sume, *Information Anxiety 2* (Indianapolis: QUE, 2001), 199.
6. James O. Prochaska, John C. Norcross, and Carlo C. DiClemente, *Changing for Good* (New York: Avon, 1994).
7. B. F. Skinner, *Science and Human Behavior* (Boston: Free Press, 1965).

chapter 1

1. David A. Kolb, *Experiential Learning: Experience as the Source of Learning and Development* (Englewood Cliffs, NJ: Prentice-Hall, 1984).
2. Howard Gardner, *Frames of Mind: The Theory of Multiple Intelligences* (New York: Basic Books, 1993).
3. Carl Rogers, *Freedom to Learn* (Columbus, OH: Merrill, 1969).
4. Ezra Pound, *The ABC of Reading* (New York: New Directions, 1934).
5. Robert Hutchins, "The Tradition of the West," in *The Great Conversation: The Substance of a Liberal Education*, vol. 1, *The Great Books of the Western World* (Chicago: Encyclopædia Britannica, 1952).
6. William James, *Pragmatism and Other Essays* (New York: Washington Square, 1963).

chapter 2

1. Alan Lakein, *How to Get Control of Your Time and Your Life* (New York: New American Library, 1973; reissue 1996).
2. Linda Sapadin, with Jack Maguire, *It's About Time! The Six Styles of Procrastination and How to Overcome Them* (New York: Penguin, 1997).
3. Jane B. Burka and Lenora R. Yuen, *Procrastination: Why You Do It, What to Do About It* (Reading, MA: Addison-Wesley, 1983).

4. Stephen R. Covey, *The Seven Habits of Highly Effective People: Restoring the Character Ethic* (New York: Simon & Schuster, 1990).
5. Dorothy Lee, *Freedom and Culture* (Englewood Cliffs, NJ: Prentice-Hall, 1959).
6. Joe Dominguez and Vicki Robin, *Your Money or Your Life: Transforming Your Relationship with Money and Achieving Financial Independence* (New York: Viking Penguin, 1992).
7. M. A. Just, P. A. Carpenter, T. A. Keller et al., "Interdependence of Nonoverlapping Cortical Systems in Dual Cognitive Tasks," *NeuroImage* 14, no. 2 (2001): 417–426.

chapter 3

1. Donald Hebb, quoted in D. J. Siegel, "Memory: An Overview," *Journal of the American Academy of Child and Adolescent Psychiatry* 40, no. 9 (2001): 997–1011.
2. Holger Hyden, "Biochemical Aspects of Learning and Memory," in *On the Biology of Learning*, ed. Karl H. Pribram (New York: Harcourt, Brace & World, 1969).
3. Richard Saul Wurman, *Information Anxiety* (New York: Doubleday, 1989), 59.
4. D. J. Siegel, "Memory: An Overview," *Journal of the American Academy of Child and Adolescent Psychiatry* 40, no. 9 (2001): 997–1011.
5. Daniel L. Schacter, *The Seven Sins of Memory: How the Mind Forgets and Remembers* (Boston: Houghton Mifflin, 2001), 34.
6. John W. Rowe and Robert L. Kahn, *Successful Aging* (New York: Pantheon, 1998).
7. CNN.com, "Ethical Debate over Potential 'Viagra for the Mind,'" March 11, 1999, http://www.cnn.com/SPECIALS/views/y/1999/03/utley.memory.mar11/#1 (accessed April 15, 2002).

chapter 4

1. G. S. Gates, "Recitation as a Factor in Memorizing," *Archives of Psychology* 40 (1917).
2. R. Rosnow and E. Robinson, eds., *Experiments in Persuasion* (New York: Academic Press, 1967).
3. William Glasser, *Take Effective Control of Your Life* (New York: Harper & Row, 1984).
4. School of Information Management and Systems, University of California, Berkeley, "How Much Information? 2003," October 27, 2003, http://www.sims.berkeley.edu/research/projects/how-much-info-2003/execsum.htm (accessed February 20, 2004).
5. John Morkes and Jakob Nielsen, "Concise, Scannable and Objective: How to Write for the Web," 1997, http://www.useit.com/papers/webwriting/writing.html (accessed February 20, 2004).

chapter 5

1. Walter Pauk and Ross J.Q. Owens, *How to Study in College*, Eighth Edition (Boston: Houghton Mifflin, 2005).
2. Tony Buzan, *Use Both Sides of Your Brain* (New York: Dutton, 1991).
3. Gabrielle Rico, *Writing the Natural Way* (Los Angeles: J. P. Tarcher, 1983).
4. Richard Solly and Roseann Lloyd, *Journey Notes: Writing for Recovery and Spiritual Growth* (Center City, MN: Hazelden, 1989).
5. Joseph Novak and D. Bob Gowin, *Learning How to Learn* (New York: Cambridge University Press, 1984).
6. David P. Ausubel, *Educational Psychology: A Cognitive View* (New York: Holt, Rinehart and Winston, 1968).
7. William Glasser, *Take Effective Control of Your Life* (New York: Harper & Row, 1984).

chapter 6

1. Adapted from Linda Wong, *Essential Study Skills*, Fourth Edition. Copyright © 2002 by Houghton Mifflin Company. Reprinted with permission.
2. Joe Cuseo, "Academic-Support Strategies for Promoting Student Retention and Achievement during the First Year of College," University of Ulster Office of Student Transition and Retention, http://www.ulst.ac.uk/star/data/cuseoretention.htm#peestud (accessed September 4, 2003).
3. Ibid.
4. Sheila Tobias, *Succeed with Math: Every Student's Guide to Conquering Math Anxiety* (New York: College Board, 1995).

chapter 7

1. Quoted in Theodore A. Rees Cheney, *Getting the Words Right: How to Rewrite, Edit and Revise*, repr. ed. (Cincinnati, OH: Writer's Digest Books, 1990).
2. William G. Perry, Jr., *Forms of Intellectual and Ethical Development in the College Years: A Scheme* (New York: Holt, Rinehart, and Winston, 1970).
3. Peter A. Facione, "Critical Thinking: What It Is and Why It Counts." A paper from California Academic press reprinted at http://www.calpress.com/critical.html.
4. Arthur Koestler, *The Act of Creation* (New York: Dell, 1964).
5. Walter Arnold Kaufman, *Without Guilt and Justice: From Decidophobia to Autonomy* (New York: Delta, 1975).
6. John Dewey, *How We Think* (Boston, D.C. Heath, 1910).
7. Quoted in Alice Calaprice, ed., *The Expanded Quotable Einstein* (Princeton, NJ: Princeton University Press, 2000).
8. Joe Cuseo, "Academic-Support Strategies for Promoting Student Retention and Achievement during the First Year of College," University of Ulster Office of Student Transition and Retention, http://www.ulst.ac.uk/star/data/cuseoretention.htm#peestud (accessed September 4, 2003).
9. Jan Carlzon, *Moments of Truth* (New York.: HarperCollins, 1989).

chapter 8

1. Lee Thayer, "Communication—Sine Qua Non of the Behavioral Sciences," in *Vistas in Science,* ed. David L. Arm (Albuquerque: University of New Mexico, 1968).
2. Carl Rogers, *On Becoming a Person* (Boston: Houghton Mifflin, 1961).
3. Thomas Gordon, *Parent Effectiveness Training: The Tested New Way to Raise Responsible Children* (New York: New American Library, 1975).
4. Sidney Jourard, *The Transparent Self* (New York: Van Nostrand, 1971).
5. Morita Masatake's ideas are discussed in David Reynolds, *A Handbook for Constructive Living* (New York: Morrow, 1995): 98.
6. Quoted in Richard Saul Wurman, Loring Leifer, and David Sume, *Information Anxiety #2* (Indianapolis: QUE, 2001), 116.
7. Peter Elbow, *Writing with Power: Techniques for Mastering the Writing Process* (New York: Oxford University Press, 1981).
8. Natalie Goldberg, *Writing Down the Bones: Freeing the Writer Within* (Boston: Shambhala, 1992).
9. Quoted in Theodore Cheney, *Getting the Words Right: How to Revise, Edit and Rewrite* (Cincinnati: Writer's Digest, 1983).
10. Theodore Cheney, *Getting the Words Right: How to Revise, Edit and Rewrite* (Cincinnati: Writer's Digest, 1983).
11. National Association of Colleges and Employers, "Recreate Yourself: From Student to the Perfect Job Candidate," http://www.jobweb.com/joboutlook/2004outlook/outlook5.htm (accessed December 15, 2003).
12. Jakob Nielsen, *Designing Web Usability: The Practice of Simplicity* (Indianapolis: New Riders, 1999).
13. LaFasto and Larson refer to their book *When Teams Work Best* in their online article: Center for Association Leadership, "The Zen of Brilliant Teams," http://www.centeronline.org/knowledge/article.cfm?ID=1884&, July 2002 (accessed January 5, 2004).

chapter 9

1. U.S. Census Bureau, "Current Population Reports: Population Projections of the U.S. by Age, Sex, Race and Hispanic Origin, 1995–2050," http://www.census.gov/prod/1/pop/p25-1130/, February 1996 (accessed January 5, 2003).
2. Dorothy Lee, *Freedom and Culture* (Englewood Cliffs, NJ: Prentice-Hall, 1959).
3. Federal Bureau of Investigation, "Uniform Crime Reports," http://www.fbi.gov/ucr/ucr.htm, 2002 (accessed January 12, 2004).
4. Stephen R. Covey, *The Seven Habits of Highly Effective People: Restoring the Character Ethic* (New York: Simon & Schuster, 1989).
5. James Anderson, personal communication, 1990.
6. Diane de Anda, *Bicultural Socialization: Factors Affecting the Minority Experience* (Washington, DC: National Association of Social Workers, 1984).

chapter 10

1. From Ann Raimes, *Universal Keys for Writers.* Copyright © 2005 by Houghton Mifflin Company. Reprinted with permission.

chapter 11

1. Frederick F. Samaha, Nayyar Iqbal, and Prakash Seshadri et al., "A Low-Carbohydrate as Compared with a Low-Fat Diet in Severe Obesity," *New England Journal of Medicine* 348, no. 21 (2003): 2074–2081.
2. National Center for Health Statistics, "Prevalence of Overweight and Obesity Among Adults: United States, 1999-2000," http://www.cdc.gov/nchs/products/pubd/hestats/obese/obse99.htm (accessed January 12, 2004).

3. U.S. Department of Health and Human Services, "The Surgeon General's Call to Action to Prevent and Decrease Overweight and Obesity," http://www.surgeongeneral.gov/topics/obesity/calltoaction/toc.htm, 2001 (accessed January 12, 2004).

4. Martin E. P. Seligman, *Learned Optimism* (New York: Pocket Books, 1998).

5. Commonwealth Fund, "Out of Touch: American Men and the Health Care System," http://www.cmwf.org/programs/women/sandman_outoftouch_374.pdf, March 2000 (accessed January 13, 2004).

6. Agency for Healthcare Research and Quality, "Men, Stay Healthy at Any Age," http://www.ahrq.gov/ppip/healthymen.htm, June 2003 (accessed January 12, 2004).

7. Albert Bandura, "Self-Efficacy," in *Encyclopedia of Human Behavior*, vol. 4, ed. V. S. Ramachaudran (New York: Academic Press, 1994), 71–81.

8. Harvey Jackins, *The Benign Reality* (Seattle: Rational Island, 1991).

9. Daniel Goleman, *Emotional Intelligence* (New York: Bantam, 1997).

10. American Psychological Association, *Diagnostic and Statistical Manual of Psychoactive Substance Abuse Disorders* (Washington, D.C.: American Psychological Association, 1994).

11. William James, *The Varieties of Religious Experience: A Study in Human Nature* (New York: Scribner, 1997).

chapter 12

1. Ira Progoff, *At a Journal Workshop* (New York: Dialogue House, 1975).

2. Richard Nelson Bolles, *What Color Is Your Parachute?* (Berkeley: Ten Speed Press, updated annually).

3. Martin Kimeldorf, *Peterson's Portfolio Power: The New Way to Showcase All Your Job Skills and Experiences* (Lawrenceville, NJ: Peterson's Guides, 1997).

4. William Bridges, *Jobshift: How to Prosper in a Workplace Without Jobs* (New York: Perseus, 1995).

5. United Nations Development Programme. *Human Development Report*. New York: Oxford University Press, 2003.

6. Charles Hard Townes in Martin Moskovits, ed., *Science and Society, the John C. Polanyi Nobel Laureates Lectures* (Concord, Ontario: Anansi Press, 1995), 8.

additional reading

Adler, Mortimer, and Charles Van Doren. *How to Read a Book*. New York: Touchstone, 1972.

Anthony, Jason, and Karl Cluck. *Debt-Free by 30*. New York: Plume, 2001.

Bandler, Richard, and John Grinder. *Frogs into Princes: Neuro-Linguistic Programming*. Moab, UT: Real People, 1979.

Beckham, Barry, ed. *The Black Student's Guide to Colleges*. New York: Madison Books UPA, 1996.

Birkerts, Sven. *The Gutenberg Elegies: The Fate of Reading in an Electronic Age*. New York: Ballantine, 1994.

Boston Women's Health Book Collective. *The New Our Bodies, Ourselves*. New York: Simon & Schuster, 1996.

Brown, Alan C. *Maximizing Memory Power*. New York: Wiley, 1986.

Buzan, Tony. *Make the Most of Your Mind*. New York: Simon & Schuster, 1977.

Chaffee, John. *Thinking Critically*. Boston: Houghton Mifflin, 2003.

Corey, Gerald. *I Never Knew I Had a Choice*. Monterey, CA: Brooks-Cole, 1982.

Covey, Stephen R. *First Things First*. New York: Simon & Schuster, 1994.

Deida, David. *The Way of the Superior Man*. Austin, TX: Plexus, 1997.

Dumond, Val. *The Elements of Nonsexist Usage*. New York: Prentice-Hall, 1990.

Elgin, Duane. *Voluntary Simplicity*. New York: Morrow, 1993.

Ellis, Dave. *Creating Your Future: Five Steps to the Life of Your Dreams*. Boston: Houghton Mifflin, 1998.

Ellis, Dave, and Stan Lankowitz. *Human Being: A Manual for Happiness, Health, Love and Wealth*. Rapid City, SD: Breakthrough Enterprises, 1995.

Ellis, Dave, Stan Lankowitz, Ed Stupka, and Doug Toft. *Career Planning*. Boston: Houghton Mifflin, 2003.

Facione, Peter. *Critical Thinking: What It Is and Why It Counts*. Millbrae, CA: California Academic Press, 1996.

Fletcher, Anne. *Sober for Good*. Boston: Houghton Mifflin, 2001.

Gawain, Shakti. *Creative Visualization*. New York: New World Library, 1998.

Gibaldi, Joseph. *MLA Handbook for Writers of Research Papers*. New York: Modern Language Association, 1999.

Glasser, William. *Schools Without Failure*. New York: Harper & Row, 1968.

Golas, Thaddeus. *The Lazy Man's Guide to Enlightenment*. New York: Bantam, 1993.

Greene, Susan D., and Melanie C. L. Martel. *The Ultimate Job Hunter's Guidebook*. Boston: Houghton Mifflin, 2004.

Higbee, Kenneth L. *Your Memory: How It Works and How to Improve It*. Englewood Cliffs, NJ: Prentice-Hall, 1996.

Hill, Napoleon. *Think and Grow Rich*. New York: Fawcett, 1996.

Hurtado, Sylvia, et al. *Enacting Diverse Learning Environments: Improving the Climate for Racial/Ethnic Diversity in Higher Education*. Ashe-Eric Higher Education Reports, 1999.

James, William. *Talks to Teachers on Psychology and to Students on Some of Life's Ideals*. New York: Norton, 1983.

Keyes, Ken, Jr. *Handbook to Higher Consciousness*. Berkeley, CA: Living Love, 1974.

Keyes, Ralph. *Timelock: How Life Got So Hectic and What You Can Do About It*. New York: HarperCollins, 1991.

Kolb, David A. *Experiential Learning: Experience as the Source of Learning and Development*. Englewood Cliffs: Prentice-Hall, 1984

Lathrop, Richard. *Who's Hiring Who?* Berkeley, CA: Ten Speed, 1989.

LeBoeuf, Michael. *Imagineering: How to Profit from Your Creative Powers*. New York: Berkley, 1990.

Light, Richard J. *Making the Most of College: Students Speak Their Minds*. Cambridge, MA: Harvard University Press, 2001.

Lucas, Jerry, and Harry Lorayne. *The Memory Book*. New York: Ballantine Books, 1975.

Mallow, Jeffry V. *Science Anxiety: Fear of Science and How to Overcome It*. New York: Thomond, 1986.

Manning, Robert. *Credit Card Nation: The Consequences of America's Addiction to Credit*. New York: Basic Books, 2000.

McCarthy, Michael J. *Mastering the Information Age*. Los Angeles: J. P. Tarcher, 1991.

McCutcheon, Randall. *Can You Find It? Twenty-Five Library Scavenger Hunts to Sharpen Your Research Skills*. Minneapolis, MN: Free Spirit, 1991.

Nolting, Paul D. *Math Study Skills Workbook*. 2nd ed. Boston: Houghton Mifflin, 2005.

Orman, Suze. *The Road to Wealth*. New York: Riverhead, 2001.

Pauk, Walter and Ross J.Q. Owens. *How to Study in College*. 8th ed. Boston: Houghton Mifflin, 2005.

Pennebaker, James W. *Opening Up: The Healing Power of Confiding in Others*. New York: Morrow, 1990.

Pirsig, Robert. *Zen and the Art of Motorcycle Maintenance*. New York: Perennial Classics, 2000.

Raimes, Anne. *Universal Keys for Writers*. Boston: Houghton Mifflin, 2004.

Rajneesh, Bhagwan S. *Journey Toward the Heart*. New York: Harper and Row, 1980.

Rial, Arlyne. *Speed Reading Made Easy*. Garden City, NY: Doubleday, 1985.

Robbins, John. *Diet for a New America: How Your Food Choices Affect Your Health, Happiness and the Future of Life on Earth*. New York: H J Kramer, 1998.

Ruggiero, Vincent Ryan. *Becoming a Critical Thinker*. 4th ed. Boston: Houghton Mifflin, 2002.

Schacter, Daniel L. *Searching for Memory: The Brain, the Mind, and the Past*. New York: HarperCollins, 1997.

Scharf-Hunt, Diana, and Pam Hait. *Studying Smart: Time Management for College Students*. New York: HarperPerennial, 1990.

Schlosser, Eric. *Fast Food Nation*. Boston: Houghton Mifflin, 2001.

Strunk, William, Jr., and E. B. White. *The Elements of Style*. New York: Macmillan, 1979.

The American Heritage Dictionary, 4th Edition.

Thiederman, Sondra. *Profiting in America's Multicultural Marketplace: How to Do Business Across Cultural Lines*. New York: Lexington Books, 1992.

Tobias, Sheila. *Succeed with Math: Every Student's Guide to Conquering Math Anxiety*. New York: College Board, 1995.

Ueland, Brenda. *If You Want to Write: A Book About Art, Independence and Spirit*. St. Paul, MN: Graywolf, 1987.

U.S. Department of Education. *The Student Guide*. Published yearly. (Federal Student Aid Information Center, P.O. Box 84, Washington, DC 20044-0084, 1-800-4-FED-AID)

Watkins, Ryan, and Michael Corry. *E-learning Companion: A Student's Guide to Online Success*. Boston: Houghton Mifflin, 2005.

Weil, Andrew. *Health and Healing*. Boston: Houghton Mifflin, 1995.

Weil, Andrew. *Natural Health, Natural Medicine*. Boston: Houghton Mifflin, 1998.

Welch, David. *Decisions, Decisions: The Art of Effective Decision Making*. Amherst, NY: Prometheus, 2002.

Winston, Stephanie. *Getting Organized*. New York: Warner, 1978.

Wurman, Richard Saul. *Information Anxiety*. New York: Doubleday, 1989.

Wurman, Saul Richard. *Information Anxiety 2*. Indianapolis: QUE, 2001.

index

Bulimia, 335
Burka, Jane, 79
Buzan, Tony, 167
Byrd, Richard E., 120

Caffeine, 351
Calendars, 70, 87, 313
Calligraphy, 170
Calories, 335, 344
CareerBuilder.com, 379
Career goals, 17, 35, 232
Career paths, 104
Career planning, 212, 370–373, 377–378.
    See also Employment
Caring nature, 45
Carlzon, Jan, 242
Car pools, 13, 97
Caruso, Enrico, 120
Cause-and-effect relationships, 228
Cervical cap, 341
Chambers of commerce, 14
Change
    of attitudes, 48–50
    prediction about, 396
    in relationships, 259
    willingness to, 44
Chapels, 13
Chat rooms, 317
Chavez, Cesar, 133
Cheating, 197
Cheat sheets, 117
Checklists, 189
Cheney, Theodore, 267
Childcare, 12–14, 148–150
Children, 148–150
Chlamydia, 339
Cholesterol, 344
Choose your conversations and your
    community (Power Process),
    300–301
Chronicle of Higher Education, 321
Churchill, Winston, 120
Citations, source, 268, 269
Civil Rights Act of 1964, 289, 292
Classes
    importance of attending, 10
    math and science, 202–207
    punctuality in attending, 173
    seating during, 160–161
    size of, 368
    suggestions for missed, 162
    taking unrelated, 366
Clubs, community-based, 14
Clues, 142, 162
Coaching, 396
Cocaine, 351
College education. *See* Higher education
Colleges. *See* Schools
Commitment
    in extracurricular activities, 15
    importance of, 4
    to new behavior, 18
    to relationships, 254–255
Commitment (Exercise), 4

Communication. *See also* Conversations;
    Listening; Speeches; Writing
    of agreements, 274–275
    assertive, 296
    barriers to, 252
    conflict management and, 254–257
    of criticism, 260
    cross-cultural, 284–287
    cultural differences, 284–287
    of effective complaints, 260
    encoding-decoding loop of, 248
    function of, 247, 250–252
    "I" messages and, 250–251, 254, 257
    learning through, 53
    listening and, 249–250
    methods of, 247
    in relationships, 258–259
    of study intentions, 81
    in workplace, 276
Communities
    activities for children in, 149–150
    online, 317
    resources available in, 14
Community colleges, 368
Compact discs (CDs), 309
Comparisons, 142
Comparison shopping, 96
Competence, 44
Competitiveness, 191
Complaints, 260
Compliments, 257
Computer labs, 13, 308, 318
Computers. *See also* Internet
    cooperative learning using, 320
    course reviews using, 192
    hardware specifications for, 309
    managing information on, 130
    student purchases of, 308–309
    tests graded by, 194
    typing notes, 169
    wasting time with, 314
Computer software, 309, 313
Concentration, 81
Concept maps, 179
Concrete experience, 34
Condoms, 340–342
Conferences, 173, 396
Conflict
    cultural differences in response to, 255
    stepping back from, 254, 255
    "you" messages and, 250–251
Conflict management
    cultural differences and, 286
    explanation of, 254–257
Consider the impact of handwriting
    (Exercise), 171
Consumer credit counseling, 14
Content skills, 371
Context clues, 142
Contraceptive implant device, 341
Contraceptive injections, 341
Contrasts, 142
Controversial issues, 273
Convergent thinking, 223

Conversations. *See also* Communication
    about planning, 93–94
    about yourself, 347–348
    choosing your, 300–301
    learning through, 53
    reciting and repeating names during, 121
Cooley, Tatiana, 130
Cooperative learning
    for math and science classes, 205
    study groups as, 191–192
    using computers for, 320
Copyrights, 316
Cornell format, 165–168
Counseling, 366
Counseling centers
    community-based, 14
    explanation of, 13
    school-based, 10
Courage, 45
Course catalog, 13
Course equivalents, 368
Course requirements, 369
Courses, short, 203–204
CPM (Critical Path Method) charts, 313
Cramming, 207
Create a lifeline (Exercise), 27
Creative thinking, 223, 224–227
Creativity
    critical thinking and, 223
    explanation of, 45
    strategies for generating, 224–227
    workplace applications for, 242
Credit cards, 98–100
Credit counseling, 98
Credit rating, 98
Critical thinking. *See also* Thinking
    about behaviors and interpretations, 357
    about controversial issues, 273
    about editorials, 151
    about information on the Internet, 312
    about instructor's ideas, 161
    about learning experiences, 126
    about master students, 53
    about procrastination, 79
    about stereotypes, 288, 299
    about success, 386
    about technology, 325
    about tests, 209
    attitudes of, 222
    concept maps for, 179
    creativity and, 223
    promotion of, 3
    strategies for, 219–222
    as thorough thinking, 218
    uses of, 217–218
    workplace applications for, 242
Critical works, 322–323
Criticism, 221, 260, 287
Cultural differences. *See also* Diversity
    in communication, 284–287
    in conflict management, 286
    in individual and collective orientations,
        302
    instructors and, 172

MONDAY ___ / ___ / ___ /

Monitor	Plan
7:00	7:00
7:15	
7:30	
7:45	
8:00	8:00
8:15	
8:30	
8:45	
9:00	9:00
9:15	
9:30	
9:45	
10:00	10:00
10:15	
10:30	
10:45	
11:00	11:00
11:15	
11:30	
11:45	
12:00	12:00
12:15	
12:30	
12:45	
1:00	1:00
1:15	
1:30	
1:45	
2:00	2:00
2:15	
2:30	
2:45	
3:00	3:00
3:15	
3:30	
3:45	
4:00	4:00
4:15	
4:30	
4:45	
5:00	5:00
5:15	
5:30	
5:45	
6:00	6:00
6:15	
6:30	
6:45	
7:00	7:00
7:15	
7:30	
7:45	
8:00	8:00
8:15	
8:30	
8:45	
9:00	9:00
9:15	
9:30	
9:45	
10:00	10:00
10:15	
10:30	
10:45	
11:00	11:00
11:15	
11:30	
11:45	
12:00	12:00

TUESDAY ___ / ___ / ___ /

Monitor	Plan
7:00	7:00
7:15	
7:30	
7:45	
8:00	8:00
8:15	
8:30	
8:45	
9:00	9:00
9:15	
9:30	
9:45	
10:00	10:00
10:15	
10:30	
10:45	
11:00	11:00
11:15	
11:30	
11:45	
12:00	12:00
12:15	
12:30	
12:45	
1:00	1:00
1:15	
1:30	
1:45	
2:00	2:00
2:15	
2:30	
2:45	
3:00	3:00
3:15	
3:30	
3:45	
4:00	4:00
4:15	
4:30	
4:45	
5:00	5:00
5:15	
5:30	
5:45	
6:00	6:00
6:15	
6:30	
6:45	
7:00	7:00
7:15	
7:30	
7:45	
8:00	8:00
8:15	
8:30	
8:45	
9:00	9:00
9:15	
9:30	
9:45	
10:00	10:00
10:15	
10:30	
10:45	
11:00	11:00
11:15	
11:30	
11:45	
12:00	12:00

WEDNESDAY ___ / ___ / ___ /

Monitor	Plan
7:00	7:00
7:15	
7:30	
7:45	
8:00	8:00
8:15	
8:30	
8:45	
9:00	9:00
9:15	
9:30	
9:45	
10:00	10:00
10:15	
10:30	
10:45	
11:00	11:00
11:15	
11:30	
11:45	
12:00	12:00
12:15	
12:30	
12:45	
1:00	1:00
1:15	
1:30	
1:45	
2:00	2:00
2:15	
2:30	
2:45	
3:00	3:00
3:15	
3:30	
3:45	
4:00	4:00
4:15	
4:30	
4:45	
5:00	5:00
5:15	
5:30	
5:45	
6:00	6:00
6:15	
6:30	
6:45	
7:00	7:00
7:15	
7:30	
7:45	
8:00	8:00
8:15	
8:30	
8:45	
9:00	9:00
9:15	
9:30	
9:45	
10:00	10:00
10:15	
10:30	
10:45	
11:00	11:00
11:15	
11:30	
11:45	
12:00	12:00

THURSDAY ___ / ___ / ___ /

Monitor	Plan
7:00	7:00
7:15	
7:30	
7:45	
8:00	8:00
8:15	
8:30	
8:45	
9:00	9:00
9:15	
9:30	
9:45	
10:00	10:00
10:15	
10:30	
10:45	
11:00	11:00
11:15	
11:30	
11:45	
12:00	12:00
12:15	
12:30	
12:45	
1:00	1:00
1:15	
1:30	
1:45	
2:00	2:00
2:15	
2:30	
2:45	
3:00	3:00
3:15	
3:30	
3:45	
4:00	4:00
4:15	
4:30	
4:45	
5:00	5:00
5:15	
5:30	
5:45	
6:00	6:00
6:15	
6:30	
6:45	
7:00	7:00
7:15	
7:30	
7:45	
8:00	8:00
8:15	
8:30	
8:45	
9:00	9:00
9:15	
9:30	
9:45	
10:00	10:00
10:15	
10:30	
10:45	
11:00	11:00
11:15	
11:30	
11:45	
12:00	12:00

FRIDAY ___ / ___ / ___ /

Monitor	Plan
7:00	7:00
7:15	
7:30	
7:45	
8:00	8:00
8:15	
8:30	
8:45	
9:00	9:00
9:15	
9:30	
9:45	
10:00	10:00
10:15	
10:30	
10:45	
11:00	11:00
11:15	
11:30	
11:45	
12:00	12:00
12:15	
12:30	
12:45	
1:00	1:00
1:15	
1:30	
1:45	
2:00	2:00
2:15	
2:30	
2:45	
3:00	3:00
3:15	
3:30	
3:45	
4:00	4:00
4:15	
4:30	
4:45	
5:00	5:00
5:15	
5:30	
5:45	
6:00	6:00
6:15	
6:30	
6:45	
7:00	7:00
7:15	
7:30	
7:45	
8:00	8:00
8:15	
8:30	
8:45	
9:00	9:00
9:15	
9:30	
9:45	
10:00	10:00
10:15	
10:30	
10:45	
11:00	11:00
11:15	
11:30	
11:45	
12:00	12:00

SATURDAY ___ / ___ / ___ /

Monitor	Plan

SUNDAY ___ / ___ / ___ /

Monitor	Plan

MONDAY	TUESDAY	WEDNESDAY	THURSDAY	FRIDAY	SATURDAY	SUNDAY

Name _____ Month _____

MONDAY	TUESDAY	WEDNESDAY	THURSDAY	FRIDAY	SATURDAY	SUNDAY

Name _____ Month _____

At your fingertips

MASTER Student

Name _____   E-mail _____

College address _____   Phone _____

City _____   State _____   Zip code _____

Course name _____   Section number _____

Class meeting time _____   Building & room _____

Class Web site address _____

School Web site address _____

Instructor _____   Phone _____

Instructor office location _____   Office hours _____

Instructor e-mail address _____

Classmate _____   Phone _____

Classmate e-mail address _____

Academic advisor _____   Phone _____

Academic advisor office location _____   Office hours _____

Academic advisor e-mail address _____

Library name and location _____   Library hours _____

Computer lab name and location _____   Lab hours _____

The **tangram,** an ancient Chinese puzzle game, is used to create images by rearranging seven sections of a square into different patterns. The cat figure below was created with the puzzle—by applying an imaginative mind, and finding new relationships and possibilities in these basic geometric shapes, you can devise hundreds of other images.

Just as working with the tangram allows you to use creative thinking, for many students learning is about putting the pieces together in as many ways as they can. *Becoming a Master Student* provides the basic building blocks with which a creative and active mind can succeed.

The Master Student logo and the icons in this book have been created using the tangram pieces. Try your hand at tangrams by cutting out the seven sections of the square below. Use the seven pieces to try to recreate the textbook icons. Then try to create something that wasn't there before. Be sure to use all seven pieces. You might start by mixing up the pieces and seeing whether you can put them back together to form a square. Take a look at some examples on page 223. When you come up with a pattern you have created, trace around the outside edge of it and see if a friend can discover how you did it.